AF522624

The Undying Light

A Personal History of Independent India

Gopalkrishna Gandhi

ALEPH

ALEPH BOOK COMPANY
An independent publishing firm
promoted by ***Rupa Publications India***

First published in India in 2025
by Aleph Book Company
7/16 Ansari Road, Daryaganj
New Delhi 110 002

ISBN: 978-93-6523-820-4

1 3 5 7 9 10 8 6 4 2

Printed in India

For my granddaughters
Siya Chakravarthy Venkatesh (13)
Ava Gandhi Vania (12)
and
Radha Gandhi Venkatesh (7)
to read, only if they wish to, when they are much older.

Mahatma Gandhi in Dattapara, Noakhali, 1946. As he emerged from a dwelling there, his attention was attracted by a dog, running a few steps past him, turning back and again beckoning. Gandhi's associates tried to drive it away. 'Don't you see,' he said to them, 'the animal wants to say something to us?' The dog then led them to the skeletons of his master and several others done to death. Painting by Manindra Bhushan Gupta (1898–1968), kind courtesy of its owner Sarojesh C. Mukerjee through the thoughtfulness of Rudrangshu Mukherjee.

Contents

PRELUDE

David Davidar, Aleph Book Company's initiator, has a sharp eye for new books. Towards the close of 2022, he came by Fintan O'Toole's *We Don't Know Ourselves*,[1] which described itself as *A Personal History of Modern Ireland*. He sent it to me, saying I might like reading it, and if I did, would I be interested in attempting something on its lines for post-Independence India?

The book's title held two keywords and thoughts: 'personal' and 'history'. The first was appealing, the second scary. Describing vignettes of independent India as I had seen or heard of them in the way of an extended adda[*] was an attractive idea. And there were around me, at home, things to encourage exactly that: fading photographs and ageing letters, some of them laminated and protected from oblivion by a vintage home remedy—pouches of tobacco leaves placed at intervals between them. This bric-a-brac from the past, growing old with me, urged: 'Say yes!'

But who was I in the India that is Bharat[†] to as much as touch the hem of historical writing even under the alibi of 'personal'? What business had I to write about the variegated republic of thirty-six states and union territories with altitudes as high as the snow-capped Kangchenjunga[‡] at 8,586 m and as low as the sea-lapped Kuttanad[§] at –2.7 metres with stories hidden in its folds—glacial, seismic, alluvial, parched, flooded, baked, and densely timbered? Did I know even one single strand of India's peoplehood, thinking its often-conflicted thoughts and speaking its myriad mind in 780[¶] languages?

I was nobody to write about India or my fellow Indians. But I could think of questions that had been with me over the years, defying answers.

Is independent India impossibly fragmented or indissolubly united?

When and where am I one among my kind, when and where utterly farq (different), ajeeb (strange)?

---

*A Bengali word suggesting 'free-floating conversation without any agenda', it has been used by Rabindranath Tagore, no less, in his novel *Jibonsmriti* with '*tete-a-tete*' given as its meaning in its English translation. (Information credit: Dr Uma Dasgupta)

†The opening words in Article 1 of the Constitution of India, now a much-used phrase, used to emphasize one or the other names.

‡One side of this third highest mountain in the world lies in Nepal, and the other in Sikkim, India.

§Covering three districts in the southern state of Kerala, the region is the lowest in altitude in India and among those few in the world where farming is done biosaline, below sea level.

¶According to the pathbreaking Peoples' Linguistic Survey of India (PLSI) carried out in 2019 under the renowned linguist G. N. Devy.

Why do I feel absolutely ghar jaisa (at home) here and totally baahar ka (an outsider, out of place), there, within the same country, my India?

Why do I, in some places, feel so alag sa (alien) that children may stare at me and street dogs snarl? No Indian should, in India, have to feel funny, bizarre, weird, unknown, alien. But Indians, many, many of us, many of 'them', do. You and I belonging to a 'majority' of some kind in one place can become, in a moment, one of a 'minority' in another. No thought has struck me, in recent times, as being 100 per cent right as Menaka Guruswamy's*: 'India is about a majority of minorities.'

Around the time I pondered these existential questions and thoughts, I was reading an essay by Ruskin Bond (b. 1934) entitled *Scenes from a Writer's Life* (1997), in which the great Anglo-Indian living in the Himalayan hush of Landour, Mussoorie, throws a shaft of light on his and every Indian's identity: 'Race did not make me an Indian,' he says. 'Religion did not make me an Indian. But history did. And in the long run, it's history that counts.'

That well-nigh decided it for me. I would give the book a try. It would not be a personal memoir; my life is not worth recounting. It would not be a history book; I am no historian. But since, as Bond says, it is history that counts, and I know, being born to a Tamil mother and a Gujarati father, raised in Delhi, taught in a 'nationalist' school and a college named after the first Christian martyr, I belonged very exactly to what Menaka Guruswamy had described India to be. And that is how this book began, a totally unremarkable person's glimpse of some remarkable events in post-Independence India that he cannot forget and has been invited now to recall.

Practical thoughts began to take shape under my fingertips on the keyboard.

'Independent India' is one thing; 'India, independent' is another. The first was a political goal, and the second, an existential condition.

Who made 'independent India'?

Its freedom fighters, of course. But then there are so many answering to that description, amazing men and women who spent years, decades, in prison with many bravehearts among these patriots getting killed in battle or being executed by the British Raj. Did they 'make' independent India as a collectivity? Or did some of them do so more than the others? There are those whom I know well who would say 'Gandhi, Gandhi. Gandhi indisputably above all others.' There are many who would say, 'The revolutionaries of Bengal, Punjab, Maharashtra, and from the deep south made the Raj quake....' And there are those who would add, 'Apart from the famous ones, the countless foot soldiers who gave the struggle its ballast.'

---

*Menaka Guruswamy (b. 1974), senior advocate, Supreme Court of India.

An incident from the early 1960s, my late brother, Ramchandra Gandhi (1937–2007), Ramu, to his family and friends, once narrated to me came to mind: 'I was travelling by train from Pilani to Delhi—a circuitous route—when at a wayside station a group of ageing men, all of them in khadi and some in Gandhi caps, trooped in. When the ticket checker came to them, they said they had no tickets on them and would not buy them. "Why so?" the gentle official asked. "Oh," they replied in delightfully earthy Hindi "Hamare kapdon se humein nahin pehchana?" (Couldn't you recognize us from our clothes?) "Hum freedom of fighters hein.... Agar aaj yah railgadi chal rahi hai to voh hamaari qurbaani ki vajah se...." (We are freedom-of-fighters.... If this train[*] is plying today, it is because of our sacrifices.) The TC let them be.' There is no doubt that those gutsy men had done more than their due for the freedom of India, been to jail, and suffered blows. Not all of them could have become ministers, MPs, MLAs, or governors. Some of them were just 'freedom-of-fighters'—often lonely, living in their memories, and sending representations to authorities for recognition, support and certainly unwealthy but with astonishing pride in having held up the national flag to the Raj's flushed face.

And who 'made' the India that it is today into its eighth decade as a sovereign state, undependent on others for food, a milk-major, buzzing with more mobile phone and smartphone users[†] than any country, barring China, an IT giant[‡] and a titan in Space?

Those who have succeeded the freedom fighters, their ideological and biological heirs? Those who have been given charge of India, its elected representatives, its judiciary, its bureaucracy, its commercial technocracy, its

---

*S. Giridhar, senior educator at Azim Premji University recalls: 'Pilani did not have a train station. So we would travel on the roofs of impossibly crowded buses from Pilani to Loharu (this station was just inside Haryana) to take the Bikaner—Delhi Express at 0140 hours—banging on windows and pleading with/threatening people to open the doors of the unreserved carriages. We never slept till the train reached Old Delhi in the morning. We were swathed in bidi, cigarette, and chillum smoke—and reasonably high from our passive smoking. Loharu, Mahendragarh, Rewari, Gurgaon...some stations are etched for ever in memory.'

†As of June 2024, China has the most mobile phones in use, with 1,610,360,000, followed by India with 1,515,971,713, and Indonesia with 385,573,398. The United States has 380,577,528 mobile phones in use. China also has the most smartphone users in the world, with over 974 million in 2022, which is almost 1.5 times more than any other country. India has the second most smartphone users, with around 659 million in 2022. (Statista)

‡According to Statista, India's IT exports in the fiscal year 2023 reached US$ 193 billion, with US$ 126 billion coming from IT software and services. In 2023, India was also the fourth largest exporter of digitally delivered services, which include education, gaming, streaming music and videos, and using computer networks to provide professional services.

formidable scientists who are now discovering means to face the huge life-changer—Artificial Intelligence? Its farmers, fishers and labourers, teachers, doctors and nurses, artists and artisans, the great stars on its screens, sports stars, media-persons, industrialists, merchants, entrepreneurs? And its soldiers on land, air, and sea?

Have all of these, we, the people of India, made the India that is Bharat, independent, sovereign, a master of the ballot, of the mobile phone, of the internet, advancing into the twenty-first century's adulthood in Cyberia, confident, proud?

But are we not responsible too, for its mistakes too numerous to count, its miseries that groan, its misfortunes that howl? Are we not the authors, in some way or other, of all that is so wrong, so utterly wrong, about it and has hurt it—like its thawing glaciers, strangulated rivers, decimated waterbodies, forests mutilated by saw-toothed machines that call themselves 'tools of development', its ancient hillsides now sliced up, with new hillsides coming up of urban refuse, plastic waste, and ceramic throwaways?

Can we possibly save ourselves from hurting ourselves? Can we save India from hurting itself?

I will not, in this book or anywhere for that matter, claim to have 'got' responses to these thoughts, for the simple reason that I have not got them. I will only do that which I can—proclaim my doubts, my misgivings about us, about India, and yet, even when admitting my honest doubt, be proud enough to recall something that happened in April 1984. Thirty-five-year-old squadron leader Rakesh Sharma (b. 1949) had been launched into space aboard the Soyuz T-11. After the launch, as he and his three colleagues, all Russians, had 'stabilized' in orbit, a satellite link connected him to our prime minister, Indira Gandhi. Looking stunning in her very carefully groomed head and wearing a single-string necklace of white and green beads, she asked Sharma a prepared question: Upar se Bharat kaisa dikhta hai apko? (From up there, what does Bharat look like to you?). After a brief preliminary, Rakesh answered the question with the first line from Iqbal's great song: Sare jahan se achha (Better than the entire world.)

And so, with my doubts unallayed, I said to myself, my country has to have in it that kuchh baat* which keeps it alive and awake.

~

As I started writing, I knew I had to acknowledge the help I have received

*'That imperishable something', the phrase that occurs in Allama Iqbal's immortal Hindustani song 'Sare Jahan se Achha Hindustan Hamara' (1904).

from persons and institutions to see some light, some way out of the questions and dilemmas that clouded my mind as a child and do so no less, now when I am old.

I start with the single biggest influence on my life, my mother's father, Chakravarti Rajagopalachari (1878–1972)[*], who was sixty-seven when I turned up in 1945 and ninety-four when he died. From him, Anna,[†] as we called him by that Tamil word, I came to perceive the idea of a fair and just Constitution, a democratic republic based on equality and freedom of speech, and of a state that values above all 'the liberty of the subject'.

From Amma, my mother Lakshmi (1912–83),[‡] came, first and foremost, a respect for two languages—the one she was born into, Tamil, and the one she grew into adulthood and old age with, Hindi. She spoke sparingly and wrote frugally but in a way that showed the place of civility in human relations and of a working 'principle': think, say, and do nothing that is not in good form or taste.

From Appa, my father Devadas Gandhi (1900–57), came a foundational love of Gujarati, both as a language and a vessel of elevated thoughts, nowhere better reflected than in the *Bhajanavali*,[§] the multilingual book of hymns from many literary and faith traditions that his father had got the musician Pandit Narayan Moreshwar Khare (1889–1938)[¶] to compile. Appa taught me to learn and sing a Gujarati version of Cardinal Newman's hymn 'Lead Kindly Light' in a double introduction to Christian devotionalism and Gujarati lyricism. This version by Narsinhrao Divatia (1859–1937)[**], 'Premal Jyoti Taro Dakhvi', he showed, could be sung in more or less the same tune as the original hymn to plangent effect. And from him, too, came the priceless and matchless 'gift' of an entrée into Tulsidas's *Sri Ramcharitmanas*,[††] which, over a one-year period, he read and recited in all its four metrical forms with me sitting by his side at home and on the numerous train journeys of his in which the family, during school holiday time, accompanied him, chaupai

*Thinker, writer, freedom fighter, statesman. The first and only Indian governor general of India, 1948–50.

†'Anna' in Tamil, pronounced Annaa with the 'n' being deep, means, literally, 'elder brother', but in some Tamil households, certainly some TamBrahm ones, the term is used for one's father.

‡Lakshmi Rajagopalachari, married in 1933 to Devadas Gandhi.

§The *Ashram Bhajanavali*, a collection of multi-faith devotional compositions in various languages and taken from different sources, first published by Navajivan, Ahmedabad, in 1922, and republished many times. Selections from the songs and hymns in it were sung or recited every morning and evening at Gandhi's ashrams.

¶Skilled and scholarly musician in the tradition of Vishnu Digambar Paluskar.

**Narsinhrao Bholanath Divatia, Gujarati poet, linguist, prose stylist, and critic.

††Epic poem in Avadhi composed by the sixteenth century poet Tulsidas, based on the Ramayana.

by chaupai, doha by doha and the two other less known metres—chhand and soratha.

From my three siblings, each very different from the other, came distinct and formative impressions of their essential natures. From the eldest of the four of us, my sister Tara, called by me and some other intimates Taru (b. 1934),[*] elder by eleven years, came the importance of passing moments, each unique and never to happen again—as in her panic-stricken rush, as a fourteen-year-old, to Birla House in New Delhi, with two-and-a-half-year-old me clasped to her bosom, to reach the room where our grandfather lay on a length of white khadi.

From the next sibling in sequence, my brother Rajmohan (b. 1935),[†] called at home Mohan, came the criticality of doing and standing up for what is right—and you know what is right, no quibbling, there—with the corollary: having the courage to pay the price that 'standing up for what is right' calls for.

In my next elder and second brother, Ramchandra (1937–2007),[‡] of precious memory, I saw, like everyone who came to know him did, a cascade of brilliant ideation in a bravura of rare freedom and equal control. When he was teaching at the University of Hyderabad, answerable to its vice chancellor, Gurbaksh Singh, the worthy gentleman asked him if he was not afraid of authority. 'Afraid of authority?' Ramu replied, 'Yes, but the authority of God and conscience—khuda aur zameer.' The VC had been emphatically excluded from that orbit.

Bibi Amtus Salam,[§] daughter of landed gentry in undivided Punjab, and ace associate of Gandhi in Noakhali, during which tour she fasted to obtain the return of a Hindu temple 'sword' captured by majority Muslims, was dear to the family as family. Once, when Ramu took seriously ill—jaundice was diagnosed—and our 'family doctor' ventured little opinions on the prognosis, Amtus bua appeared like an apparition and, touching his forehead, placed under his pillow a little packet wrapped in cloth. 'Ab theek ho jaoge...' (now you will get better), she said and, as was her wont, quietly slipped out. We saw after she had left that the packet held a copy of the Holy Quran. Ramu

---

[*]Tara Gandhi Bhattacharjee, author, linguist, artist, specializing in the processes and problems of khadi spinning and weaving.

[†]Rajmohan Gandhi, historian, biographer, teacher, and briefly, a member of parliament.

[‡]Ramchandra Gandhi, philosopher, author, teacher and interpreter of India's traditions of sagehood, approximating that station in himself.

[§]Born in the princely state of Patiala, Amtus Salam became a dedicated worker for Hindu–Muslim unity, helping recover abducted Hindu and Sikh women from West Punjab and, post-Independence, devoted herself to the rehabilitation of refugees till her death in 1985.

was up the next day, fever-free.... Superstition? Perhaps. Faith? Perhaps. Was this about India? No 'perhaps' there. India it was, India it is—a triveni, a threefold plait of superstitious belief, religious faith and—the highest forms of logic and reason. My daughter Amrita[*] once asked Ruskin Bond, the author of amazing ghost-tales, 'Do you believe in ghosts?' Said Bond sahib: 'I don't believe in ghosts, but I see them all the time.' I do not believe in miracles, but I see them all the time. Amtus bua was a miracle.

From a great teacher in my school, the tall, bespectacled, black-gowned and black-back-comb-haired original of Mr Chips,[†] if ever there was one, Awadh Kishoreji (1907–87), who taught English in Modern School from 1931 to 1967, came a love of English literature. He read aloud in class, word by careful word, step by cautious step, Sir John Hunt's *The Ascent of Everest* (1953). Awadh Kishoreji's reaching, with the rapture of an actual summiting, the words, 'And then we were on top' taught me the mysterious ways in which language can say things without saying them and not say things even when purporting to say them.

From my history teacher in school, the soft-spoken R. D. Goyal sahib (1918–2015), came to me a deep respect amounting to awe for the character of Dara Shukoh, elder brother of Emperor Aurangzeb, done to death for being liberal, learned, gentle (though also phenomenally brave and strong, physically), and being in every way deserving of the crown. Would India's history have been different if Dara, not Aurangzeb, had become emperor? I would like to believe it would have, though my historian niece, Supriya Gandhi[‡] is not so sure.

My college in Delhi, named after St. Stephens',[§] one of the early Christian martyrs stoned to death for blasphemy after he offended his hearers at a debate with diaspora Jews, gave me a sense of what freedom of thought and expression mean. Its red brick and grey sandstone cloisters had Marxist teachers and students move in untroubled proximity with the college chaplain, teachers, and students of strong Christian beliefs. In my five years there, the college had persons of such diverse views as V. K. Krishna Menon

---

[*]Amrita Gandhi (b.1977).

[†]Lead character in *Goodbye, Mr. Chips*, a novella (1934) about the life of a schoolteacher, Mr Chipping, written by James Hilton, first published by Hodder & Stoughton.

[‡]Supriya Gandhi (b. 1977), a historian of Mughal India and assistant professor in Religious Studies at Yale University, is the author of *The Emperor Who Never Was: Dara Shukoh in Mughal India*.

[§]Died c. 36 CE at Jerusalem.

(1896–1974)[*] and Morarji Desai (1896–1995)[†] speak to us with great force, and Jayaprakash Narayan (1902–79) say in his measured voice at a lecture on 'Nationalism in India Before and After Independence', at St. Stephens', within weeks of the Sino-Indian war of 1962, 'Even the Chinese are our brothers....' Not a whisper of surprise or disagreement ruffled the total silence in which JP was heard.

Another socialist who did not visit college when I was there but whom I came to know and respect was Kamaladevi Chattopadhyay (1903–88). Like JP, a natural-born leftist, she formed and held her opinions on men and matters with total objectivity. Kamaladevi gave me the example of ideology-free ideals, partyless affinities, and sanctimony-devoid ethics. And the joy of sheer autonomy accompanied by the greater joy of being chronically unpopular with one or other sections of society.

From Thomas Abraham (1927–2018), a non-devout yet firm rooted Syrian Christian, diplomat, thinker, secularist of the Nehruvian mould, my boss for four years in Sri Lanka (1978–82) and mentor for another forty, and his historian wife, Meera, I got a sense of India changing from what its Constitution intended it to be into an entity which members of the Indian Constituent Assembly would need help to recognize. 'The India that Gandhi fought for, Nehru worked for, is gone, I say,' Abraham rued time and time again. 'And I am glad I will not be around to see their memories buried.' Was he prescient? He was not. Was he hopelessly wrong? I cannot say that either.

I must also acknowledge my debt to a book illustrated by many world-class photographers entitled *Memories of Bapu*. I was a month short of three when I first turned the pages of *Memories*. Published by the Hindustan Times press, within two months of Mohandas K. Gandhi's assassination on 30 January 1948 by three bullets fired, as I learnt without fully understanding the meaning of 'at point-blank range', it filled me with horror. My father, as the newspaper's managing editor, had produced the illustrated folio in a blend of filial and professional duty. More than one copy lay around our home. The book said little or nothing of the assassin but everything that could be, through highly vivid photographs and high-voltage tributes, of the assassination. A hard thing to have to say, but my earliest memories are wrapped around death, his death, that kind of death.

---

[*]Leftist thinker, crusader for India's independence from the UK, politician, lawyer, diplomat, statesman, and defence minister under Nehru.

[†]Bombay civil servant and politician who served as chief minister of Bombay, finance minister of India and the fourth prime minister of India.

Three pictures from *Memories of Bapu* stamped themselves on my mind. One is of my father and Gandhi's doctor-associate, Sushila Nayar (1914–2001), holding the shawl that Gandhi was wearing as he fell, bloodied. The second is of a grief-stricken Sir N. Gopalaswami Ayyangar (1882–1953), India's representative at the early conferences of the United Nations, sitting next to Sir Muhammad Zafrullah Khan (1893–1985), Pakistan's representative at the UNO headquarters at Lake Success, New York. A newspaper spread in front of the two says, 'Gandhi Slain'. The third is of an unknown woman somewhere in the US, wearing a black mourning veil, weeping for Gandhi.

As I write this personal history of independent India, Gandhi looms over the words for the message that he gave to us, his fellow Indians, as India became free. Speaking to a gathering in Calcutta where he was on that day, India, he said, was becoming free, but it was also being divided, and therefore, in his words, we had cause for both 'rejoicing and sorrow'.

That ironic melding of birth and death, of joy and sorrow, seems to fit every phase of our life as a people and a nation. We may not rejoice too triumphantly, for there is, in every cause for joy in India, a countervailing reason for sadness. Nor may we grieve too loud or long for there flickers in every pang of our pain a fragile flame of faith in the 'Dispenser of India's Destiny'* holding in His or, perhaps more appropriately, Her hands, our individual and collective fates.

*English rendering of the phrase 'Bharat bhagya bidhata' occurring in Tagore's song 'Jana Gana Mana', which is India's national anthem.

BOOK ONE

THE 1940S
FRIENDS, FAMILY, AND THE FURIES

Amrit Kaur (1889–1964), the rajkumari of Kapurthala, was a friend of the Gandhis.

Anglican, anglicized but no Anglophile, a princess from the wing of one of Punjab's Sikh royal houses that had converted to Christianity, she had adapted to Gandhi's nostrums of austerity and stoicism in self-denial. When, on 9 June 1937, Lakshmi gave birth to her and Devadas's third child, Amrit Kaur somewhat cheekily wrote to Gandhi that she thought Devadas was being irresponsible. Gandhi replied, 'I agree with you that he should stop now.' But he suggested that she, not he, should advise the young man. 'They passionately love each other...cannot help themselves. I know what it is to exercise self-restraint....' And then went on to add memorably, 'Devadas and Lakshmi almost make out a case for contraceptives.'

Had I landed soon after the thirdborn, I would have been deemed the result of blind lust. But as I happened seven years later, my parents dodged that distinction. And, for some inexplicable reason, self-restraint and contraception were not on Bapuji's mind at the time. On the contrary.

At hand to be of help with his daughter's confinement, Anna, the maternal grandfather, wired the paternal grandfather, conveying the news of the birth of yet another grandson they held in common. Bapuji wired back: 'Thank God. Lakshmi and Babe have my blessings.' And in that welcoming mood, wrote to Lakshmi, 'Let the new grandson be named Govind and also Madhav. If you want to keep only one name, it should be one given by Anna.' And as on earlier occasions of the moment, it was Anna's word that prevailed in our little domesticities, with the long name Gopalkrishna duly settled on my head. It was generally assumed that I had been given the first name of the paternal grandfather's mentor, the great Gokhale.

The following year, 1946, was the British Raj's last 'clear' year.

And from the August of that year onwards, it was to be, for India's north, north-west, and east, its bloodiest.

India's south, sane, safe, and sound was, like the novelist L. P. Hartley's 'past', a different country; they did things differently there.*

Direct Action Day, called by an impatient and irritable Jinnah on 16

---

*I owe to Professor Rudrangshu Mukherjee, in a conversation, this transposition of the image of 'differently' from 'the past' to India's south.

August 1946, in Calcutta, the capital of the state of Bengal, where the Muslim League under H. S. Suhrawardy (1892–1963), was in power, saw an orgy of utter horror. The butcher's unquenchable bloodthirst, the rapist's manic craving, and the bigot's scorching torch disfigured the city and brutalized its people. The fury went on for three days. Suhrawardy, who held the Department of Law and Order, had transferred Hindu police officers from twenty-two of the twenty-four police stations in Calcutta, replacing them with Muslim officers. For the first two days—16 and 17 August—police guns remained silent as goondas from the Muslim quarters of the city held it to ransom. The governor, an Attlee-picked railway union leader, Sir Frederick Burrows (1887–1973), was not possessed of that which makes a moment memorable. He did not and perhaps could not do anything. On the third day, retaliation came from the Hindu section. And it did not lag behind the provocation.

On 17 August 1946, a calm and composed but inwardly seething Devadas got a lead editorial published in the *Hindustan Times*, castigating the Bengal's Muslim League premier Suhrawardy and Governor Burrows. Using adjectives that newspapers today would think twice before inking, it said of Governor Burrows and Premier Suhrawardy: 'He could not have been ignorant of the League preparations for a violent demonstration which had been going on in the city for many weeks. He knew the way the mind of the neurotic Premier was working.... Yet, not only did he fail to take any preventive action, he fiddled for two nights and a day while the largest city in the country burned.'[1] Incinerating Calcutta, the fire spread rapidly to other venues in the north, north-west, and further east of Bengal, obliterating all distinctions of action and reaction, attack and counter-attack.

The viceroy, Lord Archibald Wavell (1883–1950), accelerated his attempts at bringing the Congress and League to activate the newly elected Constituent Assembly and come into an interim government, which would pave the way for Britain's departure from India.

Wearied by decades of struggle, wizened by years in jail and now exhausted by protracted negotiations, Gandhi's 'band', elected now to the new Constituent Assembly of India, entered the viceroy's new Executive Council on 2 September 1946. This was, in effect, nothing less than the nascent cabinet of Independence-eve India. The Congress and Muslim League were to share de facto and de jure power. The League did not join at once, but join it did, soon enough, in what could be called a dress rehearsal for holding power in the country of Jinnah's dream and Gandhi's nightmare,

Pakistan. Jawaharlal Nehru (1889–1964),* as vice president in the council at fifty-seven, was now virtually India's prime minister-in-waiting, handling the portfolio of External Affairs. Vallabhbhai Patel (1875–1950),† Gandhi's kin-like colleague and soulmate at seventy-one, as the next most senior on that council, took charge of the portfolio of Home. And very significantly, the scholar-politician and diplomat Sir Shafaat Ahmad Khan, who had veered from the Muslim League, was included.

Ferocious focus—M. A. Jinnah concentrating on his target, circa 1946. (Devadas Gandhi personal archives).

How members of the CA, as the assembly now got to be known, could put the beastly bedlam that was happening around them to a side and settle down to a rational viewing of the short, mid-term and far future, how some of them, now termed ministers, could possibly sit around a table and deliberate on matters like external relations, finance, agriculture revival,

*Serving over nine years as a political prisoner in British India's jails, the barrister, historian, author, statesman, and first prime minister of India (1947–1964), hailed as the architect of modern India, was once described by Acharya Kripalani as the wandering lamb whom the shepherd (Gandhi) had a hard time keeping in the fold, while the other lambs stayed unmoving in the flock. Nehru was described by Gandhi as his 'heir', which made him a political son.

†The Gujarati barrister who turned freedom fighter at Gandhi's behest, serving over eight years as a political prisoner in British India's jails, enjoyed the greatest personal and political affinity with Gandhi and accepted without murmur his leader saying '...not Vallabhbhai ... but Jawaharlal' was his heir and successor. But in Gandhi's political fraternity, Patel's position was that of the closest 'sibling'.

industrial development, education is beyond my understanding. These leaders just had to be superhuman in their ability to be stoically—yogically—capable of being inside a furious cauldron and yet carry ice bags in their heads to clearly think, plan, and work with dispassion and objectivity. The Muslim Leaguers among them had a definite agenda: use the CA and the interim government to leverage the partition of Hindustan and the creation of Pakistan. The rest were bent on accelerating independence without partition if possible and with it, if inevitable.

Rajaji was asked to take Finance but thought he did not feel well enough to handle so large and daunting a department, became minister for Industries and Civil Supplies. Our life in Delhi was to be enlivened by his move from Madras—for the first time in his life—to house and house-holding in Delhi. He too, clearly, looked forward to the change and the opportunity to do what he was so practised at: ministerial office. 'I see a *Hindu* report from Delhi,' Rajaji wrote to Devadas, 'that all my colleagues have fixed up their houses!' Sardar Patel suggested to Rajaji that they might share a house in Delhi, making it easier for the two widowers to be looked after by their daughters from a single kitchen. Rajaji said he would like to move to the house on Clive Road being vacated by Sir Akbar Hydari[*] who was moving to Assam as governor. 'I like the old Ajanta painting, which old Hydari[†] had got and put up there and which young Hydari agreed to leave for me,' he wrote to Devadas.

That Buddhist cave art could link a Hindu and a Muslim shuffling official residences during riot-time is one of the minor curiosities of Independence-eve India.

But these 'ceremonies of innocence' were tempting the Devil of assassination. On 24 August 1946, a few hours after Lord Wavell announced the names on the radio, Sir Shafaat was on a walk in Simla, when a fanatic Muslim youth[‡] attacked him, leaving deep wounds on his head, chest, and neck. According to Acharya Kripalani (1888–1982),[§] this attack was

[*]Sir Muhammad Saleh Akbar Hydari (1894–1948), civil servant and politician and the last British-appointed governor of the province of Assam.

[†]Sir Muhammad Akbar Nazar Ali Hydari (1869–1941), prime minister of Hyderabad State from 18 March 1937 to September 1941 and father of Muhammad Saleh Akbar.

[‡]Some accounts say there were two attackers.

[§]Gandhi met this 'born intellectual' among 'born politicians' before any of the others who became his 'lieutenants'. Congress president at the time of India's Independence and a pre-eminent opposition leader and MP after 1947, the book *Gandhi: His Life and Thought* (Publications Division, New Delhi, 1970, from which this reference is drawn. p. 245) authored by him remains an outstanding analysis of Gandhi's ideas and action.

because Sir Shafaat 'had the temerity to accept the nomination from the Congress'. Sir Shafaat survived the brutal wounds—full seven of them—after grappling with his assailant and crawling to a rickshaw stand, from where he was moved to his home and then to a hospital. The *Hindustan Times*, in a searing editorial the next day, said: 'Is the Muslim League going to follow the Fascist and Hitlerite technique of liquidating anyone opposed to its policies and programmes? Is there no place for honest differences of opinion between Muslims and Muslims? Must everyone who does not say "aye" to Mr Jinnah's commandments be stabbed in the dark? The League cannot escape full responsibility for the dastardly attack on Sir Shafaat's life.'

If fanatic Muslim opinion did not want Muslims in the new arrangement without the League, fanatic Hindu opinion had its own take on the Hindus in the council. As a Gandhi adherent known to have wanted and worked for a détente with the Muslim League, Rajaji could not have been liked by those many who feared and had suffered at the hands of the proponents of Pakistan. Viceroy Lord Wavell inducted Rajaji into the cabinet on 11 September. Three days later, after he had moved into the home the Hydaris had vacated for him, Rajaji motored to his daughter's home. He had just alighted from the dark green Plymouth assigned to him and climbed up to our home in Connaught Circus when the car, dropping him off and turning into Curzon Road, was fired upon. It was all very fast. The single bullet, fired from the rear, pierced the hood of the boot. All of us understood this to mean an attempt on our Anna's life, as the assailant must have assumed the minister was in the car which, luckily, he was not. Would a single bullet fired on a moving car from the rear have killed its occupant in the rear seat? Possibly, possibly not. But a point had been made. The assailant was not caught, and the motive remained unestablished. But an employee from one of our neighbouring homes, whom my mother suspected was of that school of thought, rushed in within minutes of the episode, breathless, to check whether Rajaji was 'in and safe' and, on finding that he indeed was, went away as fast as he had appeared. Rajaji, unperturbed and uninterested in speculating on the event, stayed and chatted for some time and returned to his duties as if nothing had happened.

Gandhi, of course, was neither impervious to the danger nor afraid of it. On the contrary, he almost seemed to beckon it. Acharya Kripalani was not part of the council. He could judge and comment on the brutal bedlam of bigotry with greater freedom than his colleagues who were now in office. He could also analyse and comment on the Mahatma. Kripalani felt then what he was to put down in writing some twenty years later: 'In situations of communal conflict, Gandhiji could think only in terms of martyrdom. Gandhiji had a fascination for the Cross.'[2]

A readiness to die while preventing murders, rape, and hatred led Gandhi inexorably to East Bengal's Noakhali tract. Violence unleashed brutally by the mainly poor majority Muslim population on its largely better-off Hindu minority had shaken him. Attacks on the Hindu population, which started on 10 October, a day observed by Hindus in worshipping Lakshmi, the goddess of prosperity, had continued unceasingly for about a week, leaving a shockingly large number killed and many women raped. A marked feature of the pogrom was the forcible conversion of thousands of Hindu men and women to Islam.* Hundreds migrated to Bengal's west, to Tripura and Assam.

The state—undivided Bengal, its east and west together—as noted earlier, was then under the rule of the Muslim League-led government. And the British Raj's officials, from the highest to the man in the field, were doing little to either prevent the massacres or to help the afflicted. Gandhi, on hearing early reports of the horrors of Noakhali, said, 'The President of the Congress should go to Noakhali and die there.'[3] Kripalani, who was by now Congress president, typically responded by saying he had no intention of dying yet and that if he had to die, he would choose a healthier place than Bengal to die in.[4] But go to the affected areas, the intrepid soldier did. 'The Governor'† writes Kripalani, '...was then in Chittagong. On October 10, we flew to Chittagong, making a short halt at the Comilla airstrip. Thousands of refugees fleeing from the riot-affected areas had taken refuge there...When we met the Governor, he appeared to be quite unconcerned

*When the news of the killings and forced conversions appeared in the news for the first time, *Star of India*, a newspaper patronized by the Muslim League, denied any incidents of forcible conversion. However, Huseyn Shaheed Suhrawardy, while answering a question from Dhirendranath Datta in the assembly, stated that there had been 9,895 cases of forcible conversion in Tipperah. The exact figure was not known for Noakhali, but it ran into thousands, Edward Skinner Simpson stated in his report that 22,550 cases of forcible conversion took place in the three police station areas of Faridganj, Chandpur, and Hajiganj in the district of Tipperah. Dr. Taj-ul-Islam Hashmi concluded that the number of Hindu women raped or converted was probably many times the number of Hindus killed. According to Justice G. D. Khosla, the entire Hindu population of Noakhali were robbed of all they possessed and then forcibly converted to Islam. (Rakesh Batabyal, *Communalism in Bengal: From Famine to Noakhali, 1943–47*, New Delhi: Sage Publications, 2005, p. 282; G. D. Khosla, *Stern Reckoning: A Survey of the Events Leading up to and Following the Partition of India*, New Delhi: Oxford University Press. 1989, p. 68.)

†Sir Fredrick Burrows.

and at ease. [H. S. Suhrawardy] the Premier* also happened to be there. The Governor said the Premier had reported to him that everything was under control and peace and order had been restored. When we talked of the kidnapping of Hindu women by the Muslims, his laconic reply was that that was inevitable as the Hindu women there were more handsome than Muslim women.'[5] Kripalani says with his bluntness at its bluntest: 'I felt like hitting him, but I restrained myself.'

Kripalani writes that after a three-hour stay, he headed back for Calcutta, with Suhrawardy also getting a lift on the same plane. 'We were flying low. At several places, we could see smoke spiralling up from the villages, though it was afternoon. We pointed out to him this evidence of continuing arson and lawlessness. But he was quite unaffected. He was behaving like a schoolboy on a spree, taking photographs with his camera.' Kripalani's description recalls Devadas's editorial characterization of Suhrawardy as 'neurotic'.

Gandhi reached the burning, bleeding area on 7 November. Over November and December of 1946, he walked from village to village with a handful of chosen associates with only partial and unsteady responses from the Muslim majority to own guilt, atone for its crime, and restore confidence in the Hindu minority.

In the village of Dattapara, on 11 November 1946, physically exhausted and worn by a daily self-imposed ration of less than 600 calories to expiate for what was happening in Bihar, he learnt of a Hindu household of eight, including a boy of fifteen, that had been murdered. Those not killed had been converted. These included a deaf-mute who showed him, tied up in a rag, his shikha† that had been forcibly cut. As Gandhi emerged from a dwelling there, his attention was attracted by a Tibetan spaniel, running a few steps past him, turning back and again beckoning. Gandhi's associates tried to drive it away. 'Don't you see,' he said to them, 'the animal wants to say something to us?' The dog then led them to the skeletons of his master and several others done to death. What he had seen, he told a group of Muslim Leaguers, was the 'the very negation of Islam'.

The area was under 'extra' police and military cover. Suhrawardy visited him in village Madhupur on 19 November with two colleagues and suggested that the armed forces be withdrawn 'for the establishment of goodwill' and to encourage the return of those Hindus who had fled. An incredulous Gandhi asked if the government 'will name one honest Muslim to stand guarantee

---

*Kripalani uses the term 'chief minister', but at the time, the office was known as that of premier.
†Top-knot worn by Hindu men.

for the safety of the refugees returning to each village'. The query was met with silence.

It was often a one-night-in-one-village for Gandhi and his small band at this time, and the night—very cold—was spent in a hut of reeds, split bamboo, and cane. He held a prayer 'meeting' every evening, with both Hindus and Muslims attending. Not infrequently, Muslims walked out when his basic hymn, 'Raghupati Raghav Raja Ram', was sung.

Some moments of a different, less grim kind also intervened. On Christmas Day, Gandhi was in Srirampur. A Christian friend brought a soldier's hamper as a gift. It included cigarettes, which Gandhi kept aside for Jawaharlal Nehru, who was to visit him in a couple of days, with Congress president Acharya Kripalani. Nehru, on his part, brought a fountain pen for Gandhi. Nehru did not hide from Gandhi the fact that he smoked, though I doubt if he ever smoked in Gandhi's presence. Maulana Azad did and had ashtrays improvised for him in the ashram. There was a puritan in Gandhi, but there was a liberal air about him, too, which could live with human foibles as with human mannerisms. He could abide people in his circle eating non-vegetarian food, smoking, and not being teetotallers. What he could not forgive was the hiding of it and being hypocritical.

1947

'THE DAWN SO STAINED, SO STAINED'—FAIZ AHMED FAIZ

India's 'freedom' year—1947—was inaugurated for Gandhi in a village called Srirampur, where he had already spent almost a month. Leaving Srirampur on 2 January 1947, he said he would not be using any footwear whatsoever for as long as he was in Noakhali, as the ground had been 'hallowed by the innocent sufferings of poor men and women'. And then through the January and February of 1947, he was to continue the 'pilgrimage' as he now began to call it.

His associate from the Punjab, Amtus Salam, whom we have met before, had been billeted by him for communal harmony work in Shirandi village. She had, meantime, embarked on a fast against the suspected removal of a sword from a Hindu temple. The fast lasted a marathon twenty-five days. Gandhi went to her on 20 January and, seeing her emaciated figure lying on a makeshift bed, placed his hand on her head. He then asked the Muslims of the region if they would give Amtus Salam an undertaking that they would make every attempt to recover the sword and thereby help bring about unity among the communities. They agreed, and the forty-year-old, now looking twice her age, was persuaded to give up her fast, Gandhi holding a cup of orange juice to her lips.

Were the Hindus and Muslims of Noakhali getting closer to unity?

Had Gandhi succeeded in placing in the hearts of the guilty a sense of shame, in the hearts of the victims a readiness to consider forgiveness?

Manu (1927–69), daughter of Gandhi's nephew Jaisukhlal, had joined the group. In Paniala the next day, she sang a variation of 'Raghupati Raghav', modifying its second verse as 'Ishvar Allah Tere Nam / Sabko Sanmati De Bhagavan (Ishvar and Allah are both, your names / Give us, God, Right Mindedness)'. The song acquired at once a new meaning and significance, and Gandhi said that was how the song was to be sung thereafter.

While in Noakhali, in addition to his demanding work for communal amity, Gandhi embarked on what can only be described as a 'personal trip'. This was not to a village in strife but into his own inner self. He decided to test his brahmacharya. A seventy-eight-year-old testing his celibacy was, by any rational criterion, absurd. But the matter was, for Gandhi, not about reason but about his faith in himself. Asking Manu to support him in the 'experiment' as a participant, he made his intention public.

Nirmal Kumar Bose (1901–72), the Bengali anthropologist, sociologist, and freedom-activist who was accompanying him as a secretary and translator, saw the whole thing as a 'manifestation of Gandhi's questioning attitude towards his own perfection.'[1] Kripalani, ever alert to the unwisdom of things, objected at once, as did Sardar Patel. A clearly disturbed Devadas wrote to his father. It is one of the more serious regrets of mine that his letter is unavailable. Gandhi wrote to Ghanshyamdas Birla (1894–1983) who, apart from being a well-wisher of the family, was also the proprietor of the newspaper that Devadas was editing, to say: 'Devadas's letter is still ringing in my ears.... I have faith in Devadas' judgment, but then, though grown up, in my eyes, he is still a child....' He was not 'a child' as much as his child and his late mother's. The brahmacharya trial continued for a while, adding arsenal to Gandhi's detractors, dismay in his family, and confusion among many of his countless adherents. It was fellow Gujarati and eminent social worker A. V. Thakkar (1869–1951), known as Thakkar Bapa, his twin in age and temper, who managed, to the relief of many, to show Gandhi the needlessness of prolonging his self-examination when he had passed his test without any lapse and that more urgent matters awaited his undivided attention. Of these, Bihar, going up in higher and higher plumes of sectarian smoke, was the most challenging. Gandhi was taunted by the Muslims of eastern Bengal to leave them and go to Bihar to do his peace work there.

The Nehru-led interim government, with the Congress's strongman Patel handling Home, and Muslim League's smart man Liaquat Ali Khan (1895–1951) holding Finance, was a cardboard boat in a tin tub, sodden with suspicion, torn by dissension and half-sunk with the League's daily adding of irritants to its due weight of worry. The thing would have drowned if, on 20 February 1947, His Majesty's Government had not announced in the British Parliament 'His Majesty's Government's definite intention to take necessary steps to effect the transfer of power to responsible Indian hands by June 1948.' Gandhi was in the village of Bishkatholi that day, staying in the shattered home of a Hindu who had fled but returned to be able to host Gandhi. Muslim fury had reached its flame-tip in this village with a population of 306 Hindus amidst 4,694 Muslims. The house's library of books, including many handwritten texts on religious topics, had been burnt to a cinder.

Along his route to the village and out of it, posters came up on trees that said

Remember Bihar
Accept Pakistan
Muslim League Zindabad
Quaid-e-Azam* Zindabad

More telling, in some places, his path was lined by human excreta and dung, which Gandhi, using an improvised broom made of dry leaves, patiently himself removed, while 'the village crowd would stand around unconcerned and watch the fun'.[†]

Gandhi left Noakhali on 4 March for Bihar without seeing his mission in Noakhali succeed. Violence had abated, true, but not suspicion, not fear, not mutual hatred. I will be back, he said, to the bemused villagers. Tagore's great song 'Ekla Chalo Re' (Walk Alone) was sung as he walked. 'If no one responds to your call, walk alone.... If no one talks for fear, speak out alone.... If all turn away, walk alone.... Over the thorns and along the blood-strewn track, walk alone....'

Acharya Kripalani observes in tones of pained truth, 'If Gandhiji could not touch the hearts of the Muslims (of eastern Bengal), he could not plant confidence among the Hindus.' And he adds, 'What was needed in Noakhali was not a Hindu leader who was considered by the Muslims as their enemy number one. The need was for a Muslim leader, preferably a member of the Muslim League, who could have spoken to them with religious authority and told them that they had misconceived Islam...But no Muslim leader from outside, whether belonging to the League or the Congress, ever visited Noakhali.'[‡] The veteran observer in Kripalani is spot on.

In Bihar, Hindus had been merciless in their retaliatory attacks on Muslims. Estimates of the number of casualties in Bihar varied then and continue to be inconclusive. The British Parliament was told the death toll stood at 5,000. *The Statesman* put it 'between 7,500 and 10,000', while the Indian National Congress said it was 2,000. Jinnah stated that no less than 30,000 people had been killed.

It is astonishing how the dead become a count in a numbers game. The people killed in cold blood were men, women, and children. They could have been any one of those who were doing the mechanical calculating. But now, they were abstract numbers available for political interpretation. The death toll in Bihar was clearly higher than in Noakhali. The rioting had spread

---

*In Urdu, 'great leader'.

†Description by Krishna R. Kripalani (1907–92), barrister, scholar, aesthete, grandson-in-law, and biographer of Rabindranath Tagore in *Gandhi: A Life* (self-published, 1968), p. 171.

‡Ibid., p. 262.

from Patna to the villages of Bihar. In a village called Bir, Gandhi heard of an old Muslim woman said to be 110 years old having been butchered. He asked 'How could you see this before your eyes...? I will not rest, nor will I let others rest. I will wander all over on foot and ask the skeletons what happened...'[2] He was more effective in Bihar than in Bengal.

Stained at sunrise—Gandhi at the site of communal violence in Bihar, 1947. In a recurring pattern, bodies of those slain were dumped into wells. To Gandhi's left is his grand-niece Manu. To the extreme right, J. J. Singh, a US-based Indian nationalist, behind Gandhi in a collared shirt, Yusuf Dadoo, an Indian freedom and anti-apartheid activist in South Africa. Wearing a cap, next to Dadoo, G. M. Naicker, another prominent activist from South Africa. Dadoo and Naicker were on a visit to attend the Asian Relations Conference, New Delhi. Kinnari Bhatt, senior and irreplaceable archivist, Sabarmati Ashram, in a communication to the author, says: 'Date: 27-3-1947, Place: Jahanabad or [one of the seven] villages MKG visited on that day. All the images of the Bihar tour were taken by the late Shri Jagan Mehta [and] are in the album prepared by Czech photographer Jan Baros.'

With Nehru, then head of India's interim government, working overtime (and 'overhead' as well, as when in righteous rage, he rashly contemplated air-bombing Bihar's rioters), and Patel, his second-in-command, and Rajendra Prasad (1884–1963),[*] assisting, Gandhi's hands were stronger here than in Muslim League-controlled Bengal. And he had the hugely popular young socialist Jayaprakash Narayan[†] to lean on. Another priceless 'resource' beside him was Khan Abdul Ghaffar Khan or Badshah Khan (1890–1988)[‡] as he was called (as also 'Frontier Gandhi'), leader of the Pashtun in India's north-west and a passionate believer in two goals: Hindu–Muslim unity and an honourable 'settlement' for the Pashtuns in any arrangement for post-Independence India. And more than all this, he had an unalterable faith in the efficacy of non-violence.

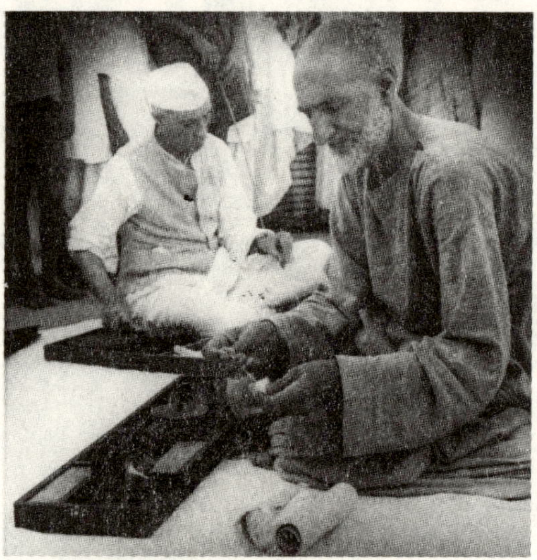

Threads of liberty–Jawaharlal Nehru and Khan Abdul Ghaffar Khan, spinning khadi yarn on Gandhi's birthday, 1947 at Bhangi Colony, New Delhi. (Devadas Gandhi personal archives).

---

[*]Gandhi first met this lawyer, journalist, and scholar in Patna in 1917 and, beginning with the Champaran satyagraha that year, he enlisted him as a lifelong associate. While Prasad's stints as Congress president in 1934–35 and 1939, president of the Constituent Assembly of India (1946–49), and the first president of India (1950–62) are the formal landmarks of his career, it is his incredible work for the relief of victims of the Bihar earthquake of 1934, outshining that of the British authorities, that must be regarded as his crowning moment.

[†]JP was imprisoned for six years (1932–34 and 1940–42) in British India's jails.

[‡]The one of a kind leader of the Pashtun in undivided India's North-west Frontier Province, later incorporated in Pakistan, was thrown clamped in jail by the British for twelve years and by Pakistan for fifteen. The founder of the Khudai Khidmatgar (Servants of God) and passionate striver for Hindu–Muslim concord is an ideological twin to Gandhi and a staggering alternative to fellow Pashtun Mullah Omar (1960–2013) of Kandahar, the fanatical Taliban leader and host, in Afghanistan, to Osama bin Laden (1957–2011).

Life gives its life-threatening diseases, the relief of remissions.

At the same time as men in Bihar and Bengal were still out bullying, knifing, clobbering, and raping, Delhi, no stranger to such behaviour itself, was the site and stage for a ceremony, at one level, of pure grace and at another, of incredible out-of-placeness.

An altogether benign and comely pageant called the Asian Relations Conference, hosted by Nehru, described as the 'author, architect and presiding genius' of the conference,* was taking place in the national capital. Such a spectacle had never been seen before in the city, at least not since the last Delhi Durbar of 1911 in honour of the British sovereign King George V. Delegates to the conference came from almost all Asian countries as did, significantly, representatives of independence movements and their opposite numbers, notably a Tibetan delegation which irritated the Chinese to no end. And there were observers from Great Britain, the US, Australia, and the United Nations.

Nehru being Nehru, he could fume and flare over the violence in Bengal and Bihar and, with no more than a blink, let his natural penchant for international affairs unfurl enchantingly. To hand, bolstering his charm and ebullience, were his sister Vijaya Lakshmi Pandit (1900–90) and his daughter Indira Nehru Gandhi (1917–84), draped appropriately for the occasion, not in coarse homespun, but in the finest silk. And offering a contrast, bringing the dust of riot-shaken Bihar to the proceedings with them, came JP with his astute and austere khadi-clad wife, Prabhavati (1906–73). A beaming Nehru was everywhere, welcoming the delegates, checking on their comfort (having arranged for them to stay with some of Delhi's aristocrats in their sumptuous homes), soothing Chinese nerves about Tibet, Tibetan egos about China, inviting all the delegates and the vicereine, Lady Edwina Mountbatten (1901–60) and her daughter, to his 17 York Road home to see artists from Seraikella present a very precious masque dance form, Chhau, squatting square-legged on the ground at the event when the sofas in the front row ran out of space.

His biggest achievement at the conference was, of course, delivering Gandhi to the delegates.

Gandhi did not have his heart in the conference, and were it not for the coincidence of Mountbatten's arrival and the invitation to come and meet him, Gandhi may not have broken his stay in Bihar to travel to Delhi.

Before arriving at the 400-year-old Purana Qila venue of the conference, Gandhi went to the twenty-year-young 'Naya Qila' (my phrase), or Government House, of stately grandeur with its 340 rooms over four

---

*The Asian Relations Conference, J. A. McCallum, *Australian Quarterly* Vol. 19, No. 2 (June 1947), published by the Australian Institute of Policy and Science.

floors connected by corridors 2.5 kilometres long, for his first meeting with Lord Louis Mountbatten (1900–79). The viceroy's press secretary Alan Campbell-Johnson (1913–98) had called in 'every accredited cameraman in the subcontinent to wait in the Mughal Gardens outside the viceroy's study for the moment'. Of the many photographs of Gandhi with the Mountbattens taken by the battery of lensmen vying for the best shot, one stood out. Campbell-Johnson describes it like this: 'Max Desfor,[*] the brilliant Associated Press of America photographer...waited until the frenzied scramble for the posed shots was over, and then, with the perception of an artist, saw that Gandhi, on turning to go back into the cool study, had placed his hand on Lady Mountbatten's shoulder. The picture was his.'

The meeting was of a preliminary nature, the two men trying to get to know and understand each other. It lasted over two hours. They decided to meet again the next day.

Moving from the Viceregal Lodge to the venue of the conference, where 230 delegates from nations as far flung as Afghanistan and Vietnam were waiting for him, Gandhi spoke with utter frankness and no hiding of India's reality—poverty, the misery of Bhangis[†] and, of course, the 'carnage that is going on before our very eyes'. Calling it 'a shameful thing', he asked the delegates 'not to carry (it) beyond the confines of India'.

Nicholas Mansergh,[‡] the historian, was an observer at the conference representing Chatham House.[§] In a confidential note submitted by him to His Majesty's Government, the scholar included some striking cameos, including one of the irascible but irresistibly engaging friend of Nehru's, the left-leaning future defence minister of India, V. K. Krishna Menon: 'Of the Indian delegation, Mrs Pandit and Krishna Menon were prominent. Of Menon, rumours were always circulating. One day, he was reputed to be in high favour with Pandit Nehru; the next, he was said to be in disgrace. In disposing of the idea of an Asian bloc, he played a decisive part. He had intervened, he told me afterwards with some satisfaction, to keep the Conference from "going off the rails". But the outstanding personality, not only in the Indian

[*]Max Desfor (1913–2018), who also took a famous photograph of Gandhi and Nehru, both seated and beaming, was to later get a Pulitzer Prize for a photograph by him of people escaping from communist forces across a blasted bridge in Korea.

[†]Sweepers, belonging to the Depressed Classes, as they were then called.

[‡]Philip Nicholas Seton Mansergh (1910–91), British historian with a focus on the Commonwealth, assembling and editing the 'monumental' 12-volume edition of historical documents associated with the independence of India.

[§]The Royal Institute of International Affairs, commonly known as Chatham House, is a British think tank based in London.

delegation but in the Conference as a whole, was Pandit Nehru. None could fail to be flattered by the time he devoted to its deliberations. He was present not only in the Plenary Sessions but also at many of the discussion Groups. He lunched at Constitution House. He personally showed delegates around the Constituent Assembly. The more cynical might talk of "Nehru fiddling while India burned", but among delegates as a whole, his already high reputation was enhanced.'[3]

If Gandhi was feted at the conference venue by Asia's good and great, he had a very contrary experience where he was staying, Bhangi Colony, the set of tenements occupied by a section of New Delhi's sweepers not far from where the viceroy resided. In keeping with the routine of his evening prayer gatherings, on 1 April, he joined an assemblage of people beside a shrine. As soon as Manu Gandhi began with the recitations from the Quran, a young man stood up, came right up to where Gandhi was seated and said, 'We will not allow the Quran to be read in our Hindu temple.' Members of the congregation pulled him back and took him away. 'My *ahimsa* will be tested here,' Gandhi said to Manu.[4]

The Mountbatten–Gandhi meeting the following day was of extraordinary importance and led to what may be called an extraordinary nothing. Gandhi made an astonishing proposal to the viceroy: Dismiss the present interim government and call the Muslim League leader and principal advocate for Pakistan, Muhammad Ali Jinnah, to form an all-Muslim government for the whole of India. Expecting the unexpected from Gandhi was normal, but this was beyond the unexpected. If only Desfor had been around to catch a viceregal jaw drop! One can only imagine the viceroy recovering from the shock before he asked, 'What will Jinnah's reaction be?' Gandhi, with his reflexes sharp as ever, plus a spoonful of wit, replied that Jinnah would say, 'Ah, it is the wily Gandhi again.' Mountbatten then asked, 'And won't he be right?' Gandhi said, 'No, I am being absolutely sincere.'

If Gandhi's suggestion was audacious, what he said in continuation was presumptuous. He said he would persuade Congress to agree. Connected to his confidence in this was his concomitant suggestion that if Jinnah declined, Mountbatten should ask Congress to form the same kind of government. Mountbatten did not throw the suggestion out of his study's windows to wither under the sun over the Mughal Gardens. He could not have done that. Gandhi was Gandhi, India's strongest leader. But the viceroy did not have to live with this troublesome démarche for long. Nehru and Patel both opposed it. The Congress's leadership did not take any time to fall in line with the two leaders. And Jinnah would have none of it. He smelt in it, not one but a whole plague of rats. Gandhi wrote to Mountbatten shortly thereafter that his plan was unacceptable to Congress and that he had left all further negotiations to the Congress Working Committee.

A moral dividend, no less, had been proposed by Gandhi for the peace and contentment of the subcontinent, and it was squandered by the lesser politics of the time. Hindu extremists' violent school would, it is very likely, have concluded that Gandhi has brought Mughal Rule back via the Mughal Gardens and decided in the logic of its ideology to punish him by death. So? Kripalani tells us, does he not, that Gandhi was ready, keen, for that 'punishment', anyhow. And he was walking, striding, singular and strong, to his Cross anyway.

Towards the end of May 1946, Margaret Bourke-White (1904–71), the forty-two-year-old photojournalist and celebrity, came to Delhi representing *Life* magazine. She photographed Gandhi, famously, at his spinning wheel, Jinnah and Nehru less so but, with her skill with camera shutters at its best, and also many scenes of Delhi in transition. The one she got of Gandhi at his charkha has become iconic, giving us Gandhi as Gandhi then was—at peace and intensely worried. Holding something of the uncertainty of the times and also serene. But it was the pictures Bourke-White took of the horrors of Partition, the mass exodus, that gave her photography of India immortality. One shot of a group inside a train has a small girl, no older than five or six, hunched on a berth, with an expression that could speak for India. She is not afraid; she is not unafraid. She is just a question mark. Bourke-White caught in her camera the interrogation mark that hung over India.

B. R. Ambedkar (1891–1956), who had earlier been elected to the Constituent Assembly from Undivided Bengal's Assembly where the Muslim League commanded a majority and re-elected now from Bombay, was, at this point, where destiny had intended this diligent student of personal, constitutional, and international law to be—at the fulcrum of law-making in and for a democratic, secular, egalitarian India, not just independent but free in the widest and deepest sense of the term.

There was little, if any, socializing between my parents and Ambedkar. I do not believe he ever visited us, or my parents, him. They do not seem to have felt anything amiss in this. My father's long-term secretary and senior journalist, R. Chandrachudan (1913–2009), told me he used to see Ambedkar, surrounded by law and history books, sitting in a corner of Milk Bar, directly below the *Hindustan Times* office in Connaught Circus, lost in deep study. No one dared disturb Ambedkar's reading; Ambedkar had no time for tattle. From an intense 'by-himself-ness' arose, ironically and awesomely enough, that political giant's inclusive vision. Even as from being 'surrounded to suffocation' came the Mahatma's 'walk-alone-ness'. As to why

Ambedkar liked this very unsnobbish middle-class eatery over the hush of New Delhi's nascent libraries, I have no means of knowing. Perhaps he just liked the place's coffee and a la carte menu of snacks, on some of which I, too, grew up—chocolate dripping ice cream sundae and oval vegetable cutlets filled to bursting with mashed delights.

Pakistan, now, was not a dream of the Muslim League for Indian nationalists to dread but a date for all of India to ring in red. It was beginning to look inevitable, unavoidable, a 'given' with Jinnah's ferocious focus.

When in Delhi, staying in Bhangi Colony, completely unguarded—thanks to his own stubborn choice—from opponents, hecklers, and worse, Gandhi met scores of visitors there, held his prayer meetings, attended events, and kept up his daily walks. These last were his equivalent of 'family time'. My siblings—Tara or Taru (13) as she was addressed by me, with a 'ben' ('sister' added as a suffix) Mohan (12) and Ramu (10) with me, Gopu (2), as I had begun to be called, joined him on those along with our parents, visiting relatives. There were many others that walked alongside, of course, and we were not special in any sense for him, but we were 'his' and he 'ours' by the accident of birth. Photographers, Bourke-White included, captured those moments of the seventy-eight-year-old 'Father of the Nation' being a plain grandfather. One such photograph by the *Hindustan Times* photographer Baburam Gupta, has me, back to camera, engaging Bapuji in the warbling nonsense grandparents love to hear from their children's children. All my siblings and others can be seen in that photograph, enjoying the rollick in a 'land' dreamily removed from the grim reality of a nation in murderous flux. Everybody is laughing in that picture. I am not sure if it is at me, with me, or about me. But everybody is laughing. Perhaps somewhere in it lurks a nervousness about the present and the future of happiness.

I remember nothing of that photographed moment. Just as well.

Mondays were days of silence for Gandhi. 'He had already begun his weekly 24 hours' silence', writes Pyarelal in *The Last Phase*, 'when Gopu arrived. So, the two had a very animated pantomime talk. Gopu set everybody, including his grandfather, roaring with laughter by mimicking his *Bhaio aur bahno, ap shant ho jaiye* (Brothers and sisters, do please quieten down)—words with which Gandhiji opened his prayer address! And so, the "family physician" had his dose of "physick" at the hands of the little one.'

A *Reuters* report from London on 23 June 1947 describing the forthcoming parliamentary procedure for the enactment of Indian independence spoke of it as a ceremony 'to give Dominion Status to nearly four hundred million people of Hindustan and Pakistan'. It went on to say, 'The Bill creating two nations, inscribed on vellum and parchment, will be drawn from a

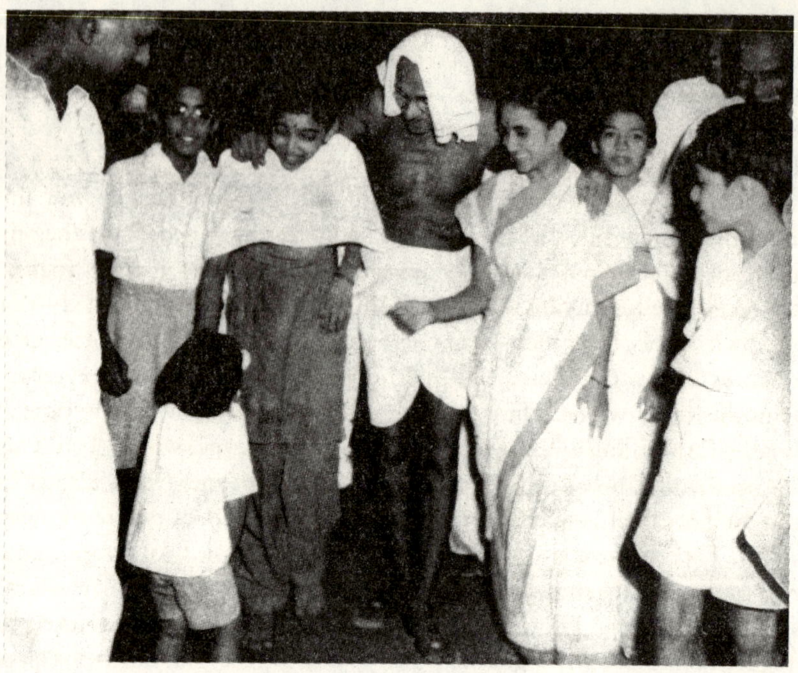

A niche for laughter—in the midst of his pre-Partition agonies, a grandfather with, to his right, grand-daughter Taru, grandson Rajmohan, to his extreme left, grandson Ramchandra and with back to the camera, engaging him, the author then aged two. To Gandhi's left is Praveena, daughter of Devadas and Lakshmi's neighbours, the Pandyas. (Devadas Gandhi personal archives).

magnificent wallet embellished with the Royal Arms in colours and gold thread....' Referring to it in his prayer meeting that evening, Gandhi said: 'The papers today talk of a grand ceremonial to take place in London over the division of India into "two nations" which were only the other day one nation. What is there to gloat over in this tragedy? We have hugged the belief that though we part, we do so as friends. And brothers belonging to one family. Now...the British will make us two nations and that with a flourish of trumpets....'

On 27 June 1947, the Partition Council, formed after Punjab and Bengal had decided to split, met for the first time in the Viceregal Lodge in New Delhi. It decided that there would have to be two Boundary Commissions, one each, for Punjab and Bengal, to draw the lines of the new boundaries. Each commission would have four commissioners, two each representing the two communities, with a common chairman who would have the casting vote.

Jinnah suggested a name: Sir Cyril Radcliffe (1899–1977). Younger than fellow barristers Gandhi (Inner Temple, 1891), Jinnah (Lincoln's Inn, 1896),

Nehru (Inner Temple, 1912), Patel (Middle Temple, 1914), and Ambedkar (Grey's Inn, 1923), the Welsh barrister, Sir Cyril Radcliffe (Inner Temple, 1924), knew his law well; India not at all. And India did not know him either. Except, that is, for Jinnah. No one objected. To Sir Cyril, who 'had never travelled east of Paris', was given the task of giving the two new nations their boundaries with each other.

Gandhi, now truly 'walking alone', very alone, was drawn to Bengal, where he had promised to return so as to get to Noakhali once again, but Bengal's capital city, Calcutta, detained him.

Partition, which had already mutilated the city the previous August after the 'Direct Action Day' pogrom of 16 August 1946, was now sizzling again. And giving the prospect a spectacular intellectual pedestal was a new book by Ambedkar. My father's bookcase had amongst its eclectic volumes *Thoughts on Pakistan*. As a bored child, running my fingers over the spines and covers of those books had been a regular and meaningless rite. I did not know, for years, the value of most of those books, and I was a total stranger to the criticality of this particular book to India's social and political evolution. I had heard vaguely of Ambedkar as a person Bapuji had some difficulties with on the subject of 'Harijans', as the Dalits were then called. Pakistan, of course, I knew of as the country that had been carved out of India to its west and east. Conversations heard by me since infancy on Pakistan, its genesis in Jinnah's supreme stubbornness, his coreligionists' loyalty to him, his deep dislike of Bapuji, and Bapuji's failure to befriend him had permeated my mind like warm ghee on a sponge-soft idli. But by the time I was about ten, I slid that book out of its place on the shelf often and turned its pages to make some meaning out of them. I might as well have been 'reading' the Indus Valley script. The author's use of the term 'Mr Gandhi' seemed odd to me at that time as I had not heard that form of address for Bapuji. The other 'Mr' in the book also seemed to me to be a strange title for the person I, as a child, had occasionally heard spoken of by elders at home by just his surname, Savarkar (1883–1966), along with those of two others—Godse (1910–49), and Apte (1911–49)—the two convicted for Bapuji's assassination.

But in another year or two, the book's import gleamed through the somewhat amateurishly printed fonts of that first (1940) edition. The following words of Ambedkar struck me as being an astonishingly lucid and elucidating formulation:

> Strange as it may appear, Mr Savarkar and Mr Jinnah, instead of being opposed to each other on the one nation versus two nations issue, are in complete agreement about it. Both agree, not only agree

> but insist, that there are two nations in India—one the Muslim nation and the other the Hindu nation. They differ only as regards the terms and conditions on which the two nations should live. Mr Jinnah says India should be cut up into two, Pakistan and Hindustan, the Muslim nation to occupy Pakistan and the Hindu nation to occupy Hindustan. Mr Savarkar, on the other hand, insists that, although there are two nations in India, India shall not be divided into two parts, one for Muslims and the other for the Hindus; that the two nations shall dwell in one country and shall live under the mantle of one single constitution....

I have not come across a more lucid riposte to the majoritarian vision of a Hindu Rashtra than Ambedkar's in this book:

> Suffice it to say that the scheme of Swaraj formulated by Mr Savarkar will give the Hindus an empire over the Muslims and thereby satisfy their vanity and their pride in being an imperial race. But it can never ensure a stable and peaceful future for the Hindus, for the simple reason that the Muslims will never yield willing obedience to so dreadful an alternative.

Steps towards a transfer of power were now, suddenly, being hurried, rushed breathlessly against a deadline that was, literally, to become a line of the dead. Fear of bloody mayhem becoming bloodier, Britain's boast of having kept India's governed in balanced order was now about to explode.

Independence was coming to India in a conflagration of furies. If *Life* sent Bourke-White to capture the birth or—as *Life*'s masters reckoned, the stillbirth—of the two nations, the British Broadcasting Corporation (BBC) sent the poet and playwright Louis MacNeice (1907–63), who had been on the BBC's senior staff, perhaps its most famous and influential member, to report on it. MacNeice, Irish and as independent as anyone can be, had written an eight-stanza poem in free verse at the height of World War II, entitled 'Prayer Before Birth'. Anyone reading it at the time MacNeice came to India would have said MacNeice wrote it for the two countries about to be born. Its opening two stanzas went:

> I am not yet born; O hear me.
> Let not the bloodsucking bat or the rat or the stoat or the
> club-footed ghoul come near me.
>
> I am not yet born, console me.
> I fear that the human race may with tall walls wall me,

with strong drugs dope me, with wise lies lure me,
on black racks rack me, in blood-baths roll me.[5]

Radcliffe, who arrived in Delhi on 8 July 1947, was given five weeks to complete his mission, the cutting up of India on its western and eastern flanks on the basis of religion. His eight colleagues on the two commissions (four of them on each, two Hindu and two Muslim) spoke as they were only expected to do from their perspectives. Radcliffe decided on most points himself, using his casting vote. MacNeice might not have met him, but MacNeice's guru in poetry, W. H. Auden (1907–73), mocked the entire exercise in a shatteringly hard poem that lampooned Radcliffe for doing what he did and then exiting on the very day the countries were born.

Rajaji, in his elliptical but fascinating diary maintained for much of this period, has the following entry for Friday, 25 July 1947:

Terribly overworked. Having Finance in addition to Industries since Monday.... New Governors names settled after long consultations these many days. Not a bright list. New members of Cabinet not yet settled. Not likely to be a bright list either....

The governorship of the about-to-be-created state of West Bengal was crucial. Deputy Prime Minister Sardar Vallabhbhai Patel first thought of fellow Gujarati, nationalist and litterateur K. M. Munshi (1887–1971) for the position. Gandhi was consulted. 'No,' he responded. 'Munshi's reputation of being unsympathetic to Muslims disqualifies him.' Rajaji, who was consulted, then suggested the distinguished Madras civilian Sir N. Gopalaswami Ayyangar, who had made a name for himself on the Drafting Committee of the Constituent Assembly. Nehru and Patel both agreed with Rajaji on that name. And, more to the point, Gandhi, who was also asked, said Gopalaswami would fit the bill. But Sir N. G. cited domestic reasons and declined. Patel then said to Rajaji: 'You should handle Bengal. You are one of the few who can.' And he said to Rajaji that he had consulted Gandhi and Nehru, who had both agreed on Rajaji's name. Most significantly, Patel added that Prafulla Ghosh (1891–1983) wanted him. The Gandhian bachelor, an admirer of Rajaji, was going to be the new state's first chief minister.

Rajaji wrote in his diary on Tuesday, 29 July:

The proposal for West Bengal Governorship has not been accepted by Gopalaswami Ayyangar. So, they asked me to take it up! What do I care what post they want me to take? So I said, yes. Nobody likes it. But it is just the beauty of Karma Yoga!

And yet, before leaving for Calcutta, he spoke to Nehru about his apprehensions. 'Don't be silly, Rajaji,' was the immediate reply. 'You can handle any job in this country.'

Chaudhry Khaliquzzaman (1889–1973), the prominent Muslim League leader, was to write in his memoirs *Pathway to Pakistan*: 'The two-nation theory, which we had used in the fight for Pakistan, had created not only bad blood against the Muslims of the minority provinces but also an ideological wedge between them and the Hindus of India.'[6] And in a very revealing narration, tells us of how Partition was going to play havoc with the lives of those Muslims who will choose to stay in India and the Hindus who will choose to not leave their homes in what was becoming Pakistan. In Khaliquzzaman's words:

> Mr Jinnah himself realised the grave dangers to Muslims who after the partition were to be left in India. I remember that on 1 August 1947, a few days before his final departure for Karachi, Mr Jinnah called the Muslim members of the Constituent Assembly of India to his house at 10 Aurangzeb Road to bid farewell to them. Mr Rizwanullah* put some awkward questions concerning the position of Muslims, who would be left over in India, their status, and their future. I had never before found Mr Jinnah so disconcerted as on that occasion, probably because he was realizing then quite vividly what was immediately in store for the Muslims. Finding the situation awkward, I asked my friends and colleagues to end the discussion.

Gandhi, housed then in a privately-owned building not without grace but in utter disrepair—Hydari Manzil, in the Muslim quarter of Beliaghata in Calcutta—was to experience joy and pain, happiness and agony plaited together, inextricably, at that hour as India became free and—divided. He was also to know and feel danger. He wrote on 13 August from Hydari Manzil to Sardar Patel, then in charge of Home Affairs: 'I...am now going to undertake a grave risk. Suhrawardy and I are going from today to stay together in a Muslim quarter. The future will reveal itself. Keep a close watch.'[7] Those four words are chilling.

The midnight of 14 and 15 August was a moment of rejoicing at the birth of independent India and a day of sorrow over the death of undivided India. Massive shifts of people having occurred in both directions—Muslims moving to the two wings of the new Pakistan and Hindus moving from

*S. M. Rizwanullah, general secretary of the UP Muslim League and member of the Constituent Assembly of India.

those into India—the air was choked with dispossession, deprivation, disease, and death.

That broad description to summarize the scene on Independence Day—rejoicing and sorrowing—is Gandhi's. He used those words right outside Hydari Manzil on the previous evening. By his choice of fellow resident in Suhrawardy, held by many as responsible for the Great Calcutta Killing that followed Direct Action Day the previous year, Gandhi was inviting grave risk to himself if also providing some safety for the controversial Muslim League leader. A seventy-eight-year-old unarmed man was sheltering the outgoing premier of Bengal in his own city. An estimated 10,000 people had gathered outside the house for a meeting on that eve, which was, in Gandhi's way of doing things, styled a prayer meeting. It being the month of Ramzan, there was a felicity to the prayer-nature of the meeting. The largely Hindu congregation heard Gandhi in silence. He spoke of the heavy burden of responsibility that was coming upon us. 'Let all those Muslims who were forced to flee return to their homes,' he said. 'If the flames of communal strife envelop the whole country, how can our new-born freedom survive?' he asked. We have this record of the talk in English as given by Pyarelal in his work—*Mahatma Gandhi: The Last Phase.* But Gandhi spoke then in Hindi, his Hindi—utterly simple, utterly true. As he spoke, a shout was heard: 'Where is Suhrawardy?' Gandhi said 'He is inside the house. He has, with my consent, kept himself away from the meeting as he wanted to avoid giving the slightest cause for irritation. But in view of the tolerance which you have shown today, I shall be encouraged to bring him to the meeting tomorrow onwards.' The scene could be from Shakespeare's *Julius Caesar*. The shout came back, stronger: 'Where is Suhrawardy?' Gandhi then gave a more detailed answer. Suhrawardy, he said, was inside engaged in ending his Ramzan fast and would appear before them presently. The future premier of Pakistan appeared after a moment, records Pyarelal, came to Gandhi's side and stood in full view of the crowd. Gandhi placed his hand on Suhrawardy's shoulder. Suhrawardy then said: 'It is Bengal's great good luck that Mahatmaji is in our midst at this hour....' We can be sure he said this in Bangla...something like...'aamaader modhye...ei muhurte...' Calcutta may love literary fluencies but it can also bring someone quickly to the point. Came the question, like a missile: 'Are you not responsible for the Great Calcutta killing?'

Suhrawardy: 'Yes, we all are.'

The questioner: 'Will you answer my question, please?'

Suhrawardy: 'Yes, it was my responsibility.'

This owning of responsibility had an effect on the gathering. 'It was the turning point,' Gandhi later remarked. 'It had a cleansing effect. I could sense it.' Responsibility. Accountability. Answerability. These are rare virtues.

Reaching Calcutta at just this point from Delhi, Rajaji wrote in his diary for 14 August: *Arrived at Dum Dum aerodrome at 1.15 Bengal time on 14th. Met by Sir Frederick Burrows and others. First sign of want of proper control. Crowds rushing in.... Thorough disorder unlike what it should be....*

Lord Mountbatten, who had been asked by the Congress leadership and would be requested by the Constituent Assembly to be the first governor general of India, was present at Jinnah's installation in Karachi on 14 August and flew back that evening to be at hand for his own, in Delhi. On that return flight, he and his entourage, which included Lady Mountbatten, could see several large fires which his press secretary Alan Campbell-Johnson was to describe later as 'beacons of ill-omen'.[8]

15 August 1947 saw Nehru as, finally and formally, India's prime minister.

In our Delhi home, the day the family had for years been taught to regard as our people's greatest goal, came tiptoeing. My brother Mohan remembers listening to the midnight chimes on the radio and the start of the historic and lyrical proceedings in the Central Hall of what was going to become India's Parliament House. Both Gandhi and Rajaji being in Calcutta on that day, the family's mind was tuned into events in that city rather than the historic ones marking the great transition in Delhi.

But even to a boy like Mohan—he was eight then—in the middle of that August, the wails of Partition's victims seemed stronger than the cheers for Independence.

In the Tamil country, the day saw a chiaroscuro of another kind. The non-Brahmin sentiment of the Justice Party, Congress's principal alternative, had turned some three years earlier at the party's conference in Salem into the Dravidar Kazhagam. With self-respect as its watchword and opposition to Brahmin domination in all spheres as its creed, the movement had been stigmatized as Raj-loyalist. Its leading light, E. V. Ramasamy (1879–1973), soon to be hailed as Periyar (the Elder), was clear in his mind that the imminence of Independence would only mean a perpetuation of Brahmin-domination through the coming into power of the Brahmin-dominated Congress and the emergence of the Brahmin-dominated Communist Party. He announced that 15 August would be declared by the Dravidar Kazhagam as a Day of Mourning. Periyar's lieutenant and future chief minister, the charismatic and articulate C. N. Annadurai (1909–69), differed. He sensed that whatever be the appeal of the non-Brahmin narrative among the people of Tamil Nadu, that of the dawn of freedom was irresistible.[9] He withheld support to Periyar's mourning call and said of the two enemies—the Brahmin and the British—there was now one less.

Rajaji's swearing-in happened at the dark hour of 1 a.m. on 15 August. Seeing the last British governor of Bengal and Lady Burrows off earlier in the morning, at 8 a.m., he unfurled the nation's flag, going up for the first time at the Government House lawns. He diarized: *Government House halls and corridors filled with friendly mobs and darshan-takers. A few thieves took advantage of the situation and stole and threw about things. The House and grounds had to be cleared with difficulty.*

The coming days were to see what Gandhi feared.

MacNeice, covering events for the BBC, saw barbarism of a kind he had not, could not have, ever thought possible—from both sides of the divide, with the Sikhs of vivisected Punjab not lagging behind. The bat, the rat, the stoat, and the ghoul were all out. As were flies buzzing around the sores of those mutilated, maimed, and killed. The screams of women and girls, Hindu, Muslim, and Sikh, were not heard by men who belonged to the faiths mentioned but in name. They were monsters. Let this be noted. No Hindu or Muslim raped. The ghoul in man did. And that ghoul is real. He seems as remorseless as he is deathless. Let no patriotism deny this: from the raped thousands of Partition, through the agony of nurse Aruna Shanbaug raped in Bombay in 1973, Nirbhaya raped in Delhi in 2012, to the medical intern raped in Kolkata in 2024, the hideous truth is that India's male population, decent and God-fearing in the main, has amongst it humanity's worst specimens of licentious beasts with the vilest claws and teeth known to creation. No sage's sermon, no hangman's rope stops him.

Who or what was responsible for the carnage and rapacity that took place in the months around India's freedom? Partition was. It was the vivisection of India that brought the beast out.

Gandhi, with Khan Abdul Ghaffar Khan alone among the others, said he was opposed to Partition and that if it were to come because the two principal parties had agreed to it, it would be over his dead body. And when it came, Jinnah was elated and—incredulous.

Rajaji went to Gandhi in his Beliaghata camp in Calcutta on 16 August. He was sensible of the peace that was then palpable in Calcutta and saw in this a miracle, as he was to describe it, of Gandhi's creation. As Manu records, this was the first time any governor was calling on Gandhi. As he would have done in Sabarmati or Sevagram, Rajaji removed his slippers at the entrance to the house and walked barefoot through the dusty frontage to the room where Gandhi was seated. 'It was their first meeting in free India,' writes Rajmohan Gandhi in his biography of Rajaji. 'The Mahatma was feeling the pain of fratricide, not the thrill of freedom. C. R. took

Gandhi's hands and held them, neither saying a word. Then they talked of possible riots and refugees.'[10]

'Riots and refugees' could be the caption for India, 1947.

Calcutta saw riots breaking out on 31 August, just a fortnight after the celebrations of harmony and freedom. A riotous mob came to his Beliaghata camp looking for Suhrawardy, hurling bricks at the house and nearly hitting him. 'Kill me, kill me,' Gandhi said to the men, shielding Suhrawardy without exculpating his roguish complicity in Calcutta's bloodbath of the previous year. Rajaji diarizes on 1 September: *Flare-up in Calcutta of murder and murderous assault and some looting. Bapu attacked by Hindu fanatic group and disturbed by the incidents of that day*. Gandhi, unsurprisingly, announced an indefinite fast. Prafulla babu was shaken. Rajaji, motoring to Hydari Manzil, asked Gandhi if fasting against goondas would have any effect. He was known for his icy logic and cutting humour. And this time, it cut deep—both Gandhi and him. Gandhi had, as was his practice in fasts, planned to add drops of sour limes or salts to his water. When responding to Rajaji's appeal to not fast, Gandhi said he had left his fate wholly in God's hands. Rajaji said, 'Why the provision then for sour lime?' He had spoken too soon, too sharp. Gandhi promptly said the provision was a sign of weakness and removed it. We can imagine the blade that must have cut through Rajaji's mind accompanied by the Tamil expression: 'Ayyo!'

The governor's diary entry four days later says: *Went round the city. No incidents.... Inspite of Acharya Kripalani got Bapu to end his fast.*

He then drafted the undertaking that two leaders of Bengal's Hindu Mahasabha, a Muslim, a Punjabi Hindu, and a Sikh signed, upon which Gandhi was persuaded to accept a glass of sweet lime from the hands of Suhrawardy. Most significantly, the Hindu Mahasabha leader Syama Prasad Mookerjee (1901–53) came and personally and most responsibly promised Gandhi that his people would go around the city to establish peace.

Gandhi's fast changed the scene dramatically. Without it, order would have taken much longer to be restored. But the governor's no-nonsense directives, with which the premier was in complete accord, played their part. Gandhi melted hearts; Rajaji, with Prafulla babu at his side, and the army and police on the qui vive held the iron ropes around the cauldron where the meltdown happened.

Gandhi, back in riot-scarred Delhi, did something on 16 September 1947 that was unexpected even by his high record of unpredictability. He addressed 500 members of the Rashtriya Swayamsevak Sangh (RSS) in his Bhangi Colony camp. Devadas had the event reported prominently in the *Hindustan Times* the following morning in an item captioned 'Gandhiji's

Advice to Sangh Volunteers' and a sub-caption 'Pakistan Cautioned Against Persistent Wrong-Doing'. It was a balancing act for Gandhi, but he did the rope-walk adroitly and—to his conscience's credit—honestly. He said, speaking in Hindustani, that he had met the RSS's Guruji a few days earlier and mentioned to him the complaints against the organization that he had heard in Calcutta and Delhi. He then told his RSS audience what the RSS chief had told him, which was a plain and clear enunciation of his position: 1. The policy of the Sangh is service to Hindus and Hinduism, but not at the cost of anyone else. 2. The Sangh taught self-defence, not retaliation. 3. But he could not vouchsafe the correct behaviour of every member of the Sangh.

The RSS congregation that Gandhi addressed had followed his meeting with the Guruji. He spoke his mind frankly. He said if Hindus believed that Muslims could live in India only as slaves of Hindus, they would kill Hinduism. Similarly, if in Pakistan, the Muslims believed that only they had a rightful place there and non-Muslims could live there only on sufferance and as slaves of the Muslims, then it would be the death knell of Islam in India. It was an unfortunate fact, he said, that India had been divided into two parts, but 'If one part went mad and did ugly deeds, was the other part to follow suit?' And he went on to say something that was vital—diplomatically, politically, civilizationally. He said: 'If Pakistan persisted in wrong-doing, there was bound to be war between India and Pakistan.'[11]

A little over a month later, war broke out over Kashmir, and the Hindu maharaja of Jammu and Kashmir, Hari Singh, facing an uprising by his Muslim subjects in Poonch, lost control of the western districts of his kingdom. On 22 October 1947, Pakistan's Pashtun tribal militias crossed the border of the state.

Margaret Bourke-White was in Pakistan at the time. Its creator and his sister were on cloud nine. 'We never expected to get it in our lifetimes,' Jinnah's sister Fatima (1893–1967), at the time the First Lady of Pakistan (the Quaid-e-Azam being a widower), told Bourke-White in Karachi, as recorded by her in her remarkable memoir, *Halfway to Freedom*. The lenswoman's studies of Jinnah in the hush of his opulent sitting room show him dressed to perfection in a suit that has been ironed to the smoothness of virgin snow, necktie in Euclidean balance, hair groomed to blade-sharp evenness and shoes—a pair of Oxford full brogue spectator shoes—polished to a gleam. They reveal the man's finickiness and, beneath that, a certain insecurity. Jinnah has to appear unflawed. 'If Fatima's reaction was a glow of family pride,' Bourke-White writes, 'her brother's was a fever of ecstasy.' The American photographer was a psychoanalyst as well. 'Jinnah's deep-sunk eyes,' she writes, 'were pinpoints of excitement. His whole manner indicated that an almost over-whelming exaltation was racing through his veins.' When Bourke-

White said some words of courteous felicitation on his 'creating the world's largest Islamic nation', the Governor General said, 'Oh, it's not just the largest Islamic nation. Pakistan is the fifth-largest nation in the world!'[12]

And she was still in the new nation when Kashmir saw what it had not seen before: an invasion. Her immediate reaction was to try to get to the scene of action. Don't! she was advised. Tribesmen are known to abduct women. 'Hordes of fanatical Muslim tribesmen,' she writes, 'were pouring in from Pakistan, killing, looting, and burning villages. A startling sweep, which took the whole Kashmiri Valley by surprise, carried the raiders to the outskirts of Srinagar, the capital.'[13] Then she describes as only a photographer could, in words, the story of a martyr to Hindu–Muslim unity who should rank among the greatest victims of bigotry and the greatest symbols of human courage. Bourke-White on Maqbool Sherwani (1928–47):

> [At] Baramulla, the townspeople told me of a young Muslim shopkeeper who had sacrificed his life rather than recant in his creed of religious tolerance. His martyrdom had taken place almost under the shadow of the convent walls, and in the memory of the devoted Kashmiris, he was fast assuming the stature of a saint. Mir Maqbool Sherwani had been a co-worker of Sheikh Abdullah in the democratic movement, and like Abdullah, he had preached the need for religious unity in the fight for people's rights...When the tribesmen invaded Kashmir and terrorized the countryside, Sherwani, who knew every footpath in the Valley, began working behind the lines, keeping up the morale of the besieged villagers, urging them to resist and to stick together regardless of whether they were Hindu, Sikh, or Muslim, assuring them that help from the Indian Army and People's Militia was on the way. Three times, by skilfully planted rumours, he decoyed bands of tribesmen and got them surrounded and captured by Indian infantry. But the fourth time, he was captured himself. The tribesmen took Sherwani to the stoop of a little apple shop in the town square of Baramulla, and the terrified townspeople were driven into the square in front of him with the butts of rifles. Knowing Sherwani's popularity with the people, his captors ordered him to make a public announcement that joining Pakistan was the best solution for Muslims. When he refused, he was lashed to the porch posts with ropes, his arms spread out in the shape of a cross, and he was told he must shout, 'Pakistan Zindabad: Sher-i-Kashmir murdabad.' It was a curious thing that the tribesmen did next. I don't know why these savage nomads should have thought of

> such a thing unless their sight of the sacred figures in St. Joseph's Chapel on the hill just above had suggested it to them. They drove nails through the palms of Sherwani's hands. On his forehead, they pressed a jagged piece of tin and wrote on it: 'The punishment of a traitor is death.' Once more, Sherwani cried out, 'Victory to Hindu-Muslim unity,' and fourteen tribesmen shot bullets into his body.

Gandhi's diligent biographer Pyarelal writes in *The Last Phase*, 'But within 48 hours of the cold-blooded murder, his dying prophecy was fulfilled, and the raiders were driven out of Baramulla with the Indian troops in hot pursuit.' Gandhi described Sherwani's death as 'a martyrdom of which anyone—Hindu, Sikh, Muslim or any other can be proud.'

Some three months later, Margaret Bourke-White was back in Karachi to resume her reportage. It was a very different Karachi, a different Pakistan, and a different Jinnah that she saw. Bourke-White writes in *Halfway to Freedom*:

> Jinnah's Olympian assurance had strangely withered. His altered condition was not made public. 'The Quaid-I-Azam has a bad cold' was the answer given to inquiries. Only those closest to him knew that the 'cold' was accompanied by paralyzing inability to make even the smallest decisions, by sullen silences striped with outbursts of irritation, by a spiritual numbness concealing something close to panic underneath; I knew it only because I spent most of this trying period at Government House, attempting to take a new portrait of Jinnah for a *Life* cover.... I was shocked at Jinnah's changed appearance—the unsteady step, listless eyes, the white-knuckled, nervously clenched hands. As I went ahead with my pictures, Miss Fatima, with sisterly solicitude, slipped up before each shot and tried gently to uncurl the desperately clenched hands.

The perceptive observer of human nature in the photographer was a political analyst as well. 'I think that the tortured appearance of Mr Jinnah,' she continues, 'was an indication that, in these final months of his life, he was adding up his own balance sheet. Analytical, brilliant, and no bigot, he knew what he had done. Like Doctor Faustus, he had made a bargain from which he could never be free.'

Gandhi was staying this time not in Bhangi Colony but in Birla House, his trusted associate G. D. Birla's manorial house on Albuquerque Road, a shout away from the house on Aurangzeb Road that Jinnah had vacated. The national capital and surrounding areas were engulfed in massacres and spewing of hatred.

In this poisoned atmosphere, there came, briefly but redemptively, a whiff of the purest air in the form of a singer. Madurai Shanmukhavadivu Subbulakshmi (1916–2004) had sung in Gandhi's presence some years earlier—in 1941 in Sevagram—and Gandhi had known of her fund-raising for the Kasturba Gandhi Memorial Trust. But this was her first 'public' appearance in a Gandhi gathering. On 6 December 1947, the then thirty-one-year-old, with her husband Sadasivam and his daughter by an earlier marriage, Radha, met Gandhi in his room. 'Bapu is busy and may not be able to talk to you,' they were told. 'But,' they added, 'you can sing.' So, sing she did, a composition on Krishna 'Ghanashyam aya re' (There comes Ghanashyam), from the film *Meera* that had made her a star. Radha danced to the song in a corner of the room, and as she did so, Gandhi stopped reading and watched and heard them attentively. MS then attended the evening prayer meeting in the lawns of Birla House. As the concluding 'Raghupati Raghav Raja Ram' was to be sung, Gandhi turned to Manu, who was about to start the prayer-song and said 'Manu, chup…Subbulakshmi ab tum gao…tum shuru karo (Manu, halt…Subbulakshmi, now you sing…'), upon which she did.

Prime Minister Nehru and Lady Mountbatten after the New Delhi premiere of *Meera*. Between Nehru and MS, in the background, the author's sister Taru. (Author's personal collection).

Gandhi had no ear for classical music, but he did for music's essence, which is lyric rapture. MS was already renowned as a singer in the best classical—Carnatic—tradition as also in the more popular zone of devotional music in more than one language. In giving her the stage that evening, Gandhi was being prescient and purposive. MS was to be a unifier, an amalgamator of India's cultures without a shred of the superior or the lofty in her. She was, like Gandhi, Hindu. Not *a* Hindu.

Gandhi had a certain regard for decorations and titles, having been awarded two, which he had famously returned. And so, something in him would have approved the fact—had he had a prescience of it—that MS would receive the highest civilian order of independent India—the Bharat Ratna—some five decades later, the first musician to do so. And that the first Param Vir Chakra (PVC), India's highest military decoration, awarded for displaying distinguished acts of valour during wartime, would go to Major Somnath Sharma (1923–47) for his unparalleled gallantry in what would be known as the Battle of Badgam, fought tenaciously at Srinagar Airport during the raid. But had he been given the chance, he would have also asked for the highest possible decoration to be given, posthumously, to Maqbool Sherwani.

1948
STOPPING THREE BULLETS IN THEIR TRACKS

Khushwant Singh (1915–2014), a lawyer practising in Lahore, was thirty-three in 1948. He saw, he heard, he understood everything, noted it all and forgot nothing. He was to become an internationally acclaimed novelist and write about what he had seen, not at once, but later and not in a dry record no one would care to read, but in a novel no one could put down—*Train to Pakistan*. It has, tucked away in it, words that say it all: 'The fact is, both sides killed. Both shot and stabbed and speared and clubbed. Both tortured. Both raped.'[1] Everyone had a sense that this was so, with many generalizations and oversimplifications like 'Muslims started it, Hindus retaliated', 'Muslims lost more lives, Hindus lost more property and women'.

On the first day of 1948, Gandhi had a Thai visitor who complimented him on India's independence. 'Today,' Gandhi said to him, speaking with great sadness, 'Indian fears brother Indian. Is this independence?' Gandhi was not meant to mentor India's diplomatic service, for sure.

When the new government decided to withhold the transfer of Pakistan's share (₹55 crore) of the sterling balance that undivided India held at Independence, he smarted. Patel saying India cannot give money to Pakistan, which it will then use to make bullets 'to be shot at us', made it worse for him. He was agitated, and then, as always happened with him, agitation led to a calm, the calm when his inner voice speaks to him—a danger signal for others. He must, he knew, fast. 'It will end,' Gandhi said in his prayer meeting on 12 January 1948, 'when and if I am satisfied that there is a reunion of the hearts of all communities.' The sterling balance issue was not mentioned. It did not have to be. But this much is known, that he called on Mountbatten immediately after the prayer meeting. During this talk, he asked the viceroy for a frank opinion about India's refusal to pay the cash balances. Mountbatten said he considered the step 'to be both unstatesmanlike and unwise'. Campbell-Johnson, who had seen Gandhi and Mountbatten conferring that evening and had made a mental note of the sequence of the fast decision, writes with great insight: 'You have to live in the vicinity of a Gandhi fast to understand its pulling power.' But even the perceptive press secretary failed to notice one important—vital—feature of this fast. It was to be, de facto, a fast unto death. He had placed no time limit on it.

Devadas was dismayed. He met his father every day, sometimes with his wife and his children as well, and could have rushed to him the day Gandhi announced his decision to fast, to vent his dismay. But the editor in him, and perhaps the chronicler, got him to put his thoughts down in a letter he sat down to write at 2.30 a.m. on the night of 13 January. 'You have surrendered to impatience,' wrote the forty-eight-year-old to his seventy-nine-year-old father and suggested that he had acted in haste. 'By your death you will not be able to achieve what you can by living.' Devadas ended with: 'I would therefore beseech you to pay heed to my entreaty and give up your decision to fast.'

There was not a hope in heaven that Gandhi, having announced his decision with the graven finality of an edict, would give up his decision on his son's entreaty. 'It is true you are my friend,' the father replied. '...I cannot comply with your request. Ram who has prompted me to go on a fast will bid me give it up if He wants me to do so.... I have only one prayer: "O Ram, give me strength during the fast so that the desire to live may not tempt me into premature termination of my fast".'

Fasts are curious things. They are undertaken by oneself for one's own satisfaction, fulfilment, sense of duty, guilt or whatever. They are also undertaken, as Gandhi's fasts mostly were, to impact someone or a group of people, to make or unmake an action, cause or cancel a decision. But they do yet another thing as well: they muck up the insides of immediate family and friends.

Patel said on Day Two of the fast, 'Let it not be said that we did not deserve the leadership of the greatest man in the world.' From the West Punjab Assembly, a legislative entity of the new Pakistan, its speaker sent a handwritten message to Gandhi sending excerpts* from its proceedings which included a remarkable expression of respect from a future prime minister of Pakistan, Malik Feroz Khan Noon, who said 'No country in the world has produced a greater man, religious founders apart, than Mahatma Gandhi.' The speaker cited Mian Mohammad Mumtaz Khan Daulatana, Punjab's finance minister, who said: 'It is our foremost duty to appreciate feelings which Mahatma Gandhi's fast reveals towards the Muslims. This (the fast) shows that there is at least one man in India who is ready to sacrifice even life for Hindu-Muslim unity.' Punjab premier Iftikhar Hussain Khan said, 'No efforts will be spared in this Province to help in saving his precious life.' And, surprise of surprises, Jinnah sent word through India's high commissioner in Karachi, Sri Prakasa (1890–1971), urging Gandhi 'to live and work for

*In Devadas Gandhi's papers with the family.

the cause of Hindu–Muslim unity in the two dominions'. Human credulity could not have had a greater tax placed on it. Rajaji, from Calcutta, said in tones of admiration, recalling the fast in Calcutta, that this latest fast had 'greater validity than earlier ones'. Demurring, Devadas wrote* to his father-in-law on 16 January 'It is embarrassing and unnecessary,' adding realistically, 'but Bapu is Bapu.'

Margaret Bourke-White was invited to dinner by Nehru on 17 January. Expecting a prime minister's dinner to be a formal affair, she managed, after a long day at work, to change into an evening dress and get to the prime minister's house on time. The atmosphere—totally informal—was stark, almost, and the menu was plain macaroni. But it was a most relaxing evening with a surprise reserved for the end. Rising from the table, Nehru said this was going to be his last meal for a while since he, too, had decided with several others, he said, to fast along with Gandhi.

But the next day, Day Six, brought relief. Over 100 representatives of different communities called on a Gandhi greatly weakened by his fast. They included a representative each of the Hindu Mahasabha and the RSS. 'We shall protect the life, property and faith of the Moslems and (undertake to see) that the incidents that have taken place in Delhi will not happen again,' they pledged. After prayers were recited, Gandhi accepted a glass of orange juice from Maulana Azad. The relief was palpable, with Nehru's being the greatest. On learning, after Nehru had left his side, that the prime minister had also fasted with him, a deeply moved Gandhi sent him a note saying, 'Now end your fast.... Live for many long years as Hind's Jawahar.' The note was in Hindi, with 'many long years' written as bahut with the u in it elongated—most probably a writing error, but the bahut spoken as it was written by him—bahuut—gave the benediction a voltage of its own.

The funds due to Pakistan, it need hardly be said, were released.

Taru, then all of thirteen, was in Birla House one day that January, when a slight drizzle prevented Bapuji from stepping out for his walk. He decided to pace inside one of the larger rooms of Birla House, instead. She joined her grandfather and, as he walked, summoned up the courage to ask him something that had long been her wish to ask (in Hindi, of course): 'Bapuji, what do you think the future holds for me?' This was in its soul, very similar to the questions in the famous 'Que sera sera' song Doris Day was to make famous in the 1956 film *The Man Who Knew Too Much*:

*In Devadas Gandhi's papers with the family.

When I was just a little girl
I asked my mother, what will I be
Will I be pretty? Will I be rich?
Here's what she said to me....[2]

Bapuji was at that time besieged by issues of existential import for him and for the country, and getting a query like this one was not designed to help him. But no. He fell silent for a while and then, with great seriousness, without vague platitudes or irritated brevity, said, precisely, purposefully in Hindi (some original expressions in Hindustani italicized with meanings given in brackets), 'Your father has very high *armaan* (aspirations) for you. He would like you to study diligently and put your studying to good account. Your father will help you go around and see the *desh, videsh* (country and the world). You will go around the world. And after you have done that, come back and take up a calling that seems you to be *sahi* (right). And make your mother Lakshmi your *adarsh* (ideal).' There was no sanctimonious talk about marriage or raising a family. Nothing about 'being a good girl'. Only a carefully wrought, carefully thought-out sketch of optimism and responsibility about her future. Somewhere hidden in that was, of course, a 'the future's not ours to see' idea, but overlaying that, there was a clear aspiration for the granddaughter but—and this is what made it so special—pointedly expressed as her father's not her grandfather's vision for her.

Right at this moment of catharsis, a group of people was silently, diligently, and methodically planning to kill Gandhi. The men fumbled on details along the way, but finally put together a plan to carry out their intent, with chilling efficiency. A non-lethal bomb was planted at the venue of the prayer meeting on 20 January to be set off at an appointed moment by Madanlal Pahwa (1927–2000), a young refugee from West Punjab. The scheme was that as the bomb went off, there would be some panic, during which two of his associates from Maharashtra, would fire at Gandhi from behind a trellis. But the scheme misfired as Gandhi controlled the crowd's nerves at once with simple, direct words, asking for composure. And by asking Manu to start singing the Ramdhun, which she did. While the bomb-planter was apprehended, the would-be assassins fled.

All India Radio, which was now recording all of Gandhi's prayer meeting speeches, recorded this one too. We used to have a gramophone record player with its snakelike needle-hold that had a spring which needed to be cranked into playing each time the record gave over. Many years later, I would play the 78-rpm gramophone record of this over and over again, to hear Bapuji speaking to the congregation in his soft, coaxing voice, interrupted by the sudden dull but clear thud of the bomb leading to an immediate cawing of agitated crows, and sounds of human voices in the melee and then Bapuji saying, with a pained laugh, 'Kuchh nahin hua hai…shant ho jayiye… (Nothing has happened…please…observe silence…)'

That 'kuchh nahin' ('nothing') was to happen as 'something else' ten days later.

'Hai bahar-e-bagh duniya chand roz
Dekh lo iska tamasha chand roz'
(Spring fleets into this world's bower to but slip away
Watch its dizzy dance through that very, very short day)

The seventy-nine-year-old repeated Nazeer's Urdu lines in what his secretary Pyarelal describes as 'a tone of infinite sadness'. This was on 29 January 1948.

It is appalling that no one, not Mountbatten, not Nehru, not Patel, not Rajaji, thought of telling each other that it is a good thing the 'bomb' was not serious, an even better thing that the bomber has been caught, but now that he has been, they must get to the bottom of the murky business. Was the man acting alone? Did he have fellow conspirators? Maybe there was a deep conspiracy; maybe this was a dry-run (as it indeed was). Now let us, they should have said, leave nothing to chance. But no. No one thought on these lines. They were great and astute administrators. But in the matter of Gandhi's personal security, they were totally naive.

30 January 1948 was just another wintry day in Delhi. Our household stirred slowly to life that morning, with Taru going to her 'Girls Only' school, St. Thomas in her white and green uniform but custom-made, by permission of the school for the Gandhi family, in khadi, not the 'mill' yardage that other girls got theirs tailored in. She was driven to school by our driver, Pan Singh, a distinct advantage, for that enabled her to have a few extra minutes at home to get groomed, the combing down and plaiting of long tresses being no small chore. Likewise, Mohan and Ramu got into their uniform, stitched by Modern School's special leave, in blue khadi, and ambled off to their school, a fifteen-minute walk away, on the leafy Barakhamba Road. They just had enough time to reach school in time for the morning assembly held in the gymnasium, with all students taking off their shoes outside, squatting four-legged on rugs, their stockinged feet stinking to the roof. The teachers, led by the dashing Principal M. N. Kapur (1910–94) and the reflective Awadh Kishoreji, were on the stage.

While Pan Singh drove Taru home as usual in the afternoon, Mohan and Ramu tarried in school because of a sporting event.

In Birla House, moving to the prayer ground faster than he usually did, for he had been delayed by a conversation with Sardar Patel, 'I hate being late,' Gandhi said to Manu and Abha* in Gujarati as they reached the prayer ground. That was his last full spoken sentence.

A jostle and the rosary and prayer book Manu was carrying had fallen as a man who pushed his way into their path gave the girl a heave.

Without a doubt, Gandhi observed this. He was hypertensive, and at that moment, his blood pressure must have spiked. Anyone's would have, seeing a girl from the family being rough-handled by some random man. And I can imagine him saying to the intruder, had he been allowed the chance, 'Kya kar rahe ho…? Yah bhi koyi tariqa hai? (What are you doing? Is this the way to behave…?)'

But he was not given that chance. For the next second, he was absorbed in the Ram that he longed to be one with. Abha, his grand-niece-in-law, a daughter of Bengal, cradled the sinking head in her lap, with Ram's name on his lips.

He had become, as Kamaladevi Chattopadhyay was to write, an icchhamarani, one who meets the end he has wished for.

Taru was minding her two-and-a-half-year-old brother, me, when a scurry of activity, more scurried than the usual, saw her parents rush out, leaving her, bewildered, to continue minding me. A few minutes later, someone ran into the house saying, 'Come, come, you have to go to Birla House…There is a car waiting for you…Bapuji has been….' Grabbing me, in a few seconds of incoherent reflex actions later, she was down the flight of stairs and into the car, which sped like lightning to where her parents had gone. The gates of Birla House had been shut tight to keep out a large crowd that had already gathered there. Sentries stood on duty. Hame andar jaane dijiye (allow us to go in), she told them, clutching me to her chest. The men, at first, refused. Mein Bapuji ki poti hun (I am Bapuji's granddaughter), she remonstrated. This had to and did work. Our parents were there, already, in the room where Bapuji had been laid on the floor. Puzzled and completely uncomprehending, I was deposited by Tara on my mother's lap.

Henri Cartier-Bresson,† who had managed to access the room with his magical camera, has captured the scene in a hazy photograph snatched from the moment of shock, grief, and stunned prayer, for no one knew what. India, perhaps.

---

*Abha Gandhi née Chatterjee (1927–95), wife of Kanu Gandhi and niece-in-law of Mohandas Gandhi.

†Henri Cartier-Bresson (1908–2004), French artist and photographer, early user of 35mm film, celebrated for 'capturing a *decisive moment*'.

Seeing the stir and hum of words floating in the air, I said, in a repeat of my old mimicry of Bapuji: Sab shant ho jayiye...adding, for good measure, Bapuji so rahe hein... (Bapuji is sleeping...) precipitating a renewed bout of muffled sobbing by those around me.

I, of course, remember nothing of all this. Family lore's stock of remembered 'footage' tells me this is what I said.

Devadas, crying like the child that he was to the man slain, kept saying, 'Wake up, wake up, please, Bapu, wake up.' Patel, in disbelief, thought he could feel a pulse on the lifeless arm until doctors told him with a grave shaking of their heads that he was wrong. It was all over. He sat, wordless, crushed. And looking, as Manu was to say later, suddenly, very, very old. Jawaharlal, the political heir to the assassinated Father of the Nation, broke down. But he was not going to forget his duties as prime minister. He went to the gates of the house and, standing on top of them, announced, for the first time, to the throng outside, including the press, that Bapu was no more.

During these moments of trauma, catharsis, and agony, matters of some immediacy had to be attended to. Devadas said Bapu's chest should not stay wrapped in the blood-soaked upper cloth. As the cloth, clinging to the chest was separated from it, a piercing cry rent the air. It was Brij Krishna Chandiwala, a devoted associate of Gandhi, who was entrusted with that unbearable task.

One person who let no etiquette or reticence come his way at that time was my uncle, Gandhi's eldest son, Harilal (1888–1948). Family lore, backed by a Gujarati newspaper report, has it that Harilal was in a tea shop in Bombay, listening to radio news that flashed the assassination. He rose, suddenly delirious, from his seat and, saying, 'I will kill the man who has murdered my father,' rushed out. Harilal, the 'estranged' son, given to drink and womanizing, rebuking and rebuked by his father, had shown the most natural reaction. While his brothers Manilal (1892–1956), then in South Africa, Ramdas (1897–1969), who with his wife, Nirmala, flew from Nagpur to Delhi, and Devadas were models of theological self-control, Harilal showed a biological loss of control. But only for a while. He went somewhere—no one knows where—and wrote out something on his father, no one knows what, and took it to the offices of a newspaper.

H. Y. Sharada Prasad (1924–2008) records the scene memorably. In the words of that rare journalist and later pillar of the Indian state's information architecture:

> I worked in *The National Standard* in Bombay then. The office of the paper was situated in Sassoon Dock in Colaba. On January 30,

> 1948, I was on the afternoon shift, which would have ended at 8 pm.... Pothan Joseph was the Editor. He told me to take charge of the edition because there was no knowing when the night Chief Sub-Editor would be able to turn up.... Joseph had told me: 'Don't disturb me until I finish the edit, which I expect to do by 11 pm.' ...The night shift Chief Sub-Editor, who was senior to me, came in well after 8 pm. But I continued to function as Chief Sub-Editor of the night shift as well. We had a very enterprising chief reporter called B.S.V. Rao. His team was able to track down the relatives and friends of Nathuram Godse in Bombay, Poona and other towns well before the police could. Our man in Poona traced a photographer who had shot Nathuram's portraits several years earlier. Luckily, the studio owner had kept the negatives, and so we were able to publish photos of the assassin...It must have been 9.30 or 10 pm. A frail elderly figure approached my desk with a sheet of paper in his hand. Irritated to be interrupted, I asked: 'What is it?' He replied: 'My tribute to Bapuji.' In my youthful arrogance, I said sharply: 'Today, everyone is issuing their own tribute to Bapuji.' The man said very gently: 'But I am his son.' I looked closer, and it was indeed Harilal Gandhi...I knew I should have left aside everything I was doing and attended to him, especially since I knew his son Kantilal in Mysore. But I was more concerned with coping with the flow of copy. I just called out to B.S.V. Rao to handle him...

Harilal reached Delhi on the day of the sanchayana—ritual collection of the ashes. Taru had stayed back and was at home when he came, weary and rail-ragged. The sixty-year-old bathed and washed his journey-clothes, without any fuss. As he was putting up his washed clothes to dry, Taru asked him if he would not like to go to Rajghat and join the family for the rite. 'No,' Harilal replied. 'Let your father and others do that...I am not worthy of that honour....' He stayed for but a few days, sharing the family's shock and grief and then announced his intention to return to Bombay. Devadas saw Harilal off at the railway station. 'This is my life, Devadas,' he said, 'wandering wandering....' He was to die shortly thereafter, the same year, in Bombay.

A new name had entered our family's consciousness—Godse, Nathuram Godse. He was spoken of occasionally but then fleetingly. Not once did I hear anyone at home say a harsh word about him, though the hideous deed was never far from the family's minds.

That Bapuji was seventy-nine years old, and walking without any thought of self-protection in the murderous atmosphere of the time to pray for human decency, for friendship without a shred of ill-will towards anyone, made his murder hideous. And with not one but one, two, three bullets pumped into him in rapid-fire sequence from near 'contact range'.

The journey of the cortège from Birla House to Rajghat was filmed and photographed by many, quite brilliantly. Bourke-White's black-and-white of people who clambered onto a telegraph pole is among the most fascinating. Cartier-Bresson was at Rajghat for the cremation the next evening. His photographs of the proceedings are made of divine tincts. One shows Brij Krishna Chandiwala facing the rising pyre in horrified agony. That one frame says it all, more than all the other photographs of the high and mighty and the simple grieving laity at the site. On 1 February, when the family went to Rajghat for the rite of sanchayana, Cartier-Bresson took some classic photographs. There is one photograph where I am playing with the sand around the now-cold pyre. I knew something had happened to 'my' Bapuji, 'something' which had made everyone cry. But I knew little more. I had, incidentally, not had a haircut for a while (Bapuji would have had something to say about that, for sure). With a long and wide swathe of overgrown hair falling over my forehead, I am playing with the sand in that picture, lifting up and then letting the grains in my hand drop in what may be called a sand-fall. Playing meaninglessly with sand-like nothings has been my life.

Ashes to ashes, dust to dust. (Photo by Henri Cartier-Bresson, Devadas Gandhi personal archives).

There is one photograph that was not taken, which, to my mind, is the biggest non-photograph or the best photograph of Gandhi's final journey that never was. Ambedkar was then India's law minister, its first. His conflicted equation with Gandhi was known, as was Gandhi's role in overcoming all differences and recommending to Nehru Ambedkar's inclusion in the first cabinet. Ambedkar was ill at the time. And yet he got to Birla House and was present there until the cortege left, accompanying it for a small part of it until his health would permit him to go no further. No photograph was taken—at least, I have not seen one—of the law minister there. Was he regarded as not important enough by the elite lens-persons?

A civilizationally acute observation on the assassination was to come from Kripalani in his classic *Gandhiji: His Life and Thought*. The professor says: 'The most cruel part of this tragedy is not only the death of Gandhiji. It is that he fell by the blow of one who considered himself a Hindu against one who had ordered his life in the spirit of the Upanishads and the Gita. The assassin has betrayed the whole history of Hinduism, which never raised its hand against a spiritual teacher for the views he held, however heterodox they were considered by a section of his people.'

A twenty-nine-year-old Punjabi called Rajinder Krishan (1919–87) was a just-arrived aspirant for a role in the world of cinema in Bombay. A thoughtful, dreamy poetry lover, he got a lucky break that year—1948—the chance to work on a script for a film called *Aaj ki Raat*, starring the then reigning queen of Hindi cinema, Suraiya (1929–2004) and the evergreen 'natural' actor Motilal. But with the assassination, he was 'borrowed' by a different muse, and he wrote a song called 'Suno suno ay duniyawalo Bapu ki yah amar kahani (Listen, listen, o denizens of this world the deathless story of Bapu)' sung by Mohammad Rafi (1924–80) which was an instant hit. This is said to have been an 'overnight' work, with the lyricist, composers, and singer working together. Be that as it may, the song went straight home. Its lines describing the end remain a reminder, a call:

Jao bapu jao bapu rahega naam tumhaara
Jab tak chamke chaand sitaare chamke kaam tumhaara
Bapu tumne praan diye aur maut ki shaan badhaayee
Tumne apna khoon diya aur prem ki jyot jalaayee

Rupert Snell (b. 1951), the distinguished scholar-teacher of Hindi and a master translator, has specially rendered this as:

Go, Bapu! Go now! Your Name shall ever endure;
As long as shines the moon and the stars, so will your deeds.

In giving up your life, Bapu, you made death glorious;
You bled for the world, and lit the lamp of love.[3]

In his governor's manor in Calcutta, the Salem vakil in Rajaji was to the fore. Taking a strictly no-nonsense court-case view of the matter, he wrote to Devadas on 2 March 1948: 'How long is Godse to be nursed and kept as a going concern? Until all the conspiracies in the world are unravelled? Please, when you get a chance, tell Vallabhbhai that I would like him to expedite the trial of this man and close the business and not be persuaded by policemen and lawyers to keep things ending indefinitely. The other cases may take care of themselves. It is not good to let things go so slow.'

Some things were moving fast. And not on the path shown by Gandhi. Nehru knew his leader's position on the atom bomb. Independent India having atomic weapons was unthinkable for Gandhi. But the new India's scientific doyens were scientists, not Gandhians. Their sense of India's future was not Gandhi's.

On 26 April 1948, Homi J. Bhabha (1909–66)[*], the pre-eminent nuclear physicist wrote to Prime Minister Jawaharlal Nehru about India's future and the role of atomic energy in that future[†]. He had plans and said, 'the development of atomic energy should be entrusted to a very small and high-powered body composed of say three people with executive power, and answerable directly to the Prime Minister without any intervening link. For brevity, this body may be referred to as the Atomic Energy Commission.'[4] Nehru did not need much persuading. An Atomic Energy Act led to the Atomic Energy Commission (AEC) which was established on 10 August 1948 with Bhabha as the commission's first chairman.

India was now moving into the era of tight secrecies for reasons of

[*]Bhabha belonged to the Parsi community of which Gandhi famously said: 'I am proud of my country, India, for having produced the splendid Zoroastrian stock, in numbers beneath contempt, but in charity and philanthropy, perhaps unequalled and certainly unsurpassed.' The description can certainly be contested on 'produced', for the Parsi are descended from Persian migrants who landed by sea on the western seaboard of Medieval India to escape religious persecution during and after the Arab conquest of the Persian Empire. But the tribute is about the handsomest and most ardent made by any Indian to Parsi India and is totally accurate in its reference to Parsi philanthropy, which has continued and taken imaginative contemporary forms in post-Independence India.

[†]See Itty Abraham, *The Making of the Indian Atomic Bomb: Science, Secrecy and the Postcolonial State* (1998); *South Asian Cultures of the Bomb: Atomic Publics and the State in India and Pakistan* (2009). George Perkovich, *India's Nuclear Bomb: The Impact of Global Proliferation* (1999); Robert Anderson's *Nucleus and Nation* (2010); M. V. Ramana, *The Power of Promise: Examining Nuclear Energy in India* (2012); Jahnavi Phalkey, *Atomic State: Big Science in Twentieth Century India* (2013).

security. The details of the workings of the AEC were declared state secrets. And a close working equation developed between Nehru and Bhabha. Twenty years younger than Nehru, Bhabha addressed him as 'Dear Bhai' or 'Dear Brother', while Nehru addressed Bhabha as 'My dear Homi'. Indira Gandhi later recalled that her father always found the time to speak to Bhabha, both because, she claimed, Bhabha brought to him urgent matters that required immediate attention and because conversations with him afforded Nehru 'warm moments of sensitivity that other people take for granted in their everyday life'. In a speech in Parliament, Nehru talked of the relationship between the 'purposes' of the proposed nuclear programme. On the one hand, he said, 'I think we must develop it for peaceful purposes,' but then added, 'of course, if we are compelled as a nation to use it for other purposes, possibly no pious sentiments of any of us will stop the nation from using it that way.'[5]

In May 1948, Devadas was part of a delegation of editors, led by Kasturi Srinivasan (1887–1959) of *The Hindu*, that travelled to London to discuss the future of the Associated Press of India and Reuters in India, as well as the possibility of setting up the Press Trust of India. Some of the delegates, like Devadas, were accompanied by their wives. Lakshmi maintained a nugget of a diary in her simple but chaste Hindi for each day of that trip; transiting in Cairo, the Indian delegates were barred from leaving the airport lounge on the Nile because, writes Lakshmi, of the Palestine 'gadbadi' (the Palestine trouble), but then India's Ambassador Syud Hossain (1888–1949) arranged for them to be given clearance to disembark. Devadas and Lakshmi met Hossain at Cairo's Shepheard's Hotel, which she describes as 'suprasiddha' (famed) and the cuisine of which was said to be 'as good as anything at Paris' Ritz, or Berlin's Adlon or Rome's Grand' and which occurs in Lakshmi's favourite detective novelist Agatha Christie's *Death on the Nile* (1937). The ambassador, a bachelor, who lived in a suite in this hotel, was known to Devadas both as a former journalist, having worked in *The Independent* published from Allahabad, and as the dashing Bengali Muslim with whom Nehru's sister Vijaya Lakshmi had eloped and lived with awhile, before getting married to Ranjit S. Pandit (1893–1944). Hossain was to die suddenly on 26 February 1949, within months of Devadas–Lakshmi meeting him—a loss to Indian diplomacy, political journalism, and Indian public life.

The diplomatic round continued with India's high commissioner Krishna Menon in London. Lakshmi writes that on 1 June, the secretary of state for Commonwealth Relations, Philip Noel-Baker (1889–1982), hosted a tea party for the Indian delegates. She says nothing beyond this, a great pity, for the Labour leader and future Nobel Peace Laureate was a man of great substance and independence. As World War II drew close, Noel-Baker, on 21 June 1938, as Labour MP for Derby, spoke at the House of Commons against aerial bombing of German cities based on moral grounds. 'The only way to prevent atrocities from the air,' he said, 'is to abolish air warfare and national air forces altogether.' What that very original man said to the Indians would have been of great interest. There can be no doubt that this meeting was arranged for the visitors through the initiative and zeal of High Commissioner Menon. Lakshmi writes that on 6 June 1948, Menon dropped in to see them at their hotel (St. James Court) at 11 p.m. and stayed for an hour, talking. Typically, he also placed his Rolls-Royce at their disposal for the drive from the Hotel to Waterloo Station when they were leaving.

While they were in Europe, Devadas's eldest brother, Harilal, passed away in Bombay. Death took him on 18 June in a tuberculosis hospital after a losing battle with life's torments. They were in London on the day, leaving for Berlin. In a tribute of tightly restrained emotion, he wrote, 'The hand of death has brought deliverance to a restless soul. My eldest brother Harilal (not Hiralal) never knew mental or physical peace in his sixty years of life.'

Meanwhile, Rajaji was moving from Government House, Calcutta, to Government House, New Delhi, to take over as India's first Indian governor general. He was sworn in on 21 June 1948, when Devadas and Lakshmi were in Berlin, being hosted in some style by Brigadier Khub Chand (1911–2003), head of India's first post-war mission to that war-swiped land, and Mrs Khub Chand, whom she describes as their host's 'khubsurat naujavan patni' (beautiful, youthful wife), punning, I think, unconsciously, on the Brigadier's name. Lakshmi writes that Mrs Khub Chand took her to see the Berlin Stadium and also to areas that now lay in ruins, including Hitler's now derelict residence. 'Shmasan se bhi bhayankar' (more fearsome than a cremation ground) is how she describes it.

On 4 July, Devadas took Lakshmi with him to Ayot Saint Lawrence, home of the great playwriter, where, over tea, they met George Bernard Shaw (1856–1950), whom Devadas knew from their meeting in 1946, when Devadas had called on him in this country home, and earlier, from 1931, when Shaw had come visiting Gandhi in London during the Second Round Table Conference.

This was, for India, wartime. Kashmir was the scene of grim ballistics. Brigadier Mohammad Usman (1912–48) of the Indian Army was, on 3 July 1948, killed in action. He was thirty-five. He, with many other Muslim officers, had declined, the previous year of Partition, to move to the Pakistan Army and had continued to serve with the Indian Army. He was commanding 50

Para Brigade when he led his men to wrest Jhangar from Pakistani seizure. He had, in March, in a written order to his men, cited the poet Horatius from Ancient Greece, saying, 'How can man die better / than facing fearful odds / for the ashes of his fathers / And the temples of his Gods?' Usman was killed by a mortar while defending Jhangar. On 5 July, Menon, who called on Devadas and Lakshmi at 11 in the night after his unending day's work, told him and Lakshmi about Usman's martyrdom. *'Brigadier Osman ke Kashmir mein ladte ladte mar jaane ki dukhad khabr mili...* (Received the saddening news of Brigadier Usman's death in action in Kashmir)', Lakshmi diarized that night.

Transfer of power—C. Rajagopalachari on arrival in New Delhi to assume duties of Governor General of India, received at the airport by departing Vicereine Lady Edwina Mountbatten, and Prime Minister Jawaharlal Nehru, June 1948. To the extreme left is Pamela Mountbatten, daughter of Lord and Lady Mountbatten. (Information & Broadcasting Department, Government of India).

Ceremonies of courtesy—Prime Minister Nehru presenting members of his cabinet to Governor General-designate C. Rajagopalachari at New Delhi airport, June 1948. Right to Left: John Mathai, Rafi Ahmed Kidwai, Jairamdas Doulatram, Sardar Baldev Singh, Maulana Azad, Rajkumari Amrit Kaur. Hidden from view behind Rajagopalachari, Syama Prasad Mookerjee.

The Constitution was being crafted at this juncture under the sharp and scholarly oversight of Ambedkar, who headed the Drafting Committee, with the initial pen-to-paper exercise having been done by the constitutional adviser to the Constituent Assembly, B. N. Rau (1887–1953)* who gave a rough draft of it to the committee for its scrutiny. With the permission—indeed, the enthusiastic approval—of Ambedkar and the president of the assembly, Rajendra Prasad, Rau had gone on a tour of Europe and the United States towards the end of the previous year to meet experts on Constitution-making. Among those he consulted was the Irish statesman and then taoiseach (prime minister) Eamon de Valera (1882–1975), who had played a prominent role in the drafting of Ireland's 1937 Constitution. Rau was given three pieces of advice by de Valera: (i) India should not go in for proportionate representation. (ii) Let the Constitution be 'flexible' in the sense that it should be amendable by a majority of Parliament because the conditions of independent India were in a state of flux. (iii) Let the Constitution of India be drafted in English, and that draft should be the

*The defining role of this exceptional civil servant, jurist, and diplomat in the making of India's Constitution has been overshadowed by the pre-eminence of the chairman of the Drafting Committee, B. R. Ambedkar.

'original text'. Ireland, said de Valera, had found Gaelic 'hard going'.

India took the first, second, and third pieces of the Irish leader's advice seriously. But neither Rau nor his chairman, Ambedkar, nor Prime Minister Nehru, in accepting the second advice, knew that the issue of amending the Constitution through the ordinary processes of law-making would become the subject of a great debate in India, which would lead to litigation and conflicting orders of the highest court in the land, and be a matter of contestation into the seventy-fifth year of the republic.

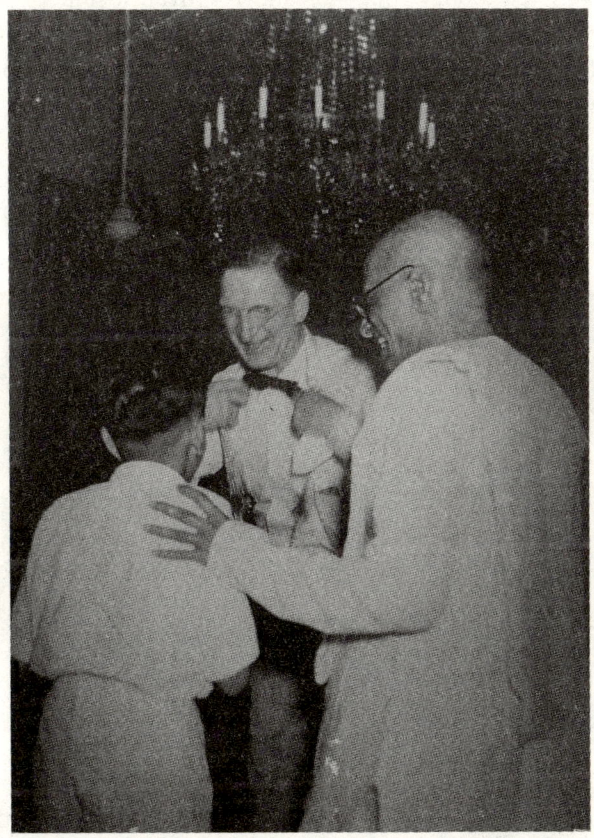

Eamon de Valera, Irish statesman in Calcutta, being garlanded by ten-year-old Ramchandra Gandhi. (Devadas Gandhi personal archives).

Rajaji was host to Eamon de Valera when the Irish statesman, now out of office, was stopping over in Calcutta on his way from Australia and New Zealand to New Delhi. De Valera was on a mission to speak to world statesmen on what he regarded as the folly of partitioning Ireland and the creation of Northern Ireland. A long-time observer of Ireland's history and admirer of 'its struggles against sectarian narrowness', Nehru had arranged for de Valera to be treated as any visiting prime minister would be. De Valera's stay in Calcutta's Government House was brief—one day and one night—but it obviously gave Rajaji a change from the routine of governorship. A cameraman captured Ramu being asked, under a grand chandelier, by his beaming khadi-clad grandfather to garland the black-bow wearing distinguished visitor.

Did Rajaji's ten-month long—or short—governorship of West Bengal, the first in the line and therefore, formative, endorse a proactive role for that office? No, for he did little or nothing with which the government of the day would have been uncomfortable. In fact, he eased the work of the government by whatever he did. Did his governorship, then, suggest that the governor should be a mere symbol of the state government, a figurehead? No, for he was anything but that. Was his governor generalship going to be any different? No.

Change of guard—Governor General Mountbatten receives his successor at the head of the grand steps, Forecourt, Government House, New Delhi, June 1948. (Devadas Gandhi personal archives).

There is something called influence. It is an effect, not a prerogative. And it comes from moral, not legal or political authority.

With Rajaji's move to Delhi, he, as governor general, Nehru as prime minister and Patel as deputy prime minister in charge of the important Ministry of Home Affairs formed a cohesive threesome, this despite the known differences between Nehru and Patel.

On one issue, all three were united: Gandhi's assassins, as and when convicted, must have their sentences carried out. Rajaji, as we have seen, had no doubt that Godse must hang. Patel could have been of no other mind. Devadas wrote to George Bernard Shaw asking what India should do with the assassin. Shaw replied on 16 July 1948, in vintage Shavian breeze: 'You and Nehru are in a delicate position as to the fate of the assassin. As the son of your father, you must say, "Pardon him". Nehru, as Prime Minister, must say, "Hang him", whatever his private view of the death penalty may be. If he is not officially and judicially hanged, he will probably be lynched. That is for Nehru to consider.... As for me, I am against all punishment as such, but no statesman can abrogate the right of civilised society to exterminate human as well as animal vermin.'

Reflecting lights—Governor General C. Rajagopalachari presenting a silver salver to Prime Minister Nehru on Independence Day, 1949, Government House, New Delhi. (Author's personal collection).

Devadas sent a copy of the letter to Nehru, who wrote to Shaw on 4 September 1948 saying: 'Devadas apparently asked you as to what we should do with Gandhi's assassin. I suppose he will hang, and certainly, I shall not try to save him from the death penalty, although I have expressed myself in favour of the abolition of the death penalty in previous years. In the present case, there is no alternative. But even now, in a normal case, I have grown rather doubtful if it is preferable to death to keep a man in prison for 15 or 20 years. Life has become so cheap that it does not seem of very much consequence whether a few criminals are put to death or not. Sometimes, one wonders whether a sentence to live is not the hardest punishment after all.'

Mohan recalls that the distinguished librarian, regarded as 'the father of library science in India' and the originator of the colon system of books' classification, S. R. Ranganathan (1892–1972), came to Modern School and addressed its students in the school's gymnasium, which used to do double-duty as the school's assembly hall and auditorium. Ranganathan had just returned from a visit to Sweden. He asked the students: 'What do you think India is known as in Sweden?' 'I felt like responding,' says Mohan, 'but chose to remain silent. Ramu, on the other, put up his hand and said, 'The land of Gandhi.' Ranganathan said, yes, that was exactly how Sweden thinks of India.

'The land of Gandhi', minus Gandhi but plus Nehru, was now groping in a new normal. Gandhi's ideals were there but were there to inspire respect, rather than be incorporated in policy.

In a letter dated 27 August 1948 to Dorothy Woodman (1902–70), the British socialist, Nehru said what sums up the state of the new nation and the state of his mind: 'I should not like to be considered as a helpless victim, pushed about hither and thither by others. To some extent, of course, we are all victims of circumstances and certainly, circumstances have not been kind to us for some time past. I am myself very critical of much that has been done in India by others as well as by me. Nevertheless, I am fully responsible for it and have no wish to disclaim that responsibility. We have fought, during the past year or more, against many evil forces, and often, one has to choose in favour of the lesser evils.'

The 1948 Summer Olympics were held from 29 July to 14 August 1948 in London (organized by Noel-Baker, who, apart from being a cabinet minister, was also an Olympics silver medallist as a runner) following a twelve-year hiatus caused by the outbreak of World War II; these were the first Summer Olympics to be held since the 1936 Games in Berlin. On 12 August 1948, India struck gold. The Indian hockey team's gold medal at the London Olympics not only gave independent India a sense of identity but also gave it a sense of quiet satisfaction in retrieving that identity in the capital of the British empire and through a win over the British team. A particular delight was the celebration of a sports star, Balbir Singh Dosanjh (1924–2020), who would go on to become a true legend of the sport. The triumph had come after many days of anxiety. The previous year, which had seen India divided, inevitably saw the composition of the hitherto undivided Indian hockey team with some of the most skilful players from Punjab—Niaz Khan, Shah Rukh Muhammad, Aziz Malik, and Ali Shah Dara, who were a part of India's Berlin 1936 Olympics squad, now choosing to play for Pakistan.

With Rajaji now in Delhi, the 'table' of the state acquired the Euclidean stability of a tripod. The family was overjoyed having Anna back in its midst.

India's polity and society were being sought to be fashioned by the trio of Nehru and Patel from their seats in the cabinet and by Rajaji from the Government House. Rajendra Prasad, as president of the Constituent Assembly, and Ambedkar, as chairman of its Drafting Committee, were simultaneously working away at the making of the new Constitution. It was an exhilarating, if also an exhausting time.

A short-lived triumvirate—Deputy Prime Minister Sardar Vallabhbhai Patel, Governor General C. Rajagopalachari, and Prime Minister Jawaharlal Nehru, Government House, Rashtrapati Bhavan, New Delhi, 1948. (Devadas Gandhi personal archives).

The Nehru–Patel divergence came into sharp play on the subject of Hyderabad's future. The Hindu majority 'princely' state was the largest among its kind in India. Its sixty-one-year-old ruler, Mir Osman Ali Khan, the nizam (1886–1967), under the influence of the militant Razakar militia of irregulars led by Kassim Rizvi (1902–70), was led to seek independent, sovereign status as a Muslim-ruled state. The idea was unrealistic, in fact, absurd on all counts. Rajaji, who had known His Exalted Highness personally from before and wanted to protect and safeguard his self-respect, was clear that New Delhi must act swiftly to settle the issue as peacefully as possible, by force if necessary. When the Razakars became belligerent, forcing Hindus to flee in droves as refugees to surrounding provinces, and night-runners taking off from random airports in Pakistan landed in and around Hyderabad, Patel, heading the Ministry in charge of States (in addition to the Home portfolio) said Indian forces should move in and occupy Hyderabad. The prime minister and the home minister differed on the approach, the Sardar leaving a meeting between the two midway. Rajaji, who was apprised, called both leaders to a meeting that very afternoon—11 September 1948—in his study in Government House. Secretary in the Ministry of States, V. P. Menon (1893–1965), who was present, records, 'It was then decided that we should occupy Hyderabad.' The next morning, the frontier was crossed, and after a four-day operation, the nizam surrendered, his ministry resigned, and the Razakar were banned. On 16 September, the nizam visited the Hyderabad radio station to announce the change in abject terms. An anomalous situation thus came to an end. Had India not moved in as it did, the Razakar would have let a foetid tumour at the very centre of India swell. Hindu–Muslim tensions across the country would have become unmanageable.

The takeover of Hyderabad was Patel's victory. He had been shown to be right on every count—the basic decision to move in, the timing, the handling of the political-cum-military part and, finally, the grace with which the now-titular head of Hyderabad, the nizam, was treated. Had Operation Polo not been undertaken and had not been successful, it may well be that Hyderabad under a nizam, manipulated by the Pakistan-backed Razakar using his personal prestige to befool the Muslim minority in India, would have become a proxy Pakistan within India. What Pakistan succeeded in doing, partially, in Kashmir, it was wholly thwarted from doing in Hyderabad. The fakery of a minority's politically untenable, ethically unjustifiable and civilizationally unsustainable rule over a majority had been brought to an end, thereby warding off a far greater Hindu–Muslim confrontation in the country. Secularism, Patel had shown, is not about tall statements but timely action with no bias at work.

But the making of a major political point took a price: Hyderabad, for the duration of the five-day operation, had to go through an ordeal of fire. Indian forces lost 42 men, with 97 wounded and 24 missing. The nizam's army lost 490 men and 122 wounded. The Razakar had 2,727 killed, 102 wounded, and 3,364 captured. These statistics mask another tragedy—murder, loot perpetrated on both sides of the divide before, during, and immediately after the operation, with women, as always, suffering privations only they can.

The high drama surrounding the armed intervention in Hyderabad against the nizam's order had put into the shade another very major and determining passage in the nation's—yes, the nation's, not just the region's—history. The area then known in the popular mind, and now, officially, as Telangana, had known what the distinguished historian of modern India, Sumit Sarkar (b. 1939), has described as 'the grossest forms of feudal exploitation... where Muslim and high-class Hindu *deshmukhs* (revenue-collectors-turned landowners) and *jagirdars* extorted stiff vetti or forced labour and payments in kind from lower caste and tribal peasants and debt-slaves'. Following the lead given by struggles in Bengal (tebhaga—24 Parganas) and in Travancore (Punnapra-Vayalar), the communist leaders and their supporters launched a guerrilla war in this tract 'affecting at its height about 3000 villages spread over 16,000 square miles and with a population of three million'. Using simple weapons like lathis and slings with stones and chilli powder, peasants formed themselves into attacking and counter-attacking bands called cheekati doralu, 'kings of the night'. The armed action against the nizam checked the communist advance at the time. But it is insufficiently realized that the beginnings of Naxalism and Maoism in India can be traced to the monstrous injustices under which the peasants of Telangana suffered at the hands of village 'mighties' nestling under the creaking regime of the nizam. Had there been a semblance of responsive governance in the region—responsive to peasants' needs—Telangana would not have needed the war which was paused by Operation Polo but which was to resurface much more menacingly in the decades ahead. Lathis, stone slings, and chilli powder were to be replaced, in the decades ahead, by sophisticated arms, transport, and radio technologies and a brutal intelligence system and punishments, including death sentences on informers and those suspected of being informers. In other words, Maoist terror.

Daughters all—C. Rajagopalachari's daughter Lakshmi (second from left) hosts to tea, in that order, Sarojini and Govindarajulu Naidu's daughter Padmaja, Vijaya Lakshmi and Ranjit Pandit's daughters Nayantara and Chandralekha, and Kamala and Jawaharlal Nehru's daughter Indira Gandhi, Government House, New Delhi, 1949. (Devadas Gandhi personal archives).

If Hyderabad holds a lesson for those who seek to subject a majority to elitist oppression, Telangana holds a lesson for those who underestimate the corrosive power of inequality.

But to return to the hush of Government House, New Delhi. A day before the start of the Hyderabad police action, Muhammad Ali Jinnah died in Karachi. The founder of Pakistan could helm the new nation for just over a year. And the circumstances of the page-turner's death were incredibly pitiful. Flown in from Murree, where he had gone for a rest cure, the ambulance which was to drive him from the Karachi airport into the city broke down. He could not be kept in a vehicle that was stifling hot and so had to be lowered onto the roadside on a stretcher, where he lay for a long while before another vehicle could reach him to take him, prone, to the governor general's home.

Rajaji and the Quaid-e-Azam had never had anything like an equation. His efforts to conciliate the Muslim League leader had alienated him from many of his colleagues and compatriots but had not persuaded Jinnah. Now, when he was governor general, he had the piquant task of responding to the death of his counterpart in Pakistan. In typical form, he picked up his pen and wrote a letter to the deceased president's sister, Begum Fatima Jinnah.

How should he address her? What should he say? Human instincts prevailed over the cramping reticence of protocol, and he wrote: '*Dear Sister, My deepest sympathy and the sympathy of all my people and my government to you and your people. May all of us be enabled by the Most High to go worthily through all our trials and tribulations.*' The creator of Pakistan had not been extolled; a sister's deprivation had been condoled. Meanwhile a happy congruence emerged between the law minister and governor general, very different, both, yet very cerebral. The ascetic head of state in homespun and the articulate lawmaker invariably in well-tailored Western-style clothes, found each others' company and conversations congenial. A photograph taken on 14 June 1948 captured that creative equation. Both must have felt then that they could work things together through reforms for India's greatness. Neither could have foretold that both, soon, would be out of office, out of Delhi, out on their different paths, which were not Nehru's path.

Law minister with the governor general (*Hindustan Times* archives).

1949
HOUSE OF POWER

My own earliest memories date from this period and to this very venue. The earliest 'picture' I have in my mind is of walking on one of the cream and red sandstone walkways of Mughal Gardens with my aunt, Namagiri, Periamma (elder mother), as I called her. Some herons or egrets, I am not sure which, walked across our path, and I tried, in boring conformity with what all kids do, to chase them, in vain, upon which Periamma asked a liveried staffer following us dutifully, to go to her room and fetch a clay heron that she had there—a gift from someone or other. It was brought within minutes. 'This one you can hold, and keep,' she said, in her quaint Hindi (I knew no other language at the time). 'It won't fly away.' The thing remained with me for decades, losing its beak first, then getting its legs to snap and buckle over until I do not know what happened to that companion of my first recollection before it was binned.

A form of nepotism—the author with his maternal aunt, Namagiri, who officiated as official hostess during her father's governor generalship, Mughal Gardens, Government House, New Delhi, 1948. (Author's personal collection).

Subbulakshmi had come in March of 1949 for a couple of concerts in Delhi, one of which, as Keshav Desiraju (1955–2021) tells us in his stellar biography of the singer, was attended by Prime Minister Nehru. Speaking after the concert, he said, 'Who am I, a mere Prime Minister, before this Queen of Song?' Subbulakshmi, with her husband and his daughters from his first marriage—Radha and Vijaya—called on Rajaji and Namagiri in Government House, and I remember watching the 'Queen of Song' in total amazement as she walked in the gardens and was photographed with all the others in her family and ours. I was all of four and could be imagining that I remember the fragrance of her jasmine floret, the whisper of perfume on her silk sari, that March afternoon. Her connection with that building was to continue till the late 1990s and climaxing in 1998, with my being again around, at age fifty-four, but more of that, later.

Family hour—the governor general with his family on a festive occasion, the author grabbing pride of place with unprotesting siblings and cousins distributed randomly. Yellow Drawing Room, Government House, New Delhi, 1949. (Devadas Gandhi personal archives).

At his father-in-law's official residence, Devadas was careful not to be identified as a live-in son-in-law, which he was not, for his home continued where it had always been—above the 'shop' in Connaught Circus. Rajaji also knew the shape of etiquette's cutlery and never bent it for Devadas and Lakshmi. His sharp-witted and sharp-tongued but uncommonly caring daughter Namagiri was officially the 'hostess' in Government House; his son Narasimhan and the family of deceased son Ramaswami were with him there, as his 'dependent' family. Devadas and Lakshmi were invited and included in events as much for being what they were in society as for reasons of kinship. Rajaji chose for himself a small room, which had been that of the vicereine's chambermaid, next to that of the vicereine's, which Namagiri moved into. A painted picture of Sri Ramakrishna came up on one of the walls of this room as did, in a beautifully carved wooden frame, that of Alarmelmangamma, (1888–1915) his wife, long since in another world.

Cherishing a gifted sister—Prime Minister Jawaharlal Nehru with his sister Vijaya Lakshmi Pandit, United Nations Headquarters, 1948. (Devadas Gandhi personal archives. Source: 'Fear Is Not a Good Companion' by Jawaharlal Nehru, London: The India League, 1948.)

This was the time when Nehru was identifying and appointing ambassadors and governors consulting Patel and Rajaji. The prime minister's very able and stunning-looking sister, Vijaya Lakshmi Pandit, had been appointed India's ambassador—the first—to Moscow. Was this nepotism? It was and was not. She had been a prominent freedom fighter and minister in the United Provinces and was unquestionably 'somebody in her own right'. But she was also Nehru's sister, and that was her first and foremost identity. Her stint in Moscow was not particularly successful if an equation with the country's top man is the test. She was unable to meet Stalin even once. When the first ambassador to the US, Asaf Ali (1888–1953), was to be replaced, Nehru sent Vijaya Lakshmi to Washington. This required finding a successor for her in Moscow.

Jawaharlal wrote to her in February 1949: 'Moscow continues to be a big headache...we feel that it might be a good thing for Devadas Gandhi to be sent there. We have not yet mentioned it to him or to anyone else, and I have no idea what his own reaction will be. Obviously, he has no experience, and he is not brilliant, but taking it in all he will be suitable. Anyway, I cannot think of any other suitable person.'

'No experience (in diplomacy)' was a correct description, but 'not brilliant' would have surprised the person being described had he come to know of it. And '...cannot think of any other suitable person' was only a default compliment paid by the prime minister to Devadas. Vijaya Lakshmi wrote to her brother saying Devadas was not suitable for Moscow. Be that as it may, one afternoon in early 1949, Nehru rang and asked Devadas to come over for a chat, bringing Lakshmi with him. This was not unusual, but its abruptness was a bit unexpected. They were received cordially by the prime minister in Teen Murti House, and after a few minutes of conversation on usual nothings, he left Lakshmi to talk to Indira (who combined this with giving laundry to their dhobi, counting the items carefully, Lakshmi recalled, as the items were bundled up) and took Devadas to a side room. The two emerged soon enough. 'What did you two talk about?' Lakshmi asked her husband in the car on their drive back home. 'Jawaharlalji asked me if I would go to Moscow as India's Ambassador.' 'Oh, isn't that nice!' Lakshmi said. 'I hope you agreed.' 'I have asked for time to think about it, but I am not inclined,' he replied.

Rajaji and Patel were told about the offer by Devadas, and both of them advised him to say yes. Patel was even more emphatic than Rajaji. But Devadas grew more and more certain that his disinclination was right. He told the PM soon enough that his heart was in running the *Hindustan Times*, and that he would not do justice to the embassy in Moscow. Nehru heard him matter-of-factly, and that was that. The offer was not reiterated, nor was it substituted by any other, and he told his sister, now packing up in Moscow, that the idea of appointing Devadas had 'fallen through'. Patel did not hide his disappointment.

A happy birthday that had no return—Sardar Patel sits for a formal photograph in the lawns of his residence, 1 Aurangzeb Road, New Delhi, on 31 October 1950, New Delhi, with his family and staff, as also Devadas Gandhi's family. Patel's secretary, V. Shankar, just behind him. (Author's personal collection).

Devadas's declining had much to do with the reason he had given to the prime minister. But it also had something to do with the Nehru–Patel rift. In Moscow, he would have been answerable to the PM, who was also External Affairs minister, but would have also been under some pressure from Patel, who, as minister for Information and Broadcasting (in addition to Home), was in charge of the publicity aspects of our diplomatic representation. Apart from his official and portfolio-based hold on our missions abroad, Patel was Patel. He thought he had a natural say in matters pertaining to diplomacy and diplomatic appointments. He could not be ignored by Nehru when he asked for Dhirajlal Desai (1908–51), the lawyer-son of the late Congress leader and legal luminary Bhulabhai Desai (1877–1946), to be given an ambassadorship. Nehru, who knew Dhirubhai, as he was called, sent him to Berne as India's minister, which was the same as ambassador—India's first in that position. Dhirubhai was Nehru's representative, but he was also

Patel's 'man' and wrote as many letters to Patel from Berne addressing him, in Gujarati fashion, as 'Bapu', reporting on his work to the home minister and as frequently if not more than he did to the prime minister and the Ministry of External Affairs. Nehru was too big-hearted (apart from being too busy running the government) to mind this. But Dhirubhai soon earned a reputation for being casual with government funds in his legation in Berne. V. Narahari Rao (1893–1969), India's first and famously vigilant comptroller and auditor general, on an inspection tour in Berne, took serious notice of accounting derelictions in the embassy and sent a very damaging report to Finance Minister C. D. Deshmukh (1896–1982) who, naturally, brought it to Nehru's notice. He sent a list of Desai's irregular spending and accounting, adding, fairly, that Desai had told him, in self-defence, that sometimes officials and non-officials visiting needed to be helped with some monetary assistance for unexpected expenses.

These were early and formative years for the Indian Foreign Service (IFS), and Nehru had 'hits' and 'misses' in his selection of persons for stand-alone non-career appointments and in his recruitments to the IFS. One great 'hit' is described below.

Decades into the evolution of the IFS, when I, an IAS 'guy', was secretary to President K. R. Narayanan (1920–2005), I was privileged one afternoon while returning from Parliament House with him to Rashtrapati Bhavan, to hear from him this account of how he came to enter the IFS to become one of the country's most distinguished diplomats: 'When I finished with LSE, Laski, of his own, gave me a letter of introduction for Panditji. So, upon reaching Delhi, I sought an appointment with the PM. I suppose, because I was an Indian student returning home from London, I was given a time-slot. It was here in Parliament House that he met me. We talked for a few minutes about London and things like that, and I could soon see that it was time for me to leave. So, I said goodbye, and as I left the room, I handed over the letter from Laski and stepped out into the great circular corridor outside. When I was halfway round, I heard the sound of someone clapping from the direction I had just come. I turned to see Panditji beckoning me to come back. He had opened the letter as I left his room and read it. 'Why didn't you give this to me earlier?' 'Well, sir, I am sorry. I thought it would be enough if I just handed it over while leaving.' After a few more questions, he asked me to see him again.' Nehru has to be credited with sensitivity and imagination in the manner in which he selected the first recruits for the IFS.

India's ambassadors-designate called on the governor general as they departed for the capitals they had been assigned. A memorable photograph has V. K. Krishna Menon (high commissioner in Great Britain 1947–52) and K. M. Panikkar (ambassador in China 1950–52) to Rajaji's right and left. A thicker density of south Indian intellection can scarcely be imagined.

In May 1949, Rajaji visited Madras and went by train from that city overnight to Tiruvannamalai, famed for its temple to Arunachalesvara, as Shiva is known there, and the stunning 800-metre-high hill just outside the town called Arunachala. No less celebrated was the place for it being the place where Sri Ramana Maharshi (1879–1950) lived in a cluster of huts going by the name of Ramanasramam. Rajaji had been invited by a Parsi disciple of Ramana, Feroza Taleyarkhan (1898–1984), to open a shrine called the Pathala Lingam within the temple set up at her initiative. He did that on 14 May, unveiling a portrait of Ramana Maharshi in the precincts. In a thirty-minute speech in Tamil, he paid a touching tribute to the sage. Swami Niranjanananda, the Maharshi's brother, attended the event and informed him of an ailment in the sage's hand, saying it was being treated. The ailment was cancer, and almost eleven months to the day, after this visit by Rajaji, the great being was to cross over.

But curiously and yet not so curiously for him, Rajaji did not call on the sage whose dwelling was just a few yards away. Why? Ramana was least concerned, and Rajaji was least worried over questions about the omission. But ordinary mortals did and still do wonder if this did not resemble the occasion when Gandhiji had driven past Ramana's hut in February 1934 without stopping. Rajaji had been with Gandhi then as his 'tour-in-charge'. Various explanations had been offered then, including the theologically-charged one that Gandhi and Ramana together would have been unsustainable in the cosmos of spiritual intelligence. But on this occasion, his not having stepped into the sage's dwelling, especially when he was unwell, bores a hole in his itinerary.

If there was a most regrettable lack of grace in Rajaji's skipping a visit to Ramana Maharshi, he gave an example of his innate warmth in another encounter. Rajaji's visit to Tiruvannamalai saw him meet E. V. Ramasamy, his friend of decades and foe of many years in those decades. EVR had sought a meeting with Rajaji in Delhi. Saving him the trouble of a trip to Delhi, Rajaji suggested they meet in Tiruvannamalai. Both were of about the same age—seventy plus—and both widowers. EVR asked Rajaji for his views on whether he (EVR) should enter into nuptials with a lady who was thirty-two and on whom he had come to rely. Details of that conversation are unknown, but later correspondence shows that Rajaji said that the reposing of trust by one of his age in one of her's had its risks. In his speech at the temple, Rajaji referred to the many years of friendship between them, despite the differences that have crept into their relationship.

He said that despite these differences, their friendship had not suffered and asked people to emulate their example. This was doubtless a handsome thing to have said, and the meeting with EVR itself had a charm to it. A little later, EVR wrote to Rajaji to say that he was going ahead with the wedding plans and would he, Rajaji, do him the friendly favour of witnessing the civil registration of the proceedings in his premises in New Delhi. Rajaji wrote back, sending his good wishes (now that the decision had been taken) but regretting his inability to do the witnessing due to the circumstances of his holding the office he was holding. There can be more than one view on Rajaji's response. EVR went ahead regardless, and the couple—EVR and Maniammal—were one of the most celebrated couples in Indian politics, with their marriage leading to a cathartic event: the break-up of EVR's Dravidar Kazhagam and the formation of the Dravida Munnetra Kazhagam*. It is my view that if Rajaji had agreed to do the witnessing—there was no precedent for such a thing, perhaps, but where was the bar?—a great healing would have occurred in the Brahmin versus non-Brahmin discourse in the Tamil countryside. And perhaps the DK–DMK split might not have occurred.

A grim issue that Rajaji had to attend to was, of course, the sentence on Gandhi's assassins. Of the seven accused, Godse and Apte were sentenced to death. With the appeal filed against the convictions also being dismissed, a mercy petition was filed for Godse by his parents, not by him. And another by thirty-five-year-old Apte's young wife, not by Apte. Manilal and Ramdas Gandhi, sons number two and three of the victim, moved for the assassins to not be hung. Their intervention was treated with respect but nothing more. Ramdas sought permission to meet Godse to 'convert' him. Rajaji wrote to Ramdas, 'I would advise you to leave the case to the hands of the Government...You should not visit the prisoner.' Harilal was no more, and Devadas did not join his brothers.

How is the editor-son of a murdered man to report the execution of his father's killers? 'As an editor, completely detached from his kinship' would be the textbook objective answer. Easier said than done. A diligent editor Devadas, he was also a passionately fond son. And it is clear that he was no abolitionist in the matter of death sentences, and there is nothing to show that he joined his brothers Manilal and Ramdas in their plea for Godse and Apte to be spared the noose. So, the son in the editor played his role in the reportage of the final days of the assassin-convicts. Governor

*The DK and DMK have maintained an equation through the decades rather like the RSS and the Jana Sangh in all its variations right up to its present form as the BJP.

General Rajagopalachari rejected on 8 November 1949 the 'mercy' petitions filed on behalf of the two. Whoever the newspaper's special correspondent was, over whose name the report appeared, I can see Devadas scripting the opening line of the report on 9 November. 'At last,' it began, 'twenty-two months after the commission of their diabolical crime, Nathuram Vinayak Godse and his co-conspirator Narayan Apte, have to mount the gallows on November 15 for assassinating Mahatma Gandhi.'

The two men were hanged in Ambala jail, where they had been held, on 15 November 1949.

A very small syndicated report on 16 November informed the reader of the *Hindustan Times* that the relatives of the two 'have been informed' of the execution. Godse was a bachelor, Apte married. His wife, Champa, had been allowed, as per jail regulations, to spend some four hours with her husband the evening before the morning execution. Godse's sister and two brothers, likewise. The report said Champa returned the next day to Poona. Even 'normal' partings within the family fold can be hard. These must have been unbearable. It must have been for reasons of 'averting tensions' that the families' request, after the cremations, for the ashes of the two was turned down. One can understand the administrative point. But one cannot miss the cobalt-cold harshness of the decision.

The Godse–Apte hangings were the first two in independent India. The law, as it stood, had worked. 'As it stood'. But India in 1949 was not where it had just 'stood'. It had become free, free of the past. The customs and codes of the laws of the past were now open for India to review, reconsider, revise, and repeal. But no, the one and only law that gave the state control over the physical body of a prisoner and the competence to kill had been invoked. And in the 'case' of one who would have everything in his power to stop that. Death had denied him the one power he used majestically over decades—the power to reject revenge and to forgive. Dead, Gandhi could not forgive, could not fast. He had died with the dying. Now, he had two dying after him for killing him. The spiritual 'perfection' of Gandhi's assassination had been given the company of the gross imperfection of his assassins' executions. 'Irony' has no equivalent that I know of in any of the languages of India.

Another companion irony may be noted in passing: the first woman to be hanged—and apparently, without sufficient proof—in the US was Mary Surratt (1823–65), a co-accused in the assassination of another symbol of ethical stature—Abraham Lincoln (1809–65).

Having Rajaji as governor general was of practical help to Nehru and Patel in political terms. His candour came in handy. In Hyderabad, on 21

December 1949, where, notably, Muslims welcomed him as warmly as its Hindu residents, a banquet was thrown in his honour by the nizam. 'Now,' said the governor general to the gentry seated at that opulent table, 'when the foreign power has been eliminated, and India is in possession of her own soul, it is not a legitimate ambition or a wise policy (for any territorial unit) to strive for isolation.' A clearer message could not have been given. It was not that of a victor but of a mentor.

Rajaji was accompanied by Namagiri on that visit to Hyderabad, and the two stayed in the nizam's Falaknuma Palace as His Highness's guests. The visit was not without its delicacy, for Rajaji was coming as the head of the Indian state, which had humbled the nizam and tumbled his administration out of its obsolete suzerainty. Family lore has it that on the guests' first evening, shortly before a banquet he threw in their honour, His Exalted Highness sent a tray to Namagiri's suite bearing a gift—a diamond-studded necklace. She naturally turned to her father for an indication on what she should do with it. The governor general had the laden tray sent back, very courteously, with the message that he thanks H. H. for his generosity, but his daughter, a widow not accustomed to wearing ornaments of this kind, is unable to accept it. Relating this to me years later, Namagiri said she had no regret at all at her father's decision but would have preferred his not alluding to widowhood. 'He could have said,' she added, 'we are Gandhi's disciples and do not own costly things.' Her alternative wording bespoke feminist gravitas and a sense of history. Daughters of the great can, at the cross-hairs of dilemmas, out-great their forebears.

A week later, he was in Shillong, the capital of Assam, where Sri Prakasa, a close friend, was governor. Some leaders of tribal groups called on him at the Raj Bhavan, and the whiff of separatism's inchoate aspirations filled the room. 'Unless,' said Rajaji to his callers, 'all of you are linked to a strong government like that of India, it is not safe. The very customs which you wish to preserve will be blown away in a storm. You cannot be strong without joining the Government of India. China threatens Tibet, and Burma is divided, whereas India is established and can defend you and your families.' Years later, Jayaprakash Narayan, trusted by the Naga and by leaders of the Muslim population of Kashmir's valley, was to say almost identical things to the same people.

BOOK TWO

1950
NO REGRETS?

The start of the year 'rang in' the Republic of India. With this, the new Constitution came into effect, giving the country its new name—India that is Bharat, and defining it as a union of states.

On 26 January, the chosen day, the nation's mood was celebratory, as is only right and natural. For our family, though, it was not exactly festooned. The first president, Dr Rajendra Prasad or Rajen babu as we knew him at home, had been a friend of the family for years. His austere nature, his hand-spun, if not also self-spun attire of 'only khadi', his sincere warmth and his outstanding command over Hindi were admired in the family. He and Appa had known each other very closely and very cordially as part of the larger Gandhi family since 1917 when, as a seventeen-year-old, Appa had been billeted by his father to work among the indigo villagers of Champaran, Bihar. And Rajen babu had been there, almost as his 'local guardian', striking a life-long friendship.

Being like family is, however, not the same thing as being family. His pipping Anna to the office of president of India rankled. Should Rajaji, the last governor general, not have become the first president? Had he not done exceedingly well as governor general, and did Nehru himself not want him to be India's first president? Yes, and yes! We never quite went along with the view that Sardar Patel did not want Rajaji to be that. Patel was a partyman, and he knew that the party overwhelmingly wanted Rajen babu, with his faultless record as president of the Constituent Assembly, to be India's first head of state.

The knowledge that more than the party, more than Patel and more than the nation's political class, it was Rajen babu himself who wanted to be India's first rashtrapati, is what we in our family had to adjust to. Anna told my mother, '...the moment I saw that Rajen babu himself was keen, I knew the time had come for me to depart...I was at peace in my mind...' And he had with Patel the following conversation:[1]

Patel to Rajaji: Jawaharlal has spoilt everything. I wanted to do it tactfully. He has rushed the matter.

Rajaji to Patel: Why are you offering me an explanation? I am not keen on the office.

In his biography of Rajaji, Rajmohan Gandhi says: 'C.R. was never to utter, in public or private, deliberately or absent-mindedly, to strangers or confidants, any word revealing a hurt at not being chosen President.' And he asks, 'Was it that C.R. concealed his true feelings with remarkable success? Or was it that he was able to look at the event with the eyes of the others involved and that he was really indifferent to the rank he held?' Rajmohan says, 'C.R. was not a saint. He knew disappointment and dejection…but…he had philosophy enough to smile both at his entry into Government House and his exit from it.' No one can put it better or more truthfully.

Kuraiyonrum illai (No regrets have I) is the opening line and refrain of a song that Rajaji penned in his later years, addressed to Venkatesvara, the deity at Tirupati. Sung regularly thereafter by M. S. Subbulakshmi in her concert to popular delectation, it fluxed with the devotion and emotion of many listeners. The words are vintage Rajaji, the emotion, the idea, classic Rajaji. But they are Rajaji as Rajaji had trained himself to be. Within that self-trained, self-restrained, self-regulated, self-denying surrenderer of his ego at the altar of his God was a human being, a father, and grandfather, with anxieties, fears, and yes, regrets at not having been able to do better by his kin, by his values, even by his faith. He was trying, and in his humble reckoning, trying successfully to subsume his regrets, to overcome them. When he says in that song that he does not have any regrets, he is telling himself that he should not have any and should have the strength of faith to not have any.

At a farewell banquet on the eve of the change, in his reply to a very moving speech by Nehru, Rajaji said: 'Sometimes the truth comes upon us with overpowering conviction. Now I realise that the greatest joy in life is to give up a thing and go.'

The ceremony in the Durbar Hall of Rashtrapati Bhavan on 26 January sparkled. It was photographed, filmed, and came, in time, to be painted. But one black-and-white photograph of the proceedings stands out. The retiring governor general has just vacated the high throne and moved to a smaller seat to its left, as the in-coming president is being administered his oaths by the chief justice, with Shavax Lal, ICS, who has been the governor general's secretary and will now be that to the president, standing to a side, lost in thought. But it is Rajaji, now literally and metaphorically, on the margins, who completely dominates the picture. How? He is looking back, turning his neck and face at an acute angle, at that moment of 'giving up,' at the statue of Gautama, the renunciate Buddha that stands behind the throne he has vacated.

Ever the objective editor, Devadas subordinated his own disappointment, and the *Hindustan Times* had for its headline the next day, 27 January: 'Delhi Goes Gay on Republic Day'. He was obviously and charmingly unaware of the connotation the three-letter word had come to acquire in the West since the time *Bringing Up Baby* (1938) starring Cary Grant handed the word over to the sense in which it now is used. One person who would have giggled seeing that headline was Lionel Fielden (1896–1974). Famously, self-professedly gay himself, Fielden had inaugurated the network of AIR in India during the late 1930s as controller of broadcasting and the first director general of AIR. Fielden was in Delhi on the day the Republic of India was born. In his riveting and hugely instructive memoir *The Natural Bent*, he says of the proceedings of the change over under the dome of Government House, soon to be rechristened Rashtrapati Bhavan: 'I got up early and went with my grandly gilded cards to the Durbar Hall, where I found Nehru and Amrit Kaur alone, fussing over the seating arrangements. They were enchantingly warm and kind and took my teasing lightly. I asked Nehru what on earth he was doing with a bodyguard, all standing round like statues and dressed up with lances in correct viceregal fashion. He said, "You wouldn't want me to put the poor chaps out of work, would you?" I felt inclined to ask him what he thought about all the poor English chaps who had been put out of work by his nationalism, but the reply was too obvious.... The ceremony that followed was an impressive transformation scene.... But to me, the most striking of all was Rajagopalachari, the retiring Governor-General. He always was my favourite man in India and still is, and I still receive his wonderful letters. That day, at the end of the thing and glittering procession, he shuffled up to the throne in a *dhoti*, clearly indifferent to the whole business, but nevertheless dominating it....'

With its first president, India also got two persons as 'firsts' of their own kind that day, both of whom happened to be Gujaratis. Sir Harilal Jekisundas Kania (1890–1951) became the first chief justice of the Supreme Court of India (which replaced the Federal Court of India established under the Government of India Act, 1935). And Motilal Chimanlal Setalvad (1884–1974) took office as the republic's first attorney general. Kania had been chief justice of the Federal Court since 15 August 1947, the last to hold that office. Setalvad had been advocate general of Bombay. At the commencement of the Supreme Court's work, Justice Kania said: '...the Supreme Court should be quite untouchable by the Legislature or the executive authority in the performance of its duties.' A noble and salutary sentiment, expressed at a turning point in India's history. Sudden and premature death was to remove Kania from the scene the following year. Setalvad was to remain in his office, despite an early reluctance to part from his practice in Bombay, for thirteen years, leaving it, finally, in 1963, with a sad feeling of being no longer wanted or valued. He had been phenomenally good, giving both the president and the prime minister his clear—and correct—view on the powers of the president. It was not within his remit to speak on the influence that a president may exert on the polity, as distinct from 'powers'.

Exactly one month later, on 26 February 1950, exercising neither his own independent powers (which he did not have) nor influence (which he had but chose not to use for demurring), President Prasad gave his assent to a contentious act. The Preventive Detention Act, 1950, was to be in force for a year but could be renewed. Under it, any person acting in any manner prejudicial to—(i) the defence of India, the relations of India with foreign powers, or the security of India, or (ii) the security of the State or the maintenance of public order, or (iii) the maintenance of supplies and services essential to the community, could be detained. There were stipulations in the Act about the duration of the detention.

Patel, as home minister, was very clear about the need for this Act, overlooking the freedom struggle's bitter experience of such detentions. He had in mind all the existential and extreme dangers India had faced in the wake of freedom, partition, the accession of states, and the communist-led movements in Bengal, Travancore, and Telangana. One of the persons detained under the Act, in Madras, early in its operation was the communist leader A. K. Gopalan (1904–77)[*] for three speeches that he had made. Gopalan filed a petition under Article 32 of the Constitution of India for a writ of habeas corpus against his detention. The matter came up before a six-judge bench headed by Chief Justice Kania. Setalvad represented the Union of India. The central point argued by the counsel for 'AKG', as the communist leader was known, was that the Act infringed the right of free movement guaranteed under Article 19 of the Constitution and that its Section 14 forbidding disclosure of the grounds of detention nullified the right of habeas corpus. Setalvad made the canny point that the Constitution should not be interpreted from the point of what an ideal Constitution should be but what the Constitution, as it stands, actually says. Does the Act violate Part III of the Constitution? he asked.

In a landmark majority order of 4:2, with each judge writing a separate judgment, the court upheld the validity of the Preventive Detention Act, 1950, with the exception of Section 14.

Between giving his assent to the Preventive Detention Act and the judgment in *A. K. Gopalan,* President Prasad raised the question as to how

[*]The case is the subject of an engaging book on Gopalan's counsel, *M. K. Nambyar: A Constitutional Visionary*, by his son K. K. Venugopal with Suhrith Parthasarathy and Suhasini Sen (Penguin/Ebury Press, 2023).

binding on the president was the advice of the cabinet. Setalvad's view was sought and came ringingly clear: The president is like the British monarch, a constitutional, not an executive head, and has to be guided by cabinet advice. The point of presidential prerogatives was not pressed by the president. Setalvad's position was to be reiterated forcibly and conclusively in 1975 when, in a landmark judgment, the Supreme Court confirmed this position. *Shamsher Singh and Another vs the State of Punjab* has settled the point.

No president has flouted Setalvad's opinion or the *Shamsher Singh* order. But every president has, I suspect, held in a sealed locket within the inner recesses of his or her heart, Prasad's doubt and—hope.

A pause in the affairs of state—a relaxed moment in the Mughal Gardens, after President Rajendra Prasad hosted Prime Minister Jawaharlal Nehru and his family to lunch, February 1950. To the extreme left is Feroze Gandhi, between the president and prime minister, Indira Gandhi, and to the president's left, Padmaja Naidu. (Author's personal collection, from the Rashtrapati Bhavan's archives).

The 1950 inauguration of the first president was to be followed by fourteen in a sound north–south variation, with the minorities well represented, though women most insufficiently. We have had, as of 2024, counting from President Prasad, fifteen presidents in sixteen presidencies, Prasad having had two consecutive terms. Thirteen of them men, and only two, women.

Irrespective of where they have come from, what their religion is, their language, their politics or their sociology, our presidents have been very

'Constitution-bound'. Some of them, rather mechanically so. No one misses anything by forgetting those among them. But some have been constitutionally correct without being craven. They have provided not an alternative helm but a supplemental plinth. The PM is the mind of the nation as a state; the president is the soul of the state as a nation. The PM leads; the president guides. The PM makes decisions; the president influences opinion.

And he warns. Not just as a right but as a duty. In his last Republic Day address, in 1967, India's second president Radhakrishnan was to warn the country and the government: 'We cannot forgive widespread incompetence and the gross mismanagement of our resources.' Prime Minister Indira Gandhi was not pleased. But the nation was sobered. India's ninth president, K. R. Narayanan, was to craft his addresses with great deliberation, speaking directly and with tremendous impact. In his address on the eve of the Republic Day, 2000, he was to say to his government: 'Beware of the fury of the patient and long-suffering people.' Prime Minister Vajpayee was not amused.

Politically, the president is weightless; ideationally, he can weigh a ton. In that office, the country has acquired an asset, the value of which can be seen in the judicious, egoless use of that office, not in 'clutching at jurisdiction', to use an expression President R. Venkataraman frequently employed. But increasingly, the trend has been for presidents, deeply grateful to the dispensation that has brought them to their high office, to prefer the quiet comfort of status over the riskier satisfaction of stature.

The office of the chief justice in India's Supreme Court inaugurated simultaneously with that of the Rashtrapati, is, likewise, of one whose influence is unmeasured but incalculable. Chief justices have attained their office by virtue of seniority, mainly, not their representative character. Yet, that feature—CJIs being reflective of the nation's diversity—has invited notice. It took eighteen years for India to get its first Muslim CJI when, in 1968, Justice Mohammad Hidayatullah (1905–92) became chief justice of India.* It took a full fifty-seven years, in 2007, for India to see its first Dalit CJI, Justice K. G. Balakrishnan (b. 1945). India got its first Parsi CJI in 2010 in Justice S. H. Kapadia (1947–2016) and its first Sikh CJI in 2017 when Justice Jagdish Singh Khehar (b. 1952) took that office. But the CJI's background is half as important as the CJI's stature. If a CJI is unafraid and, in fact, unconcerned with what may happen to her or him post-retirement, nothing can prevent the incumbent from being true to the office at its highest score on the scale. Chief Justice D. Y. Chandrachud (2022–24) brought to his office

*The eleventh CJI serving from 25 February 1968 to 16 December 1970, and the sixth vice president of India.

a height and a weight that were singularly his own, making it impossible for either the state or its litigating opposite numbers to take him for granted. His orders, alternately, impressed and depressed the state and its dissidents.

But, to return to 1950.

On the night of 14 April, Ramana Maharshi, the great sage, breathed his last in the ashram that had grown around him in the temple town of Tiruvannamalai. In a vivid report filed by its correspondent in Tiruvannamalai, *The Hindu* said, 'A meteor of unusual size and brilliance was seen exactly at the time Bhagavan Sri Ramana attained *Videha-mukti*. The devotees gathered at the Ashram were thrilled by the sight of the phenomenon and its coincidence with the sage's passing away.' A subeditor in the newspaper's head office added in brackets, 'The meteor was observed by many in the City also.' Ramana had placed little if any importance on the physical body or anything temporal, being a living example of Advaita, but his adherents across the world felt orphaned by his going. Shortly before he died, a redemptive conversation took place between the great soul and a person who was attending to him, Sivananda, who knew no language other than Tamil. Ramana said to Sivananda 'thanks' in English, and then he himself translated the word for him into Sanskritized Tamil as 'santosham', meaning 'I am happy' or, simply, 'happiness'. The metaphorical significance of Ramana's translation of the word into 'santosham' is enormous. It has to do with not wanting more. A peacock famously wailed from the roof above where the Maharshi lay. He asked, 'Has the peacock been fed?' Even as he was thanking his attendant with 'santosham' in his mind, he was thinking of what might bring santosham to the distressed peacock. Ramana's teaching, encapsulated by the philosopher Ramchandra Gandhi, my brother, Ramu, as 'I Am Thou' could not have been exemplified better. Henri Cartier-Bresson, who was present at the time, just as he had been at the time of Gandhi's assassination in Delhi, took pictures of Ramana as he was crossing over in a final silence.

Finance Minister Dr John Matthai (1886–1959), uncomfortable with the founding of the National Planning Commission had resigned, meanwhile, from the union cabinet, and a search was on for this worthy man's successor. The prime minister, pressing Rajaji to return to Delhi and help run the government, offered Finance to him but Rajaji declined. He was to go as minister without portfolio and later take up Home, with its new preoccupations with guarding the nation's security against what it deemed to be insurgents, dissidents, and, generally, 'counter-state' elements.

Rajaji's city of Madras was, at this time, revelling in its great bond with cinema. Madras newspapers had on the same front page as the *A. K. Gopalan* case story a sumptuous advertisement of a Tamil film—*Manthiri Kumari*

(1950), featuring the three dancing 'Travancore sisters'—Lalitha, Padmini, and Ragini—but more strikingly, 'M. G. Ramachandar' (1917–87) in that quaint spelling of the name of the future hero of Tamil cinema, a future chief minister of Tamil Nadu. Even more interestingly, there appeared as the maker of its 'Story and Dialogue', 'Karunanidhi' (1924–2018), also destined to be chief minister of Tamil Nadu over five times for nearly twenty years. In 1950, neither would have guessed that the Republic of India, opening that year, would see them play the politically crucial roles they were going to. Nor the role that cinema itself was to play in India outside the silver screen.

The same issue of the *Indian Express*, edited by Ramnath Goenka (1904–91), had another smaller advertisement for a Hindi film entitled *Samadhi*. This was a Filmistan production starring Ashok Kumar and Nalini Jaywant, its theme and scope being described as: 'The first picture to depict the inspiring life-story of the iconic Netaji Subhas Chandra Bose.' I do not remember seeing the film, but it had a song which I know 'by heart', as they say, as the very first Hindi film song that I remember, words, tune, the works—*gorey gorey o banke chhore, kabhi meri gali aya karo*. The acclaimed scholar of Hindi, Rupert Snell, has translated the line for me as:

> O fancy lad, so fair and fine,
> Come by my lane
> From time to time...

It is a naughty song sung by Lata Mangeshkar (1929–2022), no less, to a dance danced with unsuccessfully attempted raunchiness by Nalini Jaywant, among others.

A small news item on an inside page in the same issue gave the news that Dr B. R. Ambedkar, the union law minister, had arrived in the city (Madras) on his way to Ceylon to attend the World Buddhist Conference there on 23 May. The newspaper had obviously missed or minimized the significance of the leader's trip. He was, after another five years of study of Buddhism and attending other Buddhist conclaves, to convert to Buddhism on 14 October 1956, in Nagpur, with 400,000 followers. The significance of Ambedkar to India's Constitution-making and to its prioritization of social justice was to dawn soon enough and, with Netaji and Patel, he was to acquire a formidable afterlife stature, but the significance to Ambedkar of Buddhism and its rejection of ritual and superstition along with caste has yet to be grasped by our society being drawn now in an atavistic recoil to the revivalist celebration of past glories, real and magnified, factual and concocted.

Netaji, Patel, and Ambedkar would all three be amused, dismayed, and alarmed, in turn, if they were to see how the country adulates images of them today without bothering to study their minds and messages.

In that inaugural year of the Republic, Nehru ushered in, by a side door, as it were, a major initiative—an instrumentality for planning the nation's economic regeneration—the National Planning Commission. One person who should have been crucial to it was the astrophysicist Meghnad Saha (1893–1956), who had been known to favour a scientifically-propelled planning process for the country.

Like Ambedkar, the fifty-seven-year-old Bengali was a Dalit from the downtrodden tier called Namashudra. He had, again like Ambedkar, risen by dint of high merit and high motivation. If the law and codes of political organization came to the Maharashtrian as naturally as breath, stars and their light, peopled the Bengali's imagination. If Jyotiba Phule (1827–90) and Mahadev Govind Ranade (1842–1901) had given Ambedkar an inspired energy, two Boses gave Saha his—Jagadish Chandra Bose (1858–1937) and Subhas Chandra Bose with Prafulla Chandra Ray (1861–1944) forming a third source—Physics, Politics, and Chemistry. And neither Ambedkar nor Saha had found any inspiration in Gandhi or Nehru.

At the Republic's founding and the inauguration of the Planning Commission, the renowned physicist was not inducted into the Planning Commission despite Saha having been so integral to the idea of such a body and despite his credentials as a scientist and a conceptualizer of planned development being so patent.

'Architect of modern India' is a title that Nehru has earned. That being modern also meant being aware of the pitfalls of blinkered 'modernity', especially in terms of what that does to the natural environment, was not something anyone was talking about at the time. 'Progress' was the slogan, almost the religion, of the times. And it had its priests, its punditry, its orthodoxy. The statistician P. C. Mahalanobis (1893–1972) was, in the 'Temples of Modern India' (a favourite Nehruvian phrase), High Priest.

Nehru asked Rajaji if he would like to chair the Planning Commission. Rajaji declined. Good for him, better for Mahalanobis, best for Nehru. Rajaji would have been uncomfortable with that style of national planning from Day One and would have caused Nehru no ordinary annoyance. Patel was not asked to play any role in it. He had done his bit as only he could have done in the integration of the states, the consolidation of the civil services, and the checking of insurrections.

India's first Independence Day as a Republic—15 August 1950—had an unwelcome start. It was a Tuesday evening. At 7.39 p.m., the 1950 Assam–Tibet earthquake, also known as the Assam earthquake, shook that region with a moment magnitude of 8.6. Described as the sixth largest earthquake of the twentieth century, it left 4,800 people dead, with 1,526 fatalities being in Assam. In the words of a scholarly article:

> For no fewer than seven minutes, a length of time that must have seemed an eternity to the inhabitants, 41 tremors shook the earth. In these seven minutes, monsoon-gorged rivers burst their banks, and massive landslides blocked Himalayan valleys. Tremors then subsided. But the worst was yet to come. When these natural dams burst, the water engulfed the countryside, and rivers in spate changed their course.[2]
>
> Villages and urban centres were levelled, standing crops were submerged, and transport and communications networks were shattered. In a short period of time, the physical map of north-eastern India had been refashioned by a natural disaster.[3]

The official report drafted by the Geological Survey of India after the earthquake left no doubt about this: 'Assam is literally known as the home of earthquakes.... This region is the most unstable in India; it lies along the main boundary fault line along the foot of the Himalayas and the eastern Assam ranges and has been the scene of nearly a dozen major earthquakes during the last century.'[4]

Over seven decades after this first experience of a major earthquake in independent India, the country as a whole—seismologists, architects, policymakers, and the public—are yet to wake up to the real and horrendous truth that 70 per cent of the Himalaya could experience an extremely powerful earthquake any moment now. Any moment because, as *Frontline* tells us 'The likelihood of such an earthquake recurring in the Himalaya has been endorsed by a number of experts.'[5]

3 November 1950 saw a very different 'mountain' tragedy enacted, this time not on the Himalaya but on the Alps. Air India Flight 245 was a scheduled Air India passenger flight from Bombay to London via Cairo and Geneva. That morning, the Lockheed L-749A Constellation crashed into Mont Blanc, France, while approaching Geneva. All forty-eight aboard were killed. The plane operating the flight had been named *Malabar Princess*. Piloted by Captain Alan R. Saint, thirty-four, and co-pilot V. Y. Korgaokar, the airplane hit the face of the Rocher de la Tournette at a height of 4,677 m (15,344 feet) on the French side of Mont Blanc. Stormy weather prevented immediate rescue efforts; debris was located by a Swiss plane on 5 November, and rescue parties reached the site two days later. As a five-year-old at that time, I remember nothing of these two traumas that were, for me, firsts of their kind. But hearing about them later has made me ever thoughtful about

life and death whenever I board a flight. And ever respectful of the pilots and crew who fly all the time. And the mildest tremor strikes terror in me.

Some mail on board the Air India Flight 245 flight was recovered after the crash, and further items of mail were found in 1951 and 1952. Twenty-eight years later, on 8 June 1978, a patrol of the French mountain police found letters and a sack at the foot of the Bossons Glacier. Recovered were fifty-seven envelopes and fifty-five letters (without envelopes). The snow had preserved these through silent years. All but eight letters were forwarded to their original addressees—an extraordinary feat of tracing roots.

On 5 December came the corporeal end of the great mystic Sri Aurobindo (1872–1950). As with Ramana Maharshi, this end, too, had a devoted associate figuring in it. He asked Nirodbaran, who was attending to him, what the time was and asked for a sip to quench his thirst. Then, his biographer Peter Heehs (b. 1948) tells us, 'He plunged within.' Many will see in Aurobindo's enquiry about the time and asking for water a meaning beyond those words. That one who thought of a 'superman' future status for evolving humanity could have exited, so 'normally' is, for me, strangely comforting. Death is a democrat, and a mischievous one at that. Its valedictory alchemy can 'equalize' the brains of geniuses with those of modest intellect. The *Hindustan Times* report said of Sri Aurobindo, 'His serene appearance suggested more of one in sleep than in death.'

By this time, Sardar Patel was now ready, as he, more than those around seemed to know, for his sleep that knows no waking. As the year entered its final days, Patel's metabolic heart wavered. A weakened cardiac status did not stop him from attending to his files, his visitors, and his duties, which included travel. Change of locale, when advised by doctors, is invariably a sign of medicine losing its self-confidence. This was suggested. Patel travelled to Bombay in December 1950, seen off at Delhi's Safdarjung airport by President Prasad, Prime Minister Nehru, Rajaji, and others in the cabinet. He had earlier told Minister N. V. Gadgil (1896–1966), supposedly a 'Patelite', to remain loyal to Nehru. 'Whatever happens,' he told his loyal colleague, 'do not leave Jawaharlal.'[6]

Once in his familiar place of stay in Bombay, Birla House, he was in calm converse with the 'Other Side'. He hummed songs that betokened conclusions—'*Mangal mandir kholo dayamay* (Open the holy temple for me, O Kindly One)' by Narsinhrao Divatia and '*Hai bahar-e-bagh duniya chand roz*... (Short is the Spring of life in this world...)' by Nazeer Akbarabadi (1735–1830). On 15 December, the last month of the first year of our Republic, the great glacier, now molten beyond reversing, slid gently into the ocean of the next world.

1951
THE GAMES OF POWER

In the first 'clear year' after India became a Republic, two sons of Bihar were briefly pitted against each other—one among the people through a call for a nation-wide strike and another under the chandeliered might of the state. Jayaprakash Narayan (JP), the dashing forty-nine-year-old socialist and a credible alternative to the sixty-two-year-old Prime Minister Jawaharlal Nehru, was head of the two most powerful trade unions—the All-India Post and Telegraph Workers' Union and the All-India Railwaymen's Federation. A steep increase in the cost of living had hit the workers in these two unions, as just about everyone else. After protracted negotiations with the government yielded no satisfactory results, JP called for a strike by the two powerful bodies. The call had the potential to bring the nation to a stop. President Rajendra Prasad, father-in-law of JP's sister-in-law in terms of kinship but also JP's senior and leader in the freedom struggle, was advised by the cabinet to issue an ordinance declaring the strike illegal and imposing severe penalties on the union leaders. JP had called for a strike and 'RP' had been advised to rule it illegal.

JP now stood threatened with a jail term by a powerful pen in the hands of a leader of the pre-independence struggle, now heading his independent country. But before the iron could be struck, high and sophisticated politics came to play. Nehru said in a public appeal that as a result of such a strike, food would not reach famine-struck areas. More, that a gamble on the borders by Pakistan was not to be ruled out, and that a strike at this point was not what the country should have to experience. These two arguments and the imminence of the first general elections led to the strike threat fizzling out. JP had fired a shot, the first of its kind and ringing in its intensity, but it was deftly deflected to fall just outside the mark.

This was to have been the first labour-led initiative of its kind in independent India and also JP's opening salvo in independent India's politics. It showed him to be what he was—great in his strivings, great in his impact, but somewhere, somehow, greatly fragile. But JP was not alone in his subsidence that year.

This was also a snakes-and-ladders year in India's politics. Down the gullets of giant snakes went three important players—Purushottamdas Tandon (1882–1962), the Congress president; Rajaji, the home minister; and Ambedkar, the law minister. And a golden ladder lifted—up and up all the way—none other than Prime Minister Jawaharlal Nehru. Having made it clear that he was uncomfortable with Tandon's helming of the party, Nehru dramatically quit his membership of the Tandon-formed Working Committee, creating a tide of confusion and uncertainty, which led to more resignations from the Working Committee and then, at the All India Congress Committee's session on 9 September, that of Tandon's own followed by Nehru's election, almost unanimous—only four members out of the 295 present voting against—to that office. In voting for Nehru, were they voting against Tandon? Not really. They were voting for the leader who they knew would lead the party to victory in the elections. Tandon, the ascetic scholar and freedom fighter, was Rajrishi, the Royal Saint, but Nehru was Rituraj, the King of the Season.

Shades of Mark Antony's ancient Rome fell on Nehru's New Delhi. The *Hindustan Times* photographer captured two moments—the arrival at the Congress session of Nehru, his now trademark rosebud fastened on his jacket, accompanied by his sister, Vijaya Lakshmi Pandit, and that of the outgoing party chief, sixty-nine, looking both frail and forlorn, accompanied by his loyalists in the party. The two pictures were carried on the front page, side by side, under the banner headline 'Nehru Chosen Congress President'.

Nehru was now prime minister and Congress president. There was one thing troubling him, though. A major enactment—the Hindu Code Bill—which was meant to transform Indian society was on the anvil. It had been listed for discussion and voting in the outgoing Provisional Parliament but was causing no end of trouble to him. The cumulative result of many deliberations to make Hindu society compatible with modern mores of equality and justice as between men and women and castes, the bill was intended to change tradition-dictated norms relating to marriage, divorce, inheritance succession, and adoption. His party was with him, but he knew that in their heart of hearts, most of his partymen were very old-fashioned, status quoist. They would want change, favour reform but not at the speed the bill proposed. The 'Tandon mind-set' was widespread and was most pertinently to be seen in the nation's new president—the erudite and gentle but of firm views, Dr Rajendra Prasad. Nehru was a passionate modernizer, Ambedkar, his law minister, an impatient reformer. The two were the co-architects, engineers, and masons of the bill. But they had different timelines to work in.

Elections, being due by the end of the year to India's first Parliament, were a priority for Nehru. Super-fit, his adrenaline flowing free and fast like the Ganga in spate, he was confident of a handsome win and a confirmation of his prime ministership. Should the discussion on the bill and a possible split among his own MPs on it be allowed to muddy election waters?

For Ambedkar, far from well, advised by doctors to rest, and unsure of whether he will contest in the elections and, if so, whether Congress would oppose him, the priority was getting the Hindu Code Bill through in the ongoing session, not put off for the post-election new Parliament, something which seemed to be on Nehru's mind.

It had been thought the bill would be taken up on 16 August and passed by 1 September. But there was to be a further delay. Nehru wrote to Ambedkar: 'About the Hindu Code Bill you know we have a good deal of opposition not only inside the House but outside... We must therefore proceed with some tact...' It was while the tactful setting of the date was being worked out that Prasad wrote to Nehru on 15 September 1951, asserting his 'right to examine it (the bill) on its merits, when it is passed by the Parliament, before giving assent to it'. Nehru, startled by Prasad's position, replied the same day: '...this might involve a conflict between the President on the one side, and government and Parliament on the other. They would invariably raise the question of the President's authority and powers to challenge the decisions of the Government and the Parliament. The consequences obviously would be serious.' He must have said to himself many times that day, 'If only Rajaji had been President!' The correspondence verged on brinkmanship, Prasad saying conflict could be avoided 'if the Government and the Parliament recognise the well-established and well-known democratic institutions and their powers', prompting Nehru to remind Prasad: 'These functions have, however, under the Constitution to be performed with the aid and advice of the Council of Ministers. Any action in these fields by the President without the concurrence of his Ministers would be foreign to the entire scheme of the Constitution and would, indeed, render it unworkable.' Prasad, in a lengthy riposte, made the point that if the president was bound to act, invariably, in accordance with the advice rendered to him by the Council of Ministers and could not, under any circumstances, act otherwise, the framers of the Constitution would have made such a clause explicit in the formulations.

His patience sorely tested, Ambedkar had even agreed to breaking the bill into parts and have at least the portion on marriage and divorce getting through, but even that was not being done. On 26 September, Nehru told Parliament that the bill will be taken up later. This meant that it would be shelved until the first Lok Sabha was elected. 'I see no purpose,' Ambedkar wrote on 27 September to the prime minister, 'in my continuing to be a member of your Cabinet.' Nehru replied, typically, the same day: '...I cannot press you to stay on.' Only formalities remained. 'I should like however to express my appreciation of our comradeship during these years since we have worked together in the Cabinet. We have differed sometimes but that has not affected my appreciation of the good work that you had done. I am sorry indeed that you will be going away.' That was Nehru at his quintessentially correct and cordial. The right tone was maintained, and courtesy observed. But what was the keyword in the letter? What was the 'grade' that the prime minister was giving to his law minister who had, after doing the monumental task of piloting the drafting of the Constitution, crafted the Hindu Code Bill, which was to be a giant leap in reform? It was a 'good'. Good work! That was no compliment; it was a punch on the nose.

Was Dr Ambedkar given a farewell party by the cabinet, a lunch by the prime minister? I have not found any indication of such civilities.

Ambedkar wanted to make a statement in the house on the day he was leaving the cabinet—12 October 1951. Ananthasayanam Ayyangar (1891–1978), deputy speaker, was in the chair.[1] He said Ambedkar could make the statement but at 6 p.m. at the conclusion of the day's business. And, he asked to be shown a copy of the statement in advance. Was he acting on his own? Ayyangar's requirement was deeply resented by Ambedkar, and with good reason. Dr H. N. Kunzru (1887-1978) asked the deputy speaker, 'Has the Chair the right to exercise censorship?'[2] Ayyangar's reply was not much of a reassurance. There was no question of censorship, he said, 'but the chair has its own responsibility and could not allow irrelevant or improper statements.' Irrelevant or improper!

Ambedkar had earlier told Nehru he would like to make a statement in Parliament on his resignation. This was customary. Nehru said if that were so, he (Nehru) would also like to make a few remarks after Ambedkar had spoken. That was not customary, but Ambedkar said he would have no difficulties with that. But on the day—12 October—what he made of Deputy Speaker Ayyangar's postponing of the time for Ambedkar's statement and asking for a copy of the statement in advance was this: his statement was needed by Nehru to mull over before it was made so that he could respond appropriately to it. And who might have choreographed this operatic delay? Consider Ambedkar's description (in his statement) of Satyanarayan Sinha (1900–83), the then minister for Parliamentary Affairs: 'The conduct of the Minister for Parliamentary Affairs, who is also the Chief Whip of the Party in connection with the Hindu Code, to say the least, has been most extraordinary. He has been the deadliest opponent of the Code and has never been presented to aid me by moving a closure motion. For days and hours, filibustering has gone on on a single clause. But the Chief Whip, whose duty it is to economise Government time and push on Government Business, has been systematically absent when the Hindu Code has been under consideration in the House. I have never seen a case of a Chief Whip so disloyal to the Prime Minister and a Prime Minister so loyal to a disloyal Whip. Notwithstanding this unconstitutional behaviour, the Chief Whip is really a darling of the Prime Minister. For notwithstanding his disloyalty, he got a promotion in the Party organisation. It is impossible to carry on in such circumstances.'

The only effect of the sequence of events in Parliament that day for Ambedkar was of humiliation. After Ayyangar declined to let him make his statement in the morning, Ambedkar dramatically walked out, saying, 'I am no longer a Minister, I am going out. I am not going to submit to this kind of dictation.' And he then released the statement outside the House. He placed his resignation in a detailed setting: 'As a result of my being a member of the Viceroy's Executive Council, I knew the Law Ministry to be administratively of no importance. It gave no opportunity for shaping the policy of the Government of India. We used to call it an empty soap box only good for old lawyers to play with. When the Prime Minister made me the offer, I told him that besides being a lawyer by my education and experience, I was competent to run any administrative Department... But I have always been left out of consideration. Many Ministers have been given two or three portfolios so that they have been overburdened. Others like me have been wanting more work. I have not even been considered for holding a portfolio temporarily when a Minister in charge has gone abroad for a few days. It is difficult to understand what is the principle underlying the distribution of Government work among Ministers which the Prime Minister follows. Is it capacity? Is it trust? Is it friendship? Is it pliability? ...I have never been a party to the game of power politics inside the Cabinet or the game of snatching portfolios which goes on when there is a vacancy. I believe in service, service in the post which the Prime Minister, who as the head of the Cabinet, thought fit to assign to me. It would have, however, been quite unhuman for me not to have felt that a wrong was being done to me.'

The whole thing was done in bad form. Ambedkar had been treated shoddily. And for nothing, really. It was all about timing. Nehru was no less interested in the Hindu Code Bill than Ambedkar. He had, as we saw, crossed swords on this with President Prasad himself. But the social reformer and modernizer had a conservative party, a position-conscious president and imminent elections—the first of their kind—on his hands. The visionary chapter-turning Ambedkar had his ill-health to deal with and no certainty about where he stood vis-à-vis the imminent elections. For reasons of crossed timelines, India lost the colleagueship it needed of India's first prime minister and India's first law minister somewhere along the road to the first elections of independent India.

Devadas and Ambedkar did not have any equation worth mentioning. This is something I regret because Devadas's essentially eclectic mind (despite his foundational Congressism) would have enjoyed such an association and, withal, led to a warmer appreciation by Gandhi in his later years, of the human dimensions of the legal genius. And Ambedkar, too, would have, through such a bridge, come to view his bête noire with a measure of human indulgence. Devadas had, at his father's bidding, called on Ambedkar in London in 1931 during the Second Round Table Conference to seek a compromise on behalf of his father over the subject of the representation of the Depressed Classes in the legislatures being discussed under a new Constitution. That meeting between the two led to nothing. But all that notwithstanding, Devadas could sense the short-changing of Ambedkar in the matter of the Hindu Code Bill, and he gave Ambedkar's letters to Nehru, Nehru's replies, the deputy speaker's blocking of Ambedkar and Ambedkar's exit from the house a coverage that was very favourable to Ambedkar and then, carried his statement in extenso. Other newspapers doubtless did as much, but the *Hindustan Times,* being edited by Gandhi's son, Rajaji's son-in-law, and one who was known to be a supporter of Nehru, gave its Ambedkar coverage a certain voltage of its own.

If Ambedkar got no send-off from the ruling dispensation in Delhi, the lack of courtesy was made up for by Bombay. When, on 18 November 1951, Ambedkar returned to Bombay with his wife, Savita Ambedkar née Kabir (1909–2003), a 'well-attended welcome function' was organized for him at the Victoria Terminus Railway Station (VT) by the Bombay units of the Scheduled Castes Federation and the Socialist Party. The choice of the venue is significant, as also the agency for the reception. The VT was next to the Gateway of India, Bombay's most iconic structure. Its Gothic architecture made it a heritage masterpiece, and its quotidian function as the valve of the city's human pulsations made it what Parliament House in Delhi was not quite able to pull off—political energy. Ambedkar was, in a sense, returning from the theory of Constitution-making and law-making to the 'practicals' of daily living among ordinary citizens. The All-India Railwaymen's Federation (AIRF) was headed, as we have seen at the time, by the socialist icon Jayaprakash Narayan. Present at the welcoming event was S. K. Bole (1869–1961), a staunch Ambedkarite and one of the leaders of the Mahad satyagraha that had given Ambedkar his 'mass leader' persona, as opposed to his suit-booted Constitutionalist one. A famous photograph taken at the VT reception has Ambedkar with Bole, who was unable to find a chair in the packed-out gathering, seated on Ambedkar's lap to the merriment of all.

Ambedkar, by now, was out and could make no contribution to the polity. His conception of an aggregated Hindu Code as a modern answer to the Dharmashastras could not come to fruition within the timeframe he had in mind and, which in that shape and that time frame would have given him the credit for the new law. Its becoming law in the disaggregated form of four separate enactments four to five years later gave India the benefit of his vision and of Nehru's in a way that crowned neither of them with reformists' glory.

Rajaji, meanwhile, was also wanting to withdraw from Delhi. This was completely unconnected with the Hindu Code Bill, which he supported. But it was completely connected with Nehru's newly emerging personality—India's undisputed leader, who needed no politician's backing, only that of the people of India who, he was confident, would back him and his party—now indistinguishable—in the elections that were round the corner.

He had come at Nehru's bidding to lend some administrative gravitas to the cabinet but also because Nehru needed a Gandhi-figure to stave off Patel's strong and very Patelesque positions, which did not chime with his own. Rajaji had been neutral in the Nehru–Patel logjam with a tilt towards Nehru. But with Patel's support for Prasad in the matter of the presidency, Nehru assumed, not without good reason, that Rajaji in the cabinet would at least not be a 'Patel man' even if he was not going to be a Nehru clone. But with Patel gone, his connection with Rajaji became increasingly mechanistic, intellectual, and, one might say, aesthetic. They exchanged books, letters on books, and shared jokes. In April of that year, for instance, he sent Rajaji a book by a British author, Geoffrey Gorer (1905–85), entitled *The Americans*, saying he thought Rajaji might find it interesting. Rajaji dipped into it and found it more than interesting for the quality of its English writing 'I am reading it with zest,' he wrote to Nehru but also saying he did not think his 'increased knowledge of the interior of American minds would serve any worldly purpose.' But Nehru's choice of the book to be shared with Rajaji is in itself interesting, for Gorer was a friend of George Orwell's (1903–50), having admired Orwell's first novel, *Burmese Days,* and doubtless warmed to Orwell's views on totalitarianism, communism, and the challenges to human freedom—all of which would have struck chords with Rajaji. In any case, that the prime minister and home minister of an India reeling under post-World War disruption and then post-Partition agonies could lend and borrow books from each other and then banter about them said something about their ability to live in many worlds.

But the equation was changing and, by the autumn of that year, Nehru's visits to the Rajaji home for a chat over coffee presented by Namagiri became fewer and fewer. Rajaji became reduced from vital colleagueship he could not do without, to a good company when he had the time for it. In other words, he found himself very soon becoming a supernumerary in the national capital. Rajaji wrote to Lord Mountbatten on 8 October 1951, who had suggested that Rajaji be sent to the UK as high commissioner, even for a short while because Krishna Menon, the incumbent, was 'at the end of the tether' that he felt '...just a matchstick to light the cigarette... You throw the matchstick into the ashtray without a thought after it has served the purpose....'

He said, honestly, he was tired and deserved rest. But he also said, more pertinently, to his daughter Lakshmi, who asked him why he was leaving having only just joined the cabinet, 'I feel I am not wanted any more now.... Jawaharlal has found a new adviser in his old friend Krishna Menon.... He consults him on all matters.... Just as well....' Menon was still Nehru's envoy in London, but telephonic and confidential cipher connections were there for the adviser and advised to use.

Prasad, his gentleness and old-style gentlemanliness to the fore, and Nehru, accompanied by his daughter, Indira, were at the airport to see Rajaji off. Devadas and Lakshmi were there, of course, to wave Rajaji goodbye, as he turned at the head of the gangway with Namagiri to say yet another farewell to Delhi.

The 1947 experiment of making the cabinet broad-based and not exclusively Congress-run had run aground. The apolitical John Matthai, as we have seen, had already exited from it. Now Syama Prasad Mookerjee, founder of the Jana Sangh and head of the Hindu Mahasabha, did the same, leaving it to be an overwhelmingly Congress ministry. Patel having gone and Rajaji withdrawing, Congress too was now not what it had been. It now was Nehru's Congress.

A good thing for him because the facility of consultation, when it becomes obligatory, is tiresome business. A good thing for India too, for it could not have hoped for a more honest and true leader who was now in unfettered charge. But not good for democracy because power, like ginger, which is the best thing for health when taken in right doses, can go slicing into the head if allowed to enter the palate unchecked.

Delhi, prior to the elections of 1951–52, was a paste of that heady ginger.

But there is more to a nation's life than elections. And all was not grey and grim.

A book that was to become part of my shelf and my life, by an author I came to know and respect years later, appeared this year. I was too young to have been asked by anyone to read it, but I am embarrassed now by the fact that my family was totally unaware of this magnificent work while being occupied by books of no stature. *The Autobiography of an Unknown Indian* by Nirad Chaudhuri (1897–1999) was fat. He was tiny. The book was deadly serious. He was quirky. And it compelled a comparison with nothing less than Nehru's *Autobiography*, no ordinary book about the life of a statesman. And with Nehru's *Discovery of India*, an extraordinary book about India's history. Nirad babu was no statesman, no historian either. But his life's story, self-described as that of an 'unimportant' Indian, was going to reign over bookshops for decades as a memoir and—a 'personal history' of the times he was writing about from the perspective of unimpeachable 'un-importantness'.

Two Hindi films—Raj Kapoor's *Awara* and Dilip Kumar's *Deedar*—both about non-heroic and non-celebrity reality, hit the screen in March and December of that year and had me, among thousands, in their grip. More than the storyline and acting by the down-and-out Raj Kapoor and the matchless Nargis, it was the soundtrack of songs in *Awara* that captivated its viewers. 'Awara Hoon' (a good-for-nothing guy am I), sung by Mukesh and the song's composers Shankar-Jaikishan, had a footloose charm to it that went straight home, while 'Ab Raat Guzarne Wali Hai' (the night now steals away) sung by Lata Mangeshkar, a bewitching sadness. Few things in the world of political discourse of the time suffused the imagination of the people as these songs did. From *Deedar*, the song 'Bachpan Ke Din Bhula Na Dena'(Don't let the days of childhood fade in your memory), as tuned by Naushad (1919–2006) and scripted by Shakeel Badayuni (1916–70), moved the kid in me as also grown-ups seated around me. In his celebrated novel *A Suitable Boy*, Vikram Seth (b. 1952) would describe, some forty years later, how audiences wept unrestrainedly while watching *Deedar*. That is more than could be said of the reaction of the Indian public to the misfortunes of any Indian politician of the time—conservative, radical, or neither.

If, in the elections that came shortly thereafter, Raj Kapoor, Nargis, and Dilip Kumar had stood as candidates, they would have won hands down. The Congress party put all its intellectual hope-eggs in one basket called Jawaharlal Nehru. It was not, in its mental innards, a party of reform; its wiring was conservative. The Congress was not leftist in its heart; it was centrist, and even that not from a carefully arrived-at stance of political equidistance from opposites but out of a reluctance to put in the effort to intellect. It takes effort to dissent and energy to differ. It is more comfortable to stay unmoved. If the Congress went forward with major changes, it was because Nehru was committed to reform, and Ambedkar was not going to let anyone maintain status quo. Ideologically restive Congressmen had by now begun to part ways with the Congress, moving into the Socialist Party, which Acharya Narendra Deva, Jayaprakash Narayan, Kamaladevi Chattopadhyay, and Rammanohar Lohia (1910–67) led and the Krishak

Mazdoor Praja Party (founded in 1951), then better known as KMPP, led by the dour Acharya Kripalani, his lively wife, Sucheta, and the Andhra leader T. Prakasam (1872–1957).

This election year for the country's 360 million people was the first such in independent India, professing no single religion, no single doctrine, whether political or ideological. The only qualification for an Indian citizen to vote was age—the person, man or woman, of any or no religious denomination, of any or no caste, educated or not, propertied or not, should be above twenty-one years of age. By this calculation, 173 million Indian men and women became entitled to vote and elect their governments and their Opposition—a huge number. A bigger election had not been held anywhere in the world.

India could and did take pride in the fact that its suffrage was going to be 'universal', free, and fair.

The year of India's first election was also the year—the indelible ink used to mark voters' left forefingers to prevent multiple voting by impersonation. And the making of that ink is a story in itself. Salimuzzaman Siddiqui (1897–1994) is not a name anyone remembers in India today, barring, perhaps, those interested in the history of chemistry research. Siddiqui was a chemist working in the Indian Council for Scientific and Industrial Research in the mid-1940s when its director general Shanti Swarup Bhatnagar, asked him to help with the formulation of an indelible ink which could be used in the elections to the new Constituent Assembly that were due. He sent to him a solution of silver chromide to see if that could be developed into the required ink for use by the Election Commission of India. Siddiqui found that the silver chromide did not stain well, so he added silver bromide to it, and there was an immediate improvement in the staining power. And working on that combination, Siddiqui was able to start the process of manufacturing the indelible ink for use in the 1951–52 elections. The ink should really have been unofficially called Siddiquink. The eminent chemist was to migrate to Pakistan soon thereafter, but that story is for a different narration.

Along with the year's heroes and heroines, one tiny Nirad Chaudhuri-like, uncommonly common figure entered the scene. Arriving on the pages of the *Times of India* was the Common Man created for all times by R. K. Laxman (1921–2015). A *Times of India* edition from November 1951 had Laxman's Nehru in the election year—1951–52—pulling a cart with a giant cut-out of himself and many indolent Congressmen lolling in it. Worn out and sweat-laden, Nehru is straining at his own image of himself while puzzled and bemused citizens watch. One of them, bewildered and reluctantly sorry for the leader, is the archetype of the Common Man wearing a long coat, is bespectacled, of course, and holds an umbrella perched over his left shoulder. Laxman's shrewd, if also laid-back, Common Man was born with the first election in independent India—an apt provenance.

On 21 November that year occurred an air disaster that has ever been on our family's mind. Devadas, with a valued friend of his, the fellow journalist who started and edited the Urdu daily *Tej* were to fly to Calcutta to attend a convention of editors. Devadas got his seat booked, but Deshbandhu Gupta's was not confirmed. Unforeseen work required Devadas to cancel his trip, and Deshbandhu got his seat instead. The plane crashed near the Calcutta airport, and everyone on board, including Deshbandhu, perished. The loss of a friend twinned with the fluke saving of his own was to stay with Devadas forever.

Deshbandhu Gupta was fifty at the time and widely respected as an editor for his strong advocacy of the freedom of the press and, as a member of the Constituent Assembly from Delhi, for his insistent demand for an elected assembly in the national capital. Without doubt, he was cut out for a bigger role in national life. It is one of the traits of Indian politics that a politician is treated with deference amounting to hero worship when in his prime, but when the lights go out for the leader, a pall of amnesia envelops the person. He might well have never existed. Unless, of course, there is a bright and smart descendent who quickly dons the mantle. In the case of this outstanding politician, a career of huge promise turned literally to ashes. This was the time when new appointments were being made to ministerships, embassies, and governors' residences. Absorbed in fresh glories, India's public life had little time for regrets over the dead. In a scrapbook of rare Shakespeare quotations, Rajaji has an entry from *King John:* 'New made honour doth forget men's names.' This is exactly what happened with Deshbandhu. A college in Delhi stands in his name, but ask anyone unconnected or even connected with it about the person it is named after, and you will most likely get a blank stare.

~

Unconnected by air or rail postal networks with India, Tibet at this time was undergoing a political change of great moment. The Sino-Tibetan Treaty providing for the assumption by China of control over Tibet's external affairs, for the establishment of Chinese Military Headquarters in Tibet, the incorporation of the Tibetan forces into the Chinese Army, and for the defence of Tibet's borders by China, was concluded during this year. That this treaty was to be a major shaper of processes in Asia involving the two big neighbours was not, one may be sure, evident to those who read news reports of the treaty at that time. But was its significance caught by those who ought to have?

1952
THE MOST IMPORTANT MAN ALIVE

As it played out, independent India's first election was just about less than half an election, for less than half the number of eligible voters voted. And then the less than half of those that did vote, voted for Congress, for Nehru. This meant that a little over half of those who did vote did not vote for Congress or Nehru. But, in the first past the post system, this vote pattern gave Congress 364 of the 489 seats (and over four times as many votes as the next-largest party, the Communist Party). Nehru formed the first elected government of India with ease and éclat.

That election established five verities:

One, belying the grey prognostications of India-sceptics, it showed that India was in charge of India.

Two, vindicating the pragmatism of independent India's opting for universal adult suffrage, it showed that inside the voting booths of the Republic, the 'illiterate' Indian turns into the equivalent of a PhD, no less, in plain electoral skill.

Three, co-operating with the constitutionally-empowered independent Election Commission of India, the country showed it knew what its institutions were meant to be.

Four, vindicating India's rejection of the Two Nation Theory, it saw Hindus and Muslims voting together as one electoral college, as one political entity, and as one republican persona to choose their legislators in fearless freedom.

Five, it made electoral India an exemplar for the newly decolonizing world, so much so that it was to seek out the services of the first chief election commissioner of India, Sukumar Sen (1898–1963) of the ICS—a salute to the world's new and largest democracy.

But we must also take note, in all fairness, that five other truths about that election also emerged:

One, voter turnout being less than 50 per cent—45.7 per cent to be precise—the Indian electorate was shown to be liable to democratic ennui, a portentous sign for the future.

Two, with 55 per cent of the votes cast going to non-Congress candidates, the election signalled the fact that India's politics could play out more definingly outside rather than within India's legislatures.

Three, opposition stalwarts like Acharya Kripalani and Babasaheb Ambedkar, in Faizabad (UP) and Bombay North, respectively, being among those defeated by inconsequential Congress candidates, the elections showed that Indian voters may be persuaded by reasons other than the stature of the candidate.

Four, the elections showed the almost mesmeric influence that an individual leader—Nehru at that time—can exercise as an icon, over the Indian electorate.

Five, Calcutta, in returning from two segments of its constituent parts, two Mukherjees with diametrically-opposed ideologies in combat—Syama Prasad Mookerjee from the Bharatiya Jana Sangh and Hiren Mukerjee from the Communist Party of India—demonstrated a vital signpost—the Right and the Left would be in dramatic contestation for the future of India.

Ambedkar had stood from Bombay North, a 'reserved' seat, under the terms of the Poona Pact,* as a Scheduled Castes Federation candidate. It was a two-member constituency. He was defeated by the little-known former associate, the Congress candidate Narayan Sadoba Kajrolkar, who polled 138,137 votes compared to Ambedkar's 123,576 votes. Ashok Gopal, in his scholarly biography of Ambedkar,[1] describes how the communist candidature of S. A. Dange in the second segment of the same constituency split the votes and contributed to Ambedkar's defeat. But the fact remains that Congress opposed the chairman of the Constituent Assembly's Drafting Committee and India's first law minister in the first election that was held in India, a sorry thing. A herb of inestimable value was smothered by a weed in the garden of India's republic.

Acharya Kripalani, who had been president of the Congress when India became independent and was the first to be called upon to speak in the Constituent Assembly, was likewise opposed—a no less sorry thing. Few remember who defeated him or what contribution the gentleman made in Parliament.

For us in our family, the most 'relevant' result came from the composite Madras State, which then included parts of present-day Andhra Pradesh and Telangana, Kerala, and Karnataka, with a total of 375 assembly members. The Indian National Congress was stunned by its poor performance—reduced to a

*Arrived at after talks between Gandhi and Ambedkar under the shadow of a fast by Gandhi, this pact rejected the concept of separate electorates for the Depressed Classes (later to be designated as Scheduled Castes and Tribes) in which only members of that category would choose candidates from within the same category. The pact put on track an alternative system, which is obtained even now, the system of 'reserved' seats in which the candidates would be from that section of the population exclusively, but the voters would be from all communities. Gandhi had opposed separate electorates on the grounds that it would divide Indian society irreversibly.

minority with 152 members in an assembly of 375. It could win only 4 seats from the 29 in Malabar (Kerala), 43 of the 143 in the Andhra areas, 96 of the 190 Tamil constituencies and 9 of the 11 seats from Kannada-speaking areas. Kumaraswamy Raja (1898–1957), the incumbent chief minister, lost his own seat with five members of his cabinet (Bezawada Gopala Reddy, Kala Venkata Rao, K. Chandramouli, K. Madhava Menon, and M. Bhaktavatsalam) doing the same.

Rajaji, who had returned to Madras and settled down to reading and writing from his old house in Madras's homely suburb of Thyagarayanagar (known today as T. Nagar), was not expecting to play a political role. And so the Congress's abject appeal to him to agree to form a ministry which, the party said, if led by him, would get support from bits and pieces of the opposition in the new house and carry the day, came as a surprise. He was disinclined to start with but gave in, especially to persuasion from Governor Sri Prakasa, who said he would nominate Rajaji to the legislative council, obviating the need to contest a by-election. Nehru was unhappy about the modus and sent word saying he would have nothing to say in the Madras Congress party's choice of Rajaji for leader but would trust Rajaji to get himself elected to the legislative assembly at the earliest opportunity—something the hoary leader was not going to do.

And in a move which was doomed to be a political failure, India's first and only Indian governor general took office as Madras's chief minister. His friends were unhappy because they thought the office too small for him and incongruous after all that he had been, and his 'side-entry' through nomination seemed to lack grace. The development was undemocratic, not so much for the nomination route but because it denied the spirit of the election results its deserved culmination. The Congress was in a minority. To convert a minority status into a majority may be a fair game in politics. It was not fair to the voters of the state, who may not have voted any other party clearly to the majority and to the office but had indisputably shown the Congress the door. No party having got a majority, in all propriety, the governor should have tried to see if the next largest party after the Congress was in a position to form a government with such support as it could muster, and only if told by it that it was incapable of doing so, should he have explored other avenues. In the event, Madras was denied the chance to have a Communist Party-led ministry in accordance with the voting pattern.

In all likelihood, a Communist Party-led government in Madras would have fallen sooner than later. And the Congress could then have been right in claiming a chance to form an alternative government. That would have been honourable. What happened was clever; it was not clean. The crown snatched and slanted, sat ill on Rajaji's sage brow. He gave the state a wonderfully run administration for the few months that he was to be its chief minister, but the karma of it all was flawed. And the price for that had to be paid by no one other than the karmi, Rajaji.

Independent India's history is not just about who became what in the theatres of public office but who did what on the larger platforms of the polity. Madras, with Rajaji's stature and charisma helping it, leading to a by-passing of the spirit of the results, set a precedent. The Madras model of 1952 was to be emulated in the coming decades with jostling for office through a post-poll manoeuvre in the house, marring the essential purity of people electing their governments.

The year ended on a tense note for us in Rajaji's family on account of a development in Madras. The carving out of the Telugu-speaking part of Madras state into a separate state was known to be 'a given', though Rajaji's lack of enthusiasm for it was no secret. It stemmed more from a lack of concordance with the concept of linguistically-formed states than from any indifference to the Andhra demand per se. (At one-point Rajaji had even termed the linguistic argument as 'tribal'.) Matters came to a head when Potti Sriramulu (1901–52), an ardent nationalist apart from being a popular Andhra politician, started a fast in the city to press for a speedy division. As his foodless days progressed, the political mercury climbed, bursting over on the fifty-sixth day with the leader's death.

Andhra Pradesh as a separate entity from Madras was now a matter of time. 'The sooner it is put through, the better,' wrote Rajaji to Nehru. But Rajaji was not going to cave in on the demand for the city of Madras to go over to Andhra, or at least be a union territory or a joint capital. He even refused to countenance a demand for it to be a temporary or 'guest' capital of the new state. On 19 December, Nehru announced that Andhra would be formed as a separate state. It seems extraordinary that a step which had never been seriously opposed and, in fact, had been conceded in principle had to wait for the death of a man who held the cause to be dearer than life itself.

Political hunger-strikes or fasts have been resorted to in independent India more than in any other part of the world. This is not surprising given the tradition of fasting in India's religious history and culture as a means of self-denial, self-purification, and self-mortification. In this, as in much else, Gandhi has led the way*, starting with a fast on the very day independent

*Altogether, it has been calculated, that Gandhi fasted thirty-two times from 1915 to 1948, for a total of 148 days, over various issues and for varying reasons. This tally does not include

India was born, to grieve for the nation's partitioning and the violence that surrounded it. Two other 'Gandhi fasts' followed, as we have seen, the first, in Calcutta, from 1 to 3 September, 1947 occasioned by the riots in that city, and the second, in New Delhi, from 13 to 17 January, 1948, in the white heat of communal tensions in the national capital and the issue of Pakistan's share in the new nations' sterling balance. These two fasts of his in independent India, like his earlier ones, were for what may be called larger issues concerning the nation's and its peoples' well-being, as opposed to specific 'grievances'. Political fasts have followed Gandhi's, in a rapid sequencing of motivations and movements. JP went on a hunger strike to support the postal workers in 1949. Morarji Desai fasted for elections to be held in the Gujarat Assembly after Indira Gandhi dissolved it in 1975. Acharya Vinoba Bhave fasted famously in 1979 to make the government enforce laws prohibiting the killing of cows—a step Gandhi, sensitive to the social dimensions of the issue, would certainly not have approved of. Fasts have been undertaken in independent India over the decades for the creation of separate states (e.g. Sant Fateh Singh for a separate Punjab, Surya Dev for Haryana, Sonam Wangchuk for Ladakh), for non-territorial goals such as opposition to dams (Medha Patkar against the Narmada Dam), over river water disputes (Tamil Nadu Chief Minister Jayalalithaa went on a four-days fast in 1993, pressing for the release of Cauvery waters), protests against industrial projects (Mamata Banerjee against the Nano car project in Singur), to laws (e.g. Irom Sharmila in Manipur, against the Armed Forces [Special Powers Act], and against specific political situations. And Anna Hazare's fasts have received much notice and respect. Have these impacted on given political situations and phases? To a limited extent, yes. Have they impressed themselves on the nation's sense of political morality? Have they strengthened the fibre of public ethics, chastened an errant people, sobered an increasingly corrupt polity? Have they heightened the nation's sense of decency, of civility? Those who have fasted would like to believe they have. A dispassionate look at the trajectory of political fasts would show that fasts are now seen as 'so-called fasts' and hunger-strikes just another form of pressure tactics for 'causes' that require negotiation, not agitation. Fasts and their larger form, 'satyagraha', have been employed to further things that are nearer 'agraha' (insistence) than 'satya' (truth). With honourable exceptions, such as the protests (2011–13) against the Kudankulam nuclear plant in Tamil Nadu and the massive farmers' protests (2020–22) against

---

his fasts in South Africa and recurring abstentions from food that he observed on Mondays and other days connected to calendric causes.

three enactments which they saw as going against their and in favour of corporate interest, a good number of satyagrahas in India since Independence may be termed natyagraha, 'acting-insistence'.

The voluntary abjuring of food will be a feature of life, more in India than elsewhere, as long as food is known to gratify the one who feeds. Mortifying oneself is the logical opposite to gratifying oneself. Put differently, there will be fasts as long as there are feasts. But even as feasting, in a poor country, can seem vulgar, even obscene, so can facile fasting, in a culture that has held fasts to be almost sacred, look crude, calculated, and even cunning. Politics in post-Independence and post-Gandhi India has polished the arts of cunning, for sure. But the people of India, ever ahead of politicians in their instincts, can tell the difference between what is genuine and what claims to be so, even if their goodness is taken for a brief ride, awhile.

1953
HINDUSTAN CALLS

This sixth year of 'India independent' and its third as a Republic saw things to be glad of, things to be disturbed by.

The formation of the state of Andhra Pradesh, a long-voiced aspiration of the Telugu-speaking population of the Tamil-dominated province of Madras, belonged to the first category. It gave meaning to the concept of India being a Republic. The dismissal of Sheikh Abdullah's government in Kashmir and his arrest belonged to the second. It gave a jolt to the concept of federalism, of India being a union of states, each state electing its own government. Also, to one's faith in political partnerships. How could a leader like Abdullah, who was so manifestly a political kin of Prime Minister Nehru, become so unreliable as to be dismissed and arrested, with not enough being explained, not enough being described of the reasons for that peremptory action?

But before coming to those events, a cinematic break is called for.

I went about that time to see a film I have never ever forgotten—*Jagriti*, featuring Abhi Bhattacharya (1921–93) as a schoolteacher and the 'child artiste' Ratan Kumar (1941–2016), as one among his pupils on a school trip around the country. The song in it—'Aao Bachcho Tumhe Dikhaein Jhanki Hindustan Ki' (Come along children, let me show you glimpses of Hindustan), I have known by heart as well as I have known, say, 'Jana Gana Mana' or 'Vande Mataram' or 'Raghupati Raghav Raja Ram'. It taught me love of my country, love of schooling, and love of teachers. It was only much later when I came to know that Ratan Kumar was not Ratan Kumar but Nazir Ali and migrated soon thereafter with his parents to Pakistan, that I saw the story behind the story of that film. Nazir Ali was taunted in Pakistan into acting in a copy-cat film called by the Urdu equivalent of *Jagriti, Bedaari* (Wakefulness), in which the song got transformed into 'Aao Bachcho Sair Karaein Tumko Pakistan Ki' (Come along children, let me take you on a tour around Pakistan). Now a couple of inches taller and leaner, the Indian boy Ratan Kumar was Nazir Ali, a Pakistani, his patriotic fervour for Hindustan having been peeled off and replaced by a new sticker for Pakistan. Nazir Ali's tragic and short life need not detain us here. But this much I need to say that *Jagriti* taught me in 1954 that life travels across passports and national boundaries as air does and rivers, left to themselves, do. The lifted film, the mimed song, and the forced acting of Ratan Kumar, aka Nazir Ali, sum up the story of our subcontinent, which has turned religion and nationality into bogeys.

For me, an eight-year-old going on nine, an even more memorable experience occurred in my seeing and being overpowered by yet another film—*Do Bigha Zamin* (two bigha of earth). We know so little about others, about other sections of our society, about their ways of life, their worlds, that as an urban kid, I had no notion of what a 'bigha' meant. For that matter, I had no notion of different measures or units of land. I knew of land in terms of gardens, lawns, grounds, courtyards, groves, and even fields. But their measure in terms of parcels of land for tilling was outside my ken. So, the fact that a bigha meant a unit of land somewhere between half and one acre, nearer half than one, I came to understand only because of this film.

Based on a Bangla poem by none other than Tagore called 'Du Bigha Jomi', it was made by Bimal Roy (1909–66) in 1953 after he saw and was inspired by the great Italian masterpiece of Vittorio de Sica (1901–74)—*Bicycle Thieves* (1948) in India's first international film festival the previous year. Roy's lead actress, Nirupa Roy (1931–2004), as I was later to read, said that *Do Bigha Zamin* was one film in which she did not need glycerine to cry; she wept because the script made her eyes well up. I remember having seen the film with my mother and crying through much of it, watching Nirupa Roy play Parvati Mahato and young Ratan Kumar, of my own age, play Kanhaiya. Each song from the film embedded itself in my mind—especially 'Dharti Kahe Pukar Ke' (says the land, beckoning aloud) in the argent voice of Manna Dey (1919–2013). Acting as Shambhu Mahato, Balraj Sahni (1913–73) was 'real'; Bimal Roy's direction was about 'real' life not just in India but in all countries that stand uncertainly on the cusp of agrarian and industrial choices, compulsions, and crises. It was about the dying of imaan (honesty) in the market place of saude (deals). People do not want to see reality in cinema, it is said. They have reality surrounding them all the time...They want to see fantastic things, experience what is beyond their experience, beyond their reach...They want a brief respite from reality, a short escape.... And then I have heard it added ...Furthermore...they do not watch cinema or YouTube to think...They want to put their thinking minds off...They want to put their seeing eyes on... They want seduction, not reduction.

A very different kind of film, from an altogether different realm of India's life, released the same year, also went straight home with me. *Avvaiyar,* a Tamil hit directed by Kothamangalam Subbu and produced at his Gemini studios in Madras by S. S. Vasan (1904–69), was not about the realities of our times but another reality—India's fascination for its iconic heritage, its legends and myths, its tales from 'long long ago, oh so long ago, that I don't know how long ago'. It is said that there were three poetesses with the name Avvaiyar, but the one who thrives most vividly in the popular Tamil imagination is Avvaiyar, the court poet in Chola times and a contemporary of Kamban. Her work *Athichudi*, written for young children, has remained popular through the centuries. The theatre legend T. K. Shanmugam (1912–73) had played the female role himself on stage in a production of the same name to great effect and had come to be called 'Avvai' Shanmugam. Popular legend has it that he had two of his molars extracted to look the part. Now, in the Vasan film, the younger film actress and singer K. B. Sundarambal (1908–80) played the lead role. The film based on Avvaiyar's life made an instant impact on my tabula rasa of a mind as being about an ideal so valuable for being so ideal. Sundarambal's devotion and singing struck me as simply sublime. That the film itself might not appeal to elders, especially cynical elders, was to be understood by me much later when I read Rajaji's diary comment on it: *Saw Gemini Vasan's picture Avvaiyar. T. K. Shanmugam's play is a hundred times superior to this picture.... A lot of stock scenes of thunder, lightning and storm, of water flowing and elephants trooping and cardboard fortresses falling. Avvai is too angry and cursing...The picture is poor but when so much has been spent on it and the stake is so great how can one frankly condemn it? The music is execrable!*

Life in the raw is never far behind the fantasies of the silver screen. It mesmerizes no less than cinema. The year 1953 saw being enacted in Kashmir that which resembles a Greek tragedy in a play that, to this day, has no conclusion. An early scene in it is about death. The person dying being a man of uncommon stature—Syama Prasad Mookerjee, the Hindu Mahasabha leader who was visiting Kashmir. Mookerjee had been arrested on entering Kashmir on 11 May. With two of his arrested companions, he was first taken to Central Jail, Srinagar, and then transferred to a residence outside the city. On the night of 19 and 20 June, Mookerjee started feeling pain in the back and ran a high temperature. Dry pleurisy, which he had suffered from in the past, was diagnosed as the problem. A streptomycin injection and powders were administered. On 22 June, he felt pain in the heart region, started perspiring and feeling faint. Shifted to a hospital and provisionally diagnosed with a heart attack, he died a day later. His was a death in custody and remains to this day a mystery behind bars. Fifty-one was no age for him to go. The reaction of the premier of Kashmir, Sheikh Mohammad Abdullah, was incredible, as was Nehru's, who maintained that there was nothing in the circumstances of Mookerjee's death to warrant any suspicion of foul play. One person who disagreed was no friend of the dead man; rather, he was on a different page from his on Kashmir and many other matters—Jayaprakash Narayan. In a statement, JP said: 'It seems to me that after such a national tragedy, the least that the Indian

Government could do was to institute a proper and impartial enquiry into the whole affair. Meanwhile, it does not seem proper for the Prime Minister to pronounce judgment on such a controversial subject and attempt to whitewash the guilt of those who seem to deserve punishment.'[1]

Curiously, the Nehru who had declined to entertain calls for an enquiry into the Abdullah government's handling of Mookerjee's death, was going to act most unexpectedly against the Sheikh within days.

On 8 August 1953, Abdullah was dismissed by the then Sadr-i-Riyasat (constitutional head of state) Dr Karan Singh (b. 1931), son of Maharaja Hari Singh (1895–1961), on the charge that he had lost the confidence of his cabinet. It is notable that he had not tested and, therefore, not lost the confidence of the house, where his party, the National Conference, commanded a majority. Abdullah was denied the opportunity to prove his majority on the floor of the house, and his home minister Bakshi Ghulam Mohammad (1907–72), the chief 'dissident' was appointed prime minister, going on to rule the state for eleven years—from 1953 to 1964. Abdullah was not only dismissed but arrested and jailed for the same eleven years that saw Bakshi in power. Abdullah was accused of 'conspiracy against the state' in what has come to be called the Kashmir Conspiracy Case. It is clear that all the steps were taken at the instance of Prime Minister Nehru himself. Then, as thereafter, several theories abound as to who reported what and on what basis to Nehru to make him take this extreme and patently undemocratic step against a man who had been his close and trusted colleague, returning to his confidence in the weeks just before his death in 1964.

Kashmir was, for us at home, a distant place, almost phantom-like and covered in the mists of unknowing. None of us had visited it, nor did we have close friends from the region. But there was one link that made the events there seem close to the skin. And that was in the person of Mridula Sarabhai (1911–74), daughter of Bapuji's long-time friend Ambalal Sarabhai and, thereby, one of our Gujarati kith. Her amazing work of rescuing abducted women during the Partition furies had, in an almost natural curve, led to her interest in the travails of Kashmir. Mridula was now in complete identification with Sheikh Abdullah and livid about Nehru's actions. Had Sardar Patel been alive, she would have had some traction, for she was a close friend of the Sardar's daughter, Maniben. But now, hers was a lonely battle and one that attracted the attention of the state's intelligence machine. This stern Gujarati woman's single-minded adherence to the Sheikh's cause and her dogged support for Kashmir's voices to be heard in the national capital gave no ordinary worry to Nehru, who too admired Mridula but found her advocacy tedious and troublesome.

Devadas and Lakshmi gave the Sarabhai daughter her deserved attention but did not go beyond that. I was always in awe of this woman who spoke my father's language, dressed in thick khadi but in a cut that made her look like a ready-for-a-fight Pathan from the North-west Frontier's rugged mountains. Only a gun dangling from a belt across her chest was missing in her attire. She was a tough woman, and a no-nonsense one at that. Her close-cropped hair, her pursed mouth, and her collared long shirt fascinated and also frightened me. And I had begun to become aware of something called the 'state' sufficiently to get nervous whenever I happened to answer the occasional phone calls she made to my father. 'Are you afraid my phone is tapped?' she once asked over the phone. I do not remember what I might have stammered in reply, but I froze as she said, 'Sure, it is.' And this was in the golden era of Nehru, the roseate Jawahar.

I wondered then as I wonder even now, what it was that drew Mridula into the heart of the Kashmir issue with such passion. She wrote no memoir. The Sheikh's, published posthumously,[2] mentions her appreciatively but briefly.

On 15 August 1953, the anniversary of India's Independence, Rajaji, as chief minister, was invited by the city's leading girls' colleges, Ethiraj College, so-named after its founder V. L. Ethiraj, to an I-Day celebration. He accepted the invitation. Speaking without notes, he said some things which had the flavour of his brand of humour but also some things which pertained to marriage, constancy, and the 'duty' of girls. *The Hindu*, in its detailed report of the event on 17th, quoted the CM as saying further: 'I wish you good husbands. You cannot choose husbands. If you begin choosing you will begin to quarrel with one another. One man is as good as another. You treat a man properly; he will be good. Take care of him. You must be polite and must be able to say, "Whoever comes, I will manage him". That should be your ideal.'

Appalling! What had happened to the man who, albeit after a good deal of 'testing', had celebrated his daughter's marriage to a man she had 'chosen' after he had 'chosen' her? And did he not respect the marriage that had been solemnized by a man devoted to him—T. Sadasivam—with a woman Sadasivam chose 'by love'—the ethereal M. S. Subbulakshmi—though he was already married, 'by arrangement' to the mother of his two daughters?

Rajaji could be fascinating, he could be frustrating.

Andhra came into being towards the end of 1953.

Devadas got the *Hindustan Times* to issue a supplement felicitating the new state on its birth. Devadas must have thought about its possible ingredients and decided to ask Rajaji, the outgoing chief minister of undivided Madras, and the last chief minister of Madras to have been in charge of its

Tamil and Telugu segments, to contribute an article. But on what? Rajaji was not one to write a cliched piece of felicitation. On the contrary, he could be trusted to write something characteristically sharp like the rasam he loved. And that was a no-no. Devadas then had the bright idea that Rajaji be asked to write on a 'cultural' theme, one that would be the Tamil tract's tribute to its Telugu neighbour. And what better subject for that than the great composer of Telugu compositions to Rama, the Tanjore-based Tyagaraja? Rajaji was not amused. His private secretary, the hugely trusted and trustworthy IAS officer P. Sabanayagam (1922–2023), wrote on 23 September 1953 to Devadas: 'Rajaji desires me to say that Sri Tyagaraja was a good Tamilian of Tanjore district and that only Tamilians know how to sing his compositions properly and that Rajaji is unable to contribute an article that will hand over Tyagaraja to the Andhras.'

I cannot hear a Tyagaraja song in the sublime recordings of M. S. Subbulakshmi or in their current renderings without recalling Rajaji's astringent comment.

1954
PANCHSHEEL—PANACEA OR...?

Rajaji was, well, Rajaji. Kamaraj, the great Congress leader who had got Rajaji to become chief minister, knew that the man he had got to lead the state government would do so according to his own lights. And Kamaraj was fine with that, for he knew Rajaji would give the state a good administration and the Congress party the stable majority it needed in the Assembly and, in the bargain, a good name thereby.

What he could not have guessed is that in his self-willed way, Rajaji would present the state with a scheme for education that would land the government and the party, not to mention Rajaji himself, in deep trouble. Rajaji had said, even as governor general, in one of his broadcasts that he believed school children should take time off their text books to learn and ply the crafts and skills of their parents. But that was homily. Now, as chief minister, that became policy. He unveiled a scheme by which, for half a day each school day, each school child would learn crafts, traditional crafts. This was immediately seen as a perpetuation of caste-based vocations and, thereby, of caste itself. Rajaji was forced to resign. He had got the Congress the office it wanted after the 1952 elections, and now he was not wanted. Certainly not as the originator of a scheme which was seen as Brahminical and casteist.

The rishi in him reverted to reading and writing. But the hurt was real and was to so remain.

Devadas was at this time, in addition to his demanding duties at the newspaper office, putting his ingrained commitment to physical labour and his restorative artistry through hand work to an altogether new field: finding more and more Gandhi film footage and stringing it together for a full-length documentary film—*The Voice of India*. Words and processes like splicing, spool, subtitles, playback, dubbing, and retake, 8 mm and 16 mm entered my vocabulary. In this year—1954—Devadas took Lakshmi, my sister, Tara, and me to Madras, where we spent hours and days with family friends, Sadasivam and Subbulakshmi. Devadas got their ready agreeability to MS's recording two songs as voice-overs for the assassination sequence in the proposed documentary—'Hari Tuma Haro' a song attributed to Meerabai, and a repeated chant in an ascending scale of devotional rapture—Rama,

Rama. In these renditions, the Nightingale of India* was at her entrancing best, singing with total, self-forgetting, self-abandoning rapture.

MS's songs from *Meera* buzzed in my brain like a swarm of bees. Somehow, she got to know that two songs from her *Meera* repertory were my favourites—'Baso Morey Nayanana Mein' and 'Pyare darasana'. And she included them in a couple of chamber concerts when I was there. When that happened, I vaporized. No surprise, in season and out of it, I belted out her *Meera* songs in my shrill 'pre-crack' voice, faithfully copying every personalized inflexion, climb or glide. On this 1954 visit to Madras, I once reeled off an MS song for the unasked-for benefit of my grandfather. We were seated on sofas, face to face. Anna listened carefully, patiently, and politely and, when I finished, said, 'You sing like her.' Was I chuffed! But then, rising from his seat, he added, 'Imitation is no good.' I went *phoos*!

Nehru, in 1954, was eight to nine years into his prime ministership and in his prime. But partly because he was so indispensable and everyone feared the time when he would not be there, the question 'After Nehru who?' figured in conversations. At lunch with some visitors in Madras one day during that visit, someone raised this question. The names that found favour around the table were Jayaprakash Narayan at first place and Morarji Desai at second. Devadas ventured an unlikely name—U. N. Dhebar (1905–77). The soft-spoken but sharp-brained Saurashtrian with an incongruous toothbrush moustache that brought Charlie Chaplin rather than Adolf Hitler to mind, was to become Congress president only the following year, succeeding Nehru in that party position. And he was to be no one's fool in that seat—no small achievement with Nehru being where he was. Neither Lal Bahadur Shastri (1904–66) nor Indira Gandhi (1917–84) were on anyone's lunch-engaged minds around that table.

Devadas was then just concluding, successfully, a struggle in the horror world, dimly understood by me then, of defamation and libel in the courtroom. He had been vilified for some years from 1948 in the columns of *Blitz*, the Bombay-based journal run by the 'free, frank and fearless' R. K. Karanjia (1912–2008). With the quiet determination typical of him, Devadas filed a defamation suit in Bombay High Court. He was told libel suits are a dicey business, every calumny has to be repeated in court, with witnesses being brought in during cross-examination who make calumny turn into filth, and that the cleanest of reputations cannot wash off the dirt flung on them. But he was determined to see the thing through. A good lawyer had to be found.

---

*The 'title' bestowed on 'MS' after seeing her film Meera, in 1948, spontaneously, by Sarojini Naidu who was herself called that.

And who could that be but the barrister renowned for his professional ethics and cross-examination skills—M. L. Maneksha? A snag was immediately pointed out: Maneksha is Parsi, Karanjia is Parsi; Maneksha will two-time for Karanjia. 'He will do no such thing,' Devadas said.

I remember attending the trial for two days in 1954 and can picture Karanjia in the courtroom, with his flamboyant moustache looking both dapper and deadly. Devadas's cross-examination by Karanjia's counsel, the communist singer-actor-lawyer A. S. R Chari, was not funny. But with Maneksha's cross-examination skills working at a higher ethical elevation, the verdict came sharp and swift. Karanjia had to pay up Rs 10,000 as damages and Rs 25,000 as costs. I watched the proceedings from the wings, quivering with excitement and fear—excitement at my father's emerging vindication and fear of the power of mischief and malice. 'Will the money come to us?' I asked Appa. 'No, of course not,' he said. 'The money will go to the *Hindustan Times* because the newspaper was defamed along with me, and the newspaper has paid all the expenses.'

Bombay that year gave Devadas great compensation from the agonies of fighting defamation through a film—*Subah Ka Tara*, directed by V. Shantaram (1901–90). The entire family saw it and loved it for everything, but most of all for the lead song—'Chamka Chamka Subah Ka Tara', sung by Lata Mangeshkar and Talat Mahmood. The music for it was composed by C. Ramchandra (1918–82), and the lyricist was Noor Lakhnavi (d. 2003), but I neither knew this nor cared for such details then. Since that time, I have seen the song sequence on YouTube and have wondered how the scene of Jayshree Gadkar (1942–2008) and Pradeep Kumar (1925–2001) seated in a railway compartment, obviously a deadwood cut-out, and gazing from its windows at the morning star (a drawing board pin, no doubt) and singing the song while swaying rhythmically from one side to another could have made the impact on us that it did. But the fact is that it did. Appa asked me to sing the song for him again and again. Perhaps it reminded him of his father's favourite 'Lead Kindly Light', the great 1833 hymn of Cardinal Newman (1801–90) and its Gujarati translation 'Premal Jyoti' by Narsinhrao Divatia. The song's follow-up line, 'Tute Dilon Ka Tu Hi Sahara' (Support for broken hearts), links in spirit to the slowly emerging optimism and faith in Newman's otherwise plangent song. Jayshree, married to the film's director Shantaram, was, I later found, born in China Town, Calcutta. China Town—how come? I do not have an answer to that question.

I had little knowledge then of China, its history, culture, and political voltage. And so, when in June 1954, Zhou Enlai (1898–1976) made his first visit to India, and he and Nehru issued their joint statement embodying the Five Principles of Panchsheel, I was like everyone else, in a state of excitement and believed, genuinely, in the rightness and indeed the beauty of Hindi-Chini Bhai-Bhai—Brothers, they are, the Hindi and the Chini. That October, Nehru was in China, greatly feted and greatly impressed by what he saw of the new Communist regime.

At school, a new song 'Shanti chahiye, ab shanti chahiye…Yah Panchsheel ki pukar hai…' (Peace is what we want now, Peace…This is the call of the Panchsheel) was sung lustily by us. 1954 was a year of faith overcoming doubt, goodness enveloping its opposites—for the now. Happiness is ever for the now. Its opposite, for longer stretches.

This year saw a major step being taken by and through the law to give Indian society a contemporary sinew. The Special Marriage Act, 1954, was passed by Parliament, providing for civil marriages (or 'registered marriage') without reference to the religion or faith followed by either party. In other words, inter-religious marriages could now be gone through under this law by Indian nationals and also by Indian nationals with non-Indian nationals. This was a huge step forward from medieval to modern times. The bill was opposed by the orthodox in Parliament and outside as something that would encourage 'lust' in the guise of marriage. Its critics were from the same set that had opposed raising the age of marriage[*] in the late 1920s—no surprise there.

[*]At the time of writing the minimum age for the woman getting married is by law, eighteen, for the man twenty-one. Proposals for increasing the age for the woman to twenty-one have been facing impediments. That there should be any opposition to this patently important advance is in itself something to be regretted. No less so has been the 'Exception 2 to Section 375 of Indian Penal Code' that said 'non-consensual sexual intercourse by a man with his wife, if she is over fifteen years, does not amount to rape'. In a landmark order, had the Supreme Court say (2017) 'In our opinion sexual intercourse with a girl below 18 years of age is rape regardless of whether she is married or not', saving the nation's honour in the matter of gender rights.

1955
REMAPPING INDIA

Tulsidas's *Ramcharitmanas*, a family mainstay, occupied our thoughts in the family, as 1954 ended and 1955 began. The Reverend A. G. Atkins, a missionary who had worked for years in the Indo-Gangetic plain, showed my father the manuscript of a translation that he had done in English verse of the Awadhi masterpiece. Recognizing its worth at once, Devadas offered to publish it in the *Hindustan Times* press. The production of the book, from its typesetting and printing and binding (done by Nanhe Khan, the newspaper's pious Sunni who headed the bindery section), became for us, who witnessed its every stage, an artisanal preoccupation. Rajaji wrote a most appealing introduction to the work from his newfound free time in Madras. Why was Rajaji asked to do this? He knew no Awadhi and could not have judged the quality of the translation. He was asked because he was Devadas's father-in-law and was who he was—Rajaji.

As it happened, after his virtual expulsion from office, Rajaji was deep into the Ramayana as told by Valmiki, doing a weekly retelling of it for the journal *Kalki*, with the *Sunday Standard* soon to serialize it in English. He was, as Rajmohan Gandhi was to put it,[1] 'exercising his intellect, refreshing his spirit, cooling his resentment', doing this. He was also grimly exercised over the Cold War and its unleashing the race for bigger and deadlier nuclear weapons between the US and its allies on one side and the USSR on the other.

In the previous year, the US had carried out horrendously powerful atmospheric tests of nuclear weapons on Bikini Atoll in the Marshall Islands, one of which detonated at dawn on 1 March 1954, and was 'about 1,000 times more powerful than either of the atomic bombs dropped on Hiroshima and Nagasaki during World War II'. From his 'obscure corner' in Madras, as he described it, Rajaji shot off a letter to the *New York Times* on 4 December 1954 saying: 'Let not a false realism lead to world tragedy. Let us not accept the defeatist slogan: "It has come to stay." Let negotiation be scrapped as unworthy as well as worthless, and let the good nations begin like good men. We speak the truth irrespective of others not doing it; we are kind and honourable irrespective of the conduct of others. Let each not wait for the other, but unilaterally, let us throw all the atom bombs in the deep Antarctic and begin a new world free from fear. This is the only way to regain the Paradise we had held and which we lost in August 1945.' He ended the letter by calling atom bombs 'a threat to civilisation'.

Louis Fischer,* author of the most readable book on Gandhi thus far and a friend of Rajaji, wrote to him on 5 January 1955 to say: 'I do not think the atom bomb represents a threat to civilisation. In fact, I incline to the belief that the existence of large quantities of atomic and hydrogen bombs in both the United States and Russia precludes a third world war.' Rajaji replied to Fischer on 11 January: 'I differ from your appraisement of the evil. It is a very imminent threat to civilisation and it is a crime to be making these weapons....'

Between his getting Fischer's letter and replying to it, the Congress party met with fanfare in Avadi, a suburb of Madras, for a major session of the Grand Old Party—its seventieth. On 10 January, in that little-known place, Nehru unfurled the party's goal as being the establishment of a 'socialistic pattern of society'. Presided over by the party president U. N. Dhebar, the session had Congress's leading lights, including Maulana Azad, in attendance, with Kamaraj, the freshly installed chief minister of Tamil Nadu, being the session's centre of gravity. Nehru was on 'a high'. His visit to China the previous year and Zhou Enlai's to India, affirming the doctrine of Panchsheel, had made him something of a herald of a new dawn. And now, as he saw it, his role required a vision for alleviating India's poverty through what he regarded as the best method—democratic socialism.

A great 'Avadi picture' that has Nehru about to hurl a bolster at a colleague on the mattressed floor-seating dais and another talking to the bright and beautiful daughter of the late S. Satyamurti (1887–1943), Lakshmi, captured the event's electric atmospherics. Rajaji, from his emeritus status, was invited and, attending, seconded a resolution on nuclear disarmament. The resolution said: 'The total prohibition of the manufacture and use of atomic and hydrogen and other weapons of mass destruction as well as conventional atomic weapons such as atomic artillery is imperative if civilization is to be saved from destruction.'

The year favoured us in the family with a happy turn. The scheme of national decorations had been proclaimed, with the Bharat Ratna being named as the highest civilian honour. Rajaji, Sarvepalli Radhakrishnan, and C. V. Raman, were to get it. Namagiri packing his woollens for him, Rajaji came from Madras for the investiture, which was held at Rashtrapati Bhavan on 27 January. Called first, Rajaji walked up slowly to President Prasad's high seat and, as the president rose to place the medallion around his neck, bowed his head, offered a namaskar in an attitude that bespoke both humility and

*Louis Fischer (1896–1970) American journalist and author, among whose works is *The Life of Mahatma Gandhi*, which was turned to by Richard Attenborough into the Academy Award-winning film *Gandhi*.

self-respect, let the riband slip over his dome of a head. Radhakrishnan, vice president at the time, followed. C. V. Raman, typically of him, did not turn up, citing preoccupation with a PhD interview that he was conducting that day—an example of vanity masquerading as duty.

Nehru, on his return from a hugely successful visit to the Soviet Union where he and Nikolai Bulganin (1895–1975), premier of the Soviet Union, signed a declaration affirming adherence to Panchsheel, was conferred the Bharat Ratna by President Prasad. The president 'sprang' this at a banquet, making that gracious act the first instance of the president acting without the 'aid and advice' of the council of ministers. No one minded that! Tendentious comments have been made in recent times to say that Nehru conferred it on himself, which is both unkind to him and unfair to the president. But I must say here that it would have been good if, that very year, the Bharat Ratna had been awarded to Ambedkar as well. Prasad and Nehru lost another opportunity there to make amends to a man who had been so unjustly treated. Would Ambedkar have declined to receive it? Not entirely unlikely, but then the gesture would have been made. It was to come to him years later, posthumously, an after-thought. But no one, least of all President Prasad and Prime Minister Nehru, knew at that point that the chief architect of the Constitution of India would, Bharat Ratna or no Bharat Ratna, soon outpace other recipients in the scale of prestige enjoyed and attention bestowed on his contributions to the making of modern India.

There was no question at the time of the Bharat Ratna being awarded to anyone posthumously. That was good because how far back is one to go retrospectively—to Gandhi, Bose, Tilak, Aurobindo, Vivekananda, Ramakrishna? To the heroes and heroines of 1857? And why not to Nanak, Kabir, Surdas, Mirabai, Tulsidas, Akbar, the great Guptas, Ashoka and even the Buddha, and Mahavira? But the rules for the decoration were modified shortly thereafter, permitting retrospective application, which is a pity because the posthumous awarding has come to be applied in a way that is more about pleasing and pandering to lobbies and egos rather than to decorating contemporary pre-eminence.

Devadas's trusted colleague in the Bombay office of the *Hindustan Times*, the young, diligent and highly sophisticated TamBrahm Chandrachudan, was asked by him in the autumn of 1955 to come to Delhi and 'run' the paper's column 'Inside the States' during the absence abroad of the column's regular author Durga Das. Chandrachudan, 'Mama' as we called him, who had become family, took my brother Mohan with him on a call on Sardar K. M. Panikkar. The historian had been working with Justice Fazl Ali and

Pandit Hriday Nath Kunzru on the report of the States Reorganisation Commission, of which those three were members, with Justice Fazl Ali as chairman. The report had been submitted to Nehru on 30 September and was not yet 'out', but Panikkar, who knew Chandrachudan well, gave his callers a summary of the recommendations. The scribe knew a scoop when he found one. And the column on 2 October 1955 carried the main features of the recommendation, with the suggested division of Uttar Pradesh mentioned glancingly. Mama had been sent to be a replacement for the senior Durga Das and found himself looking at a big-time story that was coming to him from the horse's mouth. But he played his part well, sharing the fact that he had learnt of the recommendations with a trusted and highly placed friend in the ministry of Home Affairs who told him to go ahead and run it without dilating on the UP and Bombay bits and of course doing so without letting anyone know that it was the great Panikkar himself who had told him about it.

Newspapers get their scoops from chasing leads, not fishing for leaks. Here was something of a leak. And the item could be called a sleak or a sloop rather than a scoop. But, nearly seventy years on, one can look at what happened in mellow light.

Panikkar started off his independent note with a dramatic statement:

> The position of Uttar Pradesh in the Union of India is something which no one interested in the reorganisation of the States of India can legitimately overlook. It contains over 63 million people, or over one-sixth of the population of India. It is divided into 51 districts, and the average population in each district is over 1.2 million. An army of officials (nearly 260,000) is required to administer it. The uniqueness of this position will become apparent when it is remembered that the next largest State in India, Bihar, has only a population of 40 million (or less than two-thirds of Uttar Pradesh), while most of the other States have less than 30 million. In population, Uttar Pradesh is nearly equal to Andhra, Karnataka and Kerala put together, larger than the combined population of the Punjab, Rajasthan and the new Madhya Pradesh (including Mahakosal, Vindhya Pradesh, Madhya Bharat and Bhopal). The imbalance created by the existence of a State of this size in a federation seems to me to be fairly obvious. I consider it essential for the successful working of a federation that the units should be fairly evenly balanced. Too great a disparity is likely to create not only suspicion and resentment but generate force likely to undermine the federal structure itself.

Panikkar's 'UP Note' was a warning bell about the pitfalls of demographic imbalance. Nehru's government disregarded his warning, needless to say.

Appa introduced me around this time to the immortal story *Uncle Tom's Cabin* by Harriet Beecher Stowe (1811–96). This was through an illustrated classic. Frame by frame, I stayed glued to the story of this slave brutalized and yet unbent by the social hegemonies of his time. It made me see the plight of what we then called 'Negroes' as nothing else could or did. Having got to 'know' Uncle Tom, I could, as a ten or eleven-year-old, warm to Bayard Rustin (1912–87) when he came to India and visited us at home. A close colleague of Martin Luther King and a major civil rights activist himself, Rustin had been earlier to India. Like King, Rustin was an instinctive believer in non-violence as he was an intuitive Christian, subsuming Marxian ethics and satyagrahic tactics with his own political vision. I do not know if Appa was aware of Rustin's homosexual life, for which he was constantly pilloried, or whether, if he did, he did not allow his sense of sexual morality to disapprove of Rustin. In this, as in his other affiliations, Rustin's sense of human rights was ahead of time. I remember his happy and open laugh and his sunshine of a smile as he posed for photographs with us in the veranda of our flat.

A powerful American voice—Bayard Rustin between the author's mother and sister. His father stands between prominent British Quakers Muriel Lester to his left and Gladys Owen to his right. (Devadas Gandhi personal archives).

The practice of untouchability stood abolished under Article 17 of the Constitution of India, but it was in June of this year—1955—that the Untouchability (Offences) Act, which prescribes punishments for the practice of untouchability and abolishes this heinous practice, came into force on 1 June 1955. The Act imposed a six-month-imprisonment or a fine of Rs 500 for any person convicted of enforcing the disabilities of untouchability on anyone else in case of his first offence. This, in a country that had practised the evil for millennia, was what a modern commentator would call 'huge'. I do not remember Appa or anyone for that matter speaking to me about the new Act or connecting it with the other abolition in Uncle Tom's story, and truth to tell (or an honest confession to make), our family with all the inherited halo of 'Harijan sewa' over its head, did not count among its close friends, any Dalit. Not one. It had Muslim, Christian, and Sikh friends. It had friends from the black communities of the US, Jewish friends from across the world, but not one Indian Dalit.

Wouldn't Ambedkar say, 'I am not surprised'?

Our family was, of course, not alone in this. The undeniable fact is that political India will wine and dine with the Dalit, make alliances with them, and tap aquifers of votes with them, but that is about it. Liberal and educated Indian families in their 'higher' caste and class echelons, while not consciously practising untouchability any longer, prefer to keep their egalitarianism on bookshelves. Ours had *Uncle Tom's Cabin.* But I am being unfair to my father here. He had reached out, by this time, to Marcus Malik, or Itvari Hazari as his 'real' name was, an Indian Dalit émigré in London, about his memoir, *An Indian Outcast: The Autobiography of an Untouchable* (Bannisdale Press, 1951) to publish it in a parallel edition at the *Hindustan Times* press, an arrangement Malik was happy about.

In an altogether different arena, the year 1955 has to go down—or fly up—as the year when Satyajit Ray's *Pather Panchali* made its appearance. I went with Appa to its inaugural screening in Delhi at the newly constructed Vigyan Bhavan. I had, of course, never heard of the author of the 1929 novel by Bibhutibhushan Bandyopadhyay (1894–1950) of the same name on which the film was based or of Ray, whose directorial debut this was. But featuring Subir Banerjee as little Apu, Kanu Banerjee as his deeply impactful father, Harihar Ray and Karuna Banerjee as his incredibly sensitive mother was an experience I could not describe. The two figures who entered my psyche as ingots in a furnace were young Uma Dasgupta, playing Apu's elder sister, Durga, and Chunibala Devi, the family's grandaunt. For me, the first film in the *Apu Trilogy* was about Durga. Appa was silent when the lights came on and the screening ended. I have an impression he had mixed feelings about the film, as many did at the time. But neither then nor during the many decades later when I have seen and reseen the film has it ever worn on me. Each time, I see something new in it, something I had missed earlier.

It was five years since Ambedkar had left the Nehru cabinet, five years since the Hindu Code Bill had been put on the back-burner. But this year—1955—saw the passing of a key element in that bill. The Hindu Marriage Act was passed by Parliament and provided for divorce under certain conditions. This was, from the point of the woman, a significant step, empowering her vis-à-vis a husband she was loth to be wedded to.

Three other enactments, which may be said to have emanated from the discarded Hindu Code Bill were to come into being the following year: the Hindu Succession Act (1956), the Hindu Minority and Guardianship Act (1956), the Hindu Adoptions and Maintenance Act (1956). But the Special Marriages Act (SMA, 1954) and the Hindu Marriage Act (HMA, 1955) were landmarks in independent India's advance towards social and gender maturity.

What unsuitable and flawed marriages can do was seen by millions in India that year in a Bengali novel turned into yet another powerful film in Hindi. *Devdas*, by Saratchandra Chattopadhyay (1876–1938), was made into a film by Satyajit Ray's senior and peer, Bimal Roy. To be sure, the novel had been made into a film in 1936 by Pramathesh Barua (1903–51) with the dreamy-eyed singer with a dream voice, K. L. Saigal (1904–47), in the titular role. Appearing in Bengali, Hindi, and Assamese versions, Saigal's portrayal of the alcohol-sodden hero, so tragically to be re-enacted in the great singer-actor's own life, made Bimal Roy's task difficult. But his great cast with Dilip Kumar, Suchitra Sen, and Vyjayanthimala, did Roy proud.

Vyjayanthimala, all of twenty-one, was by this time, a resident of Bombay. The Tamil beauty who would become a distinguished Bharatanatyam dancer trained in the tradition of the famous Tanjore Quartet had moved to a capacious flat with her grandmother overseeing her safety in stardom. I do not remember what took our entire family to her but I do remember my father asking my sister Taru, of almost the same age as the star, to stand next to her to see which of the two was taller. Taru was not flattered, Vyjayanthimala not amused. Parents can be tiresome. Decades later, I was to ask Vyjayanthimala how working with Suchitra in the film was 'But we never met!' she exclaimed. 'How could that be...there is that famous scene when the two of you cross each other....'

'Oh, that! The two scenes were shot in different locations at different times.' And there was to be, half a century after the film's launch, and our visit to Vyjayanthimala, a Suchitra Sen moment as well. The great actress was convalescing in a nursing home in Kolkata when I called on her. Her eyes as limpid as ever, and her hair was arranged in a crown-like perfection on her pillow. 'I can never forget the pathos of your acting,' I said to her.

'In which film?' she asked in a soft voice. When I told her, she said with a sigh, 'Oh...*Devdas*...' and slowly closed her eyes. There was nothing more to be said.

Soviet Prime Minister Nikolai Bulganin and his rather more powerful colleague, the Party Secretary Nikita Khrushchev (1894–1971), visited India over an extended tour in November and December. Nehru, who had visited the Soviet Union in June of that year, went all out to give the Soviet dignitaries a reciprocal welcome.

I remember laughing my guts out at a *Times of India* cartoon by Laxman on the day of their arrival, which showed Nehru doing everything himself, from cleaning the floors, getting the welcome flowers and buntings ready, teaching dull fellow Congressmen how to cheer 'spontaneously', showing a rather obese Bharatanatyam dancer to do a 'Nataraja' dance for the visitors, spreading the red carpet at the airport and lo! welcoming dazed-looking Bulganin and Khrushchev.

While in Bangalore, on 26 November, Khrushchev made a startling announcement. On the previous day, he said, the Soviet Union had exploded a nuclear bomb which produced the effect of 1 million tonne of TNT. He said this test explosion was 'to influence the nerves of those who wish to unleash a new war'. Devadas was lavish in his coverage of the Soviet visit but got his cartoonist Enver Ahmed to draw a searing cartoon showing Bulganin and Khrushchev bursting a cracker on the 'footpath of co-existence', entitled 'Badly Timed Prank?'

I was clueless about what TNT meant and what one bomb could do to human life. All I knew was we had entered an age of horror. And so was mighty relieved that when the two visitors met Rajaji in Madras's Raj Bhavan, as the great dancer Chandralekha (1928–2006) rendered a piece to music by the eminent singer M. L. Vasanthakumari (1928–90), he asked Bulganin if Soviet Russia would dismantle its nuclear weapons unilaterally, to which Bulganin said 'No', upon which Rajaji asked if it would agree to a joint renunciation under supervision with the US, to which Bulganin said 'Yes'. Eliciting this assurance was no ordinary feat.[2]

Calcutta overflowed with hospitality as 5 million people turned up to greet the visitors. The two had never seen such a crowd before, and as people clambered onto the boot and hood of the car they were on, Soviet intelligence officers accompanying them got Bulganin to shift from an open vehicle to a closed one.

After Zhou's visit and Panchsheel, Hindi-Chini were Bhai-Bhai, but with this Soviet triumph in India, Russi-Hindi looked like something more—judwe bhai, twins.

1956
APSARA—DANCER IN THE COURT OF INDRA

In the summer of 1956, Appa had a Reuters conference to attend in London and decided to use that chance to give the family a rare treat that all but wiped out his savings—a voyage to Europe. Appa, Amma, my sister Taru, Mohan, and I (my middle brother Ramu, typically opting to stay back), boarded the P&O's SS *Strathnaver* at Bombay's Apollo Bunder to get to Vilayat.

London seized me. Vijaya Lakshmi Pandit was India's high commissioner. She invited the family to dinner at her 9 Kensington Palace Gardens residence. The dining table was laid out with silver thalis because, she must have figured, her fragile china and Sheffield cutlery would have been excessive for this very 'Delhi' family. As the food came, vegetarian for us, but in its matchless variety and high quality unparalleled, I was lost in it like a puppy suddenly shown a bounty of gleaming bones. Absorbed in the grand repast, I remember nothing of her conversation, a great pity, for she was a wit and a raconteur. Dinner over, two attendants brought a glittering samovar-like silver dish with warm water, which was gently tipped over our fingers above another silver bowl that appeared under our hands just then. I was mesmerized.

India Club on the Strand, established by our first high commissioner in London, Krishna Menon, was visited by us as often as our limited budget would allow, giving Amma relief from cooking for all of us in the Putney home we had rented from the Indian portrait painter, V. R. Rao. In the dimly lit dining room of the club, one face I remember clearly is of Bridget Tunnard (1900–71), long-time secretary of London's iconic India League, who, as I heard it whispered, was 'Menon's closest comrade and more-than-friend'. She had a remarkable face, with very stern, somewhat watery eyes and a strong chin all but covered by wisps of very thoughtful tobacco smoke. Not much talk passed between our table and hers, and I regretted that even then, at age eleven. *The Journal of Imperial and Commonwealth History* (Volume 38, Issue 3, 2010)[1] refers to an assessment by British Intelligence officer Guy Liddell, which talks of British Intelligence's sense of Menon's political views and says: 'Of more concern to MI5, however, was Menon's long-term affair with Bridget Tunnard, an India League secretary connected to the CPGB. In Liddell's judgment, Menon's relationship with Tunnard suggested "that anything of interest that Menon hears about will reach the Communist Party through her".' I had no idea then of British Intelligence or MI5 but I certainly did, of the human propensity for love—blind, one-eyed, or at full gaze.

Appa and Amma invited Marcus Malik, whose book I have mentioned earlier, to dine with us at India Club. Malik spoke little but very deliberately and in a lovely, deep voice that had more of England than of his native Uttar Pradesh. They also had over at the club, Kamala Markandaya (1924–2004), then making waves as the author of *Nectar in a Sieve*. Kamala was Kamala. In a white chiffon sari, wearing a string of very white pearls, she was made of the essences of heaven's choicest arbour. I had read my parents' copy of her book about a poor villager family in South India, avidly. Parts of it were meant for one much older, like the line in which Nathan tells his wife Rukmini about their little daughter who runs about their homestead clad in aught but innocence, 'Clothe her...It is time...'

Appa took us to Rome towards the end of the European experience. And there, we were lucky enough to crown a visit to the Vatican by an audience with His Holiness Pope Pius XII (1876–1958). The papal residence, a series of interconnected halls, each bigger than the other, with its marble flooring designed like kaleidoscope patterns, was awesome. We were all required to stand in a semi-circle and wait for His Holiness. Within moments, in a swish of silk and swirl of movement, he entered. Amma and Taru did an Indian-style namaskar, Appa and Mohan shook hands, bowing. My own bow was deep and long. I imagined blessings were raining down on me, which they probably were, for when I looked up, his eyes were smiling. His right hand rested for a fraction of a second on my left shoulder as, the next moment, he swished out of the room and all the others as well. I remember nothing of the conversation between him and Appa. But Mohan recalls his personality as being warm, though not imposing.

The Pope's granting us that interview had more Catholic sentiment in it than the Curia's diplomatic strategy. The fact that his immediate predecessor, Pope Pius XI (1857–1939), had declined to grant Mahatma Gandhi an audience in 1931 when Gandhi was passing through Rome after the Second Round Table Conference must have built up a little knot of guilt in the Vatican. Meeting Gandhi's son and his family was a way of saying, 'That was then...We are now in a different scene....'

Mohan, having been entrusted by Appa to *The Scotsman* in Edinburgh for hands-on training in journalism, stayed back. He was at the station in Edinburgh to see us all off on our journey to London to take an Air India super-constellation flight to Bombay. As the train steamed off, Mohan ran alongside it for as much as the platform's length permitted, waving. Taru recalls that as Mohan's running frame was overtaken by the train, Appa told her, 'Poor boy...he does not know he will not see me again.' She knew that this was no light comment. Appa's diabetes was doing its work relentlessly.

There were two political stalwarts who can be considered deserving of the title of 'Man of the Year' in 1956. The first of these is Babasaheb Ambedkar. His political break with Nehru now complete, he also formally broke this year from Hinduism. On 14 October, he converted to Buddhism with his wife and lakhs of his followers at a public event in Nagpur. He then travelled to Kathmandu, Nepal, for the Fourth World Buddhist Conference, where his speech touched upon Marx and the Buddha, marking the commencement of a work on the Buddha or Karl Marx. This was to remain incomplete. With diabetes, which had been detected in 1948, corroding his system, Ambedkar died in his sleep on 6 December 1956, at his home in Delhi. Prime Minister Nehru went to the residence, as did ministers Gobind Ballabh Pant, Jagjivan Ram, and a weeping Rajkumari Amrit Kaur. In a historian's tribute to Ambedkar in Parliament, Nehru described the man he had let go so easily from his cabinet and who his party had opposed in the last elections in Bombay and defeated, as 'a symbol of revolt against the oppressive features of Hindu society'. And with a frank politician's realism added: 'He was not a man of soft speech, but the very perseverance and virulence of his opposition kept people from lapsing into complacency.' The body was taken to Bombay, where a Buddhist cremation organized at the Dadar beach on 7 December, attended by half a million grieving people, offered his corporeal frame to eternity. Nehru's own ties with Buddhism are perhaps connected to his magnificent funerary assessment of Ambedkar.

President Prasad and Vice President Radhakrishnan did not go to the Ambedkar residence in Delhi, nor did the governor and chief minister of Bombay attend the funeral. Lack of grace. Also, of political insight. Prasad's and Radhakrishnan's names enjoy respect today, Ambedkar's wields strength.

The second big name of the year was that of Jayaprakash Narayan. On 12 August of the previous year, students at Patna University protesting against a bus fare hike were fired upon, leaving two students dead, one of whom, Dinanath Pande, had just got married. The students, insensate, then did something unthinkable—they publicly burnt the Indian national flag. This has to have been the first time the nation's flag was burnt in independent India. The chief minister then was the Congress veteran Srikrishna Sinha (1887–1961), and the governor was the Gandhian stalwart R. R. Diwakar (1894–1990). The students turned to JP for help. He came to the conclusion that the Sinha government, sympathetic to the interests of landlords and not free of corrupt practices, had to take the blame. He asked Nehru to get Congress president Dhebar to investigate the matter. Nehru came to Patna soon thereafter, furious at the flag-burning and at a large gathering of mobbing students, let his temper fly.[2]

JP wrote to him, 'I shall not rest until you have the truth and the people get justice...I shall be failing in my duty if I do not raise my voice....' An enquiry by the chief justice of India, Justice S. R. Das, vindicated JP's stand on the culpability of some of the police officers.

Students in another hemisphere also drew JP's attention. On 23 October 1956, thousands of Hungarian students staging demonstrations against Soviet hegemony had wafted Imre Nagy (1896–1958) to power in Budapest. Riveted by this demonstration of popular power, JP saw with horror Moscow sending its armies into Hungary, arresting Nagy. JP said this was no different from the Anglo-French action that had taken place earlier that summer in Egypt, which Nehru had roundly criticized. Nehru's silence on Hungary and then, in a speech in Calcutta, his defence of Moscow led JP to mount a scathing attack on the prime minister. 'Russia has no right to be in Hungary,' he declared. There is no doubt that embossed on India's moral currency in 1956 was JP's dissenting visage, not Nehru's sovereign one.

Nehru, keen to have independent India appear to Indians and to the rest of the world in the most favourable light, was wearying of the documentaries being made by his government's Films Division. The predictable propaganda nature of these was boring audiences at cinema houses where these documentaries necessarily preceded the main 'show'. Roberto Rossellini (1906–77), the Italian film-maker, was suggested to Nehru as someone who could be commissioned to make a series of documentaries on the new India rising on the old. Rossellini arrived in India in 1956, and among the many he met was Devadas, then deep into his own Gandhi documentary venture. I do not know what impression either made on the other.

Nehru would have, one can be sure, asked Rossellini to include in his studies for the film, much of which were in Bombay, the work that was being done by Homi J. Bhabha and his team at the Tata Institute of Fundamental Research on India's first nuclear reactor at Trombay. This was the 'swimming pool reactor', in which the core site for the uranium chain reaction is to take place is suspended in a pool of normal (light) water,[3] which had gone critical on 4 August 1956. The enriched uranium fuel rods for this had come from Britain. A jubilant Bhabha got through on the phone that day when heavy rains were lashing Bombay to convey the news. Nehru immediately made a public announcement. The 1 MW reactor was to be useful in producing isotopes and generating fundamental research for over half a century. It was given a name suggested by K. S. Krishnan—Apsara, after the dancer of Hindu mythology, in the court of Indra—a name Nehru embraced enthusiastically.

Rossellini would have presumably brought all this into his film had another Apsara not entered his life just then. More on that in the next chapter.

In August, a major railway accident in Mahbubnagar, Andhra Pradesh, killed 112 people. Owning moral responsibility for the accident, Shastri tendered his resignation to Nehru, who persuaded Shastri to withdraw it. After the launch of the air-conditioned Delhi Howrah service, which boosted his spirit, Shastri was in for another setback. On 23 November, a worse railway accident occurred in Ariyalur, Madras, involving the Madras–Tuticorin Express, causing 144 deaths. The engine and the first seven bogies had plunged into the Marudayar river while crossing the bridge over it in torrential rain, hurtling its passengers into the swollen waters. Shastri submitted his resignation once again; this time, non-negotiable. In his resignation letter, Shastri said, 'it will be good for me and the government as a whole if I quietly quit the office I hold'. The use of the word 'quietly' by Shastri invested it with a meaning all its own.

'More than the Government supporters,' *HT*'s Special Correspondent said on 27 November, 'those in the Opposition were flabbergasted when the Prime Minister broke the news in the Lok Sabha of the resignation from his Cabinet of so unassuming a Minister as Mr Lal Bahadur Shastri.' Member of the Lok Sabha from the region, K. M. Vallatharas (1901–68) of the Krishak Mazdoor Praja Party, in a rasping speech, said Shastri's resignation was of no use when the deputy minister and local official did not resign. Vallatharas singled out the Railway Board for special attention, calling it 'a lethargic organisation'. Shastri's response has to go down as something of a classic: 'I am perhaps small in size and perhaps soft in tongue, and people are apt to believe that I have not been firm with the Railway Board. Though not physically very strong I think I am internally not so weak. There are different ways of doing things....'

O. V. Alagesan (1911–92), MP for Chingleput in Madras State, was then the union deputy minister for Railways under Shastri. He happened to be in Madras on the day and rushed to the site with officials for an immediate assessment. Being from the state where the accident occurred made his position doubly piquant, and he called on Nehru to say he would like to quit as well. 'Nonsense,' said Nehru to Alagesan. 'Somebody has to run the Ministry. You have to carry on.'

1957
A THRONE AMIDST THORNS

As 1957 began—our second election year—Shastri's resignation and the moral dividend generated by it was high on political minds. Congress president U. N. Dhebar, in a smart statement, called Shastri's gesture 'a landmark in the annals of democracy'. There was another unintended side to the move. It served the cause of North–South mutuality. Shastri's response to the Mahbubnagar and Ariyalur rail accidents bespoke a reflexive concern for these southern sites.

On another plane of life, Roberto Rossellini was becoming a hot subject of conversation at home when news broke of the Italian having eloped with Sonali Dasgupta, wife of Harisadhan Dasgupta, who had worked with Jean Renoir on *The River*. The incident had acquired the proportions of a scandal, with *Blitz,* ever feeding and fed by sensational stories, highlighting the case's dramatic details. Opinion at home was not prudish, with the general sentiment being that Sonali must have had her reasons for letting the Italian wean her away from her family. 'But, what about her children?' was, at the same time, a strong if rhetorical question posed. The Sonali–Rossellini affair was the first romantic scandal I was to get to know, with all its ingredients of betrayal, seduction, and tragedy. I am relieved now, all these years later, to recall that no moral judgments were pronounced by my parents then on any of the persons involved, no characterizations typecast along the nostrums of middle-class morality.

Photographs of the dramatis personae abounded at the time in newspapers, those of the arched eyebrows of Sonali making an instant impression on my never-absent weakness for that department of female looks. If anyone was to leave Ingrid Bergman for someone else, then it would have to be one with the personality of Sonali Dasgupta. I had no idea then that eight years later, I would meet her in my sister's home in Rome and be completely wowed by her gravitas, apart from her amazing looks. Her visiting my sister and brother-in-law, then stationed in Rome where Jyotiprasad* held a senior position at FAO, has to feature in my scribbles for 1965. Taru remembers both warmly—Sonali for her amazing strength of character combined with

*J. P. Bhattacharjee (Jyotibhai, 1922–86): Illinois-trained agronomist at Sriniketan, West Bengal; head of Programme Evaluation Board, Planning Commission, New Delhi; senior official at FAO, Rome.

an impenetrable core where she was in and with herself alone, and Roberto for his spontaneous generosity and a deep fascination for Gandhi. 'He wanted very, very, sincerely to make a film on Bapuji,' Taru told me. If he had put his mind and time to it, he would have. But it is perhaps just as well that the iconic film that came to be made finally was by the more historically-driven Richard Attenborough.

As cinema goes, this year belonged, however, to no film made by a visiting cinema genius but to one of our own. Say *Mother India*, and you think at once of Nargis. And that is but right, for it was that extraordinary woman who gave the film its surpassing voltage as a political statement, an ideological triumph, and a human saga of immortal proportions. But the person whose idea it was, who made it and directed it, was Mahboob Khan Ramzan Khan (1907–64) of Baroda. A pioneer film-maker, he invested more than money in it. He invested his life's energies in it—physical, emotional, creative. If the president and prime minister saw it in Delhi, it was not just because the film was a riposte to Katherine Mayo's infamous book of the same name, which appeared and raised a storm of protest in India thirty years earlier, in 1927. It was because the film was about what a woman—in the protagonist Radha, played by Nargis—symbolizing what Mother India can do to smash exploitation and immiseration. She recalled in her role Vivien Leigh in the 1939 masterpiece *Gone With the Wind*.

Early in the year 1957, we were invited as a family, by President Prasad for lunch. The experience was greatly cherished not just because the host was who he was, the head of the Indian state but also a friend of Devadas's for decades—in fact, from 1917 when they first met in Champaran, Bihar, during the Indigo satyagraha. We were the only guests. The meal, served in the president's family apartment, was sumptuous, with the president's diminutive wife, felicitously named Rajbansi Devi (Goddess of Royal Lineage), supervising the hospitality. As in Mrs Pandit's London home, we were again treated to a great repast on silver thalis with this difference—that there was a homey informality around, the food being served by liveried staff, no doubt, but with a natural ease. The fare was delicious, ghee being prominent in the dishes, forming a little lake on the surface of each little katori.

I have only one recollection of the lunch table talk. But it is crystal clear, owing to its content. Rajen babu referred to the very recent death of Ambedkar and said, in his impeccable Hindi, that he has heard from serious people misgivings about the cause of the death. Was it due to natural causes or...? The *Hindustan Times*, in its report on 7 December 1956, had mentioned that Dr Ambedkar, though known to be a diabetic, had been in fine fettle on the day and had retired to bed in good health, working on his book on the Buddha till he went to sleep.

It is fascinating how suspicion works, as also its cousin, suspense. The word 'thriller' attached to works in the style of crime fiction is apt. Suspicion poses a huge challenge to truth, suspense to clarity. If the end has come without witnesses or in a distant venue, or if the body has not been recovered, the suspenseful looks sinister as well. The disappearance of Subhas Chandra Bose (1945, Taiwan, age 48) heads the list of unsolved mysteries which in post-Independence India and Pakistan have many notables: Syama Prasad Mookerjee (1953, Srinagar, age 51), H. S. Suhrawardy (1963, Beirut, age 71), Fatima Jinnah (1966, Karachi, age 73) Lal Bahadur Shastri (1966, Tashkent, age 62), Homi J. Bhabha (1966, air crash over Mont Blanc massif, France, age 56), Deen Dayal Upadhyay (1968, Mughalsarai, Uttar Pradesh, age 52), Vikram Sarabhai (1971, Trivandrum, age 52), L. N. Mishra (1975, Samastipur, Bihar, age 52). These have been and are likely to remain the stuff of conspiracy theories. And the list will grow.

It was now five years since the first general elections were held in the country in 1952, and it was time for the second general elections to take place. These were held between 24 February and 9 June 1957, with elections to many state legislatures being held simultaneously.

> There were 494 seats in the Lok Sabha to be filled by voters using the first past the post voting system. The Indian electorate was now master of the voting system. The Nehru-led Indian National Congress sailed into a second term in power, taking 371 of the 494 seats. The Grand Old Party gained an extra seven seats (the size of the Lok Sabha had been increased by five), and its vote share increased from 45 per cent to 47.8 per cent—all in all, an achievement to be proud of. Nehru won his own seat of Phulpur in Uttar Pradesh handsomely. The Congress was first by a huge margin of 371 seats of the 494 and 48 per cent of the votes cast,* the Communist Party of India coming second with 27 seats and 9 per cent of the vote share†. Notably, the Lok Sabha saw a good number of independents, owning no adherence to any party getting elected. Voters ignoring the giant party and also other locally significant parties and voting for independent candidates for their own personal appeal was an interesting phenomenon. Among those individuals who thus made it to the Lok Sabha on their own steam, so to say, represented a

*Nehru in Phulpur, UP, got 2,27,448 votes as against his nearest rival, Chet Ram of the Praja Socialist Party, getting 61,322.

†CPI's most famous 'result' in this election was its victory in the newly-formed state of Kerala.

> cross-section of interests and backgrounds. These included Hoover Hynniewta, a tribal from Assam, the freedom activist and peasant leader Indulal Yagnik (who had taken down to Gandhi's dictation in jail, many parts of Gandhi's autobiography) and the individualistic Naushir Cursetji Bharucha (whose hobby was driving heavy vehicles) from Bombay, the Dalit leader N. Sivaraj from Madras, the internationally-renowned clay pigeon and skeet shooter Maharaja Karni Singh of Bikaner from Rajasthan, the Marxist trade union leader of Kanpur S. M. Banerjee from Uttar Pradesh. A brilliant communist entered the Lok Sabha that year from Coimbatore in Madras—Parvathi Krishnan (1919–2014).

But by far, the most colourful arrival was that of V. K. Krishna Menon, comfortably elected from North Bombay after a mere three days of campaigning. He had won the seat even before he arrived in Bombay from New York, where at the United Nations General Assembly, he had spoken in the debate on Kashmir for eight hours at a stretch, collapsing at the end of the performance. There was no question of his constituency not electing him. But it was not just his New York speech that did it. Jairam Ramesh, in his stellar biography of the man, *A Chequered Brilliance: The Many Lives of V. K. Krishna Menon*, says, 'Nehru's altogether *sui generis* personal appeal to the voters of North Bombay to elect Menon had its effect. Menon's election vouchsafed his being inducted in the Union cabinet. Nehru offered him the Ministry of Defence, to which Menon took as to the manner born.'

Wedding bells now were about to peal at home. Jyotiprasad Bhattacharjee, my sister Taru's suitor from the time she had spent a year in Tagore's Santiniketan, had come over to our flat in Delhi, been seen by and enchanted Appa and Amma, and introduced a new stream of music appreciation in our family—Rabindra Sangeet. Appa repeatedly got him to sing two of Tagore's songs—'Pagla Hava' and 'Gram Chhada'—both of which reminded him of Santiniketan's red earth and climate. Bengal and Bengali were now integral to us. Anna (Rajaji) came, of course, for the wedding from Madras along with Periamma. As did MS and Sadasivam with his daughters Radha and Vijaya. Appa hired for the wedding the very bungalow in Lutyens' New Delhi that Anna had lived in as minister—1 York Place—and had a beautiful mandap raised on its gardens. Jyoti, hailing from an orthodox Brahmin household in Bhatpara near Calcutta, came for the wedding with his cousins. For the sartorially-confused city bred in me, watching our new Bengali relations attired in traditional flowing white dhotis and colourful saris was an instruction in a new aesthetic. Appa, planning everything to its smallest detail, got Pandit

Lakshman Shastri Joshi (1901–94) of Wai, who had officiated at his own wedding in Poona in 1933, to do the honours. And borrowing a jhoola from the Gujarat MP Balwantray Mehta's Delhi home for the traditional 'swing' song in Tamil practice, he had MS to sing it with another added—Tulsidas's 'Kahan Ke Pathik', which is about Rama and Sita as the subject of villagers' curiosity. Taru, the bride, looked totally enchanting and ethereal. An unexpected downpour of rain washed out the arrangements for the (nuptial rite) outdoors, which had to be hurriedly shifted inside. As MS sang, the bungalow was crammed with the invitees, beginning with Vice President Radhakrishnan, who sat through the entire ceremony on the floor next to Anna. Just as the ceremony gave over and everyone stepped out, a great rainbow appeared in the sky in a vibgyor of celestial blessing.

Some cameos get permanently etched in one's mind. As this rainbow appeared, my closest and earliest friend from school, Ravi, 'appeared' too, bearing a gift for Taru: a boat with battery lights that could illuminate the vessel, for a bedside lamp.

Nehru was not in town on the day, and so, on his return, a couple of days later, dropped by to greet the newlyweds and to chat with Anna. Amma knew from earlier visits of his of a sweet he had relished—laddus made of besan (gram flour). She made those and served them to a delighted Nehru, who sat and chatted relaxedly with Anna and Appa and, of course, Taru and Jyotibhai for a good length of time before returning to his cares. No politics was discussed or even thought of. Just ghar-ki-baatein—home-chat.

By the mid-1950s, unrelenting tests of hydrogen bombs by Western powers had begun to attract civil protests.

A WWI pacifist, Harold Steele[1] and his wife Shiela decided in the summer of 1957 to make their way to the Pacific Islands where a British test was due and offer their bodies as a sacrifice to the cause of nuclear disarmament and solidarity with Japanese survivors of the Hiroshima and Nagasaki bombings of 1945. Finding passages by air or sea without inviting detection and preventive arrest by the authorities was not easy for the couple, but they managed to get to India en route. On 15 May, in New Delhi, they met Nehru, noting: 'Mr Nehru wished me well, and his whole bearing and attitude of speech showed he was not opposed to my mission.' They were in Bombay at a point when Devadas was there too, as were some of us from the family. I remember sidling into the room at the *Hindustan Times*' Bombay office where the Steeles were talking to Appa. His gentle and yet strong visage made an instant impression on me, as did whatever I could gather of his mission. The idea of this man and his wife getting blown up by a bomb in the middle of an ocean frightened and also somehow elevated my sense of the human will. I had not known anyone in India attempting anything like what the Steeles were. We had, at that point, just about started our atomic energy tryst, and the ethical questions around it had not seeped in. That nuclear weaponization and atomic energy are inextricably connected had not, at that point, been quite understood. But in hindsight, I can see that Nehru, under whose enthusiastic, even excited patronage our atomic energy programme was proceeding under Bhabha, was also, somewhere in his psyche, conscious of the Faustian dimensions of it all.

The Steeles could not achieve martyrdom, but they did achieve something else—'A failed quest'. Harold Steele's dream of sailing a boat into the middle of the Pacific nuclear test zone went unfulfilled, but his vision was to inspire many others, including the new band that was to enrich environmental protest: climate activists.

I had by now, due to a combination of little exercise and much eating become nicely 'round'. Appa one day drew for me the outline of a boy's standard form. 'This is how you should be.' And then drew in contrast, next to it, something looking like a potato. 'And this is how you are.' 'Choose,' he said. All this was, of course, in Gujarati, the language in which he spoke to me—an exclusive arrangement. He spoke to the rest of us in Hindi. And that childhood training in Gujarati has stayed with me over the decades, though insufficient practice has caused my Gujarati to rust.

School was becoming for me synonymous with our teacher of English literature, Vice Principal Awadh Kishore. His teaching of poetry was of a class apart. Standing before the blackboard with a piece of white chalk in his right hand, he would recite the poems which were on the open page before us with eyes closed and the fingertips on his left hand playing with the air. The poetry of two Thomases he introduced us to has remained real for me—Thomas Dekker's 'Sweet Content' with the lines graven on my brain:

> Art thou poor, yet hast thou golden slumbers?
> O sweet content!
> Art thou rich, yet is thy mind perplex'd?
> O punishment!

Thomas Moore's poem 'The Last Rose of Summer' is not what may be called a great poem. But the way Awadh Kishoreji taught it made it, for me, one of the loveliest.

> So soon may I follow
> When friendships decay
> And from love's shining circle, the gems drop away....

One little friend I recalled particularly, as I heard my teacher recite 'The Last Rose', was a Gujarati boy of the same age as I, boarded in school in India while his parents served abroad. He would stay with the Pandyas, our neighbours, whenever he transited through Delhi, and we became vacation-time, short-duration friends. He spoke little and smiled discreetly. With a pronounced medulla oblongata, he seemed to hold a lot of wisdom in his head. One summer, a very silent Pandya household told me in quiet tones that the little guest had been on a plane coming into Delhi that crashed 'somewhere'. That friend became and will always be the gem that flew away from somewhere to nowhere or…to everywhere. Air crashes were then more frequent than they are now. And air journeys were ever something to be glad of when they brought one safely back.

Nehru visited again, his coming coinciding with another visit of Anna's. I met him as his car drove into the building's frontage without fuss and with no security worth the name. We came up in the lift that Appa had by now got installed. Looking me up and down, he asked 'Achha batao tum school mein kuchh khel-vel khelte bhi ho? (So, tell me, do you play any games in school at all?)' I hesitated and bluffed: 'Football.'

'Achha?' he asked in disbelief and, poking his finger in my belly, said, 'Tum khud football jaise lagte ho. (You look like a football yourself.)'

Born in 1900, Appa was fifty-seven in 1957. Diabetes had become a problem for him; daily insulin administered by Amma through injections, keeping it just under control. On 2 August in Bombay, where he, Amma, and I were staying during an extended summer vacation, he suffered a heart attack. It was his first and last. 'Shiva, Shiva', he intoned as life ebbed out of him and morphine injected to relieve him of pain transited him to the next world. I had scribbled in pencil on the wall just above his bed some days earlier; I do not know why, the three opening words of the hymn we all knew by heart, 'Lead Kindly Light'.

Nehru said in a message, 'Devadas was like my younger brother....' When all of us got to Delhi with his ashes, Anna heading the family, and at the New Delhi railway station platform stood, with many others, Indira. Nehru, out of town, had asked his daughter to do that. The gesture was deeply moving, and Indira herself was the very personification of caring kindness. She accompanied us to our flat, now so forlorn and full of that fragrance of joss and flowers which I associate every time I inhale it, with death. Sitting on the floor with all of us for a while, she asked me which school I was studying in. 'Modern School, Barakhamba....' I replied. She was silent for a moment and then said, 'Amiron ka school (rich folks' school).' I could not figure out what exactly she was driving at. Factually, she was, of course, right.

There was something similar about Nehru's asking me about my playing games at school and her query. But there was also a huge difference. He punctured a balloon waiting to be deflated. She made me feel like a usurious bank calling to be nationalized.

Nehru came very soon on a weekend thereafter to condole and stayed briefly talking to Anna and Amma. There was in him sadness at his old friend's going but also a resignation about immortality. As he rose to leave, Amma said to him, 'Khana taiyaar hai...khaakar jaaiye ...' (Lunch is ready, do have some food before you go...) Looking at his watch, he said, 'Mein zarur khata lekin Dehra Dun se bachche aye huen hein...intezaar kar rahein hein...' (I would have done that but the children have come from Dehra Dun and are waiting for me...) I was seeing the tender heart of a grandfather in him for the first time. It was irrelevant that the man was India's prime minister.

A week or so before he died, Appa and I had stood in Churchgate, Bombay, waiting for his car to come up from the parking lot. It was night time, and the moon was up. Gazing at it, he said to me in soft tones, 'Gopu, in your lifetime, you will see a man landing on the moon.' I found that totally impossible and said so. 'No,' he said, 'you will see....'

He was not there when, on 4 October that year, something dazzling happened in the earth's relation with outer space. Sputnik, the first artificial Earth satellite, was launched by the Soviet Union as part of the Soviet space program. The feat triggered great interest in the Soviet Union and in space programmes. What does 'sputnik' mean in Russian? Something like 'traveller', we were told, and I remember a Hindi newspaper saying whatever the word may mean in Russian, it sounds like a Hindi line ...sabut nik... meaning 'it leaves not a trace...' My excitement over the new development was turned to a different and sombre turn of mood when, after the launch, within days of Sputnik 1, its successor, Sputnik 2, went into orbit, but this time with a dog aboard. A stray mongrel from the streets of Moscow was put aboard the Sputnik 2 spacecraft, launched on 3 November 1957. The technology to de-orbit had not yet been developed, and Laika perished of 'overheating' hours into the flight on the craft's fourth orbit. Did her being on that vessel help the cause of space travel? I do not know.... I had not, at that point, any experience of being bitten by dogs (that was to happen to me three times over the coming decades), but Laika became, for me, from that point on, an obstruction to any appreciation of man's space ventures.

Like most urban children, I went through a phase when stamp-collecting was my hobby, my passion. Appa used to get a modest number of letters every day, and they used to be brought home where they were opened and kept ready for him to read. The envelopes used to become my property, along with the stamps on them, coming in rich and colourful varieties from different nations. When Appa died, my stamp collection came to an abrupt halt. I took recourse to the very pitiable and philatelically low-grade method of buying stamps from vendors to augment my drastically reduced collection. One day, someone said to me, perhaps mischievously: 'Why don't you ask Panditji to send to you a small number of stamps each month?' I was a little abashed by the thought. How could I ask Panditji? But then, a kid is a kid, and a passion is a passion. This particular kid, a future bureaucrat, was sufficiently clerical of mentality even then. I figured that my writing to the PM with such a request being out of the question, I should try a less absurd proposition and must go through the proper channels. So, getting the contact details for his private secretary, who, I gathered, was a certain Mr M. O. Mathai (1909–81), I sent to that unknown (to me) functionary my rather plaintive, handwritten request. The very next day, I got a fat bundle of stamps drawn from the envelopes of the prime minister's daily dak, hand-delivered to my house. I was, to say the least, overwhelmed. My mother believed that Mathai must have checked with Panditji and that it was Panditji himself who had ordered the thing to be sent to the stamp-collecting son of his late friend, Devadas Gandhi. But I was sufficiently 'babu minded' even then to realize that Mr Mathai could well have acted on his own, that Panditji handled the letters inside the envelopes that came to him, and his staff could do what they liked with the envelopes. I, therefore, hold it to be a pity beyond words that circumstances led to Mathai's turning into a sour individual whose reminiscences, perhaps teased out of him by Nehru-baiters, ended up as little more than potsherds of a tragic life. Mathai, like Malvolio in Shakespeare's *Twelfth Night*, was trusted and distrusted, liked and disliked, self-raised and, ultimately, self-dismantled.

I cannot take leave of this year without referring to a great novel which in 1957 got the Kerala Sahitya Akademi prize. I have read it only in the splendid translation by V. K. Narayana Menon (1911–97). The Malayalam novel *Chemmeen* was written by Thakazhi Sivasankara Pillai (1912–99) the previous year. It is, at a conceptual level, about chastity and is woven around a myth prevalent in the fishing communities of Kerala. But on a more intimate plane, it is about a relationship between Karuthamma and Pareekutti. She is the daughter of a Hindu fisherman, and he is the son of a Muslim fish vendor. Need more be said? To say anything further about the story would be unfair to its creativity. But this needs to be said and known: *Chemmeen* as a story and a cultural entity lies at the heart of India, and we owe to Thakazhi the kind of debt that is owed by English literature to Conrad or Hemingway.

1958
SCIENCE, SECRETS, AND SCANDALS

With Appa's sudden death, life for the family was placed overnight on a brink. Ghanshyam Das Birla, the Birla family's grandsire and proprietor of the *Hindustan Times*, had for decades enjoyed a close bond with my father. He told my mother and Anna that we could continue to stay in the apartment till such time as was needed for me to finish my studies. This took a load of anxiety off us, though it did make for a certain piquancy, which I did not realize at the time. At home, at about this time, a tectonic tension between two 'plates' pressing against each other—science and the humanities—was taking place invisibly but powerfully. The site of this heave was the mind of the family's most intellectually effervescent being. My brother Ramu had opted to study for his bachelor's degree in physics at St. Stephen's College. Physics was a natural subject for his study, but he was a natural student of Philosophy. The earthquake releasing the built-up pressure occurred at about this time, with the great guru of St. Stephen's College's Philosophy faculty, Sudhir Kumar Bose (1902–85), settling the issue. Bose sahib was a philosopher, not just a philosophy teacher, being a quiet master of both Western and Eastern schools of the subject. But he also had another passion that he shared with Ramu—cricket. Ramu was to famously describe to me Sri Ramakrishna's great studio photograph in which the sage stands, in ecstasy, with his right hand raised in a gesture of fingers that defies explaining except as Ramu did: 'Gopu, do you see what Sri Ramakrishna is doing? He is bowling a googly... He is saying what you see is not what is real... The real is beyond seeing...It is experiencing....'

A googly was also bowled in the public sphere in 1958. Known as the Mundhra–LIC case, in which the government-owned Life Insurance Corporation had made some questionable investments in companies owned by Haridas Mundhra (d. 2018), it was brought to the notice of Parliament by Feroze Gandhi (1912–60). Feroze was a Congressman; the Congress was in office. He was Jawaharlal Nehru's son-in-law; Nehru was prime minister. The allegations were not hot air. Feroze Gandhi prefaced his speech in the Lok Sabha on the Mundhra matter on 16 December 1957, with the words: 'Parliament must exercise vigilance and control over the biggest and most powerful financial institution it has created, the Life Insurance Corporation of India, whose misapplication of public funds we shall scrutinise today.' The keyword there was 'scrutiny'. The MP had done his homework, leading to the conscience of the state, including the judiciary being activated. A commission was appointed, headed by the distinguished Justice M. C. Chagla, to enquire into the allegations, and it found LIC guilty of wrongdoing and said, 'The Minister must take responsibility for the actions of his subordinates.'

On 18 February 1958, Nehru's finance minister, the brilliant and very aware-of-his-brilliance T. T. Krishnamachari (1899–1974), was obliged to resign on the grounds of vicarious responsibility in the Mundhra scandal. In allegation-levelling MPs being sure of their facts lies their strength. In Treasury Benches, being aware that the opposition will not level charges recklessly lies the guarantee of objective investigation. In the end, by blowing his whistle, the MP had done his dharma, by pronouncing as he did, the judge his and by putting in his papers, the minister his. And the prime minister, pushed to a corner, had done his as well. Dharma had worked its puzzling circle to the full. As for Mundhra himself, he worked out his karma in prison.

In the decades since Mundhra, allegations of scams have burgeoned exponentially. Have these been as rigorously scrutinized as Feroze Gandhi's was? No. Have all governments acted with the honest if dismayed objectivity of Nehru in the Mundhra case? No. Compared to some other ministers in succeeding decades, TTK emerges less as a wrongdoer than as one who was unlucky in his circumstances. I used to see him, in Madras, drive his own little Fiat car in the city, alone, unescorted, attending sundry events and visiting friends. When, some sixteen years later, TTK was bedridden in his son's home, Amma and I visited him. 'God will restore you to health,' she said to him. He asked through a wan smile, 'Does God exist?' When he died, a very large number, many among them Carnatic musicians who had spent a lifetime singing devotional music, gathered around his bier. 'What a loss this is to us,' said the doyen of vocalists, Semmangudi Srinivasa Iyer (1908–2003) in his Brahminical Tamil to the great violinist T. N. Krishnan (1928–2020). 'Ayyo!' the deft bowman responded, 'incalculable.'

But, to return to 1958, to affairs of state. And to another striking member of the cabinet, the very new defence minister V. K. Krishna Menon.

The year had begun with the setting up of the Defence Research and Development Organisation (DRDO) as the country's premier agency for military research and the development of its resources with a view to making the country self-reliant for its defence needs. Over 50 per cent of its defence equipment being sourced from outside, it was imperative that India should start manufacturing defence materials in right earnest. The man responsible for this was the freshly inducted Defence Minister V. K. Krishna Menon, who brought more than energy and passion to play in the matter of making India a defence equipment manufacturer of the highest class. The organization was to become, over time, a key factor in India's alertness to its safety as the originator of systems and technologies such as weapons of all sizes and capabilities, aircraft avionics, drones, artillery systems, tanks and armoured vehicles, sonar systems, command and control systems and, very specifically, missile systems.

A defence organization cannot be a haloed angel facing the cloven hooves of the devil. And in order to keep all naivete out of its processes, it has to grow its own talons and fangs. And this is where science and technology in India, as elsewhere in the armed world, has become the hush-keeper of defence preparedness. The Indian elite, not to speak of the general public, does not care to know, for instance, where the waste from the country's nuclear plants is deposited or what precautions are in place to safeguard public health from Chernobyl or Fukushima-type experiences.

Nehru, the prime minister who was alert to the nation's security, was also Nehru, the thinker who was sensitive to the opinion of the world's thinkers about India, about him. Albert Einstein (1879–1955) and Bertrand Russell (1872–1970) had, on 9 July 1955 issued an appeal to humanity in the Russell–Einstein Manifesto urging governments and peoples across the globe to recognize the dangers of nuclear weapons and calling for their elimination. With the Avadi resolution on the subject vivid in his mind Nehru, responding, initially proposed that a conference to take the initiative forward be held in New Delhi in January 1957. The conference was eventually held, starting a series, at Pugwash, a village in Nova Scotia, Canada. But, as Dadabhoy, the meticulous biographer of Bhabha, tells us, 'Bhabha was lukewarm with regard to the Pugwash movement and showed little enthusiasm for the Pugwash movement, which he believed to be inspired by 'fellow-travellers'.[1] The presence of a Pugwash spirit in India would have been welcome on many counts, not the least as an index of public awareness of the wider repercussions of our nuclear policy. But there was nothing even remotely like that around. And, of course, there were no Harold Steeles in our midst yet.

The Soviet Union, having conducted a series of nuclear tests in 1957, conducted thirty-six more in 1958, the sites being in Semipalatinsk, Kazakhstan; NZ Area C, Sukhoy Nos, Novaya Zemlya, Russia; Western Kazakhstan. Typically, Rajaji wrote to the Soviet leader Khrushchev urging a halt to tests.

On hearing of a possible new receptivity in Moscow on disarmament matters, Rajaji again picked up his pen on 27 March, 1958 to write a letter to the Soviet Union's now obvious numero uno and leader. Rajaji did not know that on that very day, the Communist Party's general secretary

Khrushchev had forced Bulganin to resign and had succeeded him as Premier.

'Dear Mr Khrushchev,' the letter written in a clear firm hand said, 'Deterrence is an absolute unreality like a figure in the clouds that will disappear when the hour arrives. As for arming for security, it is as great a fallacy. Both sides trying, each to be securely stronger than the other, is utter reductio ad absurdum. If one side is to be "secure", how can that right be denied to the other side?' And it continued, 'In this atmosphere of obstinate distrust, the only miracle that can work a sea-change is unilateral action by the more courageous side—a declaration renouncing the use of nuclear weapons of any kind.' Rajaji sent the letter to the Soviet consulate in Madras with the request that it be sent to Moscow 'By air, of course, if you will oblige.'

On 31 March, the Soviet Union announced a unilateral ban on nuclear tests. This came after it had finished its planned series of tests.

On 1 April 1958, G. Kocharyants the editor-in-chief of *Soviet Land* sent Rajaji a letter from his New Delhi office that said: 'Recognising the importance of the suggestion, emanating as it did, from a person of your eminence and sagacity, Mr Khrushchev gave careful thought to it, and while expressing his appreciation, indicated in his reply the consideration which hindered its translation into action. He however added that the Soviet Union would like to be in a position to comply with your wish.'

Kocharyants's letter is in Rajaji's family archives but the 'reply' which the editor-in-chief refers to is not. I find it interesting that the Soviet system chose to send its response to Rajaji, who was by now a political dissident, in the roundabout route that it did, not through normal diplomatic channels. But send that response, it did.

If the Soviets were anxious not to ruffle Nehru's feathers at this time, that would be wholly understandable.

Nehru and Rajaji had sparred in public over much of March 1956, on the subject of Hindi as the official language for India. Speaking in the Lok Sabha on 18 March, the prime minister said, 'One of our seniormost leaders in India and has held the highest offices and who has been a crusader for many good causes was now running a "cold war" on the language issue.

'He was speaking to a packed gathering that heard him "in hushed silence".'*

On the same day—27 March—that he wrote to Khrushchev, Rajaji replied, 'If criticism is taken in this light...then I am afraid that democracy is crumbling.'

**The Hindu*, 28 March 1958.

Rajaji took the microphone again the very next day at another meeting* in Madras. 'Democracy,' he said 'cannot be run by men of ill-temper.' The finger was pointing unmistakably to Nehru. Democracy, continued Rajaji, 'can only be run by men of equable temper and those who bear criticism.'

Reflecting on those times now, over sixty-five years after, I cannot but feel that Prime Minister Nehru was 'bearing' a great deal of criticism, Feroze Gandhi's criticism being a case in point, and that 'ill-temper' was something Rajaji also displayed, if also laced with his very special wit.

Around this time, thanks to Feroze Gandhi having dominated the news, the name 'Gandhi' attached to Nehru's daughter, Indira, began to form in me the question: 'What is it about their Gandhi and ours? My mother explained that Feroze was a 'Parsi Gandhi'; we were 'Gujarati Gandhis', and though most Parsis spell that name as 'Ghandy' or 'Gandhy', Feroze spelt it in the same way as ours. There is nothing more to it than that, she said. The strange ways of life, she ruminated, had brought together a man with the surname 'Gandhi' in touch with a girl with the surname 'Nehru', making her Indira Nehru Gandhi or Indira Gandhi. The Parsi way of spelling the name being known to none except to the Parsis, and Feroze being constantly addressed in letters and other forms as Feroze Gandhi in the way the world spelt that name, he just fell in line with the popular spelling or misspelling. There was no intention, I am sure, in his mind to create any impression that he was kin of the Mahatma. Feroze was too proud a man, too self-respecting, to want to trade under false pretences. And when Indira fell in love with him, it was not because his surname was Gandhi.

Did the confusion about the two families being related or the misperception about Nehru's daughter having married a son of Mahatma Gandhi hold political advantage for the Nehru–Gandhis? Perhaps, but not so much because 'they let the confusion work to their advantage', as some suggest, but because we as a people are historically unfastidious and unfussy. Precision, accuracy, and veracity are intellectually exhausting. Vagueness and presumption are intellectually undemanding. And so, if a Nehru daughter has Gandhi in her surname, it is assumed the father must have given her in marriage to his leader's son—simple! In any case, all this was something that did not bother me except for a very short time after the Mundhra controversy brought Feroze to my mind's radar.

**The Hindu*, 29 March 1958.

1959
SWATANTRA

As I have said, almost confessionally, at the start of this 'History', the most abiding influence on me, with all accompanying fascinations and frustrations, has been my grandfather, Rajaji. And so, when I look back at 1959, I see it first through and with Rajaji's eyes.

The eighty-one-year-old was sick at heart. Monica Felton, the most famous 'lapsed leftie' from Britain had for reasons not understood by anyone fully, taken up residence in Madras and was in regular touch with Rajaji on whom she was to write a most readable book.[1] In March, 1959, she found Rajaji dispirited and took the liberty, as only she could, of giving him an earful on that condition. She followed up with a letter on 19 March saying: 'Please conquer your gloom. You have great work to do, and it is because I have complete faith in your capacity to do it that I scold so hard.'

The state of the Congress under what he called a 'one-man rule' and of the country in what he saw as 'one-party rule' and of the world, was distressing him beyond what his training in equanimity could cope with. And then there was the growing sense of the communist world overtaking all policymaking in India, domestic, economic, and diplomatic.

The year had started, of course, predominantly, as one in which His Holiness the 14th Dalai Lama (b. 1935) came away to India, escaping from the Chinese occupation of his land. He and the 10th Panchen Lama (1938–89) had been part of my mind's memory store from their visit to India in 1957 when the country was celebrating the 2,500th year of the Buddha, and Appa had brought out a Buddha Jayanti number of the *Hindustan Times*—a rare piece of archive now. I remembered my parents telling me of the lunch they attended, hosted by President Prasad, at which, for the first time, it seemed, Rashtrapati Bhavan had a state meal arranged in the floor-seating style with low platforms for each guest.

Now, of course, it was a very different scene. News of the Dalai Lama's escape was on the radio, in the papers, with the suspense of a story in real-time we do not know the ending of. His Holiness was to say later that he heard on a small portable radio a report on AIR that he had fallen off his horse and was badly injured. 'This cheered me up,' he said, 'as it was one misfortune that I had managed to avoid.'[2] Three weeks after he exited from Lhasa in Bomdila, he was given a telegram from Nehru which read: 'My colleagues and I welcome you and send greetings on your safe arrival in India. We shall be happy to afford the necessary facilities to you, your family and entourage to reside in India. The people of India, who hold you in great veneration, will no doubt accord their traditional respect to your personage. Kind regards to you. Nehru.'

The prime minister was right. On the rest of his journey into the country that was to now be his home, thousands pressed around his convoy, shouting their welcomes. Nehru had arranged for the party to be put up, initially, at Birla House in Mussoorie, which had been requisitioned by the government. On 24 April, Nehru visited Mussoorie and met the Dalai Lama in Birla House. They talked for over four hours with the assistance of an interpreter. The Dalai Lama was candid about the talk. When the Dalai Lama said he wanted to establish his own government in exile, Nehru became rather irritated and said, 'The Indian Government could not have recognised it.' When, later in the talk, the Dalai Lama spoke of independence, he says, Nehru interrupted him with 'That is not possible!' his lower lip quivering with anger.[3]

The democrat and instinctive believer in individual liberty in Nehru was at the base of his welcome to the Dalai Lama. But there was also the historian in him which saw China and India as Asia's two great powers intended by destiny to be friends and make the continent the world's gateway to a new order. He did not want anything, including hard evidence, to deflect him from that vision. This was to prove costly. China had a different perception of its evolving role in which India was not going to be its twin but its rival.

A Keralite trimurti came to be associated with Nehru's China policy. It comprised Krishna Menon, Panikkar, and K. P. S. Menon (1898–1982); the first two have been mauled by analysts. In his excellent book *War and Peace in Modern India: A Strategic History of the Nehru Years*, that appeared in 2010, Srinath Raghavan has described in engaging detail the responses in India to China's fast-evolving presence in Tibet and the repercussions of that on our long border with the country. Raghavan says, 'K. P. S. Menon thought that China's recognition of the frontier should form part of an overall settlement on Tibet: India should not withdraw its armed parties from Tibet without securing this. In January 1952, instructions on these lines were issued to Ambassador Panikkar.' Raghavan adds that when Panikkar met Zhou in the subsequent weeks and months, the Chinese Premier spoke only of trade and cultural issues. Raghavan states that KPS's advice, which tallied with Nehru's thinking but not his action, was ignored, to the detriment of a timely settlement of the boundary issue, which stays frozen to this day.[4] The only true mandarin among them, namely KPS, was not treated this way. This had nothing to do with the Mandarinate, only with the way events unfolded and were subsequently interpreted. I believe even Krishna Menon and Panikkar have been unfairly criticized. As ambassador, Panikkar was not wrong in his assessment of our national interest. His prescriptions for the handling and safeguarding of India's border interests vis-à-vis China were unfairly judged against the events of a decade later. They should have been tested against the Sino-Soviet, Sino-Indian, Indo-Soviet, and Indo-US dynamics of the time. The dividends in terms of international credibility and India's effectiveness in the UN during the decade 1950–60 owe a lot to the fact that there was, despite known differences over the border, substantial goodwill between the two great Asian powers. Bandung, Brioni, and the great efflorescence of the non-alignment movement during that first 'clear' decade of the Cold War would have been impossible if India and China had been pitted against each other and the Soviet Union forced to take one or the other side, to the glee of John Foster Dulles, the viscerally anti-communist United States secretary of state under president Dwight D. Eisenhower from 1953 until his resignation in 1959. On 9 June 1955, Dulles declared in a speech that 'neutrality...except under very exceptional circumstances ...is an immoral and shortsighted conception'. Throughout the 1950s, Dulles was in regular conflict with leaders of the non-aligned nations whom he deemed were too sympathetic to communism, notably V. K. Krishna Menon.

Among the papers constituting our 'family archive' is a moving letter written from London on 31 March to Rajaji by Marco Pallis (1895–1989) the Greek-British author and mountaineer connected closely to the culture of Tibet and the privations being suffered by the people of that country. Rajaji sent that letter in the original to Nehru who promptly replied with an analysis of the situation that is, I believe, the clearest enunciation I have seen of the dilemmas facing India's China policy. It has a sentence which sums it up: 'The situation in Tibet is, of course, a difficult and embarrassing one for us. We want to maintain good relations with China, and at the same time, we should like Tibet to enjoy real autonomy.' He added significantly: 'The real difficulty is that many people who talk loudly about Tibet today are not really interested in the people of Tibet, but are exploiting it in terms of the cold war.' I do not know what Rajaji felt on reading Nehru's detailed reply (apart from appreciation of the prime minister's courtesy), but I can imagine him saying to himself, 'I see Krishna Menon's hand in the bit about cold war.' I should add that together with his reply, Nehru returned the Pallis letter to Rajaji.

Nehru pointedly uses the words 'balance' and 'a balanced outlook' in that letter, which bring to mind the precarious perch of a tightrope walker. His use of the word 'embarrassing' is also interesting for its total honesty. Only those with a conscience feel embarrassment. Those without it are indifferent to the delicacy of things. The Tibet issue constituted an embarrassment and a challenge. It embarrassed the decent in the diplomatic in Nehru, the philosophic and the political in him. Tibet challenged the political gentleman in Nehru to do right by the Tibet of old and by the Dalai Lama. China challenged the political historian in Nehru to recognize the reality of a new China and its seemingly revolutionary leaders.

If Nehru gave the Dalai Lama an unmistakable sense of what India's being a free country is about, a somewhat different set of events occurred in India's deep south. And there, both embarrassment and balance were found wanting in the great man.

Amrit Kaur, the extraordinary rajkumari now out of Nehru's cabinet but an MP still, wrote to Rajaji on 14 April: 'It is a tragedy too deep for tears that Congress has become utterly corrupted by power and there is no room left for free thinking or expression of opinion in their ranks. They are losing ground throughout the country and yet they do not care to turn the searchlight inwards.... How can anybody be keen either to work for or save for a government which is so totally divorced from public feeling and needs?' She closed with the lament that '...we are wandering further and further away from his (Gandhi's) ideals.'

Rajaji could not have agreed with his former associate more.

By the year 1959, Nehru had been prime minister of India, its first, for twelve years and E. M. S. Namboodiripad (1909–98), chief minister of Kerala, its first, for under three. After a so-called 'direct action' organized against the new government triggered in the previous year by its radical land reforms and education policies, Nehru decided that the EMS-led communist government of that state should be dismissed. Dismissed! And, calling the EMS government 'an astonishing failure', he did have it dismissed, using Article 356 of the Constitution of India.

EMS's government was, in point of fact, the first non-Congress government to have taken office—after the general elections of 1957—in the whole country. The world, not just India, was struck by the democratically delicious irony of a communist government having been elected to office, peacefully, emphatically, through a free and fair election, defeating India's party of the freedom struggle, the party that was ruling India and all the other states of the union, led by one whom everyone acknowledged to be the rose-bud in the arbour of the world's democrats, Nehru.

Kerala, with its high literacy and virile press, electing a communist government had made news, big news as something of a first. But not everyone celebrated. Understandably, conservatives and the religious orthodoxies in Kerala, did not. And no less understandably, India-watchers in the US's ruling establishment did not either. 'Alarm bells,' it is said, rang in Washington when Kerala's democratic choice of communism came to be known.

EMS's ministry was compact, with eleven members: C. Achutha Menon, a seasoned communist lawyer, as finance minister; Joseph Mundassery, a Malayalam litterateur, as education minister; and V. R. Krishna Iyer, the brilliant lawyer and legal activist, as law minister. And it had set about doing some pioneering things, audacious things, exactly as Nehru's Congress government at the centre was doing, in its own style.

The year—1959 was, as it happened, a landmark year for EMS. Born in 1909, he was fifty—in his prime as the first chief minister of his newly-born state. The year 1959 was for Nehru a landmark year too. Born in 1889, he was seventy—as the first prime minister of new India. Did EMS nurse and show deep resentment at what had been done to undo his election, his chief ministership? Of course, he did. Who would not? But there is such a thing as grace, as civility, as plain decency. Indira Gandhi, by then Congress president, was believed to have had much to do with the decision to dismiss the EMS government. Not difficult to believe, given that the national Emergency, some twenty-five years later, was promulgated under the Indian Constitution on her advice as prime minister to the then president under the same Constitution.

EMS said of Nehru at the time in an article for Rafiq Zakaria's book *A Study of Nehru*: 'The question "After Nehru Who?" which is on everybody's lips today is, therefore, a magnificent tribute to Nehru's incomparable role in India's political framework as much as a regrettable commentary on the inner rot of the Congress machinery.'[5]

Inner rot is no party's monopoly today.

Some do not see it when they are in it.

But some are torn by it. I would like to believe Nehru was torn between the expectations of his party and the ideals of democracy.

For us of Rajaji's family, this year was our Anna's.

Something in him broke that year, and something in him rose from that debris, with astonishing vigour and originality. His mounting criticism of Nehru and of the Congress had seemed to us, as to all who observed him, a feature of his critical mind, his sharp conscience. But this year, he showed an altogether new side of himself to him. He was eighty-one, he was sharp, he was angry. Angry at what he perceived as his long-standing friend Prime Minister Nehru's Left-ward lurch, the change of the Congress into a one-man party and of the government into a statist machine running a skin of controls and licences and quotas, stifling free enterprise and also free expression. He formed a new political party, giving it the name Swatantra, meaning 'independent', evocatively, of the freedom struggle's slogan of swaraj, freedom. Support came thick and fast from persons and groups who had felt vulnerable under Nehru's 'socialistic pattern of society' call and feared more and more state control.

On his first visit that year to Delhi, post-Swatantra, Anna sent word to President Prasad that the customary protocol of Rashtrapati Bhavan hosting the former governor general be dispensed with, as he was now a political visitor on a political mission that was aimed at the government of the day. An undoubtedly relieved Prasad agreed. But even more significantly, he told Lakshmi, his daughter, that he would not embarrass her either, she being who she was, the widow of Congress and Nehru's loyal adherent, Devadas. And so, he accepted the invitation of Sir Sobha Singh (1888–1978), the veteran builder of Lutyens' Delhi, to stay in his house, Baikunth. We called on Anna there, joined him for meals and snatched what time he could spare from his hectic schedule of political meetings and speeches. Ramu brought his fiancée, Indu, to see him. Anna was delighted and greatly taken by her, blessed their future life in marriage. That Ramu and Indu were to separate after some years is another story—'a sad story' as Indu was to put it to me many years later—and does not take away from the fact that the parents of the brilliant Leela Gandhi* were meant to be man and wife.

---

*Leela Gandhi (b. 1966) is a literary and cultural theorist, poet, and teacher, noted for her work in postcolonial theory. She is, at the time of writing, John Hawkes Professor of Humanities and English and Director of the Pembroke Center for Teaching and Research on Women at Brown University, USA.

BOOK THREE

1960
A YEAR OF SENSATIONS

I was excited in a brainless kind of way at the Swatantra Party's formation. This came with a giddy pride in Anna, awe at the eighty-one-year-old's zest, rapture over his wit and sheer dazzle at his courage. None of these emotions would stand objective tests. True, he was 'something else', but then I saw that 'else' in much larger terms than the scales of life warranted. Of the content of his politics, I understood but little. I had no thought about matters like socialism and statism, free enterprise and liberalism. Jayaprakash Narayan was also a great draw for me, struck as I was by his patent sincerity, his calm eloquence, his great looks. And yes—his sophisticated English. Clear, polished, and so, oh so, well pronounced. But Rajaji's was the more immediate pull.

After his first post-Swatantra visit, when he stayed at Sir Sobha Singh's, Anna resumed staying with us. Amma assured him she was not embarrassed, and in any case, who is to misunderstand a father staying with his non-political daughter?

Swatantra's leadership would come home, visiting Rajaji. The new party's leaders had their own appeal. 'Acharya' Ranga (1900–95), as Rajaji liked to address N. G. Ranga, the party's first president, was a warm being. Ranga gave Rajaji's new vessel the ballast of loaded paddy bags. If Ranga was about what we today categorize as organic cereals, weevils, and all, Minoo Masani (1905–98), the party's general secretary, natty, witty, and snooty, was like marzipan, choice and special, bearing the scent of The Swiss Café in Bombay situated just where Marine Drive turned into Churchgate. No surprise, the place does not exist now. Masani was not a person one could take to, only admire from a little distance. He was as superior as anyone with a sharp intellect and a tongue to match could be, but without that redeeming grace which makes superiority almost likeable. There were only two persons—apart from Rajaji—in whose presence I saw Masani's ice thaw: the Rajmata Gayatri Devi of Jaipur (1919–2009) and M. S. Subbulakshmi. Once, I told him I had devoured his fantastic book *Our India* at school. 'Oh yes,' he said, 'I know it has done well. But I have moved far from what I said in it.' Masani was referring to the great store he placed in that book by planning and the Five-Year Plans, something he now denounced with vigour as 'statist'. Masani gave the Swatantra boat its great booming hoot.

But Nehru! Was he gallantly democratic and liberal about the new party? Not quite. He denounced in no uncertain terms as 'a relic', and in one very uncharacteristic departure from his high taste and standards of public utterances, as 'a senile baby'. But on one Swatantra visit of Rajaji's, the PM turned up in our house, after a very short notice had been sent by his office. The new party's leaders were somewhat rattled by the gesture, though they tried not to show it. Rajaji was not. There is such a thing as 'for auld lang syne', the Scottish phrase denoting 'for old times' sake'. 'Hello, Rajaji,' he said as he entered the room, 'I have come to see how young you have become!' The two were together for no more than some ten minutes, one-to-one. As the PM left, Rajaji came down with him in the lift to see him to the waiting car. A black and white photograph taken by the *Hindustan Times*' lensman shows both looking tense and awkward. Democracy's graces are beautiful, but they demand a lot in their practice.

On 8 September, Feroze Gandhi died after a heart attack, his second. Feeling unwell, he had driven his car to the Willingdon Nursing Home, as Rammanohar Lohia Hospital was then called. He passed away soon after getting admitted. Nehru was shaken to the core of his being. Indira and Feroze had not made a happy marriage and should really have taken recourse to the provisions for divorce that had become available in independent India. But a son-in-law is a son-in-law, even if a truant husband.

Our home was the site of a happy event that very month, a few days later. Ramu and Indu took their courtship of some two years into the chambers of marriage. Amma went to the Nehru household to invite him to the event. Inviting Nehru was something she had to do for shared family histories, but she said to him in the same breath that she does not have the heart (himmat nahin hoti) to talk to Indira about the wedding so soon after her bereavement. It transpired that Nehru was scheduled to be out of Delhi on the day and could not attend. Anna, in the thick of his Swatantra Party work, could not come for the nuptials but did something curious and characteristically 'different'. He wrote to President Prasad to ask if he, Rajen babu, could officiate for the groom's grandfather, that is, Rajaji, and represent him at the ceremonies. Rajen babu came to both the wedding and the reception that followed the next day, staying full-time as one of the family. Kripalani and JP came, too, loyally and lovingly. Politicians might have seen in the gathering a 'coalition' of respect for Rajaji.

The year 1960 was for me memorable for something I have to be honest and unembarrassed about. *Mughal-e-Azam*, starring Madhubala and Dilip Kumar, was not a film but a sensation. I am speaking of my generation, not just of me. The song 'Jab Pyar Kiya To Darna Kya' (Why Fear When in Love?) was not Shakeel Badayuni's greatest. But Naushad's tuning of it, Lata Mangeshkar's singing of it, and Madhubala (1933–69) picturizing it as Anarkali, the courtesan in Akbar's court, made it the melodic monarch not just of the year but of the decade. And as the film's reviewer in the *Hindustan Times* put it, the scene in which Dilip Kumar as Prince Salim strokes Madhubala as Anarkali with an ostrich feather was till then and has perhaps stayed since then as 'the most erotic scene ever' in Hindi movies. I had, I must admit, forgotten the ostrich feather's little journeys. But now, reading about it again, I recall it with an immediacy that is frankly biological.

This year saw, beyond these two screen romances, a real-life story of love, rage, and murder. The case is now history, and the current generation would not be aware of it, but back in 1959–60, it held the public imagination no less than the two great films. Kawas Nanavati (1925–2003), a dashing and exemplary naval officer, had shot his British-born wife Sylvia's lover dead. What made the case sensational was his conduct, which was cool, calculated, and had a strange aura of virtue to it. After he had done the deed, Nanavati turned in his pistol and surrendered. The jury attending the sessions court held him guilty, the case going up to the high court, which found him guilty, only to have its verdict nullified by the governor who, within hours, pardoned him. It went then to the Supreme Court, which held him guilty and sentenced him to life imprisonment. After a spell in jail, Nanavati was pardoned yet again by the governor and emigrated to Canada with his wife, and their children. Every stage of the case hogged the news, and *Blitz* became its passionate reporter, its sales zooming up. 'Three shots that shook the nation' blared its mast headline.

Behind the governor's pardons for the naval officer was the discreet role of the defence minister, Krishna Menon, who had known Nanavati from the time he had worked in the High Commission of India in London during Menon's innings there. For me, this was the second major introduction to marital collapsing as a result of a third party, the first having been the Rossellini–Sonali affair. I was totally torn. Did Nanavati do something that was to be pardoned? Was Prem Ahuja—the victim—a loathsome character? Did the defence plea that Nanavati did not intend to shoot him but only threaten him, with the firearm going off accidentally in a scuffle hold water? Can Ahuja, who had just emerged from a shower with a towel around his waist, have been able to scuffle with his towel staying in place?

The greatest 'gift' from the case was its echo in the 1963 film directed by K. K. Nayyar on the story with a bewitching song (which also gave the film its title) 'Yeh raste hain pyar ke....' (Such are the ways of love....) sung by Asha Bhosle. Rajinder Krishan's lyrics for it were set to music by the gifted Ravi. It is just right that Asha was asked to sing it. She invests it with a reflection requiring forgiveness and fatalism. In the way Asha drags out certain words and pauses in it suggest an emotional intoxication that only such a condition can create. Her elder sister Lata, with her own oeuvre, could just not have sung it. The film, incidentally, went along with the 'scuffle' theory. Judged guilty by the court, innocent by the jury, made a hero by the media (*Blitz*, specifically), pardoned by the governor, Nanavati has hovered above the law in the public imagination. He slipped quietly into the other world at seventy-eight. But what of Sylvia Nanavati? Now in her early nineties and said to be living in an assisted residence as a devoted mother and grandmother, her story* has to come from her sometime, in a memoir that shakes sanctimony out of its pedestal and the truth of emotions out of its vault.

This was my last 'clear' year at school. As I look back at my time in school, I ask myself who are my peers that I remember and why.

The first of these is Shubhendra (1942–92), the only son of the sitar's most famous exponent, Pandit Ravi Shankar (1920–2012), whose daughters Norah Jones (b. 1979) and Anoushka Shankar (b. 1981) are much better known. Shubho was a gentle soul with a soft voice and a manner that suggested he knew of life more than he would care to tell. I did not know then of the strain between his parents. His mother, Annapurna (1927–2018), the hugely gifted daughter of the long-living sarod maestro Ustad Allauddin Khan (1862–1972), had a great influence on him, as I could later see, even greater than his father's. Older by a couple of years, Shubho was not in my class, and yet we got to spending much time together due to one common link: neither he nor I had any interest in sports. My closest friends in school were Ravi Nath, whom we have met from the time of Taru's wedding and Kuldeep Kachwaha, both of them shining stars in their careers, the first as a legal eagle and the second as a public sector major. Ravi and I shared few interests, but a bond grew between us, nurtured from the background by Ravi's mother, a saintly lady whose kindness extended to her son's friends like the fragrance of a jasmine stretches to anything within five feet of it. Kuldeep, though my exact contemporary, was my Hindi teacher in parallel with our faculty. His command over that language was and remains extraordinary. All three of us were very different as persons and yet were a threesome.

Rana (d. 2025), who later changed his name to Rajarshi, son of the very original politician and minister S. K. Dey (1906–89), was another very close friend with whom all my immaturities, insecurities, and confusions were shared only to be reciprocated by his own editions of the same.

---

*For a very responsibly and sensitively written account on the case and post-case years of the Nanavatis, I would refer the reader to Bachi Karkaria in *Mint*, 2 May 2017.

How friends become friends is a mystery. Why one and not another, is impossible to explain. As is friendship itself. What is that emotion, that equation, which is not derived from blood, not occasioned by professional need, not sustained by commonalities. And not prompted by that other prompter called romantic love. The latter emotion came to me in a surge for Nilima Dhanda, now Nilima Sheikh (b. 1945), married to the equally famous Gujarati painter and poet Gulam Mohammed Sheikh (b. 1937). Her later mastery of the painter's delicate brush was not in evidence at school. Did she know my feelings for her? I do not know. We were both too young for me to have spoken to her about it, but then emotions cannot remain wholly hidden.

The most prominent among my peers at school was Geeta Kapur, our principal's gifted daughter, who would become one of India's most respected art critics, and Syeda Saiyidain, the scholar, poet, diarist who would become one of the most articulate voices for communal amity and secular faith.

If friends becoming friends is a matter of wonder, friends becoming distant is no less so.

The one person I remember most vividly and with great regret over my not having tried to understand him and his situation better will remain unnamed. He was in my class. But he may have been much older. Pimply and stubbly, he would, ever so often, get an epileptic fit. It would start with a moan and end in a frenzy, the sight of which burned me up. A key or some metallic object would then be placed between his jaws. Why, I was never sure. Some said that was to save his tongue from being bitten by his grinding teeth. Others said that was a standard treatment for epilepsy. He was, I am sure, under serious medication, for he would most often be asleep in class, and no one, the teacher included, ever disturbed his slumber. There was something else too associated with him that I must recount, for it is very important. He was the loveliest human being. I do not mean physically but in his mind and heart. His smile I cannot even describe. It was an all-knowing smile, a shy and forgiving smile that seemed to say, 'I know I am ill. I know you know I am ill. I know I cannot compete with any of you in anything, studies, sports... I know...I know...I just am. I want to be nothing more.'

There was something utterly unembarrassed about him. Ever so often, he would, in class, seated in his chair, decide to unbutton his shorts, pull his penis out, and with the expression of an expert at his trade, masturbate. Everyone thought this very funny. And not a few encouraged him to do so. I would avert my eyes. And he would go the whole hog, yelling in delight as he reached his peak. I salute my school for having given him space in its ranks. But I drop my raised arm for its not having told all of us, confidentially but professionally, how to respond to our special peer. No one spoke then of mental health.* No one bothered to. What he did before everyone, all of us boys did too, in the darkness of washrooms at home, emerging from them like little choir boys with a halo over our heads but legs and hands that quivered from the secret exercise. He was, in sheer innocence, not our peer but our superior.

*Keshav Desiraju as union health secretary pioneered India's first law on the subject—Mental Health Act of 2017, bringing into focus the need for this enactment which remains to be aligned against the initial experience of its implementation. A *Lancet* study in the same year (2017) said 197.3 million persons in India endure one form or other of disorders of the mind, of which 45 million suffer from clinical depression and 45 million from anxiety. A WHO study in 2023 put the figures at 57 million (depression) and 38 million (anxiety). Clearly these figures must be taken as based on under-reporting.

1961

'TH' EXPENSE OF SPIRIT IN A WASTE OF SHAME'—WILLIAM SHAKESPEARE, SONNET 129

New Delhi in January 1961 was balmy, green, and flowerful.

President Prasad was a troubled man. He had done eleven years as president but which president, howsoever old and infirm, is above entertaining a dream for a second term? And he had enough hangers-on dangling the prospect before him. That he had drifted away from his prime minister was no secret. Nor was his expression of appreciation bordering on admiration but just stopping short of an endorsement of Rajaji's opposition to Nehru. 'All that he writes and speaks,' said Prasad of his long-standing colleague a few months earlier, 'is as acute and penetrating, as bright and scintillating, as anything that he has ever written or said.'[1]

India had a 'fairy-tale' experience this year. Queen Elizabeth paid her first state visit to India. She chose to land in Delhi, in a sky-blue dress that matched the clear blue of a January sky over India's capital. Everyone was expecting to see Queen Elizabeth II, nine years into her office with (none, she included, knew) some sixty more ahead of her, appear on the aircraft's doorway with a rim of diamonds above her head. But no, the queen had on her head something that was not a crown but not a hat either. It was more like an installation of small sky-blue pennants fluttering like the sails on a ship's masthead.

And did she gleam! A none-too-excited and somewhat diffident President Prasad, seventy-seven, in his last year in office, moved slowly and with some difficulty to the gangway and welcomed her decorously with a handshake, followed by a supremely confident Vice President Radhakrishnan, seventy-three, erect and eminent, set to become president in a year, who greeted her with affectionate courtesy and then by Prime Minister Nehru, seventy-two, who bowed just as much as British etiquette had prescribed, with a warm smile and handshake.

Amma was touched when an invitation came from Nehru to a lunch he hosted for the royal visitors in his residence. Amma recounted the event: 'Panditji was graciousness itself. There was a small line-up of the invitees, and as my turn came, he took my hand in his and introduced me to the queen like this: "How do I introduce this lady? Her late husband was a distinguished journalist, editing one of our foremost newspapers for years. She is the daughter-in-law of none other than the Mahatma himself. And daughter of a statesman, Chakravarti Rajagopalachari, the one and only Indian Governor General of India appointed by your father, to succeed Lord Mountbatten." What could the queen say to this except "Very happy to meet you." But Panditji, in a masterly way, had said everything there was to say about me in that introduction.'

Looking back, I cannot but think Nehru's gesture in inviting Amma, a nobody in protocol terms, was, before anything else, about civility and also about his sense, a historian's sense, of who the queen would like to meet. But somewhere in that invitation was an affirmation of the democratic culture he was trying to build in India.

India went all out to fete the royal couple. What was it proving? That India is hospitable? That it has forgotten or at least forgiven the excesses and, in fact, the very fact of the Raj? That it wants to have good relations with Britain as a member of the Commonwealth? Or that in the increasingly complicated relations with China, no less than with Pakistan, it values its ties with the West as much as those with the Soviet Union?

We are a Republic and a democratic one at that. But we are smitten by royals and their regalia. Diamonds and diadems, crowns and crests, titles and titularity awe us. A benign king, a kindly queen will always be a cut above the passionate MP or the committed MLA, the globally engaged prime minister. We are also and will always be deeply class-ruled. As the royal couple travelled, the wretchedly poor and semi-starved flocked around them, showing no resentment at the contrast they offered. Was that a greatness to be admired or an unawareness to be bewailed?

The band of the 39th Gorkhas struck up the national anthems of the two countries as the Queen and Prince Philip said their farewell. But this was the least challenging of the tasks that the Gurkhas of the Indian Army faced that year.

One part of India the royal visit had not covered was its northeast. There, in the hilly folds where the Nagas live, a deep discontent was spilling over. Proud of their identity, the Nagas baulked at the idea of being subordinate to anything or anybody outside of their own culture. A clash between the Nagas, who saw the Indian state as an imposition and the Indian state, that saw the Nagas as hostile, was inevitable. Towards the end of April, Captain Man Bahadur Rai of the 11 Gorkha Rifles was at the head of a platoon tasked to tackle a body of hostile Nagas. Leading the platoon at night through two Naga formations into the heart of their stronghold, he dislodged them. On 3 May, Rai was decorated with the Ashoka Chakra for his heroic action.

While the Nagas 'rebelled' and Indian Army jawans gave their lives to stop the rebellion, the rest of India remained largely unconcerned and uninvolved. The Nagas were, for most of us, a strange and distant people on the rims of India's northeastern borders whom the Indian Army was keeping in check. In check from or against what? Even that was not quite clear to us. Generally, we thought, from creating 'trouble'. There were exceptions, of course, foremost among whom being my all-time hero, Jayaprakash Narayan. He had been interested in the concerns of the Nagas and played a major role in persuading Nehru to create a separate state for them. With Nehru's consent, he parleyed with Naga leaders for a ceasefire. Staying in Kohima for months in that year, he won the confidence of both army officers and Naga 'rebels'.

I was moving from school to college that year. 'English' being the subject that fetched me my highest or least 'middling' marks in the school-leaving exams, I sought admission in St. Stephen's College's English Literature course for my BA Honours. Shakespeare was an early exposure. 'Have you read any Shakespeare?' my sister-in-law Indu, who taught Philosophy at Delhi University's celebrated college for women, Miranda House, asked me. She knew what undergraduate aspirants were about. 'Yes,' I said, 'of course.' She then asked me which plays I had read. I said, 'All of them, I think.' Unimpressed, she asked, 'Really? In which edition...' I said, 'In Charles and Mary Lamb's *Tales from Shakespeare...*' Suppressing a laugh, she said, 'Gopu, that is not the same thing. Start with reading Shakespeare's plays as he wrote them...Start with *Hamlet*.' I did as she asked me to. But if his plays—*King Lear* in particular—gripped me, so did his sonnets. Chinmoy Banerjee, one of the finest teachers of the subject in college, as also one of the cleverest, taught us the sonnets, singling out at a tutorial session, Sonnet 129 opening with the lines:

Th' expense of spirit in a waste of shame
Is lust in action...
Past reason hunted; and, no sooner had
Past reason hated

The lines made me think reflexively of something, but I checked my imagination with a 'Dirty Mind, you! This is Shakespeare...The sonnet has to have a serious meaning' only to be asked by Chinmoy: 'So...What does Shakespeare mean by "spirit"?' We were two or three of us in that session, and all of us stayed silent. 'Human semen', he said with the confidence of an oracle. We nodded in grim acceptance of the wisdom, I with relief at the revelation that mine was, after all, not so dirty a mind, the others with varying mixes of boredom and interest. I recalled my peer at school with the 'falling sickness', the very human form of 'lust in action past reason hunted'. But I am now not sure Chinmoy was right. Shakespeare has had to have had a deeper thought in mind, encompassing the gamut of human relations, with 'lust' going beyond its basic meaning to cover human greed and avarice.

Anna in Madras took it upon himself to help me 'remotely' with my BA Honours study of English literature in a way Indu, my sister-in-law, would approve. 'You should read at least a dozen of Shakespeare's plays,' he wrote to me, 'if not all of them.' And he got eleven of Shakespeare's plays in annotated form from a second-hand bookseller in Madras and sent them to me. 'Read all the plays as if they were detective stories read for amusement.' And he sent a volume of only Shakespeare's historical plays with a glossary at the end. 'This will give you,' he wrote, 'a concrete story of the Kings of England from John to Henry the Eighth.'

That an eighty-three-year-old man should engage so intensively in a grandson's education is interesting in itself, but that the man concerned was, at that time, in the thick of a demanding political battle against an entrenched political establishment makes his diversion into English literature more than interesting. But what has made, for me, Anna's deep involvement in the history of Britain's royal line and in the works of William Shakespeare memorable is the fact that here was a man who fought the British Raj with passion and spent terms in that Raj's prison taking so objective a view of the colonizer's history and literature.

Shakespeare's *As You Like It* has Rosalind affirm her love for Orlando in the line 'My affection hath an unknown bottom, like the Bay of Portugal'. That was about my only mental 'link' to the European state that had, for 450 years, no less, ruled over the small territory on India's western seaboard, Goa. And of Goa itself, my knowledge had been confined to Ram Manohar Lohia's satyagrahic actions to secure its liberation from Lisbon.

And so, when the great event of the year, the action taken by the Government of India to take control of Goa, took place, I was excited by its surface electricity, not by any sense of its historical importance. Portugal holding on to Goa and Daman and Diu was worse than an anomaly or an anachronism; it was an absurdity. It was only a question of time before the Portuguese colony returned to the rest of India in republican freedom. But India did not wait. In just thirty-six hours, land, sea and air strikes code-named Operation Vijay brought a 451-year-old rule over Goa and its enclaves to a close. Portugal had, to put it in slang, 'asked for it'. Negotiations between the Republic of India and Portugal had failed to elicit any response. Lisbon was blind to the change in times, to the fact that colonialism was now old, discredited, and all but dead. But India at the time did not cover herself with glory. The use of armed strength, utterly disproportionate with the military resources of the Portuguese regime in Goa, made the action look 'over the top'. Barring the Soviet Union, Ceylon, and a few other nations, the entire world said India had spoilt her name and lost her credentials as a nation that had won its freedom non-violently.

Communications in 1961 were not what they are today, but the fact that 4,668 personnel were taken prisoner by India—a figure which included military and civilian personnel, Portuguese, African, and Goan—was not lost on the world, nor the further detail that Goa's Governor General Manuel Vassalo e Silva (1899–1985), recognizing the futility of facing a superior enemy, disobeying direct orders from Portugal's dictator-for-life, António de Oliveira Salazar (1889–1970) to fight to the death and destroy Goa before leaving it, had honourably surrendered the day following the Indian entry. Vassalo e Silva refused to be repatriated (though his wife returned) and insisted on staying back with the Portuguese prisoners until they were all sent back.

Salazar had given Vassalo e Silva two orders. The first was to 'prevail or perish', which really meant not to surrender but let blood flow. In his words: 'The consequences of carrying out the first order of defending Goa to the last man would mean the total destruction of Goa.'[2]

The second is best described by the man himself thus: 'I was asked to shift the holy relics of Saint Francis Xavier from Old Goa to Portugal. And why did I not shift the body of the Saint? I had enough consideration for the morale of the Indian troops not to disrespect the Saint. Also, the morale of the Goans would have sunk if the body had been removed from Goa. But most importantly, if the Saint himself was posed this question, he would have certainly objected to his body being taken to Portugal.'

Without the remains of Saint Francis Xavier, Goa would have been something different from the Goa its people know. Vassalo e Silva's disobeying of Salazar has helped Goa stay Goa.

India, the land of hurts, is also a land that knows healing. Vassalo e Silva, in his eighties, was invited to India by the government and visited Goa, only Goa. He said he did not want to go anywhere else in India. He was hugged and hosted by the people of Goa in complete contrast with the treatment he got on his return to Portugal after his surrender. He had been disgraced in every conceivable way. But back on this visit to his former 'realm', e Silva said something which belongs to the annals of the highest political realism: 'The liberation of Goa was in the interest of Goans. Though Portugal ruled Goa for 450 years, this territory had always remained a part and parcel of

India, irrespective of some people who might feel otherwise. It was also in the interest of Portugal that Goa should go back to the hands of Goans.'[3]

Nehru's action was in effect not just seen as unGandhian but as politically opportunist for the action in Goa took place just days before the general elections of 1962 in which, along with the majority of Congress candidates, V. K. Krishna Menon won a resounding victory in North Bombay.

The right thing can be done in a messy way.

Two statesmen in India, risking unpopularity, criticized the action in no uncertain terms—who else but Rajaji and Jayaprakash Narayan. But more pertinently, Vice President Radhakrishnan, who was to become president the following year, disliked it. His son and biographer Sarvepalli Gopal (1923–2002) writes: '...on Goa Radhakrishnan made no secret of his dislike of military action... The action, he told the Prime Minister, was a mistake which distressed him...' Gopal adds '...and Nehru confessed that he thought and felt the same...'[4]

Goa has now been a legal part of India to which it always belonged civilizationally. What the Indian military arms did was done in obedience to orders given to them by the Government of India.

Who gained immediately? One person, certainly: Defence Minister Krishna Menon, defeating in his seat Acharya J. B. Kripalani, whose presence in Parliament would have been a democratic counter to Nehru. The irony of it all is that Menon, hugely popular in his constituency, need not have feared defeat. He would have won that seat anyhow.

Be it Nagaland or Goa, Nehru's India did what it did on its northeastern borders and on its western seaboard by its lights. But they were the lights of Nehru's, not Gandhi's India.

Rajaji, JP, Kripalani, Prasad, and Radhakrishnan were troubled by those lights.

And somewhere in the dark recesses of his lonesomeness, so was Nehru himself, though he could not show it.

Heroic Indians had fought for Goa's liberation for years prior to 1961. The valour and patriotism of Lohia, Vishwanath Lawande, Narayan Hari Naik, Dattatraya Deshpande, Prabhakar Sinari, and Mohan Ranade, who had risked personal hurt and death, is remembered in Goa to this day. But insufficiently by the rest of India.

1962
PERFIDY

The year started excitedly for India's democracy, Nehru leading his party into the nation's third general election and then to triumph. Held over six days between 19 and 25 February to elect members of the 3rd Lok Sabha, the polls gave the Indian National Congress 44.7 per cent of the vote and 361 of the 494 elected seats. Nehru held over 70 per cent of the seats in the Lok Sabha. The Communist Party came second with 10 per cent of the vote and 29 seats, no poor showing. But the star of the elections was the Swatantra Party. Fighting in a general election for the first time, it came third with 7.8 per cent of the vote and 18 seats.

Swatantra was a star in more than one sense. Its flag, bright sky blue with a white star in the middle, caught the eye. As did its new MP, Gayatri Devi of Jaipur, who had polled more votes than any of the others elected to the house, Nehru included. 'Jaypore' as she pronounced the name of her city and former state, gave the former queen of Jaipur old and new respect—old for the position she had held in history and new for her great guts in opposing the party in power and winning the first election she ever contested in what has been described as 'the world's largest landslide,'[1] winning 192,909 votes out of 246,516 cast. In an overreach by any standards of historical judgment or political realism, Rajaji described her, in an article he wrote for the magazine *Swarajya*, as a modern Rani of Jhansi. Given the violent end of that brave warrior queen (1828–58), the analogy was also inept.

There was no doubt that the Swatantra Party was a conglomerate of the rich farmer, the capitalist, and obsolete royalty—a combination that had the sparkle and sizzle of that Diwali 'firework' called the anaar (pomegranate) which goes up in a spectacular show of glitter and its brief show done, subsides without a trace.

Anna came to Delhi as the new Lok Sabha met. 'Won't you attend the first day of the Lok Sabha session and see your MPs being sworn in? It will be such a sensation,' I piped up. 'Sensation? No...that will be sensationalism.'

Nehru took his place as prime minister, elected to that office for the third time. He had every reason to be glad, but one reason more than others. He had got Krishna Menon elected, defeating Acharya Kripalani from North Bombay. Goa's liberation had everything to do with the mood of the voters who gave Menon his second victory from there, though he would have won even otherwise. And though Menon represented North Bombay, he symbolized the liberation of Goa as he entered the Lok Sabha.

Following a nuclear test by the Soviet Union in the autumn of the previous year, the US was planning retaliatory blasts. Bertrand Russell urged Nehru to send protest ships to the Pacific Ocean, where the US blasts were scheduled. Rajaji wrote to Nehru on 22 April 1962, 'If you are responding positively to Bertrand Russell's appeal, do register me as a civilian going with the "resisters".' Nehru was unenthused, both by Russell and by Rajaji. He replied to Rajaji the next day, 'That would be almost a hostile act against the United States...' But I was thrilled and wanted to sign up with my grandfather. Harold Steele's example was working in my head. My mother, knowing instinctively that little would come of the whole thing, did not want to sound unidealistic, and so she neither discouraged nor encouraged me in my fantasizing. Rajaji, meanwhile, in an article in *Swarajya*, wrote on 5 May, 'Will America stop her aid? I do not think she will. But even if that should happen, may we not say to ourselves and to posterity that we preferred losing assistance from America to losing the chance of helping the world against an evil consequence that was certain?'

No warship or any other vessel went from India to Christmas Islands, but come September and Rajaji was to board a plane, with Nehru's full knowledge and most amazingly considerate cooperation, on his way to Washington DC, to meet President John F. Kennedy (1917–63) to urge him to cease nuclear testing. For all the criticism—and it was sharp—that Nehru was receiving from Rajaji, and overcoming his scepticism about the peace mission, Nehru sent instructions to the Indian embassies where Rajaji was supposed to visit to accord to him due courtesy and attention.

Rajaji was going as the Gandhi Peace Foundation's chief spokesman, with R. R. Diwakar, the foundation's head, as the delegation's leader. B. Shiva Rao (1891–1975), constitutionalist and political thinker of eminence, was to be the third member. 'Fancy sending three stretcher cases to meet Kennedy,'[2] thought K. Natwar Singh (1929–2024), then India's consul general in New York. But he would soon eat his words, at least as far as Rajaji went.

I had to be in the frame. Flying, at no small expense, from Delhi to Bombay to see Rajaji off, I got to the international departures just in time. The governor of Maharashtra, Vijaya Lakshmi Pandit, was there, doubtless at her brother's instance, apart from her own instincts of rectitude. Sitting beside him, I asked Anna, 'Will you be meeting Bertrand Russell during your stopover in London?' 'Who?' he asked, cupping his good ear. I repeated the philosopher's name. 'Oh no,' the eighty-four-year-old said of the ninety-year-old. 'He is too old.'

Dr Thomas W. Simons, the US consul general in Madras (1957–63), had very industriously sent on 25 September a detailed telegram[*] to the US secretary of state on the delegation, in which he described Rajaji as one 'with the conviction of an ageing seer who could well qualify as another profile in courage.'[†]

And as being (in telegraphese) 'loved and feared India and respected South Asia and probably strongest anti-nuclear force and voice in Asia'. Since a lunch meeting with President Kennedy was also being contemplated, Simons added, 'Rajaji said if luncheon proposed all he wanted was a glass of milk since he wanted to talk more than eat with the President'. A 'Talking Paper'[‡] prepared for Kennedy said very pragmatically, 'Rajagopalachari is deaf in his left ear. He should be seated to the President's left'.

India's ambassador in Washington, B. K. Nehru (1909–2001) has left a vivid account of the 28 September call on President Kennedy at which he was present: 'I have had the good fortune of being present when great men have argued their points of view with each other in many parts of the world. But I have seldom seen a case presented with such lucidity of argument, such economy of speech, such felicity of language, such gentleness of manner, and such command of facts as Rajaji displayed on that day. It was interesting to watch President Kennedy's reactions, for he, too, was a great admirer of style. One could almost see his eyes open wider and wider in wonder and admiration at the frail little man who was making this masterly presentation.'[3]

Shiva Rao was to record: 'The minutes sped far beyond the allotted time of twenty-five minutes. Messengers kept coming at regular intervals with notes from impatient aides to remind Mr Kennedy that other appointments were falling behind schedule. The President ignored them all...'[4] Rajaji told his host towards the conclusion of his talk. 'If nuclear weapons can be excluded, the character of war will change. At any rate, there will not be the terrible prospect of mass destruction.' Kennedy, rounding off, said to his guest, 'I find the proposals reasonable...and I will certainly consider which of them are feasible.'

A note issued the same day by the White House recorded: 'The President said the United States is prepared to come to an agreement to ban tests in the atmosphere or in water if it is impossible to ban all tests.' This was big.

I do not know how, in the midst of a packed schedule of meetings,

---

[*]JFK Library Textual Archives JFKPOF -118a p0163.

[†]Title of book on eight US senators authored by John F. Kennedy with Ted Sorensen as a ghost-writer, in 1955.

[‡]JFK Library Textual Archives JFKPOF – 118a – 008-p0156, White House Photographs, JFK Library.

Rajaji made the time to write a letter to me on 8 October from New York.

My dear Gopu,

I am keeping wonderfully well here in America. I have seen some of the most important persons in all America. I gave good talks to them all. God has helped me to keep good health and to do my work well. Everyone I think who heard me including all the big bureaucrats were impressed and their conscience is not easy. But God keeps to Himself results.

'Everyone' included U Thant (1909–74), the UN chief, Zafrullah Khan (1893–1985) of Pakistan, who was UN president at the time, Henry Kissinger (1923–2023) (then a Harvard professor who met him over lunch), Adlai Stevenson (1900–65) then the US ambassador to the UN, Secretary of State Dean Rusk (1909–94), McGeorge Bundy (1919–96), Andrei Gromyko (1909–89), the Soviet foreign minister and very significantly, on 9 October 1962, Robert Oppenheimer (1904–67) the physicist whose contribution to the making of the US bomb was foundational.[*] The meeting with Stevenson was important, Stevenson having called for a ban shortly after the first demonstration of a successful hydrogen bomb, saying a test ban would be a small step 'for the rescue of man from the elemental fire which we have kindled'.[5]

Rajaji was particularly glad to have met Bundy, whom he described in warm terms.

Nine months later, at the end of July 1963, the US, the Soviet Union, and Britain agreed on a partial test ban treaty, Bundy describing it as 'a good first step achieved primarily by world opinion'.[6] Nehru's role in getting that treaty through was significant, in fact, defining. Did Rajaji's mission have something to do with the US's approach to it? God keeps to Himself, not just the results but also the grades.

Briefs prepared for the US President, I gathered from the one in respect of Rajaji and another for India's Finance Minister Morarji Desai, are thorough-going and written to give to the president the maximum 'dope' in the minimum wordage. Desai met Kennedy just eight days before Rajaji and his delegation. The 'Talking Paper'[†] for Desai has this nugget: 'Desai

[*]Oppenheimer called on Rajaji, who on returning to India, wrote to Oppenheimer (29 October 1962) thanking him for 'having found time to honour me with a visit' adding that 'It was an unforgettable moment for me who have been admiring you for so long'. (Oppenheimer papers, Library of Congress (Box No. 59).

[†]JFK Library Textual Archives JFKPOF – 118a 008-p0122, White House Photographs, JFK Library.

is an unusual combination of a practical Finance Minister and a Gandhian idealist. It is frequently difficult to predict whether he will discuss finance or morality.' The No. 2 in Nehru's cabinet was perceived by the US establishment as 'pro-West' and was shown in the briefs for Kennedy very interestingly and not incorrectly as one whose rival for attention and influence in the Indian cabinet was Krishna Menon, and who did not agree Nehru on issues 'that have exacerbated US-India relations' and as one 'closely associated in India with western economic assistance'. Saying that Desai's 'star will dim if that assistance falters', the brief said in a crisp sentence something that made Nehru, Menon, and Desai come alive: 'Unlike Menon, Desai has little rapport with Nehru, but the Prime Minister respects his ability.' Desai had gone to the US basically to seek assistance for India's Third Plan for development. But the visit, taking place shortly before one by President Ayub Khan of Pakistan, India's security concerns had to play a big part.

The same 'Talking Paper' alerted Kennedy to this and advised him to stress on Desai the need for India to be mindful of her neighbourhood and the problems with them escalating, leading to the diversion of funds from development to defence. I do not know if Kennedy did act on this brief and if he did, what Desai's reaction was, but the input was timely as October of the same year was to show.

By the time Rajaji returned to India, something else had happened that convulsed India.

The Sino-Indian border dispute had ignited into ballistics on 10 October and, on 20 October, Chinese troops invaded Kashmir, occupying Aksai Chin, starting the Sino-Indian war. The country's spirit was dealt a blow, Nehru's more than a blow. He had lost what Shakespeare has described in *Henry VI* as the crown:

My Crown is in my heart, not on my head:
Not deck'd with Diamonds, and Indian stones:
Nor to be seen: my Crown is call'd Content,
A Crown it is, that seldom Kings enjoy.

In Delhi, on 25 October, Rajaji met Nehru, the president, Sarvepalli Radhakrishnan, and said in a statement that Nehru ought not to be blamed for the border situation. That he had been betrayed by China, said Rajaji, was not his fault. And, he added with his own peculiar wit, 'There is no meaning in charging the enemy with cheating. It is the business of the enemy to cheat.' Coming from Nehru's foremost opponent at the time, all this was no ordinary exculpation. But Rajaji joined everyone who wanted Defence Minister Menon to go. 'Whether the Defence Minister is a good and capable person is not the issue. A large section of the people of this country have grave doubts about him,'[7] and he asked Nehru to take up the defence portfolio himself.

President Radhakrishnan was decidedly for Menon's exit. But the most reliable account that I heard at the time was that Lal Bahadur Shastri went to Nehru and said in Hindi, 'Panditji, when the officiating figure at a yagna hesitates to give a small offering, the fire extracts a big offering.' This was narrated to me by the Gandhian economist, the late L. C. Jain. The word he used was ahuti, which means a sacrificial oblatory offering. It is quite untranslatable into English. I know that in legal parlance, this account would be called 'hearsay', but I know that Jain had it on good authority. That settled it. Nehru realized that if he does not drop Menon, and the border situation worsens, the nation might well move against the prime minister himself.

On 29 October US Ambassador Galbraith personally handed over to Prime Minister Nehru a letter from President Kennedy[*] expressing his sympathy and that of his country, and assuring support, to which Nehru sent a reply[†] within hours, saying: 'I am deeply grateful...' and assuring Kennedy that such assistance India was seeking had his (Nehru's) full backing. This assurance of Nehru's was very significant and it is curious that its import has not been commented upon by political analysts and historians. Nehru was telling Kennedy something Kennedy needed to know and which could be paraphrased (in my words) thus: 'Shocked as I am, in fact, shattered. I, Jawaharlal Nehru, am in charge of my government and thereby of my country and let no one imagine that the initiative for conducting our defence in this hour of crisis has slipped from my hands to that of anyone else, the military in particular. I have not been known to seek or value armed assistance from western powers, the USA in particular, in any significant degree, but now, in this new situation, I am modifying my stand and am asking the US for arms by the exercise of my own judgment and of my own volition.'

On 9 November Ambassador Galbraith wrote[‡] to Kennedy briefly: 'One of the worst problems here is that the Chinese attack strikes the country with a very tired leader whose principles and ideas have also been shattered by the event.'

Ten days later, on 19 December, Nehru wrote[§] to Kennedy a letter that is heart-wrenchingly frank, heart-crunchingly plaintive. 'The situation that has

---

[*]JFK Library Textual Archives JFKPOF– 118a-004-p0061, White House Photographs, JFK Library.
[†]JFK Library Textual Archives JFKPOF– 118a-004-p0060, White House Photographs, JFK Library.
[‡]JFK Library Textual Archives JFKPOF – 118a-004-p0062, White House Photographs, JFK Library.
[§]JFK Library Textual Archives JFKPOF – 118a-004-p.0068, White House Photographs, JFK Library.

developed,' he wrote, 'is really desperate. We have to have more comprehensive assistance if the Chinese are to be prevented from taking over the whole of eastern India. Any delay in this assistance reaching us will result in nothing short of a catastrophe for our country,'

With the new national Emergency that had been declared, schools and colleges got their taste of the crisis through drills and training programmes. My college, St. Stephen's, got its share of the military ethos imparted to it. No institution was less military-minded than this Anglican college of which the Reverend C. F. Andrews (1871–1940) had been vice principal and where Gandhi had stayed as the guest of its principal Sushil K. Rudra (1861–1925). And its small but influential set of leftists (among staff and students) were even less inclined to anything smacking of armed training than others. But the pinkest of pink intellectuals would think the better of non-cooperating with uniformed might during times of war. And so, all of us enlisted by order, of course, in the drills. I, along with my peers, marched up and down the gravelled pathways of our college that had never known hard boots or grey and khaki uniforms. I did not mind the physical strangeness of it all, but the atmosphere that came with it was unpleasant. L-l-left, R-r-right, about-t-tur-r-n and then lapsing into Hindi, the drill-master shouted coarse words. Asking us, as part of the drill, to squat on the ground in a second's 'surprise' order, he saw me take a little long. Arrey...chutad mein baith, chutad mein... (Hey, sit on your bum, on your bum). I obeyed, burning inside. No one but no one had ever spoken to me like that before. One purely theoretical part of me asked me to step out of line and confront him, saying Sir, hukum dijiye, lekin buri zuban mein nahin. (Sir, you can give us orders, but not in bad language.) An Emergency, however, is an Emergency. Its fuel is fear.

There was also a sharp deterioration in the levels of decent converse in radio broadcasts. I heard for the first time words and descriptions of 'the enemy' I had not heard before—not on AIR. Patriotic instincts were being constantly subverted by jingoistic crudities. Our principal, S. C. Sircar (1908–76), a first-rate mathematician and superb administrator, told us we did not have to join anti-China rallies that had been called by student bodies from elsewhere. Sure enough, those organizations came and placed bangles on our gates—bangles being symbols of effeminacy. Sircar sahib was unmoved. 'They have done what they have from outside.... Let them try come in....' he said quietly. They did not.

I knew that Principal Sircar was as tough an Indian and as true a patriot as any. Most bangle-dangle nationalist actors would have fled if accosted by as much as the shadow of a Chinese soldier. It is easy to look and sound patriotic in the safe hinterland of geopolitics.

Nehru faced Parliament bravely or, I should say, stoically. Parliament, too, did not pillory him as it might have done had Menon not been moved out. Swatantra MPs led the charge in the Lok Sabha with P. K. Deo (1919–2001), the raja of Kalahandi, asking Nehru to give up non-alignment and ally with the West. Gayatri Devi, in an interjection, said if Nehru had been more aware of what was happening, we would not have been in 'this mess'. Nehru did not catch the phrase and asked for it to be repeated, which the speaker said was not necessary as what the MP had said was 'not important', but Gayatri Devi nonetheless repeated it, leading Nehru to say civilly, 'I shall not bandy words with a lady.'

The queenly MP was not alone in thinking and saying what she did. As his biographer-son Sarvepalli Gopal records[8] President Radhakrishnan, visiting the battlefront in the eastern sector, spoke publicly of the 'credulity and negligence' of the government which had brought matters to this pass. Menon had to go and did. And I, too, celebrated his departure. But in hindsight, I cannot but see the collective hound-hunt after an individual that the Menon-must-go impulse became as a form of political cannibalism.

On 21 November, China called a ceasefire along the McMahon Line, withdrew its troops from Arunachal Pradesh and saved the day for India—for the day. And wasn't a whole world of students relieved! No more drills, no more drill-time coarseness. And no more fears of the one 'order' that hung over us like a sword—conscription.

But the sense of humiliation at the hands of China was real. And it pushed our heads down. And somewhere in that atmosphere, Krishna Menon's ahuti seemed to help us lift them up a bit.

One side effect of the events of 1962 was that President Radhakrishnan emerged as a major factor in India's public life. Without transgressing the limits laid down by the Constitution and propriety, and without by-passing the prime minister in any way even once, he had established the power of presidential influence as distinct from presidential powers. His predecessor had made the president's powers an issue for general discussion and speculation. Radhakrishnan did nothing of the sort. He showed that with the required intellectual and moral stature, a president can become the nation's paterfamilias who is not ignored because no one wants to ignore him. More, a paterfamilias who is invariably heeded for what he says and writes and how he conducts himself—with unselfconscious dignity and zero desire to be 'popular'—compels attention and respect and wins compliance.

Radhakrishnan set the gold standard for the office of India's president.

Subbulakshmi came to Delhi shortly thereafter for a concert in aid of the national defence effort. I was there with my mother, applauding, as the

Nightingale of India, during an intermission, took off all the gold she was wearing—and it was not little—and donated it to the national defence fund, which was accepting gold ornaments. President Radhakrishnan invited her and her husband, and my mother to lunch. I do not know how or why, but I was included. As we came into the grand house, Radhakrishnan said he had arranged for a life-size painting of Rajaji to be made and displayed prominently. 'He was after all the first Indian to tenant this house,' he said, taking all of us to see the work in oil. The door leading to the hall where it hung was locked! 'What is this?' the president asked his staff irritatedly. 'Get it opened.' Getting keys to locks in a house that has 340 rooms over four floors connected by corridors 2.5 kilometres long is not easy. The wait was long, but it did end. As gleaming brass keys turned gleaming brass locks to open the door, Radhakrishnan bemoaned, 'See the constraints on a president!' Radhakrishnan's mother tongue was Telugu, and the language he had mastered (apart from English) was Sanskrit. But he spoke Tamil with the effortless ease of one whose best years have been spent in Mylapore and by the Marina Beach in Madras. MS and Sadasivam were as at home, talking to him in their own language in his big-domed residence as they had been there when Rajaji was governor general, hosting them in an atmosphere that was all Tamil.

Lunch was elegant, not lavish. Radhakrishnan's gracious daughter-in-law, Indira Gopal, supervising, as delicious south Indian fare was shown around the table. Her husband and the president's only son, Sarvepalli Gopal, was not present, working away, doubtless, at the Ministry of External Affairs, where he ran the Historical Records Division. It was a working day, but a president has no office hours. He is 'at work' all the time. And so, the president was in full flow. Recounting the days of the crisis, he said, 'The US Ambassador told me they are ready to fly in arms. They only need to be told, he said to me. Told! But by who? By Menon? The Malayala Bhagavati was taking his own time. We are making the list, Menon said. Making the list? I had to tell Nehru enough is enough.'

That was the first time I heard the phrase 'Malayala Bhagavati'. To this day, I am not quite sure of its exact meaning, but it was, I could see, a searing description. And one that I would never forget if also never use, for it had come from President Radhakrishnan who, as far as I am concerned, now and forever held a patent to it.

Within weeks of the Sino-Indian war, JP came to my college to give the first C. F. Andrews Memorial Lecture on 'Nationalism in India, Before Independence and After'. On the date, a fellow Stephanian and I went to JP's office in Delhi to escort him to the college for the lecture. As the car started, he asked me: 'Gopu, what, by the way, is the subject of my lecture today?' I gave him the title with a heart that had sunk into my shoes. If JP has forgotten the subject, how was he going to give that lecture? The rest of the journey in the car was spent in total silence. He was preparing in his mind the entire speech. And, my God, what a speech it was! The gods of political science and of history would have stepped down from their towers to hear it. In a slow, measured tone, he spoke extempore for the first half on what nationalism had meant in the years of the struggle for freedom—decolonization, the retrieving of self-respect, self-reliance, self-confidence with non-violent disobedience as its instrument. And in the second half of what nationalism had come to mean now—sabre-rattling, neighbour-threatening jingoism with intolerance as its fuel. He was heard in a packed hall in deafening silence. After speaking of the need for India to remember the value of Afro-Asian solidarity, he came to a sentence I thought was too much even for St. Stephen's College's liberalism to take at that point of time: 'Even the Chinese are, after all, our Asian brothers....' I was sure there would be some murmuring, if not heckling. There was none. The silence, in fact, deepened. That was JP. Independent beyond co-opting, brave beyond bullying.

1963
I SPY WITH MY LITTLE EYE

A curious political development, the significance of which to power-wielding was to be realized only the following year, occurred in 1963. And it started in the intelligent head of Kamaraj, then into his third term as chief minister of Madras. Sensing the ennui that seemed to have overtaken his party and the jaded weariness that its leaders were displaying, he put it to Nehru that the party and, through it, the country be administered a shock treatment. The Congress and the country were in need of it. He suggested that the leading members of the cabinet resign their offices and return to the party to work for its rejuvenation. And offered to resign himself. Pondering this novel idea, Nehru saw its merit and, by October, had Shastri, Morarji Desai, and Jagjivan Ram, among other seniors in the cabinet, resign as also some chief ministers. Kamaraj moved to Delhi from Madras, becoming Congress president.

The move was smart, but politics works unpredictably. Kamaraj's successor in Madras, the experienced and senior M. Bhaktavatsalam, lacked Kamaraj's verve and, in his administratively diligent but politically unstimulating incumbency, commenced the decline of the Congress in his state. In Kashmir, where Bakshi Ghulam Mohammed was surprised to see his 'Kamaraj' offer to resign being accepted, saw the start of a sequence of events that not just he but no one else could have imagined either.

On 27 December 1963, news broke out that the Moi-e-Muqqadas, believed to be a strand from the beard of the Prophet Muhammad, had gone missing—stolen, it was said, from the Hazratbal shrine around 2 a.m. when the custodians of the shrine were, like anyone else at that hour of the night, asleep. The chief minister of the state at the time, Bakshi's successor Khwaja Shams-ud-Din (1922–99), announced an award of Rs 1 lakh to anyone providing information regarding the theft. Communal tension rose like a freak fever. Cinema theatres owned by Bakshi's brothers were torched, and AIR's Srinagar station gutted. Three days later, a stunned Jawaharlal Nehru, sent the head of the Intelligence Bureau, B. N. Mullik (1904–84), to Kashmir to investigate the crime and report on the aftermath. Much more than a theft was at stake. On 4 January 1964, Mullik informed Nehru that the relic had been recovered. A relieved prime minister said to Mullik, 'You have saved Kashmir for India.' Not everything is known about the details of the recovery, but after Sayyid Meerak Shah Kashani (1895–1971), a Sufi poet and Sunni leader, identified it as the original and genuine relic, matters quietened down. Some arrests were made, but some people we do not know of need to be thanked for having averted a major communal catastrophe in India that year. How the relic was discovered will probably never be known. Mullik said the secret would remain with him to his dying day—verily the height of a spymaster's sense of secrecy between him and his Maker.

I warmed to reports of Jayaprakash Narayan's having enlisted volunteers of the Shanti Sena to help maintain law and order in the valley, enraged by the incident. JP, in a typically nuanced response, deplored the arson but congratulated the people of the valley for having restrained their anguish and restored calm. He also did what was expected of one like him: he demanded the release of Sheikh Abdullah and the return to democratic nostrums in the valley so ruthlessly dominated by the Bakshi family's ruling apparatus, which had earned the sobriquet of BBC—Bakshi Brothers Corporation.

Kamaraj's plan for rejuvenating the Congress and the travails of Kashmir apart, India in 1963, noted one major accomplishment to its credit. India's space scientists launched on 21 November its first ever rocket from a small fishing village near Trivandrum, as the town was then called. Sharp-brained and sharp-eyed technologists and rocket engineers, including A. P. J. Abdul Kalam (1931–2015), accomplished the successful launch with the help of three persons whose knowledge of rocket technology was zero but whose minds and hearts were as pioneering as those who had chosen the site for its atmospheric and ionospheric suitability (as well as its ideal distance from both China and Pakistan). Of these, two were bishops—the 'local' Bishop, Reverend Peter Bernard Pereira (1917–78) and the Bishop of Trivandrum, Vincent Victor Dereere (1880–1973), incidentally a Belgian. The third was an administrator, the district collector Madhavan Nair. These three busied themselves in acquiring 600 acres from the coastal community for the Thumba Equatorial Rocket Launching Station. India hailed the launch and the technologists behind it, as it should have done. But the two priests and the collector are not remembered quite as much as they deserve to be for what they did to make India the space major it is today.

Sixty years later, India was to announce the Indian Space Policy 2023 with the 'vision' to 'enable, encourage and develop a flourishing commercial presence in space' and spoke of its role in India's 'socio-economic development and security, protection of environment and lives, pursuing peaceful exploration of outer space, stimulation of public awareness and scientific quest'. This is no ordinary venture, no simple plan, but an audacious strategy that will make ISRO propel us towards what may be called the Chandrayaan and Gaganyaan age.

Independent India has zoomed ahead in space, but it still lacks public awareness and, more, public interest in the subject, not just to know and appreciate but also to ask and interrogate the space programme and policy. How much of the programme is beneficial to the quality of life in India? How much of it is just clubbist—designed to keep us in the high company of space majors? How much of it is actuated by supremacist pride?

The sacral and the secular coexist in India coextensively. Ironies have been India's signature.

Mullik occasions the following thoughts: Spies are as old as kings, and suspicion older, as a human emotion, than patriotism. Kautilya's *Arthasastra* and Tiruvalluvar's *Kural* explain and extol the spy's art and his science as an essential arm of the state. Spies have served tyrannical kings as also noble-minded ones. There is nothing to show that the great ethical path-finder among emperors, Ashoka, after his contrition over the havoc he wrought in Kalinga, wound up his department of spies. And spies in our republican times can be found in the state machines of dictatorial heads of government as well as in those of democratically elected heads of government. The difference is that the first type use spies to entrench themselves in power and have their friends and even their relatives spied upon no less than their enemies, whereas democrats in office put their spies to work on persons and organizations likely to be threatening the security and integrity of the state. The gross types have spies spying on spies, too, whereas the better types would risk leaving their spies unspied. (Tiruvalluvar has recommended in his *Kural*, a cap of three spies spying on spies.)

Nehru had his spies, Mullik being the spymaster. To the best of my—or anyone's—knowledge, he did not ask Mullik to whisper into his ears who was saying what about him (Nehru) and who was plotting his subversion or overthrow. The corridors of his power did not have ears, nor their corners, tongues. But his office had amongst its slats for the oxygen of awareness one that let in a steady wisp of information on the goings-on in the sewers of the state. Nehru paid just as much attention to it as it required, not more, not less. He was not a scholar prime minister for nothing.

Mullik's expertise came into play, though ineffectually, in 1963 on another crucial matter. President Kennedy wrote to Nehru suggesting that India conduct a nuclear test using a US nuclear device in the Thar desert.[1] Kennedy knew Nehru's position on nuclear tests but nonetheless suggested this for India's national security and standing vis-à-vis China, which the US had reason to believe via intelligence inputs was going to detonate a nuclear device—the first in Asia any time. Mullik and the US ambassador Galbraith, who conveyed Kennedy's letter, urged acceptance. Nehru, after consulting Homi Bhabha, who wholeheartedly endorsed Kennedy's idea, declined. Accepting the offer would have gone against Nehru's position on nuclear testing and would have strained the principle of non-alignment. But, as Bhabha's biographer says, '...it would have perhaps prevented the 1962 Chinese attack on India and served as a deterrent to Ayub Khan before the 1965 Indo-Pak conflict.'[2]

This was a classic example of secret voices being heard in quiet by the prime minister but treated on merits and a decision taken according to his own lights. Mullik would publish, amidst controversy, his own assessment of the Sino-Indian war in his 1971 work, *The Chinese Betrayal*, but after the 1962 war, the stage was set for the creation of an agency that would look exclusively into external intelligence, the Research and Analysis Wing or RAW, headed by R. N. Kao, a Kashmiri police officer with long experience in the Intelligence Bureau.

Mullik was not the first director of India's Intelligence Bureau (founded by the British Raj in 1887 as the Special Branch). He was the second, but since he started out in 1950, the founding year of the Republic, he enjoys an inaugural stature, reinforced by the fact that he was DIB throughout Nehru's prime ministership, enjoying his total confidence. Patel and Rajaji, as home minister, do not seem to have had any difficulty with Mullik either. He symbolizes the seamless acceptance by India's 'liberators' of a major agency of imperial hegemonist control over political liberties and civil rights. That those who had their letters intercepted and telephone tapped, their movements watched, and their speeches and writings reported could begin to use the same mechanisms on stepping into power shows that absolute power, before it corrupts with Actonian unerringness, desensitizes.

Is espionage essential to the working of a state? Liberals would reject the suggestion. But even India's first home minister, a star of the freedom struggle, Sardar Vallabhbhai Patel, sensed that the security and integrity of the state could not be vouchsafed without agencies that keep track of elements that are working at cross-purposes with a state's credentials to governance. And his successor, Rajaji, too is recorded as having told the British high commissioner Sir Archibald Nye, who took up with him the charge that High Commissioner Menon in London was surrounded by communists, to 'forward the names of communists working for Menon to Mullik'.[3]

What even 'illiberals' cannot deny is that the Indian state has not been able to disengage its 'spy eye' from snooping on those whom the powers-that-be of the day regard as threats to their wielding power. Just as the stick does not exist that threatens only thugs, the Indian agency for Intelligence-gathering, that does its work with no regard to the personal and party predilections of the ruling establishment, is yet to be born.

1964

...A FLAME VANISHES

Shortly after the year began, India lost Rajkumari Amrit Kaur. She was seventy-five. She was not only a freedom fighter and a trusted colleague of Gandhi and Nehru but also a pioneering health minister, having initiated mass immunization in India through the BCG vaccine. Rajaji had opposed the vaccine vigorously, in his own witty way, though he had never held the portfolio nor acquired the expertise to comment on it. If India's death rate has fallen from 45 per 1,000 in 1947 to just 8 per 1,000 at the time of writing (2024), and life expectancy has gone up from 37 in 1947 to 65 as of date, it is to no small extent because of the early start to mass immunization,* which commenced under the khadi-wearing Protestant princess of Kapurthala's health ministership. And more recently she had come to symbolize political dissent.

Amma and I went to Rajkumari's home and accompanied the cortege to Nigambodh Ghat, where she was cremated. St. Stephen's College principal Sircar sahib was there, and I remember his saying to me, as flames consumed the Protestant leader's gentle remains: 'I do not know why she left instructions for a cremation rather than a burial.... Her wishes, of course, have to be respected.... But I must confess that I—not as Christian but as just a plain observer—find the practice of burning rather extreme...violent, almost... whereas lowering the body into the earth is so much gentler.'

What is ecologically right or less wrong—burial or burning? I have never got a satisfactory answer. In a way, I suppose, the Parsi rite, now almost given up, of leaving the remains in Towers of Silence for vultures to consume would be the most 'natural', if also the most wild—talons and beaks and all.

My third and last year in college, reading English Literature as my 'main' and history as my 'subsidiary', had confirmed me as a Nehru-sceptic and, predictably and boringly enough, a Rajaji-enthusiast. Anna's continuing interest in my reading great English writing was only part of the reason for this. It was his public role as a conscience-keeper and source of a democratic

---

*Vaccinations/inoculations against tuberculosis have played a huge role in keeping the disease in check though the figure of 1,400 dying of it per day is chilling. Immunization against small pox has had spectacular results with the norm of the incidence being less than 1 per 10,000 having been held steadily since 1979. Polio vaccination has also been a success story, there having been no incidence for the last twelve years (counting from 2024), though a vaccine induced case was reported in the Northeast in 2024.

opposition to 'one-party rule' that held appeal to me. I was, thank God, sufficiently objective to see that he was not the only one playing that role.

Jayaprakash Narayan suffused my thoughts.

He was at that stage engaged in a thankless effort to persuade Nagaland's disaffected to realize that they were better off as one of the states of India rather than in any other arrangement, particularly 'self-determination'. And at the same time, telling the Government of India to do nothing that would make the brave Nagas, with their many distinct languages and proud cultural forms, feel they were tribal savages needing to be civilized.*

He also remained concerned about Kashmir, where the Kashmir Conspiracy case having been withdrawn suddenly at Nehru's behest, Abdullah and his colleagues walked free. Kashmir erupted in celebrations for the return to freedom of its most popular son and the final fall of that son's tormentor, Bakshi, disliked by all but his henchmen in the valley. Nehru sent to his friend of decades and captive of eleven years a message asking him to come to Delhi and stay with him, talking of how Kashmir and the people of Kashmir can be made to feel some happiness again. Money lavished on a person feeling wronged is useless. Nehru realized this.

Whether it was just the wisdom from a seventy-five-year-old's ebbing fireside in winter or the shock administered by China, Nehru sent his daughter to receive Abdullah at the airport and was at the portico of his house to greet his guest as he arrived. Seated together after eleven years, Abdullah noted that the 'tulip' look of his old friend had gone, replaced by lines drawn by a stroke. Let us forget the past, he told his host. Let us solve the Kashmir problem and come to some agreement with Pakistan, he said. And Nehru, listening attentively, said he agreed.

Pakistan's president Ayub Khan (1907–74) sent a message to Abdullah even as he was with Nehru, inviting the freed leader to Pakistan. Nehru encouraged his guest to accept and, in a remarkable speech at an All India Congress Committee meeting in Bombay, said Abdullah believed 'it should not be difficult for India to hold on to its values and still live in peace with Pakistan'[1], adding that India would render Abdullah all assistance in his visit to Pakistan to further the objective of a solution to the Kashmir problem that will bring India and Pakistan together.

Buoyed by Abdullah's going to Madras from Delhi to meet Rajaji to seek his blessings and then his meeting JP filled me with a sense of a great tectonic shift happening on the seismic plate of Indian politics, overcoming

---

*Ramachandra Guha's acclaimed book on Verrier Elwin is in a reverse gambit entitled *Savaging the Civilized*.

the nasty fault line of suspicion and partition. Rajaji was reported to have bemoaned the fact that Nehru was surrounded and influenced by sycophants but that it still was possible for him to do what was necessary to save the Kashmir situation.

That summer, I went with friends Jayant Das and Mohanlal Odhavji to a Quakers-organized youth conference on peace in Port Dickson, Malaysia. We were returning via the town of Penang when we heard over the car radio that Nehru had died. That he had been ailing, we knew. That he had been depressed, we knew. But Nehru—gone! I was benumbed.

In what seemed like a football field, the citizens of Penang organized an impromptu condolence meeting that very evening. Spotting us outsiders and discovering we were Indians, we were asked to sit on the stage and speak. Jayant and Mohanlal said I should do the honours. What was I to say? A conversation kept going round and round in my mind on that football field.

An Asian hero dies—Poster at Penang, Malaya, 28 May 1964. (Author's personal collection).

Tum kuchh khel-vel khelte bhi ho?
...Football.
...Achha? vaise tum khud football lagte ho...

Grief spontaneous—Penang, Malaya, 28 May 1964.
(Author's personal collection).

I do not remember what I said, but since someone had managed to gather from our local hosts whose grandson I was, he interrupted me midway and announced who I was. A kind of a moan of belonging and bereavement went up immediately, and after that, it mattered not what I said and how I said it. I was seen as my grandfathers' grandson, paying a tribute on their behalf, to their great colleague.

Was Anna attending the funeral? Jayant said he would check and said no, he is not but has issued a statement: 'Eleven years younger than I, eleven times more important to the nation, eleven hundred times more beloved of the nation, Sri Nehru has suddenly departed from our midst and I remain alive to hear the sad news from Delhi and bear the shock. The old guardroom is completely empty now. I have been fighting Nehru all these ten years over what I consider faults in public policies. But I knew all along that he alone could get them corrected. No one else would dare to do it, and he is gone, leaving me weaker than before in my fight. But fighting apart, a beloved friend is gone, the most civilized person among all of us.'

So civilized, so civil.

How Abdullah went to Pakistan and began parleys with Ayub and how, when he was there, received the news of Nehru having died, I learnt only later. That sequence is perhaps the most painfully tragic part of the histories of India and Pakistan. Nehru's death at seventy-five had brought a major initiative, soaked in remorse and dried like tears on the sleeve of hope, to naught. As Rajaji had told Abdullah, it was still possible to solve the Kashmir issue through Nehru. Would any other prime minister take the risk? Yes! Lal Bahadur Shastri would, as would from a different political page, Atal Bihari Vajpayee.

Forty-four then, and an MP from the Bharatiya Jana Sangh, Vajpayee (1924–2018), spoke in the Rajya Sabha's condolence session on Nehru; words that belong to the Hansards of legislatures but live in the annals of literature. He spoke in Hindi, of which he was master: 'A dream has been shattered, a song silenced, a flame has vanished in the infinite. It was the dream of a world without fear and without hunger. It was the song of an epic that had the echo of the Gita and the fragrance of the rose. It was the flame of a lamp that burnt all night, fought with every darkness, showed us the way, and one morning attained Nirvana... Bharat Mata is grief-stricken today. She has lost her favourite prince. Humanity is sad today. It has lost its devotee. Peace is restless today. Its protector is no more. The downtrodden have lost their shelter. The common man has lost the light in his eyes.'[2]

My sister-in-law Indu was on a train, travelling to Delhi. She said as soon as the news reached the compartment in which she was, all in it spontaneously mourned, and many began crying unrestrainedly. 'Everyone,' she said, 'everyone and at once felt personally bereaved....' Ramu was the only one in the family who was in Delhi on the day and he went. 'The crowd was huge,' he recalled. '...I made my way to the bier...And did a namaskar on behalf of my father and grandfathers...No one recognized me, but that was just fine....'

'That Wednesday,' writes the Australian high commissioner Crocker, 'was overcast, the air heavy and tense with the pre-monsoon storm which burst in the afternoon. This is the hottest time of the year in north India. The crowds took no heed of the weather. They began filing past the body as soon as they were allowed.' And he adds something which is interesting and in the context of Nehru, anachronistically so. Crocker writes: 'A little before noon, an earthquake shook Delhi.' The *Hindustan Times* reported the time of the jolt as 11.44 a.m. and said, 'Screaming men, women and children rushed out of their houses for safety. Stampedes were caused at many places along the funeral route as lakhs of people who had lined the route felt the shock. The tremor was felt strongly in the Prime Minister's House.'[3]

Nehru was agnostic. He had little patience and less time for superstitious beliefs. But people, 'ordinary' people, cannot be expected to be at the funeral of a king-like leader and have the ground beneath their feet quake without connecting the two. Crocker, no 'ordinary' person mentioning it, though, without elevating it to any meaning beyond the seismic, is only right. Tavernier and Manucci, the French and Italian contemporaries of Shah Jahan, would have done so if the ground in Delhi had trembled at Dara Shukoh's funeral. I do not want to be superstitious but cannot resist being, to coin a phrase, just plain 'stitious', and say that the fact of the 'Nehru earthquake' as it might be called, reminded me of the Biblical description of a great earthquake that occurred at the time of Jesus's crucifixion.

What would Nehru have said about this 'Nehru earthquake'? With a wan smile, slightly irritated, he might have ventured: 'Well, that is what would perhaps be best called a coincidence.' But he is known to have said, 'I am not exactly a religious person, although I agree with much that religions have to say.' In his biography of Radhakrishnan, the historian S. Gopal has given what is I believe the best description of Nehru's 'within': 'Nehru was…a reverent agnostic, without religious faith but with a religious feeling.'[4]

Two towering personalities from the south kept the ship of state from listing, if not sinking, after Nehru's death.

President Sarvepalli Radhakrishnan had no precedents to go by. No prime minister of India had died in office; no vacancy had occurred in the station. He decided quietly and without either delay or fuss that since the Constitution does not contemplate a situation when India is without an elected prime minister, no vacuum should be allowed. He told the second seniormost member of the cabinet, Gulzarilal Nanda (1898–1998), that he would swear him in as prime minister that very afternoon and did. He also made it clear to Nanda that this was an interim arrangement to end as soon as the Congress Legislative Party elected its new leader.

Kamaraj, now Congress president, bestirred himself to have that new leader elected. Strong and tough-looking like a granite hill, he conferred with Radhakrishnan and, of course, with Congress seniors and saw to it that the stature enjoyed by Lal Bahadur Shastri was quickly converted into support without there being any wrangling. Election, yes, squabbles, no.

Defeating Morarji Desai in a neat and open contest, Shastri became India's second prime minister seamlessly. But once in office, the going was not easy for him. He was painfully aware of the contrast—in physical height, in political weight, in intellectual depth. And of the atmosphere of cynical curiosity surrounding his ascent to power.

Within a few weeks of Nehru's death, on 29 August 1964, the then chief of the RSS, M. S. Golwalkar (1906–73) or Guruji, as he was called by his devotees, convened a meeting at the Poona headquarters of Swami Chinmayananda (1916–93) and announced the formation of the Vishva Hindu Parishad (VHP). Was this emergence in the afterglow of Nehru's pyre a coincidence? It certainly said a great deal about the change of times. The VHP's objective was declared as being 'to organise, consolidate the Hindu society and to serve and protect the Hindu Dharma', with plans to construct and renovate Hindu temples, press for a ban on cow slaughter, and stop religious conversion. The proximity of the two dates—Nehru's 'death day' and VHP's birthday—did not strike me then as being of any significance. In fact, the news passed me by.

By then, I was done with my BA Hons. course and enrolled in Delhi University to study the same subject, English Literature. I was lucky to be enabled to attend classes taken by the stalwart teacher of the subject and authority on Milton, Balachandra Rajan (1920–2009). He wore thick-lensed glasses and spoke with an accent that was altogether sophisticated. The author of *Paradise Lost and the Seventeenth Century Reader* seemed to me an Indian who was also strangely not Indian. And curiously Western in the way he thought and spoke, also in the way he looked. His two works, *The Dark Dancer*[5] and *Too Long in the West*[6] enjoyed iconic status by this time, but with one thing or another distracting me, I read neither till much later. But there was something about this teacher that made him very Nehruvian, very modern in an intellectual sense and very vulnerable.

Jayaprakash Narayan, who had since 1962, when he had set up an Indo-Pakistan Conciliation Group, been titling at the windmills to bring a measure of sanity in the relations between the two countries. Now, he tried to arrange a summit between Prime Minister Shastri and President Ayub Khan. His position was that the Kashmir issue had not been settled and indeed could not be settled without reference to the wishes of the people of Kashmir. When about to leave for Lahore for a meeting on 5 September 1964, a mob surrounded and screamed at him, 'Down with Jayaprakash... Kashmir is ours!' He tried to reason with them by saying he had never advocated ceding Kashmir to Pakistan, only seeking an amicable discussion to settle differences. But he was not allowed to do so.

He was just about saved from a physical attack. Agitated by this, I wrote[7] to him on 16 September 1964:

Pujya Jayaprakashji

My admiration for your courage and statesmanship—always high—has risen enormously ever since you have taken this noble and gracious stand on the India-Pakistan question. This is just to tell you that you are not alone in your mission and that there are several people who would be only too glad to help you further the cause of

Indo-Pak amity. I am young and inexperienced and a mere student. But if there is anything I can do for this work you have to only let me know. Perhaps in my enthusiasm I have only succeeded in being presumptuous. Warm regards,

Sincerely, Gopalkrishna Gandhi

He replied on 28 October 1964:

Dear Gopu,

You must forgive me for being so slow in writing to thank you for your charming letter. When abuses were being hurled from every side and the word 'traitor' was being thrown into the face, your letter, the letter of a fine young man like you, acted as a balm. Thank you, Gopu, God bless you.

You ask what you can do to help. Try make as many other young men as possible look at things with your eyes of sanity. Even if you succeed in one case, it would have been a good job done.

Do give Prabhavati's and my regards to your mother.

With all good wishes,

Yours affectionately,
Jayaprakash Narayan

An event took place on 16 October that year, which made no imprint, not to speak of impact on me. And I was fairly representative of my generation and station—English-educated upper middle-class urban youth. For a fleeting day or two, the name of a dried-up salt lake in China made news: Lop Nor, in the southeastern part of Xinjiang. China had detonated on that day a nuclear device on that obscure site. We did not realize the great implication of this test immediately and one that was going to change the face of transnational security on the subcontinent. For the first time since Independence, India now faced a direct nuclear threat. A hostile neighbour had become, overnight, a nuclear power. With this test, technically code-named Project 596 with Miss Qiu as the call sign, China was both the first Asian nation to possess nuclear capability and the fifth nuclear power in the world. To a gathering of the Politburo of the Chinese Communist Party way back in 1956, Chairman Mao had said: 'Now we're already stronger than we were in the past, and in the future, we'll be even stronger than now. Not only are we going to have more airplanes and artillery, but also the atomic bomb. In today's world, if we don't want to be bullied, we have to have this thing.'[8] It now had 'this thing'.

India did not. Homi Bhabha, was to say, eight days after the Chinese test '...atomic weapons give a State possessing them in adequate numbers a deterrent power against attack from a much stronger State. Indeed, the importance of nuclear weapons is that they enable a country possessing them in adequate measure to deter another country also possessing them from using them.'[9] He also suggested that making the bomb did not require all that heavy an investment nor would it take all that much time. He spoke of eighteen months as the gestation period. Not for us, blinkered urban literati, but for those in charge of India's policy vis-à-vis her neighbours, this was something of a bombshell. Bhabha, a Nehru favourite, was yet to establish an equation with Shastri, who, by temperament and political training, was not for making bombs. China's bomb and Bhabha's bombshell were now going to force him to put on his nuclear thinking cap over or in place of his khadi Gandhi one.

A fortnight after the Lop Nor test, Shastri signed an agreement with his counterpart in Ceylon, Sirimavo Bandaranaike (1916–2000), which came to be called The Sirima-Shastri Pact 1964 or Srimavo-Shastri Pact (also known as the Indo-Ceylon Agreement) addressing a long-standing dispute between the two countries—the future of plantation workers of Indian (Tamil) origin in Ceylon's tea plantations. Nehru had consistently maintained that these persons who had settled on the island from over a hundred years ago 'are or should be citizens of Ceylon'. His counterparts had not accepted his position but had not contested it formally or frontally either. But Nehru was Nehru, and Shastri was not Nehru, and so on 30 October, a pact was signed in New Delhi which granted citizenship to 300,000 of the Indian population in Ceylon, while 525,000 would be repatriated to India, leaving the citizenship of the remaining 150,000 Indian residents of Ceylon to be negotiated at a later point.

This was Shastri's first international agreement. It certainly led to a cordial start to his equation with Ceylon, but it also marked a new phase in India's relations with the world in its immediate neighbourhood. And that phase had hovering above it the plume of China's Lop Nor test and its meaning for the world and for Asia in particular. Ceylon had already loomed larger than life on the Sino-Indian horizon when, after the 1962 Sino-Indian war had quietened, Sirimavo made an attempt to broker peace between India and China, along with Ghana. Nehru had responded to that effort positively. And now, with the Sirima-Shastri Agreement, the relative sizes of India and Ceylon had ceased to matter. Sovereignty is independent of size. And in times of tension or need or weakness, real or perceived, being small can almost become a plus point.

That I was to get into the life of this agreement some fourteen years later, I could not have guessed at that point. But curiously, photographs of the sensitive-faced Sirima in Delhi parleying with Shastri and then signing the agreement made a strong impression on my mind. My school trip to Ceylon of 1959 had doubtless something to do with this.

1965
FIVE FEET TWO AND SO TALL

Our home was a glutton for newspapers. A thick wad of newspapers would be slipped through the front door in two or three divided reams adjusted to the gap between door and floor. The English ones were devoured by me at once, with *The Statesman* being the most coveted—an act almost of treachery against the *Hindustan Times* whose salt we lived on. That British-era newspaper was read by us with thousands of others at that time for the quality of its language, the calibre of its writers—the word-turner, Pran Chopra (1921–2013), the word-hammerer, Kuldip Nayar (1923–2018), the word-explorer, S. Nihal Singh (1929–2018), the word-spinner, Inder Malhotra (1930–2016), the word-shiner, Sunanda Datta-Ray (b. 1937). And for the views and insights of its columnists, chief among who was M. Krishnan (1912–1996), the brilliant maverick whose 'Country Notebook' took the reader on bumpy jeep tracks to the deepest recesses of India's forest world. These unforgettable journalists made *The Statesman* more than a newspaper—a vehicle of self-development. The Hindi dailies—*Hindustan* (a sister publication of the *Hindustan Times*) and *Navbharat Times* (from the Times of India group)—remained mostly unread, though the brilliantly satirical column 'Yatra-tatra-sarvatra' (Here, there and everywhere) by Gopal Prasad Vyas (1915–2005) in *Hindustan* would split my sides. His fun pieces, written with just that much naughtiness around the semi-real and semi-imaginary character of his sali (wife's younger sister), whom he found hugely captivating as compared to his gharvali (wife), who he was passionately devoted to, were riveting. Those were times when columnists and editors wrote without having to look over their shoulders for the Watching Eye.

The bias for English newspapers notwithstanding, Hindi was the 'first language' at home. Reason: my mother. Lakshmi was no author, no speaker. She was no habitue of literary circles. But her gentle command over the language that she had learnt neither needed nor permitted any mixing of words from English. She spoke her Hindi and wrote it neat, straight from her sensitive mental lexicon. And she gave to me a sense of the language's grace and expressiveness. Lakshmi translated her father's—our Anna's—commentary on the Ramayana, giving it the title *Dashrath Nandan Shriram* (Dashrath's beloved son, Shri Ram), as also other works of his, including his fables. And my teachers of Hindi at school, Ved Vyas and Vishnu Dutt, both of whom taught the language of Premchand (1880–1936), Nirala (1897–1961),

Subhadra Kumari Chauhan (1904–48) and Mahadevi Varma (1907–87) gave me a strong sense of Hindi literature's wealth.

And then there were two persons whose Hindi I came to love by just the pleasure of hearing it. Prabhavati Devi (1904–73), the stunningly articulate wife of Jayaprakash Narayan, spoke a Bihari Hindi that sparkled. The high-pitched nasality in her voice accentuated the language, as did her punctuating her sentences with laughter. 'Kaki', as Lakshmidevi (1917–1981), the wife of Martand Upadhyay of the premier Hindi publishing house of the time, Sasta Sahitya Mandal, was called, spoke her racy Rajasthani Hindi as Siddheshwari Devi (1908–77) might have sung her famous thumris—with utter abandon. If Kaki, round-faced, with head invariably covered by the red-bordered pallu of her sari, her mouth never freed from a smile of sheer innocent fun or the scent of paan, had been a writer in English, she would have given Meera Syal a run for bestseller in the relevant category. And though I did not spend all that much time with them, the Hindi of these two Devis tutored me, distance-education style.

Supervening these was a third Devi—Mahadevi Varma. Her poems, essays, and speeches held me captive like a captive who loves internment. She entered my conscious, my subconscious, my unconscious being like wine in a cask. No one, I concluded, can write like Mahadevi. Author of the timeless spaceless poem 'Mein Neerbhari Dukh ki Badli' (1935) about a metaphoric female spirit in the shape of a cloud that rises one moment only to disappear the next, she captured me through the short story 'Chini-bhai' (1943), about a Chinese vendor of silk in her native Allahabad, who starts off their association with 'Kuchh lega memsaab?' (Buy something, won't you, ma'am?). This is the greatest story I have ever read on an expatriate, surpassing for its pathos in plangent brevity Tagore's 'Kabuliwala' (1892).

And then there was, lighting up and electrifying the world of Hindi letters, Harivansh Rai Bachchan (1907–2003), now better known as the father of his son who was then known if at all in Hindi circles as the son of his father. Bachchan's pre-Independence *Madhushala* (1935)—(the House of Wine)—is a work of sheer genius. Its rhyming structure shows that rhyme has two parents—spontaneous occurrence and hard labour. One without the other will chime, not rhyme. The work, which had dazzled and dizzied generations of the young and old, was translated, post-Independence, into English by Marjorie Boulton and Ramswarup Vyas (Fortune Press, 1950) with an honest foreword by Nehru himself. But it was in his absolutely inspired translations of Shakespeare's tragedies, all done well post-1947* that HRB's

* *Macbeth*, 1957, *Hamlet*, 1969, *King Lear*, 1972.

talent took the measure of world literature. His 'ab jeena hai ya marna hai, tai karna hai' (To be or not to be, that is the question) could only come from a prodigal genius. Literary talent is a latency that unfreedom can foster or hinder, with freedom doing the same. If Bachchan could shine under the Raj, he sparkled under the Republic.

Prime Minister Nehru knew, admired, and gave official responsibilities to HRB. This was patronship as distinct from patronage, for Nehru wanted nothing in return.

Ramdhari Singh Dinkar (1908–74), the poet of patriotic fervour but also of syncretic nationalism, was taught to us at school. His 'Himalay' stirred a feeling of angst overpowering pride and then being overcome by hope. Elected three times to the Rajya Sabha, he would come by to see my father, and I watched him, my 'detailed subject' at school, in awe. On one of his visits in March 1956, Dinkar gave to him an autographed copy of his just published monumental work *Sanskriti ke Chaar Adhayay* (Culture, in Four Chapters). Part-history, part-sociology, and also, in great part, a work in literary criticism, the volume carried a foreword in Hindi by Nehru. It said in Nehru's very own sensitive Hindi, 'Whatever India is today, it has been made by the people of India in all their diversity, with all their distinctness....' Dinkar had lit a lamp unto India.

And so, when the Constitution of India's plan to wrap up English as India's official language in 1965 (fifteen years after Independence) came into effect, I felt miserably torn. I loved Hindi, hated its imperial pretensions. And being influenced by Rajaji's strong position on the subject, came soon to be irrevocably opposed to the proposed move. On 26 January 1964, the day the lifespan given to English was to come to an end, I (as permitted 'escort') accompanied Amma to President Radhakrishnan's at Home, the gracious party the president hosts on Republic Day. The veteran Hindi poet Maithilisharan Gupt (1886–1964), then a nominated member of the Rajya Sabha, was there, looking resplendent in his red tilak. The author, among many works, of two mind-wrenching long-form poems I had read and interiorized—'Saket' (1931) with Lakshman's lonely wife Urmila as the protagonist and 'Yashodhara' (1932) on Prince Siddhartha's abandoned wife—was for me a figure to be revered. That he had transmuted himself into his lead characters, both women, in these two works, speaking in their female spirits, made the works technically outstanding, apart from being intrinsically pre-eminent. Yashodhara, wife of Prince Siddharth, on seeing he has left her and their son, Rahula, says to her chambermaid, devastatingly for the future Enlightened One, 'Sakhi ve mujh se kahkar jaate...' (Sakhi, could he not have just told me before leaving me...) This is a line that will not leave my brain ever. *The Light of Asia* (1879) by Edwin Arnold (1832–1904), on the life of the Buddha and his renunciation, is a polished jewel. And Maithilisharan Gupt's 'Yashodhara', a freshly-mined gem.

Something in me impelled me to go up to Guptji, do a pranam, and then, looking at the tilak on his forehead, remind him of his statement he had made not much earlier to the effect that he was waiting for the day when the tilak of Hindi gleams on Bharat's brow. This was contrary to what Nehru said in his foreword to Dinkar. This was what Rajaji was opposing. And then, how distant and disengaged the Hindi world was from, say, the Tamil! 'Senthamizh naadu ennum podhinile' (When I hear the name of Tamil Nadu) of Subramania Bharati (1882–1921) ringing in my ears, I asked Guptji (in Hindi of course) about his 'waiting for the day...' 'Is that a good thing to happen?' He was a little nonplussed by this audacity and curiosity—a Hindi-speaking youth saying something not exactly favourable to the language. He remained silent. I did not stop there. 'Is that not a form of digvijay (land conquest) that is base compared to dharmavijay (soul saturation)?' He remained quiet again, but his silence now acquired an unplumbed, unsounded sonic retort which I imagined as: 'Get lost, you insufferable imp.' In its Hindi form, of course.

For all his sharp opposition to Hindi as the Sole Official Language move, Rajaji would have disapproved of my having confronted the great poet thus. But he could not have prevented what he said from working on his grandson's mind. Rajaji wrote a month later in *Swarajya*: 'English for unity, say I, over and over again. I shall plead for it, as long as my breath lasts, for the love I bear for my country.' Rajaji was not alone in demanding the suspension of the Constitutional directive. The Dravida Munnetra Kazhagam demanded the same, much more truculently. And that is when Prime Minister Lal Bahadur Shastri rose to the stature required of a prime minister of India. He repeated with the authority of a policy decision what Nehru had said earlier as an intention: As far as the south and east are concerned, the switchover to Hindi will not take place until they ask for it. Shastri had given Indian democracy and her federal spirit a shot in the arm.

Now, with English there, India would not become what Rajaji had warned it could be: An archipelago of nations in a non-navigable sea.

But such relief as politics might have got from this became almost irrelevant in the face of the news that on 20 March, a posse of Pakistani soldiers in disguise—ever the trademark of deceit and duplicity—had violated the ceasefire line in Kashmir. War could not be averted, and it began in true form on 5 August and saw high-decibel fighting, casualties and frenzied civil action supporting that of soldiers and airmen. September saw fierce battles. On

6 September, the Indian Army launched an attack in the Lahore sector of Pakistan, taking the Pakistan Army by surprise and advancing to the outskirts of Lahore, all but invading it. Those were pre-television times, but AIR, by its vivid broadcasts, made visual supplementation unnecessary. Heard over the air were reports that went something like: *Indian XI Corps are advancing towards Lahore along three axes—Amritsar-Lahore, Khalra-Burki-Lahore and Khem Karan-Kasur roads, overwhelming the small Pakistani force. Pakistan's 10 and 11 Divisions, deployed in the sector, have begun a series of rather confused delaying actions...But...the Indian infantry, backed by heavy armoured troops, are within striking distance of Lahore city. Some advance Indian units have managed to capture Ichhogil canal.* This was the first time I was hearing the name of that canal and of the airport in Lahore—Sargodha—and of the chilling term 'carpet-bombing'. It was not victory or near victory all the time. Came news: *A Pakistani counterattack has led to the capture of the village Khem Karan. However, a massive Indian counter-attack has managed to repulse the Pakistani forces from this sector of Indian territory.*

There is something about the imminent fall of a city in a battle that raises the war fever's pitch to delirium. There was a thrill that has to be like that at a hunt when the target is circled, and all that remains is to send the final shot. There is a thrill but also another feeling in the hunter's gut that does not like what it is doing, almost in spite of himself. We heard: *Indian advance has now moved on to capture Dograi, a town in the immediate vicinity of Lahore. It is now on the outskirts of Lahore and the Indian Army is ensured that Lahore remains under constant Indian tank fire to prepare for the main assault on Lahore city... India's jawans backed by the Indian Air Force's gnats skittled the invaders.*

That is when a ceasefire, brokered by the United Nations, was announced.

India had defeated Pakistan, without a doubt, and even when it 'left' Lahore, it was doing so as a victor that had let the city 'off'. Estimates of men killed varied, with India and Pakistan giving widely differing claims, but neutral citations gave the Indian battlefield dead as 3,000 and Pakistani, 3,800. Alexei Kosygin (1904–80), the Soviet premier, had on 4 September suggested to both Shastri and Ayub Khan that they meet in Tashkent to negotiate a truce. At that point, the war had remained confined to Kashmir and the Chhamb-Jaurian sector. With the war reaching Lahore and Sialkot, Kosygin reiterated his offer on 18 September. Sir Morris James, then British high commissioner in Pakistan, said, 'the Pakistan Army was at the end of its tether', and the choice before Ayub was an honourable draw or defeat.[1]

Devin T. Hagerty and Herbert Hagerty in the book *South Asia in World*

Politics say: 'The invading Indian forces outfought their Pakistani counterparts and halted their attack on the outskirts of Lahore, Pakistan's second-largest city. By the time the United Nations intervened on September 22, Pakistan had suffered a clear defeat.'[2]

Shastri was now a hero. India's second prime minister was the first prime minister to become both a statesman of peace and a hero in war.

Height suddenly became symbolic. Five feet two inches in height, Shastri towered over the six feet four inches tall Ayub Khan.

My eyes, as always, looked out for what my grandfather was saying. In the 30 October issue of *Swarajya*, he wrote, 'Our military answer to Pakistan's challenge was as right as it was successful. Let us never bend our necks to brute force,' adding, significantly and typically, 'But let us ever be loyal to fundamental moral principles.' He was referring, of course, to Kashmir and the need, as he saw it, for the people of Kashmir being part of the solution to the Kashmir problem. Defence of India Rules were invoked by Chief Minister Bhaktavatsalam against the publisher of *Swarajya*, and to our family's consternation, demands were made for Anna's arrest. Shastri knew better, and we heard that he called Bhaktavatsalam and said to him: 'Bhaktavatsalamji, you know of Bertrand Russell. He expresses his views freely. The British Government does not think of proceeding against him.' The chief minister got the message.

All wars have two sides to them. India knows, as does the knowing section of Pakistan's observing population, that this needless war was started by Pakistan crossing the border in Kashmir. And to that extent, this war was, for India, a 'just war'. But while a war may be 'just', every war kills humans, combatant and non-combatant, with much of that killing being wanton. And around the scenes of violence, much happens that shows man at his best and his worst.

The war had unleashed the most vicious and vile anti-India propaganda on Pakistan Radio, which AIR could not but emulate. Did the filth being spoken reflect the state of our 'real' minds? Did it give utterance to sectarian thoughts and racial prejudices that lie dormant in us, hibernating like some beast before the moment comes to waken to its appetite's satiation? I did not know the answer to this then; I do not know it now, but I suspect, very strongly, that such is indeed the case.

The Indo–Pak war of 1965 had a phenomenally important consequence which none of us, lay people, knew of then. Bakhtiyar Dadabhoy tells us: 'In December 1965, Shastri asked Bhabha to speed up plans for a PNE

(Peaceful Nuclear Explosion).... Bhabha called Sethna* and asked him to get the groups required to get the device ready.'[3] A nuclear explosion is a nuclear explosion. A nuclear test is a nuclear test. There is nothing peaceful or warful about it.

The year 1965 had pushed India and Pakistan into the nuclear age. One might say it had pushed the subcontinent into the nuclear abyss.

Dissent and war can coexist. Much depends, of course, on who is in charge of the War Room and who the dissenter is.

To our relief, Delhi asked Bhaktavatsalam to drop proceedings against *Swarajya* and, to our happiness, Shastri wrote to Rajaji in response to an advance copy of one of his controversial *Swarajya* articles: 'What you have written deserves our earnest consideration.' This was in October 1965, and in December 1965, just before Shastri was to leave for the Kosygin-catalysed Tashkent talks with Ayub Khan, Rajaji wrote to the prime minister: 'I most sincerely tender my best wishes to you in your great enterprise.' And he gave in his letter detailed advice to Shastri on minutiae as well. It was necessary, he said, to keep Kashmir out of the Tashkent agenda if the talks were not to break down and on how to set up two cooperating units in Asia—India and Pakistan—without tariffs or duties or customs barriers. Terrorism was not an issue at the time, but we can be sure that if it was, Rajaji would have been dead hard on combating it, root and branch. He was a Gandhian when it came to matters of conscience, but he was an administrator of the old school when it came to matters of governance.

*Homi Sethna (1923–2010), nuclear scientist and a chemical engineer, later chairman of the Atomic Energy Commission (India) during the time when the first nuclear test, code name Smiling Buddha in Pokhran Test Range in 1974 was conducted.

1966

'AYYO, AYYAYYIYYO!'

Ayub Khan and Shastri were locked in verbal combat for all of six days, from 4 January to 10 January. Both had authority, neither had the self-confidence which comes from total faith in having the backing of their peoples. 'Public opinion' and the worry 'What will they say back home?' hung over their heads as they talked. The urgent issues were the return by India of territories gained, and the return by both of the soldiers held captive. The important issues were the mid-term and long-term relations between the two that could normalize things between the two powers while completely skirting the central problem—Kashmir. Ayub, Sandhurst-trained Punjabi that he was, thought on his polished black-booted feet intuitively. His foreign minister Zulfikar Ali Bhutto, suave and sharp Sindhi, thought in the cloisters of his secretive mind, ratiocinatively. He counselled against conceding much, if anything, to India. Ayub, conditioned by military norms of an army that has been bested in war, wanted to wrench dignity from defeat. Bhutto, with no conditioning except that of his own sense of superiority, wanted to turn a battlefield reverse into a conference table score. Shastri's principal adviser in the talks was not his man-of-no-words foreign minister Swaran Singh so much as his principal secretary L. K. Jha, whose civil service background admitted of balance and poise in negotiation as different from bluster.

I am biased and cannot but see, in larger-than-life terms, Rajaji's 'Tashkent role' emanating as it was from the quiet of his austere book-lined room in a leafy suburb of Madras. But the chiming of Rajaji's meeting-eve advice tendered to Shastri with the text of the Tashkent Declaration[1] is not to be missed by a grandfather-smitten grandson. Nor can I, hooked from childhood on the Edicts of Ashoka, fail to see the concord-seeking emperor's spirit hovering above the text of the discord-abating Declaration. The wording of the clause about 'propaganda' was distinctly Ashokan. Undertaking to 'exert all efforts to create good neighbourly relations between India and Pakistan in accordance with the United Nations Charter', it said the two countries would aim:

To 'settle...disputes through peaceful means' and 'not to have recourse to force'.

To withdraw 'all armed personnel' no later than 25 February 1966, and to move those personnel 'to the positions they held prior to 5 August 1965', with both countries to 'observe the cease-fire terms on the cease-fire line'.

To maintain cross-border relations 'based on the principle of non-interference in the internal affairs of each other.'

To 'discourage any propaganda directed against the other country, and... encourage propaganda which promotes the development of friendly relations between the two countries.'

To return the countries' respective high commissioners to their posts and restore 'the normal functioning of diplomatic missions' while also observing the Vienna Convention on Diplomatic Relations of 1961

To 'consider measures towards the restoration of economic and trade relations, communications, as well as cultural exchanges between India and Pakistan.'

To 'repatriate prisoners of war.'

To 'continue the discussion of questions relating to the problems of refugees and evictions/illegal immigrations,' to 'create conditions which will prevent the exodus of people,' and to 'discuss the return of the property and assets taken over by either side in connexion with the conflict.'

To 'continue meetings both at the highest and at other levels on matters of direct concern to both countries.'

These decisions were described as 'pledges'. Shastri, before retiring for the day, dictated some letters. One of these was to Rajaji. 'I am sure,' he wrote to Rajaji, 'you agree with what we have done in Tashkent, and it would get your full support.' He kept the signing of the letter to the next morning. It is said that speaking to his family over the phone that night, Shastri was given an earful by some relatives for having shown 'weakness' and told that the Declaration was already being criticized in India. The letter was to remain unsigned. Jha, on returning to India, sent the letter printed on the prime minister's letterhead without its author's signature.

Late that night of 11/12 January 1966, a telephone from the newsroom of the *Hindustan Times* woke me to give the news that a heart attack had ended Shastri's life in the Tashkent dacha he was put up in. 'Ayyo!' is an untranslatable Tamil exclamation. It contains, in its normal use, myriad emotions that include shock, grief, and pain, which approximate 'alas' and 'oh no'. At a higher mental octave, Ayyo has a cousin in the much more loaded Ayyayyiyyo. I did not say Ayyo to my caller but said it to myself as I put the receiver down. My mother said we should go to the prime minister's house. She did not know the big bindi-wearing, ever-smiling Lalitadevi Shastri all that well, but she knew bereavement and deprivation. Our driver was roused, and he drove us to the shocked home—1 York Place—in the pre-dawn dark. Very few people had reached the house at that time. I will never forget the widow's bewildered and disbelieving wail that wafted across the house's hushed rooms. It was not right nor easy to stay longer than a few moments, and we drove back home in silence and in no small fear of our nation's future, losing Nehru's successor so soon after he had given us a sense of being under a benevolent and yet strong leader's protective care.

Stunned, like everyone else, Rajaji said the tragic news was 'too horrible for words' but added 'The nation will overcome this catastrophe...The soul of the departed Prime Minister has set a sacred seal on the pledges given at Tashkent.'

The Declaration, pioneering in its appearance and iconic in its content, had been overshadowed by Death. We had just witnessed a dawn with the golden orb at its most tender effulgence suddenly eclipsed by the earth's mortal orbiting.

I just had to see what was happening first-hand, and I went, later in the day, to the airport where an Indian Air Force plane was to bring home the body of the deceased prime minister instead of a beaming peacemaker. Everyone was talking in hushed whispers, and there was a ghostly uncertainty about the whole atmosphere. And more, of a kind of cowering insecurity until a plane from Madras landed and from it emerged Congress president Kamaraj. He came as a shaft of peninsular granite to replace the noodle that our nation's spine had become in those few hours.

The other scene I recall as sharply as a photograph in today's newspapers is of the late prime minister's inconsolable son Harikrishna, spreadeagled on the backseat of a limousine, his feet quivering on the front seat's shoulder, shrieking in disbelief, as his vehicle moved along with the convoy carrying his father's body. Shastri was only sixty-one. He should have had at least a decade as prime minister. But Fate's calendar only Fate understands.

Kamaraj received, as when Nehru had died, great strength from President Radhakrishnan. Constitutionally impeccable but politically savvy steps from the head of state enabled a smooth transition. Indira Gandhi, the forty-nine-year-old young minister in Shastri's cabinet who Kamaraj saw enjoyed the support of the majority of his party's MPs, was elected leader. With my parochial preferences and family ties, I wanted to see the seventy-year-old Morarji Desai installed as prime minister. He had asked, to Rajaji's applause, for a ballot this time and was given it. Desai was defeated by Indira in a clean contest. I was not a little tickled by a front-page cartoon by the gifted Rajinder Puri in the *Hindustan Times* of 20 January that showed Morarji with 32 per cent of the MP votes standing taller than all the others—five shivering party satraps standing one on top of the other, each shorter than Morarji, with the winner—Indira—standing at the very top, but shorter by herself than the loser—Morarji. Uncramped by language, uncorseted by formalities, cartoonists can say so much more and much more effectively than columnists. Desai offered Indira his support 'consistent with my self-respect', drawing from Kamaraj the retort, 'Are others not supposed to have self-respect?'

One person who was professionally shaken by Shastri's death was the chairman of the Atomic Energy Commission. Bhabha had established a sound working equation with Shastri and, as we have seen earlier, was looking forward to progressing towards a nuclear capability via a PNE that did not announce weaponization as a goal but no longer denounced it either. Bhabha's biographer says[2] Shastri had, in fact, invited Bhabha to join his cabinet as a minister but he had declined, 'preferring a scientific over a political post'. Writing to Lalitadevi on 23 January, Bhabha said, 'If there is anything that I can do to be of help to you in any way, may I request you to call on me without hesitation, as I shall deem it a privilege to do what I can in memory of Shastriji.' Few in the citadels of power bother about the bereaved family of a dead chief. But then that was Bhabha.

I might not have alluded to Bhabha here were it not for a flare in the solar eclipse. On the day Indira Gandhi was being sworn in, Bhabha was killed in an air crash. He was flying from Bombay to Vienna to attend a meeting of the International Atomic Energy Agency, having advanced his departure by a day from an earlier booking, perhaps, it was rumoured, at the instance of the love of his life, Pipsy Phiroza Wadia. The Boeing 707 *Kanchenjungha* crashed into a glacier on the southern face of Mont Blanc, killing all 117 aboard. This was the very site where, in 1950, the *Malabar Princess* had crashed. A misunderstanding between Geneva Airport and the pilot about the aircraft's position near the mountain was given as the official reason for the crash. But when a prime minister dies in a distant dacha within hours of signing a controversial agreement and his nuclear adviser is killed within days of that prime minister's death in an air crash, conspiracy theories cannot but take flight. Nor can ever return to a quiet hangar.

The next day's *Hindustan Times* had the Bhabha death in the crash as the first story. Indira Gandhi, being sworn in, took second place. That was the *Hindustan Times*' editor, S. Mulgaokar, vintage Mulgaokar.

The Northeast of India zoomed into attention that March. I must say with a sense of shame that I had not, until then, ever registered in my mind the presence on the Indian map of something called the Mizo tracts of Assam. I had heard of and knew of the Khasis, the Lepchas, and the Nagas, but not the Mizos or their Mizo National Front. That I was not alone in my ignorance makes no difference. In fact, it makes my condition the more shameful. Reports of an uprising by the Mizos and their Operation Jericho, which, demanding independence from India, captured several installations, including the government treasury in Aizawl, came in early in March, and Home Minister Nanda provided details to an agitated Lok Sabha. In what the *Hindustan Times* on 3 March described as 'one of the liveliest debates in recent years', opposition MPs took the government to task for failing to understand Mizo aspirations in good time and allowing discontent to drift into the new insurgency.

But worse was to come. In an action that was to be part of a pattern of her strong assertiveness as a protector of India's territorial integrity and sovereignty, on 5 March 1966, Indira Gandhi had four fighter jets drop bombs on Aizawl. This was the first time the Government of India bombed its own territory. The casualties were few, thirteen, but the scar went deep. It alienated the Mizos implacably. The strafing lasted until 13 March, spreading panic among the Mizos, who fled from their homes into the jungles of Myanmar and what was then East Pakistan. A greater recipe for the alienation of border people and for our troubles becoming opportunities in neighbouring countries could not have been imagined.

Verrier Elwin (1902–64), the British-born anthropologist, ethnologist, and tribal activist, friend of Gandhi and Nehru, who had begun his career in India as a Christian missionary and was, after Independence, appointed by Nehru as his adviser on tribal affairs had died in 1964, a few weeks before Nehru. I cannot help feeling had Elwin been around in 1967, he would have helped solve the Mizo issue in time and with sensitivity. He would certainly have cried 'Foul!' at the bombings.

Was Indira Gandhi wanting to show that unlike her father, but like her predecessor, she was a 'fighter', a 'doer'? And that, being a woman, she was no less of a prime minister? Be that as it may, the Mizos were to be a disaffected people until much later—1986, in fact—when her son and successor Rajiv Gandhi initiated talks and concluded an accord with the Mizos' lawyer-governor of Mizoram (by then a separate state) Swaraj Kaushal (b. 1952) playing a determining role in the proceedings.

If I learnt of the Mizos for the first time in 1966, there occurred another, happy, first from an altogether different page of our national life, an altogether different set from the stage of life. No twenty-one-year-old youth can be impervious to female beauty, but when twenty-three- year-old medical student from Bombay, Reita Faria (b. 1943), in November that year, beat fifty-one competing delegates from other countries for the Miss World title, it was national pride plus a post-teen libido that worked its magic inside me. She was, of course, all over the news space as the first Indian and first Asian to win that prize. The Goan beauty captured hearts across the board, and her photographs in swimwear, stunningly coy and yet totally decorous, and then wearing the crown put politics in the shade. There was a cleanliness to her manner, a very Indian and very unusual grace to her deportment that made her totally unique, a successor to the apsaras in the famed Ajanta frescoes.

Our high commissioner in London, Jivraj Mehta (1887–1978), a very traditional Gujarati and long-time associate of Gandhi and his wife Hansaben Mehta (1897–1995), took a little time to decide on whether or not to associate themselves with the beauty but then, after some days of prevarication, when there were comments heard on puritanism against beauty, they were persuaded, we were told, by a nudge from none other than Indira Gandhi herself, to send the winner a bouquet. The high commissioner then, to his great credit, decided to go and greet the now famous young woman from Bombay. A lovely photograph shows her raising a toast to one raised by him, seated in a two-seater's closeness. The glasses hold something dark. Was it draught Guinness? Doubtful. Ah, well.

Mulgaokar started in the December of this year a modest new weekly called *Weekend Review*, as a *Hindustan Times* offering to its readers. It was to be not 'light' but not 'heavy'. It was to be read by those with over-the-horizon sights between a Saturday breakfast and a Saturday sundowner. And he recruited for the team Sarwar Lateef, a brilliant young economist whose writing style was elegant and whose views on the nation's and world's political fates were utterly classy. As also two of the most articulate journalists—also very young—who would become big names in the coming years, Prem Shankar Jha and Suman Dubey.

With my MA exams over, I was, towards the end of 1966, in what may be called a gap between study and some work. How should I utilize it? Should I ask Mulgaokar for a perch in his new magazine?

Years ago, my father had described his junior colleague to me in Gujarati using one English word: 'Mulgaokar, with his long and drooping nose, looks like Charles de Gaulle, the great Frenchman. He is a Bohemian. And has lived many years in the West with no one as his boss. He is a brilliant journalist. Totally independent. He is the best writer in my team.' The English word was, of course, 'Bohemian'. I remember asking Appa what 'Bohemian' meant, and his saying it means 'One who believes in total freedom to live as he likes and does not care about what others might say.' That did not strike me as a complimentary expression. But I could see that Appa cared for 'his' Bohemian deeply.

I had told Amma of my intention of meeting Mulgaokar, and she was cautiously encouraging. The intention was to ask Mulgaokar if I could work during my 'free' months in *Weekend Review*. I was thinking of a volunteer's position, needless to say. With my heart in my mouth, I went down from our second-storey flat to the first floor, where Mulgaokar sat in his small but nicely air-conditioned room. My father did not have that piece of summer necessity in his room, but in many ways, Mulgaokar's was smaller and less equipped than my father's. Gone was the revolving book shelf with a massive swivel globe on top of it, gone too, the large table with its many accoutrements. Mulgaokar was poring over something when, after getting via his PA a 'come in', I entered the lion's lair. I had barely mentioned what I had in mind when he said, 'Join coming Monday. We will figure out your job description, but I will pay you five hundred rupees a month. Sorry, it cannot be more.' I had got my first job in my father's own newspaper office and, for what was to me, a princely salary. I ran upstairs and told Amma in excitement that I had got not just a 'gap' apprenticeship but a job.

I could not have hoped for a tougher and more defining first boss than S. Mulgaokar. And could not have been luckier in that my first 'job application' had got accepted without any fuss. Did my being the son of his late boss have anything to do with this? Of course, yes. Everything. I was not fooling myself. But Devadas Gandhi had not been mentioned even once. Not in a down memory lane thing nor up any other pathway either. I was the youngest and only callow recruit and enjoyed working with Mulgaokar's team under Sarwar's immediate oversight. The first issue appeared on 10 December, and was on a deadly drought that had hit eastern Uttar Pradesh and Bihar.

Suman, with another friend from St. Stephen's College who would make a great name for himself as a catalyser of volunteerism and decentralized programmes for rural development, Bunker Roy, went to report on the famine. Their reportage and photographs from the sites scalded with the fire of truth. 'The sharded earth' ... 'drought deepening into famine'...were phrases used by Suman in his dispatches that *Weekend Review* carried. And behind the reports lay accounts of astonishing work done by Jayaprakash Narayan to raise funds and alleviate distress in the parched zones.

My education in journalism was not going to be all pleasant. One day, a piece I had edited was being checked by Mulgaokar. He summoned me to the lair. I went in expecting a scowl. What I got was a roar.

'Did you change this word?

'Er...yes...'

'Why?'

'It just seemed better the way I...'

'NEVER make any stylistic changes in another's writing. Factual corrections are a different matter. But stylistic changes, NO.' My deeply cherished colleague may have forgotten the incident, but I recall Sarwar being present when the roar broke over me. But such was my colleague's tehzeeb that in total silence, he seemed to say to me, 'I have noticed and heard nothing, Gopu.'

Rajaji visited Delhi around this time, and I was delighted when he said 'Very well' to my suggestion that he meet Sarwar and his scholarly wife, Shahida. In an engaging conversation with them, he asked Shahida, not Sarwar, if their names were of Arabic or Persian origin and to explain their meanings. He was particularly taken up by the etymology of 'Sarwar' and asked Shahida in some detail about the ramifications of 'chief', which, she told him the word meant. Then, turning to Sarwar, he said, 'Do please advise Gopu to take the civil services examination, and not think of a career in journalism. He must see something of life and experience its challenges before writing about them.' Sarwar saw the old man's point.

Rajaji had told me the same, in no uncertain terms, suggesting as a possible alternative to the IAS, a career in Law where, too, he thought I would get to 'see life' and (as he thought) I would do well, especially if I was to set up practice in Madras. So, I was placed firmly on the 'IAS aspirant' track.

1967
GOODNESS TO GOODNESS

1967 was a great year for Indian democracy, for Indian federalism, for India.

This was the year India went through its fourth general elections. The people of India went to the polls to elect 520 of the 523 members of the 4th Lok Sabha, their House of Commons. They were to elect all the state assemblies as well. These were the first elections to be held without Nehru around to lead the Congress to another assured victory. It was also an election held without Shastri's war-winning presence. Above all, it was an election that was going to test the new prime minister Indira Gandhi's standing in the country. Gungi gudia (dumb doll), Rammanohar Lohia, the socialist petrel and bete noire of the Nehru-Gandhis had famously called her, in high disdain and low taste. Was she that or the secretive woman whose thoughts were in a cave of frozen ice?

The general elections were held in the pleasant days between 17 and 21 February 1967 when the winter was in retreat and spring in the air. One person who exuded confidence was Rajaji. He was eighty-eight and full of zeal, his Swatantra Party was eight years old, and both were brimming with energy as they faced their second general election challenge. Madras State was, for Rajaji, the most crucial theatre in the election because the Bhaktavatsalam-led Congress ministry was palpably passe. The DMK, led by the charismatic and scholarly C. N. Annadurai, had the crown of victory hovering above its name. All it needed was Rajaji's aged hands to grasp and place it firmly on its eager and very ready head.

Nationally, though Shastri's war had given us a sense of victory, the Tashkent Agreement was not exactly being hailed and Indira, after initially pledging her full backing to it, had by the time the elections were happening, lowered that agreement in her priorities. And, she had another tougher legacy of the war to handle: the strain of the war on the economy. The 1961–66 Five-Year Plan target of 6 per cent annual growth had been belied by the actual growth rate of 2 per cent.

Pasted to the radio, I prayed for an opposition win throughout the country. Why? For no reasons of ideology or even politics or economics. Only for the genetic fact that my grandfather was a leading figure in the opposition and my other hero, Jayaprakash, was no fan of Indira's. The Congress suffered setbacks in its Lok Sabha tallies in seven states, which included Madras, where it could win only 3 out of 39 seats, and the DMK won 25; Gujarat, where it won 11 out of 24 seats while Swatantra Party won 12 seats; Orissa, where the Congress could get only 6 out of 20 seats and Swatantra Party, 8 seats. In Rajasthan, Congress won 10 out of 20, and the Swatantra Party won 8 seats. In West Bengal, Congress won 14 out of 40, and in Kerala, only 1 out of 19. In Delhi, Congress won 1 out of 7, while the remaining 6 were won by Bharatiya Jana Sangh.[1]

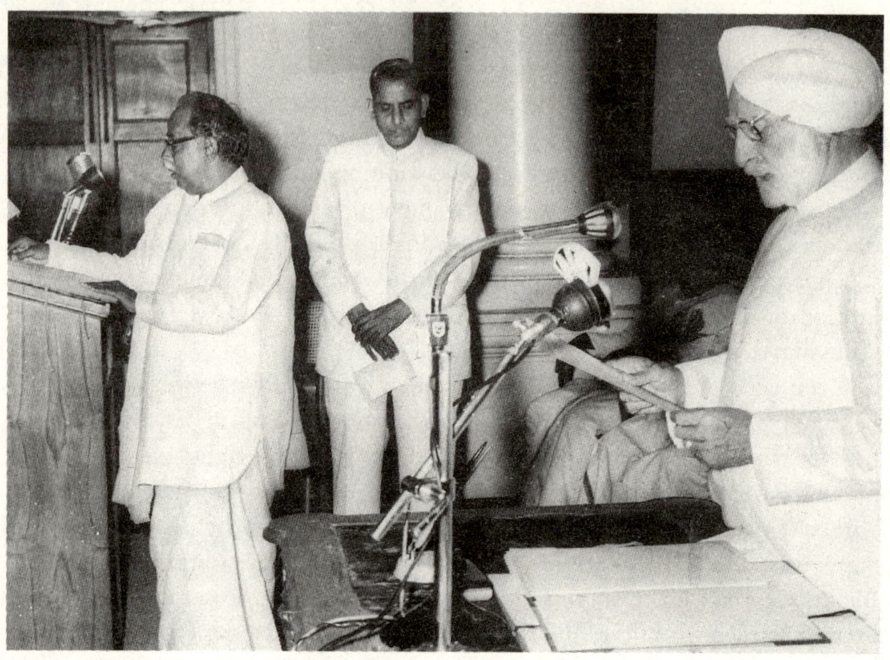

C. N. Annadurai being sworn in as the chief minister of Tamil Nadu by the state governor, Sardar Ujjal Singh at Rajaji Hall in Madras on 6 March 1967. Photo: S. Kothandaraman/ *The Hindu*.

Thirty-four-year-old Manohar Lal Sondhi (1933–2003), a former member of the IFS, very intellectual and very articulate, stood as the Jana Sangh candidate in New Delhi. I was all for him. Sheer lethargy had prevented me from getting enrolled as a voter, else I would have voted for him. But I persuaded Amma to do so, and also as many voters among friends and fraternity. Sondhi's credentials apart, Rajaji had extended his support to the Jana Sangh candidates and even shared a platform with leaders of that party in New Delhi—something I then found both natural and smart. The implications of that curious link between a liberal party and one with the views of the Jana Sangh, I was too myopic at that time, to think about. Election-time alliances are the work of panic and excitement—both of which are short-term emotions. Logic and reason are generally for the long-term. Even Rajaji, wiser than most, sharper and more principled than anyone I knew in politics, had opted in 1967 to make alliances for the short-term. Electoral adrenalins can inebriate sworn teetotallers.

The Jana Sangh's symbol was a lamp, the deepak, and I hearkened to that party's optimistic jingle 'Jeet gaya bhai, jeet gaya, deepakwala jeet gaya', meaning 'He has won, he has won, the man of the lamp has won'. The gender-specific words and thoughts behind the words did not sound wrong to me at that time. But I was not, I am sure, alone. I was elated when Sondhi won by a margin of 24,860 votes (16.3 per cent), the largest secured by anyone in Delhi. Intellectuals comprising the elite had voted for him, no less than the non-elite. Sondhi's wife, the scholar Madhuri, was the daughter of a freedom-struggle stalwart from South India, Pandit K. Santanam (1885–1949), long-settled in Lahore. That, and Sondhi's educational career in Oxford and Prague, made him totally cosmopolitan. I felt privileged when, at a semi-public meeting, I was able to go up to his dhoti-clad frame and offer my congratulations. He was most polite and completely unpatronizing, asking me about my studies, plans. He would not have minded, I thought, my becoming a fan. Were it not for my family's deep-dyed resistance to jingoistic nationalism, its revulsion from communal politics, and the permanent scar cut into its psyche by Godse's three bullets, plus, I must add, the training in liberalism received by me at school and college, I might well have allowed my distaste for the Congress's one-party ethos now fast becoming a one-family one, to make a foolish political jump.

That the incumbent Indian National Congress would retain power in Delhi was never in doubt. The question was whether it would come back to the national office wearing band-aids here and there or with serious orthopaedic plasters. It came back with a significantly reduced majority—280 out of 520, down by almost 100—with Congress president Kamaraj himself being defeated in his pocket borough by an unknown student leader. It was a shaken Indira Gandhi who was re-sworn in as the prime minister on 13 March. Swatantra doubled its strength in the Lok Sabha by 100; the party she led had also been ousted from power in nine states while losing governance in Uttar Pradesh one month after the elections. Rajaji termed the results 'a burst of health'. One-party rule had not ended in India, but its sway had been seriously questioned by 1967. The fourth general election in India raised democracy to the height that is its due. The first three had paid its debts due to the party of freedom. Now, a debt was being paid to freedom's parties.

The winter of 1967 was a period of transition for us. Amma vacated the flat in New Delhi, which had been home to the family since the mid-1930s. We had lived in it for ten years after my father's death—an arrangement which G. D. Birla, the newspaper's proprietor, had, with great generosity and affection, made out of sheer goodwill for the friend and editor he had lost. During those ten years, I finished school and college and took my IAS examination in that sequence.

My sister Taru was in Rome with her husband and children in the fascinating and enchanting world that had opened up for that family after my brother-in-law's appointment in the Food and Agriculture Organisation. My eldest brother Rajmohan was by then Moral Re-Armament's leading and (as I thought and still believe) the only credible voice. My second brother, Ramu, and his wife, Indu, were in Britain with their daughter, Leela, the future academic and poet of renown.

Completing his five years in office, President Radhakrishnan was to leave Delhi that summer for his hometown—Madras. Radhakrishnan, who had suffered a mild stroke, was seeing visitors in his bedroom, stretched out cosily on a large bed surrounded by books, some open, some half-open, some closed, face up, some face down. Amma went to make a farewell and safe-return-home call on him, and I went too. Just as we were shown in, a lady whom we knew was coming out. Her call had just preceded ours. Welcoming us with a broad smile, Radhakrishnan asked us to be seated and said in Tamil, 'That lady...you know her...poor thing...her husband lost his seat in Delhi... he has sent her to me with a request.... He should be appointed to a governorship! He...and a governor!' Radhakrishnan's voice crackled in laughter.

The sage asked me what I was doing and seemed vaguely bored when I told him I was going to try my luck with the civil services exam that autumn. We took no more than ten minutes of his time.

Having demitted office as president, he settled into his own gracious home near the Marina, to more of his books and to the plumes of Carnatic music. Among those welcoming him back was Rajaji. One might have expected Rajaji to say something in praise of Radhakrishnan through apt quotations from the Ramayana or the Mahabharata or the *Tirukkural*. But no, he said, praise of the man was unnecessary. And the unpredictable in him chose to say so in his 'Dear Reader' column in the journal *Swarajya*, through Shakespeare's *King John*, Act 4, Scene 2:

> To gild refined gold, to paint the lily
> To throw a perfume on the violet
> To smooth the ice, or add another hue

Unto the rainbow, or with taper-light
To seek the beauteous eye of heaven to garnish,
Is wasteful and ridiculous excess.

I was in Madras by that time, and Anna asked me to take that issue of *Swarajya* to the Radhakrishnan home and read the lines out to the great man. But he asked me to first rehearse the passage. 'To gild refined gold...' I went, pronouncing 'refined' as it is normally pronounced. 'Not so...' he corrected me. 'In poetic declamation pronunciation changes...Say "refined" not as in 'find' but as in 'fed'...say refin*ed*.' Perfected thus, two or three times, the poetic message was relayed to its addressee.

Radhakrishnan's successor, the estimable Zakir Husain (1887–1969), was also an old friend of Rajaji's. But Rajaji and his party opposed Vice President Zakir Husain's election on the ground that the ruling party's candidate should not get elected unopposed, not in a vibrant democracy. The chief justice of the day, Koka Subba Rao (1902–76), surprised all by agreeing to be the opposition's choice for the office and, given the electoral college's numbers, a doomed one from the start. But once again, the point was made that the ruling party should not take the country for granted. The question if a sitting chief justice should resign his office and become a partisan in the election of the president or not was moot, but the opposition was making a statement by fielding a judge as a candidate. Justice Subba Rao and his brother judges had ruled in the 1967 *Golaknath v. State of Punjab* case, that parliament could not curtail any of the Fundamental Rights in the Constitution.

A philosopher had retired, and a teacher had succeeded him after a contest against a distinguished judge. There was something noble about it all. There was no rancour, no pettiness. Above all, no hypocrisy, no theatrics. Goodness had yielded to goodness.

As with so many matters of moment, I just did not note the significance at the start this year of a set of events that have become part of the collective consciousness of independent India. A peasant uprising in the sub-Himalayan town of Naxalbari in West Bengal by a group that would be called Marxist/Maoist and its action started a rebellion among the impoverished peasants, fighting both the government security forces and private paramilitary groups funded by wealthy landowners. Most fighting by men and women who were clearly guerilla spread to the states of Andhra Pradesh, Maharashtra, Orissa, and Madhya Pradesh. Naxalism was not seen then as what it was to be seen and fought later—a war within the country for rights that were not to be opposed, for they had justice on their side, but a war being unleashed by means that were a terror and a horror. A nightmare.

The IAS exams were held in October and November. I studied hard enough for them but not overly so, having been advised that one needed to work no more for them than for an MA exam. I chose my optional subjects cautiously, English Literature accounting for two of them. My peerless teacher in the English Literature (Honours) class and mentor, Professor M. M. Bhalla (1914–68), called by us Bhalla sahib, told me, 'Gopal, you must forget your classes in college. For this exam, you need to master the answers to questions that have been posed in the exams over the last ten years. Bring those old question papers to me, and I will give you an intensive coaching from the strictly exam point of view.' I did precisely that over several sessions and, sure enough, found his advice to have been totally right.

1968
WHOSE SERVICE?

No less tough and in a very direct and personal way, much more daunting than the 'written' is the viva voce to which those who have 'cleared' the written test are called. Mine was held in March. I went to Delhi towards the end of February to be there in time for it. Amma came with me, giving me moral support, and having been invited by Indira Gandhi to the reception at Hyderabad House celebrating Rajiv's wedding with Sonia, to attend that as well. Security was not then what it now is, and on my 'escort' ticket, I went with her. It was a very tasteful affair, and despite the large number attending, it had no signs of the chaos and confusion that generally accompany wedding receptions. A long and slow-moving queue took us to the couple and to Mrs Gandhi standing beside them. There was no time to say anything beyond a word or two in felicitation, and we moved on to join the invitees. The conversation was muted, somehow, and rather self-conscious. I could be wrong, but I thought the bridegroom looked brave in his exhaustion with the ceremony and the bride the same with the added touch of a bewildered anxiety.

My viva voce, a few days later, wrung me dry. Just before it, Anna wrote to me: 'The "*yoga*" of interviews is to be straight, free and easy, not caring for results and carrying on as in private conversation.' And he added, 'Offer a prayer to *Bhagawan* before going to the interview.' I was neither free nor easy and cared for nothing but the results as I went in. The interview, which lasted only fifteen minutes—not a good sign—was anything but a private conversation. A very stern-looking tribal from the Jaintia hills of Assam, Mrs Bonily Khongmen (1913–2007), heading the panel, faced me. I was immediately struck by her presence—a confident, no-nonsense kind of overarching presence. She asked me to point out Kohima on the India map that hung on a wall behind me. Luckily, I got that right. One of the men, noting that I had read English Literature, asked me to describe Babbitry. Bab what? I had heard of no such thing. My questioner looked away in contempt. Then, I was asked to say something about the humanistic movement in literature. I was not just at sea but twenty thousand leagues under it. Some softer questions followed, and I managed to just about save my 'nose' as they would say in Gujarati. I wrote a detailed report of the interview to Anna, who, in his reply, described Babbitry and educated me about the novels of Sinclair Lewis, in one of which Babbit is a character delineating middle-class ambitions of success amounting to a vulgarity. 'However,' he added, 'it is all finished, and we need not further worry about it.' Going by my 'report', he pronounced my performance 'moderate' and said, '...we should deem it lucky if you come out within the number to be recruited. I should also not be surprised if you come off very well. It also depends on the performance of others.'

Separating myself from the experience, I could not but marvel at the sophistication of the Union Public Service Commission and the procedures for selecting future officers, diplomats, and personnel for our police and other services.

As it turned out, I got very 'moderate' marks in the interview—50 per cent. But my marks in the written tests, especially the English Literature ones, lifted my average performance up. On 22 April 1968, which happened to be my birthday, the results carried in the morning newspapers showed I had made it, with, to my delight, a couple of good friends from my college. Amma was overjoyed and hugged me with the warmth of all motherhood and single-parenting fluxing in it. I was thanking Bhalla sahib in my mind when the phone rang. It was, of course, Anna. He had seen the result in that morning's issue of *The Hindu*. 'Gopu, congratulations....'

The year I spent at the National Academy of Administration in Mussoorie was one of the most formative in my life. Dislike of the utterly meaningless horse-riding instructions and gratefulness for the superbly designed physical training along the drills perfected by the Canadian Air Force were early responses. But the chance to meet and get to know fellow probationers from across the country was of huge value. Aruna Jayaram, now known all over the world as Aruna Roy (b. 1946), has to have been the greatest of my peers at the academy. Her deep commitment to the amelioration of human distress and the advancement of human justice through mass mobilization was not, to me at least, evident then. But in her gently, strong voice, and carefully chosen few words during conversation, I could see the makings of a woman of determination. That Aruna would, with her husband Bunker Roy, become the driving force for strengthening peasants and workers in Rajasthan and making them as self-reliant as possible and, in what I regard as her greatest contribution, catalyse the Right to Information Act, I did not then foresee. I salute her guts, her stamina, and her patience, which have grown after she quit the IAS but which I believe have something to do with her early exposure to some of the ideals that inspired the best in the services.

Wajahat Habibullah, who became the first chief information commissioner in India under the RTI Act, was another star of our batch at the academy, mesmerizing all who saw him on horseback in the paddocks, as well as those who heard him sing Hindi film songs of which 'Chaudhvin ka Chand' was

Couple extraordinary—Aruna and Bunker Roy in Tilonia, Rajasthan 1983. Photo credit: Sunil Gupta.

an absolute hit. But we could tell even then that here was a probationer who would make the service proud, which he did in the way he served the cause of harmony and trust in his state of Jammu and Kashmir at great risk to his personal safety and later in the Lakshadweep Islands—a total landscape contrast to Kashmir but to which he took with effortless ease. Our island states have not entered our national consciousness, and their people have remained on the margins of our self-perception. We think of them exactly as the British and other imperialists did—areas meant for our capital formation, our tourist pleasures, our cartographic egos.

I must mention just one other contemporary. In the first week itself of joining up, a slim, fit young man with very prominent whiskers came up to me and, extending his hands, said just one word—his name, 'Muthanna'. Giving mine in reciprocation and flaunting my so-assumed familiarity with that kind of name, I added, '...Coorgi, right?' 'Coorgi?' He replied. 'No, not Coorgi...The word is 'Coorg...I am Coorg; my people are Coorgs; we belong to Coorg...' What could I say? I had been taught a lesson in culture, etiquette, and much more. Muthu and I were to become close friends despite completely contrasting personalities. He was from the army, a proud ex-captain of the Gurkha Regiment, tough as nails, gentle as a dove, a stickler for good clothing and fine eating, and, I must add, a charming friend of the brimming glass. Muthu had a brilliant career ahead in the Karnataka cadre of the IAS, but the hand of Fate, stingy with humans of quality in our midst, snatched him away when he was at the crest of his career.

My most cherished mentor at the academy was T. N. Chaturvedi (1929–2020), our deputy director. The future Comptroller and Auditor General of India and arguably the best regarded governor of Karnataka ever, he taught me everything that I or any probationer could learn about what an earlier generation of civil servants called OLQ—Officer Like Qualities. Mohanlal Odhavji, my friend from college whom we have met earlier, happened to just drop in on me at the academy one evening. We talked and talked. It became late, and by the time he left, it was well past regulation hours. The next morning, I thought I would 'just mention' this to TNC sir. 'You see, Gopal, it is not about the rightness or wrongness of this particular matter... Today, your friend overstays. Tomorrow, other guests may feel they can do the same....' I looked down at the ground, ashamed. 'No, no.... Only remember that a public servant has to always think of what his action does and means to others....'

The Kilvenmani massacre in the village of that name in the Nagapattinam division of Tanjore district, Madras state, on 25 December 1968 should have been a major subject for discussion at the academy but was not—a reflection on the academy's curricular reflexes. The burning to death of a group of around forty-four people, the families of striking Dalit village labourers by a gang, allegedly led by their landlords, was to become world news. Noticed at once by left-wing political campaigns of the time, the incident helped to initiate large-scale changes in the local rural economy, engendering a massive redistribution of land in the region.

According to eyewitness accounts, on 25 December 1968, at around 10 p.m., the landlords and their 200 henchmen came in lorries and surrounded the hutments, cutting off all routes of escape. The attackers shot at the labourers, mortally wounding two of them. Labourers and their families could only throw stones to protect themselves or flee from the spot. Many of the women and children, and some old men, took refuge in a hut that was 8 ft x 9 ft. But the attackers surrounded it and set fire to it, burning them to death. The fire was systematically stoked with hay and dry wood. Two children thrown out from the burning hut in the hope that they would survive were thrown back into the flames by the arsonists.[1]

Was this gruesome incident the result of farm-inequality created by the success of the Green Revolution? Or just yet another example of age-old caste oppression?

It was with Kilvenmani on my mind that I reached Tanjore in 1969 to take up my training stint in the state to which I had been allotted—Madras, now renamed Tamil Nadu, by a decision of the state's first non-Congress chief minister, C. N. Annadurai.

1969
TO BRAHM OR NOT TO BRAHM

Tamil Nadu was my first preference for allotment, Gujarat second, and Karnataka third. Probationer preferences were taken into account at that time by a system by which those who had ranked above a certain grade in the examination would get their first preference. I must have been in the right bracket for my preference to be honoured, but it so happened that, anxious for me to be by my mother's side, Anna sent word to the then deputy prime minister Morarji Desai about it. I was deeply embarrassed when I learnt from T. Sadasivam about this, but there was little I could do. Much later, I was told by the then union home secretary L. P. Singh that Morarji passed on Anna's message to the home minister Y. B. Chavan (who dealt with service matters), saying though Rajaji wanted me in Tamil Nadu, he (Morarji) felt I should go to Gujarat, as there were very few Gujaratis in the IAS. The home secretary apparently told the home minister that my rank justified my preferences to be honoured and that I should be allotted to Tamil Nadu, adding (as he told me) that as 'the grandfather of the grandson of the century', Rajaji's request should be honoured. So, Tamil Nadu it was.

My sense of having got what I wanted and that being my own home state seemed to me crass beyond words when I read[1] the following about someone I have long idealized. Sir B. N. Rau: Rau's career began in a most unusual way, and his constitutional outlook was immediately visible when he received his posting in his home province, in Madras. Quite strikingly, he refused to serve in Madras. As he explained to the civil services commissioner, 'Dear Sir, In regard to the province to which I have been assigned I beg to inform you that I have friends or relatives in almost every part of the Madras Presidency and also that my father possesses lands in the same province. It has been pointed out to me that in these circumstances it might be very difficult for me to perform my duties unhampered. I shall therefore be very thankful for a reconsideration of my case; and should it be possible, I request that I may be assigned to Burma.'

Following this extraordinary request, Rau was transferred to Bengal.

T. V. Antony (1934–2020) was the collector of Tanjore or Thanjavur as the district was now called. Son of the distinguished T. A. Varghese, ICS, who had been chief secretary of Madras, Antony would become chief secretary of Tamil Nadu himself. But at this point, he was the hugely active and successful harbinger of the bounties of the Green Revolution to the state's rice-rich district of fertile lands irrigated by the Cauvery and its tributaries. Antony was Malayalam-speaking but had a good grasp over Tamil and an even better grasp over the Tamil peasant's mindset.

Antony told me on my first call on him that after taking over in the collectorate, I should meet the 'HS' to learn all there is to be learnt about the working of that office. Too nervous to ask him what 'HS' meant, I later asked Appavoo, the kindly clerk who had been assigned to me—a genius of his own type—what those initials meant. 'Huzur Sheristadar,' he said, pronouncing the two words of Persian ancestry with as much respect as their aural scope permitted, and went on to explain that the HS was generally the prop and pillar of the collectorate. On my asking what the HS's name was, he said, again with respect bordering on awe: 'Parsvanathan.'

'Pars...?'

'Aaamaanga sir, Parsvanathan... Jaina'.

'Jaina? From up north, settled here?'

'Illinga sir, native. Native Tamil Jaina. Tanjore Jaina.'

Aamanga and illinga are the respectful Tamil words for yes and no, respectively.

The handsome 1896-built Thanjavur Collectorate (now a museum) had the collector's chambers on its first floor. Entering the HS's chambers located for petitioners' convenience, on the ground floor, I was in the second or third biggest room in the building. This only befitted the HS's station and rank. His masterly introduction to the Collectorate over, he paused to answer questions. I had almost none for the HS but did, for Parsvanathan sir. Answering my questions about Tamil Jainas, he said with becoming modesty that he was not a scholar of the subject but could say that they numbered a few thousand thinly spread all over the state and that Thanjavur district itself had a small but old Jaina population in the countryside as also 'many Jaina shrines'. I noted his using the word 'shrines' in preference to 'temples'.

I came away from that first meeting with Huzur Sheristadar Parsvanathan pondering the significance of a Tamil Jaina holding a Persian-origin office in the highly Saivite district of Thanjavur, of which the immensely popular collector was a Syrian Christian. Collector Antony also told me I should get hold of and read the report of the Ganapathia Pillai Commission of Inquiry on the Agrarian Problems of East Thanjavur. That, he said, would be the best introduction to the state of life in the district. He was right. The report gave a concise and precise account of the conditions of the region's agrarian population and life-cycles. The brief report made a deep impression on me for its chaste English, clear historical recounting, fair analysis, and bold recommendations for treating agriculture in Thanjavur as an industry to inure it against seasonal wage-layoffs, and for increasing the wage rates.

The intersection between class and caste in Tamil Nadu was not unique, but it was intense and called for vigilance on the part of a state that was publicly committed to egalitarian justice. My first posting in the state, being in Thanjavur, was a godsend. It brought me into what may be called the 'heart cave' of its life.

Modernizing paddy cultivation was the collector's day's chore and nightly dream. His tireless propagation of new strains of rice developed in Aduthurai, the rice research station in his district, was the talk of the state administration. Chief Minister Karunanidhi, on a visit to the district, described the collector as 'the Antony who is besotted with his own Cleopatra—agriculture'.

Antony was also a turbine of energy for something besides agriculture. Family planning was his passion, and spreading the message of the small family was his creed. That he was, as a consequence, the butt of friendly jokes did not dampen his ardour. I did not see then, but do now, that this would not have been easy, theologically, for a Syrian Christian and a devout one at that. A crucifix dangled on his chest from a gold chain at all times. Antony made me see for sure that all development would be futile if our numbers continued to grow unchecked. If our birth rate is showing signs of stabilizing today, it is in no small measure due to the likes of Antony, who made family planning a state priority at the key district level.

Soon after joining duty in Thanjavur, I was told I must, as assistant collector (Training), draw a tour programme for myself covering all the training tasks I am supposed to do and send it to the collector for his approval. So, I prepared the list and sent it with a covering line of which read something like this: I forward herewith my draft programme for your approval. The piece of paper came back super-fast with his approval and—a reprimand. 'A/C Trg to note: to your superiors you submit, to your equals you transmit, and only to your subordinates do you forward.' Hierarchy teaches its lessons. The collector's intention in sending that reprimand was to let many others who will see that note on its way to me and later know that I had been given a ticking off.

But there was another piece of vital counsel he gave me, in confidence. 'Gopal, I must tell you that ours is a very caste-conscious state. Now, I do not know what you regard as your caste. But given that you are half-Gujarati and half-TamBrahm, let me advise you, right at this starting stage of your career here, to see yourself and position yourself as a north Indian allotted to Tamil Nadu and NOT as a TamBrahm. I see from some indications that you are giving that you have a TamBrahm slant to you. Get rid of that. The sooner you do that, the better it will be for you. And one more thing: learn up about the castes of the state, which caste is dominant in which district and the like.' I followed the advice about not seeing myself and being seen as a TamBrahm, but I never quite managed to master the caste break-up in the state. A lack that has weakened me and my official effectiveness.

Amma set up a small home for me in Thanjavur town, cooking meals for me and keeping me cradled in her loving care. She was fifty-nine at the time, not a great age, but diabetes had enfeebled her, and I am, looking back, in awe of her having adjusted to what may be called mofussil life for my sake. The house was small, as I said, but new, and Amma furnished it simply but with great refinement. The only problem was the kitchen stove. There was no gas then, and we had no electric cooking systems in the house. An open chulha with a coal fire would have to be lit by her. This would take time and fill up the kitchen with smoke each time it was lit, turning her eyes red. But once it got going, it yielded the most delicious fare.

This was the year India was celebrating Mahatma Gandhi's centenary. One ingenious method used by the Indian state was to assemble a photo exhibition on wheels. A Gandhi Centenary 'Special' coursed through the country bearing these photo panels and came to Thanjavur as well. For my mother and me, this came with an additional joy—my cousin Manu Jaisukhlal Gandhi, who was on the train as, I imagine, a living exhibit, came home and also met Antony, who took time off from paddy and family planning to meet this Gandhi kin on Gandhi's centenary.

At the national level, 1969 saw the bizarre phenomenon of Mrs Indira Gandhi ditching her own party's candidate for president of India—N. Sanjiva Reddy (1913–96). She certainly had her reasons, but the optics of it all were bad. And Vice President V. V. Giri (1894–1980), a highly deserving candidate, announced his own candidature unilaterally and got the prime minister to transfer the majority of Congress votes to him on the principle of 'conscience vote'. There was little work for conscience in the whole business, only for opportunism. And, listening to radio news in my Thanjavur dwelling, I rued Reddy losing the election, ayyo, for all wrong reasons even as I could not but hail Giri winning, though for all wrong reasons.

The split in the Congress that followed, the resignation in high dudgeon of Deputy Prime Minister Morarji Desai, the nationalization of fourteen banks, and the launching of the hollow and wholly demagogic slogan of 'Garibi Hatao' (banish poverty) all marked the beginning of realpolitik in India.

Nehru had died in 1964. But his soul was buried by his own political legatees in 1969. The year in which Gandhi would have turned 100.

BOOK FOUR

1970
NO LESS HIDEOUS THAN RAPE

Amma had been given, as a departure eve gift by my father's admiring 'proprietor' at the *Hindustan Times*, Krishnakumar Birla (1918–2008), a Fiat car. She brought this over to Thanjavur and recruited a driver, a Tamil lad called Muhammad Mubarak, to drive it. Amma treated Mubarak with solicitude, and he almost worshipped Amma. And Anna was, to him, a pir—a spiritual guide or saint. He or the peon-cum-driver Hari detailed for my 'duty' would drive me from Thanjavur town to the village, Vaidyanathanpettai, to which I was allotted for training. The route passed through the temple town of Kandiyur and another town, Thiruvaiyaru, famed for its association with the saint-singer Tyagaraja, who spent his last days there.

Today, when I look back at that time, I am aware of the importance of my having had in Thanjavur a Syrian Christian Collector, a Jaina Sheristadar and a Labbay driver called Muhammed Mubarak. But at that time, over half a century ago, I was hardly conscious of that fact and drove past temple after beautiful temple, directed by a legatee of Saint Thomas, driven by a Tamil descendent of Arabs.

But, to return to Thanjavur and my training there.

Kandiyur's temple had an elephant attached to it, and one day, when a special puja was being offered at it, Doraiswami, the local revenue divisional officer, and I were invited to witness it. I was horrified, and the RDO was incensed when we saw temple minions goad the unwilling and disinterested pachyderm by thrusting sharp thongs into its testicles to make it move. 'Are you not ashamed?' Doraiswami yelled. 'If the poor beast is unwilling to do your bidding, leave him. He has his own feelings.' The callous men stopped what they were doing at once. The capture and deploying of elephants for temple service may have theological meaning in a religion that worships Ganapati, but the way the poor creatures are treated speaks poorly of human feelings. I ought to have included a paragraph on this in my tour notes and end-of-training report, but lacked the wit to do so. It is only now, as I write in 2024 that I see some hope for the beasts. A report tells me: 'In a first, a robotic elephant took the place of a captive wild elephant to conduct rituals at a temple in Kerala on February 26. On March 1, the Tamil Nadu High Court ruled that temples or private entities should not acquire more elephants in the state. Both moves are an effort to cut down on the use of captive Asian elephants in temples and festivals, so as to eliminate the cruelty that the animals are subjected to during the process.'[1] There is hope!

In Tiruvaiyaru, I saw from the car while driving through it a sight I have never been able to forget. A middle-aged man was walking ahead of a young woman who could have been his wife, perhaps a second or third one. Nothing special about that! Except that he wore a self-satisfied smirk, and she wore nothing. She was being paraded stark naked by him in what I immediately figured out was a form of public punishment. For what? I wish I knew. Perhaps for suspected adultery, a romance, or some act of individuality frowned upon by a male-dominated society. Her expression was one of utter humiliation but also of resignation. She was walking with normal steps, head held straight, and hands by her side, not trying to cover her private parts. It was all too late, anyway; she had been stripped before all, stripped of her clothes, her dignity, and there was no point attempting modesty. There are things that can be done to a woman that are no less hideous than rape. I was horrified, Mubarak no less so. But neither of us spoke a word. I was shocked as much by the passivity of the onlookers as by the incident itself. And as we drove on towards Vaidyanathanpettai, as if we had seen nothing unusual, I was shocked at my own reaction. Ought I not to have stopped the car, got out and demanded to know from the man what he was doing? Of course, I should have. But I did not. Some false sense of izzat, of not getting myself, a government official, involved in a lowly 'street matter' prevented me. I am ashamed.

I believed then and believe now that women are treated better by their menfolk in the south and the Northeast than in the rest of India. Is what I saw in Tiruvaiyaru fifty years ago likely to happen there and elsewhere today? I would say, yes, it is. But the response of the people around would not be as passive today as it was then, and an assistant collector under training is not likely to drive past such a scene now without intervening.

In January that year, Tiruvaiyaru organized what it has been doing since the 1940s—a musical tribute called the Aradhanai in honour of Tyagaraja. Musicians of note come from different parts of the state to sing the Pancharatna Kritis of Tyagaraja in the shrine beside the spot where his remains were cremated. This year, MS came with her husband and his daughters, Radha and Vijaya. Amma and I went to the event and let her divine rendering wash over our souls. That night, the four of them stayed with us in our little home. Everyone was cramped as we divided ourselves over the two rooms we had. But what an honour that was! MS was not exactly comfortable that night, and I could hear Sadasivam mama asking her how she could be helped and her saying that it was nothing, nothing at all. We lacked a dining table, and Amma had small wooden stools made for them to dine and breakfast from. The fare was simple, but with what gladness and appreciation the great musician partook of it!

Vaidyanathanpettai was a charming paddy-growing village, quintessentially a Cauvery delta habitation. Anna told me to get to know the world of the village and of its village officers intimately. He was being a super collector in this—something I did not think it wise to share with my 'real' collector, Antony. Anna's advice to me was: Give due respect to the village headman, the manigar, who is bound to be from one or other of the state's backward classes. And give due attention to the village accountant, the karnam or kanakapillai. Master his registers, in particular, the chitta, which has details of land ownership, and adangal, which has details of tenancy and cultivation. In these, he said, lie the life cycles of a village. And do not forget, he said, to get to know the psychology of the village servants who do the actual physical work with the maintenance of water ducts and bunds. The hidden sociologist in him added: 'The karnam is generally a literate Brahmin as he has to maintain the registers and is, by reason of being the "registrar", very powerful. He can do much mischief if irritated. The manigar is, as a rule, not a Brahmin but powerful in a different sense as he is ethnically strong. The rest, the village "servants", are from the lower castes. Find out if the post of nirganti still exists. It used to. The nirganti was in charge of the canals, the streams, and the ducts to those. Cultivate all of them but do not neglect the "servants" for they know life as it is lived in the village.' Anna would have made a great collector!

Sethuraman, 'my' karnam, was a teacher of teachers. Brahmin, like most karnams were at that time, he had inherited his job from his father and knew the village better than he did the lines on his palms. He was patient, understanding, and forgiving of my impatience, lack of understanding, and general airs of superiority.

I can never forget his telling me that Vaidyanathanpettai, apart from its agriculture, was also adept at weaving mats for the floor—pai—as they are called. The fibre used in the village was not the superfine variety that makes the mats of Pathamadai in Tirunelveli but was nonetheless strong without being coarse. Tempering the straw in water and then drying and plaiting it was an art. I was fascinated by the vegetable dyes that were used to colour the material and could not but hail the iridescent blue they used for a mat I got them to make (and after much persuasion, agreed to receive payment for) for me to give to Amma. She was overjoyed by the present. The mat stayed with us for years, the peacock colour fading gradually, but the mat itself remaining strong and unfrayed.

Amma wanted to get for our home a specimen or two of Thanjavur's famous iconic deity figures in vivid colours, plated and inlaid with semi-precious gems. My salary was a mere ₹350 a month, and there was no question of our buying one of the expensive types. But when Mubarak drove us to the street where the town's painters lived and worked, we got a whiff of a very different culture—utter courtesy. I had made sure that the painters did not get to know that they were talking to an IAS officer, which might have made it awkward for them to be professional in the matter of costs. Amma asked them if they would make for us paintings of Lakshmi and Saraswati without any gems, precious or semi-precious, and no gold or silver plating. Only paint, she said. Raju, the master artist, agreed at once. And in about a week's time, gave us the two works of sheer grace. The paint has not dimmed, the smile has not changed, and the grace has not fled from those two, which are, for me, assurances of divinity. If I remember alright, Raju charged only ₹200 per piece. Great art lives in India in great hands, great minds, and hearts. The poorer the artist, the richer his or her creation.

Thanjavur will be remembered by me for many things, but nothing more majestically than its great temple, the Big Temple as it is called. Big, of course, it is, but bigness is the smallest thing about it. The structure is majestic, simply majestic. The eleventh century structure for Brihadeeswara is a masterpiece of intent, design, and accomplishment, with its serenity and repose, grandeur, and beauty beng nothing like anything I have seen anywhere. That it holds a magnificent representation of the linga, ancient murals, and myriad statuary was, for me, a matter of detail. What took my breath away, apart from the towering presence of the vimana above the sanctum, was the massive sculpture of the Nandi bull. Seated with total contentment, its tongue playing with its nose exactly as any bovine's would, the Nandi at Brihadeeswara is a captivation, linking the human and animal worlds seamlessly.

1971
SIR...LOOK AT THESE BALLOTS... STUFFED INTO THE BOX...

My training year over, I was posted on my first regular assignment as assistant collector, Tindivanam, in the South Arcot District.

I remember the posting for five things: First, the elections to the Lok Sabha held in March that year, which brought Indira Gandhi to a large public ground at our doorstep. Second, the house of the assistant or sub collector into which I brought my wife. Third, a devastating fire in a village near our house cum office. Fourth, a communal flash I can never forget or forgive myself about. Fifth, the scrapping of prohibition.

The year 1971 was election year. Campaigning was in full swing in February for the polling in March, and public meetings were held there, loudspeakers blaring into our eardrums till late hours. I was returning officer for Gingee, a taluk in my sub-division and also assistant collector. And as such, supervising arrangements for a free and fair poll. This was, as I and everyone knew, Rajaji's last election. He was campaigning, in an alliance with the anti-Indira faction of the Congress led by his old rival Kamaraj, for Swatantra. At age ninety-three.

Indira Gandhi's Congress was in alliance with the DMK, then in power in the state. In other words, my grandfather was opposed to and opposing with an ancient warrior's vigour, both the party in power at the centre and the party in power in the state. I needed to be and be seen to be utterly unbiased, which, in my heart of hearts, I was not. I wanted my grandfather's side to win, to see Kamaraj installed as chief minister. But given the family 'thing' I had to be and seen to be more than simply unbiased. I had to bend over backwards to be that. I did not want any Cong (I) or DMK functionary to get a ghost of a reason to complain to anyone about me.

One of the requirements of a free and fair poll was that inside the voting booth, there should be no poster or paper displaying the image of any candidate or political leader connected with the election. My heart bled, and my eyes smarted as I ordered posters with Rajaji's face on them removed in a couple of booths. In one particular booth, the poster was stuck firm. It had to be scraped off using a tin sheet. I stood grim-faced, my fists clenched in self-mortification, as a staffer applied the sharp edge to it, obliterating the clean old neck first, then the strong chin, the thin lips, the great hooknose. By the time the scraper reached the bespectacled eyes, I had had enough. I turned and got into the waiting jeep. As it roared off, I could see nothing remained of my grandfather's image on the booth's wall. I never told him of this, but if I had done so, I do not doubt that he would have said I did right.

At a mammoth meeting on the sands of the Marina on 25 February 1971, Rajagopalachari and Kamaraj appealing to the people of Madras to vote out of office both Indira Gandhi's government at the centre and the DMK government in the state. (*The Hindu* archives).

With Congress and DMK candidates and supporters in tow, Indira Gandhi came campaigning. She was a partisan, but she was prime minister, and all the rule books required me to be in attendance, except at the election meetings she addressed. I sat at a distance from the public platform in Gingee as she spoke, with C. Subramaniam, a family well-wisher of ours now in the camp opposite to Rajaji's, his one-time mentor, interpreting her speech into Tamil. The meeting went off uneventfully, to my relief. And at the Gingee Rest House, where she stopped for a brief minute or two, Subramaniam introduced me most warmly to her: 'Gopal, Rajaji's grandson…conscientious officer…' She knew very well who I was but let CS have the satisfaction of introducing me. I got a faint smile from her.

But there was trouble in store at Tindivanam that evening. I remained in my office room, barely a hundred yards from where she was speaking, not visible but available for any need. And the need arose like this. The grounds were well lit, the amplification perfect. I had checked this out minutely. A fair-sized crowd had gathered to hear her. Suddenly, in the middle of her speech, the power went off. The venue and my office were simultaneously plunged into darkness. Utter darkness. Seconds went by, during which I prayed the power would come back. I rang the control room. The number was busy. I dispatched jeeps to find out what had happened. No luck. Seconds turned to minutes, and in that dangerous silence and dark, I saw the headlights of jeeps and cars coming on and the prime minister's convoy leave. She had abandoned the meeting about ten minutes after the power went off and driven to Cuddalore, the district's headquarters, her next stop, where she was also to spend the night. In total agitation, I followed in my own jeep. A couple of colleagues jumped into the jeep. No one spoke throughout that nearly two hours' ride. By the time we reached, she had finished her meeting. No one alluded to the Tindivanam fiasco, and I returned home, bewildered but thankful at the absence of an inquisition. No one asked me for any explanations, though I gave a report of what I could gather: the illuminations and amplifications at the ground were too intense, and the grid, unable to take the load, succumbed. Apparently, the line had been restored minutes after we left.

As returning officer in Gingee, I had a most piquant experience. As counting was on in the large hall, with representatives of all parties allowed to be present as observers, a representative of the Congress (O) came to me with a bunch of ballots that had been counted. They had all gone to the joint candidate of Congress (I) and DMK. 'Sir…Sir…Please…please just look at these…Sir…can you see the folds…They have all been pre-stamped and pre-folded and stuffed into the box…'

'How do you say that?'

'They are all sticking together….'

'Isn't it possible for one ballot paper to fall over another in the box and get, so to say, joined to the one that went before…?'

'Sir…I know that…. Of course, it can…. But then such a ballot paper would fall on the earlier one like a roof over a hut… Just one over the other…. But see these, Sir… Just see… They have been folded four-fold…four-fold… like a handkerchief…and they are like this in bunch after bunch…hundreds….'

I was struck dumb. What the man was saying was right. He was holding up for me to see bunch after bunch of such multiple-folded ballots, which had, however, been opened up from their folds and counted by the counting officers as single ballot papers. All of them had been stamped for the Indira-DMK combine. But what was I to do? The ballot boxes had all been shown to the election agents before voting began, empty and clean. Then, the voting had started. And had proceeded peacefully with election agents present from all parties. Voting over, the boxes had been sealed in front of the agents. And then stored in government venues with election agents keeping guard, day and night until they were opened by breaking the seals under the agents' gaze. How and when could anyone have insinuated pre-fixed ballot papers into the boxes and then also got the names of the voters and the ballot papers to tally....? How? I said as much to the complainant. 'You have all been there...watching...I am sorry, there is nothing I can do.' The man retreated. He looked like a crushed neem twig. My tongue tasted like one.

Nayantara Sahgal (b. 1927) writes in her biographical study of her aunt*:

1. The New Congress had won 350 out of 518 seats in the Lok Sabha.
2. The Prime Minister, who as Home Minister had intelligence, the police and the Election Commission under her supervision, told the Lok Sabha after the election on April 2, 1971, 'The complaints against the Election Commission have already been dealt with by my colleague the Minister of Law and Justice.' The Jan Sangh leader, A.B. Vajpayee, retorted, 'Not satisfactorily'.
3. '...in the aftermath of Mrs Gandhi's victory and the awe created by the pendulum swing of power; criticism died away...'

Indira's Congress and the DMK won handsomely. Rajaji took the defeat philosophically; Kamaraj was in shock for a while. 'The crowds were with us,' he said. 'But the votes have all gone to them...I cannot understand....'

In May, I was married in a match 'arranged' by my mother. Tara was the daughter of a Mandayam Iyengar couple from Bombay and granddaughter of an outstanding entomologist, M. O. T. Iyengar, on her maternal side and on the paternal side of a colleague of Rajaji's in the Swatantra Party and a senior entrepreneur, M. A. Sreenivasan. The wedding took place in Bombay according to Iyengar protocol, with the Sadasivams doing us the honour of attending and MS singing the customary song, 'Sita Kalyanam', by the bridal swing. They hosted a reception in Madras a couple of days later, to which Anna came, beaming with blessings. Kamaraj did, too, but a good two hours earlier, quietly, saying he would not like to generate any speculation about the bridegroom's political affiliations. 'He is an officer under the state.... Let him not be seen by society in the company of an opposition man like me.... Rajaji is his grandfather...that is different.' He was right. Politics makes for myopia.

*Nayantara Sahgal, *Indira Gandhi: Tryst with Power*, New Delhi: Penguin Books, 2012.

The house in Tindivanam to which I brought Tara as a bride was one long line of rooms fronted by a broad veranda on which a car could be driven room to room. It stood on the bund of a tank, picturesquely, with a stone pavilion at its middle. But the house was as old as it was handsome with the added reputation of being home to snakes, mainly water snakes, but not without some of a more venomous kind as well. These would slither into it from the tank and could position themselves on the walls, looking like one more of the many cracks. A favourite wall for snakes was in the house's best bathroom—a challenge to its user's equanimity. But Tara was not one to complain about anything that came from nature.

She was an avid bird watcher and would spend hours watching flocks of birds and singletons on the tank and its sides, mainly dabchick and cormorant. 'Orintholgy?' I asked her shortly after we set up home, wanting to sound knowledgeable. 'No,' she replied quietly. 'Not orinthology but ornithology.' I was not to be so easily bettered, and I persisted. 'Salim Ali is the great bird man, right?' 'Yes,' she said. 'But Saalim Ali is how the name is pronounced though spelt with a single "a".' I knew I was married to someone who believed in accuracy, in facts, in truth.

I was sitting at my desk one evening when I heard the town's fire engine go wailing past. This was not uncommon. But something in me felt very uncomfortable. One of those things. I got into my jeep and followed the engine. A few miles out of the town, just outside a village, the fire engine stopped, and so did my jeep, just behind. I asked the firemen why they had stopped. No road, sir, they said. Engine can't go any further. I could see they were right. The village's straggling houses were everywhere around us, the fire's glow much further back. Asking the firemen to run towards a glow, I too, started running towards it. No point, they said. The engine's hose will not get that far. There was no time to talk. Asking them to follow me, I ran towards the fire, reaching there in some five minutes. It was the village cheri, the 'lines' of the Dalit. Hut after hut was getting gutted, men, women, and children watching in a daze as their lives' possessions were getting reduced to cinder. We got hold of some cloths, the firemen produced several canvas-like sheets, and all of us started slapping the flames down. What completely stunned me was that as we, the firemen, and some colleagues of mine, were beating the fire down with our hands, men from the upper castes in nearby village streets did not move a finger. Some of them lay stretched on the pyols of their homes, dozing. The fire was accidental, and fortunately, there was no death. But this then was India. Observing caste even in the furious rages of a fire.

A few months on, in the village of Sevalapurai in Gingee taluk, occurred the death of an aged woman. So? Nothing unusual in that. But the woman happened to be Dalit, and her family decided that enough was enough by way of upper-caste strangulations of human rights and that the grandma would be taken right royally to the cremation ground like anyone else on the same pathway used by 'them upper caste folk'. This was immediately prevented by the 'uppers'. She may rot but not be allowed on our path, they said. She should be taken on the track the Dalit have always used, none other. The tension rose by the hour. I reached the village, and so did the district collector, accompanied by a police party. Both groups were determined. The law was clear. There could be no discrimination, the woman's relatives had every right to take her on the 'main' path. Let them try, and we will burn every Dalit hut in the village after the collector and assistant collector and police have left said the 'uppers'. Do not go, the Dalit said to us, till the cremation is over and we have returned home. The situation was dire. A suggestion then came for a new track to be made alongside the main one on which the bier could be taken. With the district collector present, the situation was not in my hands. The panchayat said they will fund it. The Dalit party was not happy about it but was not totally averse. At least the point that they do not have to take the bier on the bad old track had been conceded. The collector signalled his acceptance of this compromise and left.

L. Elayaperumal (1924–2005), a leading Dalit leader, came to meet me later and spoke in anger and anguish. 'What is this, sir?...two decades after the abolition of untouchability, we cannot even take our dead on the common track to be cremated?' The reading was right. What had been done was wrong in law, wrong in social morality, wrong in the eyes of justice, wrong in the scroll of time. Gandhi and Ambedkar would have frowned. I cannot speak for Collector Nambiar, who took the decision, but I can, for myself. Their frown would have been trained on me, and rightly so. The matter came up in the state assembly, and were it not for Chief Minister Karunanidhi's high opinion of Collector Nambiar, both he and I could have been in great trouble.

Before leaving the sub-division, I had a most interesting experience. Chief Minister Karunanidhi had scrapped prohibition, and we were to sell the franchise for toddy and arrack shops to the highest bidder. I was then a teetotaller and knew what Rajaji felt about it. He had gone to the CM and appealed in vain to him to keep prohibition intact. But revenue requirements prevailed. And at the sub-divisional level, I found myself required to auction the liquor shop rights. I told Anna I was torn. But he was not! 'You are an officer of the government. You have to do the government's bidding. Prohibition is a matter of principle with me, and I will oppose its scrapping.

That is my dharma. Yours, as a government servant, is to implement the new order. Go ahead and do the auctions without the slightest compunction.' Thus fortified, I found myself seated in the Gingee and Tindivanam taluk offices, enticing potential bidders to bid, bid higher, higher still...come on you there, and you...Surely you can do better than that....' I believe Tindivanam bagged a fair amount for the government's liquor coffer that year.

By the middle of the year, I was posted to the secretariat as under secretary in the Revenue Department. 'An important department,' Rajaji said. 'When you get a file, do not be in a hurry to dispose it off. You will see it will have two components: the note file with all the noting of the department officials, to which you will be required to add your own. Set that note file aside. Go first and straight to the second component, the parent file, which has all the main papers relevant to the subject. Read those carefully and in detail, and after you have mastered the subject from a study of those papers, then see what other officials are saying and say your own bit as a master of the subject. You will then find others are superficial and even ignorant of its basics.' I did not follow the advice always, being in a hurry to liquidate the pile of files in my 'in tray'. But whenever I did what he had advised, I found he was so right.

The state government was at the time vigorously pursuing socialist programmes and clamping ceilings on agricultural holdings with a passion. I was wholly in sympathy with these, having seen the grinding poverty of rural families and also the great wealth of the landed. But urban land holdings were a different category. Cutting up holdings in cities and towns to bring them to some notional 'standard' size made no sense as that would make the plots bizarre in size and shape. A different way of levelling down needed to be devised for cities.

But one levelling down was happening that year, and at the hands of the prime minister in her new avatar of socialist icon: the abolition of privy purses, as the payment to the ruling families of erstwhile princely states was called, seemed, on the face of it, a highly desirable step towards an egalitarian, post-monarchical, post-feudal order. But I recoiled at the idea. As one descended from a diwan of three Kathiawari princely states—Porbandar, Rajkot, and Vankaner, I was perhaps conditioned by that legacy. But more than that, I could see that the step was pure and simple populism, an utterly hypocritical move to appear pro-poor and revolutionary. The former princes and princesses had been granted the privy purses as part of their agreements to integrate with independent India in 1947, and later to merge their states in 1949, thereby ending their ruling rights. A word had been given to the princes—a word of honour in a strictly reciprocal scheme. And, I asked myself: were Rajendra Prasad, Jawaharlal Nehru, and Sardar Patel, particularly the last named, less committed to eradicate poverty than Indira Gandhi? Were they feudal and reactionary? Patel, who was the architect of the integration of princely state with the new union, had spoken up stoutly for privy purses. Could anyone match his role in the mergers?

To say Rajaji was deeply pained by the move would be worse than employing a cliché. He was hurt. 'Pledging themselves to break a pledge!' he wrote. 'Gandhiji would shut his ears in shame...Sardar would be as angry as he could ever be, and Jawaharlalji would be horrified and shout, "Such a thing is not done".' And in a rare departure from his norm about my being a government servant and therefore meant to stay away from his politics, he asked me to get for him Tulsidas's *Ramcharitmanas* in the A. G. Atkins version to which he had contributed a foreword. Peering through it, he located the lines spoken by Dasarath: 'Raghukul riti sada chali ayi, pran jahun baru bachanu na jayi.' For this has ever been the way of the Raghus: we may give up our lives, but not our word.[1] And citing Tulsidas in an article in *Swarajya*, he accused the Indira Gandhi government of squandering the plighted word of the Raghus of our Republic. I do not know if anyone in her durbar would have had the guts or the wit to show her the piece.

I could not but see the irony of this ancient pensioner with no savings worth the name defending princes' privy purses on a point of principle while prosperous and powerful politicians paraded their socialism by scrapping a privilege given to former royals. The hypocrisy and sham of it all was sickening. The order abolishing privy purses, after legislative and judicial setbacks to it, finally came in the shape of an amendment to the Constitution—the 26th. What was the crashing hurry? None. Only ego. The annual payout involved—Rs 5 crore—was for the government, not a large sum, and was designed to come down with each successor generation. A democrat's daughter was acting small, with a vestige of history, and doing so for the aim of looking what she certainly held no patent for—a saviour of the poor.

The transition from Nehru's to Indira's India was a shift from the age of earnest striving to that of fidgety acting, from action to drama, from the person—Nehru—being billeted to serve India to India being roped into the service of the person, Indira. India's military reverses against China in 1962 were seen as Nehru's, not the army's, failure; the spectacular success of India's military machine against Pakistan in 1971 was seen as Indira's, not its soldiers' triumph. All this was not just deplorable in itself but also dangerous as a precedent for the future.

This natak looked particularly like tawdry make-up when one saw that only a few months earlier, in the autumn of 1970, her son described by her as 'a delicate young man' with 'an enterprising spirit',[2] had been issued a letter of intent by the Directorate General of Technical Development to manufacture 50,000 'indigenous' cars at Faridabad, Haryana. As Nehru's niece and Sanjay Gandhi's aunt Nayantara Sahgal says 'It is interesting to note that the capacity achieved by established car production units during 1970–71 was 46,000.'[3] A new techno-industrial-political imperium had come into being.

Sanjay Gandhi at his Maruti workshop. (*Hindustan Times* archives).

The year ended with the Indo-Pakistan war, giving India the victory it needed to liberate Bangladesh. The photograph of the surrender has to be a classic for the expressions it captures, the body language of the winning and surrendering parties and of the AIR correspondent holding his mike to the fighters' frames. There is no gloating on the faces of the Indians, though there is a calm satisfaction in the expressions of Vice Admiral Nilakanta Krishnan, then flag officer, the Flag Officer Commanding-in-Chief Eastern Naval Command and Lieutenant General J. F. R. Jacob, Chief of Staff of the Indian Army's Eastern Command. General Jagjit Singh Aurora's great stance as he handed the pen to General A. A. K. Niazi to sign and then watched as the surrender was inked, is deeply moving. I do not doubt if an equivalent of this surrender ceremony had coincided with the lifetimes of Michelangelo or Leonardo da Vinci, they would have painted or sculpted it for posterity.

And so, like everyone in India, our little family was thrilled at our victory and at Sheikh Mujib's release and ascendancy to Bangladesh's helm. We were in Madras. Dhaka was far away. We were in India. Bangladesh was another country. But the flash of a shared joy clasped us. Somewhere in our thoughts lay the realization that the Two Nation Theory based on religion had been exploded by this war and the birth of Bangladesh. And the lonely pilgrim of Noakhali had, in an unexpected way, seen his yagna fulfilled.

Reports that Pakistani military and supporting pro-Pakistani Islamist militias had killed between 300,000 and 3,000,000 civilians in East Pakistan, leading to some 8 to 10 million people fleeing to seek refuge in India, were appalling. Some 93,000 Pakistani uniformed personnel and collaborators were taken prisoner by our army.

I could not have imagined then that in 2024, Bangladesh would become the scene of an incredible change in which, thanks to the unpopular regime of Sheikh Mujib's daughter Sheikh Hasina, that country would actually want to erase the memory of Sheikh Mujib and in the process make India not its most prized neighbour but its least trusted one, with Pakistan losing little time to befriend the people that it has trampled underfoot.

1972
NOW WE ARE BEGGARS....

'Our generals and the army,' wrote Rajaji on 1 January, 'the navy and the air force have scored a brilliant triumph...' And he was wholly admiring of the unilateral ceasefire Prime Minister Indira Gandhi ordered on the western front after the goal on the eastern had been met. And when, following Pakistan's surrender, both nations signed the historic bilateral Simla Agreement, agreeing to settle their disputes peacefully, he called it the Pact of Good Hope. Noting that the agreement was partial, he asked for a second summit to be called soon so that the people of the two countries do not 'brood over unsettled issues'.

Today, news aggresses our lives 24x7 from every direction and in multiple modes, audio, visual, and both. We have become thick-eyed and coarse-eared to it. But 'back then' when the radio was the only link with the world, its role was unique. We 'tuned into' it, literally, by a couple of moves, which led to the radio turning into a receiver with a light and a tune linking us to a voice, a real human voice, speaking to us. On 10 January, the day Sheikh Mujibur Rahman was stopping in Delhi on his way from London to Dacca, we tuned into AIR's relaying of the great meeting that Indira Gandhi had organized on the Cantonment Parade Ground of Delhi. 'India and Bangladesh will live side by side,' he declared. But the message, wholly anticipatable was less important than the scene itself. We heard in a delirium of joy the leader start with 'Madam Prime Minister...' and then being stopped by the mammoth crowd that said 'No, no, no...' and demand he switch to Bangla. An ocean of Hindi-speakers demanding that their speaker address them in Bangla! Joy! The Two Nation Theory had been thrown out, lock, stock, and bunkum! Thrill! And when the Bangabandhu complied with '...Amar bhai, boneyra...' the sky was rent by a roar of ecstasy and shouts of 'Joy Bangla!' That was the nearest I had got to a sense of freedom. Amma spontaneously went to the kitchen and made some kheer to celebrate.

What we could not see on the radio, we read in the *Hindustan Times* two days later. As Mujib ended his speech, his trademark pipe was in his clenched fist, and the crowd 'stood up to a man shouting "Joy Bangla, Jai Hind"'. And—this was something special—Indira Gandhi herself acted as the 'cheerleader' with an acclamation of 'Sheikh Mujib-ur-Rahman Zindabad!' But the *HT* report's greatest hit was in telling us that as the crowd surged to follow the motorcade, one placard had its own version of poetry and a masterful Janata understanding of geo-politics and of the region's ecological imperatives:

> India-Bangla same blood
> Ganga-Padma same flood

All my great reservations about Indira Gandhi dissolved, if only for a while, in that fluxion of history and politics. No one can be wholly flawed, even as no one can be perfect. And this was a moment of redemption for her.

The Bangladesh prime minister, Sheikh Mujibur Rahman, seen with the prime minister of India, Indira Gandhi, soon after his arrival at the Delhi airport from Moscow on 10 April 1974. (*The Hindu* archives).

As I write this, in the embers of 2024, I think of the line from a song sung by Mohammed Rafi in the film *Guide* (1965)—'Kya se Kya Ho Gaya!' (What a change, what an anti-climax!) That country's anger at Sheikh Mujib's daughter and the country's democratically elected dictator Sheikh Hasina was understandable. But not so the recoiling of that in a rollback to the nation's founder. This was appalling, as was the vandalization of Mujib's statues, the burning down of his house and the destruction of the great work of art depicting the surrender of Pakistan's military officers to India's defence forces after they had liberated East Pakistan and opened the path to the creation of Bangladesh. 'Heinous' the country's new chief adviser Mohammed Yunus called the attacks on Hindu homes and temples which followed, stoking memories of Noakhali in 1946–47. Was the new generation in Bangladesh reversing that country's rejection of the Two Nation theory? Was a new Islamization afoot in what Mujib had envisaged as a secular democratic country?

The year 1972, with Mujib being feted in Delhi, had given Indira Gandhi her 'moment'.

There was to be one more before the year ended. And all credit to her for it. The Wild Life (Protection) Act, 1972, was enacted, wholly at her prodding, by the parliament of India for the protection of plants and animal species. Until this point, India had five designated national parks. But now, the Act established schedules that protected certain plant and animal species, outlawing hunting or harvesting these species. And it extended to the whole of India.

The Emperor Ashoka, in his Pillar Edict V, listing certain types of wild and domesticated life forms and protecting them, had attempted this, famously and iconically.

This was Indira Gandhi's Ashokan moment.

Meanwhile, Madras, by October, 1972, was going through political birth pangs. The Dravidian movement suffered its second split (the first was the splitting in 1949 of the parent Dravidar Kazhagam founded by Periyar into the DK and the DMK). The DMK led by Chief Minister Karunanidhi broke as the heart-throb of millions, and DMK's most charismatic leader, the cinema star M. G. Ramachandran (MGR), formed his own breakaway All India Anna DMK (AIADMK) after opposing Karunanidhi's policies, especially the scrapping of prohibition. Rajaji was wooed by the new formation for blessings and support, and Rajaji did not disappoint it. But true to his style, he made a prediction that was to come true: 'Karunanidhi would be the loser in this business.'

On 2 October, Gandhi Jayanti, a public holiday, I had gone with him to the Gandhi Mandapam, the beautiful granite structure built in ancient Tamil style under his advisory watch during the governorship of Sri Prakasa, to attend a function commemorating the Mahatma. He told me on the longish car ride: 'Sri Prakasa and I were very clear that the mandapam should have no depiction of Gandhiji. No statue or carving should show his likeliness. This should commemorate his spirit, not his form. It is not meant to be a temple to him but to the love our pious people have for Gandhiji.'

He got down from the car slowly but confidently, as I held his left palm in my right. The actress-singer K. B. Sundarambal, of whose art he was not a particular admirer, was to sing. She greeted him with reverence and was blessed by him with affection. He knew that the gathering was almost wholly Hindu. When his turn to speak came, he spoke very briefly, thirteen short sentences which included the following: 'We should learn confession from Jesus and God-fearing from the Prophet of Arabia…Then we shall be able to act as the Gita wants us to….'

This was to be his last public speech. Felicitous that it should have been at Gandhi Mandapam on Gandhi's birthday. Chance is the best designer. I was privileged to have been present at it.

He was, in truth, now above or rather, beyond it all. And high time, too. His birthday on 10 December brought the usual stream of well-wishers and blessing-seekers.

On 25 December, Christmas day, after a brief illness and hospitalization at the city's public hospital called by all General Hospital, his ninety-four-year-old barge was ready to drift into the verge. A little earlier, he had a visitor he was too comatose to recognize. EVR, the Periyar, only a year younger, arrived in a wheelchair. Greatly shaken and almost a-quiver, the veteran looked at his friend and adversary of decades, long and lovingly. He knew the patient was in the twilight. All of us, Anna's family, offered our respect to the visitor. 'Nachchu!' he called out to Narasimhan, Anna's son, who had not heard that home name of his since God knows when. Narasimhan offered him a platter of fruit that had been brought by someone for Rajaji. Periyar accepted it with natural grace.

'Sriman Narayana charanau saranam prapadye', the chant accompanying the Vaishnava in his final moments filled the room as Dr C. Satyanarayana told us that the last mortal breath had been drawn. Periamma and Amma, with MS beside them, were a triad of deprivation. Chief Minister Karunanidhi and Kamaraj were there within minutes, as was Chief Secretary Sabanayagam, who had served Rajaji as his private secretary during his chief ministership (1952–54).

Where was the body to be laid in state? Narasimhan favoured his old residence in Thyagarayanagar for historic reasons, Sadasivam the Kalki office for reasons of space and accessibility. Kamaraj was clear: He has to lie in state in the city's biggest public hall felicitously named after him, Rajaji Hall. The chief minister and chief secretary saw the point. And so it was.

He now belonged to the margent of Time. And as we followed the hearse from hospital to Rajaji Hall in Amma's small Fiat, Periamma, who had taken care of her father for some eight decades, day after day, wept softly, wordlessly. Amma, her voice choked, said in Tamil, 'Now...we are beggars….' As the car turned into the hall, a wrenching wail, like that of a peacock, came from Mubarak at the wheel.

The funeral was a long procession that took its own time to traverse the distance from Rajaji Hall at one end of the Marina to the other, where the crematorium lay. I found myself walking between MGR, who was conscious of the attention he was getting from the populace watching, and Mohan Kumaramangalam (1916–73), union minister and son of Rajaji's long-time friends and contemporaries, the women's rights striver Radhabai Subbarayan (1891–1960) and her husband the Justice Party leader and statesman, P. Subbarayan (1889–1962). Mohan's left-wing and now Indira-dedicated politics and Rajaji's looked north and south, but the family tie was real. He spoke almost nothing through that walk, but I was drawn to his transparently sensitive face and that increasingly rare thing: a clear diction.

1973
SOMETHING ASHOKA WOULD HAVE LAUDED, LINCOLN SEEN AS NOBLE

On 1 April, Indira Gandhi launched Operation Tiger, with an ambitious aim of increasing the population of the tiger (*Panthera tigris*) in the country. Simultaneously, the tiger, more specifically the Royal Bengal Tiger, replaced the lion, specifically the Asiatic Lion, as India's national animal. This step would by itself have meant little to me but for our cherished friend, the brilliant photo-naturalist M. Krishnan. He had presented to Tara and me at our wedding a stunning photograph taken by him on 27 April 1968 of a tigress reclining majestically on a rock beside a banyan at the Kanha National Park. He took the picture seated on an elephant on a level with her, getting as close as 12 feet from her. Krishnan had spoken with unconcealed admiration of Indira Gandhi's services to wildlife. Explaining to Tara and me the wisdom of the tiger being our national animal, he said by this decision, a huge area of the tiger's natural habitat (much bigger than that of the lion, which occurs only in Gir, Gujarat) would come in for special protection. Besides, he said, the lion's symbolism is vouchsafed by it being on our national emblem—the Ashokan Lion Capital. Krishnan was as apolitical an animal as any can be, and he did not concern himself with Indira Gandhi's politics. He was glad of her interest in wildlife and her hugely pioneering steps to conserve it and protect the forests.

~

Indira Gandhi's Wild Life Protection Act, 1972, mirrored Emperor Ashoka's visionary edict on compassion to non-human life. But in the Simla Agreement also, she did something that evoked the great Mauryan. His Rock Edict XIII says, in the Kalinga war, 100,000 were slain, and many times that number perished. And 150,000 were carried away as captives. He mentions with total frankness the numbers taken prisoner—prisoners of war, we could call them—but does not say what became of them. Did they become slaves, a new helotry?

The Simla Agreement had contemplated consequential discussions on outstanding matters, the most important of that being the question of prisoners. Indira Gandhi turned very wisely to P. N. Haksar (1913–98) in early April 1973 to commence that exercise. Haksar sahib, who had been integral to the Simla proceedings, working almost singly on the final draft that came to be accepted by Prime Minister Indira Gandhi and President Z. A. Bhutto, now parleyed with Aziz Ahmed (1906–82), the Pakistani minister for Defence and Foreign Affairs and with Bangladesh's foreign minister Kamal Hossain (b. 1937), meeting Bhutto and Mujib as well. It was Haksar sahib's conceptual vision, pragmatic diplomacy, and, above all, his sense of the forces of history that led to the tripartite process ending successfully. Hardly ever, if at all, had such a massive movement of prisoners taken place from one embattled land to another through a third that had been mauled in the proceedings. Here was something Ashoka would have lauded, Lincoln seen as noble and Gandhi hailed as ahimsa in action. The Delhi Agreement of 28 August 1973 was signed by officially designated signatories, but its architect was P.N. Haksar.[1]

The United Nations High Commission for Refugees (UNHCR) supervised the repatriation of 121,695 Bengalis from Pakistan to Bangladesh, including high-level Bengali civil servants and military officers, and 108,744 non-Bengali civilians and civil servants from Bangladesh to Pakistan. India released 6,500 Pakistani PoWs, most of whom were transported by train to Pakistan. They included General Niazi, the last Pakistani officer, who was repatriated through the Wagah–Attari Border.

Pakistan's failure to repatriate Urdu-speakers in Bangladesh, not holding to account 195 senior military officials accused of breach of conduct during war and not making provision for a war crimes tribunal, remained unaddressed but the Simla Agreement was an essentially civil and civilizing accomplishment.

1974
WATCHING WITH ANXIETY

Independent India was twenty-seven years old in 1974. Old?

No, independent India was young. Twenty-seven is a young age. But God have mercy, did 'we the people' feel young? We did not. We were wan, weary, and woebegone. So many 'w's in one line. One too many. But that is how the reasons for our depressed condition seemed. They were one too many.

There was huge misgovernance. Corruption was growing. Unemployment was rising. That word—unemployment—is used so lightly. Basically, huge masses of people were without jobs, which meant the women in their families were in huge distress, and the children were undernourished, unschooled, and unkempt. And inflation—another word used routinely —was soaring. Which meant essentials, a euphemism for wheat, rice, sugar, and milk, were getting too costly for the ordinary woman and man.

Indira Gandhi had been prime minister for eight years. She had contested two general elections, winning both. The first, in 1967, by a whisker. But the second, in 1971, in a sweep. How did that happen? Was she so loved? Were her opponents so disliked? Neither. She had learnt how to win elections.

That election of 1971, as we have seen, was not fought fair. The discerning knew that. Yet, no one could prove it. That was part of the new political and electoral finesse. Do something and show you have not. Like, let 'lowerdowns' rig an election. Do nothing yourself. Let rhetoric 'rid' the poor of misery. Do nothing more. Deft at winning office, Indira Gandhi was now confident using that office, sure of her hold over the party, its funds, and its strategies. And she had beside her, as the second most powerful person in India, her younger son Sanjay. He was high on drive and low in compunctions. He had clout, with no questions asked about how he used it.

I was in a secure government job. But the salary was small. Our needs were nowhere near extravagant, but by the second week of the month, Tara, ever prudent, would say softly, 'money over'. She had to be and was wan. Amma, ever philosophic, would add her meagre savings to my modest earnings. She was weary. Hameedia, the neighbourhood department store, would cheerfully maintain a credit account for us, knowing we would pay up. But now we placed orders on the phone hesitatingly. Tara said let us stop this buying on credit. Let us pay on the spot. That way, we will know at least when to stop. But what was one to do when the wallet was all but empty and the rice and flour jars had emptied?

The previous year, the name Yom Kippur would have evoked distant images of a desert but not war. Now, reading war news sitting in Madras, its battle read like something from the Old Testament. Sinai was a faraway desert. But the oil parching that followed hit us in the gut. By March 1974, the price of oil had risen nearly 300 per cent globally and had caused the 'first oil shock'. This meant that petrol was now unaffordable. We stopped our credit account at the neighbourhood petrol bunk. We paid each time we filled the tank, litre by litre.

Bernard Weinraub wrote in the *New York Times* on 20 January 1974: 'The rising cost of oil imports places India in a bleak position as the nation is beset by inflation, political dissension, lagging growth, a spiralling population and unchecked poverty. In the aftermath of the decision by Persian Gulf nations to double the posted price of crude oil, the Indian Government remains torn by uncertainty about 1974. Food production—a key to India's stability—is expected to drop at least three million tons during the spring harvest because of the rising oil price... The cost of kerosene—the main cooking fuel—has climbed more than 50 per cent in the last two months, while gasoline prices have risen 80 per cent...Fewer cars are seen on the streets of New Delhi and Bombay, and many businessmen and civil servants are using buses for the first time.'

So, when news came of Jayaprakash Narayan comparing 1974 to 1942 and giving a call to youth to enter politics, something stirred in many young hearts. Gujarat's youth, sick of mistakes in governance and corruption in power, revolted en masse. They demanded the resignation of the then Congress chief minister Chimanbhai Patel (1929–94). A movement by the name Nav Nirman—a New Reinvention, but really signifying a New Awakening—gripped Gujarat. The rise in cost of living made those who were older seethe as they saw their young sons and daughters being arrested and fired upon. More than a hundred were killed in the outrage. And 1,000 to 3,000 were injured, and 8,000 were arrested. By March, public fury in Gujarat had reached such heights that Indira Gandhi was forced to get Chimanbhai to resign and suspend the state assembly. But she imposed President's Rule and delayed calling elections she feared she would lose. And then the rage looped over the Hindi heartland and landed in Bihar to convulse that state governed by a Congress ministry headed by a Chimanbhai equivalent in Abdul Ghafoor.

JP's wife, Prabhavati, had died the previous year. She was no automatic follower of his. She had a mind of her own, largely conditioned by Gandhi and could criticize her husband's position whenever she wanted to. And she was, often, a check on his more impulsive ideas and plans. But they were inseparable. JP had written to me in response to my letter condoling Prabhavati's demise: '...the truth is that there is nothing to console me. I have lost all interest in life, and whatever I do is only as a duty performed.'

But that 'lost interest in life' was now back in full strength, and his sense of 'duty performed' was now reaching its crest.

JP came to head a propulsion of which he said to milling youth in Patna on 5 June: 'We have to go far, very far.... You will have to make sacrifices, undergo suffering....' On 1 November, he took the struggle to Delhi. At a mass meeting in the national capital, he said Indira was no democrat. Back in Patna on 4 November, he led a 'historic march' from a jeep to paralyse the work of corrupt ministers. While being physically separated from thousands who were following him, shouting 'Lok Nayak Jayaprakash Zindabad', a two-metre lathi struck the seventy-two-year-old. JP lost consciousness. Union home minister Brahmananda Reddy (1909–94) said there had been no lathi-charge on JP, who had merely suffered a slight finger injury in a melee. 'Lying in state' acquired a new meaning.

Jayaprakash Narayan leading a protest procession against Indira Gandhi's government near Delhi's Red Fort, 1974. Behind him in another vehicle is farmers' leader Chaudhuri Charan Singh. (*Hindustan Times* archives).

When public disenchantment grows, it is natural for governments, especially when led by strong ego-driven persons, to offer enchantments as a counter. And a reliable enchanter is nationalism. Indira Gandhi in 1974 needed badly to enchant India. And she did it by an intelligent step: On 18 May, she conducted India's first nuclear test in Pokhran, Rajasthan. It was, of course, true to the prevailing style and culture of politics, called a 'peaceful nuclear explosion'. Her formidable adviser, Haksar, in an interview to *Blitz*, the Bombay tabloid which was backing her unreservedly, justified the test as something done as a step in the 'advances of science and technology'.[1] But the test was seen by India and the world as a bomb test. In 1997, Raja Ramanna (1925–2004), speaking to the PTI, would maintain: 'The Pokhran test was a bomb, I can tell you now.... An explosion is an explosion, a gun is a gun, whether you shoot at someone or shoot at the ground...' By now the former chairman of the Atomic Research Commission (1983–87) and secretary of the Department of Atomic Energy (1983–87) was a member of the Rajya Sabha, and being philosophic was befitting.

Pokhran-I revived Indira Gandhi's sagging popularity, exactly as the 1971 war had done. But one man was not taken in. Krishna Menon, ill and in hospital, sent for Indira Gandhi and 'reportedly gave her more than a bit of his mind'.[2] The old-time disarmament ideologue was to die on 6 October that very year.

Sucheta Kripalani, one of Gandhi's associates and the great Acharya's wife, was a political figure in her own right. And she was, with her husband but even more than him, a family friend. I had, over the years, been in correspondence with her over things of importance and of no importance. I wrote to her in May about the state of our politics and JP's move. I got a lively pen-picture from her in a letter dated 5 June 1974, which also contained a remarkable prescience about what was to happen the following year: 'He (JP) is now fully involved in the Bihar movement. I understand that the movement has penetrated even the rural areas. So, no one can say what dimensions it can assume. The CPI and the Government are trying to meet this upsurge in the worst possible way. One has to wait and watch with anxiety. Of course, Mrs Gandhi's luck is still holding. The nuclear blast has given her a few feathers. She can win another election with that!'[3]

That was Sucheta's last letter to me. Six months later, on 1 December 1974, she was gone. She was only sixty-six.

Three touches of grace redeemed the year for us.

First, the Magsaysay Award for Public Service that year went to MS. We were thrilled beyond measure. She had got the recognition she deserved as one who had committed her phenomenal artistry to the public weal, as her biographer and my closest friend Keshav Desiraju was to say[4] the only other Indian to have got that coveted award till that point in the category of Public Service was Jayaprakash Narayan.

Second, my brother Rajmohan got married to Usha Chandiram in Delhi, at a beautiful ceremony. Acharya Kripalani attended it, as did George Fernandes, staying throughout the ceremony. Few couples have been as fortunate in one another and as naturally meant for each other as Mohan and Usha. This was more than the start of married life. In all the amazing books on Indian and American history that Mohan has authored, Usha has been a vital participant, partnering his thoughts and offering critical and always valuable assistance. Mohan and Usha, each separately, are sui generis. Together, even more so.

Third, Tara and I were blessed with our first child. The arrival was due in the first week of October. The Bangalore obstetrician planning a Caesarean section said, 'Why not let the baby come on 2 October, Gandhiji's birthday?' 'No,' said Tara emphatically. 'If the birth was to take place naturally on 2 October, that would be a different matter... But to contrive it to coincide... No!' And so, Divya arrived on her own pathway on 1 October.

1975
LIFE NORMAL IN DELHI

'One has to wait and watch with anxiety,' Sucheta Kripalani had written to me. That was on 5 June 1974. She was referring to the political scene in India, post JP's Bihar movement and the measures being taken by Indira Gandhi to suppress it and muzzle Jayaprakash's resounding voice. She was prescient.

The violence unleashed by uniformed forces on wholly peaceful demonstrators in Patna and Calcutta and elsewhere had horrified the nation. When the forces did not themselves do the hitting and kicking, they watched goons do that, mute. In JP's words: 'Take the Calcutta incident of April 2. While thousands of hooligans milled around my car, hit it with sticks, reducing its sunshade to smithereens, and some of them got up on the hood and others on the roof and jumped and danced on it, badly damaging it, the police looked on disinterestedly...I could have been killed...I am sure this kind of thing could not have happened without the clearance of the Chief Minister and also of Mrs. Gandhi....'[1]

At a very simple and quiet dinner hosted in Madras by Rajmohan, Kamaraj was the honoured guest. Amma had made sambar-sadam[*] for Kamaraj, which he ate with relish, praising it. He spoke as always little, but he spoke, again as always, what he thought, straight. 'What do you feel, sir, about JP's movement?' Mohan asked. 'He is fighting against corruption,' Kamaraj answered. That is a good thing. I like it. I support that.' Earlier in the conversation, Mohan had asked the veteran as to who he had stood behind in the Nehru-Patel binary. 'Nehuru...' he replied, investing the first prime minister's name with a Tamil augmentation that gave it an ineffable new weight.

That something was going to happen, something sinister, could be felt by many after Gujarat had routed the Congress in its assembly elections, despite hectic campaigning there by Indira Gandhi dressed in Gujarati-style sari *and also* describing herself as a 'daughter-in-law of Gujarat'.[†] And then, as the last result from Gujarat came in, came the Allahabad High Court judgment on 12 June in which Justice Jagmohanlal Sinha (1920–2008) indicted her on

[*]A dish of rice mixed with dal in the Tamil sambar style.

[†]Her husband, the late Feroze Gandhi, a Parsi based in Allahabad, arguably knew his Gujarati but would never have claimed to be a son of Gujarat.

two corruption charges in the conduct of her own 1971 election, which she had won. He declared the election invalid and debarred her from holding political office for six years.

This was a blow to her rule, to her style of governance. The chief ministers of Haryana, Punjab, and Uttar Pradesh were asked to flood Delhi with party supporters to march to the prime minister's house to demonstrate their solidarity. And indeed, on that afternoon of 12 June, a cheering crowd of her loyalists, albeit bussed to the site, chanted 'Death to Justice Sinha', and she obliged it by making three appearances before it, pledging her determination to 'stand by the people'.

Something was bound to happen.

On 26 June 1975, I was sitting in the cool of my tree-hugged first-floor room* in the Tamil Nadu Archives in Egmore, Madras, working at the compilation of the *Pudukkottai District Gazetteer*, when a visitor told me that a national Emergency had been declared just before midnight the previous night and JP had been arrested, along with Morarji Desai, and a host of opposition leaders. The horror of it all was not manifest yet, as power lines to newspaper offices in the capital had been cut, making news transmission impossible.

That evening, the Madras edition of *Indian Express* ran its first censored front page deftly. 'Emergency is Proclaimed' screamed its banner headline. 'JP, Morarji, and other Opposition leaders arrested', said the line below it. No censor could object to that. But what the newspaper said wordlessly is what mattered. It carried a large photograph of JP smiling and doing a namaskar. It was as if he was bidding his friends in freedom farewell. I have not forgotten that front page of *Indian Express*.

The Hindu reported the promulgation of the Emergency only on 27 June. Rereading that page nearly forty-nine years on, I can see how odd the reportage was. G. K. Reddy (1923–87), master reporter and then chief of bureau at *The Hindu*'s New Delhi office, had a banner-headline front page story that said blandly 'President Proclaims National Emergency' with a smaller line that said 'Preventive Arrests: Press Censorship Imposed', leaving everything to the readers' imagination. A 'deep and widespread conspiracy' was mentioned by Reddy as the cause for the measure. A box item said, 'Life Normal in Delhi'. Only a determinedly discerning reader would have made out from the small print in the story that its body contradicted the headline by saying that several dailies had failed to come out on 26 June because of a power failure on Bahadur Shah Zafar Marg (where the office

*I was at the time the editor, *Gazetteers*, Government of Tamil Nadu.

of *Indian Express* was located). And it was through *The Hindu* of that day that I came to know of the existence of a gentleman I had never heard of before—Dr A. R. Baji, principal information officer. He had become, perhaps unwillingly, the government's mouthpiece. *The Hindu* quoted Dr Baji extensively on that page including in one story towards the bottom of the page that was headlined '676 Persons Detained all Over the Country'. The item said, 'He however declined to disclose the names of those arrested. He said the leaders were being looked after well.'

Another small front-page story in *The Hindu* of 27 June said 'Press Censorship for the First Time' with the first line inside saying it all: 'The Press in India has come under censorship for the first time since Independence'.

But it did not take long for bits and pieces of news to trickle in. JP, having been woken up at 3 a.m. and marched off to a waiting jeep, came to be known as did his now famous parting words: Vinash kale viparit buddhi (As one's nemesis nears, the intellect turns turtle).

Kamaraj was shaken. At Sholinghur, on 27 June, he said, 'I am shocked... leaders have been arrested...The radio does not give correct news... newspapers also are not giving correct news...Such an event has no parallel even under British rule...' The next day at Tiruvellore, he continued in the same strain '...I feel as though I have been left in the jungle blindfolded. I cannot visualize the consequences of the Emergency....'[2]

Tamil Nadu was ruled then by the DMK, and its chief minister Karunanidhi had fought the 1971 elections, as we have seen, as an ally of the Indira Congress. But now, things had changed for the DMK chief. On 12 July, he addressed a mass meeting on the Marina sands in Madras and, saying there was neither an internal nor external threat to India and, therefore, no cause for an emergency, called upon his audience to defend the nation's freedom.

On 2 October, in Delhi, took place a little play of power. It was the first Gandhi Jayanti in the India under Emergency. As usual, the state's dramatis personae—the president, vice president, and prime minister dutifully and artfully went to Rajghat and offered their genuflections to the spirit of the Father of the Nation. A small group of independent-minded persons sought permission to hold a prayer meeting that afternoon at the same site. This was to be a prayer meeting; no politics was involved, they said, and got the permission to so meet. Those attending included the intrepid Acharya Kripalani, the Gandhian leader Dr Sushila Nayar, and my brothers Rajmohan and Ramchandra.

Permission had been granted, but police were taking no chances. They kept vigil as the prayer proceeded. Towards its close, Kripalani turned to face the gathering and speak a few words about the Mahatma. Police immediately came up to him and asked him to stop.

'Why, why?'

'No speech allowed.'

'But I am not going to make a speech, only a discourse on Bapu...'

'Not allowed...'

Unfazed, he continued. Police moved to intervene physically. Sushila Nayar then spoke up.

'I am a doctor...I am telling you Kripalaniji is an elderly person...You should not touch him...'

The police hesitated. And then began picking up others, starting with my brothers. As Rajmohan and Ramchandra were being marched off, Kripalaniji was heard muttering... 'There is a saying in Sindhi that when a witch goes through a street destroying everything, she leaves one house untouched so as to have something for her next visit...I am that one being left out...'

Mohan and Ramu were taken to the Daryaganj police station. They had no idea then as to how long their detention was to be. Maybe hours, maybe years. Ramu recalled that among others detained, there was a small-time trader. He pleaded with the daroga to be let off. 'I was only watching...I am a supporter of Indiraji...Not only a supporter but a funder...I met Bhagatji only the other day and handed over a thaili*....'

The news managed, despite all censorship, to spread. Our cousin Sumitra Kulkarni (b. 1929), then a Congress (I) MP, heard it and, with her family-bond pulsing in her veins, rang Om Mehta (1927–1992), the minister of state for Home Affairs. 'Om, you have to release my brothers. And right now.' He must have consulted madam, who must have sensed that arresting the grandsons of Gandhi from the site of cremation was not exactly in her interest. They were freed later that evening.

But Madras experienced something it had not expected. Kamaraj, like so many, heard the news, and it did something to him, something deep and unfathomable. He was silent for a long time, and then, tired and troubled, turned in. Within a short while, a heart attack carried him away, in his sleep, to the sleep that knows no waking.

Amma and I, accompanied by Periamma, motored at once to his home. The stalwart Congressman, loyal Gandhian, amazingly efficient administrator and the man who had on two occasions saved India from the jaws of political insecurity caused by the deaths of Prime Minister Nehru and Shastri was laid out on the simple red oxide floor of his austere home. A garland of

*A pouch generally and, here, a pouch full of cash.

hand-spun yarn had been placed on his chest. People were just coming in with flowers. Some incense was sending out a gentle aroma. Lakshmi, the late great S. Satyamurti's daughter, who had been snapped in the famous photograph in Avadi with Nehru and later fought unsuccessfully on a Janata Dal ticket from south Madras for the Lok Sabha, was there, stunned. The coincidence of Kamaraj's going on the Mahatma's birth anniversary was spoken of as sublime.

But the conversation was soft, almost in whispers. We were under an Emergency.

1976
WALLS ACQUIRE EARS, SPEECH DISAPPEARS

By the time the first New Year in the Emergency dawned, Indira Gandhi's dictatorship seemed to have become part of India's destiny. Those who clung to the hopes and ideals of the Republic saw it not as part of the 'tryst' Nehru had spoken of but a cruel and vicious twist in it.

That JP was ill had come to be known. When I learnt that he had been moved to Chandigarh, first to a guest house and then to the intensive care ward of the Post-Graduate Institute of Medical Sciences and Research there, I worried that he would be basically under the 'care' of Bansi Lal, one of Indira Gandhi's deft wielders of the hatchet. And when I gathered further that JP's 'jailer' was M. G. Devasahayam (b. 1940), my gutsy fellow trainee at the National Academy of Administration, Mussoorie, I was not assured. Deva had been in the army, and I knew him to be a 'strong' administrator. I assumed he would be the kind of jailer Indira would want for her chief prisoner. It was only much later that I learnt that what happened, in fact, was altogether different.

As JP's health continued to slide, Deva drew close to his charge. JP had been in what was, in practical terms, solitary confinement. Deva was his only thought partner from outside the world of doctors, nurses, and policemen. And it was on Deva's persistent reporting of the prisoner's medical condition that he had been shifted to Jaslok Hospital, Bombay, to be treated by the eminent nephrologist Dr M. K. Mani, who virtually saved his life.

By the end of 1975, Indira Gandhi had understood that JP dying in jail or in hospital would do her incalculable harm. On 25 December, JP left Jaslok Hospital for his Patna home. Tied to a dialysis machine and isolated, but he was now at least not in jail. And true to style, he started planning action, and a Janata party began evolving in his mind.

Morarji Desai, locked up in a guest house in Haryana, ate frugally and cautiously, read, wrote, and spun khadi. He also taught some of his guards Hindi and English and remained his essential self. Asked by a minion on behalf of the prime minister if he would sign a paper retiring from politics for life in return for freedom, Desai showed the man the door.

For us in Madras, the year 1976 started traumatically. Chief Minister Karunanidhi had resisted the Emergency's impact on his state for some seven months and, as one who had backed JP's movement, had allied with JP's Janata Party initiative. Until his administration was ousted on 31 January 1976. Karunanidhi was a supporter of JP's anti-Emergency campaign and had expressed his support for JP's Janata Party. Fifty days remained for his government's tenure to end when, on 31 January 1976, he was dismissed.

At an event at Don Bosco School that day, he said, 'Most likely, this would be my final public function as chief minister.' He was out before he even got home from the function. As many as about 25,000 members of the party were imprisoned. His relative Murasoli Maran and his son M. K. Stalin were among them. The state was now under President's Rule.

The civil service is never wanting in the reflexes of adjustment. Before you could say ayyo, you were now in the new era. The Governor K. K. Shah (1908–86), switched from his cloying declarations of affection for Karunanidhi to syrupy obsequiousness to Indira Gandhi, and led the change. Chief Secretary P. Sabanayagam, a veteran of sound governance, was moved out. But something else happened, almost as if by default, which I welcomed. Two advisers to the governor were appointed, both from the IAS. They were virtually the new chief ministers of the state. One of them was P. K. Dave (1923–2006). A man of great integrity and sheer class, he brought to the state not just experience but also professional elan. Refusing to move to a 'bungalow', he opted to stay in the state guest house—almost as if to say the Emergency and President's Rule are, by definition, temporary arrangements. On the other adviser, R. V. Subramaniam, I will expend no words.

At a meeting he called of senior officers and heads of department, Dave gave us a reasoned, measured sense of what is involved in the governance of a state under the President's Rule. Most officials were sombre of mood, cautious of demeanour. Some, of course, were obsequious. One very upright and independent officer, under whom I had been privileged to serve, B. Vijayaraghavan (1936–2023), asked a question of Dave. 'Sir,' he said, 'we have served the government of Mr Karunanidhi for the last five years. It would only be natural for us to want to pay courtesy calls on the former CM and ministers and bid them farewell. Can we be permitted to do so?' Dave did not take more than a moment to reply. 'Yes, you may all do so. But make your calls brief.'

I was director of rehabilitation for much of that period, working with repatriates from Sri Lanka and Burma. And my department came under the charge of P. K. Dave. I could not have been luckier. He grasped the nuances of the repatriates' problem in a trice and gave me far greater support by way of intelligent engagement, I must say here, than I could have received from politicians. The Emergency was evil, and the President's Rule was unwarranted. But Dave was the best thing that could have happened to the state's administration.

On 15 February, Indira Gandhi came to the city on her first visit to the state during the Emergency and addressed a mammoth meeting on the Marina Beach. It was called a Unity Meet, meant to unite the different sections of the state Congress post Kamaraj. Everyone knew what Kamaraj thought of the Emergency, but he was not there! And as a garlanded portrait of his adorned the stage, the angels of truth must have laughed and wept in turns. *India Today* described the meeting thus: 'It was as if the entire population of the Madras metropolis had emptied itself on the sands of Marina Beach. In a mammoth gathering, the likes of which the city has not seen in recent years, over one million people thronged Marina Beach here on the evening of February 15 to hear Prime Minister Indira Gandhi.'[1]

Certain things even Dave could not avert. Officers are not expected to be at political meetings or rallies. But we were obliged to witness this great occasion by perching ourselves on the sprawling terrace of the Police Commissioner's Office by the sands. Her shrill voice beaming through loudspeakers is part of my stock of unfavourite memories, which just does not go away.

Governor K. K. Shah, to popular relief, ended his tenure on 16 June 1976 and was succeeded by the seasoned Rajasthan political leader Mohanlal Sukhadia, whose naturally aristocratic bearing and calm temperament were a welcome change. Sukhadia sahib was fond of his paan, and a paandaan would always be placed before him at meetings, including meetings with senior officials. He, of course, knew no Tamil, but he knew administration, having been chief minister. Governor Sukhadia and his adviser, P. K. Dave were like unintended sheaves of whole grain in a field of poisonous weeds that the Emergency was.

Attendance at government offices was punctual, prim, and proper. No one stretched lunch hour, no one loitered. And, of course, since walls had acquired ears, all tongues disappeared from corners. Files moved fast, just as trains ran more on time than before. All this was most agreeable to the public, and many said quite honestly, they hoped President's Rule in the state would last forever. But others, more discerning, knew that 'Law and Order' went together and that Order without Law was autocracy, not democracy.

Taking advantage of a constitutional provision which allowed the government to postpone elections to parliament for a year at a time, Indira Gandhi had got the elections due in March 1976 postponed by a year. That year, like a 'gap' year taken by students between school and college, was used by her to do as she pleased with the institutions and conventions of democracy. And, of course, not just by her but by her son Sanjay, who was seen by all her ministers and chief ministers as a deputy prime minister and by some as a super prime minister. His family planning drive involving the vasectomy of thousands of men and tubal ligation of women, either for payment or under coercive conditions, had become, for the government, a priority programme and, for the people, a nightmare. Seven million males were sterilized in 1976 against the pre-Emergency 'standard' target of 4.3 million for the year, according to government statistics.[2] What was a salutary programme much needed by a developing country became associated with coercion and official terrorizing.

And police excesses—to use a shameless euphemism—were an unceasing orgy. MISA, the dreaded abbreviation of the Maintenance of Internal Security Act, which had been promulgated through an Ordinance by President Ahmed on 29 June, allowed anyone to be detained without grounds needing to be produced and then no bail being given. Draconian! MISA was to be repealed in 1977, but the MISA effect could not be reversed, and the Republic of India today has other coercive enactments like the Conservation of Foreign Exchange and Prevention of Smuggling Activities Act (COFEPOSA) enacted on 13 December 1974 to prevent smuggling and black-marketing in foreign exchange is still enforced. Controversial successors to such legislation include the National Security Act (1980), the Terrorism and Disruptive Activities (Prevention) Act (TADA, 1985–1995), and the Prevention of Terrorism Act (POTA, 2002), all of which are regularly and fruitlessly criticized for authorizing excessive powers without balancing safeguards for civil freedoms.

On 10 June, after evading the police by disguising himself as a Sikh, a sadhu, and a mendicant, among others, and moving from private home to private home in quick succession, which included that of our family well-wisher Chandrachudan, in New Delhi, George Fernandes, long-time trade unionist and strident critic of Indira Gandhi, was arrested in Calcutta. And then subjected to barbarisms which came to be known to the outside world only much later. But the fact of his arrest leaked out, causing an uproar in socialist circles the world over. He was being subjected to treatment he was to describe as one 'no human being should have', in Delhi's Red Fort when Willy Brandt, then chairman of the German Social Democratic Party, Bruno Kreisky, federal chancellor of Austria, Olof Palme, prime minister of Sweden issued a statement[*] asking Indira Gandhi to reconsider what she was doing. Fernandes would say later that, but for the global reaction, he would have been done away with, and no one would have known.

---

[*]16 June 1976.

The diplomat Muhammed Yunus (1916–2001), and at that time boss at the *National Herald*, visited Madras in the middle of November 1976. In the prime minister's inner circle during the Emergency, the gentleman spoke at Rajaji Hall to an invited audience, which included us, miserable officers, on India's place in world affairs. He spoke menacingly about the Western media, crudely about just about everything else. We heard him in silence. *The Hindu* of 17 November reported his description of Western media as 'rotten, corrupt and dishonest'. Speaking of the new news agency *Samachar*, which had just started, he said there were four news agencies in India which were 'competing with each other in incompetence'. *The Hindu* very cautiously gave prominent billing to the speech. But by quoting him liberally in the five-column wide story, the newspaper did what the censor could not understand: it made Yunus look the bully he was. *Indian Express* described another speech of his to the city's Press Club as follows: 'In a 70-minute heated speech, punctuated with the use of words like "wretched", "stupid", "cheat", and "foul", Mr Yunus singled out the press in the U.K, the U.S.A and West Germany.'[3] Doubtless, the censor thought the report was 'positive'.

And in the same month, November, Indira Gandhi announced a further year's postponement. Gagged, the press could hardly comment, much less object.

1977
EPIPHANY

The Lok Sabha's life had been extended up to the summer of 1978, and Congressmen were talking of a perpetuity of Indira Raj. 'Mere elections,' Y. B. Chavan (1913–84), the minister for External Affairs, had loftily declared on 2 November 1976, 'are not democracy.'[1] But things were not going well for Indira Gandhi. Rumblings of discontent with her and Sanjay and their 'unshakable rule' were being heard by her occasionally.

Occasionally? Right. Censorship had effectively cut her off from public opinion, and the rule of fear and sycophancy had clogged all arteries of the truth, the real truth, from reaching her. When her cousin B. K. Nehru's wife, the frank-speaking Fori Nehru, told the prime minister about some of the horrors of Sanjay's family planning outrages, she actually broke down and said, 'No one tells me anything. What shall I do? What shall I do?'[2]

But she could not remain ignorant of the bad press she was getting overseas.

Prime Minister Bhutto had called elections in Pakistan. Would that not make her government lose sheen, such sheen as it had not lost, with observers abroad?

In any case, she desired appreciation, applause, validation, and legitimacy abroad. The 'foreign hand' was her bete noire or her feigned bete noire. But the foreign press was something she worried about.

She was also getting a sense of her own loyalists in the party talking behind her back. One of them said that they fear even their 'whispers' may reach her, but not 'what we are thinking'. And this she sensed. She was sharp.

And then the economic scene was worsening. This portended ill.

Pupul Jayakar (1915–97) says Indira met the philosopher Jiddu Krishnamurti (1895–1986) in 1976. 'Right action is necessary,' he advised her.[3] She had acquired a twitch in her left eye, clearly a nervous phenomenon. Journalist and biographer Sagarika Ghose suggests Krishnamurti offered to help her get over it.[4]

And she did have her astrologers. Any one or more of them might have said the time was propitious for her. Go for it. Perhaps her sleuths told her the same thing. It was safe for them to do so. One, it was something she would have liked to hear from them. Two, it was something that could well happen—who can tell with the Indian voter?—and if so, their luck was in. Three, if she lost, she would, well, have lost and would be able to do nothing to them for their wrong counsel. Convincing her she would win was a safe bet. Safe as can be.

If the lead time from the announcement to the elections was kept small, she would reckon, the jail-weary opposition would not be able to organize itself.

And so, not everyone was stunned when, on 18 January, she announced elections. They would be held in March.

With this, political prisoners were to be released. What a gamble.

~

On 30 January, Gandhi's martyrdom day, the Janata Party formed by JP called a meeting at Ramlila Grounds, the very venue where JP and Morarji had addressed the fateful meeting hours before the Emergency was declared. This time, the meeting mourned those who had died in jails during the Emergency months. Gandhi has a way of turning up!

In three days flat, Babu Jagjivan Ram (1908–86), one of Indira's senior ministers and a Congress veteran, announced he was leaving the Congress. Jagjivan Ram leaving the Congress! That was big. The gamble seemed to be going badly for her. Very significantly for us in our family, Sumitra left the Congress and joined Jagjivan Ram.

More rallies of Janata drew larger and larger crowds. And at the most famous of them all, JP thundered, quoting Ramdhari Singh Dinkar's Hindi poem, 'Sinhasan khali karo ki Janata aage aayi hai' (Quit your throne, for here come the people).

'When you stamp your vote,' he said, you will also stamp your's and the country's fate.'

The government's nervousness was becoming evident by its preventing transport from reaching the meeting venue and—hilariously—the televizing of a popular Hindi film, Raj Kapoor's *Bobby*, at the same time as the meeting. The crowds came regardless.

George Fernandes, not yet released from jail in the Baroda Dynamite case, decided to contest the Muzaffarpur seat in Bihar. He won, in absentia, by an over 300,000 vote margin from jail.

On 20 March, Amma, Tara, and I heard the Lok Sabha results over AIR non-stop. The first result to come was from Tamil Nadu, and it was of C. Subramaniam, Indira's finance minister. He had won. So, the first result was in her favour. Sitting in her small garden with the transistor radio in front of her, Amma closed her eyes and said a prayer in Hindi: Bigdi banane vale Ram, meri bigdi bana de. (Ram, mender of adversities, mend this adversity for me). Her prayer was not in vain. Result after result, coming thereafter, showed the decimation of the Congress in the north; only the south stood by Indira.

Late in the day, as late as it could possibly be stretched, AIR conceded the defeat of Indira Gandhi herself in her Rae Bareli constituency at the hands of the socialist Raj Narain, whose petition before the Allahabad High Court had gone against her, starting the whole chain of events. We were all delirious with joy.

The dictator now turned democrat, and after a meeting of her defeated cabinet, went and gave her resignation to Acting President B. D. Jatti (1912–2002).

Pupul Jayakar, known not inaccurately as India's 'cultural Czarina' and also a thinker, writer, and friend of the Nehru-Gandhis, went to the prime minister's forlorn house that night. 'Pupul,' Indira said to her, 'I have lost.' And Rajiv, standing nearby, muttered, 'I will never forgive Sanjay for having brought Mummy to this position. He is responsible.'[5]

The next day in my office, the staff which had, I could see, voted Congress looked gloomy. 'It is a shock,' said Venkataraman, one of my ablest colleagues. 'A welcome shock,' I responded, shocking him even more. I went to Fort St. George, the Tamil Nadu government's secretariat. My senior by many years and an officer I respected greatly, K. V. Ramanathan (1928–2015), seeing me cross his room called out and asked me to step in. 'What a great result, Gopal. Look at UP. She has not got a single seat there. Not one. That is democracy.'

An admirable thing happened in the city that day.

Governor Sukhadia, the principled man of honour that he was, had been getting the teleprinter reports of the results the whole of the 20th. As soon as Indira's defeat was announced, he sent for his secretary and told him he was resigning. Letter signed, he asked for his car and drove out to the airport. He was not going to stay in Raj Bhavan for another minute. His personal effects could follow.

The Emergency was officially withdrawn on 21 March. Dave immediately packed his small bag at the state Guest House and left. There were no more than half a dozen officials to see off the departing adviser, to whom cloying deference had been shown until only the previous week. Those present comprised mainly those who had never genuflected before the man who was now being carried off by a hissing train to his next post of honest duty.

Family ties going back several decades, Morarji's becoming prime minister was a matter of special value to us. During the interregnum between his becoming PM and moving into the PM's official residence, work took me to Delhi. It was natural that I should seek a call on him. But I was unsure of both logistics and protocol. I knew he had not yet moved into the PM's house, but I assumed that all the paraphernalia of staff and accoutrement would have shifted to him, and so, looking up the telephone book, I dialled the prime minister's residential number. After about four or five rings, a woman's voice came on the line.

Hello.

There was no mistaking the voice. But I asked: Pradhan mantriji ka nivas?

Nahin came the answer in a severe tone. Not stiff, not rude, just severe.

Galat number.

And before I could mumble 'Sorry, madam' or some such inanity, the receiver was put down emphatically.

She was not prime minister now. Her house, where her staff had shrunk, and she was now clearly answering phone calls herself, was no longer that of the prime minister. She was only a resident in transition.

But she was still Indira. Indira Nehru Gandhi.

Indira Gandhi's aunt Vijaya Lakshmi Pandit, who had opposed the Emergency and campaigned against her niece and the Congress during the 1977 elections, was ironically enough, deeply saddened by her niece's defeat at Rae Bareli. Mrs Pandit's daughter Nayantara Sahgal in fact writes that, when Vijaya Lakshmi heard the Rae Bareli verdict, she wept. Four months later, she went to Indira, who was literally shaking and broke down. When they sat down to talk, Indira said, 'What can I say?'[6]

'Don't say anything,' replied the aunt.

After the tortuous Emergency and vile abuses of power, the people of India had sent her back to the unlit alleys of 'ground-level' politics. She had taken away their powers. Now, they took away hers. She was not a prime minister now. Not even a prime minister's daughter. But she was Nehru's daughter and that of India. With her power gone, but with all the rights of a citizen secure. And her sense of duties as well. A sense she was going to use.

And the chance to do so, dramatically, came very soon.

On 27 May, the anniversary of her father's death, eleven villagers of Belchhi in Bihar were brutally murdered by a gang from the Kurmi/Bhumihar caste. This was classic caste warfare, in which the victims included eight Dalits and three Sunar. The human being and the politician in Indira were stirred. She resolved to go to the scene of the violence at once. The weather was against her, and the local administration unfriendly. But would she care? She said she would wade through ankle-deep and knee-deep water if no vehicles would take the road. When even that became difficult, and someone suggested an elephant as a possible 'vehicle', she said she had been on an elephant back before and would go on one. Moti, a local pachyderm, soon appeared, and there she was, on top of the bewildered beast and on top of the situation. She had travelled multi-mode to a spectacular comeback—by train, jeep, a tractor, and finally on elephant-back.

The kin of the carnage's victims were overwhelmed, her adversaries overcome. But she had not finished. In Patna, on her return trip, she stopped by at JP's home. His cynical jailer, who had sneered at his request for some human company while in custody at the hospital and said he needed none since he had doctors and nurses around him, was now his guest. And he, of course, it does not have to be said, was the ideal host, letting media photograph them and wishing her a 'bright future'. He need not have bothered. The future, at least in the short term, was going to be bright for her.

Indira had started her comeback with panache.

Tamil Nadu was not going to oblige the Indira-baiters in the elections to the state assembly, which took place in the summer. MGR's AIADMK trounced Karunanidhi's DMK in the first elections that MGR fought. And defeated it resoundingly. On 30 June, MGR was sworn in as chief minister of Tamil Nadu, becoming the first film actor to be the chief minister of an Indian state. And while being canny enough to seek good ties with the Desai government, he was not going to ignore Indira Gandhi.

By the end of 1977, Indira was becoming a force again. On 3 October, Home Minister Charan Singh (1902–87) had Indira Gandhi arrested from her 12 Willingdon Crescent residence. And why? Because, the charge said, during the election just concluded, she misused her position to get jeeps for election campaigns and another charge about a contract between the ONGC and the French oil company CFP. Nothing could have been more absurd. And nothing more suitable—more propitious—for her. She entered the police van on her own terms, taking her own time to get ready, demanding that she be handcuffed (photographers, she knew, were waiting) and then getting garlanded among slogans hailing her. After lawyers stopped her convoy from proceeding to Haryana, Indira was brought back to Delhi and interned in its Police Lines. She had a sense of the moment. She retired for the night in her cell without any fuss and made it known next morning that she had slept with nothing disturbing her state of peace. The magistrate before whom she appeared—God bless India's independent magistrates!—released her, stating that there was no evidence to back up the arrest. Indira's arrest by her former prisoners, now in power, was a botched affair. Charan Singh, to be fair to him, did offer to resign, but Morarji Desai—God bless his magnanimity—did not accept it.

1978
A LITTLE INDIA IN SRI LANKA

India had a new prime minister as the year began, and Tamil Nadu a new chief minister.

My Rehabilitation Directorate, which was aided by the centre with funds for the welfare of Tamils returning under India's bilateral agreements with Sri Lanka, was now under a new minister at the centre. And a new minister in the state. P. T. Saraswathy (1935–2009) was new to office-holding but settled into the routine of administration well. She knew, I am sure, that though her leader, our new CM, MGR, did not speak too often or too loud of his birth, the fact was that he was born in Kandy in Sri Lanka. And Kandy was where India's High Commission in Sri Lanka had an office dealing with prospective repatriates.

MGR had a sense of the repatriates' needs as only he could have. This was a great advantage to me as Director of Rehabilitation. Another advantage was that the union secretary of the Ministry of Rehabilitation was none other than P. Sabanayagam, formerly chief secretary of Tamil Nadu and my very steady, if also very strict, well-wisher.

On a visit to Madras in early 1978, Sabanayagam asked me: 'Gopal, Sunder Raj in our Kandy office is finishing his term. Will you go in his place?' I had done a little over a year in the directorate and this was placing a big trust in me. I knew I was getting something big, and said, 'Thank you, sir. Yes, I would like that very much.'

Tara was thrilled. She deserved relief from the humdrumness of being the wife of a junior administrator and a slave of his routine. I was now not just shifting jobs but moving from the control of the state to that of the centre and moving from the orbit of the Ministry of Home Affairs, which controlled the IAS, to that of the Ministry of External Affairs, which controlled all India's missions abroad. I was also changing my official persona by ceasing, awhile, from being an administrator to becoming a diplomat. (I was to be designated first secretary in the Assistant High Commission in Kandy.)

I had been working in Madras with the repatriates who had come from Sri Lanka in terms of the Indo-Ceylon Agreement of 1964 signed by Prime Minister Shastri and Sri Lanka's Prime Minister Sirimavo Bandaranaike, under which 525,000 persons with their 'natural increase' were to come to India leaving 300,000 with their natural increase to stay back. Now, I was to work with the same population that was still there and on its way to a home they did not know as home and to which they were to return by an agreement signed over their heads by two prime ministers in their bilateral wisdom.

I went to Delhi to pick up my orders, my briefings, and my bearings. This was exciting, but Thomas Abraham (1927–2018), the hugely senior IFS officer who was himself going out to Sri Lanka as India's high commissioner in a few weeks, gave me a sense of what my work would entail. He was to be my mentor in the years lying ahead and, like Sabanayagam, a father figure. But for the moment, he was a severe IFS officer giving this IAS creature a talking-to. A Syrian Christian, Abraham had spent long years in Tamil Nadu, where his uncle George Joseph had lived and worked as a Congressman and freedom fighter. Abraham knew his Tamil and his Tamil Nadu. He had also known Kamaraj very well. Moreover, he knew the problem of Sri Lanka repatriating thousands of Tamils to India.

'The agreement on repatriation—I don't know if you have studied it.... If not, do.... Master its intricacies—is a fact of life. We have to implement it with due dispatch but also with due grace. Your work will be to see to it that the agreed number coming to you for rehabilitation guidance and assistance are treated with respect. They may be wretchedly poor, but remember that in Sri Lanka, they have become or are becoming Indian nationals. Just like you or me. Do not treat them like you may treat villagers here. Treat them as you would treat any Indian national you may be meeting as an Indian diplomat in London or Paris. You get me? And do not allow the Sri Lankan government authorities to treat them like some miserable tea pluckers or peasants dependent on Sri Lankan mercy. They may be on their way out, but ensure that each of them, every man, woman, and child leaving Sri Lanka with an Indian passport, is treated with civility and gets all her or his dues. To the last penny. They have to settle all their claims and leave with all the moneys that are due to them. And not as beggars but as any employee entitled to her or his severance dues. You have to see to that. Remember that. One more thing. I hear the Kandy office has got vitiated by some petty corruption from local guys recruited to work as clerical staff. That is sickening. We cannot ask the Lankan authorities to do right by the repatriates if we are fleecing them ourselves. That wretched business has to stop. Remember that.'

And he went from there to more mundane matters pertaining to me.

'You may be an IAS guy and all that in Tamil Nadu, but remember this: you have been seconded to this ministry for one stint in Kandy, and in the Assistant High Commission there, you will be Number Two. And Number Two to an IFS chap who may or may not be a directly-recruited diplomat but an IFS–B type, a man promoted from the ranks of our ministry's clerks. In terms of seniorities and such, like here in India, he will be miles your junior. But in Kandy, he, as the assistant high commissioner, will fly India's flag, not you. You will work under him. He will initiate your Annual Confidential Report, he will disburse your pay, your Dearness Allowance, and all that. He will be your boss. Remember that.'

That was a whole lot to remember, and I left his room in a daze of admiration and awe of the man who was going to be my boss—correction, super boss, my immediate boss being the assistant high commissioner—for the next three years.

Avian icon—Renowned ornithologist Salim Ali with, to his left, Tara Gandhi (author's wife) and to her left Lakshmi Devadas Gandhi (author's mother), Madras, 1978.

Kandy was a dream, and Sri Lanka a rapture. Before we moved to Kandy, Tara and I had the honour of receiving a visit, in my mother's home in Madras, by the nonesuch ornithologist Salim Ali. I had known him from the time he had come to Pudukkottai to do a bird survey for the Pudukkottai Gazetteer, but much more significantly, he was to become Tara's guide and teacher in the coming years for her MSc. in Field Ornithology. Tara was to edit compilations of Salim sahib's works for two invaluable books. Conversations with him on this and later interactions ranged over a wide field. An admirer of Nehru for his great role and personality, he also admired Indira Gandhi, whom he described to me as 'a knowledgeable bird-watcher in her own right'. All four of us, Tara and our two daughters, Divya (then, 4) and Amrita (then, 2), loved its people, its life. My office in Kandy was situated on a hillside directly above the placid waters of Kandy's famous lake, beside which stood the Sri Dalada Maligawa or the Temple of the Tooth. Two streams of very different people wound their way around the lake every day: one, of pious Sinhala Buddhists of the Theravada school, converging on the Maligawa to seek the Three Sacred Refuges—the Buddha, the Dhamma, and the Sangha. The other converging on the very quotidian office of the Assistant High Commission of India, on the eve of their repatriation to India, of Tamil plantation workers to find a new life in the country they hardly knew. Most of them had been born on their estates in the Central Highlands of Sri Lanka and knew little of the world outside. Trepidation and resignation alternated as their chief emotions. The human dimensions, both promising and deeply worrisome, of this organized emigration, were not to be missed.

India's high commissioner, stationed in Colombo, who was packing to leave for his next assignment—Berne—was Sardar Gurbachan Singh (1923–2012). A highly professional and practised diplomat, no one could have been more different than he from the incoming high commissioner, Thomas Abraham. His were the best manicured hands I have seen, and I cannot forget how, at a reception he and his most elegant wife, Shama, hosted in India House, Colombo, he wore his whisky glass. Wore? Exactly so. As he explained to me, he used this lovely chain-held receptacle dangling from his neck for his glass, so that his hands would be free to shake hands with his guests. But there was, beneath his aristocratic mien, an earthiness to him, a very Punjabi earthiness. As a refugee himself from West Punjab to India in the post-Partition migrations (his ancestral home in Rawalpindi was now the residence of the president of Pakistan), he knew the plight of repatriates at both the points of departure in Sri Lanka and arrival in India. He also had an instinctive understanding of the demographics involved. Gurbachan Singh told me that a few months earlier, Home Minister Charan Singh had come on an official visit—the leader's first time abroad in that capacity. He had not been briefed, perhaps, or had ignored his briefings, for when told about the numbers being repatriated, he said that number was paltry compared to the daily addition to our population. Let them come, no big harm. Our intricately woven position on the subject had got rent down the middle.

The Janata government was just over a year old when, in June 1978, Charan Singh made it impossible for Morarji to have him in the cabinet. The home minister said a government that cannot bring Indira Gandhi to justice was 'impotent'. Morarji dropped him from the cabinet, but only briefly. In

November 1978, Chandre Gowda, the Congress MP from Chikmagalur in Karnataka, gallantly vacated his seat for Indira to contest from there. She contested it, campaigning as 'your little daughter' (Chikmagala in Kannada means little daughter). A slogan was coined for her, 'Ek sherni, sau langur; Chikmagalur, Chikmagalur' (One tigress against a hundred simians) and with its vivid mockery became a winning chant. Though Morarji discounted the impact of her victory on his government, the nervousness in its echelons became clear when, within a fortnight of her being elected, she was held guilty of breach of privilege and contempt of the house for having blocked a parliamentary enquiry a year earlier into Sanjay Gandhi's car project, sentenced to prison, and expelled from the house by 279 votes in favour and 138 against. Thirty-seven members, very significantly, abstained.

No former prime minister had been imprisoned for breach of privilege and contempt of the house anywhere in the world. And no member of parliament had been sentenced to jail by the house either. There were protests all over the country, and the government had managed to look petty, petulant, and more than vindictive. But the Congress seemed to be enjoying the experience, because thousands of Congressmen courted arrest in sympathy with her, and two young men, 'armed' with toy pistols and tennis balls, hijacked an Indian Airlines plane flying from Delhi to Lucknow and diverted it to Varanasi. (They were later to become Congress MLAs in UP.) Indira, too, seemed to have enjoyed the one week she spent in jail, which Sagarika Ghose tells us she described as 'a rest cure', eating frugally, reading voraciously, and practising yoga. She was out in a week.

God had given me by now the gift of two priceless friends—Godwin Samararatne (1932–2000), a Buddhist scholar who was then working as acting librarian at the Kandy Municipal Library, and Ranjan Mathai (b. 1952), second secretary at the High Commission of India in Colombo. From Godwin, I received the subtlest sense of Buddhist teaching, especially the *Satipatthana Sutta* or the teaching on Mindfulness. And from Ranjan, an example of Christian ethics with religion being hardly ever mentioned.

Godwin was a Sinhala Buddhist as far removed from Sinhala Buddhist chauvinism as Colombo is from Colorado. He spoke the Tamil of Sri Lanka's plantations as his father had worked on one. I could see in him that quintessential Buddhist who could give to the Tamils of the island—all denominations of them—that metta which alone can solve the ethnic problem in its core. With Ranjan, an instinctive Nehruvian, I discussed our political condition in India frankly. He was no supporter of Mrs Gandhi or the Emergency but was wary of the contradictions of the Janata coalition and would give me a patient hearing as I extolled Morarji's initiatives for normalizing relations with Pakistan and his reaching out to President Zia-ul-Haq (1924–88). It is, I believe, a fact that bilateral relations between India and Pakistan were as near normal and friction-free as can be during Morarji Desai's prime ministership.

Ranjan was a mine of information about the world and a passionate believer in India's destiny as a nation pursuing scientific and technological advances through strategic collaborations with countries. He found some of my thoughts romantic and over-idealistic, though his exceptional sense of conversational etiquette would not permit him to say that in as many words. He did not have any problems with India's work on nuclear energy, including nuclear and, given our regional risks, a nuclear weaponization programme either.

Where he and I were in total agreement was in our perception of north India's amnesia about south India and, by extension, the importance of our flagging the concerns of the island's Tamil plantation workers both for Colombo's and New Delhi's attention. We made natural 'pupils' of High Commissioner Abraham.

1979
TOLD HE HAD 'DIED', JP SMILED

By January 1979, Charan Singh was back in the cabinet, this time as deputy prime minister with Finance Minister Jagjivan Ram also in the same category of 'deputy prime minister'. This was not a powerful troika but a rickety table of three legs. In Kandy, I followed Indian news with trepidation. It seemed pretty much obvious that the Janata government's days were numbered.

By contrast, the island state was ruled at the time by the United National Party's J. R. Jayewardene (1906–96). Ten years younger than Morarji Desai, he was seventy at the time. They enjoyed a good rapport; both having been ousted from office by powerful women—Sirimavo and Indira. Both were extremely confident of themselves by temperament and political judgment. JR's was the more credible confidence. He was not dependent on coalition partners as Morarji was. And he was more astute.

By February 1979, High Commissioner Abraham, meanwhile, was readying for an official visit to Sri Lanka by Prime Minister Desai. The itinerary included an overnight stopover in Kandy. 'Always expect the unexpected,' he told me as we set up our arrangements in the President's Pavilion, where he was to stay.

A totally calm and composed Morarji landed in Kandy by helicopter with his host, President Jayewardene. He went into a detailed discussion with High Commissioner Abraham and me on the repatriates' issue, querying us with sharp and penetrating questions. He assured us that he will make it clear to his host that no repatriate should be rushed, that no repatriate should be short-changed and also that he would see to solid improvements in the rehabilitation deal India was offering to them.

At a domestic level, he asked to see Tara and the children and, at my request, performed the aksharabhyasa (start of alphabet writing) for little Amrita, taking her fingers and holding his pen with her hand and writing on a page from President's Pavilion stationery 'Aum' in Sanskrit-Devanagari and signing it. He told me he would visit us next day at our home and breakfast with us. But proving High Commissioner Abraham right ('expect the unexpected'), I created a small drama by slipping on a silk rug in the Pavilion and fracturing my left arm. Instead of being at the state dinner that night, I checked into a hospital where, to my embarrassment, Prime Minister Desai, accompanied by High Commissioner Abraham and a host of Sri Lankan Ministers, called on me the next morning.

Even if I had broken twenty bones, including my skull, in the ordinary course of a day, no one would have noticed, not to speak of the press. But with a PM here and what with his coming to see me in hospital, this silliest of silly acts drew disproportionate attention. This was the second time Morarji was 'hospital-visiting' me, the first having been in Bombay in 1956 when, as chief minister, he had come to see me after my appendectomy. Gujarati etiquette is Gujarati etiquette. But not all Gujarati kids turn up repeatedly in hospital as I had shown I did.

On 23 March, the nation and the world were treated to utter bathos—by the Government of India led by 'my' Prime Minister Morarji Desai. At 1.10 p.m. that day, AIR interrupted its regular programme to say that Jayaprakash Narayan had died. JP dead! That he was ailing and grievously ill, everyone knew, but no one was prepared for this news. News agencies, naturally, flashed the message across the country, and within minutes, Jaslok Hospital in Bombay, where the leader was, came under siege. Reporters, photographers, and thousands of ordinary people thronged there and tried to break through the security cordon.

Prime Minister Desai, genuinely grieved, broke the news to the Lok Sabha, which was in session, causing a grief wave of national mourning, including the suspension of parliament and the closure of schools and shops. But this was a gaffe. It is believed that the head of the Intelligence Bureau was given this wrong information, and he dutifully conveyed it to the PM. When he got to know of the mistake, the PM apologized to parliament, but the damage was not to be repaired. It is seen as part of the general way the Janata government functioned. Even its patron saint they 'killed' before his death, is how Congressmen liked to dub it. When he was told about the episode a few weeks later, they say, JP smiled. Fortunately for me, in Kandy, I did not hear of the 'death', only of the gaffe.

By July, a full-blown crisis in the Indian cabinet coincided with a sparse monsoon and something—for the first time in independent India—like a mutiny by units of the Central Reserve Police Force (CRPF). His once-deputy in Bombay, Y. B. Chavan, now moved a Motion of No Confidence against Morarji Desai, which, a hitherto Desai supporter George Fernandes decided to back. Always wanting to be PM but ever a man of honour, Morarji resigned.

President Reddy, now the centre of all attention, made the hugest imaginable blunder by turning down Jagjivan Ram's flawless claim and credentials to be prime minister and inviting Charan Singh to do so. Why did he do that? Was it about caste? Or was it prompted by President Reddy's sharing with Charan Singh the same kind of farming background?

With Indira offering 'outside support' to him, Charan Singh was sworn in as prime minister on 28 July. This was a day of utter despondency for me. And my mind kept going to JP.

'Expect the unexpected' had happened again, and High Commissioner Abraham told me we may expect this Charan Singh government to fall any day, elections to be announced, and Mrs Gandhi to ride back to office. Twenty-four is generally taken as the length of hours in a day. This time, it was twenty-four days before Indira Gandhi got her 'day', withdrew her support to Charan Singh, and saw his 'will o' the wisp' government collapse. President Reddy dissolved the Lok Sabha and called for elections in January 1980.

JP died in his home in Patna on 8 October 1979. This was just three days before his seventy-seventh birthday. The end was 'due to effects of diabetes and heart ailments', is how it was described.

At his funeral, a massive crowd converged to see his remains before they were joined to the elements. The lame-duck government in Delhi was Charan Singh's, the one in Patna Janata's. In that schizophrenic situation, the one person who used the power of intelligence and political intelligence at that was, of course, Indira Gandhi. Clad in a white khadi sari, she arrived in Patna and automatically became chief mourner. Someone who had not visited JP when he was lying critically ill as a prisoner, not even sending him a letter of concern, she was now seen mourning him. If that sight was disturbing, it was nauseating to see, walking beside her, unembarrassed, also dressed in white, her son, Sanjay. A JP supporter said something nasty to him but was quickly silenced by JP's men. They had been schooled in non-violence.

BOOK FIVE

1980
KARMA

'People get the government they deserve' is a famous quote from Thomas Jefferson (1743–1826). Modifying that with sadness, my brother Mohan said to me, 'Some governments don't deserve the people they get.' The victors of 1977 so botched the success India's masses had given to them that the vanquished of 1977 ever so easily turned the rubble of their ambition into the mortar of a restoration. Mid-term elections of January wafted Indira into power again and saw her party win 351 of the 525 Lok Sabha seats for which the electorate voted with 42.5 per cent of the votes cast.

Along with Indira retrieving the old Nehru pocket borough of Rae Bareli, Sanjay returned from nearby Amethi. He was now elected by the very people who had rejected him so emphatically in 1977. Uttar Pradesh had reanointed mother and son. Indira took the precaution of contesting from another back-up seat—Medak in Andhra Pradesh. She won from there too. Keeping the new seat, she handed her Rae Bareli seat to a relative, Arun Nehru.

If 1977 had been unbelievable, 1980 was incredible. Indira had converted defeat into victory by doing nothing but appear what she was—miserable. India hates villainy. India forgives villains. India will curse villains when they ride high. India will weep with villains when they are down. India finds tyranny intolerable. But let the tyrant go down; helping hands will lift him up—bechara (helpless), and the anti-tyrant will end up looking like a bully—beraham (heartless).

The Janata coalition had come together to oppose autocracy, illegality, and brute force. Opposing the Emergency's wickedness, it could not be wicked to the wicked. It had a halo to lose. Indira had a halo to find. And find she did, sooner than expected, dangling, so to say, on a tree in her own garden of lonesomeness to which the Janata Party had tossed it.

With JP guiding it no longer, the grand coalition of democrats morphed into a pack of incompatibles, rivals, back-biters, and back-stabbers. Indira Gandhi's road to a return was laid by the Janata Party. Leading the side that plays foul against the side that plays fair and losing, she was now leading the side playing injured against the side that has lost its will and skill to play fair or foul and ending up looking nothing but a fool. She had to win. And, of course, Fate, that eternal sprite governing India's destiny, did its bit. It took JP away and planted seeds of ambition, envy, and greed among the

Janata leadership, fertilizing the sick seedbeds with compost supplied by Indira's gardeners.

So here she was, back on the throne, but with a difference. Sanjay was now not the power behind the throne but was sitting on its arm-rest, grinning and shouting. And she did nothing to stop him. Maybe she did not want to. There were enough people telling her, including, of course, Sanjay himself, that 'this time' they are not to give 'them' even an inch-length of rope.

And how they made 'them' dance!

We were in Kandy, Tara, our two small daughters, and I.

R. K. Laxman, the greatest of all living cartoonists, and his wife, Kamala, came to stay with us at this time. The Laxmans were friends of Tara's parents from time shared in Bombay together. It was a short stay, but like his pocket cartoons, the more delightful for being that. We had to talk about mother and son. 'They will make a tough team together,' I ventured. 'She is fortunate to have her son there to help her.' The acerbic Tamilian had a corrective to offer. 'Fortunate? No, saar, she is afraid of him,' he said in that alluring Tamilization of the English honorific. '*Maartally* afraid.' This was not entirely news, only an unhappy corroboration. Who would like the idea of a mother having to fear her son?

If in 1977 it looked like the angels had come for good, in 1980 the devil was back, his forked tail adorning his neck like a garland.

On 23 June, I was talking to my daily 'visitors' in the office—prospective repatriates—and convincing myself and them that a better future awaited them across the Palk Straits, when the phone rang. Ranjan Mathai, careful as always with words and in control of the emotion behind the word, calling from Colombo, told me that Sanjay Gandhi had been killed in a plane crash. 'What?' I exclaimed in disbelief. And a moment later, a word formed itself in my mind: 'Deus ex machina'*.

The mother's courage in the face of this calamity was amazing. And her ability to bear the deprivation, both personal and political, while being where she was—India's helm—made it the more admirable. And Maneka Gandhi's poise in her agony was humbling. The thought of this young woman so rudely and so suddenly widowed, and the image of her infant son were unbearable. No one knew then the extraordinary and unusual energy she was to bring in the coming years to the subject of animal rights in India. It fell on me, ironically enough, to accept from many Kandyans spontaneous expressions of sympathy. Some of them had been led by the

*The Latin expression from Euripedes's *Medes*, means, in English, 'god from the machine' and is a plot device solving a seemingly unsolvable problem, suddenly or abruptly and unexpectedly.

surname I shared with Sanjay to assume that I had lost a kinsman.

In any case, one does not like to receive, on foreign soil, any expression of pity for one's country, be it on account of natural calamities, acts of terrorism, or occurrences such as this. One's country has to be 'up there' where it is invincible.

What was no less, in fact, even more difficult to endure was the expression of horror expressed by people one knew in Kandy at another shock—the diabolic episode of policemen blinding thirty-one undertrials in Bhagalpur, Bihar. The event was ghastly. That policemen could pin down the prisoners, gouge their eyes out with bicycle spokes, and then pour sulphuric acid on the hollow sockets was beyond belief, beyond acceptability. And Indira Gandhi's statement in parliament on 1 December about the happening befitted her station. 'What are we coming to in this country?' she said and continued, 'That anybody can do this is beyond my comprehension...I am not able to say anything more...' She also added that something must be done about the training imparted to policemen so that they 'do not become de-humanised.' That she broke down while admitting of feeling 'physically sick' made what she said not only responsible but also deeply human.[1]

The 'Bhagalpur' day in parliament was carried by Atal Bihari Vajpayee who said, in an unusual 'take' that he offered to share the blame for the malaise in society, prompting Home Minister Zail Singh to say he too, did the same.[2]

Indira Gandhi's rhetorical question: 'What are we coming to...?' was misplaced. We were not coming to something. We had been there all along. What happened in Bhagalpur showed a depravity, a streak of sadism that has existed in Indian history. Kautilya (third century BCE) prescribes blinding in his *Arthasastra* as a punishment for certain offences. And there is no doubt that Indian monarchs, sub-monarchs, and putative ones have practised the prescription, along with many others of the same type, vigorously, down the ages. In Mughal times, blinding within royalty was known, the future Emperor Shah Jahan, no less, having had his brother Khusrau blinded. What made Bhagalpur hideous in a contemporary way was that the blinding of suspects by policemen to extract evidence or from simple vendetta or as a preventive 'warning' to others had been going on for some time. Were it not for the media having got to know of this case and splashed it, Bhagalpur would have kept its grisly secret to itself for some time more.

Has Bhagalpur made this particular barbarism a thing of the past in India? It has, perhaps, as a form of unauthorized corporal punishment by law-enforcers but I cannot say with any certainty that Indian society has seen the last of this and similar forms of depravity. As long as the strong—whether authority-strong or just strong—believe they have control over the physical form of a weak person such as a prisoner, a woman, or a Dalit, torture of the vulnerable will continue. The fact that India, as a state, has not ratified its signature on the International Convention Against Torture and has not yet outlawed the death penalty speaks for itself. In this modern extension of an ancient barbarism, India is not without company.

Torture, mutilation, and legalized murder are notoriously the province of certain Islamic states. But has not the Old Testament, too, countenanced blinding as a punishment? Samson's is a famous example. Rembrandt's painting of the scene in which Samson has been pinioned down and a spoke is being thrust into his eye is a work of pain as much as of genius. Only a painter of the Dutchman's sensitivity could have thought of capturing the man's unspeakable agony in the shape of his twisted foot into which all of the man's torment is concentrated.

And so, though Bhagalpur happened in the second prime ministership of Indira Gandhi, it had little to do with who was in power in Delhi or in Patna and everything to do with the utter disregard, shown in age after age, to human life. Even the policemen who did what they did were policemen only in a manner of speaking. They were males, the dominant species, exercising their brute power. Caste was involved, class was involved, but above all, God-damned insolence was involved. And the apathy of us Indians to such happenings was involved. And do we take responsibility? Vajpayee was exceptional. And he showed—good for him and for us as a people—that his exceptional 'I accept' could make the home minister of the day say the same.

1981
AS IF GOD DID NOT EXIST

There is a phrase in courtroom Hindustani for 'acquitted with honour'—baa-adab. Indira Gandhi had been exonerated by the people of India and restored to her high station, baa-adab. I could not forgive the Janata leadership for having handed over, with pathetic cretinism, democracy to its saboteurs.

I was ruing the Indian condition from my cosy nook in Kandy when, over the spring and early summer, things happened in both countries to make what was already gloomy grim. It was Bihar again.

The state's Congress government was headed by Jagannath Mishra (1937–2019). On 30 April, Mishra, as host and prime mover, told a meeting of the National Integration Committee at Patna: 'My government has successfully combated communalism. During the past ten months, not a single incident of communal violence has taken place. My administration is determined to put it down forever.'[1] Mishra, a Brahmin, may not have been a liberal secularist by belief, but his policies and programmes in office were like those of such an emancipated politician. He made Urdu the state's second official language, a step which Muslims could not but have appreciated.

But on the day Mishra made his grand claim, just 90 kilometres away, a few hours earlier, in the town of Bihar Sharif, a nasty riot occurred between Hindu Yadavs and Muslims, leaving forty-eight dead and sixty-eight injured. The cause was the most common of causes—a disagreement over the resting place of Muslim dead. The Yadavs said they needed to protect their grazing rights on about two dozen disputed graveyards there. Rampaging marauders did not spare the local mosque, which was destroyed in a spectre that was to be re-enacted with disastrous consequences in Ayodhya in 1992. Almost inexorably, rioters moved in swarms from village to village, killing, looting, and raping.

It was as if the Bihar carnage of 1946 was being re-enacted. Reports spoke of Nooraisa, thirty, whose thirteen-member family, including a six-month-old baby, was massacred in Rupaspur village, saying in hospital: 'I don't know why they killed us. We have done no harm to anybody.... it was as if God did not exist.' It was Friday when, in Alinagar, thirteen women and children were cut to pieces while the men of their families, unaware of what was happening, were offering Friday prayers.

The state government headed by Mishra had been worse than slack.

But—hand it to the lady—Indira Gandhi, on learning of the events, got to the scene at the speed of light. Covering her face, she went to the hospital to see the bodies of the victims at the hospital. A burka-clad woman who had lost her entire family asked her: 'What was the need for you to come now when everything is over?'

Reading all this in Indian newspapers, with what face was the Indian High Commission to speak to Sri Lankan authorities and politicians about Sinhala's majoritarian mistreatment of Tamils?[2] And the need to do so arose much faster than one might have imagined. During the months of June, July, and August 1981, organized Sinhala mobs looted and burnt Tamil shops and houses in Jaffna, Ratnapura, Balangoda, Kahawatte, Colombo, and in the border villages in the Batticaloa and Amparai districts. Looting, arson, and killings then spread to the hill country, where Indian Tamils, many of them prospective repatriates to India, lived. Armed with clubs, iron rods, bicycle chains, and knives, mobs roamed the estates, burning, pillaging, looting, and killing. And while this happened, police and army units just stood watching.

Over 25,000 Tamil plantation workers were rendered homeless in the hills, and over 10,000, likewise, in the east.

High Commissioner Abraham, incensed, demanded and got an instant appointment with President Jayewardene and told him if any Indian citizen among the Tamils being attacked was touched, he would hold the government of Sri Lanka responsible. Ranjan Mathai and I were dispatched by him to the affected areas in the hill country to see the situation at first-hand and report to him. It was heart-rending to see poor plantation workers with no interest in politics, much less the politics of separatism, and with no political ties whatsoever with the Tamils of Jaffna, being made to suffer for the sole 'fault' that their mother tongue was Tamil and their religion, Hindu.

My colleagues and I were disbelieving when we heard that on 31 May 1981, after a rally held by the Tamil United Liberation Front (TULF), two policemen, Sergeant Punchi Banda and constable Kanagasuntharam, were shot and killed by gunmen belonging to an extremist outfit, People's Liberation Organisation of Tamil Eelam (PLOTE). This was a despicable act, but what followed by way of Sinhala majoritarian retaliation led by police and paramilitary men was hideous. In a pogrom that lasted for three days, the head office of the TULF party was destroyed, four people were pulled from their homes and killed, and a local Hindu temple was destroyed.

But the worst was yet to come. On the night of 1 June, another organized mob, which we may assume comprised Sinhalas, went on a rampage in Jaffna and, in a brazen act of malice, burnt the Jaffna Public Library. This was one of the most violent examples of ethnic biblioclasm of the twentieth century. The library contained over 97,000 books and manuscripts. Among the destroyed items were scrolls of historical value and the works and manuscripts of philosopher, aesthete, and author Ananda Coomaraswamy (1877–1947). This was despicable.

The people of Jaffna, Tamils mostly, are highly educated, and the library was something they prized. To put that repository of scholarship to the fire was a mean and nasty act, and whatever one may think of his later avatar as president of Sri Lanka, Mahinda Rajapaksa criticized the burning of the Jaffna Public Library as akin to destroying images of the Buddha (for Buddhists).

The year was one to lament for one more reason. The great actress Nargis, Raj Kapoor's heroine in many an unforgettable film, but none more deservedly famous as one in which Raj Kapoor had no role—*Mother India*, died on 3 May 1981. She was fifty-one. Nargis had been nominated to the Rajya Sabha only the previous year by the president on the recommendation of Prime Minister Indira Gandhi. She was to have had a term of six years there. But during one of her early days in India's senate, in the house, she felt ill and had to be rushed back to Bombay to be admitted to hospital. And then, after another spell in hospital in New York, she succumbed to the pancreatic cancer she was found to have been suffering from. She was, of course, a great actress but was also something much more. She was her own person, very distinct, very Nargis. In fact, I always felt she and Raj Kapoor did not 'match'. She was gentle and compassionate. But not in some wispy, perfumy way. She had an inner life that only she lived in. How do I say this? I have no reason to know what she felt. But her face—like that of the actress Nutan—says it. As does that of Subbulakshmi.

It was many years later that I found corroboration of my thoughts about Nargis in an entry she left behind on a page of the visitors' book in a lodge called Morgan House in Kalimpong. She had stayed there with her husband and wrote: 'If ever I want to get away from the fast and crowded life of the city, Kalimpong will be the place.... I will be gone but only to come back again.' I read and re-read those lines for their honesty and vulnerability. She signed herself there as 'Mrs Nargis Sunil Dutt'. She wanted before her name and after her name her status inscribed and announced as that of a married woman with a husband to guard and strengthen her. She wanted to go away from the fast city and also needed to not be alone.

Nargis died in a year of pogroms.

Malefic under-gods exist alongside benefic deities on the subcontinent, harassing the good and the innocent. Superstition? Perhaps. But then what explains the presence of persons like Nargis and their suffering, dying so prematurely? A biologist would say the life of an organism has its own timeline, its own forms of atrophy and folding up. It does not mean anything further. Perhaps.

1982
KANDY IS SO MUCH LIKE KERALA

This was to be our final year in Kandy, and we clung to each passing day.

We had made strong friends and learnt to love the town and the country, which had been so kind to us. Not because of its similarities with India but because, though so close to our country, Sri Lanka was so different. The topography of its central, western, and southern parts was very like Kerala's, a fact I mentioned to our Lankan friends.

Cherry George (1948–98), a delightfully witty and warm Indian diplomat posted in our mission in Colombo, was visiting us once, and I introduced him to some friends as '...Cherry is from Kerala.' This was meant to be a conversation smoother, and so it was. It was in my mind to add: 'And Kandy is so much like Kerala,' but before I could, Cherry said, 'Kerala is very much like Kandy.' Same thing? Yes, and yet not the same thing. He was not being just polite in a diplomatic way. He was being civilized. No neighbour, especially if much smaller in size, would like to be told by the biggie, 'Oh, you are just like me.' That would not be an embrace but a bear hug. Older than Cherry and longer in Sri Lanka than him, I had learnt something from Cherry.

In February 1982, India's president Neelam Sanjiva Reddy paid a state visit to Sri Lanka, which included, quite naturally, a visit to Kandy. The 'Indian Tamil' community in Kandy had organized a public reception for the dignitary and wanted to present a welcome address to President Reddy. P. T. Rajan, the wonderfully active educator and philanthropic head of the relevant association, showed me a draft of the address for comments. 'We welcome you,' it said 'to the pendant on India's necklace.' This had been said in all earnestness and out of an equal love for both countries. But I was uncomfortable with the formulation. Rajan was gracious enough to agree, not without some reluctance, to my urging to drop that line. Sri Lanka is a gem, I said to him, without being studded on an Indian plate.

In terms of our place in the world, Indians have to be among the most self-centric people. We are ancient; we love to say and be told that. We are a civilization, not just a nation; we feel good hearing that said of us. Others have learnt from us, followed us, and been disciples to the teacher in us. When that is said to us, something in us preens. President Reddy's speech writers and advisers had a very India-centric view of Lanka's heritage. Visiting the Sri Dalada Maligawa, the Temple of the Tooth, the palladium of Buddhist temporality on the island, President Reddy said, 'We in India hold the Buddha to be the eleventh avatar of Vishnu...' He meant by that to pay the highest imaginable tribute to the Great One. He was equating him with Vishnu, one of Hinduism's trinity of Godhood. You cannot get much higher than that. But to Lankan minds, the Buddha was not to be thought of as one among a dozen or so, even if that company was the choicest. The Buddha was altogether singular.

If ever a state visit was meant to be an exercise in hollow ceremonial, empty politeness, idle pleasantry, this was one. President Reddy and his entourage had dusted Lankan red carpets and given crystalware a wash. And that was about all.

Chaudhary Charan Singh, who had become prime minister courtesy of President Reddy's unilateral decision, announced his retirement from politics in April. India's elites speak generally with condescension about him. This is from ignorance, not reason. Charan Singh was shrewd, but in the way non-urban India is, with knowledge of the sky-earth connect, the way life is lived in a search for balance between challenge and response. Thanks to his knowledge of human psychology, he knew about governance and politics. His instinctive knowledge of the life of the typical peasant of rural India, of the largesse and stinginess of the weather gods, made his helming of Uttar Pradesh as chief minister meaningful. He knew his economics but not in the sense of understanding social phenomena through numbers but numbers through social phenomena. He could have, under a kindlier star, made defining contributions to India's future in agriculture, its lifeline, and in rural infrastructural augmentation, its crying need. Given a full term in office, he could have positioned India on the world's map of prosperous economies via its farmlands and rivers. He could have given India direction on how its groundwater and topsoil need to be used and conserved. He could have greened India. But politics thinks differently and acts crudely. There is such a thing as one's natural talent. Ambition and political power garbles it.

Even as the great Jat called it a day, another Indian from an essentially rural 'stock' but fantastically intellectual, amazingly skilled in his expertise—economics—moved into an office for which he was made and which seemed to have been made for him. A future finance minister and prime minister of India who would usher in fundamental reforms stepped into the pathway for that role. Dr Manmohan Singh (1932–2024) became governor of the Reserve Bank of India in September—one solid good thing to have happened under Indira Gandhi's renewed prime ministership.

Our little family, meanwhile, moved back home from Kandy to Madras. I 'reported' for postings to the secretariat in Fort St. George. The very singular chief secretary at the time, K. Diraviam, nationalist and master of Tamil literature, khadi-wearing and chain-smoking, told me, 'They said our khadi department would be the logical place for you, but then that would be too, too "pat" and so I have decided to give you a different but similar responsibility—director of Handlooms and Textiles'. And so, from working with poor tea-pluckers, I was now to work with poor weavers and mill-hands while trying to get their products into the wild and wily world of textile marketing. The work was to be more fulfilling than I imagined.

I must here, share with the reader a cameo about Diraviam. Once, landing in Delhi the proud cherisher of his language roots heard two men say to each other, pointing to Diraviam '...Madrasi...chaprasi...' In fact, they used an adjective to precede 'Madrasi' which, for decency's sake, I am omitting here. Stung, Diraviam decided that day that whenever he came to Delhi thereafter, he would wear the Tamil veshti (dhoti) and shirt, in emphatic affirmation of being 'Madrasi'.

1983
CARD GAMES

Until February of the year 1983, the name Nellie meant to me not a place but a person—Nellie Sengupta (1886–1973). I knew of her as an Englishwoman who had married a Bengali nationalist and freedom fighter and had become, in 1933, president of the Indian National Congress. Rather vaguely, I knew she was, after Annie Besant, the only non-Indian woman to have held that position. Why did post-Independence India not know more of her? An even vaguer impression told me that this had something to do with her having moved, after Independence and Partition, like a veil of mist, to East Pakistan, now Bangladesh, and had become something there, a legislator or some such.

But from 1983 on, Nellie was to mean a place, a horror. But curiously, as with the other Nellie, with East Pakistan and Bangladesh at its heart.

From the morning of 18 February, Muslim immigrants from East Pakistan in Nellie and a dozen or so other villages in Assam's Nagaon district were systematically targeted by local peasants and murdered in cold blood. Murdered? Butchered. With every imaginable piece of sharpness. Fire was co-opted to set home and hearth ablaze, and fleeing men and women were pushed into the flames with children and infants, yes, toddlers, among them.

News reports cited officials speaking of over 2,000 having been killed but of the real 'Nellie count' being much, much higher. It was said that threats held out by the immigrants to locals ignited the violence. Possible. In fact, very probable. But the scale of the reaction was barbarous.

The world has many heavens and many hells, but India is about the only stretch of the earth which holds many heavens and more hells together. It is a garden of paradise and a butcher's shop. It is both rainbow and pyre.

Why did the massacre in Nellie happen? How? Arrogance, not ignorance, was asking these questions. The arrogance of smugness, in which safety first, comfort next, and the security of the status quo have ruled my life. And that of millions of self-absorbed, self-protecting, self-seeking Indians like me.

I did not know my Assam because I did not need to know it. I did not know what living alongside a 'live' international border in the midst of bilingual strife and a binary ethnicity meant because I did not need to and did not want to trouble myself about such issues. I was safe in my sanctuary in Madras. Like the Adyar, asleep in the cradle of its banks. Of the many morbidities of India, the most common and widespread is amnesia. Of the many conditions of India, the major one is stupor, and, when shaken out of it, frenzy.

As any supposedly informed Indian, I ought to have known by now of the Assam agitation led by students and their All Assam Students' Union. AASU maintained that Bengalis in Assam, whether Hindu or Muslim, from West Bengal or from Bangladesh, were all intruders and should be expelled from the small landlocked state. I ought to have known that surrounded by poorer or more populous Indian states and now, also by Bangladesh, their concern was real. As an informed Indian, I ought to have known something else too: electoral democracy was sniffing fragrant votes in the miasma of immigrant versus local politics and that the Congress was delaying a response to the Assam agitation's demands because of this dangerous aroma.

But I did not. Typical.

Indira Gandhi was fleet. She got to the site within three days of the carnage. 'I cannot find words to describe the horrors,' she said like she had about Bhagalpur. She was being honest. She was Nehru's daughter. But she was also her party's election-plotter. And there was in her make-up a little imp called suppressio veri, suggestio falsi*. She knew, without doubt, that what she called 'horrors' could have been averted had she not, heeding party vote-sniffing, called for elections even as the Assam agitation was demanding the postponing of polls and the disenfranchising of 'immigrant voters'. Party wisdom (or call it party cunning) had told her a critical minimum of Hindu votes are and will always be with us, but if we hold elections now, in a polarized Assam, the loyal Hindu majority votes plus an avalanche of Muslim minority votes—to hell with their legal or illegal status—will also come to us and we will win. The 'resident' majority in Assam stayed off the polling, which was held shortly before the massacre, even as the Muslim 'immigrant' minority voted en masse for the Congress. If ever there was a pyrrhic election win in India, it was that for Indira Gandhi's Congress in Assam in 1983. The result of that election, in effect, spelt Nellie. The locals of that district said, in effect, 'If you do not expel them, we will exterminate them.'

Nellie was a nightmare. But Nellie is not a 'was'. Nellie is and will always belong to the present and the future. Because it is about India, the India that is a heaven and a hell, both competing and combating for its soul. It is because of that timeless conflict that a Buddha rises in it; an Ashoka reigns in it, a Mahavira, Tiruvalluvar, Kabir, Nanak, and a Gandhi make a critical difference, offer a lease to its heaven, only to be swamped by its hell. And a Nehru blossoms, the Indian summer's freak rose, and an Ambedkar miraculously opens like a lotus in a pond, both exposed to hell's torments.

*Meaning, 'suppressing the truth and suggesting the false'.

If the ruling dispensation tried the Muslim card in Assam, it picked the Hindu card in Kashmir. Elections to the Jammu and Kashmir Assembly held that summer saw Indira Gandhi come out strongly in solidarity with the most unjustly and horribly mistreated community of Kashmiri Pandits, now mainly in Jammu. Polarizing votes had lost the peace for Congress in Assam. It lost it in Jammu and Kashmir as well.

India was getting splintered along her old fault lines.

And menacingly so, in the Punjab where Jarnail Singh Bhindranwale (1947–84) had become a cult figure for Sikhs wanting an identity revival. The Akalis, traditional rivals to the Congress in the Punjab, needed a counterpoint and, encouraged by Sanjay and then by Home Minister Zail Singh, Indira Gandhi had seen in Bhindranwale that counterpoint. But Bhindranwale was not going to become someone else's puppet. He was now demanding a Sikh nation. And from within the holiest of Sikh holies—the Golden Temple at Amritsar, which had become his headquarters—armed to the teeth. He spoke fire and brimstone. Hate was being spread among Sikhs. Hatred of Hindus, of Congress, of India, an intolerable situation.

There was something about the number six that day, 6 October 1983, on the Amritsar-Delhi bus route. A luxury bus plying between the two cities. Six adherents of Bhindranwale had boarded the bus in Amritsar. As the bus threaded its way out of Amritsar's limits, two of them asked the driver to stop and, on his doing so, dragged six Hindus out and shot them dead with Sten guns and revolvers. They then took over the bus and, driving it a distance away, asked everyone to deboard and drove off in it. Brazen. Indira dismissed her own Congress government in the state, imposed President's Rule, and declared the state a Disturbed Area, with the Armed Forces Special Forces Act invoked in it.

And preparations started for Operation Blue Star.

It could have been called Operation Red Sun.

For us, deep down south, happenings in Punjab and the personality of Bhindranwale were as distant as Mongolia and Genghis Khan. The icon of the silver screen and our chief minister MGR loomed over us. He was recognized and adulated as 'Puratchi Talaivar' (Revolutionary Leader), though no one quite knew the contours of the revolution he was said to have led. In the Directorate of Handlooms and Textiles as director, I was as a shuttle in the loom of weavers and weaving. The art, as it may be called, of handloom weaving, was facing stiff competition from machine-weaving in composite spinning and weaving mills. And yet it survived, with subsidies, precariously. Government helped the weavers with a committed procurement of certain categories of handwoven saris and dhotis which had been 'reserved' in 1952 by Chief Minister Rajaji, for this sector of weavers. But when drought struck Tamil Nadu in 1983, and the cloth market turned sluggish, handloom retail got paralysed, and the shops of the Tamil Nadu Handloom Weavers' Cooperative Society, better known by its abbreviated Co-optex, which were the state-run depots for handlooms, groaned under a glut of unsold stocks. And this while farmers, without work on dry fields, lost their means of livelihood.

It occurred to me to put it to the government to buy in bulk the glut of 'janata' saris and dhotis and distribute it to suffering farmers as drought-relief. But who was 'government'? It was, in a word, Chief Minister MGR. And so, I positioned myself in a passage where he would pass on his way to discussions in the house. Seeing me, he stopped and, with a silent smile, waited for me to say something. I told him what I had contemplated. He heard me out carefully and, after no more than a moment's reflection, said in Tamil, 'Good idea. Double action. I approve.' His use of the term 'double action' for a step that would help both drought-stricken farmers and glut-struck weavers, came straight from the world of cinema. I had bypassed the Finance Department with a scheme for which he would have to find the money. K. J. M. Shetty, the finance secretary, said to me: 'Gopal, what is this? You cannot simply waylay the CM like this and get a scheme approved over my head. Not done, not done. Anyway, now that he has approved, we will issue a G.O.' Sluggish stocks of unsold handloom stirred, weavers and poor receivers of the cotton weaves got the relief they deserved, thanks to MGR's unique 'wand'.

Just about then, Co-optex's new swanky showroom in the city was ready and to be opened by the CM. We asked his office to get from him a name for the building and made a few suggestions. We did not hear from the CMO until the day prior to the opening. His decision: Thillaiyadi Valliammai Maaligai. He had decided to name it after the Tamil satyagrahi martyr of South Africa, a colleague of Gandhi's who had died in 1913 after an enervating prison term. My colleagues were in shock. What a mouthful... Who will say that long name...But there it was. At the grand opening ceremony, MGR made an impromptu speech in which he brought in the Valliamma legend skilfully and linked it to farmers and weavers of the day and, to my embarrassment, to the director.

Our home life, meanwhile, suffered a body blow. After months of silent struggles with diabetes, a cataract surgery-related eye infection, and a lung congestion, Amma slipped into a coma and, on 9 November, into her rest. All four of us, her children, were in town on the day, but it was left to Ramu, her only Madras-born child, to have the privilege of being there when she drew her last breath. With a picture of Ramana Maharshi placed by him near her, Ramu said, the end was totally peaceful. She was seventy-one.

MGR came home and laid flowers at Amma's bier, speaking of both her father and her father-in-law in terms of affection but more—knowledge of their roles in history. Many telegrams and letters arrived, condoling. One of the first was from someone I hardly knew—Rajiv Gandhi. The passing away of Devadas's wife, Rajaji's daughter, and Gandhi's daughter-in-law, being mourned by a grandson of Jawaharlal Nehru had an appositeness to it.

1984
SARE JAHAN SE ACHHA?

When all of India was thrilled to learn on 2 April that thirty-five-year-old Squadron Leader Rakesh Sharma (b. 1949) had been launched into space aboard the Soyuz T-11, I had no idea that I would ever have the great good fortune of being friends with that fantastic man. Fantastic man? I use the phrase not because his achievement was fantastic, which, of course, it was, but because, having got to know him, I can say he is a fantastic person.

I asked Rakesh about the great moment when, after the launch, as he and his colleagues, all Russians, had 'stabilized' in orbit, a satellite link connected him to our prime minister. Rakesh, seated in the middle of a circle of his fellow five cosmonauts in a tight-looking—what-shall-I-call-it—chamber, all wired up and with earphones on their ears, heard Indira Gandhi, looking stunning in her very carefully groomed head and a single-string necklace of white and green beads, ask him: Upar se Bharat kaisa dikhta hai apko? (From up there, what does Bharat look like to you?) The line must have been drafted for her, perhaps by her able and loyal information adviser, H. Y. Sharada Prasad. Rakesh answered the question with the first line from Iqbal's great song: Sare jahan se achha (Better than the entire world). We can hear a faint giggle, in the YouTube version of the conversation, for that is exactly what it was, from the prime minister. It was a good if expected question, brief, to the point, asking exactly what every Indian would have wanted to know. It was a great answer, poetic and graphic, saying what every Indian would have liked to hear. But, unlike the question, the answer was entirely unexpected in its structure—a famous quote from a famous poem.

I asked Rakesh—he was, by now, nearly seventy—in Coonoor, where we are neighbours, 'Tell me, were the question and answer premeditated?' 'Oh no,' he replied. 'I had no inkling as to what she may say or ask...When she asked what she did, I could think of nothing other than what I said—India from up there looked to me better and more beautiful than anything else on earth that I could see....'

But the Hindustan that looked so bright and beautiful to Rakesh was in dire trouble. Not many who saw the satellite interview quite knew that the previous month, the prime minister had, after much prevarication, come to the conclusion that an armed intervention by the military in the Golden Temple at Amritsar was inescapable. Only the details were required to be worked out. Throughout March and April, Bhindranwale had several—one estimate suggested eighty—Hindus killed.

I was secretary to the governor of Tamil Nadu by this point. Governor S. L. Khurana (1918–2007), a retired IAS officer who had risen to be union home secretary, had been regarded, perhaps exaggeratedly, as one of the prime minister's henchmen or hatchetmen. As a Punjabi himself, he knew the Punjab scene inside out. But as one who had done his duty by the Indian state, he was happy to be in the safe sinecure of Madras's Raj Bhavan. And I was happy to be in a sinecure to a sinecure myself, writing drafts for his speeches, which he then worked on, making me work on them over and over again.

But Governor Khurana was not going to have it easy. K. Saranyan (1936–2005), a seasoned IPS officer with the Intelligence Bureau, then stationed in Madras, kept Governor Khurana informed about the grim proceedings in Amritsar and of the ballistics of 5 June in real-time. The relieving of that sanctum from the clutches of merciless mercenaries and terrorists of the most despicable kind is a saga that has been relayed time and time again. But what I watched with horror was the demonization of the Sikh community that was slowly but unmistakably taking place in the popular mind. Were all Sikhs separatists or admirers of Bhindranwale? Surely not. I hated the fact that suddenly, a community one respected and admired as being Guru Nanak's, was now being seen as suspect and even sinister.

But the way the army, which had been instructed to use minimum force, found to its horror and its cost that the Golden Temple had become a veritable fortress of the most lethal kind showed colossal intelligence failure. Indira Gandhi had been let down by her own spooks. Butchery was replied to in kind. The fact that the sanctum had been violated by terrorists and desecrated was overtaken by the fact that the Indian Army had stormed it. If what Bhindranwale had done cut the discerning Sikh mind, what Indian forces did cut the devout Sikh heart. And overnight, Indira Gandhi became, entirely by the witchery of circumstances even she had not imagined, a hated figure in the Sikh world. When it was all done, and the message was reached to her that her troops had done what was expected of them, and of the number of terrorists slain, she is believed to have said, 'Oh God, and I was told there would be no casualties.'

One man whose position was unenviable, Giani Zail Singh (1916–94), was president of India. In a ceremonial arrangement, the supreme command of the Indian defence forces vested in him as president. But he, of course, was out of the loop in all the decision-making hours that preceded Operation Blue Star. As a Sikh and as president, Zail Singh was in an identity crisis of his own, and it was of the sharpest kind.

K. C. Singh, the highly insightful and articulate author-diplomat who served on President Zail Singh's senior staff, writes in his book *The Indian President: An Insider's Account of the Zail Singh Years* that Zail Singh visited the Golden Temple immediately after Operation Bluestar and says: 'The stench of death was in the air, as we entered the *parikrama*, the pathway that surrounds the holy *sarovar* (lake). It seemed that they had either just finished removing the bodies or some still lay trapped.' Zail Singh, back in Rashtrapati Bhavan, said as he entered his private rooms, 'disconsolately' in a low voice: 'It is a mistake made by others, but I will have to pay the price.'[1] In the event, he did not have to do so. It was the prime minister who did.

MGR and governor Khurana had a cordial equation. The governor– chief minister equation is a delicately balanced one. It should not be so close as to generate speculation, not so stiff as to suggest mutual distrust. They must not confer so long as to make people wonder 'what is cooking?' nor so briefly as to make people say 'they do not click'. And so when, on 5 October, MGR was reported to be ill and taken to Apollo Hospital, the governor was concerned as he would be, and a 'get well' message was readied and sent. But it soon became clear that the 'slight asthmatic trouble with mild renal impairment' description was not quite the whole story. Saranyan kept the governor apprised, and inside of a fortnight of MGR's hospitalization, Governor Khurana asked me to set up a meeting with the Number Two in the cabinet, V. R. Nedunchezhiyan (1920–2000), to discuss the situation. Nedunchezhiyan was in a dilemma. He did not want anyone to get the impression that he was fishing for an opportunity to be acting chief minister. And what if, as and when MGR recovered, he was told that Nedunchezhiyan had seized his powers? The governor told Nedunchezhiyan in clear terms that the Business Rules of Government envisaged arrangements to be made for the smooth running of the administration in such emergencies and that he, as governor, now was telling Number Two to put those arrangements in place. The CM's portfolios came to devolve on Number Two, and with MGR's condition becoming more and more inscrutable, no one misconstrued the arrangement.

On 14 October, the prime minister came to Madras on a flying visit. A prime minister's visit to a Raj Bhavan disembowels its life. Security men from nowhere take over. They are everywhere and all in all. And we, the regulars of the place, become outsiders, wearing badges that announce our credentials in our own place. Indira Gandhi had come for a short stay to meet party workers and state ministers. As she emerged from a rushed moment of freshening up, she asked me, as the official nearest to her walking path along the Raj Bhavan's grand staircase (she had, typically preferred walking down the stairs rather than using the lift):

'Where am I meeting the visitors?'

'In the Morning Room, madam'.

'I wouldn't know where that is.'

I realized my idiocy at once and, in silence, escorted her to that beautiful room. The meeting done, she got into her car and her retinue followed suit, each staffer running to get into his allotted car and then the entire cavalcade moving out in a torrent of dust and chaos. She saw MGR in the hospital. Doctors were being flown in from the US, and there was talk of MGR being flown to the US if needed. The state's health minister, Dr H. V. Hande, she said, should fly to Delhi in her aircraft to meet the US doctors who were arriving there and come back to Madras with them, discussing MGR's health situation on the flight.

Indira Gandhi had made a point in Tamil Nadu. She cared for it. If MGR rallied, she would have played her role. If he did not, she would have played it too, a bit differently.

But who can say who is to live and who is to go?

On 31 October, I was settling into the office's routine at my desk when Saranyan called. 'The Prime Minister has been assassinated.' 'What?' There was nothing more to be said. I went over to the governor, who was in the same Morning Room, readying to meet his daily visitors. He heard the news with shock but without any sign of grief. 'I must get on the next flight to Delhi,' he said. As that was being arranged in what seemed like a footage played at top speed, Mrs Khurana, also called Indira, came down the same staircase Indira Gandhi had used only a fortnight earlier. 'Is it really true?' she asked, without any emotion.

Seeing the governor off at the airport, I realized that governors from all states must be zooming to Delhi. Each such governor was a distinct person, but this much they had in common: they were rushing to Delhi to pay homage to the slain prime minister but more, to pay tribute to the new one. They needed to be seen by him, and their presence at his mother's obsequies 'duly' noted by him. Delhi has been and will always be a durbar. The court and courtiers change, but paying court is a constant.

When such emergencies happen at work sites, the family gets forgotten. I rang Tara at one fleeting moment during all the commotion to tell her what had happened and to ask her to get to the children's school and fetch them home. She did that, to find that parents had already begun to come there with the same idea.

There was disbelief around. There was fear as well. Was a civil war going to start?

Madras knew Punjab as distant Punjab. It did not draw the fine distinction between Sikh Punjab and Hindu Punjab. A Sikh had killed the prime minister. A Punjabi had killed the prime minister. A school run by the city's Punjab Association felt the heat.

As I got home after seeing the governor on his flight, I was glad to see all four of us: my wife, the two little girls, and I were together. And not in Delhi.

Who killed her? The little ones wanted to know. Why? Were they bad men?

It is impossible to answer questions from children. Innocence demands truth. And yet needs to be shielded from it.

For the next four days, what happened in Delhi was shaming. Shame at the murder of a prime minister by men meant to protect her. Shame at the mayhem that the murder let loose, with anything between 3,000 and 10,000 Sikhs being killed in Delhi and elsewhere by way of vengeance. Politicos, Congress politicos, were behind it; anyone with eyes and brains could see.[2] The ingenious barbarity and cunning murderousness that came out of the vanquishers was like a secret expertise waiting to be tapped.

And the new Prime Minister Rajiv Gandhi's statement that when a great tree falls, the earth quakes was just too awful, too smug, for words.

Years later, when I saw the film *Amu* about the anti-Sikh riots of 1984, I felt not just ashamed but sick at my being one of those who did nothing but tut-tut at what was independent India's version of genocide.

Are we a violent people kept non-violent by the example of our saints? Or are we a non-violent and peaceable people who occasionally let violent deeds be perpetrated by us? I really do not know for sure. I am inclined to think that the non-violent amongst us are a majority, but we are non-violent not because we believe in what the Buddha taught, what Mahavira preached, and what Gandhi showed, but because we are timid peace-huggers who do not want 'trouble'. Hindu, Muslim, and Sikh alike.

This, of course, overlooks and is unjust to huge numbers of people and non-government organizations that went to help the victims of the riots. From individuals who helped Sikhs by bringing them to hide in their homes and shielded them on trains, buses, and cars, to those who organized shelters with make-do arrangements for their food, and carried on a highly risk-laden campaign for the mob violence to be stopped, we saw humanitarian intervention of the highest order. But these minstrels of succour were those dazzling exceptions that prove the rule, which is that the vast majority of us do not riot but do nothing to prevent or stop riots.

In Madras, meanwhile, MGR's health went from bad to worse, and he was flown out to the US for treatment. When his wife Janaki appealed to everyone to pray for him, most people thought that was the heart-throb's end. But MGR would return to fight another day.

The year had not done with tormenting us.

I hid the papers from the children when news and photographs told us in the first week of December of the Bhopal gas leak and, the dying of more than 2,000 people outright and injuries of a cruel nature to the health of anywhere from 15,000 to 22,000 others. One had heard of Union Carbide Corporation as an American chemical company and a subsidiary of Dow Chemical Company, but paid no attention to what it produced. A chemical company and its factories are not fascinating subjects. But as debate mounted on who was culpable, everyone came out poorly. The company and its principals abroad for their 'Don't blame us, blame the local guys' look, the factory staff for their 'It's them, their systems, their poor supervision, not us' stance. And the administration for taking a toxic plant's presence in the thick of a city for granted.

But in Bhopal again, as in Delhi, some individuals and organizations were to rise to epic scale in the speed and dedication of their help. Just as perversion hides and is never suspected to exist until it is too late, human solidarity stays unseen and unknown to stir at a moment's notice. That is India, the theatre of strife between the hideous and the humane.

1985
A DIFFERENT NEHRU

The cynic is less visible and vocal but more populous than the cheerful in India. And his normal mode of speech is the whisper. After a period of silent waiting and watching, the cynic discovered his voice, and whispers came to be heard, suggesting that MGR had become irreversibly ill. The few photographs of him in his hospital bed in the US that we saw, it was maintained, had been doctored to make him look like he was recuperating well. And of course, popular 'diagnoses' of his medical status ranged over the gamut of morbidity. The truth was that the chief minister of Tamil Nadu, hero of a thousand fights on the screen, was battling his way to recovery.

And when, with elections announced, MGR signed and filed his nomination papers from that very hospital bed, comments swerved from his medical to his legal capacity to contest. Once MGR won with a thumping majority, all speculation came to rest.

His party, too, having won emphatically and having gone over the formality of electing him its leader in the assembly, Governor Khurana invited MGR, now back in the city, to take his oaths. They had a preliminary discussion at which it was decided that the swearing-in would be a very select affair, with none of the 'protocol' invitees being called. The idea was that MGR, whose voice had not returned to normal, may be spared the ordeal of reading the entire script and, after making an opening with the first word, 'I', go as far as he could with the text and then sign the parchment. The governor chose his small study for the ceremony, which could seat no more than a dozen comfortably. The official media alone was invited.

A smiling MGR came in, walking confidently, dressed in his customary combination of shirt and veshti, a shawl over his shoulders, and, of course, his cap, dark glasses, and big gleaming watch worn over the shirtsleeve at his wrist. He greeted the governor with great warmth and showed me the same affection that he had always shown me. I was just another cog in the official wheel, and he could have (as many do and did) breezed past the cogs. But he did not.

All was going as per plan till the moment when MGR rose and walked to the lectern, amid a blaze of flash bulbs coming on. At just that point, the electricity went off, plunging the room into darkness. The load of photographers' camera's 'leads' had proved too much for the system in that modest room. But the swearing-in went ahead with the lights of some cameras being trained on the dramatis personae. MGR was least perturbed, and no one else was upset either. The governor did not seem to mind.

Needless to say, superstition had to have its little word. 'Not a good omen,' I was told in a whisper about the electricity glitch. 'Rubbish,' I said, affecting more rationality than I possessed. 'The lights did go off, but the ceremony went on regardless and was completed, was it not?' An actor can make a fine administrator, but administrators can do with some timely acting too.

MGR resumed work in right earnest, overcoming physical and neurological hurdles, getting the matter in files read out to him, and recording his minutes in brief notes with a signature that became more and more 'normal'. There was no question as to who was the boss. His wife, Janaki, looked after him scrupulously, but one could see the tension over Jayalalithaa, his party's propaganda secretary at the time. Youth and health seek romance; illness is happier in homelife.

India's new vice president, R. Venkataraman, came on a visit around this time. I did not know him and stayed in the background. But at one or two ceremonial events, I had to be there and was introduced to him and to Mrs Janaki Venkataraman by the governor. The visit went off well in a routine kind of way. But in the afternoon of the day the vice president left, the governor sent for me and said, 'VP wants you to join his office as secretary.' He was looking distinctly irritated. 'A VP's wish is an order. You will have to go. But I have told him I can relieve you only after a substitute to you has been found here.' I was taken aback but also impressed by the etiquette of the VP. He had not uttered a word to me about his intention. He had asked my boss. That is what observing protocol is about.

The notice was short, and the family was getting plucked out of its settled routine abruptly. For Tara, who had just started a course of study of birds in the coastal region between Madras and Mahabalipuram under the renowned Salim Ali himself and was required to leave her earmarked plot of land where the study was located—this was no mean disruption. And the children would have to leave their school where they were so well settled and had made good friends.

But overarching these was another larger anxiety. We were moving into the heart of terror-borne tension. Delhi was the very centre of tensions about Sikh disaffection and its new corollary—violence. Our load of fear over this was not helped when news came on 23 June of Air India's *Kanishka*, a Boeing 747 flight from Canada to India getting blown up above the Atlantic Ocean, south of Ireland, killing all 329 aboard. It was straightaway identified as an instance of terrorism perpetrated by Sikh extremists belonging to the outfit called Babbar Khalsa. One of the victims was the distinguished Madras-based chemist Y. Nayudamma (1922–85). I had met and spoken with him only a few days earlier when he had come to call on Governor Khurana. The episode shook India. Compounding the trauma with a conjoint tragedy, Nayudamma's widow, Pavana, committed suicide. No one learning of Pavana Nayudamma's act could fail to think of the custom of sati, now mercifully and redemptively outlawed and outdated. I could also not but think of what Ananda Coomaraswamy has written in *The Dance of Shiva*: 'When the *Titanic* sank, there were many women who refused—perhaps mistakenly, perhaps quite rightly—that was their own affair—to be rescued without their husbands, or were only torn from them by force....'

We started life in the national capital with tremulation in our hearts. Today, nearly forty years on, it is difficult to imagine that emotion of fear, completely misplaced, of an entire community, the Sikhs, because of the perverse stratagem of some terrorists unleashing fear in the name of the Khalsa. But that fear was very real, as palpable as the presence of Sten gun-bearing soldiers and policemen guarding the vice president's residence where the secretary's cottage was also located. It was not nice to have to drive our children every day to school through a gate at which stood heavily armed guards. 'Do you realize the risk we are exposing our children to?' Tara asked me. 'Any one of these men, because of some frenzy or plain simple depression, can go berserk and shoot...' She was right, but I could not tell her that. I had to reassure her by talking vaguely about possibility and probability being different things and similar cant.

Delhi was a familiar city to me, having been born there and spent the first twenty-two years of my life there. But this was the first time I was seeing official Delhi from the inside. Vice President Venkataraman and Mrs Venkataraman made us part of their family from the very day that we got there. But he was a hard taskmaster! There was no resenting this because he worked as hard, if not harder than those he gave work to. For a seventy-five-year-old, he was the picture of health and energy and—a calm, unruffled cheerfulness. He was enjoying his duties because he had a work ethic which told him that one must do one's duty cheerfully.

Prime Minister Rajiv Gandhi was charm itself. I was the receiver of incoming calls on the RAX—restricted exchange—from certain privileged phone numbers for the vice president and connecting him to the caller. Rajiv would call occasionally, unfussily, matter-of-factly and, of course, courteously. And he would invariably have a word or two to say to me, which was more than many bigwigs cared to do.

Freedom's warriors—Then vice president, R. Venkataraman with fellow freedom fighters at Rashtrapati Bhavan, Independence Day, 1986, the author, then secretary to the vice president, in attendance. (Author's personal collection).

But even as my admiration for his leadership grew, my view of one of his colleagues dimmed steadily. Arun Nehru (1944–2013), former president of the paint company Jenson & Nicolson and newly inducted minister of state for Home Affairs handling security matters, was a cousin of Rajiv's. Throwing his weight about came naturally to him. Portliness combined seamlessly in him with arrogance. And most people saw him as Rajiv's alter ego. Poor Rajiv.

The vice president had gone on a brief tour once, and I had, of course, accompanied him. When we returned, a very crestfallen team of our office colleagues called me aside and said, in whispers, that the VP's office room had been broken into. 'Broken into?' I asked in disbelief. 'With all our security apparatus?' Yes, they explained. 'We have all been fooled. A posse of men claiming to be from the telephone department with ID cards and all came to see our phones to make them "tamper proof". They said they had come on a day the VP was away in order to not disturb him. So, we let them in, and they spent a few minutes and went away as quietly as they had come. But after they had gone, we felt some doubts and checked with the telephone authorities, and they said they had sent no such team and would never do that without proper coordination. No one is able to say who it is that came....'

I reported this to the VP, who was as surprised as all of us. Within an hour or so, in drove Arun Nehru to tell us with the smile of a smart alec that it was he who had arranged for this 'sanitizing' to be done. 'You see how easy it is for anyone pretending to be an official to enter the VP's sanctum sanctorum? Your security is the pits. You are all sitting ducks. Pull up your socks.'

Tightening the vice president's security apparatus may have been Arun Nehru's intention. But his achievement was something different: letting us know who was Boss. Telling us who called the shots in Delhi. Telling us who the centre of power was. I was fairly disgusted. The VP, in jest, called Arun Nehru 'Boss'. That the man relished being called that only added to my disgust.

His clout was only to increase because in May, over two days, transistor explosives exploded across much of North India in buses and trains. A hundred or so were killed, and many times that number were injured. It was, of course, the work of the same set of terrorists howling with hate over Operation Blue Star. The objective went beyond retaliation. It was to spread fear and hatred and, in the arising miasma, thrive on it. In his passion for reaching accords with disaffected sections of society, Rajiv did the most audacious of his outreaches—to the Sikhs by means of the accord signed by the head of the Shiromani Akali Dal Sant Harchand Singh Longowal (1932–85) on 24 July. Among other steps, it extended the ongoing enquiry into the 1984 anti-Sikh riots to Bokaro and Kanpur, removed restrictions on the recruitment of Sikhs in the army, and granted Chandigarh to Punjab. But Sikh extremists denounced it at once.

On 15 August that year, Rajiv Gandhi made his first speech from the Red Fort. This was the custom-decreed Lal Qila address to the nation, broadcast and now telecast live early in the morning on Independence Day. An invitation to the event received by an official is virtually an order to attend, and so, with the VP's permission, I went to it. Rajiv's speech in Hindi was as good as speeches go. When he referred for the first time to his mother, saying that she would have been making this speech had she not been 'snatched away from us', there was a collective and silent sigh. And when he announced a historic development: an accord that had been signed only a few hours earlier in the pre-dawn hours with the student leaders of Assam, which could bring the agitation and the tensions underlying it to an end, there was genuine appreciation. He also spoke of our neighbours and said India would be in discussions with Sri Lanka's leaders on the ethnic issue in the island in an unlikely venue: Thimphu in Bhutan. Rajiv said he hoped this exercise would lead to peace and 'end the tension in the south'. No one could have guessed at that time that Rajiv's own destiny was going to be linked with that 'south'.

Speech done, flag unfurled, and the national anthem sung, Rajiv sped away in his convoy with the speed of terrestrial light, other cars in the cavalcade following him in what my brother Ramu was to describe as 'scared rabbits scurrying away'. But the prime minister had good reasons to take every care.

The Thimphu talks that Rajiv mentioned had started in July and were tortuous. President Jayewardene's brother, assisted by three lawyers representing the Government of Sri Lanka, conferred with delegates from leading Tamil organizations, including the Liberation Tigers of Tamil Eelam (LTTE). They were two irreconcilable groups. The Tamil delegates, with great differences of their own, put together four principles, which came to be called the Thimphu Declaration, which no sovereign government of Sri Lanka could have accepted. These were recognition of the Tamils of Ceylon as a 'nation', of the existence of an identified homeland for the Tamils of Ceylon, of the right of self-determination of the Tamil 'nation' and of the right to citizenship and the fundamental rights of all Tamils of Ceylon.

Barring the last, the official delegation rejected all outright, and on 18 August, the talks were declared to have collapsed.

Rajiv was also having some trouble, as I could see, in forming what may be called a clear Indian position with the veteran diplomat and foreign policy adviser G. Parthasarathi (1912–95), whom his mother trusted, not being among his trusted counsellors and there being no substitute to GP readily available.

Vice President Venkataraman knew GP well and had a better appreciation of the Sri Lanka imbroglio than most, but rectitude held him back from proffering opinions. He devoured my novel on Sri Lanka's plantation workers *Saranam*, which came out at this time. 'Too many characters in it, Gopu,' he said frankly. 'I got lost tracking them.' But I was chuffed that Khushwant Singh reviewed it most generously.

On 20 August, two Sikh youths fired shots point-blank at Sant Longowal, president of the Akali Dal during the Punjab insurgency of 1980, killing him on the spot. Rajiv's was no easy mission. Peace-waging hath its trials, and Rajiv was a peace-warrior.

1986
WHO RULES INDIA?

The beginning of the year 1986 showed Rajiv in the worst imaginable light—at least in the eyes of contemporary observers. Shah Bano Begum (d. 1992) of Indore, Madhya Pradesh, was divorced in 1978 by her husband, who, after having lived with her for fourteen years and having five children with her, took a second wife and threw Shah Bano out. She filed a criminal suit in the Supreme Court of India, in which, after a much-observed sequence of hearings, she won the right to alimony from her husband. This was seen immediately by liberals, the Left, and the Hindu Right as a major achievement for human rights, marital equity, and for the advance of social reform. A contrary response from Muslim opinion had to and did come. Scholars of Islamic tradition and practice, authorities on Muslim Personal Law, clerics, and politicians, including MPs, asked for the verdict's nullification, citing the Holy Quran in order to show that the court was reversing Islamic law.

Overall, majority opinion in India was that the Supreme Court having pronounced in the matter, that was that. Within the prime minister's own office, his director for Minority Affairs, the wise and reflective Wajahat Habibullah himself, advised Rajiv that the government need not involve itself in the matter, the Supreme Court having spoken. But Rajiv Gandhi's government passed a law that nullified the judgment. The jury, that is out on whether Rajiv did this to 'appease' minority opinion or not, will never return with a clear answer. But I can see the point made powerfully and with detailed cross-referencing by Mani Shankar Aiyar[1] that what Rajiv did was to give credence to Islam's own specific provisions for the maintenance by the ex-husbands of divorced women or, in the absence of that, by the Waqf Board's specified duties towards such women. Rajiv was to win no fans by what he did, and lose not a few. Arif Mohammed Khan (b. 1951), then a minister of state, was so upset by the enactment that he resigned, being hailed then and ever since for setting a rare example of a Muslim opposing an enactment that was meant to, ostensibly, protect Muslim custom.

If Rajiv was seen as having appeased Muslim opinion in the Shah Bano case, he found himself being seen as doing the very opposite, as a corrective, almost, in another theatre of India's complex life. So as to create a favourable wave in the Hindu vote pool, it was alleged that the locks in the disputed Babri Masjid–Ramjanmabhoomi structure in Ayodhya were opened. A local court in Faizabad, on 1 February 1986, had vacated a stay order passed in 1949 that the status quo should be maintained at the site. And so, the locks were opened, and thereby, so were the floodgates of the controversy that was to lead to the demolition, in 1992, of the Babri Masjid.

Did Rajiv Gandhi know about the opening of the locks? If he did, it would be a matter of shame. If he did not and the locks were opened without his knowledge, then it would be a matter of embarrassment to him that a Congress ministry in the state—Uttar Pradesh—should be so brazen as to take such a patently dangerous step without as much as keeping the prime minister informed.

Wajahat Habibullah, whose word carries honour and integrity, has written that on a flight to drought-hit Gujarat later that year, he asked Rajiv why and how he allowed such an appalling thing to happen. Rajiv said to Habibullah that he had given no such orders and had come to know of it only after the whole thing had been done by Vir Bahadur Singh (1935–89), the chief minister, apparently at the instance of Arun Nehru.[2] The chief minister, who owed his office to Arun Nehru, either assumed that any word from him would reflect the thinking of the prime minister or regarded Arun Nehru to be big and accredited enough to give him such an instruction. Vir Bahadur went ahead and had the locks opened.

So, to my mind, it is clear that it was the cousin who, with an eye to electoral victory with Hindu votes surging in, and in order to counter what Rajiv had done in Shah Bano, got the infamous thing done.

Rajiv Gandhi was not only a transparent prime minister but also a trusting leader. He dropped Arun Nehru from his position as minister for Internal Security. The damage to his image had been done, though, and it was incalculable.

Rajiv's efforts at bringing a measure of agreement in Sri Lanka on the Tamil question were as necessary as they were difficult. And it is noteworthy that in his Red Fort speech on 15 August 1985, he said he hoped that the talks on Sri Lanka that were going on in Thimphu, Bhutan, would ease tensions in 'the south'. Not many in India's north were particularly interested either in Sri Lanka or, indeed, in India's south. P. V. Narasimha Rao, in fact, said to an Indian scholar-diplomat, 'I know for a fact that our Tamils do not care at all for the Sri Lanka Tamils; in fact, they hate one another, but they are using the situation solely for political purposes without giving the slightest thought to the broader implications.'[3]

The wise leader and future prime minister was not entirely right. Indian Tamils were concerned about their co-linguists and co-religionists in Sri Lanka and were not pretending to be affected by the violence perpetrated on them. But they were not for terrorism as an answer, or for that matter, violence of any kind. They wanted a fair and a quick redressal of the Tamil grievances. And Rajiv Gandhi's policy of pressing Colombo to negotiate with the Tamils, supporting the territorial integrity of Sri Lanka, opposing the demand for an independent Tamil Eelam, opposing terrorism, refusing to allow any terror outfits from Sri Lanka to operate from Indian soil found general resonance in Tamil Nadu.

On 19 February 1986, no less than eighty Tamil farm workers were killed[4], allegedly by Sri Lankan Army personnel, in the town of Akkaraipattu in the Eastern Province of Sri Lanka, and their bodies burned. The farm workers were reportedly threshing the paddy fields when troops appeared from the nearby jungle. The women at the site were let go, but the men were rounded up, their hands tied, and shot. The bodies were then piled on top of the dry rice harvest and burned. This was one of the most gruesome acts of state violence on an ethnic minority committed in Sri Lanka. It was now for the LTTE, the most violent of the Tamil organizations, to return violence with more ferocious violence.

The LTTE, we have noted, was not going to keep quiet. On 3 May 1986, twenty-one people were killed and forty-one injured when an Air Lanka flight set to fly to the Maldives blew up at Colombo airport.[5] The LTTE was clearly trying to impact the world through this attack on a plane that was packed with tourists from all over the world.

Taking strategists' advice and that of policy and preparedness planners in the Ministry of Defence, Rajiv Gandhi approved a purchase at this time of field guns from Sweden, which was going to dog him, defeat him, and dethrone him. At the time, no one outside of the rarefied world of defence strategy really took much notice when, on 24 March, a contract was signed between the Government of India and the Swedish arms company Bofors for the supply of 410 155 mm Howitzer field guns.

But all external threats apart, Rajiv stared, at this point, at Punjab's deteriorating situation. Would there be a return of widespread terror? Some 200 extremists having regrouped in the Golden Temple, would another Operation Blue Star become necessary? In an exercise that stood in marked contrast to Blue Star, Rajiv sent commandos from the National Security Guards, and 700 troops of the BSF into the complex on the evening of 30 April and, in twelve hours, completed the operation with only one dead. Punjab's director general of police, K. P. S. Gill (1934–2017), led the operation and was hailed as 'Super Cop'—a title that was to be his crown and his cross in the coming years. Punjab's Akali chief minister Surjit Singh Barnala (1925–2017) was fully on board.

Vice President Venkataraman was consulted by Rajiv frequently, and to the best of general knowledge, President Zail Singh not at all—a most unnatural state of affairs. RV's punctiliousness made him accessible to the PM, but he was correct and prudent enough not to extend his advice unsolicited.

Working with RV was a joy and an instruction. One of the 'time-pass' roles assigned then to the vice president was to be the chief guest representing the Indian state at the national days of different countries observed by their resident ambassadors and high commissioners in Delhi. I would invariably accompany RV to these very pleasant and very weightless gatherings. Being 'on duty', I could not sip a drop of the many spirits that moved around in dainty glasses nor partake of the high-end refreshments at ease. But this deprivation was made up for by being able to sit in on the conversations that often ensued.

At a reception held in the Chinese embassy that year to mark Chinese National Day, I saw the veteran communist leader E. M. S Namboodiripad standing by himself in a corner. I went up to him and, offering my respects, asked if he would care to meet the vice president (who, as per norms of protocol, was seated at a fixed point and not mingling). EMS immediately said, 'Yes, yes', and I had the privilege of conducting the living legend of India's Left to where RV was seated. On seeing EMS approach, RV sprang lithely to his feet, and the two spent several minutes in pleasant conversation. On our drive back, RV said, 'What are we before this giant of a man! He had inherited a big tharavad (family estate) but gave up everything for his cause, everything', stressing the 'v' impactfully.

No latent Congressism was allowed by him to come in the way of this admiration. There was in RV an instinctive fairness. It is not as if he did not have his preferences, even prejudices. He did, but he kept them furled when observing his public duties and his private courtesies. The vice president is, by virtue of his office, chairman of the Rajya Sabha. In that role, he was equally cordial and equally firm with members from across the benches, pulling them up for inadvertencies as much as for intentional misconduct, especially during Question Hour, the hour that he scrupulously spent in the house. Prolixity, additional supplementaries, 'irregular' Calling Attention Notices, and Adjournment Motions were summarily put down. 'Nothing will go on record, nothing...' was heard in the familiar high-pitched voice whenever decorum was broken or a levity exercised. Members doing a 'walkout' would hear 'All right...attendance is optional...' making the MP feel and look utterly unheroic. Predictably, RV earned the left-handed title of 'headmaster'. The only time I have heard anyone anywhere ask someone to 'Get Out', was when, in his chambers in Parliament House, RV told the Congress MP Kalpnath Rai, who was going on and on about something that was wholly improper, RV lost his proverbial cool and with a gesture to match shouted those two words at Rai who exited at once.

That the relations between President Giani Zail Singh and the prime minister were under strain was obvious. Gianiji was a warm human being, but in politics would not go down as a saint. Rajiv was a gentleman, if ever there was one, but in politics, he knew enough to not be seen as a monk. Congress MPs, sensing the tension between the two, kept away from Rashtrapati Bhavan, and ministers did not call on the president to brief him, which was a normal and standard thing to do.

Gianiji's travels abroad on state visits became negligible, and RV being asked to travel overseas became the norm. But two years into Rajiv's prime ministership, Gianiji seemed to have decided that enough was enough. And an opportunity to show his mettle came to him in the shape of the Indian Post Office (Amendment) Bill, 1986, which would authorize the government to intercept personal mail. Gianiji refused to sign it. There is a phenomenon in the US called the 'pocket veto', which can be used by the president. Gianiji did not refer the bill back for reconsideration, a procedure that would have been constitutionally valid, but with the proviso that if the government resubmits it to the president, he will have to accept it. Gianiji just had the file put in a cupboard and kept the bill pending. He had neither approved it nor sent it back, unsigned. He had consigned it to indefinite limbo. There is no time-cap prescribed for the president's decision on a bill. Rajiv and his cabinet could do nothing. It stayed there, nestling between life and non-life, until Rajiv was to lose his office, be succeeded by V. P. Singh after a bitter feud, ultimately to be withdrawn by the V. P. Singh cabinet.

RV was aware of this, and the constitutionalist in him was irritated. When a bill has been passed by parliament, no president can sit on it, is how he viewed the matter. But the democrat in him was not for the censorship of mail either. And I, for what it was worth, was delighted that a bill as draconian as this had been stalled. Who would want government, which means some clerical meanie, poring over one's private correspondence? It is one thing that Rajiv, being a decent man, would not have mail intercepted, but as the locks in Ayodhya had shown, Rajiv was neither omniscient nor omnipresent. Gianiji had, for reasons of personal pique as much as democratic hauteur, done a smart thing. And RV, shortly to become president, was not going to un-smart him. He, too, did not sign it.

Morarji Desai, now in almost total retirement in Bombay, was never far from my thoughts. How could he be? I owed so much to him. And so, when on 3 August a news report said he had got a death threat from terrorists who also said they would blow up his Bombay apartment, Oceana,

I worried for him. He was now out of power. Was his security detail, if any, good enough? Replying to a letter of concern from me, in which I also told him about my working for RV, the veteran sent me a lovely little postcard:

> Oceana, Subhash Chandra Bose Road, Bombay
>
> 5.9.1986
>
> My dear Gopu
>
> I was very glad to receive your letter of 3rd today. I am not at all worried by the threat as nothing worries me. I am glad you are with the Vice President. He has much experience and is a nice person. I hope you are all very well.
>
> With affectionate regards,
>
> Morarji Desai.

1987

THE RIGHT MAN IN THE RIGHT PLACE

A. P. Venkateswaran (1930–2014), India's foreign secretary, was a man RV had admiration for. He had known Venkateswaran's father, A. S. P. Ayyar (1899–1963), a highly regarded writer, dramatist, and judge in the Madras High Court. Venkateswaran, diplomat that he was, thought on his feet and spoke as he thought—without edits. His publicly expressed negative views on Rajiv's policy on Sri Lanka had irked Rajiv, and another contretemps about a visit by Rajiv to Pakistan in connection with SAARC led the PM, in a press conference in January, to say that there would be a new foreign secretary very soon. Venkateswaran put in his papers within minutes.

RV did not like Rajiv's action. 'This is not the way…' he said and asked me to tell Venkateswaran, 'I would have expected nothing less from a son of A. S. P. Ayyar', which I did, adding my own words of disappointment and regret, as one whose parents had also known Ayyar. But I believe RV advised Venkateswaran to turn his resignation, which would have cost him his pension, into voluntary retirement, which protected it. Did RV discuss the matter with Rajiv? Most likely, he did, for the issue was hot, and RV and Rajiv did talk about a wide range of matters. But I do not think RV would have criticized Rajiv for what he had done. RV knew what was worth the candle and what was not.

For me, 1987 was valuable for the gift of a cherished friendship that it brought. Vikram Seth's first novel, *The Golden Gate,* had appeared the previous year. But I read it in the opening weeks of 1987, completely mesmerized by its verse, its storyline, but above all, by the deep pathos underlying it. Liz Dorati in it is an all-time figure of tragic beauty. There was a dinner at which I found myself seated with Vikram. Chatter flowed from heavily made-up faces with the ease of wine. I sent him a note after it, telling him how great the impact of his book on me was. Beginning what was to be a lifetime friendship—not worth measuring in its frequencies or its intensity but a lifetime thing alright, like the deepening wrinkles on the forehead. Vikram replied:

7 Teen Murti Lane, New Delhi 110011

February 2

Dear Gopal,

Thank you for your very kind and affecting letter of a few days ago. It was good to meet that day, for all the lacquer and loquaciousness.

To meet a reader who sees through the light-hearted surface of the book to the sadness beneath is rare for me. Most people say they are amused by the book but few that it moved them.

Thank you once again.

Vikram

I do not know and have not bothered to ask Vikram if he knew Rajiv. It is more than likely he did, if only as an alumnus of the same school, The Doon School. It has been very civilizing and, in a strange way, very reassuring about 'God in his Heaven and all being good down on earth' to see 'Doscos' as they are called by themselves (gamely) and others (somewhat cynically) remaining steadfast in friendship through their lives. Rajiv's immediate contemporaries there, such as Mani Shankar Aiyar, Sekhar Raha, and Vivek Bharat Ram, all of whom I know well, have been true-as-true-can-be friends of Rajiv, which includes being frank with him. And the Dosco I know best and cherish inestimably, Ramachandra Guha, much junior to Rajiv, has, of course, been an unsparing critic of the family rule that has come to characterize the Congress. One Dosco I have never met, only spoken to over the telephone, is Rajasaheb Vikramsinhji, the former maharaja of a tiny, once-princely state in the Panchmahal district of Gujarat called Jambughoda (jambu—the jamun tree, ghoda—horse). I rang him to find out something about his old estate's motto or insignia, 'Satyameva Jayate' (Truth alone prevails), which preceded by decades the same motto adopted by the Republic of India. Drawn from the *Mundaka Upanishad*, it is a remarkable motto for India to have, as it does not valorize the country (as many national mottos do) or turn abjectly to godhood (as many also do). It is a philosophic motto proclaiming confidence in the unassailability of truth. That the royal house of so small a state could have such large a thought-span was impressive.

The summer was ugly that year.

Meerut saw Hindu–Muslim riots in the town's suburb of Hashimpura seeing a horror in blood. Forty-two Muslim men were killed in this quarter by policemen on or around 22 May. By the police? Yes. By uniformed men of the state's Provincial Armed Constabulary (PAC) who were without doubt acting under some higher-up's instructions.[1] The youths, agricultural labourers, were working at a site together. They were rounded up and taken in a lorry to the outskirts of the city, shot dead in cold blood, and their bodies dumped in a nearby irrigation canal. Ongoing riots in Meerut, with a 36 per cent Muslim population, had tested the cops' patience, but this was no punishment. It was about power. The bullets were police ammo, and the fingers that sent them flying were those of policemen. But the impulse came from much more than that. It came from venomous spite, official hubris, and sheer political insolence mixed with communal conceit.

Rajiv Gandhi reached the scene on 30 May. Accompanying him was his joint secretary, Wajahat Habibullah. A throng of people met him at the Government Circuit House. Barring one, an MLA who spoke little if anything, there was no Muslim among them. The PAC had seen to it that only Hindus would have access to the prime minister.

Wajahat records: 'Taking me aside, Rajiv asked me to tour the city, specifically the Muslim Mohalla affected by rioting and report to him the inputs of the Muslim leadership.'[2] What Wajahat saw was nightmarish. The killings were cold, calculated, and cruel. Rajiv acted speedily, but he was the prime minister of India, not the chief minister or chief secretary of Uttar Pradesh. He gave the wheels of law in the district of Meerut a heave-ho, but he had to leave it to others on the spot to keep it turning. And did they turn?

Nearly thirty years later, the Tis Hazari Court, Delhi, on 21 March 2015, acquitted all sixteen of the accused in the massacre case of 1987 due to insufficient evidence. The Uttar Pradesh government announced in May of that year, 2015, a compensation of ₹5 lakhs for the family of each victim.* At first, the man wields the firearm; after a while, the firearm begins to wield the arm.

In the early weeks of 1987, when Rajiv was beginning to lose the 'Teflon' looks of zero controversy, the political air in Delhi was rife with rumours that President Zail Singh might 'dismiss' Rajiv and instal some minister or Congressman in his place. The names of Arun Nehru (unbelievably) and party seniors V. C. Shukla, Ashoke Sen, and Arjun Singh were floating around. I had no clue that RV, too, had been approached by some Congressmen who told him that he had to only agree, and they would get a sizeable number of Congress MPs to back him. RV apparently showed them the door but had to meet President Zail Singh, who, in the meanwhile, had asked to see

*On 31 October 2018, Justices S. Muralidhar and Vinod Goel of the Delhi High Court, hearing an appeal, sentenced all the accused to life imprisonment.

him. RV said not one word to me about what the president had said to him—absolutely correct of him.

Gianiji's increasing hostility towards Rajiv came to be seen and noticed in many ways that were not 'mainstream political' but were not without political overtones.

Netaji Subhas Chandra Bose's birthday is on 23 January. In Kolkata on that day, Gianiji said: 'The Indian media has always built up some families while others have been completely ignored. Sons and daughters of national leaders like Mahatma Gandhi, Sardar Patel and Subhas Chandra Bose, who laid their lives for the country's independence, have been totally forgotten.' He said, 'The Indian media…' but it was clear whom he was targeting. He followed this up by extending an invitation to Netaji's daughter, the distinguished Hamburg-based Austrian economist Anita Bose Pfaff (b. 1942), to visit Delhi and stay at Rashtrapati Bhavan as his guest. When she came, he had a function organized in her honour, to which my sister Taru (Tara Gandhi Bhattacharjee) was invited as well. This made quite an event in the Mughal Gardens—an obvious way of telling the Nehru–Gandhis that there were other 'famous descendants' in the country. Neither of these two invitees was in the least politically inclined, but they could not, once there, miss the president's point.

By May-June, it was clear that RV would be Congress's candidate in the presidential elections due in July. At the portico of the vice president's house, receiving a Congress delegation that came to formally seek RV's consent, I thought party veterans like P. V. Narasimha Rao and Kamlapati Tripathi (1905–90) looked like bride's uncles coming to seek the bridegroom's benign agreeability. Among much hilarity and joie de vivre, the consent was sought and given. RV was an Iyer. The Left fielded the esteemed Justice V. R. Krishna Aiyar (1914–2014). 'Iyer v/s Aiyar', RV v/s VR the unequal contest was to be. And a gentleman v/s gentleman as well. The pioneer of judicial activism and master of unexpected turns of phrase was a sore loser, but a person intellectually difficult to oppose. Congress asked RV to undertake a nationwide tour to campaign, as Krishna Iyer was expected to. RV declined. 'I will have to speak for my candidature versus Justice Krishna Iyer's. That in itself will be unpleasant,' RV explained. 'But more importantly, when the country is plagued by so many divisions, what is the point of a future rashtrapati going about dividing the presidential vote?'

RV won resoundingly. And with a major propriety observed—a worthy opponent defeated with his great prestige held intact.

The night before his swearing-in, I knocked at the Venkataramans' apartment door to brief him on a few matters of procedure for the coming big day. 'Yes?' came his high-pitched voice. With the help of Mrs Venkataraman, he was putting some of his personal effects together for the move. As we were talking, a bulb on the ceiling of the room exploded, scattering glass splinters all over the carpeted floor. Bulbs giving up the ghost due to long use is not uncommon. Ever open to 'signs', the mishap was, for me, unwelcome. Not so for the president-to-be. As I made some noises about the quality of bulbs and Mrs Venkataraman looked mildly irritated, RV beamed.

Beamed? Precisely so. 'Wait, wait,' he said and, with a few quick steps, went to a chest of drawers and returned smiling, with a dinky gadget in his hands. 'This picks up glass splinters,' he said with the excitement of a child. And in no time, the seventy-seven-year-old was on all fours, the battery-operated thingummy purring all over the carpet, picking up the sharp pieces of the shattered bulb. Neither the man who was to become First Citizen in a few hours nor the First Lady-to-be thought of omens, signs, or superstitious auguries. Believing in a Supreme Power and the Advaitic teachings of Adi Shankaracharya, as represented in our times by the ascetic Ramana Maharshi and Chandrasekharendra Saraswati, the Paramacharya of Kanchipuram (1894–1994), they had little time for astrology.

I was told by him that I would be moving with him seamlessly from his vice-presidential office to his presidential one, as joint secretary to the president. 'We have to find a replacement for the present secretary to the president,' he said and asked me for names. I gave him a few. But he was to make the selection of his own.

One of the first recommendations made by Rajiv to RV in his new role as president was to induct M. L. Fotedar (1932–2017), a confidant of Rajiv's and bete noire of the former president Giani Zail Singh, as a cabinet minister. RV agreed without any hesitation, but S. Varadan, the outgoing secretary to the president, felt this was a bad start. RV had shown that the president-PM friction of Gianiji's time was over. It was too early in the day for RV to have expressed his disapproval—if he did disapprove—of Fotedar's induction, but I wished he had done so. Fotedar was an impressive political falcon. Rajiv had need of his sharp eyes, sharper talons. Even princes of singular veracity in India have needed that bird perched on their wrists for a sense of security. But as president, RV's attention was meant for the nation's, not the prime minister's, political comfort level.

Meanwhile, Rajiv was sewing up the major Indian Peace Keeping Force (IPKF) agreement with Sri Lanka. Inspecting a farewell Guard of Honour in the President's House in Colombo on 30 June, where he had gone to sign the Indo-Lankan Accord the previous day, one of the ratings lined up for the ceremony, Vijitha Rohana (b. 1965)* swung his Lee-Enfield rifle and brought it down on the prime minister of India. I have given his full designation in the foregoing sentence because it helps us understand the seriousness of the occurrence. It was a narrow thing. Rajiv's presence of mind and quick physical reflexes had made him duck just as the guard had begun to move. This was an unprecedented incident and made the Lankan hosts red-faced. Was the man mentally disturbed? Was he part of a bigger conspiracy? He was Sinhala, needless to say, and disapproved of the accord under which Indian troops were to come into the Island as peacekeepers. Is it possible that had Rajiv been hit more grievously and had fallen, immobilized, some more attackers would have joined the assailant and killed him? The man was overpowered, and Rajiv emplaned as per schedule.

The news shook everyone in Delhi. Given the attack on him, RV decided that he would go to the airport to receive Rajiv as he returned to the national capital. The bureaucrat-pedant in me mumbled the word 'protocol' to him and 'He is fine, sir...The injury is said to be trivial,' with the intention of dissuading him from going to the airport. RV brushed the idea aside with less than contempt. And issuing a moving statement praising Rajiv for 'waging peace' and facing the risks of that, RV was there on the tarmac to receive Rajiv.

If the phone rings, waking you up at an odd hour, something coils up in one's guts. This has to be about that curious thing called intuition. When the phone rang in the wee hours of 24 December that year, I knew it had to be bad tidings. The caller was A. Padmanabhan (b. 1928), chief secretary of the Government of Tamil Nadu. 'Gandhi, sorry to be troubling you at this hour, but I have to convey to the president the sad....'

MGR had been ill, but his death was unexpected. He went very swiftly after a heart attack he suffered around 1 a.m. Receiving the tidings at that benighted hour of the screeching owl was deeply disturbing. The news was deeply saddening for me, personally. MGR's almost shy smile, his generous pat on my back, and his words, so few and therefore so expressive, all came back in a flood. But I was not supposed to wallow in my thoughts. I had to convey the news.

President Venkataraman took no time in deciding that he would go to Madras at once to pay his homage. This time, I kept my thoughts about presidential protocol to myself. He was, even otherwise, to have gone to

*Court-martialled and sentenced to six years, Rohana was, however, pardoned by President Premadasa after two and a half years. He is said to be an astrologer now.

Madras later that very day for a public event—ironically, the inauguration of a medical university to be named after MGR. The departure was advanced suitably. Now, the visit became exclusively a condolence visit. The president going to condole a chief minister's death was not standard protocol. But MGR was MGR, and, more pertinently, RV was RV. As we have seen, he knew when the protocol was to be observed and when it was to be breached. Politics has a grid with vents that no politician misses, and no non-politician can ever fully see or understand.

Rajiv Gandhi reached there separately, a little earlier, and with the spontaneous grace which was typically his, went straight to Rajaji Hall, where MGR's body lay in state and then to MGR's residence to condole the death with Mrs Janaki Ramachandran.

We landed in a melting pot of mass grieving, administrative tension, and political uncertainty. Who would succeed MGR? J. Jayalalithaa (1948–2016) was no ordinary claimant to the prize, but she was, at the time, out of the ruling establishment's favour. MGR's widow, Janaki, a novice to politics but the keeper of MGR's conscience over the years, was there. The two Js were poised to split the party in power. Jayalalithaa was the propaganda secretary of the AIADMK, a position MGR had created for her, and as such, she had locus standi. And Janaki was chief mourner.

Displaying the stamina of a woman of will, Jayalalithaa stood unbudging for hours at the head of the slanted platform in Rajaji Hall, where MGR's body was lying. Members of his family and his adherents who disliked her bore this, grinding their teeth.

Seeing the man who had been more kind to me than any other political leader in my entire career in Tamil Nadu lying in his final sleep, I said a quick and silent nanri, ayya (thank you, sir) to him before being nudged by random politicians to get a move on.

Tamil Nadu, the land of intellectual venturesomeness, is also the home of emotional meltdowns. Nowhere else is the phenomenon of self-immolations on political issues and at the time of great leaders' deaths known in quite the way it is in that state. The act has a vivid name in Tamil—ti-kulippu, meaning fire-bathing. Thirteen persons fire-bathed themselves to death in frenzied grief over MGR's death. Nobody pressured them to do this. They acted wholly of their own accord.

The practice goes back, say Tamil Nadu scholars, to ancient times. But in more proximate calendars, it can be traced to the anti-Hindi agitation that shook the Bhaktavatsalam government in 1965. A twenty-seven-year-old married man and father of an infant daughter had set himself ablaze in Tiruchirappalli after leaving a note saying, 'I plan to die to protect Tamil.

One day, my goal will be met.' Six more had followed him in the fiery protest.[3] So, it is not just the cult of personality but something else, something inexplicable, that must lie beneath the phenomenon. I have been unable to understand or explain it.

1988
BHARAT RATNA

The year began 'greatly', as one might say in Indian English, for Tamil India.

MGR was conferred, posthumously, the nation's highest civilian decoration, the Bharat Ratna.

RV had decided at some point in the hours that followed the news of MGR's death that he would have this done. Traditionally, the names for the Bharat Ratna are decided by the president and prime minister in consultation. RV obtained Rajiv's concurrence with no difficulty. A thought crossed my mind when I learnt of the president's decision: two stalwarts of the Dravidian movement, MGR's seniors, both, and regarded by him as mentors, had not got the Bharat Ratna, posthumous or otherwise—Periyar and Annadurai. The conferring of the Bharat Ratna on MGR posthumously superseded his seniors. It would, of course, be accepted by all in Tamil Nadu with no criticism because it was coming in the wake of his death, almost as part of the obsequies. But it would raise demands in the future for the decoration to be conferred on those two and others as well, such as Karunanidhi himself.

This was a pedant's thought. Pedants are ants. Bureaucratic pedants are ants who think they are scorpions. To be sure, their tails do have a tiny sting, but, alas for them, the points carry only minor acids, no real venom. Their moves are of no consequence. My rumination on the Bharat Ratna was pointless.

When emotion rules and when political personages with their instincts buzzing guide them to take audacious decisions, they go right ahead regardless of what officers may murmur. RV had dealt with bureaucrats all his working life. He knew what to get from them and what to discard. 'MGR was a patriot,' RV said to me, 'who served the people of Tamil Nadu without ever questioning the sovereignty of the nation. He called his party All India Anna DMK....' The announcement of the Bharat Ratna for MGR on the eve of Republic Day, 1988, was welcomed in Tamil Nadu by most. But *The Hindu*, notably, which reported it prominently on its first page on 26 January, refrained from writing an editorial on it.

This was the first time that RV was approving the full list of Padma awards. He did not have much trouble doing so as the names, which had come with Rajiv's approval and, in some cases, at Rajiv's instance, were impeccable. RV suggested some names himself. In sports, Viswanathan 'Vishy'

Anand (b. 1969) and Mohammed Azharuddin (b. 1963) got the Padma Shri. In music, Umayalpuram Sivaraman (mridangam, b. 1935), Zakir Hussain (tabla, 1951-2024). In dance, Sudharani Raghupathy (Bharatanatyam, b. 1944), Bikash Bhattacharya (1940–2006) for painting and, delightfully, Mario Miranda (1926–2011) for cartooning. In the Padma Bhushan category figured the unbelievably supple and puissant Odissi dancer Kelucharan Mohapatra (1926–2004) and the scholar-biographer B. R. Nanda (1917–2010). I was gratified to see the Padma Vibhushan go, albeit posthumously, to the all-time great Hindi writer Mahadevi Varma.

I have dwelled earlier on this reclusive woman, who spent almost all her working life in Allahabad, writing the most stunning prose and poetry and painting as well and her short autobiographical story *Mera Chini Bhai* (My Chinese Brother) about the classical 'outsider', a Chinese vendor of silk who has become friends with Mahadevi and calls her his 'sistal'. Mrinal Sen made a powerful movie based on the film, *Neel Akasher Neechey* in 1959, which, with Hemen Gupta's 1961 film *Kabuliwala* based on Tagore's story of the same title, helps us see the absurdity of our latent xenophobia.

Mahadevi got the Padma Vibhushan, as I said, posthumously and if some fans of hers worked for it, so much the better for great writing. But the lobbying by others (none of those mentioned) for these awards had been sickening. Letters, phone calls, and whispered pleas came from people who sometimes were deserving of it but who vitiated their case by abject appeals.

On the same day that MGR had passed away, an interim cabinet headed by the most senior minister in the MGR ministry—the then finance minister, Dr V. R. Nedunchezhiyan—was ushered in by Governor Khurana. But the going was not to be smooth. MGR's one-time fund manager, long-time confidant and later a minister, R. M. Veerappan (1926–2024), backed the apolitical Janaki Ramachandran (1923–96) to step into her husband's shoes and lead the party and the government. The Nedunchezhiyan-led interim cabinet resigned quickly thereafter, and even as Jayalalithaa sulked and strategized, Khurana once again moved swiftly, swearing in an eight-member cabinet headed by Janaki Ramachandran with, predictably, Veerappan being the Number Two, and also the leader of the house. The departed chief minister, the new chief minister, and the challenger to her were all stars of the silver screen, and the events all had the look and feel of an exciting thriller.

Before the year ended, a memorable occurrence gave President Venkataraman and his team happiness, suspense, relief, and rapture in quick turns. The prestigious Chukha Hydel Project in Bhutan, a major India-assisted venture, was being commissioned and the President was to attend the event, with His Majesty the King of Bhutan, do the honours. It was proposed that

M. S. Subbulakshmi should be flown to the event and sing an invocatory song or two. To everyone's delight, she and her husband, T. Sadasivam, agreed. But, as Dalip Mehta, a valued friend and senior diplomat, at that point, joint secretary in the Ministry of External Affairs 'in charge' of India's relations with Bhutan, Nepal, and the Tibetan communities in India, recalls (in a personal communication to the author, dated 14 January 2025):

> President Venkataraman was not too happy that the Nightingale of India should visit Bhutan at all because of the altitude and whether it would cause her any health problems. But once she agreed and agreed enthusiastically, the decision was made and MS accompanied the president on his state visit to Bhutan. During the visit a trip had been arranged to fly to the Chukha Hydel Project which then was a major Indian assisted project. The entire entourage was to fly to its destination, a makeshift helipad, in two M-8, I think they were, Indian Air Force helicopters. The president, his family, the King of Bhutan Jigme Singye Wangchuk, the Indian Ambassador Nareshwar Dayal, and other senior officials went in the first chopper, while MS, her husband, and one of her daughters along with Siddharth Singh the COP, myself, and a few others flew in the second. The first chopper landed without a problem but the second, with MS on board developed some mechanical problems which caused considerable delay and the weather too took a slight turn for the worse. The president became very agitated as there was no communication between the second chopper and those that had already landed (There were no mobile phones at that time). The president feared the worst! We in the second chopper also became very agitated and did not know how to inform the president as to the cause of the delay. Finally we did take off and landed safely to the great relief of all concerned. The king kept his calm but later told me of the acute anxiety he felt not knowing what to inform the president. After MS sang a couple of bhajans she then sang, in Dzongkha, the local language of Bhutan, a popular hymn that wafted magically over the mountains and surrounding valleys. It was an unforgettable experience and our president could feel the palpable joy of all those present. After the lunch that had been arranged we all returned to Thimphu much richer by the experience.

I was in that second helicopter and remember the experience Dalip has recalled so vividly. I shudder now at the thought that the chopper could have malfunctioned mid-air and come down with the Nightingale on board.

Thanks to the Grace that guarded her, it all ended well. The most abiding memory of that entire episode is, for me, MS, facing the snow peaks, rendering of 'Nagendra Haraya', the hymn to Shiva, which with its evocation of that lord of the snows, was ethereal for its sublime appositenesss.

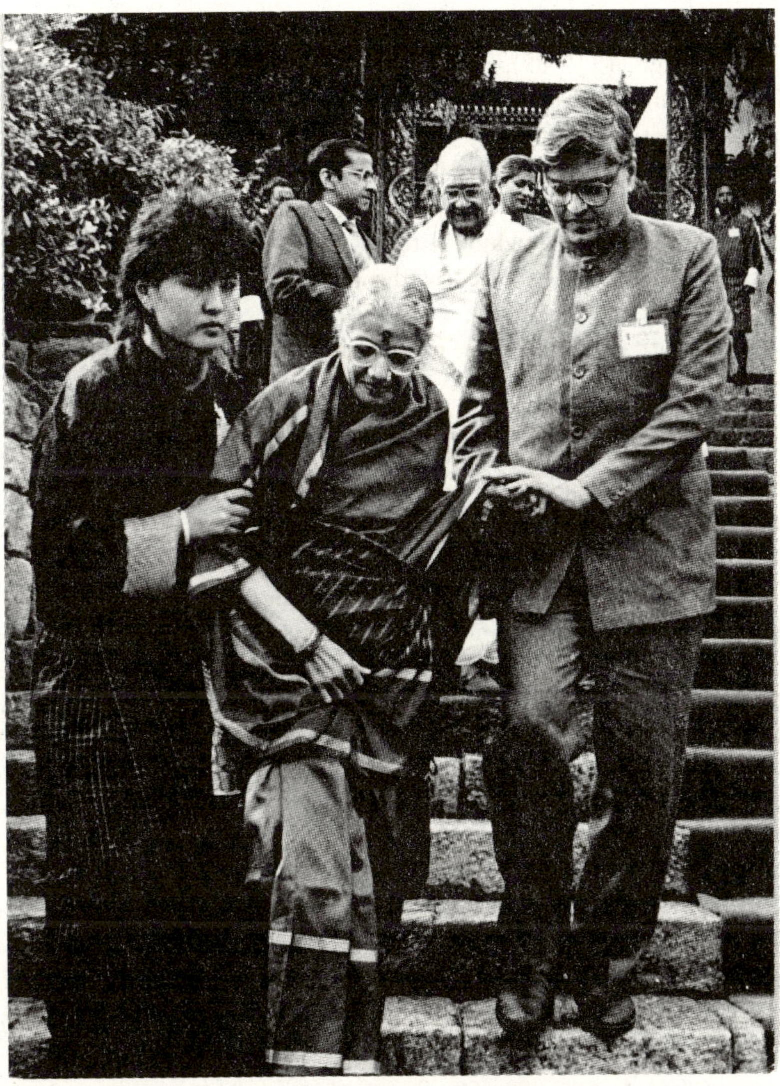

Nightingale of India flies to the Himalaya—M. S. Subbulakshmi at Thimpu, Bhutan, October 1988, after a concert. To her rear is her husband T. Sadasivam. Helping her down a steep flight of steps, the author, then joint secretary to President R. Venkataraman. (Author's personal collection).

1989
JUSTICE

The shadow of a Sikh loomed over Rashtrapati Bhavan as the new year began.

Kehar Singh (1935–89), an assistant in the Directorate General of Supply and Disposal in New Delhi in the Government of India, had been sentenced to death, along with Satwant Singh (1962–89), in the Indira Gandhi assassination case. Satwant Singh, with Beant Singh (1959–84), had fired several bullets, killing Indira Gandhi. Beant was killed by other security guards present on the spot, but Satwant Singh was taken in. His role was clear. He was a co-assassin and would have to get the punishment the law prescribed and the courts decreed.

Every court involved in the proceedings found Kehar Singh guilty, and President Venkataraman, as advised on file by Rajiv Gandhi's cabinet, turned down the mercy petition filed by the convict summarily.[1]

During these tense hours, I got a call on behalf of His Holiness the Dalai Lama, asking if I could meet him. He was visiting, staying in a hotel. My brothers knew the Dalai Lama well, not I that much. But then he had 'placed' me, joint secretary to the president, as the youngest brother of Rajmohan and Ramchandra Gandhi. I could sense that he wanted to say something 'official' to me, so I sought and got the president's permission to meet HH.

I went dutifully to HH, bowed as always, and told him how honoured I felt that he should want me to meet him. HH was kindness and grace itself. He enquired about my brothers' and my welfare and then said: 'You see...I have been thinking of this matter of the death sentence on...' and he turned to his aide for the name... 'Yes, Kehar Singh... I do not know the legal position, you see, but as a Buddhist and as a follower of your grandfather's teaching of ahimsa, I feel, you see, that India should, in the name of the Mahatma, not hang the man.... Can you, you see, convey this to the president?'

I went straight to the president, who heard the account without reaction.

Hours before the execution, irascible lawyer Ram Jethmalani (1923–2019) and high-voltage lawyer Shanti Bhushan (1925–2023) argued before the Supreme Court for two hours to persuade it that the president had not applied his mind on the mercy petition. The five-judge bench led by Chief Justice R. S. Pathak declined to intervene. Jethmalani said: 'If this court can't intervene, then it is not just my client who will hang tomorrow. Something much more vital will die. It will not be Kehar Singh who will be hanged;

it will be decency and justice.' Shanti Bhushan said, 'In fact, the court must decide whether a man should ever be sentenced to death on the basis of circumstantial evidence alone. Circumstantial evidence can never remove that last lingering speck of doubt about a man's guilt.'[2]

The matter had drawn international notice. The International Commission of Jurists appealed to the president to grant clemency to Kehar Singh: 'The International Commission of Jurists is profoundly disturbed by the rejection of pleas for mercy which have caused deep concern among the jurists throughout the world. As appears from the judgment, the only substantial evidence on which his conviction was based was that he had talks with Beant Singh on various occasions, but there was no evidence as to the contents of those talks. We beseech you to exercise your right and power to have regard to the merits of the case in order to prevent what might be a terrible error of justice.'[3]

The president was unmoved.

That night, while I was at dinner with the family, the phone rang. It was the ace lawyer Soli Sorabjee. 'Gopal, sorry to be disturbing you at this hour, but you have to help. Please tell the president that even at this late hour, he can intervene. He can ask for a stay of the execution until he has reviewed the matter.' I told Soli there was no point, the president was not going to review the matter. But I asked the Rashtrapati Bhavan telephone exchange to check with the president if he would take a call from Soli. Futile.

The next morning, 6 January 1989, Kehar Singh and Satwant Singh were hanged at Delhi's Tihar jail on a scaffold that was put up for the purpose. Reports said his last words were 'Bole So Nihal, Sat Sri Akal'. The scaffolds, reports said, were demolished immediately after.

RV, of course, was his usual self—spruce, diligent, working away at his desk that morning. Kehar Singh was a file disposed of.

Rajiv was beset by Bofors, an increasingly hawkish opposition, and a snappy press. He did not realize what many had begun to sense: his government's days were now numbered not because its five-year term was drawing to a close, but because his popularity had shrunk, his credibility had shrivelled, and the chances of his returning to power had slimmed beyond redemption.

Vishwanath Pratap Singh (1931–2008) had emerged as a new force, personifying integrity and courage and a new brand of honesty. He had, in addition, a reputation of efficiency and intelligence in the running of ministries. Officers respected, even admired him. RV's secretary and my boss, Prem Kumar, himself a man of great probity and efficiency, had been commerce secretary when V. P. Singh was commerce minister, and he told me how much he respected his former minister. V. P. Singh was also known as one who had tossed his prince's lifestyle—he hailed from the principality of Manda in Uttar Pradesh to become an ardent egalitarian. His chief ministership of that state was known as one that had few controversies and no scandals attached to it.

So, Rajiv was in trouble, deep trouble. And election-eve trouble.

Bofors was soon on all political minds and in all media discussions of current affairs. I never thought then nor have ever since then that any monies had been transferred by the Swedish manufacturer of that machine to Rajiv Gandhi. But some money had moved, like the Northern Lights in a wispy dance proceeding on an inky sky from nowhere to nowhere. Where it landed and to what purpose it was put was a mystery. *The Hindu*'s N. Ram, one of India's foremost journalists, who was to become a beacon of strength for the safety and security of working journalists worldwide and for freedom of expression, alerted the nation to questions that needed answering in the deal.

As the heat rose on Bofors, RV, who, as a former defence minister, knew all about defence purchases, kept his thoughts to himself. V. P. Singh's resignation as defence minister had electrified the opposition and the nation. He had, in the presidential election, despite his new role, voted for RV, who made no secret of his admiration for V. P. Singh's integrity and honesty. 'He is emerging as an alternative to Rajiv,' RV once told me, and in his typical style, added, philosophically, '...all right.'

Meanwhile, Prem Kumar was due to retire, and RV wanted him to be given an extension so he could be there to assist during the elections and its aftermath—government formation. He knew Prem Kumar would give him assistance of gold standard. He sent to Rajiv a proposal for Prem Kumar's extension. But now it was Rajiv's turn to do a Zail Singh-like pocket veto. He did not agree, he did not decline. He just kept quiet. Perhaps he had been told of Prem Kumar having worked with V. P. Singh. The retirement date came, but no orders on the proposal for extension. RV got the message, and RV being RV, he was not going to see if this candle was worth it. Prem Kumar, scrupulous to a fault, after taking a meeting, his last as secretary, on the planting of trees on the president's estate, demitted charge and slid with the grace of a bird migrating to another clime.

T. N. Seshan (1932–2019), than whom the god of governance has not created a more potent self-loading, self-ejecting, self-directing cannonball, was then a very strong environment secretary to the government and also advising government on internal security. RV, who knew Seshan well as a 'Madras civilian', asked him for advice on who may be appointed in Prem Kumar's place. Seshan suggested an excellent name: P. Murari, also an IAS officer of the Tamil Nadu cadre, the most genial of men and the most congenial of secretaries. If Prem Kumar was an admirer of V. P. Singh, Murari was, it so happened, an honest admirer of Rajiv Gandhi. RV was relieved but was also sure that Murari, with his training in Fort St. George's rigorous mores, would give him strictly correct assistance and ensure that all presidential prerogatives would be exercised correctly, recorded accurately and be not only right but also seen to be right.

With the elections to the Lok Sabha announced, RV's presidential instincts were to the fore. He read up precedents, Indian and British, for all contingencies. He also knew that all reading and preparations help that much and no more. Ultimately, contingencies call for contingent responses.

My brother, Rajmohan, who had been critical of the Rajiv Gandhi government over many issues, was working then at the Teen Murti Memorial Library when V. P. Singh all of a sudden arrived there and reaching him among the book racks, asked him to spare a minute. Stepping out, Rajmohan was surprised to be asked out of the blue if he would agree to contest against Rajiv from Amethi. Rajmohan was surprised but not, I think, overwhelmed in any sense. Thinking hard and deep, he agreed to do so. This was big news: Gandhi versus Gandhi and, in a further tweak, 'Real Gandhi versus Fake Gandhi'—a most unseemly juxtaposition, making Rajiv's surname to which he was entitled by paternal descent, a put-on thing to fool the public. This was wrong, in poor form. Rajmohan could not stop his campaign managers from using that line. He had, all said and done, been put up against Rajiv Gandhi because he was a Gandhi, Rajmohan Gandhi. The contest became the most watched contest of the election. And watched not just within India but by media elsewhere as well.

At this point, Rajiv was said to have been advised, doubtless by the lesser minds of his party, to ask my sister Taru to choose 'any safe constituency anywhere in India' to contest from there as a Congress candidate. I do not know how true this is, but a phone call to follow up on did come to Taru. It was from M. L. Fotedar. Taru, who had no idea who Fotedar was, asked: 'Kaun?' (Who?). Fotedar gave his name again. This must have come as a shock to the party strongman. He repeated the name. Taru could still not get it and then asked, 'Spelling?' Fotedar might have been near collapsing in shock. He spelt out his own name, perhaps for the first and last time in his life. The message was received, reflected on, and was replied with, 'Sorry, this I cannot do.' Tara Gandhi Bhattacharjee, an acknowledged authority on khadi with a knowledge base on that craft scarcely equalled, a master of Hindi letters, widely travelled and hugely sensitive to matters historical and civilizational, would have been an asset to the Lok Sabha. But she also was—is—a woman of exceptional veracity who would do the right thing only for the right reasons.

With Rajmohan now contesting against the prime minister, my role as joint secretary to the president was not enviable. English has words for every situation or almost. Piquant is the word to describe mine in Rashtrapati Bhavan. My situation was more piquant than piquant. RV could sense my difficulty. When I said to him that people might think I am using my position in his office to advance my brother's case, RV said, 'No, no...nothing of the kind. In any case, you do not handle political files. When government formation is happening, Murari will put up the relevant papers to me. No one can fault you.' The problem had to turn serious. And it did.

On polling day in Amethi, goons began rigging the election with brazen dare. Booths were captured, and voters intimidated. Police looked the other way. Worse, at a melee, police opened fire, and Sanjay Singh, campaigning for himself and for Rajmohan, was injured, not all that slightly.[4] Was Rajiv aware of this?

Not much after, I decided in the integrity of my loneliness that I should go on leave for the remainder of this election phase and right up to and beyond government-formation. I conveyed this to RV in a note. 'Approved,' he wrote on the page in his neat hand.

The days that followed were miserable for me. Friends would ring and commiserate, making me feel worse. Our cherished friends Mala and Tejbir Singh one day took me and Tara to their farm, Panch Peelu, for just a change. A sweeter gesture could not have been made.

After the results came in, with Rajiv winning Amethi but losing his majority in the Lok Sabha and RV inviting V. P. Singh to form the new government, a saga ended. RV followed constitutional proprieties meticulously. He first asked Rajiv, as leader of the single largest party in the new house, if he was willing and able to form the next government and on Rajiv expressing inability, then turned to V. P. Singh. RV consulted legal experts with Murari, his rock-like support during this delicate transition.

Rajmohan's defeat was seen as a moral victory. Meeting former president Giani Zail Singh around that time, he was told by the Giani, 'You lost, but because of the way you lost, at least 30 or 40 Congress candidate all over the country lost their elections.' (The elections having been staggered, there were phases after the one in which Amethi figured.)

On 2 December, V. P. Singh became prime minister of India, leading a coalition led by his Janata Dal and supported very contradictorily by the Bharatiya Janata Party (BJP) and the Left.

From my leave-perch at home, I watched the swearing-in ceremony on television, with the drama of Devi Lal coming within a whisker of the prime ministership, as the nation gasped in disbelief, and then with great good grace yielding the place to V. P. Singh, as the nation sighed in relief. The next day, the phone rang at home. It was the president. 'Gopu, the drama is over. You can return.'

But the drama had not quite finished.

The appointment of Mufti Mohammad Sayeed (1936–2016), the Kashmiri leader who had joined the Rajiv Gandhi government in 1986 as minister of Tourism and in 1987 quit the Congress party to join V. P. Singh's Jan Morcha, as home minister, the first Muslim to be appointed to that office, thrilled me. This was secular politics in action; that Mufti was controversial in his home state and that he was deeply distrusted by Farooq Abdullah, the incumbent chief minister of J&K, made little difference. A Muslim as home minister of India was big-ticket news. Rajmohan told me he was delighted too by the message that V. P. Singh was sending by that one gesture to all of India and to the world.

But the joy, naive and simplistic as it was, was short-lived. Within a week of the new cabinet assuming charge, Mufti's daughter, Rubaiya Sayeed, a twenty-three-year-old medical intern, was kidnapped in Srinagar by separatist militants from the Jammu and Kashmir Liberation Front (JKLF).

Moosa Raza (1937–2024) was chief secretary of J&K at that time. With a rare raconteur's gift, the Tamil Nadu-born civilian says in his book *Kashmir: Land of Regrets*, 'I had come to Delhi for some meetings on 6 December, 1989...and had an appointment with the home minister on the afternoon of 8 December.... When I reached North Block at 4 p.m., the minister's P.A. told me they had just received the news that his daughter had been kidnapped.[5] When I was ushered in, the minister was on the phone.... He waved me to a seat in front of his desk.... When he put the phone down...he was calm and collected.... The only thing he said was, "I would not have been so anxious had they kidnapped my son..."'[6]

The kidnappers demanded the release of five jailed members of the JKLF. Raza was to play a key role in the negotiations with others, wheels turning within wheels, and T. N. Seshan, who was the lame-duck cabinet secretary at the time orchestrating everything from Delhi, telling Raza on 13 December that 'the state government...(should) ensure the safe release of the hostage without any injury to her....' This was an order. Raza took it to mean the only thing it could mean: 'Do whatever is needed to secure her release.'

'Would this have been done if the girl was not a VIP's daughter?' was the question on most minds. VIP children do bear a cross, even when kidnapped. Noblesse oblige of a kind. True, but a most dangerous precedent had been set. When the swap happened, and Rubaiya was released, RV rang the home minister and congratulated him on the return of his daughter. But I know he was not amused. He regarded the swap and the release to be a cop-out. But Kashmir had more happening to it within the next few days.

Several kidnappings followed, including the infinitely tragic one of forty-eight-year-old H. L. Khera, the general manager of state-run Hindustan Machine Tools, who was killed and had his body flung to a random site in Srinagar. RV writes in his memoir 'This sent shock waves throughout the country. The relatives of Khera castigated the government, saying in the case of Rubiya Sayeed, it had conceded the demands of the terrorists, while in Khera's case, it left him to his fate.'[7] Farooq Abdullah, who had opposed the swap plan strongly, had consistently predicted this. Years later, Raza asked Seshan what lay behind his instructions of 13 December and got the answer, 'The game was much bigger…The target was much higher.' Seshan did not elaborate. He was, by then, the chief election commissioner of India.

BOOK SIX

1990

IF THERE BE A FIELD OF WAR ON EARTH, IT IS HERE, IT IS HERE, IT IS HERE

Kashmir entranced Emperor Jahangir and, gazing at the Shalimar Gardens, he recalled the famous words in Persian: Gar firdaus bar roo-e zameen ast, Hameen ast-o hameen ast-o hameen ast (If there is a heaven on earth, it is here, it is here, it is here). That line could well be redone now, with sadness: Gar maidan-e-jung bar roo-e zameen ast, Hameen ast-o hameen ast-o, hameen-ast. (If there be a field of war on earth, it is here, it is here, it is here)

For the very reason that the rest of the country was divided over the kidnap-swap and fearing more kidnaps-swaps as a result of this precedent, streets in Srinagar, Anantnag, Sopore, and Baramulla burst into delirious celebrations. Wajahat Habibullah, ever the balanced observer and restrained commentator, writes, 'The astoundingly widespread celebration by separatist JKLF supporters in downtown Srinagar streets was a foretaste of the uprising that was now imminent.'[1]

V. P. Singh had left the state to Mufti, who had left it to his loyalists in the Valley. He wanted to take no chances with Farooq. Within weeks of Rubaiya's release, Governor Krishna Rao, who enjoyed a cordial equation with Farooq, was sacked. He was to be replaced by the one man Farooq did not want to see in Srinagar. Jagmohan Malhotra (1927–2021) had been governor there from 1984 to 1989, well-liked in Jammu and well-disliked in the Valley, and of course by Farooq and not by Farooq alone. This appointment was Mufti's doing. As soon as Farooq heard of it, he resigned with the result that the state had vacancies arising simultaneously in the positions of governor and chief minister—an unprecedented situation. Paramilitary forces were sent to the state to control it, and they did so with the only means at their disposal: force. The day after Jagmohan was appointed, to cite Habibullah again, '...panic-stricken CRPF firing in Gawkadal in January precipitated a full-scale insurgency and the exodus of Kashmiri Pandits. I learned of at least fifty people killed at Gawkadal, although survivors claimed a death toll of nearly 300.' The state went into a spin that had to end in direct rule by Delhi, which meant rule by Mufti.

But who rules for ever or even for very long?

The outwitters are always outwitted by their own tribe.

The country was preparing for and getting engulfed in two battles, one trying to outsmart the other. So quick-to-move was action against reaction, that one could not know which was the action, which the reaction.

Deputy Prime Minister Devi Lal, whom President Venkataraman remembered as the one who insisted on calling himself deputy prime minister at the time of his swearing-in when propriety and protocol required him to take his oaths as 'minister' (and later be designated as deputy prime minister), and his son Om Prakash Chautala, the chief minister of Haryana, made Prime Minister V. P. Singh think of stratagems to take the wind from the senior Haryanvi's sails.

The implementation of the Mandal Report was done at least partly, if not wholly, to outwit Devi Lal. He hoped, not illogically, that the move to suddenly brighten the prospects of OBCs across the country would so consolidate and galvanize different segments of society as to make Devi Lal's politics look small. But then, before that could happen, and before V. P. Singh could ready himself to face the backlash in terms of upper caste resistance to Mandal, the BJP and Hindutva forces, already planning the rath yatra to Ayodhya, gave an impetus to the great push to Ram's birthplace.

President Venkataraman, committed as he was from his early days in Congressism to social justice and the removal of caste-based injustices, could not but be supportive of Mandal. But he was aware too of this thing called 'right steps for the wrong reason'. And he could not but rue the haste with which Mandal was being taken forward, leading to the attempted self-immolation of a college student—Rajeev Goswami. If Mandal hit a roadblock, the rath yatra to Ayodhya, which the BJP stalwart Lal Krishna Advani (b. 1927) had commenced, did too. Bihar chief minister Lalu Prasad had him arrested at 4 a.m. on 23 October 1990 in Bihar's Samastipur district, adding new political dynamics to the demand for a temple to Ram being raised where the Babri Masjid stood.

The BJP had to and did withdraw its 'outside support' to V. P. Singh's government, Atal Bihari Vajpayee motoring to Rashtrapati Bhavan to give the letters to the president. According to Neerja Chowdhury in her book *How Prime Ministers Decide*, Congress loyalists moved fast to have Rajiv Gandhi installed as prime minister in V. P. Singh's place, with defectors from Janata Dal and the Congress's MPs backing him, and when M. L. Fotedar went to RV at this time, the president told him that he was ready to install a Congress-led ministry 'immediately', but only if it were led by Pranab Mukherjee, not Rajiv. Presumably, Chowdhury heard this from Fotedar.[2]

President Venkataraman was not free of political likes and dislikes. He was not infallible. But as president, he was too conscious of what posterity would say of his veracity, his sense of objectivity, his impartiality, to make a proposition that was not from out of his 'headmaster's textbook'. But Neerja Chowdhury writes from notes kept meticulously by her.

The inevitable happened, with V. P. Singh losing the confidence motion in the Lok Sabha on 7 November 1990, followed by the constitutionally unimpeachable process of Chandra Shekhar, who staked his claim and produced names and numbers of MPs—64—just enough to win the president's invitation to form a government, being called upon to shoulder the responsibility. Rajiv supporting Chandra Shekhar from the outside was no reassuring arrangement, but then it was an empirical fact which no president could ignore.

At the veteran socialist's open-air swearing-in at the forecourt of Rashtrapati Bhavan on 10 November 1990, the president's secretary, P. Murari, did the honours of calling out the names while, as joint secretary, I did the subordinate clerical honours of handing over the signing quill to the new prime minister to sign the register of office with. Chandra Shekhar, no novice in politics, no greenhorn in public life, was still new to high office. Reaching where he had long wanted to, he was yet excitedly nervous. His hand was in a mild tremor as he picked up the stylus, dipped it in the ink-pot, and before he could put the nib over the paper, let a drop of the black ink fall on the broad open page.

It is difficult at such moments for the most dogged rationalist to be unaffected by such a 'sign'. I have no idea what Chandra Shekhar felt, but I stepped back, in my bandgala affair, to my position in the line-up, feeling distinctly uneasy.

1991
'YEH KYA HUA HAI?'

Four months and a few days after Chandra Shekhar had become prime minister with Congress support, the grand old party withdrew that support. Those months may be said to be one of the most mysterious in post-independent India, for no one quite knew what was happening. The balance between the coalition and the 'outside support' being given to it was and will ever be the subject of many theories and interpretations that ranged from envy on the part of Rajiv at Chandra Shekhar's rapid progress on a solution to the dispute at Ayodhya, to plain and simple lure of a return to office by a Rajiv-led ministry with support from defectors coming out of both the Singh and Shekhar camps, and pique at what seemed like surveillance of Congress party premises by government sleuths. Fotedar was busy as busy can be to see fault lines and create them, if need be, in the ranks of MPs in other parties so as to give Rajiv the critical mass of MPs needed to stake a claim to a new cabinet formation.

But the math did not add up, and in March, as Shekhar was readying the budget, Rajiv announced he was withdrawing his party's support to Shekhar. He had opted for the imponderables of yet another election to those of an unreliable partnership with disparate MPs. The inevitable followed, with Shekhar recommending the dissolution of the house and elections, both of which President Venkataraman could not but accept.

And 'the 1991 elections', as they came to be called, were held a mere sixteen months after the previous election. Over 500 million eligible voters were to once again elect their government—no welcome exercise when no leader seemed to have national stature in the sharply polarized and fractious environment caused by the OBC and Ayodhya controversies. 'Mandal–Mandir' was the popular name given to the choices faced by the electorate. And with the shadow of what was being seen as Rajiv's miscalculations over Sri Lanka. A weary and wan campaign commenced in the summer, supervised by the chief election commissioner, the redoubtable T. N. Seshan.

The nation's scene by mid-May was like this: the country's general elections were midway through their course. Shekhar was a caretaker PM. Extremely emotive issues were floating in the air, tugging at India's caste and creed moorings. The president was head of a state in flux. And yet, in strictly constitutional terms, there was a government in position, a cabinet in office, a PM heading it. Rajiv was, again, in strictly constitutional terms, a former PM and a candidate in the elections to the Lok Sabha.

21 May 1991.

Tara and our elder daughter, Divya, had gone on a trek to the Pindari glacier in the Himalaya. Amrita, our younger daughter and I, after dinner, watched a Hollywood movie, *Child's Play*. This was a horror movie full of gore and multiple slayings, decapitations, and every imaginable monstrosity enacted in direst detail. I was glad when the thing got over a little after 10 p.m. Amrita was fast asleep in a trice, but the monster scenes kept turning in my mind. Foolish, I said to myself, letting a silly film occupy my brain.

I was just beginning to drop off to sleep when the phone next to my bed rang. The time of the night being what it was, this was unusual and disturbing. It was Murari, the president's secretary. 'Rajiv has been killed,' he said, 'blown up in Sriperumbudur by a suicide bomber. His head has been severed....' The drowsy brain mixes words, scenes, and images. The lurid film had not left my brain when Murari's words entered it. On my asking some incoherent questions, Murari said, '...a few minutes ago...Seshan rang and told the president'. Seshan's office at that election time had invested him with powers and prestige out of the ordinary.

There was no time even for shock. I went over to the staff rooms, woke up Urmila, our diligent housemaid and, saying there was an emergency, and I had to rush to the president, asked her to be with Amrita, who was, of course, fast asleep. Dazed but very responsible, she told me to go unworried; she would take care. Our house—19 Willingdon Crescent—was just a two minutes' drive away from the gates of Rashtrapati Bhavan, and within about ten minutes of Murari's call, I was in the President's Study. There RV was, his interrupted sleep not fully out from face and eyes, looking both rattled and alert. Standing near him was Murari, on the qui vive, and a little to a side—Seshan. A kind of euphoria had possessed the civilian, a surge of power, a suffusion of energy. Through the silent pauses and phone calls coming in and being made, I gathered that Seshan had got the news from his election staff on duty in Sriperumbudur, had immediately dialled Rashtrapati Bhavan, demanded to be put through to the president and succeeded, broke the news to him, rang Murari as well who got to the president in no time, ringing me in the same hectic minutes. Seshan himself got to Rashtrapati Bhavan super-fast.

There were just the four of us in that study for the next many agonizing moments, before others, relevant to the crisis, came in and went. At one tense moment Seshan motioned to me to move with him to an alcove between the study and the adjoining Yellow Drawing Room, just about 12 feet away from where RV was seated. With wide eyes and shovelling hands, Seshan spoke in whispered urgency. He said he felt the election process needed to be stopped straightaway, the nation's security be brought under swift and strict control, and that he was ready to play his role beyond his office of CEC and, if RV thought fit, could serve as the country's home minister.

~

RV meanwhile got through to Sonia Gandhi over the telephone. His words to her, coming in spurts of grief and wisdom, were brief. He must go, the president said, to Sonia's house. The president's convoy was assembled within minutes by the military secretary and other staff who had all by now converged.

Seshan, in a state of high tension, also left. There was a tender moment as he said to me, 'Please ring my wife and tell her not to be worried, I will be contacting her soon.' I rang Mrs Seshan, the wonderful Jayalakshmi Ammal, ever supportive of her husband, ever stoic, and gave her the message. She was as understanding as ever, as cordial as always. As suddenly as he had seemed to me a control-freak, fishing in troubled waters for a trawl of power, Seshan became a simple householder, worried for his wife, who worried for him. We are many identities, each one of us within one body.

RV could not reach Sonia in her house. A not very large but very vituperative crowd went for his convoy, smashing window screens. It turned back with some haste, with the crowd giving it chase for a while. If an infuriated Delhi was targeting Sikhs in 1984, a maddened Delhi in 1991 could well—who knows?—go for any Tamil in sight. RV returned, well past 1 a.m., looking most troubled and grieving; he sat down in his seat with a sigh. Within a few minutes, the aide de camp announced that Prime Minister Chandra Shekhar and Cabinet Secretary Naresh Chandra (1934–2017) had arrived. Lame-duck and 'caretaking' his prime ministership might have been, but the MP from Ballia and now PM was composed. In measured words, he said to RV that what should not have happened had happened but that everything needed was being done to contain the crisis that had just arisen. And Naresh Chandra! I can only say my pride in the civil services soared as I heard him tell RV: 'Sir…the tragedy is unimaginably great, but let me assure you every step is being taken to contain the crisis. There is no need for any panic, no need to pause the election process. The borders are being watched for any unusual activity. And if I may say, sir… The person killed was a young and charismatic leader with long years of service ahead of him. But he was a former prime minister, not the prime minister. The prime minister here, Chandra Shekharji, as you have yourself explained, is prime minster in every sense of the term and is heading a government that is in total control of the situation and will handle any fallout, internal or external, with total confidence. India is secure. Please be assured.'

I have never heard another phrase more gratefully as Naresh Chandra's that night of howling jackals: 'India is secure.'

RV was assured.

I recorded in my diary for that day: '*Shattering news of RG's assassination at about 11 p.m. followed by a whole night with President and Bob (Murari) and others. CEC present throughout; bossy and trying to "take charge". Cab. Secy. picture of calm confidence.*'

I managed to return home briefly to check on Amrita. She was a little puzzled upon waking to a home from which her mother and sister were away and without her father near. The staff had by now heard what had happened but had spared Amrita the details. I told her as much as was necessary and shifted her to the home of friends, for I knew I would be busy the whole day. During this hectic hour, the phone rang. P. V. Narasimha Rao was on the line, calling from Nagpur airport. He was on his way to Delhi and wanted to see the president straightaway on landing. 'Gopal, yeh kya hua hai?' (Gopal, what is this that has happened to us?) is how he began. 'Sir, itihaas ne karwat badal li hai' (Sir, history has shifted position), I replied. 'Yes,' said the man who had moved southwards, almost bag and baggage, reconciled to a life of political reclusion if not anonymity, having been denied a ticket for the elections by Rajiv. I said I would let RV know at once that he, PV, wanted to see him post-haste. But as more calls kept coming to my home number from every conceivable political specimen in creation, I sped to my office.

Deaths in India are magnets. Every manner of metal, precious, semi-precious, base, rusty, alloy, tin, is drawn to it. And funerals are a moving mound of emotions mixed with some open and many more concealed motivations.

The *Hindustan Times* of 22 May 1991 said with disarming innocence, in a PTI report headlined 'Seshan meets President', that the CEC met the president 'within hours of the assassination' and that 'it is understood' that the meeting 'took stock of the poll situation' and the 'security environment in the country'! I did not doubt then, nor do I now, that PTI was fed this benign interpretation. The election process was not interrupted or altered. But the Congress party's profile changed unrecognizably. Machinations of the most unseemly kind saw Congress hefts seeking or, rather, scrambling for sudden parries at power. Wisely, sagaciously, Sonia Gandhi declined to take Rajiv's position of Congress president, a move that led others to imagine they could run the party in her name. And within a week, during which he had met RV, P. V. Narasimha Rao was elected president of the party.

Meanwhile, unable to halt the elections, Seshan decreed a long deferment of the dates for the polls in the second and third rounds of polls from the one concluded on 20 May to 12 and 15 June. He said in an interview that these dates had been 'dictated' by the government. Prime Minister Chandra Shekhar nailed it in an emphatic denial. Why would Seshan be doing this? Only Seshan knew. V. P. Singh and I. K. Gujral called on RV on 15 June to complain about the EC's 'strange' practices.

RV was to say in his memoirs that Seshan did his work impartially and firmly but that 'During all these charges and counter-charges Chief Election commissioner Seshan maintained an unnecessarily high profile, holding Press Conferences every day, giving his views on all issues and hurting people by his brashness.'[1]

The election process went ahead, on dates and in the manner dictated by Seshan, and the nation heaved a sigh of relief when it gave over on 15 June with Congress candidates in the seats that went into polls after the assassination, winning on a sympathy tide, including among them, Mani Shankar Aiyar in Mayiladuthurai, Tamil Nadu, who was looking at a rout, winning comfortably. On 18 June, the results showed Congress winning 232 of the 521 seats and becoming the single largest party in the Lok Sabha. Rao, with Sonia's nod, was the clear leader of the Congress Legislature Party and future prime minister. At this point, the veteran administrator, now out of office, P. C. Alexander (1921–2011), rang. 'Gopal...you know I have been close to PV. He has asked me to be around at this time.... He needs some trustworthy people to be there nearby. You know Delhi.... And at some point, when the dust has settled, I will need to see the president....'

'Yes, of course, sir....' I said. Alexander was, I knew, a lightning conductor of a civilian, just the kind of person who should be consulted by leaders for sheer maturity of advice. Rao and Alexander confabulated on likely names for the new cabinet, with Finance being a key portfolio. Naresh Chandra, still the cabinet secretary, told Rao of the parlous condition of the economy. The next finance minister would have to be a magician. Alexander suggested the names of I. G. Patel and Manmohan Singh, who was then chairman of the University Grants Commission.

Rao asked RV for advice. RV said both names were good but he was more inclined to the age-senior IG. So, IG was asked first, and upon his declining, Manmohan was asked. Not asked so much as told, albeit very respectfully. And on 21 June, exactly a month after the Rajiv assassination, a minority Congress government took office with P. V. Narasimha Rao as prime minister, no troublesome deputy prime minister, and a somewhat dazed but very 'held-together' Manmohan Singh as the country's finance minister.

Even he, with his perceptive oversight, may not have reckoned with the reality that, at that time, 'India had enough foreign exchange reserves to pay for just two weeks of imports.'[2] Prime Minister Chandra Shekhar had taken an International Monetary Fund (IMF) loan in early 1991. Now, with our credibility with the IMF lower than ever, it needed a second tranche.

PV, who had held almost every major portfolio at the centre except Finance, was now doing one of the most daring acts in India's finance history. And under the advice of Manmohan Singh. As part of this 'bailout deal' with the IMF, India pledged as collateral 20 tonnes of gold to the Union Bank of Switzerland and 47 tonnes to the Bank of England and Bank of Japan. The World Bank promptly sanctioned a structural adjustment loan of two components—an IBRD loan of $ 250 million to be paid over twenty years and an IDA credit of SDR 183.8 million (equivalent to $ 250 million) with a thirty-five-year maturity. In the formal wordings, the president of India was the borrower. Gulp! RV had been finance minister, and he had a sharp, sensible finance mindset that was never so rash as to jump into the deep-end and never so conservative as to stay in the shallow. He measured the levels of risk and hope with prudence, proceeded with diligence. He took pride in the fact that India had never defaulted on her repayments to the IMF. Now, at this point, our finances had plummeted to such a low that we stood on the brink of our first failure to pay up. And so, he had no difficulty in appreciating the only method in which that contingency could be, for the time being, averted—the pledging of our gold reserves. He felt that 'between the evil of defaulting and that of selling gold, the latter course was prudent', but he did get from the RBI Governor S. Venkitaramanan (1931–2023) an important clarification: the gold being transferred was not the gold held by the RBI as backing for the currency but confiscated gold. This was quintessential RV—the prudent risk-taker.

But this emergency room-like action apart, with his ace adviser and financial crisis-manager Manmohan Singh, Prime Minister Rao had launched schemes that would make India 'internationally competitive[3]', and remove 'the cobwebs that come in the way of rapid industrialisation[4]'. This meant, essentially, doing away with large chunks of what Rajaji had, years earlier, dubbed the 'Permit-Quota-Licence Raj'.

Rao's financial team comprised, under Manmohan Singh, Montek Singh Ahluwalia (b. 1943), P. Chidambaram (b. 1945), and Jairam Ramesh (b. 1954). Entirely comfortable with Manmohan Singh's helming economic reforms and structural change, RV was not so with the other three for different reasons. He said of Montek, 'He is perhaps very intelligent, but I find he does not know India.' Here, RV was being hasty. What does 'knowing India' mean?

Montek knew his India no less than those who may look like they have walked through the dust of India's villages or the grime of her cities all their lives and he may have studied in an elite college, Delhi's St. Stephen's and then in Oxford. But had not K. R. Narayanan and Amartya Sen studied abroad? And did Montek's near-exact contemporary, the brilliant Marxist, Prabhat Patnaik not do likewise? Did they not 'know India'? One could argue with Montek on policy but not question his suitability for the office he was moving into. But there was one area in which Montek could be said to have a deficit—his first language was English. His second language was also English. As was his third. But what good English that was! Rajaji, in 1963, speaking at St. Stephen's College, had occasion to hear Montek speak from the presiding chair. 'I have rarely heard such good English,' the old English literature buff said in his speech, of Montek's brief oration. Clearly, Rajaji did not regard proficiency in English a handicap in an Indian.

Jairam Ramesh was for RV a 'Rajiv boy', whose oeuvre had little to do with RV's DNA—again an unfair dismissal, for RV had not held R. K. Dhawan's proximity to Indira Gandhi a minus mark in the loyal Punjabi. And Jairam, an IIT-Bombay alumnus, a widely-read technocrat and intellectual was no Dhawan-type man Friday. As to P. Chidambaram, RV associated the brainy Chettiar* with G. K. Moopanar, RV's bete noire in TN politics—a 'given' I could never understand nor ever felt interested in understanding.

Tamil Nadu politics could not but, and did, take up much of RV's time. Tamil Nadu MPs and MLAs, old and new, sought time and met him non-stop. It was said he had, in the dismissal of the DMK government, 'colluded' with Rajiv and Chandra Shekhar (who depended on Rajiv's numerical support in Lok Sabha). This was unfair, for whatever be RV's views on Karunanidhi and the DMK, he was not going to risk his image of an impartial president for the sake of some retrospective score-settling in Madras. But that be as it may, Jayalalithaa stormed into office for the first time in June of 1991, ending the President's Rule in the state, and starting her first term as chief minister. She had held no public office earlier. She now moved up to and held the highest one in her state. She did so as to the manner born with the word coined, it would seem, for her—aplomb. On Janaki fell the title to MGR's

*The Chettiar (also known as Nattukottai Chettiar or Nagarathar) are a Tamil mercantile community famed for expertise in commerce, banking, and moneylending. Traditionally concentrated in the Chettinad region of Tamil Nadu, they are prominent in philanthropy and the patronage of the fine arts and in the building of several temples, colleges, and universities, of which the most prominent is Annamalai University, near the temple town of Chidambaram. The community, which has over the centuries ventured overseas in the pursuit of trade, is currently said to number about 100,000 persons.

real estate; on Jayalalithaa, the mantle of MGR's political estate. And with Congress and Jayalalithaa's party being in alliance, Madras held Delhi's hand in parliament, with Delhi holding Madras's hand in the legislative assembly.

PV's slender numbers in the Lok Sabha would have unnerved any politician, but PV knew his math. He was a political polymath. And he had in this a guide only he communed with—his intuition. Within days of becoming prime minister, the first Congressman from outside the Nehru–Gandhi family to do so, he sent to President Venkataraman a proposal to confer the Bharat Ratna posthumously on Rajiv Gandhi. The party wanted it, the government had to set the ball in notion. And PV, too shrewd to sound discordant, went along. President Venkataraman, who had proposed to Rajiv to give it to MGR posthumously, could not but warm to the idea. Indeed, if the thought had not crossed the collective mind of the Congress, RV would have proposed it himself as a natural and fitting sequel to the assassination, like an Amen after a prayer. Nehru and Indira had been conferred the Bharat Ratna by Presidents Prasad and Giri respectively, in their lifetimes, and Lal Bahadur Shastri after his death, by President Radhakrishnan. RV's giving it to Rajiv posthumously had an inevitability to it as well as a felicity.

The ceremony on 6 July, not even fifty days after Rajiv's death, was deeply poignant, with Sonia coming to receive the medallion and parchment with a poise in sorrow that was moving and impressive. As prime minister, PV arrived after Sonia had been conducted to her lonely seat. He sat down in the chair earmarked for him and then, with agility and verve, went over to Sonia to offer his respect, the respect of the present to the past. Power is about the present.

PV showed his sense of power when he followed the Bharat Ratna on Rajiv with another proposal, this time not pushed by the party. The prime minister sent to President Venkataraman a proposal no Congress prime minister had sent and no non-Congress prime minister either. He proposed that the Bharat Ratna be conferred posthumously on Sardar Vallabhbhai Patel. This was chastening for Nehruvians, of which RV himself was one. But could RV have demurred? He could not have. Not when the person concerned was the Iron Man of India. Patel was beloved of the nation. He was not beloved of those whose beloved was Nehru. And here now was Narasimha Rao, a non-Nehru–Gandhi family Congress prime minister whose grateful memories of the 1948 Operation Polo, which was dubbed a 'police action', in Hyderabad, which had merged the former nizamate with India were strong, asking the president of India to give Patel, in death, what had been given to Nehru and Indira in their lifetimes and at the height of their incumbencies as prime minister, and then to Rajiv in his death.

Six days after the investiture for Rajiv, this other one for the Sardar came to be held on 12 July under the same dome, with the same paraphernalia. His grandson, Bipin Dahyabhai Patel, received it from the hands of President Venkataraman during a ceremony which former prime ministers V. P. Singh and Chandra Shekhar also attended.

In August, Rao was to do another unexpected thing. He proposed that the Bharat Ratna be awarded to a bete noire of the Nehru–Gandhis, former Prime Minister Morarji Desai. The award was approved by President Venkataraman and announced on 24 August, but RV was not pleased. The logistics of an investiture for the Bombay-based and none-too-mobile ninety-five-year-old were pondered over. RV was unwilling to go to Bombay, where it was suggested, he could confer the decoration at an event in Raj Bhavan. When he was told Desai would be unable to go to Raj Bhavan to receive it from his hands or those of the governor, 'Let it be sent by post,' he said. This was not quite in keeping with RV's innate sense of courtesy. But the most evolved of beings are entitled to have some peccadillos. Ultimately, the medallion and parchment were sent across to Desai's home through a joint secretary. Lok Sabha saw a spirited debate on the subject on 27 August. L. K. Advani from the Right called it 'a graceless act', and Rabi Ray from the Left criticized it roundly. In an unbelievably weak response, minister Arjun Singh promised the house that he would 'bring all these things to the notice of the prime minister and suitable steps would be taken'.

1992

A CIVILIZATIONAL COLLAPSE?

The prime minister's Bharat Ratna 'monsoon' spilt into January 1992. On the 22nd, one day before the birth anniversary of Netaji Subhas Chandra Bose, came the announcement that the Bharat Ratna was to be awarded to that great son of India, posthumously. And, simultaneously, on Maulana Abul Kalam Azad as well. Their twinning did not make much sense. They had hardly seen eye to eye within the Congress. But then the PM was picking the ripest fruit from the tree that bore no Nehru mark on it. And that was the sense behind the announcement. President Venkataraman, an admirer of both the leaders, approved the recommendation easily, but no one was excited by it, and certainly, the Bose and Azad families were not. But somewhere on the subtle tablets of public consciousness, a point was being made: another discovery of India was in progress.

Netaji's family respectfully but emphatically declined to participate in this celebration of the great man. His daughter, the economist Anita Bose Pfaff, was clear in her reaction that her father could not be a recipient of a belated medallion. Netaji's grandnephew, the historian, teacher and politician Sugata Bose (son of Netaji's nephew Sisir Bose), was to tell* me, 'The entire family led by my father categorically refused the offer of the Bharat Ratna in 1992. My father, my aunt Anita, and all others felt that the Mahatma, Netaji, and Gurudev were of a stature far higher than could be properly honoured by a state-awarded Bharat Ratna, and they should be kept above it. Hence, the award was not conferred or received by anyone. (Narasimha Rao may have been well-intentioned, but that was not the right way to honour Netaji.)' The larger Azad family (he had no direct heirs) was hard put to come to a collective cogent response or decide on who should receive it. So, no one from the Maulana's household attended the investiture held on 2 February. The medallion and parchment were sent[1] by post to a nephew of his, located in Calcutta, who was too infirm to travel to Delhi—Noordeen Ahmed.

1992 was the last year of President R. Venkataraman in office.

And it was to be my last in the IAS—a fact of sub-zero importance to that limb of government for which individual officers are mere digits. But of some importance to me and my family. I had done twenty-four years

---

*Communication dated 4 September 2023.

in the service of government and could seek voluntary retirement and was determined to do so for a simple reason: once RV demitted office, I would have to revert to my cadre, Tamil Nadu, which was no problem because Tamil Nadu was my state, Madras my home town where I had family and friends and associations—of which MS and her husband Sadasivam were foremost. What was problematic for me was that I would have to be an officer under Chief Minister Jayalalithaa. Her brief meetings with me when I was secretary to Governor Khurana were always cordial, if also brief. I dimly knew then something I was to come to learn by bitter lessons later—that a colleague or a boss can be a friend, but one should never let a friend become a colleague, a boss, or a subordinate. That way lies the end of friendship. Jayalalithaa was not a friend, not even an acquaintance, but a wisp of mutual courtesy hung over our equation, which I did not want to dissipate.

RV understood me perfectly when I told him of this. 'But what do you propose to do after Rashtrapati Bhavan?' he asked me. I said I could try to get a teacher's job in a school within the J. Krishnamurti system, or I could seek to join a publishing house. He was not quite convinced of the wisdom of either of these choices and said he would like to think about the matter, and asked me not to rush into putting in my voluntary retirement papers.

Just then, as my good fortune would have it, Dr L. M. Singhvi (1931–2007), our high commissioner in the UK, wrote to RV asking him if, on RV's demitting office, I could join the newly-established Nehru Centre in London as its director. This was to be a venue for Indo-British dialogue at academic and cultural levels, bringing men and women of distinction from both countries together. RV asked me to accept this without the slightest delay. Things moved rapidly, and with my appointment coming through, I put in my papers. Cabinet Secretary Naresh Chandra asked me: 'Gopal, why do you want to leave the service? We can send you to this London assignment as a serving IAS officer.' I thanked him and said, 'Sir, this is a plum posting, and I should give something up before taking it. It would not be right to keep my lien in the service and go to this job.' He smiled minimally, said little after that. But I knew here was a man who wished me, someone miles his junior, well, because that is how he was—decent, civilized. He was big made, broad-minded, large-hearted.

I was on a 'climb'. But what of Tara? She had to leave a fulfilling job she had at the World Wildlife Fund (WWF) in Delhi because I had been 'posted' to London, a decidedly attractive thing for me. But she, and our daughters had to make deep adjustments in their professional and academic calendars because I was on a 'climb'.

Meanwhile, India–Pakistan relations, never unstrained, were getting tested with the agitation for the Babri Masjid in Ayodhya to be razed gaining momentum, and the JKLF trying to cross the LoC. J. N. Dixit, in his seminal book *India-Pakistan in War & Peace,* says of this period in the two countries' relations: '(Shortly after 3 February when he met our Prime Minister Rao in Davos) Nawaz Sharif (b. 1949) gave a call for a strike all over Pakistan "to express solidarity with Kashmir". The strike was observed on 5 February with the total support of the Pakistani Government. The very next day, the National Assembly of Pakistan adopted a resolution critical of India on the issue of Kashmir and reiterated support to the separatists. Anti-Indian activities did not stop here. JKLF cadre attempted to cross the Line of Control on 11 and 12 February. Fourteen people were killed, and nearly 115 people injured in this attempt. Nawaz Sharif sent six Ministers of his cabinet to mobilise international opinion against India on the Kashmir issue.'[2]

And in the midst of all this, on 25 March 1992, Pakistan won the World Cup, beating England by 22 runs to become global champions for the first time. After Imran Khan got the last Englishman out, Ravi Dayal (1937–2006), sensitive friend with a brain as sharp as the bidis he smoked in preference to over-packaged cigarettes rang me and suggested that it would be good if President Venkataraman sent a message of felicitations to his counterpart in Islamabad. Ravi was an independent publisher, not a dyed-in-the-wool diplomat. Persons like Ravi can be expected to get such fresh ideas.

Aftab Seth was joint secretary XP, that spooky sounding abbreviation standing for nothing more innocuous than 'external publicity'. I rang Aftab not just as one joint secretary to another but as a friend of many years, going back to a shared college and a shared probation at the Academy of Administration, Mussoorie. Aftab said: 'Gopal, that will be a coup.' Armed with that 'credentialled' opinion, I asked the president if he would consider the suggestion. His face lighting up, he said, 'Yes, yes…very good …' A good draft came from the MEA. To my surprise, the president toned it up, repeating 'victorious' twice. Our high commissioner in Islamabad at the time, the late Satinder Lambah (1941–2022), author of a major book, *In Pursuit of Peace: India-Pakistan Relations Under Six Prime Ministers*, handed over President Venkataraman's message with one of his own to its addressee. Not everyone in the Ministry of External Affairs was exactly pleased. Certainly, Foreign Secretary J. N. Dixit was not. In his book mentioned earlier, Dixit was to say, 'Thinking back, I wonder whether such exchanges between heads of state serve any useful purpose. In my opinion, they only serve to increase the scepticism of public opinion in both countries about the incongruity of it all.'[3]

So, was RV's gentle message and intervention a futile step by the canons of diplomacy? Perhaps, yes. Did that message have any long-standing impact on India–Pakistan ties? Of course not. But at that particular moment, when everyone was heated up, his message did seem like a coolant air. Were it not for an independent citizen—Ravi Dayal—suggesting this and an imaginative diplomat liking the out-of-the-box suggestion, President Venkataraman's receptive and sporty mind may not have considered sending that message.

I was now getting ready for the move to London. The Nehru Centre in London was a creation of the Ministry of External Affairs, via its Indian Council for Cultural Relations. Administratively, it came within the purview of the High Commission of India in the United Kingdom. And so, the director of the Nehru Centre came also to be called 'Minister Culture' placing him in the same genre as its ministers Economic, Press, Security, and so on.

On 30 April, my last day in the office, I went to President Venkataraman to say a formal goodbye, though I was to see him again before leaving. He was reminiscent. 'You knew all my friends,' he said. 'There was the Rajaji link...That made things easy...' And then he added, 'Poor PV has no such help.' He was not quite right there. PV's private secretary, the amazingly learned and wise Ramu Damodaran, was all that I might have been for RV, plus much more, as he was a skilled diplomat and aided the prime minister in all his diplomatic work very pointedly. I told Ramu that this was my last day at work and would he be so kind as to convey my respects to the PM and my thanks for the London appointment. Within minutes, I got a call back to say the PM would meet me and asked if I could come over. He was working at files that surrounded him as he sat on a low settee. He continued to study his papers, barely looked up at me, and, of course, did not smile. That was him. The manner meant no indifference, much less discourtesy. It only meant a manner. 'So...you are off to London,' he said, continuing to gaze at his file. That was not a question. So, after saying my thank yous, I said I hoped to make the centre a venue for scholarly activities, with the performing arts taking second place. He signalled his approval of that. I then posed my worries about a suggestion that the centre can receive private funding, which I feared would create 'integrity' problems for it. 'Private participation is now necessary and is to be the pattern for such work,' he said. And, as to my worries, he said, 'As to the integrity part of it, Gopal, with you at the helm, no one will have any doubts about funds being used as they should be.' He wrapped up the five minutes' talk with 'best of luck'. I need that, I said to myself as I did a namaskar and left.

Dr Karan Singh suggested that it be called the Nehru–Gandhi Centre. I always defer to age, a habit ingrained in me from family training, but I had to demur. I said there were two problems with his suggestion: First, Gandhians would say it should be the Gandhi–Nehru Centre, not Nehru–Gandhi. Second, sceptics will say, 'Which Gandhi is the Gandhi in this Nehru–Gandhi Centre?' And I added, 'Maharaja, it would also not do for Gopal Gandhi to introduce Gandhi into the concept.' He did not demur.

The president and Mrs Venkataraman hosted a farewell dinner for us on 29 May. A seven-year association was ending. 'I will leave my papers to you,' he said to me. 'Nothing to be published in my lifetime...' On 2 June, a brief ceremony was held at 10 Janpath where Sonia Gandhi handed over a set of Nehru books for the Nehru Centre. Dr Karan Singh and Natwar Singh were there, as also Foreign Secretary Dixit. Describing to Mrs Gandhi the plan for the opening programme on Dadabhai Naoroji, I said we would put up some photostats of archival documents. She responded with just one word: 'Photostats?' I knew that plan was flawed. Photostats are not what such a centre should be displaying. We have to be original.

Reaching London with Tara on an Air India flight on a glorious summer noon was heavenly. The South Audley Street premises of the High Commission, where the centre and our flat were located, was large and airy and, thanks to the liberal self-confidence of the former High Commissioner M. K. Rasgotra (b. 1924), had been re-conditioned to true Edwardian norms of interior and exterior heritage. Among neighbours in the building, we were to have the brilliant diplomat Talmiz Ahmad, the incredibly sharp and equally warm P. S. Raghavan and their families. We could not have asked for more. Dr Singhvi welcomed me in India House that very afternoon, very warmly. I saw, to my great relief, that neither he nor his colleagues had any time or inclination to interfere in the running of the new cultural centre. I was what I wanted to be: my own boss left free to devise the calendar of programmes within a sparse budget, to be held accountable for all faux pas and mistakes, and to be by no means credited solely for any successes as the High Commission's work was, after all, a team effort.

The centre got off the ground astonishingly well, with a celebration of Dadabhai Naoroji on the occasion of the centenary of his election—the first of an Indian—to the House of Commons. Nani Palkhivala (1920–2002) and the Rt. Hon. Mark Lennox-Boyd (b. 1943), minister of state for Foreign and Commonwealth Affairs were the speakers at this inaugural programme. Over the year, outstanding 'Indianists' from British academic institutions, writers and poets, and visiting Indian musicians like Pandit Ravi Shankar and Ustad Ghulam Mustafa Khan (1931–2021) gave programmes.

In November, matters pertaining to the dispute over the Babri Masjid in Ayodhya were entering a vital legal phase. Prime Minister Rao was hoping the Supreme Court would give his government the receivership over the mosque and thereby control over it, so he could protect it legally and constitutionally, unconstrained by the powers and predictions of the BJP government that was ruling Uttar Pradesh with Kalyan Singh (1932–2021) as chief minister. But he was circumvented. Vinay Sitapati was to record twenty-three years later: 'The Supreme Court started hearings in late September. Kalyan Singh—through his lawyers—swore to protect the mosque. The Supreme Court chose to believe him and dismissed Rao's request for receivership.'[4] The ground was set for an epic betrayal, an epochal denouement. But even though the diplomatic bag brought me newspapers from India, and I read them avidly, somehow, the imminence of what was to come eluded me. The demolition of the Masjid on 6 December left me disbelieving. The reader will bear with excerpts from my diary for certain glimpses of that December.

Monday 7 December

After 30 January 1948 this I think is the darkest moment in India's history.

Tuesday 8 December

India continues to burn. The number of casualties mount. Massacre of the innocents.

Wednesday 9 December

Unexpected TV recording session for Channel 4 in the evening. Tariq Ali programme. I am unused to this kind of thing and fare badly. Off-mood completely. The violence in India overshadows everything.

Thursday 10 December

Are we on the brink of a civilizational collapse? I have said (on Channel 4) we cannot collapse. We are an ancient, tolerant people. Pray that I will not be proved wrong.

Friday 11 December

Office work amidst feeling of gloom over events in India. The 'score' now nudges 1000. Think of a New Year card with picture of Nehru announcing Gandhi's assassination and his moving tribute because of the reassurance in it of 'light'.

Monday 14 December

Visit St. Martins and Trafalgar Square for candle-light gathering in support of peace on the sub-continent.

I was no diplomat. My diplomatic assignment in London was a pottage of a historical overhang (the centre having been conceived as part of Nehru centenary plans), cultural over-decking and diplomatic over-spreading. But as the prospect of being with intellectually and aesthetically stimulating persons in London was appealing, I had seized the chance and was enjoying the experience. But Ayodhya was a new factor. I wanted to open the subject for a free-ranging discussion. My colleagues were chary of this. And rightly so. I was soon to find that the brazen act was being 'matched' in Pakistan. Some reaction there was bound to be, but what unfolded there was unacceptable. J. N. Dixit was to record: 'The Indian Airlines office in Lahore was set on fire by a mob on 7 December. The residences of Indian officers and staff at Islamabad and Karachi were subject to stone-throwing. On 7 and 8 December, a number of temples, churches and gurdwaras were destroyed by Pakistani mobs on the rampage. The culmination was the ransacking and burning of the residence of Indian Consul-General Rajiv Dogra in Karachi, with government connivance.'[5]

Dogra, a gifted raconteur and sensitive writer with a scholar's interest in modern Indian history, was to write later a most engaging book. It is remarkable and admirable that in this book, he relates many experiences and anecdotes but does not say anything about the harrowing experience he and his family went through. 'A few weeks after the Babri incident,' he says, 'I happened to be at a dinner with Benazir. Suddenly, out of the blue, she asked me, "Is India at the point of breaking up?" "Why do you presume that?" I enquired. "I am not saying that. It is your Prime Minister [Narasimha Rao] who said so," Benazir replied.'[6]

On 19 December, which was a Saturday, I was levitating in a dream-world after lunch when a phone call from my colleague P. S. Raghavan brought me sharply back to terra firma. 'Sorry to disturb you on a weekend but...a letter-bomb has gone off in the hands of an India-based assistant in India House.... Security has to be beefed up....' Terrorism, retaliatory and furious, was now knocking at our doors.

Visitors to the centre and hosts of friends asked: 'Could this not have been prevented? And once the demolition started, could it not have been stopped?' I did not know the answers to these questions then and do not know them now.

1993
THE QUAKING EARTH

An echo of the Ayodhya trauma and its aftermath, meanwhile, came to be heard in the other end of the country, Goa. At a session of the Indian Science Congress in Panaji on 4 January 1993, C. Subramaniam (1910–2000), the governor of Maharashtra, addressed the delegates. He had been invited not just as a governor but as an elder statesman whose contributions through science in the making of the green revolution had been immense. CS, after the formal event was over, relaxed over a private tea with some of the scientist-delegates and said, as the conversation proceeded, to the chief concern of the nation, 'Why are we trying to pretend nothing has happened in Ayodhya and that the nation is not facing a crisis?' Thinking aloud, he then went on to say that Prime Minister Rao was 'wasting too much time attending unimportant functions' and cited an instance when, during a visit to Nagpur, Rao 'accepted five invitations in a single day'. Subramaniam added he felt Rao had burdened himself with too many responsibilities and was guilty of centralized decision-making. All this was not unusual in a private conversation, but CS did not realize that there was a journalist present. Marcellus D'Souza, the news editor of the Panjim daily, the *Herald*, had got a scoop. He placed the conversation in the front page of his newspaper the next day. A furious Rao asked for CS's resignation and, on getting it, recommended its acceptance by the president, who accepted it. I wish he had not. He had, after all, known CS for much longer than he had known PV. He could have asked PV to think it over and given CS a gentle word of caution. CS became, in a sense, an Ayodhya casualty.

I was most saddened because I respected CS greatly and looked upon him as one of the makers of independent India, for it was he, as the union agriculture minister, who, with key scientific and organizational support from the formidably knowledgeable and innovative M. S. Swaminathan (1925–2023) helmed its green revolution, and got us out of what was called 'ship-to-mouth' dependence on food imports. Rao was prime minister and in so high a position that he could have ignored the report totally and perhaps, when he next met CS, twitted him about it. But the ego, when pumped up, can make big men think small. The incident was regrettable for another thing. It shook the confidence one should have in conversations with members of the fourth estate that are not meant for publication. One such successful scoop can extinguish many insightful conversations that people in positions of responsibility can have with journalists—a mutual loss.

Quite incredibly, by this time, Prime Minister Narasimha Rao was exuding confidence. In January, he did a demolition of his own—he reversed the nationalization of banks that Indira Gandhi had carried out in 1969. The Reserve Bank of India announced a licensing for private banks. Wisely, he did not touch the working of state banks.

Bombay and Ahmedabad were, at the same time, going into a communal frenzy. Diary entry for 9 January: *Am asking myself: What is this business of purveying Indian culture when the country is burning?* Diary entry for 11 January: *Wake up very early morning. Howling wind in the chimney place symbolizes my thoughts. Deeply troubled over the scene in India. Is India cracking up?*

The High Commission, having left it to me, I convened a discussion entitled 'Ayodhya and After' on 21 January 1993 with stellar participation. Alan Campbell-Johnson (1913–98), who had been Lord Mountbatten's press adviser in Delhi during the transfer of power, the Rt. Hon. Michael Foot (1913–2010), who was known as the best Labour prime minister that Britain never had, Ben Kingsley (b. 1943), the acclaimed actor, Judith Brown (b. 1944), the historian and biographer of Gandhi, were among those who spoke with passionate concern for the future of tolerance and peace on the subcontinent. Kingsley's presence was, for me, very special. As he held out his hand to greet me, I noticed they were large, warm, and, in a strange way, compassionate. I told him so, to which he said he had heard others say the same and, in fact, describe them as 'healers' hands'. And healing was indeed what India needed. No one had any illusions about what had happened. But no one was prepared to lose hope. India was not just a country out of any old or new atlas. It was the land the Buddha had trod.

But worse was to come.

My diary entry for 12 March: *Maria [Couto] rings around 11 a.m. to say bombs have rocked Bombay. I ring Mala [Singh]. She confirms situation is bad. I lose all interest in work, in the evening's programme [at the centre] and yet it must go on. P. Chidambaram speaks well. Audience impressed. Dinner at home for P.C. Bombay dominates conversation.*

Dixit writes: 'Nawaz Sharif indulged in the formality of sending a message of sympathy to our Prime Minister Rao on the Bombay blasts. Preliminary investigations, however, established by 17 March that the blasts were orchestrated by the ISI of Pakistan, which utilized Dawood Ibrahim, the Memon family, and their criminal associates to heighten the already tense communal atmosphere in India born of events in Ayodhya...I spoke to Foreign Secretary Shahryar Khan over the hotline on 17 or 18 March and gave him advance information that preliminary evidence indicated the involvement of Pakistan in these bombing incidents. As expected, he responded by saying that this accusation would not be acceptable to Pakistan and that if there was any genuine evidence, it should be conveyed to Pakistan. After obtaining evidence from the Maharashtra state government and from our own concerned agencies, we passed on the information, with documentary proof, to High Commissioner Riaz Khokhar, on 23 March.'[1]

On 25 March, I had the personal satisfaction and the centre, a professional one, in hosting a very cherished event—a reading by Vikram Seth from his just-published masterpiece *A Suitable Boy*. The hall was packed, many standing outside and on the stairway. The novel had had huge pre-publication publicity, including, I am sorry to say, ill-advised hints by the publisher that the book would get the Booker. An elite gathering had come, and Vikram, nursing a bad throat, read most effectively and when, at one point, had to pause because his voice was feeling the strain, accepted a lozenge that Baroness Shreela Flather (1934–2024) passed to him. 'A commercial break,' Vikram quipped as he put the soother into his mouth, to much merriment.

London-based Salman Rushdie (b. 1947), as the most outstanding writer in English of Indian origin at the time, should, normally, have been the first invitee. But what is normal when it comes to life in and about plural India? The High Commission had kept a studied distance from the author of *Satanic Verses*, the 1988 book that had enraged Muslim sentiment the world over, including in India, which became the first country to ban the book. A British journalist told Rushdie the day after the Seth book launch that he (Rushdie) had not only not been invited but that High Commissioner Singhvi had made an unfavourable comment about him. This was, of course, pure fiction. Rushdie was understandably angry, but then, I was told, when the actual conversation was conveyed to him, he was reassured—'big' of the man, India in London runs its own rumour mills with agility.

I have mentioned Maria Couto (1937–2022). A teacher and writer, she was much more. She and her husband Alban Couto (1929–2009), who had been in the IAS, were now in London, he working with the Commonwealth Secretariat, and she enriching the intellectual and literary life of the metropolis. The security-ringed Salman Rushdie was among their friends. Maria and Alban invited Tara and me over for a meal in their home, with Salman being the only other guest. Our conversation was most pleasant and full of reminiscences. Towards the end of the evening, he said he wanted to visit India, which he missed dearly. The Indian High Commission was, under instructions from Delhi, not giving the author of *The Satanic Verses* a visa. He also expressed disappointment at not being invited by the Nehru Centre 'not just as a speaker but even as an invitee....' I heard him say that without comment, for I knew that our giving him a visa was out of the question. There was another occasion not long thereafter when I met Rushdie again, unexpectedly. The celebrity author of *The River Sutra* and *Karma Cola*, Gita Mehta (1943–2023) was hosting a reception on 6 May (which happened to be our twenty-third wedding anniversary) by Random House for her husband Sonny Mehta (1942–2019) editor and the editor-in-chief of the New York-located Alfred A. Knopf. Rushdie, who had been famously published by Mehta, was there, for once not the centre of the party earth, which, at that party, Sonny was. We met up. Narrowing his bespectacled eyes, Rushdie wasted no time on 'courtesies'. He asked me directly if he could come to meet me to discuss a visit by him to India. I told him that given the Government of India's position on his book, his visiting me about that would be a fruitless exercise. He tensed up and said, 'You guys piss me off.' With that, he turned abruptly and was lost in the gathering.

Rushdie had said all he could say by way of contrition for any hurt caused. And he was living 24x7 under a very real threat of being murdered. And he wanted to, like anyone would, get to return to his homeland, which was a free country, a democracy, secular, plural. Rushdie deserved every consideration. But there was also this thing about public order. If he were to come, the likelihood of there being violence, even killings, was high. Was it worth taking such a risk? I wish I could have made him see that.

My diary entry for that day: *When will he understand? But he has reasons if anyone ever did for feeling discriminated [against].*

An event of great significance passed us by at the Nehru Centre, and I hold my ignorance of international affairs squarely responsible. Thanks to a thought shared by our skilful and insightful diplomat Shivshankar Menon (b. 1949), then India's Deputy Chief of Mission in Tokyo, with Prime Minister Rao and Foreign Secretary Dixit, a process of negotiations had started between India and China on the border issue the previous year. Menon, on being asked for his opinion on whether India and China could possibly negotiate on the subject, said something that I can only call profound. He said after Tiananmen Square and US pressures on China mounting, Beijing needed to concentrate its strategic resources to bolster its own internal strength and that while it would be unrealistic to expect it to change its hard positions on the boundary dispute, Beijing might be amenable to discussing an agreement to maintain peace and tranquillity on the border. This led to Menon soon being appointed to the desk in the Ministry of External Affairs dealing with China, from where steps were taken to bring into being exactly such a treaty.

On 7 September 1993, during Prime Minister Narasimha Rao's official visit to China, the Border Peace and Tranquillity Agreement (BPTA) came to be signed by China and India, both agreeing to maintain the status quo on their mutual border pending an eventual boundary settlement. This did not lead to a resolution of the boundary question between the two countries but was to keep the Line of Actual Control (LAC) between India and China largely quiet and 'cool', unlike the Line of Control (LoC) between India and Pakistan which has been as hot as any border can be, with cross-border terrorism, infiltrators, and actual ballistics.

If I had had the wit to spot the importance of this agreement immediately after 7 September, I would have requested West Bengal's chief minister Jyoti Basu (1914–2010), who was visiting London and coming to the centre to speak on something like 'India-China relations, an Indian Marxist looks ahead'. And something tells me he would have agreed.

Jyoti babu came to the centre on 21 September and spoke to a packed hall on the subject I had suggested: 'A Bi-Centenary Reflection on the Permanent Settlement of 1793'. Through his heavy-lidded eyes, he went through the exercise of reading his prepared speech without pausing even to take a sip of water (which had been kept ready for him beside the lectern). I could see his long, single-tone reading well-nigh put many in the hall to sleep. But as soon as he finished, and a polite applause was about to start, the charmer in West Bengal's veteran leader folded the written text, looked up and speaking straight to the audience said: 'I must tell you frankly, I did not write the speech that I have just read out.' A thunder of applause broke out at this disarming candour and drowned his next sentence: 'A serious scholar I know kindly wrote it for me. I, of course, endorse every word in it.'

The scholar in question was Utsa Mukherjee Patnaik (b. 1945), the distinguished economist and with her husband, the celebrated Prabhat Patnaik (b. 1945), a friend of decades. My purpose in having the occasion marked by a speech from one of Jyoti babu's stature was not just to flag a major landmark in India's agrarian history but to also give a discerning audience in London the chance to understand the dilemmas faced by India post the green revolution where a new divide was likely to be created by those farmers who could afford the cost of high-input greening and benefit from its yields and those who could not. And, incidentally, raise a discussion on the pioneering land reforms instituted by the Left governments in West Bengal and Kerala, where the progressive miniaturization of holdings due to the laws of inheritance were creating new problems for the benefits of those very reforms.

On 30 September, as I was making arrangements for a lecture that evening by the historian and Churchill biographer Professor David Dilks

(b. 1938) on 'Does the Commonwealth Have a Future?' came a call to tell me that Maharashtra had suffered a major earthquake centred around Latur early that morning and that thousands were reported to have died. Cancelling the reception that had been planned after Professor Dilks's talk, my thoughts now turned to what the duty of a centre like ours was in the face of this calamity.

Lata Mangeshkar, the melody queen of the Indian screen, was in London at the time and came to the centre to speak on 'Maharashtra ki maati' (the Earth of Maharashtra) to, needless to say, an overflowing house. She did not say anything that would stoke pity, anything that might be sentimental. Of empathy, there was no shortage, but it was of an empathy with pride in the resilience shown by the survivors, the strength of their spirit, their determination to look ahead.

A question-and-answer session followed, and here is where Lata had to rely on her own instincts. One questioner asked her what she would like to be reborn as. Lata did not take more than two seconds to say, in Hindi, 'Reborn? I do not wish to be reborn at all.' The house came down with spontaneous and loud applause.

1994
WHY IS OUR LAND THE THEATRE OF TRAUMA AFTER TRAUMA?

Kashmir was high on India's political agenda as the year began. And India's reputation as a country that cared for human rights was at stake around the world.

The High Commission's political and information wings were responding to the situation 24x7, not I or the Nehru Centre, our remit being different. But at gatherings at the centre, after the events gave over and our invitees prepared to leave, it was only natural that we would hear them say, for instance, on 20 January when New Delhi's architect Edwin Lutyens's hugely insightful daughter Mary Lutyens (1908–99) spoke on Annie Besant: 'That was a great talk.... Amazing she is...at her age...such sharp recollections.... By the way... sad, isn't it, the Bij...Bij......' and I would find myself completing the word for them. '...You mean Bijbehara.... Yes, truly sad that violence should mar life in that vale of beauty...'

On 27 January that year at 11 a.m., Kupwara, a border district town in the Kashmir Valley, saw the Indian army open fire, killing twenty-seven persons and injuring thirty-eight. This was to lead to a storm of protests, and British media was active in commenting on it.[1]

And then, on 28 January, after a talk by Deborah Swallow, the hugely knowledgeable curator of the Indian and South East Asian Section of the Victoria & Albert Museum, an attendee saying, 'That was a treat, Mr Gandhi...Thank you, thank you very much indeed.... But you must be worried about yesterday's events in Kashmir, right?' Truth to tell, I had not heard of Kupwara's agony of the previous day and looked either a fool or a knave hiding the 'truth'. The gentleman nodded knowingly as he departed, educated about Indian art and aesthetics but unconvinced about Indian policies and practices in its northernmost Himalayan state. On 22 February, the Lok Sabha and Rajya Sabha did something that had not been done earlier by the Indian Parliament. They unanimously passed a resolution saying, 'The state of Jammu and Kashmir has been, is and shall be an integral part of India and any attempts to separate it from the rest of the country will be resisted by all necessary means.' The sentiment was not new, but this was the first time that parliament was saying so in so many words. The resolution also said, 'India has the will and capacity to firmly counter all designs against its unity, sovereignty and territorial integrity.'

The resolution noted 'with deep concern Pakistan's role in imparting training to the terrorists in camps located in Pakistan and Occupied Kashmir, the supply of weapons and funds, assistance in the infiltration of trained militants, including foreign mercenaries into Jammu and Kashmir with the avowed purpose of creating disorder disharmony and subversion'. It condemned 'the continued support and encouragement Pakistan is extending to subversive and terrorist activities in the Indian State of Jammu and Kashmir'.

Prime Minister Narasimha Rao was visiting select world capitals in the summer of the year, and it was important that his government's resolve on Kashmir, backed by every section of political thought in the country, be on the table when he did that. But before that major event, I had the responsibility of arranging another that had nothing to do with politics or policy. But it had everything to do with a VIP—Nirad C. Chaudhuri.

We have met him in the previous section. But this time, it was different. His rivetingly-produced 1994 edition of Henry Yule's *Hobson-Jobson* (1886) had just come out. For sheer brazenness in the descriptions of ribald specimens of that genre, his introduction in it is not to be equalled. I doubt if any Indian publisher would venture to publish or republish it. It is hilarious and utterly risqué. Nirad Chaudhuri laughs his guts out through sample after sample. There was an event at the Nehru Centre, London, around the book. I went to Oxford and motored with him to London for the function. Nirad babu was dressed to perfection as a British country squire. I was educated during the drive on European history, Western literature in general, and the two World Wars. When we reached the Nehru Centre, and he emerged from the car, placing his hat on the great dome of his head, picking up his brass-knobbed cane, he asked me, 'Where is the cloakroom?' It took me a second or two to figure out that he meant the loo and conducting him to that destination, alerted my wife, who had arranged for Nirad babu to join us for lunch, after the programme, in our flat above the Centre's hall, that the great man had arrived. To my 'Sir, may I offer you a glass of wine?' he reacted with, '"Glass of wine?" What is that? You do not offer a glass of wine. You should ask whether you might offer a drink and mention wines, giving the precise names of the wines, white or red, or as an alternative, cider or beer, then again, ask if it might be lager or draught...not some "glass of wine"....' As we settled down over lunch, I was quizzed about the Sanskrit for 'mango' and the difference in Urdu between be and ba.

To a casual observer, all this would have seemed like 'showing off'. It was, in truth, nothing of the kind. Nirad Chaudhuri was the very personification of learning. But of a learning that was its own fulfilment, its own destination, journey, and climax. In ancient Greece, Nirad Chaudhuri would have been surrounded by fawning students, in old Persia by a host of besotted murid. In Nalanda of yore, by novitiate monks intent on mastering grammar, syntax, and prosody at his feet. But he was in a world that was too impatient, too much in a hurry for knowledge to have time for his learning. His lecture, as another guest said, was not a lecture but a performance. He was brilliance personified.

The prime minister's official visit to the UK began on 13 March. On 9 March, a motion was tabled in the House of Commons over the signatures of fifty-four members, barring three Liberal Democrats, all but one, Labour MPs, welcoming him with these words: 'That this house welcomes the forthcoming visit of the Indian prime minister, Narasimha Rao, on 13 March; applauds Britain's historically excellent relations with India which make it the second largest investor in that country; notes the participation of a wide range of leading British and Indian companies in joint ventures; congratulates those British exporters which have developed increased trading links with India.' It then went on to say '[This House] further welcomes Prime Minister Rao's determination to ensure the highest standards of respect for human rights and the establishment of the National Human Rights Commission; expresses the repeated and gravest concern that the continued reports of human rights violations, massacre and rape by occupation forces of the Indian army in Indian-held Kashmir have nonetheless escalated in recent months; calls on Her Majesty's Government to be equally vigorous in supporting United Nations resolutions of 1948, 1949 and 1960 which uphold the rights of the Kashmiri people to self-determination through a United Nations-supervised plebiscite, thereby fulfilling the explicit commitment made to the people of Kashmir by Lord Mountbatten, the last Viceroy of India.'[2]

One Conservative MP was among the signatories—Gary Waller (1945–2017). He was also, at the time, chairman of the House of Commons Information Committee, making his joining up that much more notable. This was an unwelcome note to start the visit on. But both the Indian and British establishments were familiar with lobbies and their activities. Obviously, Pakistan's High Commission in London had been busy and must have congratulated itself on this motion.

The PM came to the Nehru Centre on 15 March, spending well over an hour there in discussion with a stellar group of academics and others that we invited to meet him. The group met him around a table. He had a prepared address, which he read out but to which he kept adding impromptu extempore bits which rather prolonged his speech. To my shock, I was suddenly asked by the high commissioner to say a few words about the centre. This was not on the programme, and I do not know how I managed to do it without loss of face.

In July, we were delighted to be able to receive Jyoti babu once again. He came this time, on 11 July, to inaugurate an exhibition of paintings of Calcutta's nineteenth-century buildings by the hugely gifted British pencil artist John Nankivell (b. 1941). Amrit Wilson (b. 1941), the feisty London-based 'writer, journalist and activist who since the 1970s has focused on issues of race and gender in Britain and South Asian politics, mounted a demonstration outside the centre, protesting what was described as the West Bengal government's human rights violations. I did not think the Left government in that state attracted such a charge, but then, in London, one learns! City Police alerted us quite nonchalantly about the planned demonstration. They would handle it, they told us, but they would not prevent it. I was worried because I did not want my senior guest to feel the slightest discomfort and did not want a much-cherished programme at the centre to be disrupted. I was unnecessarily worried because the police did indeed handle the demonstration well, allowing the protesters to gather at a spot a little distance away from the entrance from where they raised slogans. It was all most civil, most democratic. Just before Jyoti babu reached, a valued friend, Richard Blurton (b. 1952), in charge of Indian collections at the British Museum, came up and said to me, 'Gopal, you look worried. Do not worry. A demonstration outside one's doorstep in London is actually a stylish thing to have.' I could not have been more reassured.

Rajmata Gayatri Devi of Jaipur, a daughter of Cooch-Behar, who spent many months each year in London, was invited and came a little earlier than Jyoti babu. 'How good to have you with us, Rajmataji,' I said to her. 'Do join Jyoti babu when he has a cup of tea with the artist.' The ageless queen of taste thought for a moment and then said, 'I don't think I will. He does not like me, and I don't think I like him either.' There goes the Feudalism v/s Marxism binary again, I thought to myself, but when the chief minister arrived, the rajmata went up to him most graciously, greeting him in Bangla, which he reciprocated in Bangla, of course, and the two had a brief but most cordial chat about Calcutta, heritage conservation, and Nankivell's art.

August brought a different gloom. It was plague this time.

Why is our land the theatre of trauma after trauma? The question was idle.

The outbreak was of bubonic and pneumonic plague in south-central and western India and stretched from 26 August to 18 October 1994. The number dying was 56 out of 693 suspected cases from five affected states as well as the union territory of Delhi.[3] These numbers were not benumbing, but the experience of Surat, the Gujarat town that was most affected, was. On the night of 21 September 1994, as news of the plague spread, stocks of tetracycline vanished. Patients in hospitals started fleeing, fearing infection. What followed was described as 'the biggest post-partition migration of people in India with around 300,000 people leaving Surat city in 2 days for fear of illness or of being quarantined'.[4]

Reports had come of Surat having experienced a flood just before the plague outbreak and that large numbers of rats had been washed up, dead, from its sewers. It was believed that this started it all. Rats! Fleas! In such contemptible beings lies the power to kill humans en masse. The Black Death of the fourteenth century, which wiped out half the population of Europe, and the bubonic plague of 1896/97 in Bombay with its political repercussions caused by the policy of 'search and segregation' would make for worthwhile reflection. There were numerous Surtis among the nearly 800,000 Gujaratis in the UK, and their involvement in plague relief operations was only natural. But I resisted the thought of doing a programme on the Surat plague. We should not get to be known as the Nehru Centre for the Study of South Asian Calamities.

In retrospect, I realize this was a mistake because the resilience of Surat and Gujarat in overcoming the crisis, with Surat getting to be spectacularly cleaned up under Suryadevara Ramachandra Rao, an IAS officer, as municipal commissioner of Surat, was something to celebrate and share. Rao, a Telugu-speaker serving in Gujarat, transformed Surat into one of the cleanest and greenest cities in India, getting the city rated as the second cleanest in India, after Chandigarh, by the highly regarded Indian National Trust for Arts and Culture (INTACH).

1995
MYSTIFYING MILK

On 10 April, Morarji Desai died in Bombay. He was a year short of 100. I did not arrange a memorial meeting for him. I should have; I am ashamed I did not. Not just because he was a former prime minister of India, its first non-Congress one, and a fearless defender of democracy through the Emergency that Indira Gandhi put the country through, but also as a man of personal integrity, and great administrative acumen, parliamentary etiquette and, above all, political ethics. Also, for a personal reason—he had been very kind to me, personally. Why did I not? Who stopped me? No one. Just my warped nerves. I thought of and settled all the centre's programmes by myself, with total autonomy. But commemorating Morarji was something I did not want to do without checking with the high commissioner, and did not want a no to stop me. The leader's 1959 entry in my autograph book—nirbhay bano (be fearless) mocked me. Memories glided through my head, but none so sharply as of a conversation I had with a friend who was making fun (predictable, trite) of Morarji's auto-urine therapy. 'The guy drinks his own urine...' to which I said (adapting Lincoln and his shoe-shining) 'Whose urine should he have drunk—yours?'

The internet had come to India in 1986 but with only limited reach. With the launch of the Educational Research Network (ERNET), it was something which the sequestered elite among a few educational and technological institutions, like the five IITs and the Indian Institute of Science in Bangalore, alone knew about—a closed fist of the learned or acharya mushti to use a phrase from Sanskrit or Pali, denoting privileged and unshared knowledge. This was going to happen as any idea or trend 'whose time has come', but the new tool had much to do with something else that had also 'come'—Prime Minister P. V. Narasimha Rao's technologically active mind.

Being strictly non-technological, I made little sense of the new development beyond seeing its potential as a speedier means of communication. That it would revolutionize the way people and institutions connected not just with each other but through something called cyberspace with a whole universe of knowledge 'up there, somewhere and everywhere' was beyond my imagination. As were the operational complications that would soon beset the great new technology in India through connectivity delays, disconnections (as frequently as every three minutes), and high charges.

I did not even dimly perceive the rise of the software industry, India's undersea cables, which would become the largest in the world. That the internet was to become a formidable facility for communication, information, and creativity but also a form of dependence, of huge trespassing into privacy and the bewildering problem faced by its millions of users by sudden official internet bans, which the central and state governments are empowered to do.

And as my office very tentatively, even timorously, began using the computer which came to be installed there around this time, I stayed off it.

About a month and six days after the internet had been launched in India, and the country had taken a gigantic leap towards a new age in science, the country was treated to a bolt of contrasts. Let me quote the journalist Suzanne Goldenberg from her report in *The Guardian* of 22 September 1995: 'Before dawn on 20 September 1995, a worshipper at a temple in southern New Delhi made an offering of milk to a statue of Ganesha. When a spoonful of milk from the bowl was held up to the trunk of the statue, the liquid appeared to disappear, apparently taken in by the idol. Word of the event spread quickly, and by mid-morning, it was found that statues of the entire Hindu pantheon in temples all over India were taking in milk.'

Within hours, thanks to old and new technologies of communication, the 'miracle' had spread all over the country and to the Indian diaspora the world over. Superstition and communication had rarely, if ever, combined thus to impact human thought and behaviour, if only briefly. Before one could say Ganesha, the adored and adorable deity, had his likenesses being spoon-fed with milk. If many said the God was not interested, many said he was drinking it up with gusto. 'Rational' and religious men and women, including one might add those employed in the world of science and technology, were crouching around Ganesha images, spoons and ladles of milk in their hands, which either trembled in excitement and fervour or in doubt and dismay. The London correspondent of the *Hindustan Times* filed a story that said, 'The crowd at the temple swelled to hundreds as the news spread. Those who came included a large number of professionals, doctors and engineers', and added, 'Some sikh families also visited…'[1] This was interesting, given Southall's fame as a Sikh stronghold. Suzanne Goldenberg, then serving as the South Asian correspondent of *The Guardian*, a journalist I did not know personally but for the integrity and professionalism of whose work I had unbounded respect, filed a splendid story which *The Guardian* carried on 22 September entitled 'India's gods milk their faithful in a brief miracle'. More need not be said about it. Tim McGirk, Delhi correspondent of *Independent*, filed a similar story saying: 'From Calcutta to Canada, from Southall to Singapore, millions of Hindus say they witnessed a miracle. In temples, houses, and village huts, statues of the elephant-headed god, Ganesh, and Shiva, the destroyer, were drinking spoonfuls of milk. Yesterday, in New Delhi and other Indian cities, the dairies ran dry. All the milk had gone to the gods.'

Scientists ascribing the phenomenon to normal capillary action may or may not have convinced the faithful, but by the next day, the frenzy petered down. That London saw a big draw of milk cans in the suburbs with sizeable Hindu residents that day is about the only thing that could be said, finally, of this twenty-four hours' wonder.

Subrahmanyan Chandrasekhar (1910–95), the Indian American theoretical physicist who shared the 1983 Nobel Prize for Physics with William A. Fowler for '...theoretical studies of the physical processes of importance to the structure and evolution of the stars', died on 21 August at the age of eighty-four. This was a huge loss to the world of theoretical physics, of course, but also to the climate of scientific research, globally.

I had no physics in me. His telling the world that large stars, bigger than the mass of the sun, do not, as is assumed, burn out to become white dwarfs but contract indefinitely into denser and denser black holes seemed to me to be something that may interest astrophysicists but made no difference to human thought or life. And yet this Lahore-born TamBrahm making it to the US to win a Nobel was something to be proud of. And I could not but feel a nationalistic pride reading an obituary by Leon Mestel in *The Independent* on 'Chandra' on 24 August 1995 that described him as one who made Newton come alive. And a tribute in *The Guardian* of the same date by the physicist and radio astronomer Sir Bernard Lovell (1913–2012) describing him as one who has had 'a major impact on international science in this century'. That Chandrasekhar's expertise in hydrodynamics had led Robert Oppenheimer to invite him to join the Manhattan Project at Los Alamos, but he declined to do so, I regarded as a fortuitous thing. It would have been a great pity if this transformationally illumined mind had become associated for all time with the making of that killer bomb.

Chandrasekhar's interest in Shakespeare and Shelley had made me warm to him sufficiently to seek to read his lecture 'Patterns of Creativity'. I was not surprised when a galaxy of scientists agreed to speak at a memorial meeting for Chandrasekhar at the Nehru Centre on 27 September, starting with the astronomer royal Lord Martin Rees (b. 1942) and including Sir William McCrea (whose research on the composition of the Sun and on star formation led to the development of the big bang theory), Professor R. H. Dalitz (known for other key developments in particle physics: the Dalitz plot), Professor Raymond Hide (professor of physics at the University of Oxford), Professor Donald Lynden-Bell (British theoretical astrophysicist, the first to determine that galaxies contain supermassive black holes at their centres, and that such black holes power quasars), with Stephen Hawking, no less, sending a message which was read out. Few programmes left me feeling a deep sense of gratitude for the chance given to me to be part of a programme of linking India and Britain at the level of high scholarship.

I have mentioned Chandrasekhar and the Manhattan Project. I did not know then what Bakhtiar K. Dadabhoy in his biography of the founder of India's nuclear programme Homi J. Bhabha says of India's first Prime Minister Nehru[2]: 'When Oppenheimer lost his security clearance in 1954, it was presumably on Bhabha's intervention, that he was invited by Nehru on more than one occasion to visit India and to stay in India...and even immigrate if he so wished. Oppenheimer declined because he felt that it would not be proper for him to leave the US until he had been cleared of all charges.'[*] Nor did I know then that over much of the year—1995—Prime Minister Rao had been mulling over ardent suggestions from scientists working on India's defence preparedness to take the country's researches and progress in nuclear science towards weaponization and, specifically, towards a nuclear test. Negotiations were on at the time over the Comprehensive Nuclear-Test-Ban Treaty (CTBT) to ban all nuclear explosions, whether for military or peaceful purposes. India was firmly opposed to the CTBT as it was patently discriminatory. Having tested in 1993 Prithvi-I, the missile that could, as Vinay Sitapati says, 'carry a nuclear load to Islamabad',[3] the scientists were impatient. But Rao was not sure. The consequences of an economic sanction that would immediately result, and of unpredictable responses (in terms of a counter-nuclear step) from Pakistan and China, made him think deep and long. But not conclusively. He ordered near-final steps to be taken for a test which US satellites picked up, and so when President Clinton rang him on 21 December to ask him about these, he said elliptically and with typical Indian circumspection: 'There is right now no plan to explode. But yes, we are ready. We have the capability.'

There were no Chandrasekhars among our atomic physicists. In the event, Rao did not 'explode'. The privilege was to belong to his successor, Atal Bihari Vajpayee, some three years later.

October was a month of some personal importance for me.

On the 17th of that month, at an event in the Nehru Centre, High Commissioner Singhvi drew me aside and said: 'Gopalji, I need to congratulate

---

[*]Josh Levy, PhD, Historian of science and technology, Manuscript Division, Library of Congress, in a communication to the author, says: 'Kai Bird (coauthor of *American Prometheus*) has also recently referenced Nehru's overtures to Oppenheimer to immigrate to India.' (ref: Container number, J. Robert Oppenheimer Papers, Manuscript Division, Library of Congress, Washington, D.C.).

you. You are being appointed our High Commissioner to South Africa.' I was somewhat dazed by this and must have appeared so to him, for he went on to explain. 'I met Narasimha Raoji in Delhi, and in the course of our conversation, he said that the high commissioner in Pretoria, M. K. Mangalmurti, was retiring and he was looking for a successor to him. He asked me for suggestions, and I thought of you. He immediately agreed and issued instructions to take this forward. You will soon be informed of this by the Ministry of External Affairs. They are seeking Pretoria's agreement.' My brain could only think of saying 'Thank you, Uchchayuktaji' (as I addressed the high commissioner in Hindi) as we went into the hall for the programme. It is only towards the later part of the evening that my daze gave way to excitement, which I shared with my wife Tara and the children at home. They were happy for me, though this meant that Tara would have to give up her assignment with the Commonwealth Science Council, a pity, for it was interesting her and was remunerative—something our young family was grateful for. She could have said she would rather not come with me to Pretoria, and opt to continue with her Commonwealth Secretariat job. She could have got a suitable visa if she had wanted to, and found herself private accommodation. I waved away the thought, and in so doing waved away her autonomous decision-making. For me she was my wife, a high commissioner-designate's 'spouse'. Her place was beside me, adding social standing to my official status, and indeed, making me seem somehow culturally and in terms of 'public appearances, complete'. Others she spoke to about her choice and dilemma also said to her: 'History, don't you see, is making Gandhiji's grandson India's high commissioner to South Africa where Gandhiji became what he was...Your place is with him...Yes, your job is important but the South Africa posting is history...' And so history well-nigh made short shrift of her own story as a person in her own right, her own self-respecting individuality. From being a valued member of the Commonwealth Secretariat's team, she was now a 'spouse', to deck herself for receptions, as hostess or guest, smile and shake hands, sometimes return hug for automatic hug, peck for ritual peck. Her fascination and her specialization for birds and bird life had been caged. A golden cage, sure, but still, a cage. I had become an Ambassador Extraordinary and she? An Appendage Oh so ordinary. Did I care? To be fair to myself, I did. And felt sorry about the whole impact-on-family thing. But appointments to high places are intoxicating. You lose balance, perspective, proportion. You become very 'high'.

My selection for the important diplomatic assignment was clearly part of PV's growing distance from the Nehru–Gandhis and their political circle. He was telling them by this appointment that South Africa was, for India, the land which 'made' Gandhi and that it was right that a Mahatma Gandhi-descendant should go there, not one who belongs to or owes anything to the Nehru–Gandhi circle. PV did not decide or decide not to decide without his own reasons unless political compulsions forced him to do otherwise.

I have mentioned Dr Singhvi telling me that he had suggested my name to PV for the Pretoria post. I think, in hindsight, that Dr Singhvi might have over-construed his role. PV had his own reasons giving him his own ideas aided, very likely by Ramu Damodaran's alert mind. Vice President K. R. Narayanan had, earlier, suggested to PV the name of Ramu's father, the veteran diplomat A. K. Damodaran for the first incumbent in the Pretoria post, but PV had not accepted the suggestion. PV had erred there for A. K. Damodaran, with his deep historical insights, would have been more than outstanding in that position.

1996–97
RAINBOWING A NATION

The year opened distastefully, like car grease on the tongue. A scam of huge proportions suggested senior politicians across party spectra and bureaucrats in high offices had their murky hands deep in a hawala (foreign exchange laundering) till. The story shocked India and rocked its faith in its leaders. A couple of brave journalists had blown the lid off the story after a militant in Kashmir had led sleuths to the trail. Prime Minister Rao went full blast into a chase, but not with the credibility he would have had if his own record had been free of suspicions of malfeasance. The 'Jain Diaries', as they came to be called after the diarizer and apparent mastermind Surendra Jain, were the primary documents containing names of beneficiaries. The BJP leader and statesman L. K. Advani, who was named in the diaries, resigned as MP immediately, saying he was acting on the dictates of his conscience—an honourable and wise thing to do, as did Sharad Yadav (1947–2023), both managing thereby to stabilize their reputations. Eventually, the case collapsed in court because the records produced (including the diaries) were found to be inadequate as evidence. But great damage had been done to the probity quotient of public life.

March and April of 1996 were months of election fever in India. This is one fever that is willed by the Constitution, got going by the Election Commission of India and enjoyed—not endured, but enjoyed—by the patient, India's electorate of men and women above eighteen. Curiously, Narasimha Rao was confident of getting a renewed mandate and of ruling India for another five years. But the country's mood had shifted from a post-assassination wave of grief for Rajiv's Congress to a post-scams tide of cynicism about Rao's Congress.

Seshan, who was chief election commissioner at the time of the May 1996 elections, describes the results tersely, factually: 'The election produced a hung house. The Congress and its allies just garnered about 140 seats. The United Front managed a tally of 179 seats and elected the Karnataka leader, H. D. Deve Gowda (b. 1933), as its leader. The BJP and its allies Shiv Sena, Samata Party, Haryana Vikas Party, and the Shiromani Akali Dal had a tally of 194.'[1]

As leader of the largest group, Vajpayee was invited, in strict propriety, by President Shankar Dayal Sharma (1918–99) to form the government. This was the first time the BJP was going to form the government at the centre, and the party too would have liked it to do so, but its dependence on a disparate alliance was impractical. Vajpayee was the very epitome of decorum when, upon realizing he could not command the confidence of the house, resigned on the thirteenth day after being sworn in. Seshan continues, 'The United Front finally came to power with the external support of the Congress. Gowda became the PM.'

The months after summer were better than their predecessors, though Narasimha Rao's exit from office was, for me, a very sad thing. This was so not just because I had joined my office in London by his 'approval' and was now scheduled to move to Pretoria entirely by his initiative, but because I saw him, with his finance minister Manmohan Singh, as one who had saved India's economy from falling over the precipice of fiscal collapse.

The elegantly goateed Inder Kumar Gujral (1919–2012) I thanked God to see, was the External Affairs minister in this new cabinet. He brought a weathered wisdom to that ministry, if also a not wholly warranted air of 'I know the ropes'. He genuinely wanted to make and leave a mark as one who healed sores rather than as one who deepened them. A difficult task and certainly a more thankless one. The culture of 'Yes Minister' prevented his officers from advising him frankly and in his interest against naming his vision for a peaceable neighbourhood the 'Gujral Doctrine'.

With his erudite and gifted wife Sheela (1924–2011), he had the most winning of honest-to-goodness Punjabi ways—a hug where a double handshake would do, that close and long clasp of hands when a normal handshake is what is expected, a 'how are you?' said softly and with a caring one-to-one tone that vaporizes the formality of that unmeant ritual of a question. His repertoire of Urdu versifications was an asset, placing him in the same league as Vajpayee and V. P. Singh in their mellower creativities. I was to see him let his temper fly at a meeting of regional heads of mission, but I saw that as a put-on act for mere effect.

It was somewhat later that I learnt from my brother Rajmohan that when the file about my appointment was recirculated to the new minister for confirmation, Gujral paused and rang my brother. He said to him, 'Your brother, Gopal, was approved for the High Commission in Pretoria by Narasimha Rao sahib.... But you are the elder brother, and I think in all fairness you should have the chance to go there.... Please tell me if you are interested.... If so, I will change the appointment from Gopal to Rajmohan....' Gujral sahib was aware of the old verity of brothers being not always well-comported and wanted to check if that was true in the case of these Gandhi brothers. My brother took no more than a second to thank Gujral sahib for the gesture but said no, he would not like to take his younger brother's place. And Gujral sahib took no more than another second to approve the proposal that was before him.

The agrément from Pretoria came around the time of this transition, followed shortly thereafter by the announcement of the appointment. My friends in the High Commission felicitated me; those colleagues I did not know so well or who had not cared to know this 'outsider' were sullen and silent. Envy is in human nature quite normal, but in Indian official nature, more than normal—almost a rule.

I was levitating. The prospect of being in the country that 'made' my grandfather (as he himself declared), that made Mandela, that was the most happening place in the world at that time, was no small joy. Kathleen Raine (1908–2003) has a poem.

> Within the ring there lies an O,
> Within the O there looks an eye,
> In the eye there swims a sea,
> In the sea reflected sky,
> There shines the sun,
> Within the sun a bird of gold.[2]

I was seeing that bird.

Kathleen Raine was happy for me but sad too, over my leaving. She was a mystic in her own way, and at a farewell dinner at her modest yet warm and cosy home, she brought out a set of pebbles from a cabinet—runestones, she called them—and asked all of us in the family to choose one each and then interpreted our fortunes from them, almost as if in an indoor game but not entirely so. When it came to my turn, she said, 'Gopal, you are now stepping into history.' Anyone going as an ambassador to Mandela was stepping into history's presence, and so I left her prediction at that.

Kathleen was a mystic poet, but mystic first and poet only thereafter.

She had a way of divining thoughts and going behind those thoughts to what may be called one's inner life. Once, earlier, when visiting Kathleen in her cosy nook on London's Paulton's Square, Tara complimented her on the little garden that fronted her home. Kathleen pondered what Tara had said and responded with 'You don't have a garden.' Tara said that was right but she lived in a lovely flat in a great area—Mayfair. 'But,' Kathleen continued, 'you don't have a garden.' Coming from her and in the context in which it came, 'garden' became a metaphor for the inner space and the still centre that a person, especially a woman needs for herself beyond the overplayed role of homemaker.

Poet Kathleen Raine at home. (Author's personal collection).

Tara had moved with me and our children to a series of residences some of which came with large lawns and was to move into more such. But Kathleen's 'little garden' was for the nature-lover in Tara 'something else'. It was where she could stretch on the grass, crunching an apple, find music in a frog's croak, art on a beetle's back. I could not share those enthusiasms of hers, preferring the delusion of 'a life of the mind', in the hush of a book-lined study and in the ageing aromas of old letters tucked away in drowsy folders.

Kathleen, who knew and loved both her garden and her books had a practical suggestion to make to me. She said I must meet her friend, the Afrikaner writer, farmer, and soldier Colonel Sir Laurens van der Post (1906–96). 'He knows South Africa rather well,' Kathleen said as she took me to meet him. 'You may not agree with all that he has to say, but he will be well worth hearing.'

Sir Laurens was ninety and would die later that very year. So, I was lucky to have been able to meet the famous novelist and his wife—who was deeply stricken with Alzheimer's—in their flat. Farmer and soldier were good descriptions of the tall, rugged man who greeted me with a mellow and slightly withdrawn warmth. I did not have to ask too many questions. The political leaders of the new South Africa came in for unequivocal criticism, beginning with Mandela himself. The man who came in for his most withering comments was Bishop Desmond Tutu. I will not write the words he used for the Nobel laureate, anti-apartheid crusader, and glowingly good human being. But I was interested by his unqualified praise of Inkatha chief Mangosuthu Buthelezi (1928–2023) as a mature and trustworthy leader whom I should get to know for a fuller understanding of South African affairs.

In mid-June of 1996, I went to Delhi, as is the practice, before heading for Pretoria to make protocol calls and be briefed at the Ministry of External Affairs. I started with a call on Foreign Secretary Salman Haidar, an old and prized friend. We had travelled together as members of official teams accompanying the then vice president Venkataraman, whose secretary I was, and Salman, chief of protocol. There could be no tougher protector and symbol of India's diplomatic image, her status, her stature than Salman. No ambassador stationed in India or visiting officials from abroad could take any liberties with him. But at the same time, among friends, close friends with whom he shared an ecology of viewpoints, he could laugh at official and human foibles and at simple, funny situations.

He was talking to a visitor as I was shown into his room. He asked me, expressionlessly, by a gesture of his hand, to take a seat at a slight distance. As soon as he was done with his visitor, he beckoned me to join him and said icily, 'So...Congratulations.' That was not exactly Salman. Not a little surprised at his manner, I also said 'thank you' somewhat coldly, serving frost to ice. 'You know,' he then said, 'you have been selected for the job for the wrong reasons....' I figured out at once what he meant. He was displeased by my appointment not because I was 'non-career' but because he was convinced, I had been appointed because I was a grandson of the Mahatma, whose links with South Africa are a matter of our shared histories. 'Today's South Africa has moved beyond Gandhi,' Salman continued, 'and it wants to deal with India not out of historical sentiment but in hard self-interest.' 'Sure,' I said, 'but in that case, Salman, why did you not stop the appointment? You could have. You had the authority to do so, the opportunity as well when Narasimha Rao left, and a new government came.'

'Let us leave that where it is....' he continued. 'You have been appointed, and it is all done.' It is all done! Too late! I felt like spilt milk and got up to leave. My meeting with the foreign secretary, I told myself, had been a disaster. But I had despaired too soon, for Salman got up too and, coming up to the door, stepped out of the room with me. As I held out my hand to say goodbye, he switched to Hindustani and said...'Acchha to bataao, aaj raat ka khaanaa kahaan khaa rahe ho...?' (Right, so tell me, what are your dinner plans for tonight?) I said Vice President Narayanan had kindly invited me to dine with him. With some dates- exchange, he asked me to dine with him on 27 June. As I climbed down the curved cream and pink stone steps to the ground floor of MEA's headquarters, I realized that inside his office, Salman was the foreign secretary; outside the door of his office, Salman was Salman. And that is only right. My diary entry: '*Salman at his complex best. Starters are spiced, dessert very sweet.*'

A foreign secretary is not the ministry's chief publicist (as he is thought to be) but its conscience-keeper. And that conscience has to be about negotiation, discussion, and dialogue. Not about belligerence, bellicosity, or ballistics. A Foreign Office is not meant to be a shadow War Office. A foreign secretary is not an alternate defence secretary. A foreign secretary must quell, not fan the fires of prejudice; must douse, not inflame suspicion. By definition, diplomacy must explore the scope for peace in the noisiest rumbles of war, it must excavate solutions from the deepest seams of voltaic furnaces. Today, when the acids of suspicion have overrun the channels of foreign policy and the iron of retribution or, to use Shakespeare's great phrase (*Henry IV*), 'revengement' has replaced the alloys of negotiation in diplomacy, a foreign secretary cannot be an applicant for the Nobel Peace Prize, but he cannot afford to look like an unstarred general either. Salman was such a foreign secretary.

And so, when I showed up at Salman's home for one of the most sumptuous dinners a gourmet can serve to a guest, we talked and talked till late into the night about things that one can only expect from a foreign secretary of Salman's mettle and a human being of his class—what representing India means. When we were done, Salman, in his white pyjama-kurta, walked me to the car and, as I was about to enter it, gave me a hug and said softly, 'Achha Gopal...Khuda Hafiz.' I could not have asked for more. Sometimes, when the eyes mist over, they do so with just a hint of pain. The pain of gratitude for human goodness.

Prime Minister Deve Gowda was aware, I am sure, that Delhi's 'smiling pickthanks and base newsmongers', to use another Shakespeare phrase (*Henry IV*), were sniggering at the rustic manner of this 'son of a farmer' even as they bowed and scraped when they were before him. But he let that be. He knew that his office could fly from him as swiftly as it had flown in. He just wanted to do an honest day's work on the day given to him in Delhi. I was expecting my call on him to be brief, matter-of-fact. It was that. But I was in for a most pleasant surprise. He said to me, perhaps with an input from MEA, but with his own directness, 'Remember that you are representing India in South Africa, not in Indian South Africa.' I craned my neck to catch the nuance better. 'What I mean is that the African South Africans should feel you are India's ambassador to them, not to the Gujaratis and Tamils and Telugus there.... Mingle with the Indians there, of course, listen to them, their problems.... But your priority is not them.... Your priority is South Africa, Africa....' I could not have hoped for a clearer mandate.

As advised by the ministry, I called on Dr A. P. J. Abdul Kalam, then chief scientific adviser to the prime minister and secretary of the DRDO, in his office in South Block. The future president of India was cordiality itself but had little time to spare—a healthy reflection on his priorities. He had a faint sense of who I was, having been introduced to me by Dr V. S. R. Arunachalam (1935–2023), his predecessor in DRDO, when the two of them had come to meet President Venkataraman at the time of their handing and taking over. Having asked me a couple of questions about my background, the big man expressed some interest in my being Tamil-speaking and asked me to see fellow Tamil, K. Santhanam (d. 2021), his estimable colleague in DRDO. The nuclear physicist with a formidable record of work for fifteen years at the Bhabha Atomic Research Centre, Trombay, spoke with knowledge and insights about the nuclear weapons programme of apartheid South Africa and of Nelson Mandela's nuclear 'rollback'. Santhanam told me with the twinkle and smile of one who knows that there was more to the rollback than appeared on the surface. It was from him that I first heard of Pelindaba and of the African Nuclear-Weapon-Free Zone Treaty, also known as the 'Pelindaba Treaty'. The treaty had opened for signature on 12 April 1996 in Cairo, Egypt, and entered into force on 15 July 2009. The treaty required all parties to apply full-scope International Atomic Energy Agency safeguards to all their peaceful nuclear activities, thereby entrenching nuclear disarmament, nuclear non-proliferation, and the peaceful uses of nuclear energy.[3] Santhanam told me of a book by two investigative journalists, Peter Hounam and Steve McQuillan, called *The Mini-nuke Conspiracy: Mandela's Nuclear Nightmare*, which had been published only the previous year, 1995. He said the book talked of F. W. de Klerk admitting in 1993 to the world that South Africa's apartheid regime had secretly built six atom bombs but vowing, however, that all had been destroyed. Santhanam said the authors suggested that this was not quite the case and that President Mandela, with his earnest commitment to a nuclear weapons rollback, faced a nightmare. Santhanam said the book was in limited supply but that he had managed to get a copy and would send it to me. But in the rush of things that could not happen.

There was no doubt in my mind that Mandela's rollback was what it was and that he had reversed apartheid South Africa's deadly sport with nuclear weaponization. The Treaty of Pelindaba is there for all to see. As a result, South Africa, the only African nation to have had nuclear weapons, gave them up in 1989, and Libya stopped its nuclear weapons programme in 2003. Now, I knew there were no nuclear weapons, not just in South Africa but on the entire continent of Africa.

What I did not know then is that we had reached and were standing on the tip of a nuclear test ourselves, with Narasimha Rao, shortly before the elections of 1996, having given what Vinay Sitapati[4] and Neerja Chowdhury[5] describe in tenterhook detail, as the near-final seven steps to 'Go Ahead, Explode'. The departing prime minister had urged his immediate successor for thirteen days, Vajpayee, to lunge into a test, which Vajpayee might well have done had he not had to resign for want of a parliamentary majority. Deve Gowda and Gujral had been fully briefed about the preparedness but decided not to test.

I was going as high commissioner to a country which was cherished by India and which, in turn, held India close to its heart. I responded to the emotive and well-grounded slogan that I was to hear: India–South Africa: Two Struggles, One Freedom, which bespoke a historical verity. But I knew too that India-South Africa, Two Friends, Many Differences spelt the more contemporary truth. My task was not going to have the tensions that would accompany an Indian diplomat being posted to China or Pakistan or to any other proximate neighbour with shared borders and unshared perceptions. And yet, there could be issues pertaining to global issues, like the NPT, trading interests, and unpredictable matters in which differences could—and did—arise. South Africa had, under Mandela, enthusiastically signed the NPT. India had not and would not.

Mandela, I could see, was being not just the skilful politician but also the deft diplomat in bringing the warring factions of South Africa's Black African sections to negotiate. From the moment he was released, two things happened simultaneously within the country: euphoria among the great majority who supported him across all ethnic divides, even if not all were in the African National Congress (ANC), and deep unease among those who had assumed he would rot in jail forever, and therefore, had become passive or active collaborators of apartheid. Inkatha, led by the Zulu chief Buthelezi being the major player in the latter game. Result: barbaric Black-on-Black violence, with Inkatha unleashing terror on ANC or thought-to-be ANC supporters in Inkatha-dominated areas. The violence did not take long to be reciprocated. And Mandela was torn. But Mandela being Mandela, did not give up. He was determined to snatch negotiated peace from the fury of the flames, resolved to craft a concordat between the emerging Black African leaders and the departing White players. This meant trusting the good sense, basically, of de Klerk and Buthelezi.

We in India were luxuriating in the great relief at his release and imminent assumption of authority, marvelling with the rest of the world at Mandela's greatness as a man free of bitterness and all that, without quite realizing his challenges. He was a mix of Gandhi, Nehru, and Patel in the 1946 lead-up through riots and senseless killings to India's Independence. And with

Inkatha playing Muslim League. When de Klerk and Buthelezi both joined his new government, he had achieved in the power-sharing part, at least, what Gandhi could not.

Pretoria was incredibly lovely. The air and the light were pure in a way that was new to me. The trees seemed to be happy, the birds ecstatic. The high commissioner's residence was spacious but not overly so. And the chancery at 52 Schoeman Street Arcadia, was exquisite. A lean and clean red-brick affair, the vintage structure had that indefinable but unmistakable quality—grace.

I had an extraordinarily able colleague in the mission—Talmiz Ahmad, the deputy high commissioner. We had known each other over the years thanks to our mutual friend, Ranjan Mathai, who had been in college together with Talmiz in Pune. Talmiz and Bhagwant Bishnoi, another highly dependable colleague from the Foreign Service, gave me a vivid portrait of the different political players in South Africa and the other diplomats stationed there.

It was a modest room in which President Mandela, assisted by senior officials from the Ministry of Foreign Affairs, was standing as I entered, on 6 August 1996, ceremonially, with my daughter Amrita (Tara having had to be away in Delhi to oversee our elder daughter's admission in university), Talmiz, and two other colleagues. As I advanced towards the great man, I might have appeared calm enough, but was excited and tense beyond description. My pulse beat fast, and arrhythmically. And that mysterious phenomenon called fasciculation made mini-waves under the skin on my face. No one noticed, thankfully. The Letters of Credence having been handed over, I was asked to begin my speech. I read out all of it, containing names of stalwarts in the struggle and of Indian leaders who supported it with passion. I had the feeling when writing and then while reading my speech that I was overdoing the historical bit and was neglecting contemporary economic and technological opportunities and strategic interests. But I was wrong. Mandela heard me with attention. And when his turn to speak came, he used the written text before him and also improvised. With almost his opening sentence, Mandela made our shared histories the pivot of his speech. He said relations between South Africa and India began in 1861 'when the first Indian labourers, as they were called at that time, arrived in this country'. And then said, 'But the most significant date was 1894 when your grandfather established the Natal Indian Congress.' Mandela followed that with a description that made an immediate and lasting impression on me. He said the Natal Indian Congress (NIC) started by Gandhi 'was the first organised and disciplined political movement in the country'. Mandela specified three achievements of that movement: One, it laid the foundations of the modern liberation movement. Two, it fought for the rights of the community by peaceful means. Three, it introduced the powerful weapon of non-violence.

Accredited to President Mandela's South Africa—After the presentation of his credentials as high commissioner to South Africa, Pretoria, 1996. To the extreme left is Abdul Minty, veteran South African diplomat, to the right is the author's daughter, Amrita. (Protocol Department, Government of South Africa).

Mandela then said, moving away from his prepared speech, that in my speech, I had left out mentioning Judge Mahomedali Currim Chagla (1900–81), the great Indian jurist who introduced a resolution on behalf of India at the UN, opening a debate against apartheid in South Africa. Mandela said this was a 'wonderful development because it focussed the attention of the international community on the evils of apartheid'. Towards the end of his remarks, he returned to the subject of Gandhi: 'I am very happy to welcome,' he said, 'the descendant of a man who, as I have said, introduced the first organized and disciplined political struggle in our country.' That succinct observation was, to my mind, the best possible synoptic description of Gandhi's value to South Africa. And for me personally, it was invaluable as it brushed away in one sweep my reservations about having been chosen for the job 'for the wrong reason'.

After the credentials ceremony, as per practice, there was to be a brief tete-a-tete with the president. But since the speeches had exceeded the time given for them, the chief of protocol announced with quiet finality that the tete-a-tete was dispensed with, and the Norwegian ambassador-designate, who was next to present credentials, was waiting to be called in. As Amrita and I hastened to leave, Mandela asked me about the Nehru–Gandhis: 'How are Sonia and the children?' They were well, I answered. 'Send them my best wishes,' he said. As I stepped out of his official residence to the bright, pure Pretoria morning as high commissioner of India to South Africa, I could not but think of the man who had served several months in jail in that very city with his son, Harilal. And who had been hailed by the president of a liberated South Africa as a pioneer.

Mandela was heading a government of national unity, though in the election of 27 April 1994, his party, the ANC, had obtained a majority of seats in the national assembly and was fully within its rights to form the government on its own. He asked the party of the apartheid era, the National Party (NP) and the ANC's rival in KwaZulu Natal, the Inkatha Freedom Party (IFP), to join the cabinet. He invited other parties to join the cabinet, too, disregarding their poor numbers in the national assembly. Most notable for me was the presence of four Indian South Africans in the cabinet—the flamboyantly charismatic railroad engine of a leader Jay Naidoo (Communications), the sage Daimler-like Dullah Omar (Justice), the brainy strategist Benz-like Mac Maharaj (Transport), the suave Merc-like Valli Moosa (Constitutional Development). And the Pahad brothers Aziz and Essop, the first a deputy minister and the second a counsellor with Deputy President Mbeki, both batteries of packed power. The appointment of two distinguished Indian South Africans—Ismail Mahomed (1931–2000) and Frene Ginwala (1932–2023) to the positions of chief justice and speaker of the national assembly, respectively, was the double cherry on the cake. I have not known a more perceptive person than Ismail, who is, at the same time, a mine of human values, or a more confidence-inspiring and no-nonsense born 'captain' than Frene. Mandela was asked by African colleagues in his party, 'Madiba, how come there are so many Indians in high places …? More than proportionate to their numbers…' Reply, classic Mandela: 'The number of Indians in high positions [in the new South Africa] is not proportionate to their *population* but proportionate to their *contribution* to the struggle [for our liberation].' The reader may vocalize the italicized words in her mind to catch his emphases.

And then there were MPs from the community who were able and passionate about the new republic, my cousin Ela Gandhi (b. 1940), my uncle Manilal Gandhi's daughter, being foremost among them. Her understated but adamantine virtues of steadfast commitment to justice and non-violent change were incomparable. Ela could have got a ministership for the asking. But she was her grandfather's granddaughter—valuing duty above office. Ahmed 'Kathy' Kathrada (1929–2017), who had been imprisoned after the infamous Rivonia Trial and served prolonged incarceration on Robben Island and Pollsmoor, was in the Parliament, a sage and wise figure. He had declined a ministership, saying he did not join the struggle to 'get positions'. Indres Naidoo (1936–2016), a grandson of Gandhi's colleague, Thambi Naidoo (1875–1933), made for a striking presence in the senate. Indres had served a ten-year-long prison term with Mandela in Robben Island and suffered cuffs and kicks at his jailers' hands, one episode of those impairing his hearing irreversibly. These were inspirational figures. Men and women with values that I only associated with India's leaders under Gandhi.

Just as Gandhi was called by millions in India 'Bapu' (meaning father), Mandela was addressed by his people as 'Madiba', a title of respect derived from his Xhosa clan name. Wanting to delve into its etymology some more, I learnt that in Xhosa, the title also meant 'deep lake'. There was something impenetrably calm about Mandela, something unfathomably deep. Saintliness is not a political quality. But if some of it is to be found in a politician, it is not at the expense of intelligence. An alert innocence is not a weakness in that polluted province; rather, an asset. Being that much rare, it stands out and commands respect.

I had no idea then and did not get to know until several years later of the inconspicuous presence at that time of the Guptas. That this Saharanpur family, which set up a hardware business named Sahara after its town of origin, was to become all-too-powerful and be seen in terms of 'state-capture' was reserved for later knowledge. The Guptas never came in contact with me, or if I saw them anywhere, they did not enter my conscious or subconscious mind. They were not quite as major in 1996–97 as they were to become, or perhaps the High Commissioner of India held no attraction for their goals.

But I did meet more than once Vijay Mallya (b. 1955), who was civility itself. No airs, no crudity of the kind one associates with the nouveau riche. He dropped no names of Indian or South African VIPs. In fact, he spoke very little. When I learnt later of his style of living and working in India, especially in the leisure and airline sectors, I could not match what I heard with what I had seen of the man in South Africa. Mallya had just bought United National Breweries when I met him in 1996. The company sold sorghum beer across the country, mainly to lower-middle and working-class customers. This was an Indian investment venture in South Africa, and the High Commission had to wish it well. I was and am no teetotaller, but I felt sick in the pit of my stomach as India was taking coppers out of poor South African pockets for booze and profiting from the process. I used to see among the dead-drunk or drugged, sprawled on roadside kerbs, more Black African men and Coloureds rather than White or Indian. These were the down-and-out people who had, most likely, no regular job or a precarious income from physically demanding jobs. They had consumed their beer from large containers, or cannabis, heroin, ecstasy, mandrax, or the like and consumed in public locations. This was exactly like in Indian cities. To feel sorry for them, I knew, was a superior and arrogant thing to do. But what else was one to do? The only consolation I could get was from the fact that if Mallya did not put affordable beer in the market, his customers would probably drink illicit stuff and turn to illicit drugs and court death. Mandela, in his very first inaugural address in 1994, had flagged alcoholism and illicit drugs as major social ills.

Neither India nor South Africa had, at that time, a sound and rational liquor policy. The extreme of imposing prohibition has been tried and known to be flawed since it breeds corrupt practices apart from illicit brewing. Its opposite—leaving the whole sector unregulated to the caprice of the market hurts the poorer classes in the gut and the families of those who drink. A Muslim vigilante group called People Against Gangsterism and Drugs (PAGAD) had just been set up, creating problems in its wake since it often took the law into its hands and being what it was—an ethnic organization—it raised new problems. The most gnawing aspect of the drug menace in South Africa, as my colleague Talmiz Ahmad lucidly explained to me, was that those who were caught were the last or last but one in the illicit drug chain of drug peddlers, drug pushers, drug barons while the drug lords remained hidden and safe, far away. The ending of apartheid had meant the ending of South Africa's isolation and the relaxing of surveillance along its international borders. Ironically, this had encouraged illicit drug trafficking and, by grim extension, the further spread of irresponsible male behaviour leading to sexually transmitted diseases, notably HIV/AIDS, which had first made its appearance in the country in 1985.

With the dismantling of apartheid and democratic trust replacing autocratic fences, a pyrrhic tax had to be paid. Drugs and drunkenness led to the breakdown of standard inhibitions, and rates of HIV reached pandemic levels. Before partnerships could arise between civil society and state agencies, South Africa was in the grip of a first-class HIV/AIDS crisis. In January of 1996, the year I got to the country, South Africa was gearing up for the Africa Nation's Cup. The country's national soccer team, Bafana Bafana, announced it would contribute to the AIDS Awareness Campaign by wearing red ribbons at all their public appearances during the series. But state policy on the subject was beset by varying views on the economics of it. On 5 July 1996, the health minister, Nkosazana Dlamini-Zuma, attending the 11th International Conference on AIDS in Vancouver, said: 'Most people infected with HIV live in Africa, where therapies involving combinations of expensive [anti-retroviral] drugs are out of the question.'

An AIDS drug, Virodene, was put out in the market controversially, and in February 1997, the Health Department supported the drug, stating that 'the "cocktails" that are available for the treatment of HIV/AIDS were way beyond the means of most patients'. Parliament had previously launched an investigation into the procedural soundness of the clinical trials for the drug. The South African government 'refused to provide life-saving antiretroviral treatment (ART)'[6] for a long time. In India too, where the first HIV/AIDS case occurred in 1985 and then spread elsewhere, it was only in 2013 that the government announced its intention to provide free ART at government hospitals and then again only to people living with HIV/AIDS in the six high prevalence states and in the city of Delhi.[7]

Mandela's 'problems of state' were compounded with problems at home. I heard, like all others, of his 1993 divorce case against Winnie Mandela (1936–2018) with great sadness for him. He needed healing at home to be able to do the great reconciliation he was trying to effect in his country. And that was denied him. Winnie's life had been a mess. But the wild ways she took to, through the menacing guards that she had employed, were appalling for their wanton violence and brazen criminality. Mandela's dignity and honesty in court when he said she had not shared his bed after his release and that he wanted 'to get rid of this marriage' were heart-wrenching. Mandela was a family man, and in the early years of his jail term, he pined for Winnie and the children. But her ways could not be hidden from him. All this, when I heard it, made my regard for him that much greater but also laced it with great sadness.

Not long thereafter, I called on Chief Buthelezi. The home minister was civility personified. I could see there were many Buthelezis in the man. And no one could say which was the real Buthelezi. Perhaps not even Buthelezi himself.

Was Gandhi irrelevant now in South Africa? Worse, was he a remote irritant? This question haunted me as I saw the moth-eaten condition of Gandhi's famous Tolstoy Farm near Johannesburg. I visited the site repeatedly, and every time I went, I saw the structures of some of its old rudimentary sheds further reduced in size by the work of diligent vandals. Coming in very matter-of-factly, they carried away pieces of timber, rafters, door and window frames. There was no way the local administration could have superintended these venues; they were uninhabited, with no owner-occupant in sight. Phoenix, the Gandhi settlement near Durban, was no better, despite being near where the amazingly intelligent and perceptive Sita Dhupelia and the hugely inspiring and brave Ela Gandhi, Manilal Gandhi's daughters, lived. 'Sarvodaya', the dwelling used by Gandhi and Manilal and Sushila Gandhi's residences, were in a shambles—the work, again, of vandals. The poor and unemployed Black African communities near these sites were not acting deliberately against Gandhi, of whom they knew next to nothing. They were helping themselves to the material remains of properties that had once been used by Indians better off than they, and now had no occupants. True, they knew they were breaking laws, and true, too, that Ela was doing her utmost, almost single-handed (though she would say she had many persons of all communities helping her), to tell them of the heritage of the place the need for solidarity among the various populations of South Africa, of ubuntu (non-violence).

In Durban that September, I was glad to have been able to do something else as well. Driven in her small car by Ela herself, no less, I paid my respects at the grave of John Dube (1871–1946), Gandhi's African contemporary and neighbour in the sense that Dube ran his Ohlange Institute from very close to Phoenix. Dube, who, after a stint at the Booker Washington-run Tuskegee Institute in the USA, was to found this with the same objectives—Black progress through education and entrepreneurship. Dube, who was to go on to found the African National Congress later, met Gandhi in 1905. Even as the visionary African spoke with admiration of his new Indian acquaintance, Gandhi wrote in *Indian Opinion* words of frank appreciation about this African pioneer. Ela also drove me to another grave, that of Chief Albert Luthuli (1898–1967) in Groutville. Luthuli was a passionate believer in non-violence, winning the Nobel Peace Prize in 1960. He never met Gandhi but knew and was a friend of Gandhi's son, Manilal. Luthuli's commitment to non-violence had brought the two close together. I knew of that well, though I was to come across more references to it only later, such as described by Mandela. To Richard Stengel, who was working on a biography of Mandela in the 1990s, Mandela said: 'The Chief [Albert Luthuli] was a passionate disciple of Mahatma Gandhi, and he believed in non-violence as a Christian and as a principle... Many of us did not... because when you regard it as a principle you mean throughout, whatever the position is, you'll stick to non-violence... We took up the attitude that we would stick to non-violence only insofar as the conditions permitted that.... Our approach was to empower the organisation to be effective in its leadership. And if the adoption of non-violence gave it that effectiveness, that efficiency, we would pursue non-violence. But if the condition shows that non-violence was not effective, we will use other means.'[8]

Meeting on 8 September with the chief's highly spirited daughter Albertina Luthuli (b. 1932) by her father's gravesite, I called on the chief's ninety-two-year-old bed-ridden widow the next day in Albertina's home. This was a most moving experience. In between the two Luthuli meetings, I had my first meeting with the KwaZulu ANC leader Jacob Zuma (b. 1942), a future and highly controversial president of South Africa. I could not have anticipated then the weird career that lay ahead of this man, his financial and personal crises. Nor did I know that Albertina would one day, thirty years on, be publicly critical of President Zuma and be one of 100 ANC stalwarts signing an open letter calling for reform in the ANC, and attend several civil reforms and protest decisions of Zuma's government.

On 13 September, I had to call on President Mandela to hand over a letter from our prime minister seeking South Africa's support for our candidacy for a membership (non-permanent) of the UN Security Council. For the five seats that were being contested, Africa had one, and, thanks to African coordination, there was only one candidate—Kenya—while for the Asian seat, there were two candidates, Japan and India. This was, therefore, a matter of some prestige and tension. Ordinarily, such letters would be handed over to the Foreign Office for onward transmission to their high destination. But I wanted to do better—diplomatic ego, nothing else, and a desire to be patted on the back in Delhi for having got an audience with the big man for this task. There was little hope for India to defeat Japan. I do not know why we had to stick our neck out and court so prominent a defeat. But then, it is not for diplomats to question why. Mandela heard me out non-committally. He was by nature and instinct circumspect. And, by now, was sufficiently groomed in diplomatic ways as well. I did not expect him to make any commitment, either, but having said my piece on the subject, I had enough to put into my report to MEA. As I was taking my leave, Mandela said, 'And...High Commissioner...tell me...this name...Your prime minister's... Gowda...I can't understand it...Where is he from...?' I told him that Prime Minister Deve Gowda was from Karnataka, the state of which Bangalore is the capital, and that he hailed from what he himself called 'peasant stock'. As for the name, doing some fast thinking, I said, 'Madiba, the name Gowda is like the Tamil name here...Gownder or Govender...' His face brightening in recognition of that well-known Tamil South African name, he said, 'Ohh...I now get it...Gownder...Gowda...' For Nelson Mandela, leader of the rainbow nation of South Africa, a minor ethnic mystery had been solved, and a new fibre of a new hue added to his repertory of population groups.

The election was held on 21 October. And as feared, for the single seat of the Asian Group, from the 181 ballots, Japan polled 142, against India's 40. It was all very demoralizing. But then, as far as diplomatic missions go, within the larger disappointment lay either the further humiliation of the host country also having been among those who voted against India or the saving grace of it having voted for India. To me and my colleagues' great relief, South Africa had voted for India.

Not everything about India and South Africa was happy. On 16 November, news came of a Panamanian vessel, M.V. *Cordigliera*, with nearly thirty Indian crew, sinking on 14 November off the East London coast near Durban. Reports said the vessel placed a distress call to Durban Radio at 10.30 p.m., reporting a leak in a hold and urging immediate assistance, but before that could be arranged, the freighter sank off Port St. Johns with the loss of all lives on board. Families in India of the men on board were unconvinced that they had drowned. This was natural but was infinitely sad as there seemed no hope that they had survived. I could get an appointment at short notice in the Transport Ministry with a Captain Dernier. He held out no hope. I agreed that there was no chance of anyone having survived, but couldn't something be done to reach the wreck and see if the dead were there and could be counted? I asked. No, he said. I escalated the matter to Minister Mac Maharaj, a good friend. But he, too, pleaded helplessness. There were only one or two skilled divers who could go so deep into the sea, and they were not in the service of the government and would need to be hired at exorbitant rates. In any case, it was too late. I accepted defeat but not without saying that if the crew had been European or American or even, say, Japanese, the divers would have been hired, and those crews would not have been left underwater to turn to coral. Racism outlasts liberation movements in subtle ways.

Deputy President Thabo Mbeki (b. 1942) and his charismatic wife, the feminist activist Zanele Mbeki (b. 1938), visited India in December. It was a droll affair, that visit, with everything going to plan and nothing major achieved except for the adumbration of common 'strategic interests' and the signing of a memorandum of understanding on cooperation in the field of defence equipment. Vice President K. R. Narayanan, who was Mbeki's counterpart and host, saved the whole thing by his engaged and engaging conversations. Prime Minister Deve Gowda hosted a lunch, which went well enough, with the PM being a frugal talker and good listener. The VP sparkled in his gentle way at the banquet he and Mrs Narayanan hosted for the Mbekis.

At Bangalore, Mbeki visited the Infosys campus and was quite captured by what he saw and what he heard of its founder,

N. R. Narayana Murthy (b. 1946). The enterprise had floated an initial public offering (IPO) in February 1993 with an offer price of ₹95 (equivalent to ₹690 or US$ 8.60 in 2023) per share against a book value of ₹20 (equivalent to ₹140 or US$ 1.80 in 2023) per share. And to start with, the IPO was undersubscribed, needing to be 'bailed out' by US investment bank Morgan Stanley, which picked up a 13 per cent equity stake at the offer price. But one could see that IT had begun to soar in India by now, with Infosys and Wipro being the formidable 'twin towers' of the new technology.

For me, the visit was made memorable by one incident alone. And it had nothing to do with India–SA bilateral relations or India–SA congruences in multi-lateral matters. And the incident went like this. A visit to Agra on 5 December to see the Taj was planned, as expected. I got to the great monument minutes before the distinguished couple's car arrived. The designate guide, like all guides, was suitably excited, and as the car doors opened and the couple stepped out, the guide stepped in front of all present and said, 'Welcome Excellencies! Welcome to the teardrop on the cheek of time, as Rabindranath Tagore called this mausoleum…Welcome! Here lie the great Emperor Shah Jahan and his beloved Empress Mumtaz Mahal, who bore him fourteen children…' At this revelation, Zanele Mbeki froze. 'Fourteen children did you say?' 'Yes, Your Excellency, fourteen, all fourteen from the same mother, Mumtaz…And Your Excellency, she died bearing the last, the fourteenth.' That was enough for the South African visitor. 'I am not going in,' she said and proceeded to get back into the car. As the guide's mouth dropped and everyone tensed up, Thabo went up to his wife and spoke. He must have told her something to the effect that all this was about a time long past, that her not going into the precincts would be interpreted as a diplomatic contretemps. Zanele, with great reluctance, agreed to step into the heritage site but, throughout the tour, said not a word. The light was fading as the visitors went around the monument, and it bore a sadly ethereal look, heightened in my mind by Zanele's thought process.

I took my hat off at her strength of conviction. Child marriage and premature child-bearing in India today are not what they were in medieval times. But they have not gone. Post-partum haemorrhage, which is what probably killed Mumtaz, is also not what it was when institutional childbirth services were unknown. But who can deny that marriages are still arranged in India before the right age for child-bearing? Who can deny that the mother-to-be in India is not as consensually associated with the rites of procreation?

Zanele and Thabo Mbeki at the Taj Mahal. (Author's personal archives).

The Indian cricket team, captained by Sachin Tendulkar, visited South Africa in the last week of December. I know next to nothing about the game, but being what and where I was, duty required me to witness the opening of the first test in Durban. Our team had stars in it. Besides Tendulkar himself, there was Sourav Ganguly, Mohammed Azharuddin, Javagal Srinath, Anil Kumble, and Rahul Dravid. I was conducted by the South African hosts to the cricket equivalent of the theatre's 'green room' where the players were readying for the match. Going in there was the stupidest thing to have done. They were in no mood for niceties, and an Indian high commissioner was the last person they wanted to spend any time with. They were surly, distracted, tense. I could not blame them. I beat a hasty exit and took my place in the stadium to witness a humiliating defeat by our team at the hands of the hosts captained by Hansie Cronje.

Krish Mackerdhuj, the Indian South African chief organizer behind SA cricket, hosted a dinner at which he seated me, very imaginatively, next to Cronje. The weather had been dicey, and everyone was hoping the matches would survive the weather. I asked the SA captain: 'Tell me, Mr Cronje, in this day and age of superfine technology, should cricket be left so vulnerable to the vagaries of weather? Cannot it be protected against rain and damp by some device, like indoor stadiums, so that the game does not have to be abandoned midway?' Cronje was thoughtful for a few moments and then said, 'No...I do not think that would be right...Cricket is meant to be like life...It must take the rough with the smooth...Life is not always smooth...' I was deeply touched by that comment and remembered it with a pang of sadness as well as admiration when some three years later, in 2000, a conversation between Cronje and Sanjeev Chawla, a bookie, over match-fixing allegations led to the great South African all-rounder with three other players, Herschelle Gibbs, Nicky Boje, and Pieter Strydom, being implicated and after an enquiry by the King Commission, being banned from any involvement in cricket for life. I was sad beyond words that a cricketer who had spoken with such deep philosophical reflection to me should have had to run into the 'rough' and that, in cahoots with an Indian.

It is an irony that South Africa should see India and Indians as being symbolized at one level by Gandhi and another by the likes of the Gupta brothers and Chawla.

When, in June 2002, I learnt of Cronje's scheduled flight home from Johannesburg to George having been grounded and then his hitching a ride as the only passenger aboard a Hawker Siddeley HS 748 turboprop aircraft which got caught in poor visibility in clouds, crashed, killing him, at age thirty-two, and the two pilots instantly, I was grieved beyond words. Air crashes and conspiracy theories are ever twinned, and I am not surprised that some have said Cronje was murdered on the orders of a cricket betting syndicate. But I would like to believe that he was overtaken by what he had described to me as the roughness of life.

The Bangladesh High Commission in Pretoria was then headed by an acting high commissioner who made a request in January 1997: Can we help get an appointment with President Mandela for a visiting special envoy of President Sheikh Hasina? I said I would try, and when I did, it was given straightaway. The only condition was that I should accompany the visitor—Mr Valiur Rehman. The Bangladeshis had no objection. Sheikh Hasina had sent a message to Mandela to grace the twenty-five-year celebration of the formation of Bangladesh. When the visitors had said their piece and Madiba had given them a careful hearing, he drew me aside to a separate drawing room and said he wanted to visit India and could I set the process in motion. I said I would, of course.

Just as I began naively to imagine that there was a very special relationship between Mandela's government and India, came a report (March 1997) that South Africa was to supply arms to Pakistan.[9] Rusty Evans, who had served the apartheid regime but had been retained by Mandela as director general in the Foreign Office, said in the report that the sales 'had been made' but they were 'defensive' material.[10] I had never heard of weapons of that unidirectional description.

By the time Mandela assumed office, South Africa had become the tenth largest arms producer in the world, with approximately 800 arms and arms component manufacturers employing a workforce of 50,000.[11] The apartheid regime that had held power until 1994, had given Armscor, the state-owned arms exporter, a free hand in finding lucrative markets irrespective of the human rights records of the buyers. With the Mandela-led ANC government coming to power in May 1994, a new era of responsible arms trading practices was being worked out when, barely four months after the Mandela government took office, in September 1994, an arms-related scandal broke. A commission of enquiry, known as the Cameron Commission, was appointed to investigate South African arms exports and propose policy reforms, and it recommended an interdepartmental cabinet committee to implement the new policy. This National Conventional Arms Control Committee (NCACC) had the able and integrous former law professor in Ireland, Kader Asmal (1934–2011), as its chair.

I went with my defence adviser Virendra Singh to the defence headquarters in Cape Town to ask what it was all about. The discussions were bumpy. According to the report that I have mentioned, Pakistan was 'close to sealing a 600 million Rand ($165 million) export contract for the supply of missiles to Pakistan'.[12] I was told that the proposed supply of these missiles followed a commitment made to Pakistan by the apartheid regime, and a bilateral agreement could not be revoked. We were able to prise an assurance that nothing more would be finalized between South Africa and Pakistan behind our backs. But securing prior information of a deal is not the same thing as securing cancellation of the deal, which we wanted for the reason that we did not want South Africa to be pulled into an arms bazaar in South Asia. I went to Cape Town the next day to meet Defence Minister Ronnie Kasrils (b. 1938) on the issue, but my aim was to meet Kader Asmal, which I did at Cape Town airport, where he and I found ourselves, waiting to board separate flights.

Asmal was someone I valued greatly for his erudition, his puckish sense of humour, and his total transparency. He knew that I knew that the new arms policy included sensitivity to the existence of internal or regional tensions or armed conflict in the recipient countries. He heard me with great care and told me that he would bear our concerns in mind.

But little comfort was to be had. Pakistan was doing its work as diligently as us. The SA–Pak defence deal did make the SA–India MoU on defence cooperation seem obsolete.

And as a telling backdrop to this was the fact that South Africa was actively engaged in achieving an extension, albeit conditional, of the NPT, while India refused to sign it until it was firmly linked to an overarching process of nuclear disarmament by all nuclear powers. At meeting after meeting, I had to address this difference in our nuclear policy.

So, did all this show that Salman Haidar was right when he said South Africa today is about its sovereign national interest, not about historical sentiment? It was undeniable that key Indians saw South Africa now as the land of grand business opportunities rather than as the land of great heritage sites associated with an austere Gandhi. In other words, of commercial pragmatism over ideological idealism.

Meanwhile, Mandela's visit to India, initiated entirely by him, was to materialize at the end of the same month, March. The director general in the President's Office, Jakes Gerwel, was an academic and anti-apartheid activist who enjoyed Mandela's total confidence and commanded wide respect. I had more than one session with him about the visit, and during one of them, I told him of the request from the Bharatiya Jnanpith that President Mandela present that year's award to the great Bengali writer and social philosopher Mahasweta Devi (1926–2016). I was only performing a duty. The request had come, and my ministry had no objection to it being placed before Mandela, but I did not expect it to hold any interest for the president of South Africa. To my delighted surprise, Jakes said the idea was excellent and one that Madiba would respond to positively. The programme was included in the itinerary.

I reached Delhi ahead of him to be at the airport in my allotted place, with the welcoming VIPs on 27 March 1997. 'You are a South African,' he said to me as he shook hands with the welcomers, including me, loudly for all to hear. 'You should have flown in with me.' Could a diplomat have asked for more?

The Jnanpith ceremony went off spectacularly well, with Mandela saying disarmingly, 'I had to be here because, in my previous visits to India, there was no opportunity to meet with writers…' Mahasweta Devi was, of course, quite pleased, but being the kind of person she was she remained totally self-possessed and mindful of all she stood for in terms of human rights, tribal rights, women's rights and, above all, the rights of a free thinker and writer. The author of *Hajar Churashir Ma* was being honoured by Jnanpith and at the hands of Nelson Mandela, but she was also conferring a distinction to the occasion, which only she could. The Ramon Magsaysay Award was to come to her the next year.

Sitaram Kesri (1919–2000), the Congress president, with some Congressmen, called on Mandela, a political formality as the Congress was supporting Deve Gowda's government very crucially from the outside—an unstable arrangement which makes the government of the day wholly and pathetically dependent on the outside supporter. Mandela was polite with his white-capped caller, who seemed to have nothing to talk about except Gandhi, Gandhi, Gandhi. That he had some rather drastic political plans forming in his mind no one could, at that point, have guessed.

Mandela's meeting with Prime Minister Deve Gowda was a singular success, with the PM speaking from our side forcefully and expressing our warmth for South Africa generously. The climax of the visit was the signing of the Red Fort Declaration by Mandela and Deve Gowda on mutual cooperation in bilateral and multilateral forums. Tortuous negotiations on the text preceded its finalization, with South Africa's High Commissioner Matsila raising many objections and Jakes Gerwel skilfully sorting them out to everyone's satisfaction.

Within a month of Mandela's return, Deve Gowda was out of office. Kesri had withdrawn his party's 'outside support'. Why? Many reasons were being presented, but they could all be substituted by one word—'whimsy'. My diary entry for 11 April 1997: '*TV shows the voting in the Lok Sabha and Deve Gowda's statesmanlike subsidence. Kesri's is an unpopular, even despised, victory.*'

For 12 April: '*The UF government under Deve Gowda has fallen. Will another Cong-UF coalition emerge?*'

Congress, having tasted the 'outside support' power-play, I could see it leveraging its influence and, when annoyed, pulling the rug from under the prime minister's feet. It was now enjoying this role, no matter what the games did to the nation's stability and to its political economy.

Whether because he sensed the national mood or for other reasons, Kesri had the good sense to agree to support from the outside another UF government led by the outgoing minister for External Affairs, I. K. Gujral. I breathed a very 'local' sigh of relief as Gujral's sense of India–SA ties was sound. I was also reassured that under the new Gujral-led government, I would not be disturbed from Pretoria. National calendars are ever translated into personal almanacs by those in the service of the government.

Pietermaritzburg, the town where, in 1894, Gandhi, on his rail journey from Durban to Pretoria, had been ejected from his compartment, changing the course of his life, now had a mayor of Indian origin—Omar Latiff

(1954–2015). A man of great refinement and equal wisdom, he took it upon himself to arrange an imaginative event: Mandela should travel on the same rail journey, and so should the Indian high commissioner, namely, I, and at a function in the town, President Mandela should confer the freedom of the city of Pietermaritzburg on Gandhi posthumously, and I should receive the key and the parchment. Mandela accepted the idea immediately, and the event took place on 25 April. I should say this was the most memorable day of my short stint in the country. For Tara and me, travelling with Mandela on the train and spending most of the day with him, talking and reminiscing, was an unforgettable experience. Mandela spoke movingly, and a speech I prepared with great care was appreciated beyond my expectations. To quote myself would be insufferable for the reader of this book, and so I shall not do so. After the momentous event was over, Mandela offered us a lift on his special presidential aircraft back to Pretoria. This was an unprecedented and unexpected gesture. But I remember it for two occurrences. The first: as the plane was about to land, Mandela lifted the blanket he had covered his legs with, folded it carefully fourfold into a neat little bundle and then, holding it in both his hands, gave it to the stewardess, an Afrikaner lady, as gently as he would or anyone would, an infant wrapped in swaddling clothes. This was the president of the country, showing courtesy both to the blanket and to the stewardess. Most passengers on flights leave the blanket in a mess on the seat as they leave. The second: When we landed in Pretoria, the president's car drove up to the tarmac. Ours was parked a little behind. As we all came down, he turned and asked me if a car had come for us. I pointed to it and said, thank you, Madiba, there it is. At this, he came up to Tara, linked his arm to her and, walked her (and me) to our car and, on reaching it, kissed her hand as she entered it and then turned and went to his own waiting car. Gandhi had been given the freedom of the city of Pietermaritzburg by the president of South Africa, and by this simple, personal gesture, Nelson Mandela had placed on that act the stamp of a personal, familial bonding. Mohandas Gandhi, I prayed, had watched the whole sequence.

But beyond these reflections, another significance of the day's proceedings became clear to me a little later. Gandhi had been ejected from his seat in the train in apartheid South Africa. Now, a hundred years later, the president of a new, liberated South Africa was giving a ride on his special aircraft to free India's high commissioner and his wife.

On 1 July 1997, I completed a year in South Africa. My diary entry for the day: '[*The year*] *has sped. It has elated. It has frustrated. But it has been the most important year of my life.*'

That month, a cyclical change took place in Rashtrapati Bhavan. President Shankar Dayal Sharma, ending his five-year term, was succeeded on 25 July by his almost unanimously elected successor, K. R. Narayanan. This was, in my reckoning, a great development for India. KRN was not only to give India the long-delayed privilege of having a Dalit as its president but was also to bring to his office an extremely modern mind of great erudition and judicious discernment. His knowledge of international affairs as a diplomat of many decades' standing and a deeply reflective thinker was to be an additional asset for India.

On the evening of 9 August, I got a call from President Narayanan himself. 'Hello Gopal, when are you coming?' he asked without any preliminaries. I, as usual, mumbled some inanities. He then said, 'I have been without a secretary all these days since moving here.... Some kinds of tasks have to be performed by a secretary alone. They cannot be delegated to anyone else.... Try to come and join as soon as you can....' I then mumbled some more inanities. He then said, 'I have spoken to the prime minister, and he has agreed.' There was nothing further to be said or mumbled. KRN had effectively transferred me out of Pretoria to the president's secretariat. And that was that. But something of a former ambassador to many capitals in him made KRN add: 'I know it will be a wrench for you to leave South Africa.... You are doing well there.... But I promise to get a good ambassadorship for you after you have spent some time with me here...'

The only accommodation given was that I was allowed to stay on until a visit to South Africa by Prime Minister Gujral was over. 'Why are you taking Gopal back?' Mandela asked the PM. He said the only thing he could, 'Our president wants him; I am helpless.'

On 4 November, I called on President Mandela to bid goodbye. It would be downright pompous of me to say what he told me. On 13 November, Tara and I reached Delhi and returned to the precincts we had left in 1992—Rashtrapati Bhavan. Reporting to President Narayanan for duty was a privilege. 'Ah, so you have come....' he said to me. 'Good.' A banquet was held shortly thereafter for a visiting dignitary to which former prime minister P. V. Narasimha Rao was invited. At the pre-dinner gathering of guests in the Ashoka Hall, when PV saw me, he asked me to come and sit beside him. As I did so, he said with unconcealed annoyance, 'What happened? I did not send you to South Africa for you to come back like this so soon.' I told him my return was not of my making but was in obedience to orders. He was unconvinced. 'Anyone can be secretary to the president here.... I had hand-picked you for Pretoria.... Anyway....'

1998

I, KOCHERIL RAMAN NARAYANAN....

From the very start, Bharat Ratna, the highest civilian decoration in India, was a matter decided between the prime minister and the president. Prime Minister Gujral suggested to President Narayanan that Abdul Kalam be accorded the honour. Though Gujral would never have gone for a nuclear test and did not, he admired Abdul Kalam's skills and valued his help in 'hosting' the system's operational innards within his reach, keeping the keys to the 'chamber' with him all the time. President Narayanan had no particular difficulty with the proposal. But in a conversation around that time, he said to me, 'I think we should now also think of a Bharat Ratna outside the architecture of the state and of politics.' And he asked me for suggestions. With my knowledge of the world of music being dominated by the personality of M. S. Subbulakshmi, I mentioned her name. Narayanan responded positively. He asked Gujral for his opinion, mentioning his own inclination for it. Gujral had, of course, heard of MS. But the sharp politician in him made him think of a 'popular' name. 'What about Lata Mangeshkar also?' he asked. Fortunately, Narayanan realized that the uniqueness of the first Bharat Ratna going to a musician should go to someone who belonged to the same plinth as the Bharat Ratna's early recipients. He responded with, 'That is a good name...but maybe a little later... not at the same time as Subbulakshmi.' And so, both proposals came and were immediately approved by the president, along with one for Satyajit Ray (posthumous).

On signing the parchment for MS, he said to me, 'Let me speak to her....' She came on the line from her home in Chennai and had to be told of the decision in slow, measured terms so that she understood it all. This took a little explaining, and my communication services were enlisted. She was, as in everything she said and did, totally dignified and subdued. That she was grateful was, of course, obvious. The president then said, 'I would like to inform Chief Minister Karunanidhi also.' I connected him to the CM, who was elated. That the Bharat Ratna was going to a daughter of Tamil Nadu and one as illustrious as her, and, very pertinently for Karunanidhi, a daughter of an illustrious member of the community of Melakars or what used to be called the Devadasi, to which he himself belonged, meant a great deal to him. He did not conceal his joy.

At the ceremony, MS sparkled as only she could. In the photograph of President Narayanan placing the ribbon bearing the medallion around her neck and giving her the parchment, he looks as grateful as she. The jejune practice of the giver and the receiver turning to look at the camera at the crucial moment had not started. The camera was for the investiture then, not the investiture for the camera.

MS stayed with us on that visit. Tara and I invited some persons knowledgeable about Carnatic music to meet her over lunch that day. At the investiture, I asked Abdul Kalam sahib if he would be free to join, and he readily agreed. So, both Bharat Ratnas honoured us that day. She and the missile man had sat together during the investiture. To my amusement, when at lunch he entered the room, she turned to me and asked in a whisper, 'Gopu, tell me clearly, who exactly is that person?' I wish I could have told her he was a future president of India. N. Ram, visiting from Chennai, was another distinguished invitee at the lunch and engaged the scientist in conversation at length, but so little was the presence of the just-decorated scientist noted and so unseen as special, that it occurred to no one to have the two in converse photographed. Time is, among other things, quite a joker.

On Congress withdrawing support to Gujral's government over the DMK and its alleged links with the LTTE, it had to fall. Gujral took this in his stride, with great dignity, though he was, one could see, very hurt.

Neither the Congress nor the BJP were able to garner the numbers required to form a government. And so, the outgoing prime minister Gujral recommended dissolution of the house, a recommendation which the president accepted without any difficulty as Atal Bihari Vajpayee and the Congress also recommended the same.

Narayanan was a Nehruvian. His temperament and training made him secular. The BJP's politics was not his politics, nor its worldview either. But Narayanan was also, again by his natural bent, a fair man. And so, when, around 20 February 1998, Uttar Pradesh's governor Romesh Bhandari (1928–2013) dismissed Kalyan Singh's BJP government for having lost its majority following defections and installed a Congress ministry led by Jagdambika Pal (b. 1950), in a fast-moving sequence replete with high drama, he felt disturbed. It made no difference to him that the sacked ministry was a BJP one. Was the sacking right and constitutional? Had the governor observed all the procedures for ascertaining the loss of majority by Kalyan Singh? The courts were moved by Kalyan Singh and ruled in his favour, leading to Kalyan Singh forcing his way back into his old office. Jagdambika Pal acquired the distinction of having been chief minister for just one day. It was all a mess. Bhandari's action had come in for universal condemnation, and demands grew for the governor's recall. Bhandari did not put in his papers.

And Narayanan did not press the point. He had let the public know what he felt duty bound in the matter, and that was enough.

The elections gifted the country a house that was not just hung but hung, drawn, and quartered. Counting started on 2 March and soon showed that the BJP on its own got 182 seats, the Congress by itself, 141, but both the BJP and its allies and the Congress and its allies, even after counting-in the United Front, fell well short of the required 272 seats. A series of bomb blasts in Coimbatore, believed to have been masterminded by Pakistan's ISI, from which the BJP leader L. K. Advani escaped narrowly, led to the decimation of the DMK in Tamil Nadu. An immediate fallout of the results was that Sitaram Kesri lost his presidentship of the Congress. 'Serves the man right,' P. V. Narasimha Rao might well have said, recalling his own ouster the previous year from the same position. With Jayalalithaa of the AIADMK, which had done well in the elections, offering 'outside support' to the BJP (not before some dramatic demands had been made by her as a quid pro quo, which Vajpayee rejected as unworkable), the coast was clear for Vajpayee to be sworn in as prime minister, leading a minority government. When President Narayanan's formal invitation to Vajpayee to form the government was issued, UP governor Bhandari resigned—an act that would have been very seemly when Kalyan Singh had been reinstated.

At the swearing-in at Rashtrapati Bhavan's forecourt on the dazzlingly clear morning of 19 March 1998, Vajpayee looked distant and philosophical. He was, I am sure, conscious of the extreme vulnerability of the cabinet in view of his fragile numbers in the house and his precarious dependence to Jayalalithaa's whims. Her party had won 30 of the 39 seats it contested and so she asked for and got four cabinet berths, including (for Thambi Durai) the Ministry of Law and Justice, very important for her in view of the cases she faced. She had asked that Dr Subramaniam Swamy be made finance minister. He certainly had the skills and expertise for that portfolio and, in her sights, deserved a top slot because of the solidarity he had demonstrated for her. But Vajpayee was determined to keep him out and did.

On the day the Vajpayee government took office, E. M. S. Namboodiripad, the veteran communist leader and former chief minister of Kerala, passed away in Thiruvananthapuram. The eighty-eight-year-old icon of democratic dissent and socialist ardour, despite so-called disadvantages such as shortness of height, a stutter, and very impaired eyesight, had exceptional personal charisma. EMS had campaigned tirelessly in the elections just concluded but fell ill shortly thereafter. President Narayanan was deeply saddened when he got the news. Not that he had been close to EMS. On the contrary, during his own election to the Lok Sabha from Ottapalam, Narayanan had been targeted for unfair criticism by CPI(M) party cadres. He once told me that it has been said of him by election campaigners from the Left that his long years in the Foreign Service have distanced him from his roots, that he does not know even how to wear a mundu or eat with his fingers. But Narayanan, who had told me of this, was just too evolved as a human being to bear these pettinesses of election time in mind. He went to A. K. Gopalan Bhavan, the CPI(M) headquarters in the capital, to offer his tribute to EMS. The president of India going to a political party's office was not standard practice, but EMS was EMS and Narayanan, Narayanan.

Accompanying him to that venue and watching him sign the condolence book surrounded by red flags with the hammer and sickle was, for me, one of the high moments of my tenure with him. Vajpayee, just a few hours old in his office, sent a good message—perhaps his very first in his new role. But Narayanan penned his tribute with much thought. He described EMS as 'a social theorist of the highest order and originality' and 'an educator of people as well as their leader'. For EMS's life to be examined and extolled so cerebrally—and concisely—by Narayanan showed a very Keralite intellectual poise.

Before two months had elapsed after Vajpayee's becoming prime minister, he did what the outgoing Narasimha Rao had asked him to do in 1996, on his first taking that office. He gave the signal for underground nuclear tests to be conducted in Pokhran, the site of the nuclear tests conducted under Indira Gandhi's command in 1974. President Narayanan had been apprised of the possibility by the national security advisor (NSA) Brajesh Mishra. On 11 May 1998, a little before 4 p.m., Mishra rang me to say three tests had been carried out and could I inform the president. No one, he said, had been told of it yet (although it would have been picked up by international satellites at once). The president was pleased with the news and at once issued a statement congratulating our nuclear scientists team. EMS would have most certainly opposed the test. But that is neither here nor there.

Trained to despise nuclear testing from my teenage, I kept thinking of what my grandfathers would have said. 11 May happened to be the birthday of my closest friend, Keshav Desiraju. We were to have met up in the evening. But after the president's statement had been issued that afternoon, I rang Keshav in his office. 'We have burst the crackers,' I told him. 'No!' he exclaimed, 'that is so...so...' He did not have to complete his sentence. It was Buddha Jayanti. 'Gopal, before we meet up, can we go to the Buddha Vihara at the Birla Mandir?' And so, my wife Tara, Keshav, and I went to that shrine as part of his birthday 'celebration'. I can never forget his very

Vedic namaskar—saashtanga*—before the serene image of the Buddha there. For whom or what he sought absolution, only he knew...and the Shakyamuni.

Vajpayee had, for the moment, but only for the moment, silenced all critics in the opposition and carpers in his coalition as well. On 13 May, two more tests were conducted. The country was jubilant. The world was cynical. Pakistan, expectedly enough, responded with a diatribe but, on 28 May, carried out five underground tests of its own. Deterrent parity in mass death-dealing had been established by what was being seen as a Hindu bomb in India and a Muslim one in Pakistan. Indira Gandhi had, in 1974, most definitely tested to strengthen herself politically as much as to strengthen national security. The same story was re-enacted in 1998 by a beleaguered Vajpayee. But did the Indian polity realize the price for that political aim? Weaponization of the deadliest and most competitive kind imperilling human life, giving India and Pakistan the distinction of being called 'the most dangerous place in the world'.

Prime Minister A. B. Vajpayee at the Shakti-1 test site in Pokhran in Rajasthan on 20 May 1998. Photo: Shanker Chakravarty/*The Hindu*.

Jayalalithaa was stilled but very briefly. She came up with a fresh list of expectations, of which the chief was the dismissal of the Karunanidhi government. Vajpayee did not say yes to her; he did not say no. But even with Pokhran-I to V under his belt, he knew his government's days were

*Literally, a prostration.

numbered. As did the president. As 1998 wore on, so did the Vajpayee-led motley coalition government, despite endless differences among the allies. Though out of power in her state, Jayalalithaa had 18 rock-solid MPs in the Lok Sabha, on whose support the BJP relied. In return, she demanded that the union government withdraw all the criminal cases that Karunanidhi had filed against her. Did the laws allow that interference by Delhi? They did not. But did Jayalalithaa care? She threatened, from time to time, to withdraw her support to the Vajpayee government.

In September, Bihar became the centre of political activity. And not an ordinary one at that, for it involved President Narayanan and the Vajpayee government. The government of Bihar was being described as dysfunctional, 'non-existent'. It being on the defensive in numerous court cases was going against it.

The spirited, now-jocund, now-sombre, never-say-die Lalu Prasad Yadav had lost his office of chief minister of Bihar in 1997 amid allegations of corruption, and in July that year, had stunned the political world of India by seeing to it that if he were to leave, his wife, Rabri Devi, would succeed him. This was considered a joke, a poor one at that. That she was duly elected leader by the party that held a majority of the legislative assembly and was legally and constitutionally entitled to that seat, that office, that position of power was not taken seriously. That a wife, merely because she was the former chief minister's wife and not a formally educated woman at that, had become chief minister through the back door was what was being said.

And by this time that year, 1998, Rabri Devi's government was in deep trouble. The precariousness of her numbers in the house apart, her government was being criticized for its standards of governance. In September, the union cabinet recommended to President Narayanan that the government of Rabri Devi be dismissed and President's Rule imposed under Article 356 of the Constitution of India. Crucial to the recommendation was the report of newly-appointed BJP-affiliated Governor Sunder Singh Bhandari, citing financial mismanagement and poor law and order. Governor Bhandari claimed to have sent a 'foolproof' case for the government's dismissal.

The governor's assessment may have been foolproof, it was not Narayanan-proof. The president read the cabinet's recommendation line by line, word by word. Those of us on his staff who had gone over the text and made our own comments on it did what we were meant to do, like fact-checkers in any newspaper office. But the president's appraisal of the recommendation was his own. He studied it and reflected on it in silence, without anyone butting into the process. He had done the same about a year earlier when Prime Minister Gujral's UPA government had recommended the dismissal of the BJP government led by Kalyan Singh in Uttar Pradesh. And just as he did then, so he did now. He returned the recommendation to the government for reconsideration. There was no politics to his decision. There was only fairness, Constitutional fairness.

Wordsmith—President K. R. Narayanan goes over the draft of his address to the nation, Rashtrapati Bhavan, 1998, New Delhi. To his left is his press secretary, T. P. Seetharam. (Author's personal collection, from the Rashtrapati Bhavan's archives).

Law and order failures, financial mismanagement, and misgovernance are bad. But they do not amount to a constitutional breakdown, the sine qua non for President's Rule. This was his clear, simple reading. There can be political democratic responses to those situations, but Rabri Devi did not call for unseating on the grounds of a failure of the constitutional structure. This was a protection he was giving not to a chief minister but to a constitutional principle, a protection he was duty-bound as president of India to give.

And while initially, the Vajpayee cabinet was rattled by his decision, just as Gujral's had been, it decided in its maturity to accept the point. It did not press for the dismissal. It did not repeat the recommendation which the president, under the Constitution, would then have had to accept. *The Hindu* carried an editorial on 27 September 1998 entitled, 'Well done, Mr Narayanan', while the *Hindustan Times* entitled its editorial 'Not a snub, a favour'. How a favour? The editorial said that an eminently dismissible government would have donned the mantle of martyrdom had it been dismissed. In the event, it stayed on until the logic of democracy brought about a change. So, the president had done the union government a favour.

It was not to do a favour to anyone that President Narayanan did what he did. It was to do the right and proper thing without fear or favour. He was undisturbed by the criticism that had come briefly his way from the BJP. He was unelated by the encomiums that came to him from the supporters of Lalu Prasad and Rabri Devi.

'I, Kocheril Raman *Narayanan* do solemnly affirm that I will faithfully execute the office of President…' he had promised the nation. The affirmation of a virtuous man is no less weighty than swearings in the name of God.

Honouring brilliance—Amartya Sen, after receiving the Nobel Prize for Economic Sciences, 1998, arrives at the Rashtrapati Bhavan, New Delhi, for a dinner hosted in his honour by President Narayanan. (Rashtrapati Bhavan archives).

Before 'taking leave' of this year, I must record another 'MS Bharat Ratna' cameo and, from it, lead on to another of the same gem. A day after the medallion had adorned her name and added lustre to its own fame, Pandit Ravi Shankar came calling on her, in the highest form of artistic etiquette. Seated on a small sofa in our study room, she saw him enter and said, reading his mind like an x-ray machine would read any limb, in English: 'Next time, you!' The maestro's amazingly sensitive face lit up in a lovely mix of sheer modesty and pure delight. The same year—1998—saw the Nobel Memorial Prize for Economic Sciences conferred on Amartya Sen. President Narayanan was very glad of this and decided to propose to the Prime Minister that the Nobel laureate be honoured by the Bharat Ratna, a suggestion that found no resistance with Vajpayee. Sen was to get it the following year, with none other than Ravi Shankar. MS's prophecy had come true. But before that felicity, on a visit to India—his first after the Nobel, Amartya Sen was hosted by President Narayanan to a dinner to which the president invited not the protocol-mandated big names alone but academics, politicians with an interest in matters economic. Amartya Sen in Rashtrapati Bhavan that evening, as K. R. Narayanan's guest, was a sight that Harold Laski would have liked to see. and Nehru would have hailed. On duty at the event, I thanked my stars for the chance to see Sen and Narayanan at the same table.

1999
BLOODY, BLOODY BEASTS. BLOODY BEASTS

The year 1999 began horridly.

Graham Stuart Staines, a fifty-eight-year-old Australian Christian missionary, and his two sons, Philip (10) and Timothy (6), were burnt to death in Odisha by members of a vigilante group, the Bajrang Dal.

Staines had been working among leprosy-afflicted persons, mainly of tribal origin, in Mayurbhanj, Odisha, since 1965. Hindu groups had accused him of converting people to Christianity and introducing tribals to 'beef and brassieres'. On 22 January, Staines was travelling to the village of Kendujhar with his sons, who were on a holiday break from their school in Ooty, when they decided to spend the night in Manoharpur in their vehicle. Gladys, his wife, and daughter were not with them. That night, about fifty people set the station wagon alight, burning the three Staines inside to death. The men slunk away into the night after the deed was done, leaving the charred bodies to be found in the morning, clinging to each other. As the news came in, I went, dazed by the horror of it all, to President Narayanan with a draft statement. He had heard of it, of course, and touched up what I had suggested to make it one of the strongest statements to have been issued by him, describing it as 'a monumental aberration of time-tested tolerance and harmony'. He said, 'The killings belong to the world's inventory of black deeds.' Describing the murderers as 'a blot on our collective consciousness', Prime Minister Atal Bihari Vajpayee sent three cabinet ministers to Odisha to probe the incident and then set up a Supreme Court enquiry into the matter. Dara Singh, the leader of the mob, was to be sentenced to life imprisonment.[1]

Four days later, on 26 January, at the Republic Day reception at Rashtrapati Bhavan, I went up to Rob Laurie, the Australian high commissioner in India (1997–2001), and offered my own personal contrition as an Indian over the tragedy. I said, 'High Commissioner, I am going down on my knees before their memories.' He heard me in civil silence. Christians were, around that time, being made the subject of hate speech in India. And no one was more pained by this than Vajpayee.

His government had just about completed a year and a few weeks in office when Jayalalithaa withdrew her outside support to it. She arrived in Delhi on 12 April and was met by her 18 MPs and Subramanian Swamy.

The BJP, which until recently had been meeting her on arrival, boycotted her this time. She told media-persons that she had come to take 'the final step of withdrawing support to the Vajpayee Government'. She said that she would meet leaders of 'like-minded secular parties' including Congress president Sonia Gandhi to evolve a viable alternative government.

Her stay became the talk of the town, as reports had it that Jayalalithaa had checked into the Chandragupta Maurya suite at the Maurya Sheraton hotel, along with nearly two dozen security and secretarial staff and forty-eight pieces of baggage. It was later clarified by her party that the forty-eight pieces included the baggage of her entourage. After meeting many opposition leaders and speaking over the phone with Sonia Gandhi, Jayalalithaa called on President Narayanan at 11 a.m. on 14 April with her letter of withdrawal, looking tense and relaxed, nervous and confident in turn. Handing over her letter withdrawing support to the Vajpayee government and exchanging a few words in pleasantries, she left regally with a new glowing elan. She, an out-of-office state-level leader, was bringing the government of India down.

President Narayanan was in discussion with legal experts who advised that in view of Jayalalithaa's withdrawal of support, he should ask Vajpayee to seek a vote of confidence in the Lok Sabha. Punctilious, Vajpayee did so on 17 April. His minister for Parliamentary Affairs, Pramod Mahajan (1949–2006), phoned as many MPs as he could, including Mayawati's BSP MPs and even some 'disgruntled' Congress MPs to vote for Vajpayee.[2] But with the BSP, after promising him its votes, switching sides at the last minute, and the Odisha chief minister Giridhar Gamang, an MP still, voting against him, Vajpayee lost by one vote—269 to 270. I watched the proceedings on a TV in my office, as the president was doing from his. Vajpayee had lost, and his government had fallen, but no party was in a position to form the next government. Sonia Gandhi's overconfident claim, made from the forecourt of Rashtrapati Bhavan, that she had the support of 272 MPs coming to grief, with Mulayam Singh saying his MPs would not back her,[3] President Narayanan dissolved the house, as he had to, and asked for fresh elections in September-October.

But before those could be held, Pakistan forced a bitter war on India—the Kargil War. It was, as became apparent later, a war that was not just forced on India but on Prime Minister Nawaz Sharif as well, by the head of Pakistan's army, General Pervez Musharraf. Very young officers and men of the Indian Army who had never been in battle before, plunged into the war with stunning valour. This time, officers were in the lead, it is said, at the insistence of the soldiery, as what was involved was climbing uphill on peaks occupied by Pakistani soldiers. And these officers were among the 500

Indians left by the war, martyred. By July, India had managed to recapture the strategic points, and Pakistan withdrew to its earlier positions along the LoC.

Vajpayee entered the elections as the head of a war-victorious leader and, as he had to, won emphatically, his alliance winning 300 seats.

Jayalalithaa had, unbeknownst to her, done him a favour. Rashtrapati Bhavan is like a pop-up book. It slumbers when the nation is unexcited by politics or untroubled by cabinet intrigues. But come election time and cabinet-formation time or a crisis that seems to question the cabinet's poise, its elegant cut-out pops up from the sleeping pages of the book. We were not surprised when Vajpayee's list of proposed ministers was slow in coming. Gone are the days when the strong prime minister-designate would, perhaps in consultation with one or two confidants, draw up a compact list and send it to the president for his approval. Now, before he could celebrate his victory, he needed to consult his confidants and peers and rivals within the party, the grumblers, mumblers, and number-tumblers who had a potential to become thorns in success' soft tissues. He also had to reckon with the veto power used with inscrutable grimness by the BJP's ideological senior—the RSS. After Vajpayee's list had reached Rashtrapati Bhavan and all was set to operationalize it, the RSS contacted him with a couple of modifications.

The subtle sophisticate Jaswant Singh, who was widely expected to become finance minister and figured conspicuously in the list that had come, was disfavoured by the RSS. Vajpayee sent word saying we should disregard the list that had been sent and await a fresh one. When it came, Jaswant Singh and Pramod Mahajan were out of it.[4] Advani, of course, continued in it as Number Two. Unsurprised and unannoyed, a cool President Narayanan approved the revision, and the president's printing press then got to work on printing the parchments with all names correctly put in, and, I should add, in complete secrecy, for there should be no leaks that could imperil the balance that had been achieved.

On the crisp morning of 13 October, Atal Bihari Vajpayee was sworn-in as India's prime minister, for the third time. A photograph has him seated alongside Advani in Rashtrapati Bhavan's forecourt, looking mildly amused, contemplating his fingertips as his team gets inducted.

Omar Abdullah's name had come in the list of prospective ministers of state as 'Omar Farook'. And that is how it was printed. Without any fuss, matter-of-factly, he said he was Omar Abdullah, not Omar Farook. And was called accordingly. In accordance with custom, after the president was seated in his high chair, I walked up to him, bowed, and sought his formal permission to commence the proceedings. He gave it, again by custom, with a slight nod. Returning to the rostrum where my microphone was, I started by saying, in Hindi, 'Shapath Grahan', meaning 'Swearing-in Ceremony', and then proceeded to call out the names, beginning with that of Vajpayee. The ceremony went off uneventfully. At the end of it, a Sanskrit and Hindutva enthusiast complimented me for starting the ceremony auspiciously in Vedic terms with 'Shubha Mangalam' meaning 'Blessed Beneficence'. When I corrected his impression, he was disappointed. Rangarajan Kumaramangalam, who had crossed over from the Congress to the BJP and was becoming a minister, was accompanied by his gifted wife, Kitty. After the ceremony was over, she came up to me and said, 'Gopal, you were aglow... How do you do it?' I said it was the white suit and the bright sunshine that glowed, not I. And both of us laughed aloud. I recall this with a pang of pain because Rangarajan was to die the very next year, at age forty-eight, of acute myeloid leukaemia (blood cancer) and Kitty, tragically, in 2021, at the hands of a laundryman and his accomplices in a maniacal and petty instance of robbery.

The year 1999 was to leave as horridly as it began, with a sharp kick in our abdomen. An Indian Airlines Flight, IC 814, an airbus carrying 176 passengers, flying from Tribhuvan International Airport in Kathmandu, Nepal, and headed for Indira Gandhi International Airport in Delhi, India, was hijacked by five masked Pakistani militants of the Harkat-ul-Mujahideen (HuM). This was shortly after it entered Indian airspace at about 5.30 p.m. IST on 24 December. After changes of mind and changes of manner by the hijackers, it was flown to several locations before landing in Kandahar, Afghanistan, after a stopover in Amritsar and Dubai, where it managed to get refuelled. While it was in Amritsar, India had a last and golden chance to halt its progress. Jaswant Singh (who had, by now, been inducted into the cabinet as minister for External Affairs) tried in Amritsar to have the aircraft blocked by getting a lorry parked in front of it and surrounding it but was not backed up by the chief minister (Parkash Singh Badal) who feared that any such action might lead to the hijackers harming the passengers. And so the aircraft made it to Kandahar, which, at the time, was controlled by the Taliban. The hijackers released 27 of 176 passengers in Dubai, fatally stabbed one and wounded several others. Taliban militiamen fighters encircled the aircraft to prevent any Indian military intervention. Vajpayee was, like everyone else, shaken by the brazenness of the hijack and the audacity of the demand—securing the release of terrorists held in prison in India—fellow HuM members Ahmed Omar, Saeed Sheikh, and Masood Azhar and a Kashmiri militant, Mushtaq Ahmed Zargar. Later accounts speak of Vajpayee having turned sullen and silent while contradictory advice was poured on him. There were those who said India should not give in to this blackmail. There were others who said public opinion in India was agonizing over the fates of the trapped passengers and the panic in their families. Finally, it was decided that Jaswant Singh would fly out to Kandahar with the prisoners and release them in Kandahar in exchange for the passengers on board the hijacked plane. The hostage crisis ended after seven days, with the jury left permanently out on whether the exchange was right or wrong. The three released terrorists have not been silent since then; their names linked to other terrorist outrages, such as the 2001 Indian Parliament House attack. President Narayanan was the last person to say to a prime minister and a cabinet fighting the flames of a terrorist attack that they should take time off from their urgent deliberations to keep him informed of what was happening. Nor was he one to take a continuous neglect by the cabinet of his prerogative and duty. Prime Minister Vajpayee met the president only on 30 December, fully one week afterwards, after the deal had been agreed to. This was the first meeting between them after the hijacking of the plane on 24 December. He was 'confronted with a fait accompli to avoid having to answer awkward questions'.[5] But he did his own fact-checking sufficiently well to gather that the cabinet had been numbed as much as the nation was by the crisis. That Defence Minister George Fernandes came back to New Delhi from his tour in northeastern India only the night of 27 December, that the chiefs of the defence services—General V. P. Malik, Air Marshal A. Y. Tipnis, and Admiral Sushil Kumar—were called in only on 28 December, and that political leaders outside government were informed of Jaswant Singh's going to Kandahar after he had taken off, and then also, without any details of the 'deal'. On 31 December, Vajpayee said in his address to the nation: 'The hijackers had demanded the release of 36 terrorists. We were able to substantially scale down their demands.' This was not accepted by everyone. Pakistan's role in the hijacking of the flight was becoming clearer by the hour, with the Pakistani origins of the hijackers, as well as the role of Pakistani officials posted in Kathmandu, coming to light. I find it impossible to fault the Vajpayee government over the IC 814 incident. It is easy to say we should never have agreed to the exchange. But placing myself in the government's shoes, I can see that the hijackers, being who they were—death-defying and death-dealing desperados—could have easily killed every single passenger, one by mangled one, minute by bloodied minute, asking for their demands to be fulfilled. 'Are you releasing our men?' 'No?'. Okay, here, one passenger down.' 'So…Are you releasing?' 'No?' 'Okay, here is the second….' And so on, until the plane was littered by the dead and the dying. They would then have killed themselves. Had India not done a 'deal', would India have forgiven Vajpayee and Jaswant Singh for the massacre of those innocents? Would India not have laid their deaths at the doors of the government? Of what value are a few terrorists, it would have been said, before the 176 passengers and their families?

I cannot blame Vajpayee for the deal. One of two lesser evils is very often the choice we face, whether in policy-making or in life's larger theatres. And I believe President Narayanan's position was the same. On the last night of the millennium, I turned in, saying a blur of confused prayers for our dear land and its bruised, battered life. But also thanking God for reuniting all but one of the passengers on that plane with their families. And finding no words of solace to offer to the widow of twenty-five-year-old Rupin Katyal, freshly married, who was returning with his wife after their honeymoon in Kathmandu and who was stabbed to death by the hijackers. Bloody, bloody beasts, I said to myself. Bloody beasts, not wanting to further sully my mental language further at that moment, so delicately poised between one millennium and another, by using a similar word beginning with a 'b'.

BOOK SEVEN

2000
THE CONSTITUTION, DEMOCRACY, SECULARISM, AND FUNDAMENTAL RIGHTS

The *Hindustan Times* reported (1 January) that informally, the decision to release the hijackers had been taken on the night of 29 December: 'The militants-for-hostages swap was decided collectively by Prime Minister Vajpayee, Home Minister Advani, External Affairs Minister Jaswant Singh, Principal Secretary to the Prime Minister, Brajesh Mishra, the Director of the Intelligence Bureau and the Secretary of the Research and Analysis Wing late on Wednesday (December 29, 1999).'[1]

President Narayanan, an alert 'diplomatist' antenna within his brain receiving and transmitting signals, alerted Vajpayee and Jaswant Singh on the criticality of naming Pakistan and telling the world what and where we stood on terrorism. Not that they were unaware, but nudges work to speed, ginger, and sharpen action. On 3 January, Prime Minister Vajpayee formally accused Pakistan of being behind the December hijacking of IC 814 and urged that Pakistan be declared a terrorist state.

On 6 January, four men based in Kashmir were arrested in connection with the hijacking. Discussion on the whys and why-nots of the incident went on, with former prime minister Gujral saying, 'Although the Prime Minister rang up to say that [Jaswant] Singh was going, he did not breathe a word of the deal that had already been struck with the hijackers. He told us half-truths.'[2]

President Narayanan's speech in Parliament on 23 February 2000 had forty-nine paragraphs dealing with almost every aspect of governance. The hijack came in for passing mention in these lines: 'Irrefutable evidence has been provided by the Government about the Pakistani origins of the hijackers as well as the role of Pakistani officials posted in Kathmandu. We sincerely hope that Pakistan will reverse this policy of hostility towards India so that normal relations could be restored.'

Curious it was, that a traumatic, even cathartic, experience that convulsed the nation and brought it close to a meltdown should have finally got condensed into one of the smaller paragraphs in a forty-nine-paragraph-long speech. Doubtless, each word in that paragraph had been through microscopes of phraseology. The government would not have appreciated

Narayanan cavilling at the wording. But Narayanan did what a constitutional head of state could. He made his antenna thrum in unqualified relayings to the government. The very next day, 24 February, a review of national security was ordered, citing the report of the committee on the incursion of Pakistani-backed forces into Kargil. The report, going by the popular name of Subrahmanyam Report, after the head of the committee, the renowned international affairs expert and defence strategist K. Subrahmanyam (1929–2011), had exposed serious shortcomings. The committee had recommended a new 'national security planning and decision-making structure for India in the nuclear age'.

There was something else that was giving President Narayanan cause for worry. Admiration for the Constitution and a sense of affiliation with its spirit was, for him, an ardour amounting to a passion. And so, the Vajpayee government's interest in getting the Constitution 'reviewed' by a committee, as reflected in the draft for his address to Parliament, did not sit well with him. The Constitution, he believed, was not infallible and was open to amending. But then only by Parliament, not at the instance of a government-appointed committee. Yet is there anything wrong in a government appointing a committee to study the Constitution and suggest changes in it in the light of experience? The point was moot. But Narayanan's apprehension was about a 'review'. That was an omnibus approach, making the Constitution's supremacy as a whole subject to a reconsideration, a reappraisal—an audacious thing to attempt. And so, he did what was within his scope: he touched up the draft paragraph expertly, delicately. It finally read as follows (with the words in italics reflecting President Narayanan's thinking):

The Constitution, which India adopted fifty years ago, has served us well. It has been a reliable guarantor of parliamentary democracy, secularism and fundamental rights, which all of us cherish. It has also inspired the spread of democratic consciousness in our society, empowering dalits, adivasis, backward classes and women and making our system of governance more participative and progressive. While keeping the basic structure and salient features of the Constitution inviolate, it has, however, become necessary to examine the experience of the past fifty years to better achieve the ideals enshrined in the Constitution. The Government has, therefore, set up a broad-based Constitution Review Commission. *The recommendations of this Commission will be presented before Parliament, which is the supreme decision-making body in Indian democracy.*

Without the benefit of Narayanan's thinking, the unitalicized parts would probably have been all the speech said. Thank God for an alert president with a humming antenna, a sharp eye and a sensitive pen.

President Bill Clinton's visit to India was imminent. Shortly before the visit began, a suggested draft came from the Ministry of External Affairs for his use in the banquet speech. President Narayanan, in one inspired sitting, tore through the MEA draft and virtually rewrote the whole thing.

Brief thaw in hoarfrost—President K. R. Narayanan introduces his wife Usha Narayanan to US Secretary of State Madeleine Albright, Rashtrapati Bhavan, New Delhi, 1998. To the left, President Clinton and India's ambassador to the US, Naresh Chandra. (Rashtrapati Bhavan archives).

The preliminary round of discussions that he had with Secretary of State (the first woman to hold that office) Madeleine Albright (1937–2022) was frosty. An obituary of the lady was to say: 'Admirers said she had a star quality, radiating practicality, versatility and a refreshingly cosmopolitan flair.'[3] Her meeting with President Narayanan showed she also had a beam of steel in her, a cold steel. Narayanan, who had wanted to be apprised about the Jaswant Singh-Strobe Talbott talks on non-proliferation and was dissatisfied with what he was told by way of briefs, expressed himself forcefully to Albright on what he called 'India's sovereign options' but kept his franker views for when he was to be face-to-face with Clinton. Their discussion was prosaic and went on expected lines. In his banquet speech, President Narayanan came with total confidence to his punchline: 'Mr President, we do recognize and welcome the fact that the world has been moving inevitably towards one world.... But, for us, globalization does not mean the end of history and geography and of the lively and exciting diversities of the world.

As an African statesman has observed to us, the fact that the world is a global village does not mean that it will be run by one village headman.' There was an audible silence as he said this, but the one-time socialist and now minister Sushma Swaraj, sitting diagonally opposite me, looked at me, gestured and through a mischievous smile, signalled her total approval of President Narayanan's words.

More was to follow. Narayanan ended his speech by quoting the famous American thinker Henry David Thoreau: 'It takes two to speak the truth—one to speak it and the other to hear.' I have no idea what Clinton thought, but as the invitees to the dinner left, I heard Jaswant Singh voice his disapproval of Narayanan's speech and wonder if there should not be a practice of having banquet speeches being vetted by his ministry.

Clinton's speech at a joint sitting of Parliament was a fantastic success. He got repeated ovations during it and a prolonged standing ovation at the end of it, with MPs from all parties jostling around him to shake his hand. I must admit that despite my great satisfaction and pride at my president having said what he said, I could not but admire the words of the visitor: 'I believe that the greatest of India's many gifts to the world is the example its people have set from Midnight to Millennium. Think of it, virtually every challenge humanity knows can be found here in India. And every solution to every challenge can be found here in India as well: confidence in democracy, tolerance for diversity, a willingness to embrace social change. That is why Americans admire India....'

India knew all that was known about the 'Lewinsky affair',* but it was not going to let that come in the way of its appreciation of Clinton. President Narayanan, in a comment prior to Clinton's arrival, said to me he was not worried about Clinton having had an affair with 'some woman'. His problem, he said, was that Clinton did what he did 'in the Oval, right inside the White House....' I had laughed at that and sort of agreed with Narayanan. But hearing and seeing Clinton in our Parliament House, I forgot all the negatives associated with the Lewinsky story. Clinton was a winner. And on nuclear non-proliferation itself, as one who was and continues to be repelled by the very thought of nuclear weaponization, I could not but applaud Clinton's comment made elsewhere on his visit: 'Only India can know if it truly is safer today than before the tests.'

---

*A sex scandal involving President Bill Clinton and Monica Lewinsky, a White House intern.

US President Bill Clinton addressing the members of Parliament at the Central Hall of Parliament House, in New Delhi on 22 March 2000. Photo: Kamal Narang/*The Hindu*.

'They are calling me a Cold Warrior,' President Narayanan said to me. 'Where is our sense of sovereignty?' He was, of course, saying this with his knowledge of thirty-six Sikh men massacred, even as Clinton was visiting India, in Chittisingpura village in Kashmir's Anantnag district.[4] The gunmen's identity to this day remains unestablished, but to everyone who is aware of the phenomenon, was clearly the work of Pakistan-based terrorists.

In April, the country was seized by a natural disaster—severe drought in Rajasthan and Gujarat. Exactly a century earlier, in 1900, a drought had ravaged Gujarat. This time, an unprecedented crisis of drinking water and fodder scarcity gripped Saurashtra. Rivulets went dry, wells stood parched, ponds sharded, baked. On 23 April, criticized for doing 'too little, too late' about the severe drought in Rajasthan and Gujarat in the north-west, Prime Minister Vajpayee sent out a televised appeal to the nation for donations to help. IAS officers at that time had only a modest salary, and it was not possible for us to make a donation of any significance. But reading reports of the 4,000 villages and about 125 towns reeling under the scorching skies, the fact that I was ensconced in the assured comforts of non-stop water-supply, with fountains in the Rashtrapati Bhavan playing ceaselessly, one in the shape of serpents spewing water, another like snail-shells doing the same, stung something deep within me. Maybe, I thought, I should go quietly and incognito to Saurashtra and experience the trauma there. It was, after all, my ancestral region.

Tara was not exactly impressed. Impulsive, it seemed to her, and self-fulfilling. She is wise. But I could not give up the idea. The president agreed to let me go for a week. I set out in the first week of May for the village of Kundaliya, in the Vav taluk of Gujarat's Banaskantha district. It lay on the India–Pakistan border. Karsandasbhai, the sarpanch, took charge of my orientation at once. Standing on the very hot soil, wearing a pair of closed sandals made of tough hide, a bright turban, a loose-fitting cotton apparel on his torso, with many folds in it and strings rather than buttons, and a dhoti, he pointed north and said, 'Aa baaju Rajasthan,' (On this side lies Rajasthan) and then wheeling towards the west said, 'aney aa baaju—Pakistan.' (And on this side—Pakistan). Utterly matter-of-fact, non-judgemental. No GPS could have done better. The sky and ground blazed, blinded.

My work among the salt of the earth, which is what the villagers were, as they did drought relief chores, involved building a bund to store rainwater as when the rains came, by digging the earth in allotted chokhadis (plots), each of which was assigned to a gang consisting of men, women, and some 'grown' children as well.

I found myself in Gang 29. Lifting headloads of not-very-soft mud was excruciating for one who had done nothing of the kind ever. Doing so, pretending to feel no strain, was even more difficult. The sense of camaraderie at such a work-site is something no desk-bound urbanite can imagine. The villagers took to me, and I to them. Sleeping under a tree, doing the nature stuff out in the open behind a bush, and bathing by a hand pump were all minor changes from my routine of metropolitan blessings.

By Day 2, I began being called by the Gujarati name for father, 'Bapu'. Not having shaved for two days, I had grown a stubble and looked old enough for that paternal title. One day, I asked a group of women working on the hard plot, 'Is this chokhadi not very hard to work on?' One of them replied, 'No, Bapu, the chokhadi is not hard, our kismat is hard.' An elder said to me: 'This life is written for us from above.'

On one of the evenings, as I sat around with some fellow earth-diggers at dusk, I saw and heard, at a slight distance, a bullock cart decorated with festoons filled with celebratory women and men moving out of the village. From within it, a small girl's voice wailing rang out. What was happening, I asked. 'Oh,' I was told, 'that is a wedding party...The girl is wailing as she is leaving her parental house for her sasuraal (in-laws' home) for the first time.... She will come back after five days.... It is natural for the bride and her mother to cry on this occasion…. It is also a custom…' As a father of two daughters, I choked and could not sleep properly that night. I tried telling myself that this is what happened to my grandmother when she was married off at thirteen to my grandfather of the same age. Perhaps this little girl will be perfectly happy in her new home. Was she not too young to be flung into marriage, non-consensual motherhood, followed by the possibility of being coerced into female feticide and infanticide? My esteemed friend, the outstanding lawyer Ashok Desai, had told me of how in Gujarat, the old practice had not yet gone of new-born baby girls being made 'dudh-piti' (milk-drinking), a reference to their being suffocated in a bucket of milk. I knew of the imbalance between males and females in Gujarat but was too overwhelmed by the kindness of the villagers to discuss this sensitive subject with them.

The UN's Population Fund was in the coming months to condemn the Government of India 'for its lack of commitment to tackle the imbalance between numbers of males and females (960 women to every 1,000 men) in the country' caused, in its words, by 'the feticide and infanticide of baby girls'.

My Kundaliya visit was essentially a self-fulfilling indulgence which drew from the hospitality and time of the village. It left me richer for the experience but the village poorer for whatever it spent by way of time and attention and, not to forget, the expense on hosting me for meals. What I gave in return was negligible. I am sure when I left it, the village quickly forgot all about its curious visitor.

Reliance Industries advertisements were all over the state. Like millions of Indians, I had, of course, heard of Dhirubhai Ambani (1932–2002) and, as a Gujarati, felt quite proud of the man's achievements that had made his company the country's largest private venture. But I did not quite realize then the importance of Reliance Industries announcing its plans to enter the new information technology sector, which was to become the driving force of India's modernization. There is something natural about an entrepreneur with a genius for bold ventures wanting, through its new subsidiary, Reliance Infocom, to lay fibre optic cables to connect the top 115 cities within India to the internet. But that this venture was soon to go global and would see to the laying of submarine cables in the sea connecting continents, even Reliance's brainpower may not have known then.

Before going to Kathiawad, I had reminded President Narayanan of his promise to me that he would have me appointed to a diplomatic mission once he had settled into his new office. It was now two-and-a-half years since I joined his office and more than midway into his term. He was as good as his word and put it to Lalit Mansingh (b. 1941), the foreign secretary, that I should be kept in mind for an ambassadorship. Lalit, a classically fine diplomat and faultless friend of sobriety and good sense (apart from master of a chiselled English), asked me if I had any country in mind. I mentioned to him that I had always had an audacious desire to serve in our mission in Beijing but that, having worked in Sri Lanka from 1978 to 1982, had a feeling for that troubled country as well. The island was at that point in high tension, with the LTTE doing its ferocious worst. Lalit noted that in his characteristically understated manner.

On 10 May, he got back saying MEA had proposed my name for Rome, but the PM had said Colombo, which was falling vacant, was more important and I should be asked to go there, and if I did not want to do that, 'Rome would be made available.'

I was asked to make a quick choice between two venues to go to as head of mission: Rome and Colombo. (The Hague was also mentioned as a third possibility.) I mentioned this to the president, who said immediately, reflexively: 'I cannot advise you to take Colombo. It is a volatile place. You had better take Rome.' Tara and our daughters said, with natural spontaneity, that I (and they) deserved a posting with no security hassles, and I should choose the Italian capital. But I knew that my going to Rome would be and seen to be a pole-vault from ease to rest, whereas Colombo would be and be recognized as a change to hard work plus real danger plus the risk, almost guaranteed, of flopping.

On 11 May, External Affairs minister Jaswant Singh came to Rashtrapati Bhavan to brief the president on his forthcoming China trip, and after the meeting was over, I asked EAM for his advice. He said, after a moment's reflection, that in Colombo, I would be able to make a contribution because of my associations, which I would not be able to in Rome. 'God willing,' he said, 'you will be able to assist India play its part, keeping the confidence of all parties.' Later that day, I called on Brajesh Mishra in the PMO. He said the PM felt Colombo would be a weightier position for me. The next day, I told Tara it seemed inevitable that I should head for Colombo. Her reaction was as could only be expected. When I rang Rajmohan to tell him the same, he said, 'Bless you, precious brother.' On 12 May, at 10.30, the very start of the office's day, Lalit Mansingh rang:

'Have you decided?'.
'Yes, I accept Colombo'.

'I congratulate you. You will make a contribution. You are bound to do very well there.' Straight after my talk with Lalit, I went to rashtrapatiji, who was in his apartment, getting ready to come down to the office. He immediately held out his hand and said 'Congratulations.' I took his extended hand in both of mine and then touched my head. 'You have a golden touch,' I said. 'I need it.' He said, 'You never know. Sometimes, the choice of a tougher option turns out very well, and you could do very well there.'

The suspense was over, but not conversations about the decision, which had got its share of publicity in the media.

My former boss in Rashtrapati Bhavan was cross with me. 'Do not go to Colombo,' said RV. 'You are being made a sacrificial lamb. You have been a success in every job you have done. No Indian ambassador can succeed now in Colombo. And you will certainly not. You are courting failure. The Tamils there will have very high hopes in you. And when they find you are unable to help, they will curse you.' But after hearing out my reasons, he gave me his blessings. Mrs RV had a slightly different take and said, 'God will protect you, Gopal. You work hard wherever you go. You will work hard there, and people will see that you are doing so. You may not be able to leave Sri Lanka soon. You will earn a good name there.'

Meanwhile, the long-planned state visit to China from 28 May to 3 June by President Narayanan was falling into place, coinciding with the fiftieth year of the establishment of diplomatic relations between the two countries. Narayanan chose a politically representative and talented team to go with him and Mrs Narayanan that included Petroleum Minister Manohar Joshi of the Shiv Sena and MPs—Sushma Swaraj of the BJP, Somnath Chatterjee, Nilotpal Basu of the CPI(M), Suresh Kurup of the CPI. Among journalists accompanying he invited N. Ram, at the helm of *The Hindu*.

President Narayanan knew his China, not just from his time as ambassador there (1976–78) when he had been selected by Indira Gandhi to be the first ambassador resuming that level of representation after the Sino-Indian War of 1962. He knew it from his early years in the Ministry of External Affairs when, in 1964, he served at the China desk, from where he wrote a defining note on India–China ties. The first Chinese atomic bomb had been tested that year at Lop Nor. In his note, the forty-four-year diplomat had examined the possible consequences of the Chinese acquisition of nuclear weapons and suggested that the only option open to India was to go in for a nuclear programme of her own for a credible minimum nuclear deterrence. Y. D. Gundevia (1908–86) was foreign secretary at the time, and I do not know what his response to it was, but his note was generally received with unenthusiasm at the time. Later, in April 1970, when China sent its first satellite into orbit, Narayanan resubmitted his 1964 memo to the Indian foreign secretary, T. N. Kaul (1913–2000), for another examination in the light of our neighbour's growing prowess in the skies and from the skies. In

1970, Narayanan was a director in the Policy Planning Division (PPD) of the MEA. He had said in that note: 'The PRC has achieved a dramatic feat of sending up an earth satellite.... The real departure for China took place in 1964 when the first Chinese atomic bomb was exploded at Lop Nor.... The arguments used in the [1964] paper remain fresh and relevant even today; in fact, they are more relevant today than in 1964. I am, therefore, resubmitting this paper for your perusal.'[5]

It is not impossible, though somewhat improbable, that China's technologically savvy sleuths were aware of Narayanan's views as expressed in his notes or as spoken of diplomatic chatter in New Delhi. But there is no doubt that the Chinese system must have done its homework on Narayanan before welcoming him as a state guest. And this would have included taking note of Narayanan's statement in his speech at the Tata Institute of Social Sciences, Bombay, on 5 May 1979, in which he said: 'If one examines China's border claims against India, it will be found that they impinge directly upon the geographical and strategic unity of India. The claim to Arunachal Pradesh, which may or may not be a mere bargaining claim, will, if realized, have the effect of detaching a vast chunk of territory from India and crippling India politically and strategically. And the Chinese occupation of parts of Ladakh, seen against the political background of Beijing's support for self-determination for the people of Kashmir, implies a threat to India's unity and security in its strategic north-western region.'[6]

Considering this, the significance of the immaculate welcome accorded to him outside the Great Hall of the People in Beijing on 29 May 2000 was not to be missed. In the talks that followed immediately, President Jiang Zemin was warmth personified. My diary entry for the day:

> *JZ carries a subtle mind behind his uncreased face. He is relaxed and warm in his words welcoming the 80-year-old President of India as 'an expert in State and diplomatic affairs'. Describing himself in the conversation as 'an engineer in mechanics and dynamics', he arrived at the crux of his thoughts—the position of the U.S.A. in the world. He said as that engineer, he knew that 'one pole—unipolarity—is not practical.' Rashtrapatiji responded by saying to his host that he was 'not only a mechanical engineer but a social and political engineer.' Rashtrapatiji excelled himself in presenting the Indian case and in responding to comments and queries. The accompanying MPs are thrilled by his performance.*

Jiang hosted an elegant banquet before which the eminent violinist Vidvan L. Subramaniam (b. 1947) gave a recital with the much younger Chinese conductor maestro Li Xincao. Numerous courses, with special ones for vegetarians like me, were served and taken away without the slightest fret or noise. So different from our clanging tensions at Rashtrapati Bhavan.

The president held talks the next day with Li Peng (1928–2019), former prime minister and current chairman of the Standing Committee of the Peoples' Congress. A hardliner with little patience about matters like human rights, Li spoke little, raising his very striking black eyebrows every now and then when listening to his guest. Chinese phrases and word-constructions carry great meaning. And so, when Li spoke of India as 'a great country', a notable change was said to have been made from the standard Chinese description of India as 'a great neighbour'. The meeting I personally valued the most was with Prime Minister Zhu Rongji (b. 1928), an intellectual of no mean standing. He spoke of 'differences left over by a third party' and of there being 'more than a touch of India in the Chinese civilization'. Rashtrapatiji described him as 'an economic genius'. Our ambassador Vijay Nambiar was an exceptionally good explicator of China and Chinese ways. What made him valuable was his being able to take his own stature lightly and his office as something that was stimulating rather than overwhelming. He had an amazingly able and pleasant deputy in Vikram Doraiswamy, endowed with a sense of very Stephanian humour, much to my relief. Vikram was later to become high commissioner to Bangladesh and the United Kingdom.

President Jiang, as was to be expected, had the Dalai Lama on his mind and spoke of 'the Dalai clique and other anti-China groups [who] may exploit his [Dalai Lama's] presence in India'. Jiang was expected to and did express appreciation of India's position on Tibet and of the Government of India's 'prudent handling' of the activities of the Karmapa*. Jiang said he hoped 'India would not permit the Dalai Lama to engage in anti-Chinese activities'. In measured words, President Narayanan reiterated the Government of India's position that Tibet was 'an autonomous region of China' and that the Dalai Lama was 'a religious, not political leader'. On the Karmapa, he said he would 'not be permitted to indulge in political activities' and that it was 'up to him to decide what kind of future he wishes'.[7]

President Narayanan proposed a new mechanism for promoting bilateral relations—an Eminent Persons' Group, which would supplement the work of the governments and make recommendations. With President Jiang readily supporting the proposal, the two sides (in the words of a report in *China Daily* of 30 May 2000) 'agreed to set up a forum featuring eminent figures from both sides to promote cooperation and mutual understanding'. President

*Ogyen Trinley Dorje, born 26 June 1985.

Narayanan had said to N. Ram in a conversation broadcast by Doordarshan and AIR: 'There has been no change in India's need for living in harmony and in cooperation with all our neighbours, including Pakistan and, of course, our big neighbour China, and others. This is India's need, if I may say so, and India's policy also has been in that direction.'

The most human moment in the entire trip was the president's meeting with Guo Qinglan (1916–2012), the octogenarian wife of Dwarkanath Kotnis (1910–42), the legendary Indian doctor who, with four other doctors, had served in the Indian medical mission in China in the war-torn years, from 1938, dying in 1942. There was more than a protocol moment to this. Narayanan knew the value of gestures, but he valued human beings for their own sakes. And he saw China as a vast collection of humans who bore no ill-will to India, only a sense of India's grandeur in history.

There are, to put it simplistically, in fact, naively, two Indian reactions to China. The first is one of instinctive and instant suspicion, which can be called 'the 1962 syndrome'. Intense scepticism and an unabating competitiveness are its ingredients. The second is one of cautious observation, calibrated studying and a willingness to be receptive about its endeavours to emerge from its dire circumstances while confronting a hostile international environment. An existentialist belief in coexistence rather than confrontation as the natural equalizer in international relations is its active component. Narayanan belonged to the second category. But he also was Indian enough and a pragmatic Keralite enough to believe India must not let China's ambitions nibble at India's territorial integrity or trifle with her sovereignty. He put his nuanced view across skilfully.

A visit to the Great Wall was natural. Climbing up to it and standing at a vantage point, I looked at its curving length, awed. The wall looked like a sated serpent, asleep for now but capable of being awakened into a red-eyed rage by something as tiny as a pebble falling on it. Dalian and Kunming were visited, the first a sterile city aping New York with tall buildings and vacant lots between them, and the second a sample of potted ethnicity.

Back home on 3 June, preparations began for leaving home. 7 June brought news of an LTTE bombing in Colombo, which killed fourteen, including the Industries minister Gunaratne. On 13 June, B. K. Nehru (1909–2001) rang from his retirement home in Kasauli: 'Gopu, are you being fired?' What could I say to that except—'I am firing myself, Uncle Bijju.'

That evening, I called on the EAM. The tough-thinking, tough-speaking Rajput was superb. In less than twenty minutes, he gave me the sharpest official picture of Sri Lanka: 'The ground position is better. The Sri Lanka Army's morale is higher. Chandrika is a woman of courage. She has lost her husband, suffered an attack on her person, seen a military reverse. And yet stands firm. She said to her demoralized army chiefs, "We must fight back." She means to do that.' I asked the EAM if there was any chance that Pirabakaran would be receptive to suggested solutions short of separation. 'No, none,' he replied. 'For him, a solution is not the solution. For him, a perennial confrontation is what is needed. He has had so many people killed that he cannot compromise without inviting revenge from those whose near and dear have died. He has to keep the conflict going in order to survive.' I then asked him what instructions he had for our mission in Colombo. He then said something which was very important and was to guide my functioning for the next two years. 'We should not pivot our mission and our representation on Jaffna, the Tamils and LTTE. There is so much going on between us and Sri Lanka. There is the Buddha. There are cultural links with Orissa, Andhra, Kerala....' And then he added, almost as an aside, 'We should bring back some laughter and joy in our mission there. It has too much gloom.' I then asked him a candid question: 'Will the fact that I am half-Tamil be a disadvantage to the mission?' The reply was swift. 'Not in the least. Please put that thought away as useless baggage.'

I went south in early July, officially for a briefing at ISRO, Bangalore, where its chief, Dr K. Kasturirangan, gave me a startling satellite image of the island in its proximity to our Tamil coastline, but personally, for a visit to Sri Ramanasramam, Tiruvannamalai, and for a call on MS amma. At the foot of Arunachala, by the asramam, I did a circumambulation of the hill with Captain Narayanan,* who has been doing that for years. 'We do not walk,' he said to me, 'we are walked.' May Sri Ramana Maharshi 'walk' me through Sri Lanka, I prayed.

'Unakku onnum aahaadhu' (Nothing will happen to you), said MS amma to me in her Chennai home on 6 July. She had just given me a sumptuous breakfast. 'Sariya iruppe' (You will be fine). 'Bhagavan unne kaappaatuvar' (God will protect you). A shadow of concern crossing her ineffably beautiful face—she then said in a lowered tone, 'Irunthalum nee num kuzhanthai thaane.... Adanaalai kavalai irukku.... Praarthanei seyhiren...' (But since you are, nevertheless, our child... so there is a worry......I am praying)... A worldly mother-figure taking over, she added, 'Unne Delhi-liye oru periya velai koduthirkalaam...Yennamo...sariya poyittu vaa...Ange ponathum kaayitham podu...' (They could have given you a bigger position in Delhi itself....

*Captain Narayanan joined the Indian Navy in 1966 as a short service commissioned officer and served for seven years, later joined the Merchant Navy, serving as chief officer and captain for 17 years, coming to Sri Ramanasramam for good in February 1992; he passed away in 2009, aged 63.

However.... Go and return safely.... And drop me a line on reaching....) While leaving, I told her how, despite the riskiness of the job, some people thought I was being rewarded with another cushy job. Pursing her mouth, she controlled her anger and said 'Bhagavan avaale parthuppaar!' (God will take care of them!)

'So you are off!' Sonia Gandhi said to me when I called on her on 11 July. We discussed a host of things—the Gujarat and Rajasthan drought, the variations in life between the northern and southern districts of Tamil Nadu, Tiruvannamalai and Sri Ramana Maharshi (about whom she did not seem to have heard), the difference between Sri Lankan and Indian Tamils on the island. She asked detailed questions about the India–Sri Lanka 1964 and 1974 Agreements.

'I would like to think I am going with your good wishes,' I said as I was leaving. 'That goes without saying,' she said. 'All the best to you.'

I told myself this was the widow of a man slain by an LTTE terrorist. Her composure and objectivity, the absence of any personal pique or resentment, were a marvel.

At the Ministry of Defence, I gathered that the military prognosis for the Sri Lankan government now was good, the LTTE having lost 1,000 men—too much for it. Its arms deliveries, especially of spares, had also dwindled. I was told by a person dealing in security affairs 'Follow the rules 1-10. Not 1-9, not 1-9.5, not 1-9.9. But 1-10. And if you do that, you should be okay.' Scary, that was. But even if I was to somehow manage to squeeze myself into that scale, what about the family?

As Tara did most of the packing and clearing, her book *Birds and Plant Regeneration* came out. Its publisher, Ravi Dayal, personally brought copies over. 'Am I being fair to the family? In my wanting to be "useful", to "do well", am I jeopardizing the family?' I wondered. I had no answer to these questions.

21 July was a red-letter day for me. Prime Minister Atal Bihari Vajpayee met me at 5 p.m. The meeting lasted for all of fifteen minutes at his residence. I recorded the gist of that all-Hindi conversation (I could not have spoken to that master of Munshi Premchand's language in any other). I give excerpts in an English rendering, barring the opening line:

PM: Aayiye rajdoot mahoday! (Welcome Mr Ambassador!)

GG: Pranam, Pradhan Mantriji, that designation has been bestowed on me by you.

PM: When is the departure to be?

GG: Next month. In mid-August. I was there twenty years ago. For four years. Even back then, it was you who had sent* me. I had gone with Morarji bhai's blessings.... An ambassador by himself can do nothing.

PM: That is not so. We have many expectations of you.

GG: It is generous of you to say that.

PM: ...Well then, my best wishes...

RV had us—the whole family—over for a farewell dinner on 23 July. He loved us. Mrs RV thought of us as of her children. A spry ninety-year-old RV gave me a brief resumé of the Sri Lanka-LTTE problem. He recalled the Indo–Sri Lanka Agreement and the IPKF's role from the time when he was president. RV said, and I quote from my diary entry for the day:

J.R. Jayewardene was under great pressure from the insurrectionist JVP in the south. He needed to disentangle the SL forces from the north to take on the JVP in the south. He did that the moment the Indo-Sri Lanka Agreement was signed. He crushed the JVP revolt, saved his government, saved his own life. And put the northern burden on the donkey's back—our Indian back. And no sooner did that happen, we found ourselves being attacked by the very people—the LTTE—whose cause we had espoused. Prime Minister Premadasa actually was giving arms to the LTTE, the Sri Lanka government's sworn enemy—to attack the IPKF! Look at the irony. And as soon as Premadasa became President he packed us off! Now the position has become so intractable that one can fairly say there can be no solution until Pirabakaran is alive.

I marvelled at his lucidity and up-to-date-ness.

J. N. Dixit, our most famous 'former high commissioner to Sri Lanka' and very likely to be the most celebrated ever, was the very embodiment of generosity. I could not have guessed then nor he that he was going to be, in four years from then, India's NSA. Hosting (in his words) 'a big dinner' for Tara and me at the India International Centre, he preceded that with a lunch one-on-one at The Chambers, Taj Mansingh Hotel. Pointing me to a discreet corner where our conversation would be beyond other customers' curious eavesdropping, he gave me the most precise and personal insights. I recorded in my diary only that which was outside what he said in strict confidence, his extraordinarily penetrative eyes saying as much as his words:

*Vajpayee was then minister for External Affairs in Morarji's cabinet.

'The justness of the Tamil demands should not be lost sight of. You must keep at it all the time, while fully supporting the unity and territorial integrity of Sri Lanka. Don't announce your personal engagements too much in advance.'

I called on Defence Minister George Fernandes the same afternoon. Seated behind a very large desk at the far end of his very large room, the 'RM' (raksha mantri), as he is called, gave me a very 'Georgian insight' with precise instructions. Again, I recorded in my diary that which may not be called 'classified': '*We are committed to the territorial integrity of Sri Lanka. We cannot support a break-up of that country. In the late 1980s, in Stockholm some LTTE cadres met me. I told them so. They were not pleased. They said to me "We shall see." But they have just demands. These cannot be ignored by us. We have to encourage the Sri Lanka government to concede the maximum.*'

Chandra Shekhar, our former prime minister, was kind enough to meet me in his home on 25 July. 'You will have to press for justice for the Tamils,' he said. And then told me how in 1990–91, when he was prime minister, he had warned the then chief minister Karunanidhi about LTTE cadres in Tamil Nadu and advised that he call all those suspected of LTTE links and threaten them with deportation. He was not heeded, Chandra Shekhar said. Apparently, his advice reached, verbatim, Pirabakaran's hideout in Sri Lanka. Chandra Shekhar felt that this could not have happened without Karunanidhi's knowledge. It is my feeling that here Chandra Shekhar was going by his sleuths' interpretation. If word of his advice to Karunanidhi did indeed reach the LTTE supremo, it is because Pirabakaran's ears were as long as his qualms were short. But he was not discouraging me from going. Nor disapproving of the appointment. A gutsy man, he was not going to transmit nervousness. He gave me his best wishes and came out of his room to see me off. Small things stay in my memory. As we left his modest room together, he turned off the lights and fans—a sign of self-regulation so becoming in a former prime minister of India and so unexpected in that station.

I called on former prime minister Narasimha Rao the next day. 'Congratulations,' he said grimly. The conversation that followed was an admonition. My diary reads:

> *'I need your blessings, sir.'*
>
> *'Having congratulated you, let me tell you this posting of yours is wrong. If the government wanted to consciously make a wrong choice it could not have done better. Your Tamil connection will be a handicap to you. The Sinhalese will misunderstand you right from the start. Your successes will therefore be tiny, your failures will be portrayed in exaggerated scale. Nobody who wishes you to succeed*

would have given you this posting. You will be regarded as having a Tamil bias. I am sorry if I am being brutally frank.'

I give him the background to my posting, and my having virtually 'asked for it'. I tell him I know he speaks from concern for me and from a unique knowledge of politics and diplomacy. Perhaps, I say, I am under an unlucky star! That touches him and he says 'What I have said is what I have analysed in hard objective terms. But that is at that level. The fact is you are going. Nothing more is to be done about it. I thought the posting had been foisted on you. I now find it has been foisted by you on yourself. The fat is in the fire. But let me tell you that despite all the minus points that I have just described you are bound to do well. You will do well. Even the Tamil factor—who knows?—may turn to your advantage. You have my good wishes. You are welcome to stay in touch with me if you want to consult me over anything. Any time.'

This and RV's were about the toughest and most practical briefings I could have got from anyone. RV had sketched the background for me, and PV the foreground. I could not have asked for more. This extended account of conversations around my departure for Colombo is given here for two reasons: one, to say that those days, the Vajpayee days, were such that a high commissioner-designate could meet former prime ministers and a former president from outside the ruling party circles without fear of being misunderstood. Two, that India's political class at the highest level was interested in a neighbouring country's welfare for its own sake, not because of its implications on India. That consideration was not absent, but it was secondary to an intrinsic interest in the neighbour.

Dr Manmohan Singh gave me time on 28 July to see him in his office in Parliament House. We spent some forty-five minutes together, with him asking questions and making observations that revealed an exceptionally close knowledge of Sri Lankan affairs. My diary entry:

MS: What would you advise Congress to do or say?

GG: Congress should be transparent and should say the two things that need to be said with equal emphasis: we are committed to the unity of Sri Lanka and believe that the only way of vouchsafing that unity is to give the Tamils of Sri Lanka a sense of confidence and of equal participation.

MS: What do you feel about Natwar Singh's comments on India making a military intervention?

GG: I have the greatest respect and affection for Natwarji, but a military intervention by us would be and be seen as India fighting the Tamils, not the LTTE. We will end up messing our hands and alienating not just the SLTs but also the people of Tamil Nadu, who, though ordinarily unenchanted by the LTTE, will not remain neutral in the context of brutalities against SLTs.

MS: Gen. Kalkat said much the same thing to me.

As I took leave of him, Dr Manmohan Singh said, simply and sincerely, 'God bless you.' I was not expecting this particular formulation from him. But it seemed typical of him when I thought upon it later. He was transferring the right to bless me to the Almighty.

R. Rajagopalan, a senior Tamil journalist based in Delhi, who had in the past written a very negative story about me in the journal *Junior Vikatan*, was kind enough to throw a reception in my honour at India International Centre the same evening. His guest list was stunning: Chandra Shekhar, G. K. Moopanar, Sitaram Kesri, P. Upendra, Subramaniam Swamy, the acting Sri Lanka high commissioner, among many others. A cameo I recorded in my diary entry for the day: *At Rajagopal's dinner, I joined Chandra Shekharji, who was talking to the acting Sri Lanka high commissioner and Subramaniam Swamy. Subramaniam Swamy told the acting Sri Lanka high commissioner: 'To talk to the LTTE would be to legitimise it. Don't do it. It is a terrorist outfit. The PLO is not like that. It has not killed its other leaders or other Palestinian leaders. If Chandrika wants to, let her declare Sri Lanka to be a federal state unilaterally. That will take the wind out of LTTE's sails.'*

There is no doubt the diplomat would have reported this snatch to his headquarters. I did not then and do not now agree with Dr Swamy on all matters. But on the subject of Sri Lanka and LTTE, he has been amazingly consistent on the side of a civil solution and against the monster called terrorism. There need be no surprise that he has needed security cover.

Preparations and packing took a break on the last day of July when, in the evening, Divya, our elder daughter, said to me I must accompany her and our younger daughter, Amrita, and Tara to see a film—*Kandukondain Kandukondain* starring Tabu (b. 1971) and Aishwarya Rai (b. 1973). I liked the film, based on Jane Austen's first novel, *Sense and Sensibility*. A. R. Rahman's music and the absence of gratuitous violence were a joy. It also had none of the obscenity that goes with much of Indian cinema. Director Rajiv Menon (b. 1963), who I was to get to know later, with his brother Karun Menon, had made a really good film. Tara was as taken by the lead actor Mammootty (b. 1951), as was the film's heroine. But even while seeing the film, I was not able to leave Sri Lanka aside. Bala, as Major Bala, is an IPKF officer who loses a leg while fighting in the jungles of war-torn Sri Lanka, caused by an explosion triggered by Tamil militants.

Vaiko[*] came to see me on 3 August. He was with me from 5 p.m. to 8.30 p.m., something of a record by way of visitors' visits for me. He talked almost without pausing, giving a history of the ethnic discord in Sri Lanka from Chelvanayakam's[†] days to the present, giving cameos of his association with Pirabakaran and others. I could not but admire his commitment and his risk-taking. He could have died when he went furtively to Sri Lanka in 1989. I told him he had filled information gaps in my knowledge and that I do not believe in labelling or typecasting people. Each plays a nuanced role and makes a subtle contribution. I told Vaiko, he had a role to play, a role in the evolution of Sri Lanka's polity, as a keen student of its history and political dynamics. But, more significantly, I said to him that he should remember DMK gave up secession as a policy in 1962. Today, Tamil Nadu is politically important in India, operating the levers of power in Delhi. He should note that, I said. I do not think I convinced him.

Former prime minister I. K. Gujral and Mrs Gujral hosted Tara and me to dinner on 10 August, receiving us at the portico and then seeing us off. This is what is called tehzeeb, in Hindustani. He gave me a perspective that differed only in nuances from that of Jaswant Singh, Dixit, and the RM. 'No point talking to LTTE. We should shed all the formal tears, of course. But the fact is they are just not interested in talks. Maanenge nahin (They won't listen). I was in London recently, and Puri[‡] told me that when he was flying Pirabakaran back after ISLA, Pirabakaran told him, "How can I agree to peace? I have the blood of so many people on my hands!" Peace will have to be found minus Pirabakaran. He will never agree to anything less than Eelam. The solution...has to come without him. We must be advocates of the Tamil cause but not of Eelam, not for the LTTE as we know it. Chandrika is the best bet for Sri Lanka and an asset to us.'

A person I was very keen to meet, Murasoli Maran, the most prominent DMK member of the Vajpayee cabinet holding the important portfolio of Commerce, gave me time for a call on 4 August. My diary entry:

---

[*]Tamil Nadu politician, (b. 1944) for many years in the DMK and member of parliament, founder and general secretary of the Marumalarchi Dravida Munnetra Kazhagam (MDMK).

[†]Samuel James Veluppillai Chelvanayakam (1898–1977) Sri Lankan lawyer, politician and Member of Parliament, founder and leader of the Illankai Tamil Arasu Kachchi (ITAK) and Tamil United Liberation Front (TULF), described by Ceylon's Tamils, as 'Thanthai Chelva' (father Chelva).

[‡]Hardeep Puri, then deputy high commissioner in London.

MM: Trouble is nobody knows Pirabakaran's mind. Nobody is in touch with him. And he has no political deputies—they have all been assassinated.

GG: Pirabakaran would now rank himself with Arafat and Mandela.

MM: Yes, and at one time, he was wandering in Kodambakkam.

This made it clear to me that Chandra Shekhar's impressions about Karunanidhi were not based on facts.

In Chennai, on 13 August, the day before Tara and I flew out to Colombo, I was given twenty minutes by Chief Minister Karunanidhi. Climbing up the steps to his room in his Gopalapuram home, I thought of what Chandra Shekhar had had to say and whether what I hear from the man himself would bear some relation to the former prime minister's impression. Karunanidhi was in a sombre mood. His remarks were far from being LTTE-leaning. I noted: '*K rues continuing militancy in SL. Says P will never have a change of heart. Parting words to me: Jaagiritahiyaaha irungal...* (Take every care/ Be ever so careful....)'

Feeling wretched and torn about having to leave our daughters, who were studying, behind, Tara and I boarded a flight from Chennai to Colombo on 14 August 2000. Men in transferable jobs become mindless minions of their careers. Their 'progress', their 'success', their images as hard-working officers is their priority. They fail to think of the impact of their 'moves' on the family. They do not see that in the happiness and security of their wives and children must lie their progress and success in that which is bigger than their jobs—their life. They take the family for granted, bundling it into trains, planes, and other random modes of transport as if they were chattel or cargo, while they proceed to earn their 'good names'. From the shaken alphabet of the family's fortunes are the glowing records of successful civilians and diplomats made.

We were in Colombo an hour and a half later. The highly cerebral and insightful Sibabrata Tripathi, our deputy high commissioner, and his wife, the poet Jayshree Misra, were at the airport to meet us. We were returning to the island after eighteen years. But everything about the place was familiar. The residence itself, which we had visited many times in our earlier stint in Kandy as guests of High Commissioner Thomas Abraham and Meera Abraham, was a place we related to at once. Our predecessors in the house, Shivshankar and Mohini Menon had left the place gleaming, and the Tripathis had stocked the fridge with every conceivable essential and delicacy. We went round the house together for an hour, a bit dazed at what we had relinquished back home and what we had stepped into where we would be, God willing, for some two years.

A Guard of Honour presented by the Indo-Tibetan Border Police (ITBP) on duty to 'secure' the high commissioner and his family and the residence itself reminded me of the instruction given to me: Alertness, not 9.9, but 10.

15 August dawned on us before we realized it. The Indian tricolour was duly hoisted by me in the morning before an invited gathering at the India House garden, Siba assuring me that my not having presented my credentials yet did not matter and being 'designate' was enough. I read rashtrapatiji's speech, which I had been through many times in its evolution in Delhi. We were hosted to lunch—bara-khana—by the ITBP men in their barracks just behind the house. Salt of the earth in fearlessness that they were, they also were the most skilled cooks and generous hosts. Dedicated and sharp-eyed, they inspired admiration, confidence, and more—they made one feel proud and grateful. At 5 p.m., they piloted and escorted me to the official residence of Foreign Minister Lakshman Kadirgamar (1932–2005). I saw for the first time how, at traffic signals and traffic hold-ups, they jumped out discreetly from their jeeps in a fraction of a moment and took up positions, armed and totally alert, around my car, jumping back as soon as it was time to move on. So, this is how it is going to be now on for you, Mister High Commissioner, I told myself. This is not the leafy, sleepy Colombo you knew but the Colombo where you may sleep with one eye open, if that is possible.

Our discussion had to and did then turn to the LTTE. My diary entry reads: *[LK] said they are and remain opposed to dialogue. The Norwegian initiative continues but they have told us LTTE are not in a mood to read the draft Bill [on devolution]. Balasingam, who only reflects his master's voice, has said, 'Sometime in the future we could look at talks but for the present our sole interest is the recapture of Jaffna'. We can expect them to do something towards that any time now.*

I asked him about channels with LTTE. He said: *'[Joseph] Pararajasingham of the Tamil United Liberation Front (TULF) got elected to parliament from Batticaloa with a huge margin—4,000 votes—and his democratic credentials are high. He represents the LTTE's way of thinking in the TULF and is opposed to the Bill. Perhaps out of fear [of Pirabakaran]'.*

Both Kadirgamar and Pararajasingham (1934–2005) were to be shot dead by the LTTE in 2005, Kadirgamar as he emerged from a swim in Colombo and Pararajasingham as he sat with his wife at midnight mass on Christmas day in Batticaloa—a grim end that I would not have been surprised to hear in 2000 if some futurist had told me of it.

Arumugam Thondaman (1964–2020), grandson of the late leader of Indian or 'estate' Tamils, S. Thondaman (1913–99), came to see me on 17 August. He was general secretary of the Ceylon Workers' Congress and a minister. Large built, with sharp eyes not unlike those I was to notice much later in the great bowler Muttiah Muralitharan, he stayed for an hour. I liked the frankness with which he said: 'I had been a party boy....'

Tamil United Liberation Front (TULF) MPs, representatives of Lankan Tamils, called on me in a group the next day. They were led by the sixty-seven-year-old R. Sampanthan (1933–2024), who, though not an MP himself at that time, was TULF's leading voice. 'Sam' was a hardy survivor in Sri Lanka's blood-smeared politics. If he were in Chennai, not Colombo, and I was meeting him for the first time and hearing his gift with words, I would have said he is a Mylapore lawyer. I give it below as transcribed in my diary with my silent reactions, unspoken but strongly felt, given in brackets:

> *'TULF does not approve of violence but regards LTTE as an outfit that has made sacrifices and suffered' (You do?)*
>
> *'We hope to bring it [LTTE] round' (Good luck).*
>
> *'But at the moment, it is the assault on Jaffna that obsesses them. Nothing else. (And you are with them in this, aren't you?).*
>
> *'For years, the Colombo regime with the Sangha has trampled upon Tamil aspirations.' (I am not unaware of that).*
>
> *'We are a nation and a nationality.' (Now, where have I heard something like that before?)*
>
> *'PCBK has taken some bold decisions. But her own people are sabotaging her efforts.' (I know of the first part of what you have said; want to know more of the second).*
>
> *'Mahinda Rajapakse told the Sangha he would get 3 MPs to vote against the Bill though he himself would be constrained to vote for it.' (Interesting).*
>
> *'The elections will be difficult for us, but we will contest, including in Jaffna.' (Wish you well, gentlemen, not just electorally but...).*
>
> *'The PM's statements are dangerous. He is talking the language of destruction. We do not want anybody or any organisation 'destroyed'. (Sure, you don't).*

I could see that Sam was saying some things for me to hear, some for Pirabakaran to gather from Sam's colleagues in the deputation, especially Joseph Pararajasingham. He was being as cautious as he could be. Caution is a product of fear, and fear is a primordial mechanism for self-protection. I could not blame him. In his position, I would have done the same.

Would it have shocked me to know that two of the MPs who called on me that day were to be killed by LTTE tigers before long? No. That was how things were in the country. And one of the MPs who came had replaced in parliament two MPs who had been assassinated by the same blood-thirst.

I was told President Chandrika Bandaranaike Kumaratunga, PCBK or CBK for short, would receive my credentials on 22 August afternoon. The new ambassadors of China and Japan were to join me in the same ceremony, one after the other. But all dressed up in my achkan and churidar, I waited for the chief of protocol to come to India House to escort me to the president's house. Minutes passed, and then hours, and no CoP! Messages were sent and questions asked with rising worry until the good man came and apologized profusely, saying a political crisis of the worst imaginable kind had engulfed the president, with three of her coalition ministers belonging to M. H. M Ashraff's party, the Sri Lanka Muslim Congress, threatening to pull out. They had been offended, CoP said, by a remark made by one of CBK's ministers belittling their political base. Any routine political matter, he assured me, would not have led the president to delay the ceremony, but this was an extraordinary one, and would I please not misunderstand a postponement to the next morning. I said I had no choice and that I hoped the crisis would blow over by the following morning. It did, and three of the most major Asian countries—India, China, and Japan—had their envoys duly present their parchments to the sovereign head of Sri Lanka on 23 August 2000, after a due wait. Credential ceremonies are great levellers.

My predecessor, Shivshankar Menon, also had to wait for his credentials beyond the appointed hour. Shankar is among the few diplomats, very few, I should say, who impresses at first sight, impresses more on getting better acquainted, and moves from being impressive to being altogether a wonder to know, hear, and read. I was stepping into shoes far too large for me.

PCBK had, I saw, flair. Not tall and certainly not short, not heavy and certainly not slight, she carried her power with her like someone would perfume. She held an air of immunity about her as a peacock does its crest. But her essentiality lay in her very expressive face, which, though constrained by the loss of sight in one of her eyes after the bombing, could be warm and cold, soft and harsh, depending on what it beheld. She looks like she is permanently empowered and eternally detached about it. Whether because of her near-miss with death or something deeper, she seemed to have a feather-touch of the other-worldly about her, to be aware in a deeply Buddhist way of the ephemerality of things.

For the credentials event, where the designate envoys of India, the world's largest democracy, China, Asia's most powerful country, and Japan, the world's techno-cultural icon, no less, were to present their letters of credence, PCBK was dressed as she might be for an informal Sunday morning. Kadirgamar, suited and booted, and her secretary Balapatabendi, similarly attired, stood on either side of her as I was announced.

When the postponed credentials ceremony was over, she sat down to talk with me without aides for nearly an hour. The diary reads:

> *She is determined to meet her challenges but also has more than a touch of detachment about her. 'If I am still around' and 'If I am back' etc., when talking about future plans. We discuss the interior décor of the Presidential Palace, archaeology, Buddhism, and then come to the political situation. She is hard as nails about the United National Party. In fact her ire is reserved for Ranil Wickremesinghe [b.1949] and the U.N.P., not for Pirabakaran and the LTTE...*

This was a get-to-know meeting, and telling me that she would soon set up a more relaxed conversation, PCBK rose to conclude the engagement.

Her elder sister, the thrice-married and divorced Sunethra (b. 1943), came home for dinner that evening. My diary entry:

> *What a vivacious person! Lithe and so very bright. No one can say she is 56 or 57. More like 40. 'Some of our predecessors have been very good,' she says. 'But some very bad.'*

Ratnasiri Wickremanayake (1933–2016), a long-time member of the Sri Lanka Freedom Party, had become prime minister just a few days before I landed in Colombo. All power resided in the president, but a prime minister was prime minister, and protocol required I seek an early call on him. The veteran was warmth personified and as unaffected as any prime minister can possibly be. He rather surprised me by an unexpected sounding-out:

'Excellency, can India sell to us 63 tuskers for our devales*?'

One does not say no to a prime minister too lightly, and I did not. Moreover, there was a certain dignity to the request. He was not asking for a gift of the tuskers. He was offering to buy them for his country's Hindu–Buddhist shrines.

But I could barely conceal my amusement at the prospect of sixty-three Indian pachyderms coming across the Palk Straits in a flotilla of wobbly boats and landing seasick in Talai Mannar. The image invoked Captain

*'Homes of the Gods' votive temples with Hindu deities that are scattered throughout the island, Kandy, Kurunegala, Uva, and the Sabaragamuva provinces, including the south of the island, having a good number.

Hathi leading his rag-tag animal parade in the *Jungle Book* film. Diplomatic-speak has many pockets with soft inner linings, and so I said: 'Mr Prime Minister, India–Sri Lanka cultural affinities are many-splendoured, and I will certainly find out. But I must share with you the fact that there is a strong environmental lobby in India that may not be pleased by the idea of elephants being sent out of the country in so large a number. Nevertheless, please rest assured, I will check this out.'

Reflecting on Wickremanayake's request later, I realized that it had a larger salience. Like India, Sri Lanka faced what in environmental circles is called HEC, human–elephant conflict, in which the shrinking of the natural habitat of its elephants is in conflict with farmers whose crops are routinely decimated by hungry elephants and who, in turn, try to eliminate the destructive mammoths. But even without HEC, as Sukumar Raman, the foremost elephant specialist in India, explained: 'The Sri Lankan elephant population suffers from a general lack of tusks among its male elephant population (only about 2 per cent of male elephants on the island possess tusks as opposed to over 90 per cent of males in southern India having tusks).'[8] A historical tradition thus grew for Sri Lanka, seeking to import tusked male elephants and because of the tradition of the sacred tooth relic of the Buddha being carried by a tusker.

The elephant had provided some passing relief from the other entity that was, in reality, the island's main concern—the 'tiger', LTTE's ferocious weapon, 'burning bright in the forests of the Sri Lankan night' (to adapt William Blake's words). The highly mature and insightful Norwegian ambassador in Colombo, Jon Westborg (b. 1946), came with Erik Solheim (b. 1955), the chief negotiator in Oslo's ongoing initiative, to meet me on 30 August. They were being fast; I was only fifteen days' old on my job. My diary entry for the day: '*I am most impressed by ES. His face is that of a truly good man who is also very intelligent. He tells me LTTE is prepared to discuss E minus*[*] *proposals, but at the moment, the ceasefire is paramount for them.*'

This was consistent with what Kadirgamar had said. The Norwegians were trying to set up a face-to-face with Pirabakaran in the forests of the Wanni to get a sense of his thinking and to persuade him to talk about a solution short of separation. Few believed they would get to meet the man, and fewer that even if they did, he would have any patience with E minus solutions. And this scepticism was shared by India, by my colleagues in our High Commission and by me. But committed as we were to a negotiated settlement and to being broad, if not enthusiastically, supportive of the

---

[*] A package that is for substantial devolution of powers but short of Eelam.

Norwegian initiative, we were guardedly encouraging of it.

No one can be wholly 'institutional.' No one can cease to be oneself.

Sri Lanka's polity was now divided into two unequal groups: the first, larger group, which believed the LTTE was, by its very DNA, separatist and would never negotiate anything less than Eelam. The only answer to LTTE is a military answer. The Buddhist majority, most political parties led by the ruling SLFP, and the uniformed services belonged to this. And ironically, so did the Buddhist priesthood. The second, smaller, group believed that the military option was a bitter one, exacting a toll on everyone, and that, given the high communal barometer, it should be considered only if every possible chance for a negotiation has failed. A minority among the Buddhist majority, a minority of political parties (chiefly the TULF), and a slender sliver of the political and intellectual class belonged to this. The SLFP in its own DNA belonged to the first, though PCBK and Kadirgamar did not want to renounce the path of talks. The chief opposition party, the UNP, in its own DNA, was not averse to this primarily because it could afford to do so, not being in office.

The island's Muslims were unaffiliated to either, their leaders preferring neutrality's safety to affinity's risks.

So, to turn to collective nouns, there were many a cast of hawks in the country and a few flights of doves. What I wanted to see around me was a parliament of wise owls who could move their heads in a complete circle to view the whole scene. But what to talk of a collectivity of that great bird, I could not spot even one.

I called on Sirimavo Bandaranaike, the eighty-four-year-old grand lady, by prior appointment in her Rosmead Place home, the very dwelling where her husband had been assassinated in 1959. She was seated like a queen in the drawing room. Her forehead, broad and unwrinkled, was a thing of beauty. It set the determination on her face plus a consciousness that she had been 'something'. She had not let the stroke she had suffered get the better of her. She spoke in a soft voice with perfect cogency, asking, 'How is Delhi?', 'How do you find your quarters?' Recalling India House as 'a large house with a lovely garden', she wanted to know if the 'divided lawn at the rear' had been unified, as suggested by her. She was happy to learn that it indeed had been. 'Do please visit it,' I said. 'I will be glad to do so,' she said. There was only one very sweet, very tender indication of her mind having slipped just a bit when she asked me, 'How is Kamaladevi?' The great Indian revolutionary and friend of Sirimavo had been dead for twelve years.

Anuruddha Ratwatte (1938–2011), a cousin of Sirimavo, was a classic Ratwatte. Having been a big-brass army man, he had moved to politics and was, at the time I reached Colombo, as deputy minister for Defence, the de-facto minister for Defence, whose portfolio was held by PCBK herself. He told me matter-of-factly that LTTE hostilities would resume and 'we will see things happening in the next few weeks'. The Sri Lankan Army was in poor shape. As General Rohan Daluwatte (1941–2018), chief of defence staff, told me separately, the SL Army stood at 118,000, but 25,000 had deserted over the last two years.

Back in India House from the very depressing visit to the Defence Ministry, I returned home and joined my daughter Amrita, who was visiting us fleetingly for the best thing in a family's life: aimless conversation. In the middle of it, she suddenly asked me a question I could not answer then and have not found an answer for ever since.

'Is the world,' she asked, 'a good place or a bad place?'

I could hardly tell her it was a good place, given what was happening around us. Nor could I, as a dad, tell her my depressing fear that it was not.

Anuruddha Ratwatte's grim prognosis was proved right sooner than expected. Elections to parliament were announced to take place on 10 October. On 10 September, exactly a month prior to the polls, the LTTE struck—in Batticaloa and Amparai, killing a ruling alliance candidate.[9] The LTTE said the government should have announced a ceasefire with the elections and had not done so, and, therefore, it had no option.

While I was getting more and more into the demands of work, the family was having a hard time. On 14 September, I wrote in my diary: '*Have I made a terrible mistake coming here? The family is scattered. When will I know?*'

On 15 September, a suicide bomber set off a bomb at 10 in the morning near the Eye Hospital at Maradana.[10] But so inured had Colombo become to the dance of death that PCBK could send word that I should see her. Over an hour's conversation, totally relaxed, warm and in no hurry whatever, she reminisced.

'I have seen two, in fact, three tragedies. The first was my father's death—assassination—then the death in a car crash of my fiancé, then Vijay*....'

As I left, she said, 'One of these days, I will invite myself over to your place for an Indian meal.'

The next day, I got a call to say Minister Ashraff had been killed in a helicopter crash. I had met him only the other day at a diplomatic reception at Hotel Galadari when he had been very warm, embracing me in good three-shoulders Islamic style, speaking in Tamil, and promising to meet up soon. The atmosphere was so weird that I took the 'crash' hypothesis with

---

*Her husband, Vijay Kumaranatunga (1945–88).

a pinch of salt. But the motive remaining unclear, the salt soon dried and flaked off my fingers. At his grief-struck home, his son Aman and his colleague Hakeem said Ashraff had a premonition. Aman said, 'We had all gone to dinner the previous evening...and father recapitulated his recent actions and seemed thoroughly contented...A look of contentment was on his face as if he had completed his task....'

What had been completed? Only God knew.

Norwegian ambassador Jon Westborg met Anton Balasingham (1938–2006) in London a couple of weeks earlier. 'They are still interested in a dialogue but will not reveal much of their inclinations until after the elections', he said. My diary entry: '*P needs to be told that he does not have a hope in hell or heaven of (i) carving a secure territory for Eelam (ii) administering it self-reliantly, and (iii) obtaining even one country's recognition of it.... He needs to be told he is global in his technology, his communication systems, his procurement of supplies. But that he is not global in his image, his prestige. He is not in the same league as the history-makers. Mandela, Arafat have had several nations and world organizations supporting them. For the matter of that, Gerry Adams, too, has had some people here and there saying Adams should be talked to; he has a viewpoint.*'

As a personal suggestion of mine, and making it clear that it was exactly that, I said to Westborg that Norway should take note of the fact that Pirabakaran has, miraculously, one Indian 'hero' who could work as a role model—Subhas Chandra Bose. Pirabakaran perhaps has only a rough knowledge of Netaji. He may not be aware of the fact Netaji's only child, his daughter Anita Bose Pfaff, is a teacher in Germany. Perhaps Anita Bose could be asked if she could contribute to the process? She is not in politics herself (her husband is a Social Democrat MP), but she is a politically aware person. She has political chemistry. I also mentioned Captain Lakshmi Sahgal of the Rani Jhansi regiment, who was a frontline colleague of Netaji. Perhaps Sahgal, a completely non-establishment former combatant-in-jungles (who is Tamil-speaking besides), could also be associated? Nothing came of my suggestion regarding the Bose–Sahgal women. Whether or not Westborg conveyed it, Pirabakaran was not listening, and the Norwegians were trying to make him listen to more urgent nuts and bolts issues. The important always gets overtaken by the urgent in politics. Always.

India is a difficult country to represent abroad.

It fills one with pride, and the very next moment makes that pride vanish.

And on 29 September, news came that former prime minister Narasimha Rao had been found guilty of corruption in a bribery scandal dating from 1993.[11] This was being hailed by the press as a signal that high rank in India does not provide legal protection. I hailed the news not at all. I remembered the vote-buying case involving allegations that, in 1993, as PM, Rao tried to influence a parliamentary vote of no-confidence by bribing four lawmakers of a group of MPs from Jharkhand. Rao's then minority government had defeated the no-confidence motion by a narrow margin—265 votes for him to 251 against. The four Jharkhand MPs had made a difference. Congress legislators were jubilant but, as Vinay Sitapati writes, 'the Prime Minister gestured with both hands but offered no comments.'[12] Had he personally bribed MPs to vote for him? Most unlikely. But his party had gone all out to survive the motion, and there is no doubt that 'all out' meant the use of Vitamin M as money had come to be called. That was the political culture now. That Rao was someone who had been consistently kind to me, I could not forget, and I penned a personal letter of concern and regard to him. I did not keep a copy; I wish I had.

2 October has been a day of reflection and prayer for our family.

But Bapu was far from my thoughts on this 2 October as, hastening to a call by Kadirgamar, I went to his home. For two hours non-stop, he spoke of the national scene. True, the SL Army was having its troubles, and the LTTE was now retaliating with full force.

That night, I rang my brother Ramu in Delhi. He was at his usual venue—the India International Centre. Speaking to him on this anniversary was a balm to my soul.

At the Korean National Day reception on 3 October, Defence Secretary Chandananda DeSilva (1937–2015) told me with a distinct tone of despondency that LTTE 'had not failed' in their latest offensive. Gone was bravado, gone even confidence. He said they wanted naval surveillance to strengthen quickly and decisively. This was duly conveyed to Delhi. In the ultimate analysis, an ambassador is a sender of messages and a receiver of instructions. That these are sometimes in coded cyphergrams gives them a sense, wholly superficial, of practising a secret and vital rite.

Sunethra Bandaranaike (b. 1943), was at the reception, the brightest spark in the gathering. Elections being in the air, everyone wanted to know what the president's extremely canny and politically ambiguous sister had to say on them, though few dared to ask her. Speaking to her 'generally', I was mindful of an account, wholly credible, I had heard: forty-one-year-old SWRD Bandaranaike married twenty-four-year-old Sirimavo, seventeen years his junior. Heirship was a matter of concern to the not-so-young couple. In 1943, Sirimavo and SWRD had a daughter—Sunethra—their first-born. Their second child, born two years later, in 1945, was again a girl. When it was time (1949) for their third child to arrive, the father-to-be chose to stay away at Anuradhapura, ostensibly at work (he was minister for Local Administration) but also perhaps to propitiate the Blessed One. On hearing the tidings that a son had indeed been born, he rushed back to Colombo and strode joyously into the house shouting, 'Where is he? Where is my ratana-puta (gem-son)?' As traditionalists hailed the arrival of Anura, the Bandaranaikes' male heir, Sirimavo, presumably, breathed a sigh of relief.

I called on Anura later that month. A lovable man, rotund, double-chinned, never far from a tear or a laugh, he was completely exempt from airs. Anura was now with the UNP, opposed to his sister, the president. He was contesting from Horagolla, the family seat. Anura had a large residence, comfortably but not luxuriously furnished. We chatted for the better part of an hour over tea and Lankan short eats. I was cautious enough to not speak of family politics but conversation on the election scene was unavoidable. Anura told me he felt the UNP would do marginally better than his sister's party and alliance, 'by 10-15 seats, not more'. I thought his prediction was a deft combination of optimism and realism. I was intrigued to find an almost verbatim report of our conversation in a Sinhala newspaper the next day. Media-persons must have pestered the 'gem-son' for news-gems.

On 10 October, election day, I was in my office talking over the long-distance phone to Leela Ponappa, joint secretary in the MEA 'in charge of Sri Lanka', so to say, and a valued friend, when Deputy High Commissioner Siba Tripathi came into my room, which was unusual, as he would not if I was taking a call. He had heard a rumour to the effect that Sirima had died a few minutes earlier on the high road from Horagolla, where she had voted, to her Rosmead Place home. Siba, hats off to his connectivity, had got this from a newspaperman whom he knew at the very stretch of the road where she had died. I conveyed this to Leela, who must have been the first person anywhere outside Sri Lanka to have heard this. I left for Rosmead Place without waiting for confirmation. An ambulance parked outside the house said it all. The family had not yet reached to see the body being brought out of the vehicle and into the house.

Sunethra was the first to come. 'Your mother has stepped into history,' I told her. 'India mourns with you.' She responded in silence with a grief-drenched hug.

PCBK arrived minutes later. Her cars were silent, no hoot, no flutter. The two sisters embraced in tears at the doorstep. Seeing me, PCBK turned towards me. I went up to her and said her mother's extraordinary life had had an extraordinary end. 'She was no ordinary woman,' PCBK said. Anura arrived last. He had been campaigning for the UNP. Disconsolate, he broke down in Sunethra's hug. The only one to collapse in grief was the departed woman's son. Her daughters were made of stronger stuff.

Sirima had motored to Horagolla to vote in an election in which her only son was standing from a party opposed to that of her daughter, the president. Opposing him from the SLFP was a relative, also a Bandaranaike. At the booth, I gathered she needed help to cast her vote. She was asked by the election officer who she would like her vote to be registered for. She managed to say just one word, slowly, 'Ban-da-ra-na-ike'. It is anybody's guess which Bandaranaike was privileged to receive the last vote cast by the world's first woman prime minister—her son or her party's candidate.

I suggested to Leela over the phone that it would be good if Rashtrapatiji were to ring PCBK and condole. A written message was preferred. But it came super-fast and was well-worded. Leela rang to say she had only sent him a basic draft and that he had worked on it to make it 'vintage K. R. Narayanan'. India's vice president Krishan Kant (1927–2002) and his wife came for the funeral. Holding the rank he did, he outranked all others present. But at the site, I was told no one was being allowed to place flowers on the cortege. This was difficult to explain to the VP, who having come specially expected at the very least to be able to 'offer due respect' at the bier. A quick solution had to be found. And a 'garland' made of khadi yarn (basically a spinner's hank) that I had brought with me 'just in case' solved the problem. No flowers but a hand-woven garland, in the tradition of Mahatma Gandhi, is to be placed on it, I said to the officiating priests. PCBK was consulted. And yes! This was exceptional, and an exception was made. Krishan Kant came up and did the needful, completely unaware of the few minutes of tension that had preceded his 'due respects'.

That was a time when the news was still newspaper news, not 'online.' The diplomatic bag brought in newspapers from India twice a week, and I devoured them, responding to the good and bad and indifferent in them as they required.

The 24th of October was a traumatic day. A massacre took place in the prison at Bindunuwewa, Badulla, resulting in the deaths of twenty-six (some reports claim twenty-eight) Tamil political prisoners. Initial reports spoke of a mob of Sinhalese having perpetrated the foul deed, but it turned out later that the murderers had been brought in a truck and disappeared after they had done the deed. The prison had been established to house former LTTE cadres. Of the 26 killed, 2 were under the age of 21, and the rest were between 21 and 30.[13] Once the massacre started, it was reported, police personnel posted there refused to intervene to stop it—all too familiar a story.[14]

30 October brought stories of communal disturbances in the central

highlands where estate Tamils are concentrated. Talwakelle and Ginigathene were badly affected by arson and looting. I urged the MEA to have a statement issued condemning the atrocities. But Delhi thought it better that I call on PCBK and convey to her India's views in the matter. This was, for me, deeply disappointing. I felt that the whole of Sri Lanka, not just the government, must know that any traumatizing of the Tamil minority in Sri Lanka troubles India. With its proximity to Sri Lanka, India cannot be unmoved as say, Korea or Peru can. But instructions are instructions, and I dutifully sought an appointment with PCBK, which, of course, I got quickly enough.

A cameo needs to be recounted. Ushered into her study before she came, I noticed the simplicity of the room—a large but not remarkable writing desk, a sofa arrangement, and shelves with some pictures. Two captured my subjective attention at once: First, the Bandaranaike family with Jawaharlal Nehru and Indira Gandhi at Temple Trees, the Sri Lankan prime minister's residence in 1957. They are all standing in a row, Indira next to SWRD and Sirimavo next to Nehru, whose hand rests on the shoulder of young Anura dressed in a traditional sarong like his father. Chandrika stands with her sister, Sunethra, coyly. The second is of PCBK with President Nelson Mandela, taken in Oslo in the early 1990s. I was gazing at these when PCBK, entering without any fuss from a door behind me, said, 'Hello, Excellency!' I turned and reciprocated. She came up to the Mandela picture, took it down to give me a better look at it, and then wiped it with her hand. A film of dust transferred itself from the glass on the frame to her hand. 'My staff are supposed to wipe these pictures every Saturday,' she said, wiping the dust off with a tissue. Ama, an aide, materialized and relieved her of the browned piece of paper. 'Look at this,' PCBK said to the help, 'look at the dust...' The dust of running a house sat on her hands as naturally as that of running the country.

We then settled down to a one-and-a-half-hour-long conversation. 'I was horrified,' PCBK said to me, 'by Bindunuwewa. I was on the phone that day, though I was down with the flu, to tell the officers to quell the violence or face the sack.' Towards the end of our talk, she said she was 'battle-fatigued' and was planning a month's break outside the country. She asked me to tell Delhi she wanted to stop over there on her way back to talk to the PM. I said I would act on that.

Erik Solheim, meanwhile, had met Pirabakaran in the Wanni and came with Jon Westborg to brief me about it. The man had set no preconditions, they said. This, according to them, was a hopeful sign. But on 4 November, Kadirgamar, who asked me to meet him, said, 'Don't expect a ceasefire' and described the Norwegian interlocutors as 'messengers...taking and bringing messages....' But on my part, I saw the Norwegian initiative, and I wanted us—India—to be more 'with it'. Not that India was not encouraging to the Norwegians, it was, but just that—encouraging. It was not backing it with what may be called any enthusiasm. It had known of the LTTE's ways for far too long to think a Nordic team could change the tiger's stripes. Delhi, it seemed to me, was neither warm nor cold to the Norwegians; it was 'room temperature'—waiting for events to shape themselves and bring success or failure or a stalemate, with no bets taken and so no risks either. If the initiative worked, we would have the satisfaction of saying, 'Did we not wish them well?' And if it flopped, we could say, 'We always feared that.' This, I felt, may be smart but not 'big'. And what was needed now was bigness.

Did we not want strife to have a constructive pause, if not end altogether? A truce is not the same as peace, but especially if it is truly reciprocal, is it not better than continuous warfare in terms of lives saved and destruction averted? If the Norwegians want to help bring the proceedings to some sort of a quietude politically, I felt we should encourage them more than we are doing.

Beyond the immediate issues, I often asked myself a larger question: 'Why, and how, of all countries and persons who could be bridges, Norway? What is really behind their interest? And, in typical Indian cynicism, is there some chakkar (inner deal) if not a gol-maal (sinister design) in it?'

I could think of some explanations:

The Norwegians love tussling with challenges. They want to strive against the odds and summit their targets. Therefore, it is that they have produced two of the world's greatest explorers—Fridtjof Nansen (who reached a record northern latitude of 86°14' during his Fram expedition of 1893–96), and Roald Amundsen (who, with five others left in June 1910 on the ship *Fram* and reached Antarctica in January 1911). Conflict resolution and arduous rock climbing have some similarities.

Alone among the Nobel Prizes, Alfred Nobel (1833–96) endowed the Peace Prize in Oslo, Norway, the other ones being sited in Stockholm, Sweden. Norwegians regard 'peace' as their specialization and the Nobel Peace Prize as their very special gift to the world. Without any arrogance but with self-assurance, they want to be known as the world's foremost peace-makers, somewhat like the Japanese would not mind being known as the world's best camera-makers.

Though nominally a Christian country, Norway is very laid-back on the subject of religion. This makes Norwegians peculiarly suited to mediate among groups of different ethnicities and faith-traditions. They cannot be suspected of evangelism, overt or covert.

And though in NATO, and despite being an arms-manufacturing and arms-exporting nation, Norway is not looked upon as a weapon-minded or weapon-brandishing member of that body. Besides, they have the added advantage of being a European power that is wholly unstained by any colonial or imperial history.

Being lucky enough to have no belligerent neighbours, no insurrectionist elements within their society, and no ethnic divisions of its own, Norway has that which few countries have—a great deal of free time to dabble in other peoples' affairs and problems!

They would not be distressed if regarded as failures as much as they would being regarded as light-weight 'not-to-be-taken-too-seriously' do-gooders whose work 'can do little harm' even if it does 'little good.' Unfortunately for them, this last reputation was hovering over their work in Sri Lanka. Peacemakers may be the blessed of the earth, but theirs is a lonely patch of blessedness.

Solheim and Westborg met PCBK in the first week of November and came directly thereafter to brief me about what transpired between them and the president. To brief me? What an egotistical way of saying they came to apprise the Government of India. Its accredited representative in Colombo could have been a recording machine.

My diary for 5 November 2000 says:

> She saw the pictures [of Pirabakaran and them in the Wanni] and said, 'This is not him, it is his double,' but later agreed it had to be him. The important thing is P did not contradict Erik Solheim when he made it clear that Norway was not discussing matters outside the framework of the unity of Sri Lanka, that Norway was not discussing separation. Therein lies hope, however slender.

Slender indeed it was. Pirabakaran may have let the Norwegians talk to him and be photographed with them, but he did not let up on death-dealing.

The LTTE's seaborne operations, through 'sea-tigers' as they called themselves, were becoming a serious matter for both Sri Lanka and India. Arms smuggling by LTTE through deep-sea routes was a challenge. I went mid-November to Delhi for consultations at which our chief of naval staff Admiral Sushil Kumar (1940–2019), an expert in hydrography and amphibious warfare, gave me details of our role. Sushil Kumar had a deceptively north Indian name for one who was Nagercoil-born. As a Tamilian from its coasts, he knew our southern seas from the inside, so to speak. He was uniquely suited to address the issue at hand. And I learned a great deal from our conversation. The Sri Lankan naval chief Tissera had just visited India and was, as Sushil Kumar put it, 'very happy and all charged-up', as a result.

Sushil Kumar educated me about the surveillance being put in position and said it would 'extend up to the Andaman and Nicobar area'. We had just sold to Sri Lanka our off-shore patrol vessel (OPV), the INS *Sarayu*. Re-named with wit and imagination SLNS *Sayura* ('sea' in Sinhala) the 101-metre-long vessel carrying the Bofors anti-aircraft gun was, with other OPVs, to intercept and sink many LTTE boats.

We were participating in Sri Lanka's security needs without direct involvement, and we continued, of course, to be 'well-wishers' of the Norwegian peace effort—a classic Indian stance in which India was both present and absent, material and subtle, tactile and an abstraction.

Outside of my official meetings, I called on Congress president and leader of the opposition in the Lok Sabha, Sonia Gandhi. Reflecting on this later, I cannot but note that there was no 'problem' about an incumbent envoy of the BJP-led government seeking and getting an appointment with an opposition leader. No one misunderstood the move; no one objected. Meeting Sonia Gandhi in her large and airy book-lined study has always been a very workman-like and focused experience. There is both a sense of her being unhurried and also a no-time-to-waste manner about her. You ask and say what you wish to and get measured, almost ready-to-print answers. She does not pretend to know more than she does. When she does not know something, she says she does not know it. And she is not afraid of asking basic questions. There is courtesy, correctness, and no deficit in what may be called the civil graces. But there is no small talk, not to speak of gossip. Above all, she is very frank, honest, and candid with her opinions.

Sonia Gandhi was well-informed on Sri Lanka matters, appreciating both the volatility of the scene and the now-strong now-weak prospects of dialogue. 'There seems to be some opening there,' she said. But my conversation with her was, as it had to be, primarily on Indian political affairs and her party's. Sonia Gandhi was refreshingly candid. The Congress, she said, had been so used to being in power, to be able to command things, that it was uncomfortable being out of it. And whatever it did was not being given the coverage that was due by the media. She said with honest puzzlement, 'My visits to rural India are always a success. There is much enthusiasm. But it does not always get translated into votes.'

She was to enter a contest for the party's presidentship, with a senior Congressman, Jitendra Prasada, contesting against her. There had been reports of violence used against him, with discussions on the 'intolerance' within the party of opposition to 'the family'.

My diary entry:

> *I offer my congratulations in advance over her re-election as Congress President. 'We will know [the results] on the 16th. It is a huge process. An all-India election conducted with small resources.' I tell her it is good she said [Jitendra] Prasada's contesting her was 'not dissidence'. She says, 'Of course, we are a democratic party.'*

As I left, I said to her that I valued her good wishes and needed them. 'You have them always,' she said, coming up to the door to see me off.

Back in Colombo, Norwegian ambassador Westborg called on me to say Pirabakaran had agreed to 'suspend terror' though not the war if the embargo on the Wanni was lifted. The Sri Lankan government, he said, was looking at the proposal. The man was being his brutal self and asking a sovereign government to accept his terms at the point of the gun. And what, if you please, were the 'terms'? He will not explode bombs in civilian venues, not assassinate MPs, not terrorize innocents along the borders of areas under his control! But will not ease up on the war itself, thereby keeping the SL Army engaged. Great concession! Yet, this was more than Pirabakaran had ever offered to do and would save some lives for sure. Delhi, I felt, should encourage this, though being sceptical and silent with just nominal sounds of appreciation made logical sense.

In Pirabakaran's Heroes' Day speech (his equivalent, if you please, of a head of state's Throne Speech), he offered unconditional talks but called for de-escalation and the creation of 'a conducive atmosphere'. I worked on a translation into English and analysis of the speech with the help of an ace colleague, R. Swaminathan, of the IFS. In my transmission to headquarters, I compared it to his Heroes Day speeches of 1998 and 1999. Kadirgamar, who asked me to see him on 6 December, talked about the speech and said he had an English text which was good but wanted my recension, which I was happy to share with him.

I told Kadirgamar in my 6 December meeting with him of a few openings that were discernible in Pirabakaran's speech: 1. The absence of invective against PCBK. 2. The toning down of rhetoric. 3. The non-insistence of troops withdrawal. 4. The treatment of Jaffna as a metaphor rather than as a military objective. He noted all that, but 'some people', he said, 'talk about confederation. But confederations take place between two or more sovereign states, not between a unit of a state and that state'. Kadirgamar then said something which I could see was aimed at startling me, 'Besides, a confederation here would be unfriendly to India. It would destabilize India. So that is out. What, then, is there? There is the Indian model—the powers enjoyed by the states. There is no need to go beyond the Indian model. We can't—we don't have to—go beyond that.'

I apprised him of the Mizo National Front in Mizoram, of GoI's accords with the Bodos, the Rajiv–Longowal Memorandum of Settlement, and the Assam accord, which included the Karbi Anglong Autonomous Council and the North Cachar Hills Autonomous Council. Kadirgamar knew they would do well to study all those.

He had wanted to go to Delhi to discuss the gamut of problems and take a brief holiday with his wife in Shimla, which he had never been to. We arranged for that happily, including a stay at the hill station's best hotel, where he wanted to be able to swim in a warm-water pool.

Pirabakaran meanwhile conveyed to the Norwegians through Anton Balasingham (as reported to me by Ambassador Westborg) that the Sri Lankan Army was escalating the war and that India's sale of 'a warship' (*Sayura*) to the Sri Lankan Navy with other military equipment seemed to run counter to the peace process and the Norwegian initiative. Apparently, he wanted to know if India was no longer interested in 'a peaceful settlement' and also if the US was with India in its changed stand. The man's questions had a fearsome logic to them, and I wondered if Delhi would do anything to clear his doubts.

I stayed firm with what EAM Jaswant Singh had told me: There would be 'no military component to India's relations with Sri Lanka' (meaning no direct participation in the war) and that India 'can and should contribute to the mental labour required for filling-in the space between Eelam minus and Devolution plus'. This needed to be announced officially by Delhi, loud and clear. And Delhi was not doing so. It was silent.

Blabbing when silence is called for and remaining silent when we should say something is an old practice of the Indian elite.

On 21 December, Pirabakaran declared a month-long unilateral ceasefire as a 'goodwill measure to facilitate the peace process'. A statement on their official website said orders had been issued to all units and combat formations of the LTTE army to 'cease hostile military actions against the Sri Lanka armed forces from midnight 24th December 2000 to midnight 24th January 2001'. The announcement also said the LTTE was prepared to extend the 'period of peace' if the Sri Lankan government responded 'positively by ceasing armed hostilities against our forces and takes steps to implement the Norwegian proposal of mutual confidence-building measures.'[15]

2001
WORDS AS DIPLOMACY—SRI LANKA

2001 opened to a Sri Lanka dangling on the tusks of an elephantine contradiction: there was in force the ceasefire called by Pirabakaran on one side and a war being fought by the state's army on the other. And within that dangle swung another incongruity: the Norwegian peace process was in action but with neither party really identifying with it and the government of India maintaining a cordial aloofness to it all. Delhi was never going to let Tamil sentiment within the country feel it did not care, never going to make Lankan Tamils feel abandoned by it. Nor was it going to let the Sri Lankan government feel that India was not with it in immobilizing LTTE terror. It had been scorched by that ogre, had it not? Rajiv Gandhi had been badly, really badly, butted on the shoulder by a Sinhala naval rating leaving President Jayewardene speechless. He had been blown to bits by an LTTE cadre, leaving Pirabakaran celebrating.

When has state policy been easy, diplomacy smooth sailing? I wanted the peace process to proceed. Which civilian did not? And so, Delhi's prudent wordlessness and Colombo's ambivalence irritated me. I, too, 'swung'—between irritation at peace doves not being launched and a realization that those doves on taking wing would, more likely than not, be blasted to smithereens. But I was too accultured by Jayaprakash Narayan's way of thinking, too much in awe of Nobel Peace Prize-winners, to subordinate risks of peace-making to the safety of prudence. Pirabakaran and the LTTE were no less an anathema to me than to anyone else, and I knew also that even if I was viewed as a 'peacenik', I was, at the start and end of the day, India's high commissioner in Colombo and as such a high target for LTTE's bullets or mortars. But I wanted, perhaps egotistically, during my tenure in Colombo, to pursue two objectives, both of which had, in principle, my government's nod: one, help get Sri Lanka's Tamils their due, and two, take the peace process further.

Moral perspectives and pragmatism have ever been at loggerheads in India's foreign policy options. Prominent examples include India's response to the Soviet Union's action in Hungary and China's moving into Tibet (during the Nehru years), Soviet actions in Czechoslovakia and then in Afghanistan (during Indira Gandhi's innings), Rajiv Gandhi's sending armed forces to the Maldives and Sri Lanka, both steps being essentially guided by considerations other than 'moral'. They bear out the statement of the veteran Indian diplomat and political thinker P. N. Haksar: 'In the real world of politics, even in countries which claim to follow Jesus or Buddha, moral arguments do not carry weight.'[1] PCBK was in London, and Kadirgamar was in Shimla at the time. He went into a tizzy of coordination between Shimla, Colombo, and London with the calm expertise that was his own.

'We may be failing,' Ambassador Westborg said to me on 1 January, 'but if we do, we will start all over again.' Kadirgamar, back from his India visit, came with his wife Suganthi to call on Tara and me on 3 January. Coming at 7.30 pm, they stayed for two hours and forty-five minutes. We did not ask them to stay for dinner, not having prepared for it, and not being informal enough to ask them to stay on and join us at a simple home meal. But over drink and snacks, a most relaxed conversation was had. He was full of appreciation for the visit to India and, in particular, the holiday in Shimla. He said the water in the pool was exactly of the temperature he wanted. Knowing how things do not always work to plan in my dear country, this detail was very gratifying. He said Indian security arrangements everywhere, and in Shimla too, were discreet and effective. He said on his return journey, they stopped over in Bangalore, where he said he had his 'best audience ever' with Sri Satya Sai Baba. A crystal Ganesha, he said, materialized, glinting in the air, and was given to Suganthi. 'Things will settle down in Sri Lanka,' the sage told Kadirgamar. 'Can't tell you when, but they will.'

It was not yet six months since I left the president's Secretariat to take up my assignment in Colombo. There had been many moments, even in this short spell, when I wondered if I would not have been better off in my job in Delhi rather than in the melting pot of political strife, terror, and war that Sri Lanka was. President Narayanan had not filled up the post of secretary after I left, and his industrious joint secretary, Shumsher Sheriff, was holding the fort with ease. A few days later, Leela Ponappa, during a phone call on official matters, said a story had appeared in *Indian Express* that said President–PM relations had improved after my departure from Rashtrapati Bhavan, that I had been the spoiler in RB–PMO relations and that with Sheriff, 'an affable and accommodating person managing affairs, things had never been so good between President Narayanan and Prime Minister Vajpayee'.

All capitals breed gossip. Delhi does so with a panache of its own.

On 23 January 2001, the LTTE announced an extension of the ceasefire by another month. There was both relief and mystification. Why is this ostensibly good thing happening when there is no reciprocity being shown by Colombo? Are we missing something? Be that as it may, the announcement did give a push to the Norwegian peace process, and to that extent, I welcomed it and advised Delhi of my reasons. Our Republic Day—my first in Colombo—was approaching. The response to our invitation for the customary At Home was overwhelming.

On the 26th morning, it looked like it could rain, and so we cleared up the main rooms to shift, if need be, the At Home indoors. I rang my sister Taru in Delhi that noon. I was in for a shock. She told me an earthquake* had jolted Delhi, of which the epicentre was believed to have been in Gujarat. Later in the day, more news came in—500 dead, then 1500. Should we cancel the reception? Ideally, yes, but we would not be able to call each and every invitee in time. We just went ahead with nothing changed. It poured in the afternoon, drenching the awnings we had installed in the lawns. By 5.30 pm, it cleared as guests started arriving even before the appointed hour of 6.30 pm. Within the next half hour, some 800 had arrived, including ten or more ministers. Most had learnt of the earthquake, and congratulations on the Republic Day and commiseration on the earthquake mingled in natural contradiction. Life is not simple. After the guests had gone, I spoke to more than one contact in Delhi and Gujarat to ascertain details of the tragedy. It was worse than I had thought.

A US$ 100 million credit line to Sri Lanka had, meanwhile, come to be finalized, and the signing was due on 29 January. One may have felt good if the money was diverted to Gujarat instead, but if we did that, we would be resiling from an international obligation, and that would not be right. Dharma is another word for dilemma. The signing went off as scheduled without much media coverage, which was a blessing.

The earthquake would not let me be. The fact that it had ravaged Gujarat made it that much more personally affecting for me. As a palliative for my troubled head, I sought time for a call on Arthur C. Clarke (1917–2008), the English science writer, science fiction writer, undersea explorer, and passionate promoter of the idea of space travel. He had migrated to Sri Lanka in 1956 to pursue his passion for scuba diving, and had lived in Colombo ever since. The eighty-three-year-old received me in a wheelchair in his spacious and busy-looking office-cum-residence. My diary entry:

> *ACC says 'Ceylon is a little India—without its hassles'. I gently remind him of the ethnic conflict in Sri Lanka. His facelines change and he agrees but I can see he does not want to discuss politics. Nor do*

*The 2001 Gujarat earthquake, also known as the Bhuj earthquake, occurred on 26 January at 08.46 a.m. The epicentre was about 9 km south-southwest of the village of Chobari in Bhachau Taluka of Kutch District. Measuring 7.6 on the Richter scale, it killed between 13,000 to 20,000 people, injured another 167,000, and destroyed nearly 340,000 buildings.

I, not with him. He tells me how sorry he is about the earthquake. 'I spent three weeks in Ahmedabad,' he tells me, 'speaking at the Vikram Sarabhai place.' ACC shows me a letter from the Indian scientist Krishna Dronamraju [1937–2020] of Houston, in which the latter puts forward the theory that the 26 January earthquake could have been triggered by anti-India people manipulating the fault line. ACC says such a malevolent act is tectonically possible but, like germ warfare, is likely to recoil on its perpetrators. It could be that such an idea has crossed peoples' minds in the US and Moscow. ACC is an admirer of S. Ramanujan and says it is good Ramanujan 'keeps popping up in other peoples' work'.

And then, wheeling his mobile chair to a bookshelf, Clarke pulled out a copy of his *Richter 10*. Giving it to me, he said the book starts in Delhi. When standing on the balcony of his hotel room, he felt a movement under his foot and asked an attendant if there was a metro under the hotel. He was then told that, no, what he had experienced was an earthquake. I asked the famous writer to inscribe the book for me, which he gladly did. I told myself I would invite him over, but with one thing and another, that never happened. Reading the gripping book authored by him and Mike McQuay, I realized its importance. An earthquake at 10 will leave nothing undestroyed. And it is not something that can happen only in a book of science fiction. The solution prescribed by the story was not, however, something I could accept—nuclear explosions deep inside the fault lines in order to 'spot-weld' them.

Donations for the Gujarat earthquake relief flowed in copiously. It was a delicate thing, a 'big' country receiving help from a 'small' one. But the help came spontaneously, mostly from people of Indian origin, and gave the donors a sense of participation in the earthquake relief. The Bohra community was particularly generous, giving LKR 1 million. The All Ceylon Hindu Congress gave LKR 2 lakh, and a Hindu group from Jaffna gave LKR 1 lakh. PCBK rang on 14 February and asked me to see her. She handed over a draft for US$ 100,000 and a token consignment of garments, all of which she had personally taken the initiative to put together.

As the world rushed to Gujarat's and its devastated city Bhuj's succour, the government of Gujarat moved to spend US$ 1 billion for the reconstruction and rehabilitation of the city and the rehabilitation of about 300,000 families.[2] At that point, India had not decided, as it was to a couple of years later, to decline foreign aid on the grounds that it could look after its needs—a decision I could not understand, for receiving support in distress is not a sign of helplessness but of solidarity.

Assistance poured in from across the globe. The USA sent relief materials worth US$ 5 million. George W. Bush (b. 1946) had become president only twenty days earlier. The Labour government in the UK led by Tony Blair (b. 1953) offered £10 million and dispatched a rescue team containing specialists skilled in locating trapped casualties still buried under collapsed buildings.

Japan, that earthquake-prone nation, sent US$ 3 million in financial aid and ¥101.4 million worth of relief supplies and equipment. Curiously, that handsome gesture came from a government headed by maverick Prime Minister Yoshiro Mori (b. 1937), said to have 'the heart of a flea and the brain of a shark'.[3]

All help, national and international notwithstanding, the work of rescue, relief and reconstruction had to be done by the government of Gujarat, and there, the Keshubhai Patel BJP government fared poorly. Loss of nerve, confusion, and lack of local leadership delayed the start of rescue and relief operations. Public anger mounted as it dawned on all that poor quality construction, with clearances given without due verification of stability or quality through a nexus of corrupt officials and contractors, is what made a deadly earthquake deadlier in its impact.[4]

The RSS's cadres arrived on the scene with the speed only that organization can show and started relief operations to public admiration. It has to be said to that organization's credit that it showed reflexes expected of a responsible public authority. Today, one can say Gujarat rebuilt its devastated sites well and with future safety in view. But India, as such, has learnt no lessons. An earthquake of the severity of the Gujarat earthquake of 26 January 2001 occurring anywhere any time in India will have the same disastrous fallout, the same panic and loss of nerve will occur, the same rage. We are earthquake-prone and earthquake-dumb, deaf and blind. We will be earthquake-ravaged as well unless we take steps to mitigate the impact. There is no Arthur C. Clarke amongst us to shake us out of our languid callousness.

PCBK was to make an official visit to India in February.

Preparations for such visits are for any diplomatic mission, back-breaking in terms of the briefs that have to be prepared, proposals made for programmes, visits, calls, meetings, gifts, receptions, and banquets. The appetite of the 'dealing desk' in the ministry for background data, foreground projections, character sketches, etc., is insatiable.

The next three days were spent in South Block with my colleagues at the Ministry of External Affairs, principally in its BSM Division, dealing with Myanmar, Sri Lanka, and the Maldives. Leela Ponappa, the 'dealing' additional secretary, ever a model of efficiency, quick-thinking, quick-acting, and clear-headedness, was, besides, a south Indian with a natural connect to the issues involved. But unlike me, not being Tamil, she was altogether free from any lurking biases. I had given her more than one occasion to tick me off in each of which, I always saw in hindsight, she was right, and I was wrong. But in the absence of sustained and consistent clarity in policy, the division's skills had to be deployed on the nitty-gritty rather than the larger picture.

On this eve of PCBK's visit, the division was pressuring itself with the minutiae. I did not underestimate the importance of detail, but detail should have its place, and the larger picture should have its own. I hectored Leela, the director Banashree Bose, and the under-secretary Manish Chauhan about our need for clarity in options.

Although a member of the IAS, not our Foreign Service, my postings abroad (Sri Lanka twice, the UK, South Africa, Lesotho, Norway, and Iceland) have made me have much more to do with the MEA than any other ministry in the Government of India. And so, my own deep and broad IAS stripes notwithstanding, I have come to respect and admire the IFS and our MEA enormously. The IFS, just like the IAS, has the standard stock of sniping aunts, sullen uncles, and scheming cousins. But its sense of shared goals, a common ethos, an unwritten code of dos and don'ts, a deference to the foreign secretary as captain of the ship that could be called SS *Jahaz-e-Hind*, the IFS and MEA are unique.

PCBK's visit to Delhi placed my fingers on Delhi's Sri Lanka pulse.

Contrary to my apprehensions about our policy on the peace process, Prime Minister Vajpayee and External Minister Jaswant Singh were clear. The dog-eared formulation about India wanting the 'legitimate aspirations of the Tamils of Sri Lanka' to be addressed was given a new propulsion in our wanting Colombo to negotiate a settlement within the unity and sovereignty of the state, yielding the maximum it could to the demands, through the Norwegian initiative. There was no ambivalence.

On 22 February, I met a person for whom my regard has been steady and growing. Arun Singh (b. 1944), once a deeply cherished member of Rajiv Gandhi's council of ministers as RRM or ṛaksha rajya mantri, minister of state for Defence, was now security adviser to minister Jaswant Singh. I met Arun in his South Block room 161, which was smaller than the one his PA may have had when he was RRM. I had no idea if Arun was a 'defence' hawk in the MEA and would take a hard line on matters in which the MEA mandarins would be doves. Regardless of that, I just told him in plain words what I thought. Arun Singh does not waste his words, and even if the security adviser had expressed himself on the subject, I was not going to record what he said in my diary or in a recounting such as this one. Suffice it to say, Arun Singh was hugely sensitive in his response, totally pragmatic.

PCBK met the PM with only the two ministers present. The two high commissioners—the distinguished archaeologist and academic Senake Bandaranayake (1938–2015) and I—were excluded. Diplomats are held above their station in their own estimation, only to be put in their place by political reality. We joined the principals at the lunch that PM hosted for PCBK. The food was choice. But not the conversation, which was all about pleasantries punctuated by long silences or rather long silences dotted by some remarks. The spells of zero-conversation were really taxing. I wonder what the visitors felt. Indians love to talk. What happens at meal time when there is someone 'different' at the table?

President Narayanan hosted PCBK at dinner, preceding which there was a most elevating conversation. He made an unusual point, a political theorist's point, to his visitor: 'Talks are valuable because the process of engaging in talks requires the other side to reason out its stand and that can be a softening exercise.' An unusual take! But then, our president was an unusual man.

PCBK had, on the day she arrived, made an unusual request to me. 'Can I see a classical dance performance?' The lead time for arranging any such unplanned programme was short. She went one step further. 'Like by...Leela Samson. Possible?' I could see her taste was impeccable. Leela Samson was an outstanding exponent of Bharatanatyam, schooled in Kalakshetra, Chennai, in the great tradition of Rukmini Devi Arundale. I knew and esteemed Leela, but it was not for me to set this up. Heading the Indian Council for Cultural Relations was a good friend, the experienced and convivial diplomat Himachal Som. But this time, he chose to be institutional. 'This kind of thing is not on. She cannot say, "I want to see so-and-so dance." She can say she wants to see an exposition of dance. She cannot lay down who the dancer should be. Leela is not an ordinary artist. She may not be here, may not be free. In any case, why should she oblige? I cannot snap a finger and say, "The President of Sri Lanka wants to see you dance and so—Dance!" No. I will not do it.' I must grant the man had a point, though it was as brittle a point as an over-sharpened tip of a pencil. And it broke. Himachal did ask for and get Leela's acceptance. A stunning performance it was that PCBK witnessed. What is more, the MEA arranged to have our prime minister himself attend the very exclusive hour-long performance. Himachal, of course, deserved to and did get full credit for swinging the whole thing.

Immediately after the dance programme, followed a dinner hosted by High Commissioner Bandaranayake in his gracious residence in Chanakyapuri. The guest list was high-ranking, as it had to be, with J. N. Dixit being in my view, the most interesting invitee. Not the most popular Indian high commissioner in Colombo but easily the most vital, insightful, and defining ever, he was quiet for much of the evening, PCBK being polite to him. The most voluble guest was General Amarjeet Singh Kalkat, who had been in overall command of IPKF operations in Sri Lanka and was the last to leave Sri Lanka's shores on 24 March 1990. As the evening progressed, the hero from the Indo-Pak wars of 1965 and 1971 recounted the IPKF's work and on what should be done now, politically. PCBK, of course, heard him, rapt. Kalkat's narrative was extremely relevant for her, and who could deny the absolutely heroic role of the IPKF against every possible odd and that of Kalkat himself? At the end of the meal, as we left the dining room, I asked PCBK if retired generals in Sri Lanka could wax eloquent like this in front of visiting heads of state. She just smiled in response. I could see she was quite pleased with what she had heard. If India's political and diplomatic leadership had urged her to sue for peace, a retired general had vivified a likely military route to trounce Pirabakaran. Typical of India, she must have felt.

The official message, however, was clear: India wanted a solution based on the Eelam minus and Devolution plus (E- D+) approach. PCBK was happy with the visit; she told me as she emplaned, a parting Delhi 'gift' of mild hay fever notwithstanding.

It had long been my ambition to visit Jaffna. I had been talking of Jaffna, Jaffna, Jaffna, war, war, war. It was time I saw the place. It had also been long since an Indian high commissioner had visited the north. Conditions had not been conducive. And even though there was nothing that could be called peaceful now, there was something of a pause that encouraged me to go, and I had two reasons other than the desire to go there. One was a request from C. B. Muthamma (1924–09), the first woman to join the IFS. She wanted me to go there and meet her ailing sister, C. B. Rengamma, with whom she had virtually lost touch. Rengamma was a gynaecologist who was reputed to have delivered every living person in Jaffna town less than half her age. The other was a warm welcome from Swami Chidrupananda. I had urged this monk, loosely connected to the Sri Ramakrishna Mission and who ran an ashram at Point Pedro near Jaffna dedicated to Srima Sarada, to arrange for me to visit it and participate in a prayer to Sri Ramakrishna. I did not ask Delhi's clearance for the visit as I thought it was not necessary, the whole of Sri Lanka being my 'beat'. The visit had, of course, to be coordinated with the authorities in Colombo, who arranged for me to fly out, on 3 March, to Palaly airport in a SL Air Force aircraft with a small two-man security team drawn from the ITBP contingent in India House. Siba was all encouragement. I gave him the keys to my safe of classified papers before I took off from Katunayake airport at dawn on a turboprop twin-engine military transport aircraft. The plane, which had no seats, only two benches facing each other, shook throughout the brief journey, making my ears go numb. After breakfast at the army commander's chalet 'Lion's Den' at Palaly, we drove in a jeep to Point Pedro. My diary entry:

> *Past many bombed and emptied areas, reach PP in 40 minutes and spend an hour with Swami Chidrupananda who is a bhakta of Saradama in particular. He chants beautifully to satisfy my request. Leave for Jaffna via the ghost town of Chavakacheri. I have never seen anything like it. On both sides of the road, building after blasted building. Roofs shattered, walls pitted, and collapsing. The devastation has been caused almost entirely by SL forces when they re-took Chava from LTTE. Some of the buildings are gracious structures. Now their ruins speak of a departed time. Homes, shrines, medium-sized and even large temples, chapels, schools, colleges, boutiques, hair-dresser kiosks, tea kades, sports centres, all brought down, all a-tumble. Mile after mile of devastation. At the end of the Kaithadi bridge I find striking large temple-front, quite derelict. I cannot just pass it by. I ask for the vehicle to be stopped and step inside. The once-temple had been converted into a bunker and is now not in active use by the military. Only some sandbags stacked up here and there. In one side shrine an empty Coke bottle sits on the sanctum. Stone pillars with some valuable mythological carvings have been attacked, several bas-relief panels knocked off. The roof has gaping holes in them. Ganesha carvings dominate the pillars. In the main sanctum which has been stacked with sandbags, I find three books lying in a corner. The Bhagavad Gita in Tamil is right on top. 'What is this book?' my escort Col. W. A. R Gunawardene asks. I tell him what it is, my voice quite choked with rage. I return to the vehicle with the thought: if Buddha shrines in Bamiyan are being destroyed, well, it serves the Sinhalese right. Then I am ashamed of the thought. We drive on. More devastated bridges. We pass at Kaithadi, a Home for Elders—totally derelict. I stop again and go in. At the entrance on the floor lies a register of inmates with Ponnambalam Ramanathan's picture on the cover. There is a large hall inside. Covered with dust and debris. On the walls are several framed pictures: two of Sri Sathya Sai Baba, one of Vivekananda, one of Christ, one of Gandhi and Nehru—the famous smiling one, and several of gods and goddesses. At the entrance gate is a mutilated trishul. Are all*

these personages and gods forgiving what has happened or are they asking for some reparation? We go over the Navathuli bridge. Mixed heronry everywhere, jabbing about for fish and crabs...

Jaffna town is about the most charming town I know. Its roads in straight lines at right angles are sparklingly clean. No litter anywhere to be seen. But the thinness of human movement was noticeable and spoke for itself. I called on Rengamma in what had been her home, a fine old-style stand-alone structure, but now more the dwelling of her farming-carers. From the diary: '*She is far gone into Alzheimer's. But she has a classical face, sharp features set in an expression of aristocratic hauteur. She reciprocates my namaskaram...Her daughter, mentally handicapped, is also present. What a torment! I place SLRs 5,000 in Rengamma's caretaker's hands and take my leave.*'

I wanted to visit Jaffna district's main Hindu temple at Nallur, but I could not have gone in without my two security guards, and they would, like me, have had to remove their shirts to go in. That was not something I wanted them to have to do. So, with them, I offered my obeisance to the vel, the great spear that represents Kandaswami, the presiding deity, from outside.

After seeing the government agent (collector) of Jaffna who wanted to import goats from India, the Anglican Archbishop of Jaffna, who talked of the urgency of peace and said the government must make the move, I went to see the Roman Catholic Bishop of Jaffna. He was out, but the priest in charge of Kopay was present and showed me the ravaged Jaffna cathedral, where Sri Lankan military missiles had come tearing through the asbestos roofing. Staying overnight in Jaffna was an exercise in faith. The place was simple and comfortable, but I must confess that, after a delicious meal of thosais made of unrefined rice, I dropped off to sleep with more than one prayer for my safety and that of my two security men in my mind.

Early next morning, Nadarajah Raviraj (1962–2006), the very personable human rights lawyer and mayor of Jaffna, came with two TULF MPs—Mavai Senathirajah (1942–2025) and one other. They heard me out as I described PCBK's visit to India and the message India has given to her, namely, that political discussions were irreplaceable. On the way to Palaly to take the flight back, with Mayor Raviraj leading our jeep in his Austin, I saw two statues—those of the great leader Chelvanayakam and the Tamil poet of poets—Subramania Bharati. Chelva's was next to the ravaged Jaffna public library and the burnt-out municipal building. Bharati's stood at a road crossing, looking like it needed a coat of paint. Though assassinations were by now part of the political reality of Sri Lanka, I could not have guessed that this young mayor would, some six years on, be assassinated in broad daylight in the heart of Colombo by unknown killers. Back home, late that night, Siba Tripathi rang to tell me that a Tamil radio had said I had visited Point Pedro to see an Indian warship!

A thought crossed my mind. Was I wise in wanting to go to Jaffna? Was Colombo wise in letting me go there? There were three reasons why it did. First, it did not want India to think that it could not arrange for its HC to visit the north. Second, it figured that at this point, the LTTE would gain nothing by killing the Indian HC. On the contrary, it would lose at once the little credibility it was gaining in the world's eyes and squander the chance of getting supplies into starving Wanni. Third, if, God forbid, the LTTE did the foolish worst, what would happen? The peace process would collapse, and Sri Lanka, with Indian backing, would go all out into intensified warfare—something the hawks wanted, craved, and the LTTE, at this point, was not prepared for.

I, of course, sent a detailed report to Delhi on my visit. Did the MEA approve of my venture? Did it think of it as an adventure and an unapproved one at that? The high commissioner for India being bumped off in Jaffna by some unidentified shooter zipping past on a mobike would have been a horribly messy thing—for India, for Sri Lanka, for the peace process. And, I shudder to admit, for Tara and the girls. In making that trip to what had been a war-zone I was being the HC who was egotistical enough to try what his more sensible predecessors had not, and it was plain circumstantial luck that brought him back in one piece to Colombo, to India House, to his gloriously flapping flag on its pole, with his salt-of-the-earth ITBP detail, safe.

Siba, a relieved deputy, returned to me the keys I had given to him before leaving with his typically wry half-smile. He was concealing a strong urge to say, 'Thank God you have come back safe, sir.' Beneath Siba's almost cynical exterior was a deeply emotional soul, as his poet-wife Jayshree knew well. A hundred guesses would not have led me to know then that this rock-solid king of plain words was to die within a decade after being India's ambassador to Madagascar and high commissioner to Kenya at the hands of the Emperor of Maladies.

Sri Lanka unveiled, on 8 March, an LKR 75 billion defence budget for the year 2001. A little earlier, Pakistan had announced an aid of US$ 20 million to Sri Lanka to procure 'vital arms' for its war effort against the LTTE. This was militarization. At a dinner in India House, I told Batty Weerakoon, a long-time Trotskyite and MP, and a man I liked greatly for the twinkle in his eye, the smile on his lips, 'There is no such thing as a clean arms deal.' On 13 March, speaking in Parliament in the budget debate,

Weerakoon spoke of charges of corruption against Chandrika's government and quoted me about there being no such thing as a clean defence deal. Weerakoon need not have immortalized me in Sri Lanka's parliamentary proceedings, but I did not regret having said what I did. Curiously, the next day, I learnt of the *Tehelka* expose of bribery allegations in our Ministry of Defence. Two days later—15 March—George Fernandes resigned in the scandal, which threatened to bring down the government. Opposition parties stalled the workings of parliament for a third day on 16 March even as media released sting footage on the internet, showing government members from the MoD and other senior figures accepting bribes from bogus arms dealers.[5] India, at this point, did not look pretty, which meant we from the high commission were avoiding questions, and my comment to Batty Weerakoon began to look like wicked prophecy—not for Sri Lanka but for my own country.

I was genuinely sorry for George Fernandes, as I had felt for Narasimha Rao. Whatever may have happened, my heart told me, must have happened 'lower down' in the MoD; George would have had no hand in it. The old-time socialist could be faulted for other lapses like political judgment, opportunism even, but not for corruption. He was not one to take bribes. And I recalled the sage advice he had given to me on the eve of my departure for Colombo about the importance of talks in any solution.

There was every indication that Sri Lanka was militarizing like never before while 'staying in talks about talks'. One thing that had to be said in Colombo's favour was that it was not doing anything in secret. It wanted to not lose in battle (who would?) and wanted the LTTE to not win the talks (that would be unequal). Fair enough.

London's banning of the LTTE, along with nineteen other terror outfits, was a long time coming. And rightly so. But the timing of it was something I had told Linda Duffield, the British high commissioner, needed to be calibrated to the peace process. She agreed with me but was not able to impact policy in London, which wanted swift action. We had banned the LTTE in 1991 and could not but approve London's step. PCBK, while transiting in Delhi from her visit to London, late March, who was met by Foreign Secretary Chokila Iyer at the airport, told her that the ban had come 'thanks to India'. EAM told me to request Colombo to 'desist from repeating what was partially true at best incorrect at worst, for we did not single out LTTE in any demarche to London'. So, if this was partially true, what was that partial truth? Just this, that we had told London that it was doing the right thing in banning terrorist organizations as terrorism is anathema to India. Diplomacy is not double-speak, but it can be single-speak with side whisper or multiple whispers within one word. Selective deniability and universal proclaimability are the two blades of the pair of scissors that we call external affairs. And who in Kautilya's land can say this is not in the nation's interest?

I welcomed visits from knowledgeable Indians, which were outnumbered by visits from other kinds—tourists who embarrassed, harassed, and made big holes in our time (and allowances). One welcome in-transit visitor came on 28 March. Minister of state for Commerce and Industry at that point, Omar Abdullah and I lunched at Taj Hotel's airport lounge, Habiba, overlooking a lagoon. At thirty-one, Omar was our youngest minister at the time, and I, at fifty-six, checked myself from acting even remotely patronising or avuncular. He was, after all, a minister in the government of India and I, a mere representative of the government. But his total freedom from airs and engaged questioning made me regard him as an ideal future minister for External Affairs (which he was to become—minister of state—a couple of months later) and repeat my set piece: despite all our messages for peaceful solutions, Sri Lanka is militarizing like mad and will create problems for us in the future. We cannot participate in its militarization or compete with China and Pakistan in this. But we can do something better—make China and Pakistan's military marketing redundant by advancing the peace process. As I was saying to him that Sri Lanka should not become a battlefield, Kfir jets zoomed out from the airfield right next to us. Omar could not have got a better sense of what I was saying. My diary has a short line: '*He sees the point.*'

On 20 April, Foreign Minister Kadirgamar asked me to meet him. I was low in spirits about my country, with Parliament being rocked by opposition demands for an investigation into arms deals, our northeastern region of Darjeeling crippled by an indefinite general strike called by the Gorkha National Liberation Front (GNLF) over an attack on their leader, Subhas Ghising (1936–2015), and sixteen Indian soldiers having been killed by Bangladeshi forces in border skirmishes with indications that they had been tortured before being murdered.[6] I went hoping Kadirgamar will not even mention these horrors to me, for I would have nothing to say.

From my diary: *As we talk, I hear two reports in quick succession. SLFM continues regardless. Beyond thinking momentarily of a piece of metal having fallen on another, I, too, think no more upon it. SLFM talks of this and that and showing me his collection of walking sticks including a silver one given to him by President Narayanan when he called on Rashtrapatiji in New Delhi, he sees me up to the car. Later, as I am dining, he rings to say, 'Gopal, both those reports we heard but did not "notice" were gunshots.'*

Apparently, a security guard of his had fired off a shot accidentally, and another had panicked and returned the shot. Luckily, no one was hurt. I expressed my relief and, complimented him on his ability to stay cool, and said he was meant to bring peace to the country. But the whole thing left me feeling very uneasy in the gut. Was it all really that accidental? Was someone trying to psych out SLFM? Or the Indian high commissioner? If so, who? Or was I letting my imagination run riot? Perhaps. But facts are facts. Where my car was parked and where Kadirgamar saw me into it was no more than a couple of feet away from where the shots went off. That 'accident', had it occurred a few minutes later, would have had a different voltage. And though Kadirgamar had barely noticed the thing when it happened, he was sufficiently affected by it to phone me and tell me about it. I am sure he did not sleep too easily that night. I certainly did not.

A bullet with Kadirgamar's name on it was already, really, there, somewhere in LTTE's arsenals, throbbing impatiently for its moment.

LTTE did not extend the ceasefire. On 25 April, the LTTE announced from its headquarters in Wanni that there would be no further extension. My diary reads: '*I am sad beyond words. I had told GoI again and again that we must tell the Sri Lankan government that its escalation is dangerous. If only they had listened!*'

At a grim meeting in my office, Siba said tersely that 'security in charge in Delhi' should be informed. 'For our security to be tightened?' I asked. 'Aapki,' he replied in one telling Hindi word ('Yours'). He was right.

The Sri Lanka Army launched on 25 April, the no-nonsense sounding Operation Agni Keela 'to expand its control over the Jaffna peninsula'. More than 100 were killed, 300 wounded on the first day itself. It was at war, a unilateral war. The LTTE had been observing a unilateral ceasefire. And both had at the same time been talking about talks while asking, 'What are we talking about?'

Sitting that evening in the rear veranda of India House, gazing at the spread of lawn that Sirimavo Bandaranaike had remembered so fondly, I nursed a glass of single malt as I might a blind wound on my shins. All the birds of the garden had fallen silent or gone to roost. If the lone owlet that used to hoot from time to time was around, it was silent, too. Chiku, our good old stray from London, lay curled up by my ankles. The ITBP boys were in their barracks, ready to hit the sack but equally ready to jump into action if called. Tara, who knows when I need her to talk me out of my sulks and when I need to be left alone to mope, had decided to just let me be. In that soft state of wistful brooding, I asked myself: so, has all that had been sought by the Norwegians and encouraged in varying degrees by India come to naught? Were PCBK and Kadirgamar playing at peace while plotting military conclusions? Getting advice from us and arms from Pakistan? Was the cunning carnivore holed up in the Wanni, aware of this reality, doing the same? Getting advice from Norway and arms from just about everywhere where they are on sale? Were all the peace process sceptics in Delhi right after all, and I the olive-wreathed clown in the pack?

Ayyo, ayyo, yes, it seemed to me. Exactly so.

A major political chapter, meanwhile, had turned in India. In mid-May, the ruling BJP suffered defeat in five key state elections, losing ground to the opposition Congress (I) party in Assam, Kerala, and Pondicherry. In Tamil Nadu, a coalition allied to Congress (I) swept to power, making Jayalalithaa, with a conviction for bribery[7], chief minister there for the second time. In West Bengal, the communist Left Front returned to power, continuing its record as the world's longest-serving elected communist government. Much as I had come to like and, in fact, revel in the leadership provided to India's mission in Colombo by Vajpayee and Jaswant Singh, my Congress DNA was pleased at the grand old party's showing in the polls. But I was sincerely sorry at Karunanidhi losing to Jayalalithaa in Tamil Nadu. She would hound him, I knew. But what good news from Kolkata! Jyoti babu being back was just great.

In Delhi on 22 May for consultations on the subject of arms sales, the LTTE's demand for de-proscription and the Letter Rogatory in the Rajiv Gandhi assassination case that I had been asked by the Ministry of Home Affairs to hand over to Colombo.

It was a sign of the spaciousness of that time that after my official meetings at the MEA, I could, the same evening, call on Congress president Sonia Gandhi. I sought no one's permission to do so, though I knew that our Intelligence Bureau's tabs on 10 Janpath would convey to those concerned the fact that I was among those who had called on her. No one seemed to have been particularly bothered. I certainly was not, as I was not going to share any official secrets with her, nor was she interested in knowing them. In my thirty or so minutes with her, I found her as interested in Sri Lanka as when I had called on her last before leaving for Colombo. The subject of her husband's assassination and Pirabakaran's extradition must have been on her mind, but, bless her etiquette, she did not touch on that at all. I told her, on my own part, though, that I thought there was a certain revisionism taking place within the LTTE about the assassinations of Rajiv, of the senior politician and MP Appapillai Amirthalingam (1927–89), of lawyer and human rights activist Neelan Tiruchelvam (1944–99), and the bombing of the Trincomalee harbour in 1994, none of which furthered the

Tamil cause. She heard me without comment. I congratulated her on the assembly election results and said I hoped Jayalalithaa's second helming of Tamil Nadu would be better than her first. While talking of the Left's victory in West Bengal, I could not but say to her that it was a pity Congress could not get itself to support Jyoti babu for the prime ministership in 1998. She said the CWC was against it, and she did not want to overrule it, though as Congress president, she could have. Anyway, all that is history, both of us said almost together.

Full as I was of Sri Lanka, yet I could not but absorb with a sense of deep satisfaction the news that came the same day that the Vajpayee government had extended an offer of talks on Kashmir to Pakistan's president General Pervez Musharraf. In a nuanced move that had Jaswant Singh written all over it, we had also ended India's six-month unilateral ceasefire in the disputed region. We wanted talks but were not giving history away.

Back in Colombo, on 28 May, I called on Kadirgamar. He spoke long as usual and grippingly. He had a way of speaking that held you. His eyes, which were wide, would get wider as he spoke, and his hands, which were small, would use their fingers to great effect. I could never miss the ring with nine gems that he wore, which, as he told me, Sathya Sai Baba had materialized and given to him.

But the times were not right for peace anyway, either in India or in Sri Lanka.

On Saturday, 30 June, Tara, Amrita, and I were shopping in Colombo's enchanting boutique for handlooms and handicrafts called Barefoot run by the grand dame of all exquisite fabrics, Barbara Sansoni, when my security detail brought the car phone to me saying the foreign minister wanted to speak to me urgently. Apologizing for the weekend intrusion, Kadirgamar said a document was on its way to me and could I meet him in the afternoon to discuss it. Having read it, I met Kadirgamar to hear him. The document and he spoke of an air attack having commenced earlier that morning on the Jaffna peninsula following a heavy build-up by the LTTE. The argument was most unconvincing, and I told Kadirgamar so. Our official spokesman used the phrase 'deep disappointment' and expressed India's reaffirmation of our commitment to peace. Media in Sri Lanka carried this prominently.

Sri Lanka was not, at this point, at the top of MEA's or PMO's attention. Pakistan was. Vajpayee wanted a breakthrough. The newly positioned president of Pakistan, Musharraf, being invited to Agra for talks was a huge step in faith. PCBK, who invited me to see her on 30 May, was full of praise for Vajpayee's invitation to Musharraf and said she would like to speak to him and felicitate him.

I did not bother the MEA too much over the rest of May as I knew Pakistan was occupying its thoughts. On 17 July, hopes for a new era in Indo–Pakistani relations were dashed when the Vajpayee–Musharraf summit collapsed on the Kashmir issue. Musharraf was clearly the spoiler, not that everyone on our side was exactly rooting for a deal. For me, this was most disquieting. Vajpayee could claim to have checked the Pakistan misadventure in Kargil, though at the cost of far too many precious soldier and officer lives. And yet he had extended his hand of friendship to Islamabad. I was proud of that and felt deeply saddened by the breakdown at Agra.

An invitation came to me around this time to speak at the National Defence College in Delhi on the Sri Lankan situation. Siba, whom I consulted, said I should accept, which I did, flying from Katunayake airport to Delhi on 22 July. On 24 July morning, Siba rang early in the morning to say Katunayake airport had been attacked by LTTE, with as many as eleven aircraft damaged in a daring pre-dawn operation. Apparently, a dozen or more operatives had sneaked in the previous evening through an open drain that ran along the tarmac and, after disabling electricity mains, had carried out the attacks.[8] This was clearly a message that I imagined was saying, 'If you think you can flatten us on the ground by bombing us from the air, we can cripple your airpower by merely crawling on the ground. We are tigers by day and cobras by night.' Colombo had been talking about LTTE's preparations to attack Jaffna when, in fact, LTTE was preparing with cool meticulousness a disabling of Katunayake.

My two-hours talk with a Q&A at the NDC later that morning went surprisingly well, thanks to my having prepared intensely for it. I spoke that evening to my cherished friend from London days, P. S. Raghavan, in the PMO, who said Dr L. M. Singhvi had written to the PM suggesting that I be appointed to our mission in London or New York. Well, well, I thought and decided to think no further about it.

The next day, 25 July, I was lucky enough to get a morning flight out to Colombo via Chennai, where I went to see MS, radiant as ever. I did not hear that day of something dreadful that had happened in Delhi that very afternoon. I learnt of it only the next day, in Colombo. I am sure I had passed the gate of her house on my drive from India International Centre, where I was staying, to the airport hours before she was killed. Famed 'Bandit Queen' turned MP Phoolan Devi had been assassinated by a masked gunman at the gate of her New Delhi residence on 44 Ashoka Road. She was all of thirty-seven. None of her bodyguards could save her. Finally, it was neither a bandit nor a queen but a woman whose so-called fame had led her from a life of dacoity and bullets to politics that fell to an assassin's bullets. I had the chilling realization that Sri Lanka was not the only country nor Colombo, the only city where people—MPs included—can be surprised by murder at their doorstep. I also had this worrisome thought: is India becoming lawless? Are guns floating around our country with mercenaries and gunmen everywhere hireable to kill at will? Indira Gandhi, our prime minister, had been similarly shot dead in 1984 at the gates of her house very near to where Phoolan Devi had been killed. Both assassinations showed that on the Indian subcontinent, it is dangerous to have enemies and dangerous to be prominent. Bodyguards help, but only up to the point their prarabdha or destiny permits.

The flight from Chennai to Colombo, a Sydney-Colombo flight diverted to Chennai, was the first to land at Katunayake after the trauma. Its provisions had run out, but we were grateful for the cold crispies served to us by an apologetic crew. As we descended and curved over Colombo's coconut groves and marshes, I looked out for a possible sniper still out there. The plane landed smoothly but taxied slowly, hesitantly, not wanting to ignite a cracker left behind by the night-riders. Reaching India House and returning to the family for a hot meal was like reaching a seam of life that was blessed. Tara, Divya, and Amrita looking after our house guest Sonal Mansingh seemed like they were made of substances above those that make up the earth.

That day, a milestone day for me, I was talking to a visitor in my office when our Chokila Iyer rang. After a few moments of 'pleasantries' (which I always find very tedious when it is clear that they are mere fillers before the real stuff of the call comes), she said, 'The reason why I am ringing you is to ask if you're willing to go to London.' This did not come altogether as a surprise to me as Raghavan had hinted as much to me. I said I would, of course, be willing to go to London and would be honoured to do so. Back home for lunch, I told Tara, who was not exactly thrilled. It had just been a year since we came, and to disrupt our household so soon again.... Yes, I know, I said to her, but now that the girls seem to be poised to go and study abroad.... Once again, my 'career' turn had come as a fait accompli to her, as it does to millions of wives in India. The man of the house calls the tune. The wife... Shortly thereafter, I was informed that the president had approved my appointment, the agreement from London had been received, and the foreign secretary telegraphed the formal announcement. In due propriety, I informed Kadirgamar. 'Oh,' he exclaimed, 'that will be a catastrophe for us! Why is Delhi being cruel to Sri Lanka? You were hand-picked for the job.' And then, in a change of rasa, 'London is, of course, a big honour for you, a richly deserved one, if I may say so.'

In the macabre theatre of terror, we were doing no better than our 'small' neighbour. On 1 October, thirty-eight people were killed in what was described as 'a concerted attack on Indian government buildings in Srinagar, Kashmir'.[9] Aping Pirabakaran's modus, a Pakistani suicide bomber from the Jaish-e-Mohammad detonated a government jeep packed with explosives at the entrance of the buildings, while the outfit's operatives disguised as policemen entered the complex and began firing. Had Jaish observed the Katunayake procedure? The All Parties Hurriyat Conference of Muslim separatists and the Pakistani government both immediately condemned the attack, but the Indian government accused the Pakistani authorities of collusion.

On 24 October, President Narayanan signed into law the Prevention of Terrorism Ordinance granting extra powers to the police in an effort to combat terrorism, as well as allowing the detention of suspected terrorists for up to three months without charge. The ordinance made it a duty for people to report suspicious behaviour.

Diwali 2001 fell on 14 November, which is Jawaharlal Nehru's birthday. As in Pretoria five years earlier, I had a bust of our first prime minister sent to us for installation at the foyer of the High Commission. It is a sign of the large-mindedness of the people and of the times that the government of India then was not a Congress one, nor was it a Congress one this time. And on both occasions, I kept Delhi informed. This time around, I had myself mentioned my idea to EAM Jaswant Singh, who had no problems with it. PCBK agreed, despite her preoccupations with electioneering, to unveil it. She was only forty-five minutes behind time—something of a record! But it truly was a marvel that she came. As did her sister Sunethra and brother Anura. PCBK's extempore speech was of the expected very high standard.

Sunethra, who, though not being in politics, has a sharp political sense as well as a deep self-identification with her parents' party, told me a few days before polling day, 'We are losing.' I placed far greater weight on that than on many an 'expert' opinion that said more or less the same thing. On 5 December, polling day in Sri Lanka, a People's Alliance (PA) reverse was definitely in the air. It was not 'Will UNP get a majority?' but 'How big will UNP's majority be by itself and how much with its partners?' The results came fast: UNP—89; PA—62, but with allies getting counted both ways, Ranil had a slender majority. Chandrika did not protract matters. She swore him as prime minister on 9 December. We had arranged for our prime minister's letter of felicitation to be ready, and I handed it to Ranil Wickremesinghe almost immediately after he had assumed office. He told me he wanted to visit Delhi as soon as Delhi would receive him. I conveyed this to Jaswant Singh, who at once said, 'Of course, he will be more than welcome.' Thanks to our standing with everyone concerned, the High Commission of India got to see the names and portfolios before the world did. Late that evening, Kadirgamar asked me if the foreign minister had been named. When I told him yes and that it was Tyronne Fernando (1941–2008), he said, after a pause: 'Well then, Gopal, good night.'

PCBK was not going to deny herself the counsel of this ace mind. She appointed Kadirgamar as her adviser on foreign affairs, a most felicitous step. Not for him as much as for her and for Sri Lanka.

On 13 December, I was exercising on the treadmill in Colombo's Taj Samudra hotel when I saw BBC say on the TV screen in front of me Parliament House in Delhi had been attacked by five terrorist gunmen wearing Indian ordnance uniforms. They had reached the site in a vehicle bearing false stickers of the Home Ministry and Parliament. They were spotted first by Kamlesh Kumari Jatav, a woman constable of uncommon bravery, who was shot by the gunmen, succumbing to her wounds on the spot. Carrying AK47s, grenades, and grenade-launchers, they killed six police officers and a gardener and injured nearly twenty. All the gunmen were killed, some doubts remaining on whether they also tried to kill themselves, as the vest of one of them exploded when he was shot.[10] Here was an audacious emulation on Indian soil of the Katunayake siege, not just in India's capital city but right in the sanctum of its parliamentary democracy.

No parliamentarians were hurt, though some hundreds of them, including the vice president of India and chairman of the Rajya Sabha Krishan Kant and Home Minister L. K. Advani, were inside the great Edwin Lutyens-created circular building of pillared majesty. The government blamed the attack on two Pakistan-based Kashmiri militant groups, Jaish-e-Mohammad and Lashkar-e-Taiba, the former of which had attacked the local government centre in Indian-administered Kashmir in October. It had been a close shave. Our VP and HM could have been going out or going in at that moment and been killed. Or Prime Minister Vajpayee, my own Minister Jaswant Singh. And Sonia Gandhi, likewise. Horrors.

No embassy can hope for its home country to always be the object of admiration or awe. But it does not want it to be the object of ridicule or pity in the country of accreditation. Better be unnoticed than noticed being in the dumps. As I stepped out of the gym in the India-owned and India-run hotel in Colombo, I did so feeling miserable. How was one to look hurt on the shin but not harmed in the face? How was one to say we have not been tonsured, only tousled? Difficult, when the brazen terrorist gang had shown us to be not merely vulnerable but naive, getting taken in by stupid stickers and stolen uniforms? Were we looking like something of a cud-eating holy cow mauled by hyenas? No, sir! I schooled myself. We are to say, 'We got 'em. All five of them. And we know where they come from. We will now go for and get their bosses. We'll show 'em, we will.' This didn't quite sound like me, but then which diplomat has to sound like himself? He is paid to, meant to, and expected to sound like his government.

Even as I drove out, I got calls. The first was from former Foreign Minister Kadirgamar expressing shock and solidarity and also, to my slight annoyance, asking me for 'inputs' for PCBK's official reaction. Ranil Wickremesinghe, the new prime minister, also rang with the same spontaneous sentiments and also asking what his government should say. He had no less reason than PCBK to worry about Pakistani reactions. On a high, he was now in a position from which he, too, would be dealing with Delhi, Islamabad, and Beijing. I suggested to the prime minister that the word 'condemn' would be apposite.

Both, I might say, without any egoism, acted on my suggestions solicited entirely by them, without any modifications.

The Ministry of External Affairs, I knew, would be convulsed with messages flowing and speeding out on how this crisis was to be handled. Pakistan was clearly connected with the outrage; there was no doubting it. And so, for a while, the MEA's higher echelons would understandably be wholly Pakistan-preoccupied and in no mood to devote attention to Sri Lanka. But even as, say, the liver continues to function when the body has been stricken with, say, a stroke, the BSM Division of the ministry was 'there' for our mission. Colombo's messages would be quickly read in the Division, noted for being concerned enough, filed.

Tension between India and Pakistan escalated rapidly, with the Indian government accusing its Pakistani counterpart of supporting the terrorist attack on the Indian parliament. The threat of war between India and Pakistan suddenly loomed large, and both sides massed forces along their common border.

2002
WHEELS WITHIN WHEELS—NORWAY

On 2 January 2002, there was an exchange of mortar fire across the LoC in Kashmir. And we now had the curious experience of Sri Lanka, with a host of the world's nations expressing the hope that India and Pakistan will avoid armed conflict. British prime minister Tony Blair came visiting both capitals. Some leaders of the groups believed to have been involved in the parliamentary attack being arrested in Pakistan, it seemed only right that our Prime Minister Vajpayee should declare that war was 'unnecessary'.

By this time, I should normally have started packing for London, but London it was not to be. I will never know why and how, but the appointment was cancelled, the hugely gifted diplomat Ronen Sen (b. 1944), who had been named for our mission in Islamabad, being appointed instead of me. It was left to Jaswant Singh to speak to me with candour about the whole thing. With a Rajput's sense of honour, he said to me, 'Could it have been done better? The answer is "Yes". Who is responsible? I am.' And thus, taking the blame upon himself, he proceeded to tell me exactly what and how that 'what' happened.

I have never quite been persuaded by the saying 'Everything happens for the good.' But let me say Ronen Sen was suited for the London job in a way I could never have been. I was to do not too badly for myself without London, but he certainly went on to be a sterling quality high commissioner in London. With him there, everything happened just right for India's representation in the UK. Ronen was then to go on to become one of India's finest ambassadors to the US, playing a role as only he could have in the finalization of the 123 India–US civil nuclear agreement of 2005.

At yet another meeting with Jaswant Singh in his very cramped office in Parliament House, I asked where I should be headed if anywhere at all on his map. He spoke in his very Rajput-style Hindi. Apke kile ki jo divaarein girin hein unko humein phir se khadi karni hain. (The walls on your fort that have fallen, it is our duty to raise them up again.) He wanted to waste no time on the sequence of events. He asked me to say where I might wish to go in London's place. I had to think fast and realistically. I knew Oslo was being vacated by my old college contemporary, Nirupam Sen, who was coming to replace me in Colombo. So, I said 'Oslo'. EAM picked up the phone and, speaking, I imagine, to the foreign secretary, said, 'Gopal Gandhi is here.... We need to give him a posting.... I have discussed the matter with him. Please move to have him appointed to Oslo. Thank you.' That was classic Jaswant Singh.

So, Fridtjof Nansen's country it was to be. But before I went to Oslo, life had more things to show for itself in Sri Lanka and in India.

On 27 February, after fifty-nine Hindu pilgrims were killed in a fire aboard a train in Godhra, Gujarat, one of the worst incidents of communal violence in India started. The violence in the city of Ahmedabad left over 500 Muslims dead.[1] On 28 February, a mob attacked the Gulbarg Society, a lower-middle-class neighbourhood in Chamanpura, Ahmedabad, with most of the houses getting burnt and at least thirty-five victims, including a former Congress member of parliament Ehsan Jafri being burnt alive.[2] From my location in Colombo, I could not find out then what emerged later about President Narayanan's intervention. As was only to be expected, he wrote and spoke directly to Prime Minister Vajpayee, requesting him to send the army. His letter to the PM was ordered, much later, by the chief information commissioner, acting on a petition, to be placed in the public domain, but the Delhi High Court overruled the CIC and the contents of that communication remain veiled. The court cited Article 74 (2) of the Constitution, which bars courts from going into the advice tendered by the council of ministers to the president. Does that bar work in the reverse also? I would say it does. The intent of that Article 74 (2) is that President–PM interactions should be privileged. I know the value of that protection. Those two dignitaries must discuss all they need to, in conditions of confidentiality, so that maximum frankness marks their discussions. If those two (and, likewise, governors and chief ministers) are not to discuss matters of state candidly with no holds barred, afraid of 'leaks', then how are the two offices going to work together for the nation's benefit? A president should be able to tell a PM that such-and-such minister is useless, or that such-and-such step being contemplated is dangerous, or that s/he has heard of a certain development that can affect the stability of the state or the security of the country. If each such conversation or correspondence is to be made public during the process of that discussion, then decisions will get vitiated. The operative part of their talks can always be set out in official statements issued later by mutual consent.

But that position of mine did not prevent me, like just about everyone, from wondering what the pressures were on Vajpayee.

One clear result of President Narayanan's intervention was that he came to be ruled out for a second term in office. The opposition Congress and the Left encouraged him to contest. My brother Rajmohan urged him to do so because 'our core values and our Constitutional values are under threat'. KRN had apparently appreciated the suggestion.

Tara and I were in Bangalore at the time, making arrangements for our younger daughter Amrita's wedding, which was due to take place on 3 March. And so, on the first two or three days of the violence, we remained almost entirely uninformed about it. Giving a daughter in marriage is a deeply moving thing for her parents. Something of oneself goes at the proceedings of a daughter's wedding. That your daughter suddenly belongs elsewhere is an unbearable thought and feeling. The moment of the couples' departure after the wedding is utterly unbearable, and it is only the exhaustion caused by the multiple tasks at hand, the greeting and welcoming of guests, that steers one through the mental churn.

Former president R. Venkataraman and Mrs Venkataraman came, a gesture that we would remember forever. 'Gopu, why didn't you tell me about the London problem?' he said to me. 'I would have spoken to Vajpayee and seen to it that you were sent there.... Anyway...All right....' That was typical of him. And then he moved to where the bride was and gave her his blessing in loadfuls.

From Colombo came Lakshman Kadirgamar and his wife, as did Minister G. L. Pieris. Calling from Colombo to felicitate us, Ranil said it was something that both the Lakshmans had come (G. L. being Lakshman too). The greatest blessing came in the presence of my sister Taru and my brothers Rajmohan and Ramchandra.

On 4 April, Prime Minister Vajpayee, on his first visit to Gujarat after the riots, made a landmark speech appealing to both the Hindu and Muslim communities to end the spiral of violence and said that the 'shameful events' in Gujarat were a 'blot' on India.[3]

Within a few weeks of that, PCBK visited Delhi to deliver the first Madhavrao Scindia memorial lecture organized by the *Hindustan Times*'s chief, Shobhana Bhartia. Kadirgamar came with her. I was, of course, there on duty to 'cover' the visit. The speech said nothing that was new, but she put whatever she said well. The Scindia family came and called on PCBK formally to thank and invite her—a gesture which went down very well with her. 'Such good-looking people,' she remarked.

It was again an index of the spaciousness of the times that the BJP government of the day, whatever its leaders may have felt, did not discourage or, in any way, disfavour PCBK coming to Delhi for a Congress party-inspired event.

Prime Minister Vajpayee hosted a lunch in her honour. As it turned out, this was to be, for me, no ordinary lunch. It started out, as on the last occasion, with large gaps in conversation, Jaswant Singh trying his best to fill the silences. At one point, PCBK suddenly asked: What is the situation in Gujarat like?' The PM, after a moment's reflection, said, 'Ask the Home Minister.' Mr Advani said with candour, 'Things are bad though better.'

PCBK: Have there been deaths?

LKA: Yes, 800, of which 180 due to police firing.

Sombre reflections—President Narayanan ruminating about his own future to the author, Rashtrapati Bhavan, New Delhi, 2002. (Author's personal collection).

Vajpayee now intervened but with just two words: 'Gandhi's Gujarat.' Eyes turned to me. They had to. PCBK then asked me: 'Gopal, did you hear that? The PM said 'Gandhi's Gujarat'. 'Yes,' I responded, 'I heard that.' What else or more could I have said? But her bold question showed up in a trice our prime minister's thoughts. That Vajpayee should have said what he did, albeit in a two-word sentence that had little syntax but much meaning, to a visiting dignitary from overseas was no small thing. As lunch gave over and everyone rose to depart, the PM passing by me said, 'Gujarat jal raha hai...' (Gujarat is burning). I said to him, 'Agar vahaan kuchh karne ke liye aap mujhe aadesh dein to mein tayyaar hun' (If you instruct me to go there to do something, I am ready). I did not expect any such instructions nor get them. But it was enough for me to hear my prime minister, a person for whose sense of right and wrong I had real respect, say to me what he did.

PCBK called on rashtrapatiji, who was this time looking frail, slow of movement, and sounded weak of voice. To my surprise, he told PCBK, 'My term ends in July.' After her departure, standing at the North Court's magnificent archway, he asked me, 'When are you going to Norway?' With the London fiasco in mind, I said, 'I am reluctant to make plans.' He laughed gently, and asked when my elder daughter Divya's wedding was to take place.

On 4 May, militants attacked an army base in Kashmir, killing thirty-four people and leading to a sharp rise in tensions with Pakistan. Speaking in the Lok Sabha on 15 May, our prime minister said: 'We will have to retaliate.'[4]

Vikram Sood and Jyoti Sinha, Stephanians both, and then, working with our Research and Analysis Wing (R&AW), came to Colombo on a two-day visit to clear certain issues. It was, for me, refreshing to share perceptions with these two seasoned officers frankly. Jyoti and I, exact contemporaries in college and good friends, were meeting after a long time. I told them of the need for greater coordination between R&AW and the MEA for contradictory instructions to us in the missions created difficulties. As we talked, on 21 May, came news of the killing of the moderate Kashmiri separatist leader Abdul Ghani Lone. Vikram Sood said after Lone's killing, 'India will have to go ahead with elections in J&K whether free or fair or not.' So, we seemed to be back to square one and a 'hot war' seemed inevitable,

On the same day as the Lone assassination, Vajpayee began a five-day visit to Kashmir. In his speech on 22 May, he said that 'a new chapter of victory and triumph will be written in the history books soon'. I must confess I could not make out the import of these words.

Ranil, accompanied by his wife, Maithree, made his first visit to India as prime minister in June 2002. I flew out with him, Bangalore being the first city visited after a transit halt in Chennai. And Whitefield, the location of Sri Sathya Sai Baba's ashram, the site of the first programme in his itinerary. I accompanied the couple to Whitefield, outside the city, where an audience had been arranged. I was seeing Sai Baba for the first time—a valued moment. An excerpt from my diary entry for 9 June 2002:

> *SSSB is a diminutive man, with his famous black mane of hair sparser than I imagined. We are seated in a small sitting room. He walks in gently, saying [as everyone rises]: 'Baitho, baitho' (sit, sit), and asks for names. There is a childlike manner to him. Every now and then he scribbles something in the air with his right hand, closes his eyes, places his forefinger on his forehead as if to concentrate. He asks Maithree, 'Do you want some divine ash?' When she nods he says: 'Dekho, dekho' (watch, watch) and rubs his right hand in the air for a couple of seconds and some vibhuti appears. He places it in Maithree's hands and then, charmingly, gives her a loose leaf from a scribbling pad to transfer it into. He wipes her hand (which had held the vibhuti) with his kerchief. A little later he materialises a navaratna ring for Ranil and a chain for Maithree with a pendant depicting Lakshmi. He has a word for most, asking a security guard standing on duty to sit with the words: 'We are all the same'... Says '...peace will come, definitely, in a month or two. By July or August all will be calm, peaceful.' He then asks 'How is Chandrika?' Ranil indicates the president of Sri Lanka is well. His maturity in responding to the reference to his arch-rival is impressive. He says not a word in disparagement direct or indirect of her...*

Delhi lavished its proverbial hospitality on the visitors, with calls on Ranil by Home Minister Advani and External Affairs Minister Jaswant Singh and a full-scale meeting with the PM followed by the customary lunch. As I left, I told him my innings in Colombo had drawn to a close, and I will get to Norway by September. He responded to this with a short laugh, which I could not interpret.

During the return transit halt in Chennai on 11 June, at the governor's banquet, Chief Minister Jayalalithaa had a one-on-one conversation with Ranil. He recounted it for me and for the record. She said to him: 'I have no problem with the peace process, but I have my reasons to ask for what I am asking, just as you have yours for your position.' This was Jayalalithaa at her characteristically blunt and crisp. She was implacably opposed to the LTTE and wanted Pirabakaran's extradition. As she prepared to leave, she turned to me and said, 'It is good to see you again and here in Raj

Bhavan....' She had not forgotten our brief but significant conversations in that building back in 1983 and 1984, when MGR was stricken and she at a crossroads. 'Please keep in touch,' she said as she wheeled out of the hall with regal steps.

By mid-June, it was time for the names of candidates for the election to the office of the president of India to emerge. KRN would not have been disinclined to consider a contest if P. C. Alexander was going to be the BJP's candidate. Having been governor for over twelve years in three states, his credentials for the nation's highest constitutional office were impeccable. And politically, PCA's being a Christian from Kerala made him a 'good' successor to KRN, a Dalit from the same state. I believe PCA would have defeated KRN, but not everyone wanted another south Indian, and that too, a Malayali, to be the next president. Chandrababu Naidu, the Andhra leader, spoke of the need for a consensus and indicated Vice President Krishan Kant, whom Naidu had worked with when Kant was governor of Andhra. Agreeing, Vajpayee phoned the gentleman to ready himself for it. But with the twists and turns of politics being what they are and a war psychosis building up against Pakistan, a surprise name sprang up from literally outer space: A. P. J. Abdul Kalam. It was a name none could have thought of and none could have any objections to. Congress remained undecided for a while, but only for a while. BJP warmed and puffed up to the name like a phulka.

I had, many years ago, asked Tara's cousin-in-law, the space engineer Aravamudan (1936–2021), a long-standing friend of Kalam's, to describe him to me. 'Kalam is an aeronautical engineer by training,' Dan (as we called him) said. 'He has a great specialization—he has a knack for organizing team-efforts, team-work, team-spirit.' Soon, Kalam's name had caught on. I recalled MS amma asking me at lunch after the two of them had received the Bharat Ratna in 1998: 'Gopu, tell me exactly, ivar yaar...? (who is he?) No one would have any difficulty in answering that question hereafter. KRN announced that he was not a candidate. I have no idea how the change of plan was put to Vice President Kant and by whom. Vajpayee would have been hard put to explain it.

After Dr Kalam had been to Delhi and things had been tied up for his candidature, and he returned to Chennai, I rang him and left a message. He rang back. The conversation in mixed English and Tamil, as recorded in my diary, went like this:

APJK: Vanakkam saar.

GG: My respectful felicitations.

APJAK: Ungal blessings enakku irukkarudaa? (Do I have your blessings?)

GG: Paripurnama (In abundance).

APJAK (repeating it to himself and others who may have been with him): Paripurnama. I would like to discuss the set-up in Rashtrapati Bhavan with you,

GG: Any time.

APJAK: When are you returning to India?

GG: August.

APJAK: Oh... Augustaa? (Oh...in August?) Phone le pesalaamaa (Can we then talk over the phone?)

GG: Yes, on this very number.

I later rang and told his devoted secretary Sheridon that should Dr Kalam so desire, I could come to Chennai and meet him there.

Abdul Kalam was elected on 15 July by the designated electoral college comprised of the members of both houses of the parliament and of all state assemblies. Put up by the ruling NDA coalition, he got the support of the opposition Congress, having called on Congress president Sonia Gandhi and sought her support, and of most other parties. Kalam was the third Muslim to be India's president and the third Tamilian to occupy that palace, the first Tamilian to have done so being C. Rajagopalachari, as India's first and only Indian governor general. It was Kalam's unlikeliness that ensured the people of India taking to him as they did from day one and right up until the last day of his incumbency. He was a technologist, a man who the people of India saw as the creator of missiles that could zip off and smash our enemies, Pakistan particularly. Also, they saw him as the man who had assembled our nuclear bombs (which he had not) that had made us members of the world's superpowers. The South loved him as he was from the South, spoke English with an unembarrassedly heavy Tamil accent, and spoke zero Hindi. The North loved him as he carried no anti-North or anti-Hindi baggage, being, as people wrongly thought, completely innocent of politics. His lack of intellectual airs, a political manner and, as anyone could see, a very small wardrobe comprising no more than one or two blue collared shirts and a couple of pairs of very ordinary trousers made him refreshingly different, made him 'one like us', for millions. Being a Muslim who was vegetarian and was said, not without some optimism, to be an adept veena player, made him just that much more untypical and so that much more original. But above all else, the missile-man's artfully artless hairdo made him an instant hit. He was simple; he was quirky; he was naive; he was unique. He had an intelligence that was different, a modesty that was distinct, a manner that was all his own.

Prime Minister Atal Bihari Vajpayee had delivered to the people of India a president no one expected to see installed in an office that was associated with the scents of the freedom struggle, the notes of scholarship or—the guiles of politics. The interesting thing about all this was that Kalam knew this. He knew his assets. And in the five years that lay ahead of him in his gilded office, he meant to use them deftly. With his Chaplinesque gait, his quizzical expression, his unusual turns of phrase, he was going to be, in the corridors of power, not a cat among pigeons but a man speaking of a dazzling future among men with dim histories.

I had worked with two presidents, both of whom had also been from the South—R. Venkataraman and K. R. Narayanan. But I knew the day Kalam became president that my great bosses would be remembered only by historians of the presidents of India, but this president would be remembered by the ordinary people of the country as no other president would be. Auto-rickshaws would carry his photographs; small eateries would put them up on their walls.

Twelve days after Kalam was elected, on 27 July, Vice President Krishan Kant died of a heart attack. Prarabdha, one might say. But no one can be blamed for thinking that a man who had been deprived of the presidentship of India that had been offered to him by the prime minister himself, dying within days of his disappointment of a heart attack, was going to suffer a medical breakdown.

In Colombo, Foreign Minister Fernando came dutifully to the High Commission and signed the condolence book that we had opened. Duty marked all the ceremonies that accompanied Krishan Kant's obsequies. Kalam himself, of course, visited the vice president's house to condole. He had already learnt the form his new office called for.

PCBK graciously hosted Tara and me to a farewell dinner on 29 July at the President's House, at which guests included ambassadors of the US, China, Japan, the Kadirgamars, and some mutual friends. She was even more candid in her conversation with me than usual and expressed her fears of a possible coup.

'What,' she asked, 'would India do if that happens?' This was a tough one and was not to be ducked. I said India would be most unhappy and would convey its feelings unambiguously. I also reminded her of India's intervention in the attempted coup in Male. But at the same time, I also said I did not believe such a thing would happen, the public reaction would be great and would be a deterrent.

I was to meet her once before I left the country.

A day prior to President Pervez Musharraf's arrival, Prime Minister Ranil and his wife, Maithree, hosted Tara and me to a farewell dinner with the other guests, including the US and Norwegian ambassadors. He had just returned from a brief visit to the US. Ranil said, in his discussions at the White House, President Bush told him the US 'felt comfortable' dealing with democracies and so wanted to be friends with India, but at the same time, it did not want to anger Pakistan. Ever the one-track-minded diplomat, I put it to Ranil that in any joint statement being issued with Musharraf the next day, they had better leave out references to Kashmir or to India–Pakistan matters, keeping the text bilateral. Ranil said he would see to that.

My word to Ranil was neither superfluous nor spoken in vain. The banquet hosted by President Chandrika for President Musharraf on 31 July, to which, like all heads of missions stationed in Colombo, I was invited, was my last engagement in Sri Lanka—a piquancy if ever there was one. The Pakistan president's speech touched, sure enough, on Kashmir. He said the Kashmir issue must be solved in accordance with UN resolutions 'and the wishes of the people of Kashmir'. This was, to say the least, rich coming from the architect of the Kargil invasion. As he left, all guests were introduced to the visiting dignitary by PCBK. As my turn came, President Musharraf looked me up and down and said I had 'height', and that two high commissioners of India he had seen in Islamabad—S. K. Singh and J. N. Dixit—did not. The only response I could summon was stony silence. Neither 'SK', nor 'JND' would have let such a snide remark pass without a telling if also polished retort. After Musharraf's limousine drove off, I told PCBK that her speech, in which neither Kashmir nor India figured, was important for what it said and for what it did not. She then bid me a most fond farewell, having also sent tokens of friendship earlier the same day for us to India House.

As Tara and I left that gorgeous residence for the airport in the evening on 1 August, the ITBP unit presented a Guard of Honour and, lining the driveway as the car pulled out, said in unison, 'HC sahib ki jai! Gandhi sahib ki jai! Madam ji ki jai!' And then added 'Jahan bhi hon khush hon, hamari duaein apke saath hein' (May happiness attend you wherever you are. Our wishes are with you!) Did they say this each time an HC left? I think so and hope so. But I knew from the jawan's faces and the timbre of their voices that they meant every syllable of what they said. We had been welcomed to the house by ITBPs bravehearts two years earlier, and now were being seen off by them. They had kept us safe. Putting their lives on the line, as Divya once told me when I had been short with one of them, they had kept us from harm's way.

The previous year—2001—a truly great film had captured audiences in India—*Lagaan*. In many ways, it was a twenty-first- century avatar of *Do Bigha Zamin* and *Mother India*, but gentler, mellower, as it fused two of independent India's fascinations—cinema and cricket. Its lead song, 'Ghanan Ghanan' (lyrics by Javed Akhtar and composed by A. R. Rahman), about dense clouds (ghanan meaning dense), was magical, bringing to life the desperation of a rain-parched earth for the mercy of the clouds. The song also has words to the effect that the earth is ours, as is the sky. It seemed absolutely right for us to play and sing and dance to it, as Divya wed Rustam Vania on 25 August. Rustam's father was Parsi. And so the nuptials had some charming Parsi elements to them, including the substitution of coconuts by eggs in the ceremony where they are smashed to invoke blessings. The Parsi priests and our own Hindu ones blended seamlessly. Rustam and Divya were to move out of their marriage later, but their daughter Ava, a joy to them and a boon to Tara and me, will be keen, as she grows up, to know of her parents' wedding day. The wedding took place in the same exquisite venue just outside Bangalore, Tamarind Tree. Prime Minister Ranil Wickremesinghe and Minister Milinda Moragoda came to it. On the day previous to the wedding, I rang H. T. Sangliana (b. 1943), Bangalore's commissioner of police, to request him to not stop the traffic on the road for the Lankan PM too much ahead of his arrival. Each invitee, I said was as important for us as Prime Minister Wickremesinghe. The tough Mizo commissioner, and future MP from Bangalore was unmoved. And sure enough, not just were many invitees held up, but so was the bridegroom's car itself till the Lankan convoy had passed. And I remember Sangliana (who was not among my invitees) in the context of that wedding more than those friends who attended, many of them embarrassed and apologetic for being late to arrive. Indian authorities love their powers of veto.

Ranil, of course, would have had no problem with the traffic being allowed unhindered by his convoy. But VVIPs in India are generally immune from any discomfort, not to speak of regret at their beflagged vehicles sailing past humanity held up by their privileged category. More often than not, VVIP security and arrangements in independent India are about status than security.

In Delhi on 6 September 2002 for consultations prior to leaving for Oslo, I met the minister of state for External Affairs, Digvijay Singh (1955–2010). Digvijay talked relaxedly of this and that and shared an anecdote about President Musharraf. During the Pakistani leader's visit to Delhi, he had been appointed minister-in-waiting. As their car neared Tees January Marg and the site of Gandhi's assassination, Musharraf asked Digvijay why the road had that name. Digvijay told him why. He then asked, 'Was Gandhi shot or stabbed?' Digvijay said he was shocked by the level of Musharraf's general knowledge and of the quality of briefs prepared for him by the Pakistan Foreign Office. It was inconceivable that a high-ranking Indian visiting Pakistan would ask if the Quaid-e-Azam had been assassinated or died of natural causes.

Bihar and Bihar's socialist traditions were strongly represented in the MEA at this time, with Digvijay Singh as MoS and Yashwant Sinha as EAM.

It was a pleasant thing to see in Yashwant Sinha's office a portrait of Jayaprakash Narayan on the wall. I complimented him on that—something he reacted to warmly. 'We will pluck you out of Oslo,' he said to me as I was leaving, 'when something suitable comes up.' NSA Brajesh Mishra was cordial as always, because of which I could presume to tell him I had a contribution to make in London and hoped that when the time came for it, the government would not lose sight of me. To this, he said, 'You are assuming we will still be here.' General elections were still two years away, but the NSA had his input and intelligence, both of the systemic kind and his own.

We reached Oslo in the second week of September, with the greater part of our luggage missing. It took a couple of days for the airlines to track and reroute the three suitcases to our doorstep in the quiet city's even quieter suburb of Vinderen. My anxiety was not so much about the baggage carrying our clothes and suchlike as about the one box that had in it precious family archives, including original letters from my grandfathers to the family. These had, accompanied me over my different postings in India and abroad. I cannot describe my great relief when that particular bag was delivered. I hugged it as inconspicuously as I could as I took it into the comely residence.

Oslo was not and has not been ever regarded as a serious diplomatic station. The last ruler, or maharao as he was called, of Kutch, Madansinhji (1909–91), was the first ambassador of India (1957–60) to Norway. I think he rather liked being called le maharao de Kutch, for that is how the Royal Ministry of Foreign Affairs designated him on its lists.

The maharao was a logical choice for Oslo, given that Norway was a monarchy. How he was received by the palace and the Royal Foreign Office, I would not know, but it is very likely that some hurried studies must have been conducted on the relative importance or otherwise of the principality in Gujarat, surmises drawn. Madansinhji was a tennis buff, knew the great legendary great French champion Jean Borotra, and having represented India at the Davis Cup in 1936 and at Wimbledon in 1937, where he played doubles, became friends with Franjo Kukuljevic the Yugoslav tennis player as well. This aspect of 'le Maharao' is bound to have held appeal to his Norwegian hosts.

Another Indian ex-royal whom Nehru had inducted into the foreign service was Apasaheb Pant of Aundh (1912–92). An altogether different kind of 'prince', Apasaheb had democratized the polity of his state much before Independence and won the appreciation of Gandhi himself. Nehru asked him to go to 'the continent of dawn', Africa, and not just open India's mission in Nairobi but also get into the momentum of Africa's burgeoning aspirations for independence. Pant was an intellectual presence with a great fascination for the yogic science of Suryanamaskar, placing him in a class by itself.

It is said you have been too long in Norway if it does not seem excessive to spend 800 kroner on alcohol in a single evening of countless Skål!, clinking glass with glass.

Not long after Apasaheb, there came to Oslo (1968–70) Ambassador Nootaki Venkatesh Rao. The Hindi phrase 'hazir-javab' (of instant wit) may be said to have been coined for him. Asked if there was an Indian equivalent to Skål! he coined on the spot a lovely alternative—Chiranjeevi!, saying India did not have the same kind of tradition in drinking spirits as Scandinavia but had always known of alcohol, which was imbibed with cheer and good wishes, the word he had coined reflecting it.

During the National Emergency (1975–77), India's ambassador in Oslo was the brilliant leftist thinker and writer K. S. Shelvankar (1906–96). 'Shelley', as he was known to friends and admirers among whom I counted myself, was a sensitive soul and an incisive writer who had represented *The Hindu* in London for nearly three decades. How one of an intellect as subtle as his, of a conscience as clear as his, could be purblind to the Emergency and represent India at the height of that monstrosity is something I cannot fathom. Haksar, the leftist philosopher and diplomat, was, as Indira Gandhi's principal secretary, in the same position. And the two were good friends.

Indira Gandhi then sent a third ex-royal to Oslo as ambassador, Rajkumar Dorendra Singh of Manipur (1934–2018). A quintessential politician, he had been chief minister of Manipur during the national Emergency and, after Indira Gandhi's return to power, was rehabilitated in the Oslo posting but only briefly—1981–82—when politics drew him back home.

But to my mind, the finest Indian ambassador Norway has ever had was L. N. Rangarajan. This scholar of scholars served in Oslo from 1989 to 1992 in the post-Rajiv Gandhi years. Rangarajan's translation of Kautilya's *Arthasastra*, with a brilliant introduction, is a landmark book, the kind of which has no forerunner, no peer, and is unlikely to have a successor. Ambassador Rangarajan was also a great skier, using that mode of locomotion to go from home to office and back when snow lay plentifully on the sidewalks. A quintessential ambassador of India and a role model.

I have lingered on this diplomat because of my regret at the diminishing levels of intellectual capital in India's administrative and diplomatic echelons. That this has coincided with the arrival of the digital age could be accidental, but the falling off of books from bookshelves and their place being taken by portable wires and chargers (not to forget that indispensability, the 'mouse') makes me think that browsing overtaking reading is the culprit. The reading, thinking, and contemplative Indian is not to be found among officers of government now. Not as naturally and in the numbers as they used to be. Why should I regret that? Does a well-read, reflective person make a better civil servant? I cannot say that. But a well-read and reflective person is likely to better appreciate the human condition than one who has never read Tiruvalluvar, Kabir, Tulsidas, Shakespeare, Dickens, Orwell, Tagore, Premchand, Bharati, Mahadevi Varma, Thakazhi, Karanth or, in our times, Khushwant Singh, Nirmal Verma, Amrita Pritam, Mahasweta Devi, Perumal Murugan.

The hush in our new setting in Oslo was in great contrast to the hustle of Colombo. And I decided to settle into some study and writing in the hours of leisure that Oslo would yield. I bought Henrik Ibsen's works to start with and immersed myself in it. Having seen Satyajit Ray's *Ganashatru*, based on Ibsen's *An Enemy of the People*, I devoured that play and found it strangely disturbing. It seemed like an eternal play, cautioning us about a danger that can happen anytime, anywhere, but especially in my country.

In 2002, Norway was peaceful by all standards, with fifty-five-year-old Kjell Magne Bondevik, a Norwegian Lutheran minister and leader of the Christian Democratic Party, as the country's prime minister. The country's economy, with its unparalleled offshore oil, was booming. It had no enemies, no rivals worth the name. One might say the country was boringly 'normal'. But an ambassador's mental ecology is not made by the place where he is posted as much as by the state of life back home.

September and October saw elections held in the state of Jammu and Kashmir in an atmosphere of tension. I remembered what IB chief Vikram Sood had told me of elections, 'free and fair or not' in Colombo. It was a relief to see that these elections were free and fair, a great and much-needed corrective to the 1987 elections[5], which had been thoroughly rigged. The fact that 1.7 million voters, representing 43.7 per cent of the registered voters, used the electronic voting machine (EVM) for the first time in the state was noted across the world, which lauded the fact as a victory, despite calls for a boycott by separatists, of the ballot versus the bullet. The result saw a surprising defeat of the National Conference and of the government led by Farooq Abdullah. The NC, which had dominated the state for over forty years, did emerge as the single largest party but failed to get a majority of the 87 seats. A coalition government was formed by the People's Democratic Party and the Congress by means of a curious compromise in which PDP leader and former union home minister Mufti Mohammad Sayeed would be chief minister of Jammu and Kashmir for three years, followed by Ghulam Nabi Azad of the Congress for another three years.

The National Conference had won 28 seats, the Congress 20, and the PDP 16. Even by coming together, the parties number two and three were short of the party number one. But cobbling together support from other successful MLAs, they formed the government. In strictly democratic terms, NC should have been asked to form the government, but it would have been voted out in the legislature by the combined opposition. And so, the anomalous and piquant arrangement was witnessed by the leader of party number three, becoming chief minister. This opportunistically mathematical sequel to free and fair elections was becoming India's norm, power being the crystal goal, with all that power carries—chiefly, financial clout through patronage and crony capitalism. In my thinking a vicious circle was now the order in elections—astronomical sums raised from not very voluntary donations are spent by candidates and parties on the campaign, the victors have to return the sums to the donors, and that is done through patronage and through crony capitalism. Losers, too, do well because they may have failed to win seats, but some of the money raised by them stick to their pockets. Behind and along with all candidates in an Indian election is an unseen candidate: Mr Money. Whoever else wins or loses, Mr Money is ever victorious. That said, the fact that India's conflicted 'crown' had seen a relatively clean election overshadowed all other considerations. And in Oslo, I was happy describing three Indian successes in the J&K elections: first, not a bad voter turnout despite calls for boycott by separatists, second the expert first-time use of EVMs by the electorate, third, a democratic change of government.

The 18th of September was Credentials Day for me. The seniormost ADC to His Majesty King Harald came to the residence to fetch me in a six-door car from the Royal Palace. I had never been in one before and felt squeamish rather than anything else as the ocean liner-like vessel sailed through the city's streets, occasioning mildly amused curiosity among onlookers. Royal guardsmen presenting a Guard of Honour at the entrance reminded me of the credentials ceremony that used to take place at Rashtrapati Bhavan. The ambassador-designate in New Delhi would arrive in a car and then, at the entrance, transfer to a horse-drawn buggy and ride up in that coach to the Forecourt, where a guard of honour would be presented, after which he would be conducted to the Ashoka Hall, where the resident would receive him—an altogether immaculate ceremony. In the mid-1990s, the practice was simplified, the buggy-ride being done away with. What was achieved? Nothing, I would say. If the earlier arrangement was high on pageantry, the revised one was low on atmosphere. What we think of as simplification is often only robbing a jewel of its gems to expose its hollow sockets.

A spruce man in military uniform, the king greeted me in his elegant study with a formal handshake and, after the parchment had been presented by me with a slight bow and received by him with a warm nod, motioned me to a seat in front of his desk. Speaking English with the merest trace of an accent, he described Norway to me as 'a small country with a long strip of land which if turned round would touch Naples'. To its north, he said there was really nothing between it and Japan!

The king brought up the Sri Lanka peace process and said, 'There seems to be some hope at last, and they have stopped killing.' To my relief, he did not ask me pointed questions about the Gujarat riots, just saying sagaciously, 'Your part of the world has had its troubles right from the beginning, has it not?' And again, to my relief did not mention Kashmir or Pakistan. He had been briefed well by his Foreign Office, and of course, he knew in his bones what to say to itinerant diplomats. At exactly the fifteenth minute, he indicated to me that it was time to close and pressed a little bell that opened the room's door to which he led me. My diary entry for the day describes him, truthfully, as '*the perfect recipient of letters of credence*'. I could not have guessed that the sixty-five-year-old king had serious health issues—cancer of the bladder and cardiac insufficiencies—facing him. His prowess at yachting and military service had served his physique well.

During all this, Norway remained actively engaged in the Sri Lanka peace process, with Erik Solheim briefing me constantly for updates needed by Delhi. Prime Minister Ranil Wickremesinghe, visiting Oslo for discussions on a Donors' Conference for Sri Lanka to be held in Oslo, came over to the Indian embassy residence with his Ministers G. L. Pieris and Milinda Moragoda and restated his government's readiness to talk with LTTE on a federal solution short of Eelam, provided LTTE eschewed all violence. India's formulation that any accord must be acceptable to all sections of the Lankan community remained at the heart of the peace process—something we could draw satisfaction from.

On 15 December came news of the BJP's triumphant return to power in

Gujarat, with Narendra Modi at the helm. If asked, at that point, whether Modi would be the next prime minister of India, I would have said, 'Modi? No, I doubt it.' Not because I thought the Congress would dislodge the BJP from power (which it was to do) but because I imagined, so wrongly as it turned out, that the BJP's MPs would find a successor to Vajpayee from among themselves. The gods of politics had a different plan. A future prime minister of India was inching towards Delhi, unbeknownst to most except, I think, to himself. The Gujarat results, I must say in the frankness that ink on paper demands, surprised me. I had imagined the March riots would have appalled 'Gandhi's Gujarat', to use Vajpayee's expression, and it would want a change of government. I was wrong.

On the evening of 16 December, a cold day, a white Oslo greeted Afghanistan's president Hamid Karzai. Norway's President Bondevik hosted a banquet in his honour at Akershus Fortress. Resident heads of mission were invited, and I attended it, dutifully. My diary entry reads:

> *'I have spent many pleasant years in India,' Karzai says to me as I introduce myself. At dinner I am seated near Zalmay Rassoul, National Security Adviser in the transitional government of Afghanistan, a medical man (nephrologist), tells me Pakistan is sustaining Taliban and sending them into Afghanistan and to Kashmir systematically. 'They are doing so on both sides.' He says the US would have liked to be harder on Islamabad but cannot 'since it needs Islamabad for Iraq'. He also says in his view Musharraf is not in control and is engaged in a struggle for survival. In an after-dinner chat, Karzai tells me to convey his regards to Prime Minister Vajpayee. He also asks 'What is the position about the elections in Gujarat?' How can I give him my honest thoughts on that? I tell him BJP has won resoundingly. He does not respond but asks: 'Will that improve stability and cohesion in the state or make it worse?' I say the majority is huge, and the newly elected government should be able to give stability and reassure all those living in the state that they are—whether of the majority or minority community—entitled to equal protection of the law.*

A little earlier that month, a Special Court in New Delhi convicted three Kashmiris of planning the December 2001 attack on Parliament House and sentenced them to death. Norway shrank from violence, was repelled by terror. But Norwegian sentiment was also viscerally opposed to the death penalty.

Did India matter to Norway?

I did not want to delude my bond with my country by saying it did.

But I could not ignore some clear signs of how and what India meant to Norway. Or, to be specific, to certain sensitive Norwegians. And I have to say with no bias operating and in all objectivity that Mohandas K. Gandhi had much to do with this.

One of my early calls was on Geir Lundestad (1945–2023), the erudite director of the Nobel Institute and secretary to the Nobel Committee. I had never had any time for the view that Gandhi should be given a retrospective Nobel Peace Prize. Those who aspired and lobbied for this were well-intentioned but did not realize that Gandhi's effectiveness in the cause of peace did not suffer from not getting that medal. When I said this to Lundestad, he said, 'The Prize has suffered, been impaired by the omission.' He then showed me around the institute and took me to the Committee Room where Gandhi had been passed over three times—in 1937, 1947, and then in 1948. He then asked his secretary, a gentle lady in her fifties, to take photocopies of the Nobel Committees' proceedings on Gandhi's nomination for me to keep. These were, of course, in Norwegian. While rolling the photocopier, she said to me, 'I am very happy to meet not only the Indian ambassador but the grandson of the great ommitment.' I loved that phrase of her own coinage. It seemed to me much more effective and determining than 'omission'. And coming from a simple Norwegian, it meant a great deal to me. Leaving the handsome premises of the Nobel Institute, it occurred to me that its walls could do with a painting of Gandhi or a quotation from him. But the thought went as fleet as it came.

Another experience of the 'India that is Gandhi' came via a statue and its maker. The statue was of Haakon VII (1872–1957), the Danish-born king of Norway from 1905 through World Wars I and II. As Hitler closed into Norway, the Norwegians having done their best to resist the invaders, Haakon was advised to flee. A photograph captured the moment when the king ran with determined steps to his escape, his famous hat firmly on his head. When a full five years later, he returned, Haakon stood on the front deck of his ship with that very hat held by him against his heart. This returning Haakon had been captured by a great sculptor, Nils Aas (1933–2004), in a statue that stood in front of the Foreign Office in Oslo.

Very keen to meet Aas, I got an appointment with the great man that I cherished no less than the credentials at the palace. Taking my hand in his large palm, he said slowly but clearly, 'I do not speak good English. I am glad to see you.' A little later, as we settled down to some tea and 'spice cookies' made by his wife Kristine Reintz, he said, 'India…Oh, India…It is so huge.... We are small....' And talk turned to a subject I half expected. Raising his arms over his head as if carrying a palladium on it, he said, 'M-a-h-a-t-m-a G-a-n-d-h-i.' He intoned the name rather than say it. And then added, with hand movements suggesting bewilderment, 'But...but he did not get the Nobel Peace Prize.' Aas seemed to regard this as inexplicable. Responding to a sudden thought, I said, 'Perhaps you may sculpt him.' 'Aa-h,' he said, as if that would be more than an assignment, a sacrament.

We met a couple of times after that, once at the embassy residence over a meal. As he came into my study, he at once noticed what most people would have missed—a framed picture tucked away in a corner of a hand holding a pen. He wanted to know whose hand that was. When I said it was Gandhi's, Aas went up to the picture, lifted it up and, seeing it carefully, asked, 'Is it possible...can I have ...a copy of this picture?' I sent him one not long thereafter, but just in time, for within weeks, the great sculptor was gone.

Tara, a nature conservationist by instinct and an ornithologist by training, had known of the extraordinary philosopher of 'deep ecology', Arne Naess (1912–2009), much before I even heard of his name. It was from the historian Ramachandra Guha that I first learnt of the ninety-year-old as one who has been greatly inspired by Gandhi. He had carried out a satyagraha, no less, against the concept of dams. Along with a large number of protesters, Naess, in 1970, chained himself to rocks in front of Mardalsfossen, a waterfall in a Norwegian fjord, and refused to descend until plans to build a dam were dropped. The demonstrators were carried away by police, and work on the dam did not stop. But Naess had launched Norwegian environmentalism's activism. He talked with feeling about Gandhi and also about India. Inevitably, the subject of nuclear weapons came up and, to my surprise, I found him optimistic and, given the present pace of disarmament talks, even naive. 'Over the next two hundred years,' he said, the world will come so clearly to realize the ridiculousness of war that it will banish it.' May your prophecy come true, I said to myself. As we left, Naess challenged me to an 'arms hold' and defeated me, thirty-three years younger than him, flat. His Viking arm was far too strong for my Vaishnavite one. His non-violence was that of the strong.

India meant, for most Norwegians, Gandhi. This was both a matter of pride for us in the embassy, but also some discomfiture, for it required India to be judged by moral yardsticks. In October, representatives of Statoil, the Norwegian state-owned multinational energy company, met me and said the ONGC had let them down in an agreement they had agreed upon. I was shown correspondence which showed the ONGC had conveyed to Statoil even the date for a signing ceremony. At the last minute, a joint secretary from the Ministry of Petroleum told them the whole thing was 'off'. This was not on, they said. Just not on. What could I say except that I will check the thing out. I understand that a government can come to know something which makes it necessary to go back on a bilateral understanding. But to shut the door on it without assigning reasons and do so at the last minute does India no good. How could I continue lobbying the Norwegians for support in our legitimate aspirations to a permanent seat in the UN Security Council when we cannot tell them why we are backing off from a simple agreement?

I was put to a 'Gandhian test' not much later when three earnest, wise, and focused persons representing Physicians Against Nuclear Weapons called on me to express their concern on the India–Pakistan nuclear situation. I gave them, with poor conviction and poorer persuasion, our side of the story of how China went nuclear, its basic track record vis-à-vis India's, of Pakistan's nuclear programme, of our having announced a no-first-use...etc.

But as we make missiles—Agni and Prithvi—to deliver our bombs to farther and farther distances, we keep Gandhi out of our thoughts.

On Christmas day, a quiet holiday, I read up Raj Chengappa's *Weapons for Peace*. A racy account of India's nuclear programme from Nehru to Vajpayee, it was a fascinating read. A frank admirer of the Indian bomb, he writes in it about the history and processes of its creation with awe. I was impressed by Raj's awe but horrified by the object of that emotion.

The end of a year and the beginning of a new one is nothing but one date changing to another. Yet so entrenched are the optics of a calendar, so deeply inked in our minds the four numerals making up a year that sentiments overtake one. As 2002 ended, I felt like speaking to an elder, a wise Indian senior, and offer my respects and invoke a wand of blessing. So, on 27 December, on impulse, I dialled Narasimha Rao. He came on the line very quickly. I wished him a good new year, but he characteristically disposed of so-called pleasantries in one second and came straight to the point. 'How are things in Sri Lanka?' I gave him a brief idea of the general situation, the outer profile, as it were. He asked probing questions. I answered them to the best of my ability and scope. He ended the conversation with, 'You must succeed.' I could not quite make out what he meant by that 'must.' He did not say 'will succeed', which would have been a blessing and a prophecy, or 'should succeed', which would have been a kind of wish, but said, as enigmatically as he typically was, 'must'. The ambiguity notwithstanding, I felt deeply humbled by the acuity and mental application of this man who had no need to trouble himself with the conditions in another country, a detail in India's external affairs, an ex-prime minister who was not being consulted either by his successor or, for that matter, by his own party on matters of importance. And yet did trouble himself to do that. How many would, in his place? Why, how many in actual positions of responsibility would be as interested in the subject except as an obligation?

There was one 'takeaway'—an unlovely figure of speech belonging to the vocabulary of cash-and-carry eateries—from my brief talk with Rao sahib. While the Sri Lanka peace process mediated by Norway was on, an Indian ambassador in Oslo had but one value: as a witness and withal a cautious contributor of encouragement to that process. India–Norway bilateral ties came only next and then again only mildly, in order of importance.

2003
SURJEET, SHATRUGHAN, AND SHIV SHARMA IN OSLO

The year started for me with troubled ruminations on the peculiar times we were in, the war-clouds over the Gulf, more than anything else.

My visceral antipathy to war and war machines came to the fore again at a dinner that very evening hosted by a UNDP official. A very interesting Vietnamese gentleman was also present. He was from the judiciary. I have the following diary entry: *'He laughs and talks wittily, but when the host talks about napalm bombs, he says, simply, "Oh, don't tell me about that. I have seen...children without eyes...don't tell me about it..."'*

I was in a very anti-war mood when India's war-readiness took up all my thoughts. On 4 January, the Cabinet Committee on Security met in New Delhi. Any meeting of the CCS is important. Its composition: prime minister (chair), defence minister, finance minister, external affairs minister, with the cabinet secretary and the NSA attending, makes it, in fact, the most important such in the country. The meeting was thus attended by Prime Minister Vajpayee, Defence Minister George Fernandes, Finance Minister Jaswant Singh, External Affairs Minister Yashwant Sinha and, most significantly, by the nuclear doctrine's author, NSA Brajesh Mishra.

The master-strategist and deeply cerebral Mishra, we can be sure, was the moving force at the meeting. The summary described India's nuclear policy in terse, unambiguous terms and gave its aim as 'building and maintaining a credible minimum deterrent'. Its immediate next line gave a new decision, not a one-time or episode-related decision but a binding one: nuclear weapons will be used in retaliation against a nuclear attack on Indian territory or on Indian forces anywhere. This amounted to saying two things at once:

1. India will retaliate against a nuclear attack with its nuclear arsenal.
2. India will not use its nuclear weapons before another.[1]

This was, in effect, a warning and an assurance. A 'No First Use' policy had earlier also been announced by Prime Minister Vajpayee in a Draft Nuclear Doctrine after the 1998 nuclear tests. But now, four years on, NFU was being cast in stone. Also included in the CCS's announcement were three other decisions: India will not use nuclear weapons against non-nuclear states, it will continue its moratorium on nuclear tests, and remain committed to a nuclear weapons-free world through global, verifiable, and non-discriminatory disarmament.

All this was manna for me, and I was resolved to spread the word among officials in my host government and among fellow diplomats. But I knew too that if they were to read the doctrinal statement carefully, they would not miss some non-pacific tones that were also contained in it. The doctrine also said, in addition to India's 'retaliation to a first strike' on it. It will also retain the option to retaliate with nuclear weapons in the event of a major attack against India or Indian forces anywhere by biological or chemical weapons. The statement said such a retaliation by India 'will be massive and designed to inflict unacceptable damage'. No one, friend or adversary, could object to these intentions. They were such as any sovereign country would want for its security.

China had announced their NFU, being the first nuclear weapons country to do so. But Pakistan had done no such thing, nor had nuclear weapons NATO member states. The Soviet Union had, briefly, under Leonid Brezhnev, gone NFU but then later dropped the abjuring. So, in 2003, India was the only country in the world after China to be an NFU country. And who was to say when China would go back on its NFU policy? In some ways, Pakistan emphatically saying no to NFU was easier to live with than uncertainty about China's NFU.[2]

How binding was India's NFU going to be on successor governments in New Delhi? Would Vajpayee's self-restraint be like Emperor Ashoka's about war, violence, and hatred that elevated him but found no adherents in his own successors? These questions were natural and admitted of no clear answers. So, I was both pleased and befuddled about NFU and the 4 January statement. The desire to keep all options open had led to that statement qualifying NFU with that ballistic line about massive and unacceptable damage from India to any party that led a major attack on India. Who was to determine what 'major' was? The prime minister of India or the Nuclear Command Authority that was formed under the same doctrine? And within that NCA, by the Executive Council headed by the NSA or the Political Council headed by the PM?

In the flash micro-seconds of a 'major attack', how were these two councils to get to work? What was meant by the words 'massive' and 'unacceptable'? Was India saying it could handle through nuclear retaliation a joint challenge from Pakistan and China at one and the same time, with non-state agencies complicating matters with nuclear terror? And did not the different qualifying clauses in the doctrine make its NFU announcement conditional? It also seemed like the doctrine was Brajesh Mishra's skilful weaving together of competing perceptions in India's political executive and its military and diplomatic bureaucracies.

The questions nagging my mind made its doctrine look like a patchwork quilt with gaping holes in it, through any one of which an inspired act of nuclear terrorism could creep in. That would leave us debating whether non-state terrorism constituted provocation enough for nuclear retaliation and if so, against whom. At the end of the day, I was clear that India's NFU palliated the pacific instincts of some Indian moderates and no one else and left the rest of the world as sceptical of the nuclear future of South Asia as it always has been.

The diplomatic bag brought 'dak' and newspapers from India once a week, and it was, therefore, a little after *The Hindu*'s 5 January 2003 issue appeared that I got to see that newspaper's report on the CCS announcement and an accompanying editorial. The report by C. Rajamohan made a crucial point. 'The Government also mentions that it has "reviewed and approved" alternate chains of command for retaliatory nuclear strikes in all eventualities". This is a reference to a situation in which the Prime Minister may be incapacitated during a crisis. But the CCS did not reveal how the power to press the nuclear button will move down the political chain in the event of such a contingency.' *The Hindu*'s editorial echoed Rajamohan but speculated that this silence was perhaps determined by the need for secrecy—the alternative chain, by being disclosed, could be targeted and destroyed by the adversary at first strike. The *Hindustan Times* of 5 January said what I had also surmised, namely, that it was Jaswant Singh who, in the CCS, insisted on an alternate chain of command being put in place for the 'apocalyptic' situation when the highest decision-making body is either wiped out or rendered inert.

Brahma Chellaney, a redoubtable strategy expert said in *HT* with relief that he was now seeing the government ready with a credible minimum deterrence. Several scenarios involving the first enemy strike wiping out India's civilian/political leadership, the prime minister's 'incapacitation' being a euphemism for it, flitted through my imagination, and I wished I could ring Rao sahib again and ask him what he thought of it all, but I could not do that. Not because he was 'history' but because such a thing, in protocol terms, was 'not done, just not done'. Besides, I was the great missile-maker President A. P. J. Abdul Kalam's envoy to King Harald of Norway, bomb-tester Prime Minister Atal Bihari Vajpayee's representative in Oslo and had to take the CCS decision and its statement exactly as they were, with my troubling thoughts lodged supine in my nut of a head like the kernel in a walnut.

At that point, I had no idea of the phenomenon of Artificial Intelligence gestating in the womb of the future and how, in no more than two or three decades hence, AI could place before the world the possibility of AI becoming part of not just a nuclear weapons delivery system but of any order of belligerence, making the arrangements made by a pre-AI era CCS look like a fire brigade drill.

But one thought has to be shared here. When every stripe of 'informed' Indian opinion was discussing what the CCS's action meant and what it did not in terms of national security and defence and retaliation, and was going into what manner of devastation could visit India's political and military chains of command and what decapitating blow our retaliation could comprise, one 'player' was forgotten: the innocent victim. The fact that millions of innocent lives would be lost in the nuclear collisions, blown out of existence without their having had the chance to say anything about the war or the weapons of war. And then, perhaps even worse, millions more would die slow deaths caused by radiation. Disputes over territory can have an aggressive side and an aggrieved side. But wars over those disputes can have only deaths upon deaths, sudden or slow. War corpses are not good or bad corpses. They are the remains of children, women, men old and young. A nuclear war, like any war but only more than any other type of war, is about killing en masse; its victims are about dying en masse, dying in a flash or dying in degrees. No report or editorial on the CCS's nuclear doctrine that I read had anything to say on nuclear mass-deaths. But I was being a fool to have looked out for innocence in a doctrine that was dealing with the opposite.

I was a fool many times over in another foolishness as well. If India's politico-military elites were looking at the doctrine for what it meant in its technical interstices, the vast majority was totally disinterested in that detail. That majority wanted India to be a military more-than-equal of its adversaries, Pakistan in particular. And the vast majority in Pakistan, I was sure, wanted the same, in reverse. The behemoth called the Indian urban middle-class was, in the matter of India's military options, like giddy boys on a Diwali night intoxicated by the sight, smell, and sounds of sizzling crackers, deafening 'bombs' and hissing 'rockets' that competed with those being sent off into the polluted sky by other children in the neighbourhood, while their fathers and uncles played rummy and made or lost money while tipsy.

At about the same time, I had to reckon with another Indian 'image' that was most troubling. An agreement was in the making between India and Norway in the environment sector. Keen to introduce in the draft agreement a clause that insulated tenders being called from corrupt practices, it had proposed a clause on the subject. This was in itself unexceptionable, but the way the draft clause was worded made India look like a cesspool of corruption. Delhi, naturally, objected to such a suggestion or insinuation appearing on parchment. Discussions on the agreement, therefore, broke down. Oslo now wanted to resuscitate the agreement and modify the wording, and I was asked to convey this to Delhi in my discussions in the Foreign Office. I had no illusions about corrupt practices in India, but as India's ambassador, I was not going to let a bilateral agreement paint India as a shady partner while Norway was bathed in the cleanest sunlight.

Norway was not a cricketing country, but it could not have missed the 2000 India–South Africa match-fixing scandal in which Mohammed Azharuddin and Ajay Jadeja were banned from cricket for life and five years, respectively,[3] or the 2001 Ketan Parekh securities scam, or the more recent stamp paper scam. Norway had certainly not missed reading reports of the 2002 Taj Heritage Corridor case where the then chief minister of Uttar Pradesh, Mayawati, and a minister in her government, Nasimuddin Siddiqui, had been charged with corruption.[4] This was a charge, not a conviction, and, for all one knew, Mayawati was not guilty. But the Taj Corridor project, intended to upgrade tourist facilities near the Taj Mahal, something all tourists would have benefited from, was now controversial. If India could not insulate its greatest heritage icon and one of the seven wonders of the world from the taint of corruption, what was left of its image as a protector of its heritage and a tourist destination? All this for India's missions abroad was deeply humiliating. And going to the Foreign Office meeting on the Indo-Norwegian environment agreement contract, I was in what may be called the dumps. Around this time, the local press in Norway—robustly independent though funded by law by the state—was reporting the Statoil corruption case about that company's misconduct and extensive use of bribery in Iran between 2002 and 2003 in order to secure lucrative oil contracts.[5] It was my unpleasant task to remind my Norwegian interlocutors that graft was not exclusive to any country, and contractual texts would have to place responsibility for ethical conduct equally on both contracting parties. But the overall effect of the episode was distasteful. That India should have to defend itself against the odour of corruption was hugely embarrassing.

The Mahatma came to the rescue of one's morale at this time, once again. Shyam Benegal's film *The Making of the Mahatma* was just out, and we arranged a screening to which the diplomatic corps was invited, with state secretary Widvey as Chief Guest. My diary entry:

> *MKG is such a miracle worker! There is a strong and spontaneous applause at the end of the film. The Chinese Ambassador holds my hand for a long time and describes the film as 'an experience.' The Pak Ambassador is thoughtful and asks: 'Sir, "Vande Mataram"*

ka matlab kya hai?' (the song having been sung powerfully in the film). The Japanese Ambassador asks if the baby mid-wifed by the young Gandhi in the film is my father (which it is). I ask the South African chargé d'affaires to sit next to the chief guest, as the film is as much about South Africa as it is about India, and to join me in the goodbye line-up. Kasturba is the true heroine of the film. Seated beside Tara, I cannot help feeling that inconsiderateness to the wife has not left the family, while nothing like MKG's compensating greatness mitigates it!

I had been wanting to call once again on Geir Lundestad, director of the Nobel Institute, who had spoken of the omission to give Gandhi the Nobel was an omission, a mistake and had left the scheme 'incomplete'. I did so on 3 March, and said to him that my call had nothing to do with the government or the embassy of India and that I was speaking entirely in my personal capacity. I had heard, I said, of the institute's idea of starting a Peace Centre on a large area with new architecture and landscape. Would a bust or an oil portrait of Gandhi made by Norwegian artists not be a fitting thing to display here? Lundestad, a historian and a man of decency and practicality, heard me very carefully, thoughtfully, as I continued: 'I have never been in favour of a Nobel for Gandhi posthumously and in any case, the Nobel rules preclude that. But if the institute were to commission a work of art on Gandhi for its new premises, a negative would become a positive. Lundestad said, 'I will reflect on this. It is a delicate matter. But it will, I know, add to our credibility. It will be a rectification.' I then said, 'As the lowest common denominator, there could be an engraving in bas relief with a quotation from Gandhi.'

By 20 March, war had broken out over Iraq. Bush, asserting the USA's superpower status as 'a given', had had his way with Blair's Britain following suit. No one was convinced that Saddam Hussein posed a threat to the US, that if he had nuclear, biological, chemical weapons in quantities the US alleges, this war was the only way to dismantle them. On the contrary, if he did possess them (as if the US and Israel did not), he would probably deploy them and hurt innocents. I was disappointed with the Indian position, which did not even name the US, and I lamented the lack of consensus in the UN Security Council.

Meanwhile, India and peace were to get a jolt around the same time. Armed militants from the Lashkar-e-Taiba came dressed in counterfeit military uniforms to Nadimarg in the Pulwama district of Kashmir between 11 p.m. and midnight and shot twenty-four Kashmiri Pandits. The victims were eleven men, eleven women, and two small boys, one of them two years old. They were lined up and shot and killed by the gunmen. India openly proclaimed Pakistan's complicity.[6] Sometime before this, I had accepted an invitation to dinner from Shahbaz, the Pakistan ambassador. Should I send word saying, in light of Nadimarg, I am sorry, I cannot attend? Perhaps I should have done that. But I went, telling myself that Shahbaz and I were small men, mere envoys of our governments, who have been civil to each other. Neither of us spoke of Nadimarg, confining ourselves to the big issue of the time—Iraq and the war Bush had unleashed. I ate frugally. But when the dessert came—a lovely creamy kheer made by Shahbaz himself—I could not look at it. I left the delicacy cold on the plate and hastened my departure. I doubt if my over-nuanced gesture was even noticed.

Neighbouring Iceland was covered by our mission in Oslo. In early April, Tara and I took a flight from Oslo to Reykjavik to formally present credentials to President Olafur Ragnar Grimsson (b. 1943). 'It's like landing on the moon,' she said, as the aircraft touched down at Keflavik airport. There was no natural vegetation in sight nor any buildings of note. We could see only small houses with corrugated roofing—ideal for an earthquake-prone area. The wife of the Indonesian ambassador-designate also travelling with us said, 'They look like Lego houses.' And we could see very, very few people. But gosh, what beauty lay in that austerity!

Elections to the country's parliament—Althingi—were due the next month, and the country's role in the Iraq war was at the heart of public discourse. Gunnar Gunnarsson, the permanent secretary of state, said to me in response to a question that the war will be a factor in the election. He said opinion polls showed that more than 80 per cent of the people of Iceland were against the war. This could affect the prospects of the present coalition. He did not ask me what Indian public opinion was about the war. If he had, I would not have had a clear answer.

Iceland's ties with the USA were—and have remained—closer than close, Keflavik serving as a US air base. The US had four F-15 jets stationed there. The Iraq war had burst upon the world; Reykjavik was technically in the war, if not at war. At my meeting with Minister Counsellor Olafsson, I asked if the US would need the Iceland government's permission if it intended to use its base in Iceland for purposes of its war. He did not answer my question directly.

A Cadillac from the president's house drove us to the incredibly modest white home of Iceland's head of state. When, in fact, the car slowed down in front of it, I thought it had developed a mechanical fault. But no, it had slowed down to turn into a house that had no compound walls, no guards.

Two liveried sentries stood at the door. I was conducted to a hall where President Grimsson was positioned to welcome me and receive the letters of credence, which he did warmly and conducted me to the study for a tete-a-tete. Tall, slim, and with a full head of white hair, he exuded confidence but no conceit. He straightaway came to the subject of India. He said he respected it as no other country in that region. And he said something that struck me as original. 'Now that the USA has instigated a war on Iraq in the pretext of installing a democracy there, the importance of the voice of the largest democracy in the word should be recognized and heard.' He was choosing his words in the full knowledge that I would be conveying them in a message to my principals immediately after the ceremony. President Grimsson then went on to bend protocol to host a reception for Tara and me, completely outside the requirements of the ceremony. He invited to it about a dozen India-related and India-interested persons. In free-flowing remarks made to me at the reception, he said he would like our rashtrapati to make a state visit to Iceland. And then, in a gesture reminiscent of me of President Mandela, spoke warmly of Sonia Gandhi. He had played host in Iceland to her, Manmohan Singh, and Natwar Singh when they visited Iceland in 2001—'a diplomatic risk' as he put it to me. His own state visit to India the previous year was a success in protocol terms, deepening his feelings for India. On my part, I acquainted him of the unremitting pattern of cross-border terrorism in India, a phenomenon which he understood instinctively.

Having heard of Iceland's geothermal reserves and of how naturally heated underground water was piped to homes at that welcome temperature, I was grateful to India's honorary consul in Reykjavik, John Arnalds, for taking me to the fascinating Science Institute of the University of Iceland where the professor of Chemistry Professor Bragi Arnason (known as 'Professor Hydrogen') gave us a presentation on the allied subject of Iceland's hydrogen project for vehicular fuelling. Back in Oslo, I rang and spoke to President Kalam about President Grimsson's keenness to invite him to Iceland and about Iceland's advances in hydrogen research. He listened most attentively. I tried to be as correct and precise in my use of scientific expressions as I could—no easy thing for a non-scientific person like me. I told him about the geothermal resources of Iceland and about the term 'geyser' having come from a place, Geysir, in Iceland. When I said that underground water in Iceland can be as hot as 150 degrees Celsius he was taken aback and asked, '150?' He then asked me a question that pleased me to no end: 'Is it true that Iceland has developed a method of earthquake prediction?' This was an interest that I had looked for in policy-makers, planners, administrators, and even geo-physicists in India and found wanting. I told him of their ability to predict volcanic eruptions and take steps for evacuating households in time.

The great advantage of having a scientific mind in Rashtrapati Bhavan became for me clear, for the first time. No one in the Delhi of that time other than President Kalam would have taken any interest in what I was conveying. In the summer of 2003, it was only President Kalam who had a ready ear for this matter of crucial importance for India—earthquake anticipation. I was encouraged thereby to take the matter of India-Iceland collaboration on seismic matters forward. I did not ask, or shall I more truthfully say, I did not have the courage to ask the person most popularly associated with India's underground nuclear tests if those tests could trigger earthquakes. After all, Pokhran was very near and, in tectonic terms, almost identical with the epicentre of the Kutch or Gujarat earthquake of 2001. I have no doubt if I had asked that question, President Kalam would have said something like 'Absolutely not' and added, 'there is no empirical data to establish any such connection'. This much I knew then and have known, generally, that bomb-positive minds will never deny such a connection, and bomb-negative ones will never cease affirming a possibility. But plain, simple common sense says if something like a nuclear bomb creates a crater that causes tremors, even if 'mild' and 'fleeting', the earth with all its built-up faults, fissures, and frustrations is not going to be a forgiving sponge for all time, absorbing in philosophic silence every hole punched in its innards as a matter of maternal duty to its human offspring. I was to have the chance to ask him a question somewhat later, but to that, I will come a little later.

A tense and time-consuming part of an ambassador's time is taken up by VIP visitors from home. Not a few among them regard an Indian Embassy as a tour operator, hotel-keeper, shopping helper, food guide, and, not often, food provider and, above all, emergency-solver. All of which being done as a matter of selfless service performed in true Bhagavad Gita spirit 'with no expectation as to results'. In June, I had a visit in Oslo by fifteen, no less, legislators from Uttar Pradesh of different parties led by the very erudite, soft-spoken, 'old-style' gentleman speaker of the UP assembly, Keshari Nath Tripathi (1934–2023). And going by past experience, I anticipated fifteen problems. Contrary to my apprehensions, the Hon'ble MLAs were the very epitome of guest etiquette and showed great interest in Norwegian matters, asking very pertinent questions. Among the MLAs was the leader of the opposition, Mohammed Azam Khan (b. 1948), who managed to leave a folder of his on the Scandinavian Airlines (SAS) flight out from Oslo to Stockholm. Though most civil when talking to me about the loss, he said to our mission in Stockholm that the mission in Oslo should have done more to try to locate the lost folder. I spoke to SAS customer service, who said the aircraft cleaners do not come under their supervision, but they would try to locate it. That was all we could do, but that was all that was needed to give our mission in Oslo a thumbs down for the Hon'ble MLA. Operational hazards do not spare embassies, legations, or chanceries anywhere. But they seem to delight in tormenting India's missions.

From another end of India's political spectrum came a most fascinating visitor—Harkishan Singh Surjeet (1916–2008), general secretary of the Communist Party of India (Marxist). At eighty-eight, he was totally alert, and what is more to the point, gave me a fascinating picture of Indian politics on the eve of general elections. My diary for 8 July 2003:

> *No tremor of hand, no forgetfulness, no garrulousness. He gives me on his own and quickly, over a cup of tea, a synopsis of the Indian political scene as he sees it: Communalism is the main question. What kind of country do we want? Secular or Hindutvic? For this, it is necessary for secular parties to come together. Congress under Sonia is coming round to the pre-election coalition idea. Manmohan Singh is in contact. An honest postman. Even Mulayam has been brought around. Jayalalithaa in Tamil Nadu remains unpredictable, but we have been assured through a reliable source that she will not go with BJP. Sharad Pawar has to keep up a show of independence to not lose his base in the sugar belt but is no longer harping on the 'foreigner' issue and has agreed to let it be till after the polls...*
>
> *On Sonia Gandhi: 'She has emerged as the only leader in the Congress. No one can challenge her. She is the chief. She sent Arjun Singh to me. I told him to advise her to come to terms with like-minded parties.'*
>
> *On LTTE: 'Unreliable. Want autonomy of the 1953 Kashmir type? Bad for Sri Lanka, bad for us.'*

I could not have got more from a professor of political science. I accompanied the veteran down the small flight of stairs from my first-floor office to the parking lot below. Surjeet nearly tripped while going down the stairs, and I just about held him back. And he was on his way to Sweden, Iceland, and Canada!

India's next general elections were now looming on the horizon. And anything done, even in the international sphere, would be done with election impact in view. And so when, on 25 July, Shahzad Rana, a Norwegian of Pakistani origin, came to our mission with Sunniva, his Norwegian wife, for a visa to go to Pune to adopt an Indian child, my office had to refer the case to me. If both the applicants had been Norwegians of Norwegian origin, the visa would have been granted after standard verification across the counter. But the man's Pakistani origin made the whole thing complicated. Asked by me to give some details of the child proposed to be adopted, the couple said it was a girl named Purnima. Thinking of all ramifications, I decided to grant the visa but gave a bit of unsolicited advice: do not change the child's name. Let her be Purnima always, and help her learn of the country of her origin in the fullness of time. They accepted this with grace.

If this couple had come exactly a month later, on 25 August, the mission's attitude would have been less objective and mine less sanctimonious. That day, as Tara and I were hosting West Bengal governor Viren Shah (1926–2013) and his wife, Anjani Shah, who were on a Scandinavian tour, to lunch at home, came a grim report from Mumbai. Two vicious bombs had gone off in parked taxis, killing 54 and injuring 244 people. One of the bomb explosions was at the Gateway of India, the other in the jewellery market called Zaveri Bazaar near the Mumba Devi temple. Both the bombs, detonated by remote control, had gone off during lunch hour. Pakistan-based LeT was blamed for the act seen as revenge for 'anti-Muslim' riots in India.[7] Viren bhai, of clear BJP persuasion but quintessentially a Mumbaikar, anger streaked on his elegant, bearded face, said: 'These people have to be taught the lesson of their lives. Until we do that, this will go on....'

In a bizarre mutuality of contradictions, Pakistan-originating terrorism was feeding its ideological opposite—Hindu majoritarianism. Terror-triggered polarization could well divide the Indian vote on Hindu–Muslim lines. Equally, any of the last-minute reasons I have mentioned could change all of that. The Indian voter votes by instincts that could be driven by deep-seated memories of hoary vintage or by provocations, evocations, and concoctions less than a few hours old.

With elections on his mind, cinema star and star politician Shatrughan Sinha (b. 1946) visited us in October 2003. He was coming as shipping minister with an IAS batchmate of mine, D. T. Joseph, who was secretary shipping. Six feet two, 'Shotgun' was charm, wit, jokes, ease of manner, personified. Mimicry was, I found, a side forte which illumined his own brand of serious political comment. What appealed to me most was his frank, open nature. At his meeting with the Norwegian Trade Council, the thespian minister started by making a few remarks and then, pointing to Joseph, said, 'I am only the banner; my secretary Joseph is the film'—a delightful gambit. But the same vein of humour crawled to the brink of a faux pas when, in an interview to the newspaper *Dagbladet*, intending to pay an honest compliment, he said, 'Norway has no pollution and almost no corruption.' Driving with the minister to see him off at the airport, the conversation turned to Jayaprakash Narayan, who Sinha said had inspired him. He says he was at the Rajghat ceremony in 1977 when the new Janata leaders took their vows to carry forward the legacy of the Mahatma. He said the air was rent with a 'gaganbhedi' (sky-piercing) slogan—Andhere ka ek prakash, Jayaprakash Jayaprakash!' (The only light in our darkness—Jayaprakash, Jayaprakash!)

Sinha was no intellectual, sure, but what a supple mind he had—connecting the past with the present politically, humorously and most important, wisely. Sinha did not say who he thought would be the winner in the ensuing elections, but he was not brimming with any over-confidence about the NDA's chances.

November brought to Oslo the visit of some music 'greats' from India—the santoor father-and-son geniuses from Jammu, Pandits Shivkumar (1938–2022) and Rahul Sharma (b. 1972), and Pandit Hariprasad Chaurasia (b. 1938). Music stars are also stars. Fans turn them from art to ego. The santoor wizard Shivkumar Sharma and his son Rahul Sharma, also a most skilled player on the santoor, came with the grace of Kashmir around them, and its delicate beauty. Panditji, who does not look sixty-five, told me his father, Uma Dutt Sharma, was director of music at AIR, Jammu, but working at AIR's station in Srinagar as well. Coming across this instrument—santoor or shata-tantri (hundred-stringed)—in the Valley where it was used for playing folk tunes, his father tasked his son, Shivkumar, to see if it could be adapted for classical music. Shivji worked at this for a while, reducing the strings to ninety-one, and became a maestro. Shivji and Rahul played at Jakobskirke (Kulturkirken Jakob), Oslo. They were creative elegance itself, barely touching the board with their walnut-wood plectra working like mothwing flutters. Their rendering of Vachaspati was, to use a cliched phrase, incredible. Their tabla player, Vijay Ghate (b. 1964), was something! No player of the tabla can avoid the influence of the wizard Zakir Hussain. Without Zakir's trademark shock of dangling curls, rolling shoulders, Loris-eyes, and pouting lips, Ghate nonetheless created an aura of his own. His climaxes drew repeated applause to, I felt, Shivji's slight annoyance.

But Ghate checked himself when he came on stage next with Hariprasad Chaurasia. Donning a rupee-coin sized tika and a silk blue kurta, Chaurasia was enchanting, but not before some side-action from him by way of asking the tanpura player (a Norwegian woman) to move back, his table player (Ghate, again) to move forward, and the person handling the sruti box to move sidewards. Panditji played a Malkauns with greater zest than feeling, the duet between Ghate on the tabla and Panditji on his flute showing the diaphragms sinking in defeat to the ascending fluidity of the reed. Ghate's humility-in-defeat and the master's grace-in-victory were a sight for the gods. Oslo was, briefly, in India's pocket, and we who had done nothing towards this artistic coup stepped out into the Oslo cold like proud peacocks, imagining crown-plumes riding high on our freezing foreheads. Without doubt the Norwegian audience had come to hear the duo with the haunting music of *The Call of the Valley* (1968) reverberating in their ears. That album of Hindustani classical music with Shivji (santoor), Hariji (flute), and Brij Bhushan Kabra (guitar) about a day in the life of a Kashmiri shepherd could not but resonate with them.

Indian art, like Gandhi, ever comes to India's aid abroad, whether on shivering snows or on simmering sands.

I could not but wonder, though, whether the Norwegian youth Christian Ostro had heard *The Call of the Valley* and been impelled by it in 1995 to go to Kashmir, a fatal step. The twenty-seven-year-old had come out to India after a manner of Europeans drawn to 'the East' and been captivated by Kerala, where he tried to learn the dance form Kathakali. And then decided to visit India's northern extremity before returning home. He was among six western tourists and their two guides kidnapped in the Anantnag district of Jammu and Kashmir on 4 July 1995 by as many as forty militants from the terror outfit Harkat-ul-Ansar. Their ostensible aim was securing the release of militants in India's custody, including the mastermind Masood Azhar. Christian was decapitated by his captors. Norway knew, as the world did, that the ghastly deed was the work of terrorist brutes, but the location being what it was—India—the Indian state remained, for Christian's family, accountable to it.[8] For it, *The Call of the Valley* was superseded by A Cry from the Valley. And the tragedy was we could not help. God has given serpents fangs, alligators teeth, and tigers claws. But He has given Man in his inscrutable wisdom a mind so depraved in its cleverness as to put the violence of the animal worlds in the shade. The lesser being's prey to appease hunger. We torture and kill not to survive but to satiate our base instincts.

Kashmir bled even as it crowned India. It wept even as it adorned India. 'If ever Paradise...' was ever so painful to speak about.

Towards the end of November 2003, a ceasefire along the Indo-Pak line in Kashmir was announced. Pakistan had taken the initiative this time, linking the ceasefire it announced to Eid-ul-Fitr. India had to respond in a positive spirit, and it did so. Norway's secretary general in the Foreign Office, Lindstrom, said to me somewhat tongue-in-cheek, 'This is not the first time you are having a ceasefire,' but added, 'I hope this time it stabilizes.' The same hope was expressed by the ambassadors of Egypt, Iran, and the PLO, whom I rang to greet on Eid. (I left a message for Shahbaz, the Pakistan ambassador.)

On 10 December, Nobel Day, Tara and I attended the Nobel Peace Prize ceremony. The winner, Shirin Ebadi of Iran (b. 1947), in her very singular speech, spoke out against the patriarchal regime in Iran and said that it was a male-dominated society, not Islam, that sanctioned discrimination against women. But the punch in her speech was reserved for the US. She said what I wished an Indian, particularly an Indian official, would have and could have said:

> Why is it that some decisions and resolutions of the UN Security Council are binding, while some other resolutions of the council have no binding force? Why is it that in the past 35 years, dozens of UN resolutions concerning the occupation of the Palestinian territories by the state of Israel have not been implemented promptly, yet, in the past 12 years, the state and people of Iraq, once on the recommendation of the Security Council, and the second time, in spite of UN Security Council opposition, were subjected to attack, military assault, economic sanctions, and, ultimately, military occupation?[9]

I could see US ambassador John D. Ong was not pleased. Einar Hagvaag, the correspondent of *Dagbladet* told me that when he asked Ong for a reaction to Ebadi's speech, the ambassador said, 'I have to leave' and exited. A business executive who had served as an employee of B. F. Goodrich Co., known for manufacturing rubber tyres of quality, Ong was a Reagan-time figure of importance in Washington, DC, and now represented the Bush regime in Oslo. He had an exaggerated sense of his own importance, that of the US embassy in Norway and of the US itself. He was the only ambassador in Oslo whose limousine went about beflagged. All other ambassadors flew their countries' flags only on three occasions—when they went to the palace, when they went to the opening of the Storting on its ceremonial opening by the king, and to the Nobel Prize event. On all other days and occasions, they rode in cars like anyone else. But Ambassador Ong's Lincoln had a flag-rod on either side of the bonnet.

On 31 December 2003, the last day of the year, I went per custom to the palace to sign the book of respectful greetings for Their Majesties—a fine diplomatic rite. My car bore the Indian national flag, and at the entrance to the palace, tourists and bystanders watched the flagged cars go in. They did not, I think, recognize the flags, mine included. Nevertheless, it felt good to watch the 'tiranga' catch the public eye. It was amazing how much that small rectangle of cloth could mean and did mean to me and to any

Indian. My diary for the day reads: '*I feel a sense of pride all of a sudden in representing all that lies behind that flag and I find myself signing the book in Hindi* (I add the name and title in English, of course).'

I have always thought that ministers and other official functionaries in India riding in cars with flags fluttering on their bonnets and red lights whirling on the roofs look very presumptuous and strangely undeserving of the honour. The funny thing is the occupants just do not realize that the arrangement does not enhance their dignity. It only makes them look comic in their sense of self-importance. I was to come to ride routinely in a flag car as governor of West Bengal not long thereafter. It was left to me to very often instruct the Raj Bhavan staff and traffic personnel, on an ad hoc basis, to furl the car flag as I went to certain places where the flag was not going to be appropriate—as, for instance, when I went out, as simply as I could, with no sirens blaring in the pilot car, for a haircut or for a quiet meal in a restaurant or to friends' homes or for medical consultations. But independent India has made its high functionaries dependent on these tokens of office for the fulfilment of their sense of self-importance. I believe only the president of India should have the privilege of flying the national flag on the presidential car and then again, only on certain specific occasions like at the president's swearing-in, the annual opening of Parliament, riding in state to the saluting base on Republic Day. Of course, when on state visits abroad, the car bearing the president of India must fly the national flag.

This step in self-restraint will also serve to bring an end to the pernicious practice of political party functionaries flying their party flags on their vehicles. When this is done by those belonging to the ruling party, the traffic police get intimidated, as does other vehicular traffic—clearly an undemocratic thing. The national flag, meant to symbolize the nation's pride in itself has come to signify in independent India the flag-flier's own pride and conceit.

2004
PRIME MINISTER VAJPAYEE SUBMITS HIS RESIGNATION

As the New Year began, I said to myself, I have seven more months to go in Oslo. And after that?

Tara and I had discussed our future and decided that it would be best if we settle down in retirement either in Bangalore, near where our daughter Divya was located or in Chennai, our traditional 'base'. I would need to supplement my pension with some earnings. N. Ram, a friend of years, now heading *The Hindu,* told me, at my instance, that I was most welcome to write for his newspaper after returning. When I said to Tara's uncle, M. A. S. Rajan, that I was thinking of retiring in Bangalore or Chennai and becoming a columnist, he said, 'I see a different picture in the crystal ball. Nobody will let you off so easily.' And then added, 'When are you becoming a governor?' My diary entries from the time: '*Little does he (Rajan) realize how irrelevant I am to the powers that be—neither a nuisance to be placated nor an asset to be utilized.*'

On 30 January, the anniversary of the Mahatma's assassination, I had an interesting visitor. Aamir Shaikh, a long-standing city councillor in Oslo, of Pakistani origin. His wife, an Afghan, was an MP. Shaikh said he wished to organize a Peace Concert to celebrate the recent India-Pakistan initiatives on ceasefire and peace. 'Duniya Hindustan-Pakistan ke jhagaron par hasti hai' (the world laughs at Hindustan-Pakistan squabbles), he said. They had got PM Bondevik and the foreign minister to accept the invitation. I could see that the Norwegian leaders had done so for reasons of vote-bank support no less than for reasons of peace in South Asia. Recommending my acceptance, I asked Delhi for instructions. I could not have gone without Delhi's nod.

On 6 February, Shahzad Rana, the Pakistani-origin Norwegian and Sunniva, his wife, who had come seeking an Indian visa to go to Pune to adopt an Indian child, came calling. And brought with them Purnima, the girl they had adopted. My suggestion to them to keep her name had been partially accepted. The child was named Nima Aurora. A sprightly two-year-old with a strong will of her own was perfectly at home with her parents and was at ease with her parents and their language. I was more than reassured about the rightness of my decision on their visa application when they said to me their experience with the orphanage in Pune had been good and that they hoped to go there again after some time to adopt another child, a sibling for Nima. Of such things is an ambassador's life fulfilled.

Pakistan was hovering around my thoughts in Oslo. On 9 February, Shireen Mehrunnisa Mazari, head of the Pakistan Institute of Strategic Studies, spoke at the Norwegian Institute of International Affairs (NUPI). Very different in her personality from her namesake, Shirin Ebadi, she gave a restrained and responsible presentation, which was an establishment affair, showing Pakistan to be a model of rectitude, politically, diplomatically and in every other way. I had to and did respond by way of a seven-minute intervention, which seemed to me to be effective enough from the point of view of India's stand on cross-border terrorism, among other matters. The distinguished economist, political scientist, teacher, international civil servant R. Sudarshan, was then serving in Oslo as Policy Advisor for Justice and Governance in the UNDP Oslo Governance Centre. He attended the meeting and later that day told Tara and me that I should be a Permanent Representative of India at the UN. I took that as a great compliment coming from him but also as something that was as good if not better than such an appointment because it made me chuffed and with no work having to be done,

Summer is mango season in India and Pakistan. And mangoes have their following the world over. For some reason, I could never fathom why India's soft diplomacy could not deliver choice mangoes in good shape and in good time to its missions abroad for distribution among the host population and its leaders. Pakistan, on the other hand, had perfected the art of having mangoes selected when they were just about ripe, not quite ripe, and packed in straw beds with great care and transported in superb cardboard or fibre containers to world capitals so as to arrive when they are just ready for the table. When Pakistani mangoes arrived in Oslo in the early summer of 2004, and their Indian equivalents did not, I was ashamed to feel a trifle jealous. Envy over mangoes! A poor emotion by any consideration. But then there it was—emotions as sour as our mangoes that had not arrived. And so, when at a diplomatic sit-down lunch at which Pakistani mangoes were served to the great satisfaction of Ambassador Shahbaz, I ate them in silence. But when Shahbaz went on at some length to extol Pakistani mangoes' flavour, succulence, and aroma as if the great fruit grew nowhere other than in his country, the petty peer in me could not but join the conversation. I said, 'These terrific mangoes live up to the generic scientific name of the fruit—*Mangifera indica*[*].' I stressed the indica to the limit of its acoustic

---

[*]India is the world's largest mango producer, accounting for 45 per cent of global mango

scope. It was now Shahbaz's turn to eat the fruit in silence.

India–Pakistan relations have another important non-political and non-diplomatic player: cricket. The willow and the red orb become intensely political weapons, cricket-watchers unrepentant chauvinists bringing into stadia and into distance watching platforms non-cricketing and un-cricketing crowds, who mutilate the spirit of the game. In early January 2004 came the announcement that India would tour Pakistan in March that year. Responding to India's security concerns in Pakistan, the Board of Control for Cricket in India sent a three-member team in February to assess the situation. The team reported that it was 'satisfied with the (security) measures being planned by Pakistan'. Delhi's 'go-ahead' followed, and India entered the Test series, never having won a Test on Pakistani soil, playing five One Day International matches and three Test matches against the Pakistan cricket team.

At the Tunisian National Day in Oslo on 22 March, when everything hung by India's performance at the fifth and final match in Lahore, India's cricket tour of Pakistan was the subject of some jollity in Pakistan ambassador Shahbaz's chat with me. Rahul and Priyanka Gandhi had gone to Pakistan to witness the first match in the series and been shown a lot of respect. On returning to India (while the cricket series was still on), Rahul had announced he would contest the forthcoming election in India from his father's seat. I said to Shahbaz that the izzat shown to Rahul in Pakistan may have bolstered the young man's self-confidence. 'Okay,' Shahbaz responded, 'blame it on us!' Shahbaz then said to me there was 'strong speculation that Prime Minister Vajpayee will come to Lahore to see it'. 'Okay,' I said to that, 'if you lose in Lahore, blame it on Vajpayee's presence!' India, captained by Sourav Ganguly and Rahul Dravid, went on to win the ODI series 3–2 and the Test series 2–1, with Virendra Sehwag being named Player of the Test series and Inzamam-ul-Haq of the ODI series.

SUM, the Centre for Development and the Environment at Oslo University had, on the same day as the Tunisian National Day, invited visiting Professor Joseph E. Schwartzberg (1928–2018) of the University of Minnesota to speak on the subject of which he is regarded an authority—Kashmir. I could see he had made a deep study of the physical, demographic, religious, linguistic, and cultural diversity of Kashmir, not to mention its politics, as a justice

---

production, with Uttar Pradesh and Andhra Pradesh being the biggest mango-growing states within India. The fruit has 500 known varieties in India, of which rare grove-specific types like Imampasand may be called royals, the Hapus or Alphonso an aristocrat, the Banganapalli, Chausa, Safeda, Neelam, Dussehri, Malgova, courtiers, and Langra the reigning democrat. The mango, *Mangifera indica*, is India's national fruit, as well as Pakistan's, while Bangladesh has chosen the jackfruit from the tree *Artocarpus heterophyllus* for the honour.

and peace activist and scholar of cartography. A solution, he said, has to be and can be found if there is political courage on both sides. It will be, he said, a hard sell for both sides, but a give-and-take is the only way out. He ruled out an independent Kashmir as an option, though he said, in his estimation, some 80 per cent of the valley's population wants it. In a private talk with me, Schwartzberg said the Chinese border in the Ladakh region and on the Tibet–Baltistan border was undelimited, much less demarcated during the British Raj, and the Chinese got from Pakistan what they did in 1962 only that which they had claimed all along, and not as a 'gift'. He also added, by way of anecdotage, that Zhou Enlai had offered to Krishna Menon accommodation in NEFA in our favour if we agreed to an adjustment in Aksai Chin, but Menon refused.

All this was not exactly 'news', and I felt (though I did not say so to the professor) that only a BJP government in India, led by someone with the patent transparency and earnestness for peace of Vajpayee can do the 'give-and-take' with Pakistan over Kashmir and with China over our two borders. No Congress government can ever attempt to do so for fear of right-wing rage, chauvinist consolidation, and ensuing electoral rout.

As May began, India was in election mode. Tara and I got our postal ballot papers for the New Delhi Lok Sabha constituency. Ajay Maken (b. 1964) was contesting the seat for the Congress against the veteran civil servant and sitting minister Jagmohan. Service loyalties should have made me vote for Jagmohan, but my sense of the importance of secularism in India was predominant, and for all my admiration for Atal Bihari Vajpayee, Jaswant Singh, and Yashwant Sinha, and my respect for Brajesh Mishra, on 5 May 2004, sitting in my office, I cast my vote for Maken. As, I believe, did Tara (I never asked her to vote one way or another). In my mind, I had no doubt whatsoever that we had voted for the losing party, that the NDA would come back to power, Vajpayee would be prime minister again, and, at the end of my two-year term in Oslo in September, I would be heading home. But by the time the process was over, one kept hearing that the NDA was faring badly and that anti-incumbency was hurting the Vajpayee government. Keshav Desiraju was keeping me telephonically updated.

My diary entry for 12 May 2004:

A day of lull for us, with polling over (except for Andhra) and counting not yet taken up. The non-NDA people will make a spectacle of themselves before they make a credible alternative if their numbers merit the President's consideration. The Communists can be expected to play a constructive and responsible role.

For 13 May:

Keshav rings early morning to tell me Congress and allies are leading in a majority of seats. As the day proceeds, the leads are consolidated, and by the evening, Prime Minister Vajpayee submits his resignation. The Left, with its largest tally ever of 60 + seats in the Lok Sabha, announces its support for a Congress-led government at the Centre. The Congress Working Committee meets to chalk out its strategy. A day to remember.

I was sad at the defeat of my minister, the EAM, Yashwant Sinha. I drafted later that day by fax, my resignation to the prime minister and the EAM. This was what propriety required of a political appointee.

18 May:

Keshav rings to tell me of an extraordinary development. Sonia Gandhi has declined to be PM! Congress workers go into hysteria outside her home. Congress MPs in a meeting in Central Hall plead with her but she is firm. She refers to her 'inner voice'. This is remarkable. Her renunciation makes her critics look like perverse pygmies, but she does not even name them. She only talks of her decision as being irreversible. She has added inches to her stature, has retrieved morality from politics, done what is absolutely right. It was her right to be a candidate for the election, to be elected MP, leader of the Congress Parliamentary Party. It was her duty not to exercise her right to be PM. She has made history.

19 May:

Manmohan Singh is emerging as her replacement. A better man, more decent, intelligent and honest is not to be found in Indian politics. But will the sycophancy of Congressmen, the craven family-worship and cultism of that party allow him to function as he—or any PM—should? Much will depend on Sonia's own attitude. Her renunciation of yesterday makes me feel that she will be consistent and conscientious enough to let Manmohan be PM in every sense of the term. But there will be endless tale-carryings, back-biting...

On 25 May, the new sixty-eight-strong council of ministers led by Manmohan Singh was sworn in. I sent three letters to Delhi—the first in Hindi, of course, of thanks to Atalji and to Yashwant Sinha. The third, containing my resignation, to the new PM. The new external affairs minister, Natwar

Singh, lost no time in sanctioning a year's extension in Oslo to 'buffer', he said to me, the time between now and my 'next appointment' under the new government.

My deeply cherished friend, V. K. Ramachandran, was then heading the Land Board in Kolkata. The installation of the new government having been completed, VKR and Chief Minister Buddhadeb Bhattacharjee discussed the succession to Viren Shah in the Raj Bhavan, Kolkata. VKR raised my name and in a meeting with the new prime minister, Buddhadeb proposed it to him, Manmohan Singh accepting the suggestion straightaway, saying to them, 'We also want that he be given such a responsibility.' Parallelly, Sitaram Yechury (1952–2024) had spoken to Sonia Gandhi with no negative response from her, even if there was no clear endorsement of the idea.

Sonia Gandhi clearly was supremely powerful and had the veto. Her nod meant assent, her silence, 'undecided'. I gathered she wanted me in one of the Nehru group of institutions rather than a Raj Bhavan. I also saw that 2006 being the next big election year in the states, Congress would want tried and tested party-hands in Raj Bhavans, not so-called independent-minded civil servants. It was a Nehru institution for me or nothing.

On 7 October, in a classically autumnal Oslo, I got a call from External Affairs Minister Natwar Singh. To my shame, I assumed it was about me. It was not. 'Who is the Nobel going to?' he asked. I recalled immediately the press speculation about Musharraf and Vajpayee sharing it. But I told Natwar, 'My gut feeling is we can discount that speculation. 'Us mein kuchh nahin hai...' (There is nothing to that...). 'Can I tell that to Mrs Gandhi?' he asked. 'Yes, you can,' I said. I said further to Natwar, '...If the organization that denied it to Gandhiji...' and he completed my sentence '...and to Jawaharlal Nehru and then give it to Musharraf and Vajpayee...When now it is we who are talking to them...' In the event, the prize went to the Kenyan environmentalist Wangari Maathai (1940–2011)—a relief!

Oslo in the autumn is incredible. Its reds and rusts, golds and yellows, among the greens are an enchantment. And on clear days, the sun filtering through the filigree of leaves is bewitching. On 12 October, at the Spanish National Day reception, I had a good conversation with Chen Naiqing, the Chinese ambassador. I told her how in the morning Tara and I gloried in the sun's illumination of the treetops around our garden and on the slowly swaying Chinese red flag. It was, I told her, a wonderful sight. Ambassador Chen was clearly happy to be told about this. She said to me by way, I imagine, of a reciprocal sentiment of warmth that she knew I had been very active in promoting Norway–India relations. I took that as a big compliment.

Later that same day, I wrote to Geir Lundestad, director of the Nobel Institute, about my suggestion made to him orally and entirely in my personal capacity that a suitable quote from Gandhi be inscribed on the walls of the institute or its new Peace Centre. I also sent him a quote from Gandhi: 'The way of peace is the way of truth,' from a 1920 article in *Young India*. That evening, the Nobel Institute organized a 'One Year After the Prize' lecture by Shirin Ebadi. I was seated between South African ambassador Ismail Coovadia and Pakistan ambassador Shahbaz. Talking of this and that, before the function began, Shahbaz said to me that before General Zia's plane was to take off at Bahawalpur, two baskets of that region's famed mangoes had been loaded on to the aircraft, unchecked. The bomb that ripped the plane, killing Zia, is believed by some to have been among the mangoes. When I said to Shahbaz that there are suggestions that Mossad may have been involved, no one, Shahbaz, said has been able to solve the mystery. Neither he nor I referred to the charge levelled in Pakistan at the time that India had a hand in it. I did tell Shahbaz of Zia's phone call one evening—1988, it must have been—when I was joint secretary to President R. Venkataraman. The president was not available when Zia rang, and the president of Pakistan then asked to be put through to 'the secretary' and was connected to me. Zia's warmth was something. He asked me if I was a Stephanian, and when I said I was, he, a Stephanian himself, promptly moved on to 'yar' terms. No admirer of Zia, Shahbaz then said to me, 'A Stephanian? Oh...You should have kept him there....'

Shirin Ebadi, in her speech, made no bones about her personal safety at the hands of the conservative ultras in Iran but said that if no one could force her to wear the hijab, no one could tell her to not wear it either. Fantastic, that was. Truly independent. Ebadi got a standing ovation, the Nobel Chairman Ole Mjos (1939–2013) saying in his vote of thanks, 'We thank you; we admire you, we are proud of you, we love you.' Lundestad, at the function, told me he had received my letter about the Gandhi quote. I did not reiterate the suggestion, as that would have been overdoing the good thing. But I wished the Nobel Institute would see this as a way of getting over its bad conscience about Gandhi's not getting the Nobel depute being nominated five times—in 1937, 1938, 1939, 1947, and 1948.

I was in Delhi mid-October 2004.

The Sonia Gandhi–Manmohan Singh equation was a power-equation requiring great tact and forbearance. Her renunciation was as genuine as any can be. But she also had a sense of responsibility, of accountability and of what is best described in Hindi as javabdehi—answerability. To whom? To her party and to her constituents, the millions of voters who had swept her party to power. Each state and, for that matter, every single parliamentary constituency has its own local reasons for voting as it does. But taken in the main, the 2004 election victory was that of the Congress party led by her. It was her victory. But she was also 'led'. She was in her own words, led by her inner voice, which said, 'You will not be prime minister.' It did not say to her, 'You will retreat to a cave of your own.'

By mid-November, I was informed that my going to Kolkata's Raj Bhavan now awaited only formalities. Tara was happy for me but full of anxieties. 'Promise me,' she said, 'you will not accept anything beyond this governorship.' Who was giving me anything beyond this? Even this, I told her, remained to be formalized. She was convinced Kolkata was coming through, altering our lifestyles, ending all privacy, imprisoning us in panoply and worse, in security cages. 'I am not realizing my dream,' she said, of the two of us living regular lives in Chennai and working from home—'you writing and I doing my nature stuff, instead of all this'. And then added, making me quite numb, 'I don't want to live in the shadow of guns.'

Rashtrapati Bhavan's communique issued on 3 December. Buddhadeb rang to say if I reached Kolkata on 14 December, I could be sworn in the same day. Former prime minister Gujral rang and said, 'I do not know how good it is for you; it is good for the country. Sometimes wisdom dawns here. Congratulations.' On 6 December, I called on His Majesty the king. He asked me if I had enjoyed Norway and said he was sorry to see me go. On 10 December, Chinese ambassador Chen gave us a farewell dinner, a most elegant affair. At a round table for fourteen, one person did all the serving of immaculately prepared and presented dishes with vegetarian options for Tara and me and the British ambassador Mariot Leslie, also vegetarian.

11 December brought news of MS amma's death in Chennai. A divinity had passed from our midst. The end, I was told, was peaceful. So we think. How do we know what she passed through? Keshav, dearest of friends, rang on 13 December, my last day in Oslo.' We are blessed,' he said, 'to have been alive at the same time as MS.' And then said, 'So your Oslo phase is coming to a close. Look after yourself and Tara. Greater things beckon.' I told him I know what really beckons me: Arunachala. Whatever else happens or does not, may my end be in Arunachala. Not necessarily at the site but in union with it.

Tara and I landed in Kolkata on 13 December 2004 in the morning. This was an exhilarating moment for me, a tense one for Tara—there were too many guns around. I held my euphoria concealed, she her apprehensions. Chief Minister Buddhadeb Bhattacharjee met us at the foot of the gangway, holding bouquets, one for each of us. A line-up of ministers greeted us, each one of them introduced to me by the chief minister. As Tara moved as inconspicuously as she could to a side, I 'took' a guard of honour with all its crisp automated elegance. We then drove largely in silence to Raj Bhavan, where, after a few hours of recovery from the intercontinental flight, I was sworn in.

Walking past a photograph of Rajaji, West Bengal's first governor, heading a gallery of photographs of former governors was a churn. I felt absurdly unworthy to follow in his line, a miscreant almost. But crossing the photographs of some other incumbents of the office, I recognized politicians and ex-civil servants of both the worthy and toadying kind, and I felt less unworthy.

I had sent word that I would like to take the prescribed oath in Bangla and had the relevant text with me, in Bangla and Devanagari characters, but acting chief Justice Ajoy Nath Ray (b. 1946) turned my suggestion down 'to avoid complications since there is no authorized Bangla version'. I felt rather disappointed at the time but later realized that it was just as well. What had prompted me to want to take the oaths in Bangla? Love of Bangla? Love of Bengal? Yes, of course, but also another love—of myself. I wanted to make an impact on my first appearance and be applauded as a Bangla-sevak (servant of Bengal) when I was, in reality, a servant of my own ego.

I was an appointee of the UPA and its ally, the CPI(M), both flawed by the indelible ink of political machinations, but I was expected to and was about to swear myself to being impartial. But I was also expected to and wanted to help the new alliance, which had been voted to power nationally and was in position in West Bengal. Help it how? By looking away from wrongdoing? Or being frank?

The acting chief justice was attired for the occasion. Custom had made Their Lordships in the Calcutta High Court adhere to wearing a big wig at ceremonials, and something in me rather enjoyed seeing him in one and a red coat, looking like a Raj character straight out of a Merchant–Ivory period film, while I in my khadi dhoti-kurta affair, looked like a good nationalist. The optics quite perfectly suited the occasion and fulfilled my fantasies. Jyoti babu's presence, in his trademark crisp dhoti, was a great honour. He spoke little, but whatever he said, he said from the core of 'wishing well'.

Buddhadeb introduced me, at the ceremony, with very special intent to Anil Biswas (1944–2006), general secretary of the CPI(M) in West Bengal. I had heard of him from V. K. Ramachandran as a determining figure in the state's political life and perhaps the chief minister's closest friend and confidant. I did not know then that the two were of the same age, both born in March 1944, just one day apart. That made both of them one year and a bit older than I was. Anil babu, too, spoke very few words, the sign of a good former journalist who observes better when silent. I could sense layers of political experience within him, compacted into a firmness of will that extended politics into sociology and ideology. I said to him I hoped we could meet regularly, to which he nodded in what was neither concurrence nor indifference. I did not know then, nor could anyone have, including Anil babu himself, that he would die in just over a year, of a brain haemorrhage, robbing West Bengal of a politician who knew the state's biochemistry like no one else, and robbing Buddhadeb of a thought-partner who could keep confidences, especially about their fellow comrades.

My sister Taru had come from Delhi to bless me, as had my brother Ramu, a rare thing, for he was not one to attend ceremonials and public events. 'Amar boro bon (my elder sister),' I said, introducing her to Buddhadeb, 'she met my late brother-in-law, Jyotiprasad Bhattacharjee, in Santiniketan.' 'I know', he said. 'Amar mejo bhai (my middle brother),' I said, introducing Ramu, 'he is a teacher of Philosophy and taught for a while in Santiniketan....' 'I know,' Buddha babu said again. The chief minister, I could see, had done his homework about his new governor.

I felt then what I was to feel throughout the rest of my five-year tenure in the state, which was that in Buddhadeb Bhattacharjee, I had a chief minister I could respect, trust, and work with in complete assurance. The sharp conflict between us over Nandigram was still over two years away, and although that was to vaporize the cordiality with which we started out, it would not in the slightest reduce my feelings for him. But even in the white heat of Nandigram, I understood that whatever negativity he felt towards me was driven by state-level political compulsions and ideology obligations. But more of that later.

VKR was away in Addis Ababa, but his scholar-wife, Madhura, and their precocious son, Madhav were there. 'They are waiting for you,' Buddhadeb told me, 'in the Prince of Wales's sitting room.' Tara and I met the mother and son in arrears of love, seeing them as we were after years.

The UPA-I government headed by Manmohan Singh, led by Congress helmed by Sonia Gandhi had, in West Bengal's CPI(M) government led by Buddhadeb in his early years as chief minister and in his second term in office, an ideal backup for the success of its coalition arrangement. My appointment was seen in Kolkata as that of a Left-leaning liberal former civil servant who enjoyed the concurrent confidence of both governments. I was a kind of coalition figure in myself, not a 'party' Congressman but of Congress lineage. Certainly not a communist of the classical or neo-classical kind, but one who had touched a seam of trust in communist leaders. My surname certainly stamped me, but it was generally known that I may be a Gandhi by reason of birth but was not a Gandhian in any hide-bound sense of the term, was not a teetotalling, khadi-wearing ascetic. I looked forward to living in the grand manor built in 1799 to imperial proportions. If my grandfather, a rishi of a man, could live there as governor, so could I, no rishi by any standards. An agreeable ambiguity surrounded my incumbency.

That complications awaited my time in West Bengal was not unknown to me. But it was more clearly known to others. At a function two days after my swearing-in, acting chief justice Ray said to me within earshot of Law Minister Nisith Adhikary (d. 2024) and many judges 'Any time, governor, that I can be of any help on any matter…one-to-one…I am available. I am saying this before witnesses….' I knew Adhikary would have noted this and would convey it verbatim to the CM. In offering 'help', the seniormost judge in the state was being honestly considerate. He knew that the CPI(M) had its own priorities while the law its own. Justice Ray hinting to me that I could have run-ins with the government on points of law was something I noted. But had the Congress also not played politics with the judiciary? Acting justice Ajoy Nath Ray happened to be a son of Justice Ajit Nath Ray (1912–2009), the controversial Supreme Court judge whom Indira Gandhi, during the national emergency, had elevated to the office of chief justice, superseding three judges. Did not the Congress regard Indira Gandhi as a Mother Goddess on par with, if not superior, to Justitia, who, blindfolded and holding the scales of justice, upholds its moral energy?

Determined to see only congruence and no dissonance between the centre and the state, I visited Delhi the same evening that Justice Ray had offered his 'help', and I had ruminated on the nature of the help I needed to take and to give. I was not disappointed. Home Minister Shivraj Patil (b. 1935), no favourite of the CPI(M) on account of his religiosity, told me that 'more than from other quarters, it is from Congress' that I may expect complaints and requests for redressal and that I should act 'fairly and do right without fear or favour'. The reason for this, he said, was, 'If it were otherwise, the prestige and credibility of the governor would suffer, and it would not be good for the image of the Congress either.' And he had helped me enormously.

I met Prime Minister Manmohan Singh that afternoon. He spoke about the pressures that would devolve on me. 'Congress persons have their grievances,' he said ruefully. 'They will come to you with their grievances.' And he was frank about the CPI(M). 'It has a certain way of doing things…. Even rigging elections….' I responded by saying, 'I will do the right and proper thing….' He then said, 'The chief minister is a very good and reasonable man,' a sentiment that I warmly endorsed. 'You enjoy the confidence of both the state and centre,' he said. He had sent, under clear party pressure dyed-in-the-wool Congress persons to various Raj Bhavans—Pratibha Patil (b. 1934) to Rajasthan, Balram Jakhar (1923–2016) to Madhya Pradesh, Nawal Kishore Sharma (1925–2012) to Gujarat, Buta Singh (1934–2021) to Bihar, Rameshwar Thakur (1925–2015) to Odisha, R. L. Bhatia (1920–2021) to Kerala, S. M. Krishna (1932–2024) to Maharashtra.

'You bring a fresh mind to the work,' the PM said to me and, humbling me with his trust, added: 'Do feel free to write to me on any national matter you want to. I would like you to take an interest in national issues beyond your state.' He was different from most others in his party, very different. Which is why Sonia Gandhi could rely on him. She had chosen him not because he was a good example of the typical Congressman who was loyal but because he was a good example of what the typical Congressman is not but was still loyal to the party and to its President.

Sonia Gandhi was frank. When I thanked her for having endorsed the idea of my appointment, she said, 'I wanted you to help with the institutions—IGNCA and Teen Murti. But when I learnt that you were keen on a governorship....' Keen. That word was scorching but scorchingly true. I was keen on it. That I was not tongue-out and mouth-watering keen, had not begged for it, did not take away the fact that I was keen. Some covet positions tail-waggingly, some do so looking solemn. I was the latter type. So, I did not contradict her but offered to assist with those institutions in any manner I was capable of. I suggested to her the highly cerebral historian Mukul Kesavan (b. 1957) for the Teen Murti job. She had heard of him, she said, and then described that place sadly as 'a dead house', and said, 'I am sure Panditji would not have wanted it to be so.... People like Sharada Prasadji are not available now, and that is why we were banking on you....' The Congress president did not say anything of her own on West Bengal's Congress party except to say when I referred to it, 'You know our people in the West Bengal Congress....' I was left to surmise the meaning of that quizzical comment, which I did. I mentioned no names. Nor did she. The only person discussed was Buddha babu. 'He has a more modern...more open mind than others,' she said very perceptively.

I came away from my call on her, aware that her heart was not in my appointment, but her civility had made her go along with what the chief minister and prime minister had both wanted. Former Presidents R. Venkataraman and K. R. Narayanan, my former bosses, were affection itself. 'You have succeeded Rajaji,' RV said to me.' Now, you must also go on to succeed me as president of India.' What could I say in response? I just shut my eyes and did a namaskar. I was undeserving of any such honour. And how Tara would dislike the constrictive and life-destroying trappings of that guns-enclosed position! RV's wife, Janaki Venkataraman, came into the room just then, addressing me as 'Governor ayya!' and, holding my hands in hers, said, 'But, for us, you will be our son only.'

KRN said, 'Governorship is not difficult as such, but West Bengal is a tricky state.' He was alluding to the incipient tensions between the alliance partners and ruminated: 'If Congress had let Jyoti babu become prime minister (in 1998), the Congress–CPI(M) relations would have matured.'

I should, in all propriety and basic good manners, have called on P. V. Narasimha Rao but failed to. He had been ill, making my omission that much more unforgivable. And so, when on 23 December I heard of his having passed away, I cursed my callousness. I owed my first major appointment—high commissioner to South Africa—to him. If it had not been for his putting me on that high road, I would not have been sitting under the high dome of Kolkata's Raj Bhavan. He had placed me in that league. I had received from him, on my appointment to Kolkata a lovely letter of felicitations from him. Fie, fie! It was several years later that I gathered from Vinay Sitapati's biography of the big man that he had suffered physically and psychologically towards the end, especially when he lay dying in hospital. We are not a grateful people. We are a forgetful people. And I had proved myself to be another shining example of the ilk.

India faced two pulls—that of poverty, which demanded aggressive interventions, and that of social stagnation, which required equally radical measures. Because these two were not easy to deliver for any government, I felt left-of-centre policies pursued by Congress and its allies had over the decades to resort to shamelessly populist theatrics of the Indira Gandhi type, climaxing in the appalling national Emergency of 1975–77. And likewise, the same compulsion made BJP governments and their allies palliate mass grievances on the economic and social fronts by appeals to religious sentiment. The reality of immiseration and social decadence had made independent India the stage for political histrionics, which were a variant of our age-old fascination for pageantry, theatrics, and melodrama.

Would the honest-to-goodness Manmohan Singh and the good and honest Buddhadeb Bhattacharjee be able to rescue India from the intoxicating influence of carefully choreographed obfuscating poverty and backwardness? This was the thought in my mind when a shock from another veracity shook India—that of nature.

I had been through several rounds of discussions in Norway with geologists and seismologists on the threats faced by India from the earth's crust. And had also interiorized some of the data given to me there on tsunamis. But like all of my fellow citizens, I was unprepared for what hit our southern coasts on 26 December. News of Car Nicobar having gone underwater and of the Marina beach in Chennai being lashed as never before was traumatizing. Tara and I rang family and friends and were comforted to learn they were safe. Tara told me, as only she could have, that after I had finished being dazed and traumatized, I could perhaps ring Buddha babu to check what West Bengal (which had just about escaped being lashed) could do to help areas in distress. West Bengal was a cash-strapped state, and it was no easy thing for the chief minister to rush aid from the state's own condition of want. But he told me the following day he was sending Rs 78 lakh worth of materials—tarpaulins, clothes, and foodgrains to the Andamans. Buddha babu was not, on the face of things, a sentimental man, and I would have been the last person to say 'Bless you' to my Marxist chief minister, but in the 'Thank you for doing what you are doing' that I said to him I did pack in all the blessings I could muster.

Amitav Ghosh (b. 1956), whose fame as a novelist and historian was to rise to immense heights shortly thereafter, was already being lauded for his great novel *The Hungry Tide* that had appeared earlier that year. Amitav was in Kolkata when the tsunami struck the Sunderbans—the scene and site of Amitav's novel. Amitav describes with a sharpness of evocation the destructive power of a cyclone affecting the Sunderbans and giving an indifferent people a lesson in nature's actions. The tsunami was an uncanny and this time real enactment of what Amitav had described in *The Hungry Tide* and I rang him to ask how he could be so prescient.

On 27 December, I read of a woman being stripped and tied to a tree at Haripal, a village in Hooghly district. This was utterly disgusting, and I told Jasodhara Bagchi, chair of the West Bengal Commission for Women, to investigate it. This cruel rite of humiliation and degradation of women by male brutes is widespread in India. And is specifically directed at Dalit women. Crimes against women in West Bengal were less than they were in many Indian states, but they were not negligible, and that was not how it should be in the province of Raja Rammohun Roy, Ishwar Chandra Vidyasagar, and Swami Vivekananda.

2005
RAJ BHAVAN, KOLKATA

The new year began badly with the sudden death of the NSA J. N. Dixit. This was a terrible loss for the PM, who trusted Dixit implicitly and needed his blunt advice, which was invaluable. And I lost in him a true friend and guide. Dixit knew his strength and could be merciless with cowards, crooks, and careerists. But he also had it in him to be stunningly helpful to people from all divisions and classes of society, the recipients of his kindness never forgetting their debt. But there were to be those who had been groomed by him, who owed everything to him, doing a U-turn in loyalties. This is human nature, but in India, the natural pattern has been perfected way beyond its original energy. I was relieved that Dixit's position was taken by his deputy, M. K. Narayanan (b. 1934), whose sharp mind had been further sharpened by a nimble alertness that observed and absorbed more than was apparent. And for me, again, a personal satisfaction, for I had known him for decades and admired him. Dixit was a diplomat with a cop's instincts; MKN, a cop with a diplomat's insights.

On 11 and 12 January, we had a visit by the PM and his most highly observant and, therefore, highly aware wife, Gursharan Kaur. Governors value visits by presidents and prime ministers for one reason more than others: they get a chance to motor with the VVIP, as per protocol, and talk to them uninterruptedly and for longish durations, one-to-one. The journeys to and from the airport are especially valuable. There is, of course, the very distinct possibility of the cars being bugged and the conversations being taped or tapped by agencies one may guess at but not be sure of. With my brief stints in our missions abroad, I had become aware of this risk but never allowed it to come in the way of my conversations with visiting VVIPs—'Let them listen.... I am not saying anything subversive or unbecoming,' was my attitude.

The prime minister had his stock of official engagements, but over a meal which had just him and Gursharanji, Tara, and me, he asked: 'Gopal, what do we do about Pakistan?' I was not quite prepared for this and so gave him a somewhat uncogent if spontaneous answer: 'Sir, perhaps history expects you to break the Gordian knot.' He then asked a couple of more questions on how this rather romantic picture of mine could be operationalized and listened to my tentative suggestions with a seriousness that humbled me.

The meal was a one-hour affair, simple in every way. The advisory we got on the Singhs' dietary preferences was a model of simplicity, unlike those

Raj Bhavans and embassies are used to, complicating matters beyond belief on what may or may not be served. They ate un-fussily, appreciatively and with great courtesy being shown to the serving staff apart from us, the host couple. Tara and I were relieved but not surprised.

What I took away from that visit was the call they paid on Jyoti babu; I motoring with the PM and Gursharanji with Tara. Congress–CPI(M) links in the running of the UPA government were at the top of their minds. As befitting their ages, the PM asked Jyoti babu for 'advice to the UPA government'. 'We, both of us,' Jyoti babu said to PM, 'have to be patient.' PM agreed. The two parties must stay together, Jyoti babu said, 'because the BJP is not dead'. This was the first time that I heard BJP being spoken of in the entire trip of the PM. He never once referred to the party that his party had ousted or the former PM Vajpayee. There is something called culture.

On the return drive to the airport, PM said to me, 'Your appointment has been one of the most fulfilling for me....' I was, of course, chuffed by this—who would not be? But more than that, I realized that he was telling me that he had ensured that something he wanted had been done, that his will had prevailed over that of the party, and this, in the state of affairs then prevailing, was no simple thing. He may have been an accidental prime minister and may be constrained by both the dharma of coalitions and the karma of Congressism, but he was Manmohan Singh—a gold coin in a heap of much-thumbed lead. And the pile knew it.

On 24 January, Tara and I invited Jyoti babu over with two young admirers of his, both industrialists. I had been told that one of them had said 'somewhere' that 'the governor is our man'—a description that revolted me. And so, when seeing the young man off, I told him of what I had heard and that if true, he should know that I was nobody's man. He said he had never said any such thing and may have only said he knew me and that his simple statement had been enlarged and distorted into what was communicated to me. I accepted the explanation at once.

Darjeeling is West Bengal's crown, and I took an early opportunity with Tara to visit it, our children accompanying us. The beauty of the Himalaya there and its own calm made Darjeeling and its environs heavenly. A day after we reached, staying in the loveliest of Raj Bhavans anywhere, our children woke us at 6.30 in the morning saying the Kangchenjunga was out of the mist in all its glory. Tara and I rushed out to the terrace to see its resplendence. '*Nothing like it in Europe or anywhere,*' I wrote in my diary. '*With dawn's gold shimmering on the mountain's silver slopes, it is a jewel.*' Nepal and India may be said to share the glory of the mountain—the third tallest in the world—with three of its five peaks being directly on the

Nepal–India (Sikkim) border, giving it an Indian 'side' and a Nepali one.

But Darjeeling's politics was far from resplendent. Subhash Ghising, who had led the Gorkhaland movement in the 1980s and was now chairman of the Darjeeling Gorkha Hill Council, regarded himself as king of the area. He was nothing of the kind, but he was something nonetheless. What was that 'something'? A local leader who wanted to be left alone to do as he liked with the region, but also a politician who did not want to and never tried to weaken Darjeeling's ties with the Republic of India. He was, to that extent, very different from certain other leaders of the Northeast who had dreamt of 'separation' before realizing that their dream was a waste of everyone's time. Ghising was, however, no democrat and brooked no rival. He was stubbornly refusing to have elections to the council, due to be held. Buddha babu urged me to impress upon Ghising the need for elections.

When the Gorkha leader called on me, I saw at once that he had one of the sharpest minds that I had encountered. Two beady eyes, restless as marbles, reflected his mind. Choosing to speak in Hindi but lapsing into effective English from time to time, he painted a horror story about the role of the ISI in Nepal. He said ISI planned to dethrone the king of Nepal via Prachanda*, then dethrone Prachanda and gain control of Nepal for Islamabad and Beijing, and do a repeat of this in Bhutan and Sikkim as well. Darjeeling, in such a situation, he said would be unimaginably critical to India. The situation is a 'burning' one; he said elections to the council should not be held and that he must continue to be chairman of the council in an open-ended way. Over another meeting, I said to him he was a patriot, recognized and valued by India as such. He has not encouraged separatism, has not encouraged a Cyprus-like Enosis sentiment in the Gorkhas. But he must also see that he does not lose out as one who failed democracy in Darjeeling. Zidd (stubbornness) I said to him in Hindi was not good. At this, he smiled. Continuing, when I said, 'And so, elections....' he interrupted me, 'those are secondary.' I said, 'They may not be of the same level as principles like India's security and sovereignty and Gorkha pride, but still, even though procedural, they are fundamental, not secondary, in a democracy.' He did not contradict me. Buddha babu, who was going to parley with Ghising in the national capital, was strengthened, I think, by this. But Ghising's story was to take twists and turns.

I could not lose myself in Darjeeling's politics to the neglect of Darjeeling's lifeline, tea. I was shocked to learn from Rajah Banerjee,† owner of the

---

*Pushpa Kamal Dahal (b. 1954), alias Prachanda (meaning 'fierce'), thrice prime minister of Nepal.

†Author and horse-rider, Rajah or Swaraj Kumar Banerjee (b. 1947) is reputed to have sold the most expensive tea ever in a tea auction.

Makaibari organic tea estate, that while Darjeeling produced 10 million tons of tea, it sold 40 million tons! How, I asked, is that possible? This was because, he said, Germany, the principal importer of Darjeeling tea, blends it skilfully and sells it in its multiplied quantities as Darjeeling tea—a practice he said must be challenged in WTO.[1] Makaibari tea was exceptional, even among high-grown varieties. Makaibari 'Darjeeling' tea sells at a record price of around Rs 1.12 lakh per kg, and the Makaibari tea estate is recognized as the producer of one of the most expensive teas in India. Tea is liquid gold. And is savoured by the rich and poor alike, only in sips that taste different in their different origins. And so, its monetary value is a riddle in a way solid gold's is not. Whoever owns the estate must earn its profits, even as he must bear its losses. Fair enough. But are the profits, when they accrue, reasonable, or do they go through the roof? And who taxes those? The centre or the state concerned? And what of the plantation workers? Are they paid anything like a wage that matches the owners' income? These questions would have been dismissed by plantation owners during the British Raj, even if they had been asked. But now they are not asked with the impatient insistence they call for.

For most visitors to Darjeeling, including and especially those from other parts of West Bengal, Darjeeling is a resort, a hilly 'change', a piece of the Himalaya to escape to in the summer. That its people have a life of their own, a perspective of the rest of their country and fellow citizens we do not realize. On my walks around town, I would pass a small kiosk that sold trifles, including, alas, snacks in non-biodegradable wrapping. The owners' little son, Swayam, as he was called, became a friend, following me with laughter in his eyes and voice for a little distance. 'How are you?' he would say and answer the question himself: 'Fine, thank you.' This banter became a regular feature, and I would look forward to Swayam's greeting each time I stepped out, praying inwardly that Swayam should grow up into a 'fine, thank you' resident of Darjeeling, registered voter in West Bengal and citizen of India. Was that asking for too much?

The 'local' residents of Darjeeling, I noticed, were better dressed than others in the state. I asked, in confidence, a Gorkha boy who was speaking to me frankly about his poor circumstances if the jacket he was wearing had cost him a great deal. He smiled and said (in Hindi, of course), 'Sir, don't get the impression that we kids necessarily own what we are wearing. When going out, we borrow each other's clothes and try to look decently clothed.... We have a lending library of clothes....' This was funny in its own very sad way, but what another boy told me introduced me to a grim reality of the hill district and, I realized, of the whole of our Northeast. He spoke, choking, of his brother being a drug addict. As he spoke, I thought of the 1971 Hindi film that had gripped me—*Hare Rama Hare Krishna*, in which Zeenat Aman (b. 1951) plays the role of a drug addict and her brother played by Dev Anand (1923–2011) goes looking for her in Kathmandu to which place she has moved with a bunch of hippies. That film, with its eponymous title song, came vividly to life as I heard this young Gorkha speak of his brother lost to drugs and worse.

Substance abuse is imperilling independent India's youth who, either due to poverty or ironically due to an excess of wealth and leisure, are chortling into that pit. There has been nothing near the nationwide movement against this sickness that we need to rid our future of its menace. What, I said to myself, does it matter if elections to the Gorkha Council are held on time or not? What does it matter if Darjeeling remains a district of West Bengal or not, if its youth are going to slide into a drunken or drugged daze?

Two youths, luckily for my equilibrium, showed me a different, happy picture. Tara and I were walking down to Lebang, where the 6th Grenadiers are located, when she spotted some rare birds from the species—sibia and yuhina—which delighted her. And a little further on, we came across two handsome youths carrying on their shoulders dhunkis, the wooden mattress fluffer that makes the most beautiful twangy sound when used. I asked them where they were from, for they looked like they did not belong to these hills. They were from Chhapra in Bihar, they said; their names were Nizamuddin and Firoz. I just described them as handsome. But that is an understatement. They were uncommonly good-looking and reminded me of the great song in Kamod about Ram and Lakshman that Pandit Kumar Gandharva (1924–92) used to sing—'Muni padakamal bandi dou bhrata....' They said they walked over large areas in the hills where razais (quilts) are used in order to fluff them, charging Rs 85 for doing an old razai and Rs 550 for making a new one. These two were migrant workers, but not of the kind that wander unemployed looking for any job, but skilled men with a skill to use and create work from. May your tribe increase! I said to them wordlessly. And may you stay safe in times where being not local is a vulnerability and being of a community like yours can become a different challenge. Dou bhrata muni...is a dhun, and here, with Nizamuddin and Firoz, it joined a dhun that came from a dhunki.

Back in Kolkata in time for the opening of the West Bengal assembly—my first experience of the procedure—I went through the draft of the address that I had to give. As per custom, this speech is intoned by the governor, but the words are the government's, not his. Just as in the case of the president's speech at the opening of parliament. It was a draft I had no problems with, reciting as it did the government's achievements over the foregoing year and indicating its plans for the coming weeks and months. But I noticed a paragraph that mentioned Pakistan and ISI in it. I felt this foray into external affairs was not called for in the governor's address. I rang Buddha babu to suggest this, and he immediately saw the point and agreed to delete the paragraph. But when I saw the printed version, I noticed the portion had not been deleted. I rang Buddha babu again, and to his credit, he said, 'I am to blame' and agreed to make the deletion even at that late stage—a handsome response becoming of a big man.

Assembly Speaker Hashim Halim (1935–2015) called on me, as custom required, ahead of the opening. A communist and party member for decades, Halim had been speaker since 1982 and saw at least five governors through assembly opening ceremonies. He was more than frank. He said many of the MLAs were 'loafers' who may stoop to anything, including throwing eggs, tomatoes, and stones at the governor, and that I should be prepared. I wouldn't say I liked his description of the MLAs, but said I was ready for some unruliness. He then related the experience of Governor Nurul Hasan, the portly scholar who had been governor of West Bengal from 1986 to 1989 and then again from 1990 to 1993. Halim sahib said an MLA moved up to Governor Hasan as he was entering the hall, snatched a pen from the governor's achkan pocket, and jabbed it into his tummy. I was not going to show any emotion at this revelation and did not.

On the day of the opening, I noticed that the printed text had indeed been attended to as I had wanted, but in a way that made the matter worse. Instead of having the booklets reprinted, pieces of paper had been pasted over the para meant to be deleted in each copy, drawing instant attention to it! It was too late for me to react, and of course, as Halim sahib predicted, a dozen or so Trinamool MLAs, all of them then in the opposition, raised slogans and placards as I entered. I read out the speech regardless and did not take the noisiness personally. Buddha babu later told me over the phone to ignore this. 'I will handle this if it comes up in the assembly; lay the full facts on the table.' Very responsible of him this was. I have related this experience here to illustrate the fact that governors can take up any doubts and misgivings they have over the wording and contents of the legislative address to be made by them, and chief ministers, if they are of the reasonable and pragmatic mindset of Buddha babu will take the governors' thinking in the right spirit. The coarsening of governor–CM relations has had its impact on the governor's address to the assembly in recent years—a most regrettable and avoidable thing.

2006
RAJ BHAVAN, PATNA

Bihar had an interesting governor at this time, Sardar Buta Singh. I had interacted with him at the time when I was secretary to President Narayanan, and issues pertaining to the formation of government were occupying the president's mind. Buta Singh was then out of office, but rightly prided himself on his expertise in matters constitutional, having been home minister under Prime Minister Rajiv Gandhi and at the heart of governments for decades. I respected his acumen and his articulation.

Buta Singh's Dalit background enhanced my respect for him and his accomplishments. As governor of Bihar, at this point, he had become controversial for his very patent bias against Nitish Kumar, who had, with BJP MLAs backing him, staked a claim to chief ministership. Governor Buta Singh clearly wanted Lalu Prasad's team to hold that office. But Nitish Kumar had the numbers, and there was absolutely no way he could have been kept from becoming chief minister. But the veteran Congressman in Raj Bhavan demurred. He claimed that 'horse-trading' of MLAs was taking place and recommended the dissolution of the house and the promulgation of the President's Rule.

The union cabinet accepted the recommendation—a crassly partisan decision which the prime minister must have been pressured to sign—and sent the papers to President Kalam, then on a state visit to Russia to sign.[1] Reluctantly, it is said, he signed it. The matter was taken to the Supreme Court, which quashed the promulgation and ruled in favour of Nitish Kumar, with Buta Singh being obliged to resign. I was told that I would be acting as governor of Bihar till such time as a substantive replacement to Buta Singh was identified and appointed.

Chief Minister Nitish Kumar and his cabinet, all of them singularly correct and cordial, gave me, a UPA appointee, a movingly warm welcome. They could have been just correct. But they went beyond, including the BJP ministers in the cabinet.

I told Nitish babu at the airport that I wished to visit JP's home and pay my respects to his memory as soon as possible. Visiting JP's house, which was also associated with his late wife Prabhavati for the work she did from there for khadi spinning and weaving by poor and unemployed women, was, to put it in a cliché, a pilgrimage. The room where he died was spartan, but not in some monastic sense. It was bereft of any accoutrements of well-to-do-ness because it was a middle-class home with no pretensions either to a 'wannabe' upper class or an ashramic simplicity. It was utterly real, utterly genuine. It was like JP was, simply true.

Nitish babu was astute, urbane, and relaxed. Working with him from January to June was a singular pleasure. There was more than one occasion when I returned an ordinance for his reconsideration. There are ways and ways in which a governor can return an ordinance he is uncomfortable with. He can do so with hauteur. He can do so with civility. Nitish babu accepted my suggestions on ordinances every time without fuss. One was tricky as it involved disabling Lalu Prasadji from heading the Bihar Sports Association. The vice-like grip of politicians on sports bodies is an old plague in India. Politicians want to tap into the youth base of those associations and, of course, into the finances they generate. Nitish babu agreed with me that the reform need not be hustled through an ordinance that was meant for contingencies of an urgent 'can't wait' nature. This was big of the man.

Opening the inaugural session of the Bihar assembly with him as leader was, for me, a great experience. The draft speech in excellent Hindi was a pleasure to read. There was not a single interruption. Rabri Devi, as leader of the opposition, heard me with attention and great personal dignity. When Nitish babu felicitated me on this, I said to him that I did not deserve the credit for the speech was not mine, it was his. Nitish babu's answer disarmed me. He said the smooth passage of the speech was due to what he described as my 'vyaktitva' (personality). I knew, of course, that there was another reason: they were giving a certain respect to me as the Mahatma's grandson. That was the long and short of it.

March is a problematic month in the world of superstitions, and it lived up to its reputation in so far as the UPA was concerned. Strains between the Congress and its important partner, the Left, emerged this month over the agreement for cooperation signed by Prime Minister Manmohan Singh and President George W. Bush for India–USA nuclear interaction for civilian purposes. This was still 'early days' as the US Congress had to consider and approve it—something that could not be taken for granted. At our Indian end, too, the going was not smooth. NGOs sceptical of nuclear activity in India and all those who were suspicious of US intentions, which prominently included the Left, opposed the deal instinctively. The point being made by the Left was: will India be able to safeguard its sovereignty against US demands for guarantees? And hints were thrown for a reconsideration of support for the Congress-led coalition. President Kalam was solidly for the deal. Manmohan Singh felt confident enough to go ahead with the idea. He was committed to it as the country had not seen him dedicated to anything else. An energy surge could be discerned in him when he spoke of the proposed agreement.

He was prepared to stake the stability of his government on the issue—a serious position that was going to be put to actual test not long thereafter. My views in the matter were of sub-zero importance. I saw the point of the deal, that nuclear energy was a renewable form of energy, after all, and if India were to be unshackled from nuclear energy use restrictions imposed after its nuclear tests, it could use that nuclear energy to replace its dependence on non-renewable fuels. I could see that. Still, my personal worry was that the 'safeguards' and 'guarantees' that Manmohan Singh could be trusted to honour might be flouted by a future government. In this, I was being like hard critics of the deal in the US Congress. Bush explained in a very Bush way the importance of the energy concord: 'Listen, the whole purpose of the advanced energy initiative is to end our dependence on oil, and as we develop technologies that will enable us to do so, we look forward to working with India so we can achieve the same objectives. Dependency upon fossil fuels causes particularly during times of shortage, prices to rise in both our countries. And it's in our interests that we share technologies to move away from the era of fossil fuels...It's not an easy job for the prime minister to achieve this agreement, I understand. It's not easy for the American president to achieve this agreement. But it's a necessary agreement. It's one that will help both our peoples.'[2] This made sense to me, and I began to see more clearly the pith and purpose of the imminent deal.

But when Manmohan Singh went on to say: 'I have met the president a number of times, and on each occasion, I have admired his vision, his resolve, and his commitment to strengthening our bilateral relations,' I thought he was overdoing the good host's role. And I squirmed when Bush said: 'And, oh, by the way, Mr Prime Minister, the United States is looking forward to eating Indian mangoes.'

Bush's visit sharpened the terrorism threat. On the eve of his arrival, Bush was 'presented' with two terror strikes in Pakistan—one outside the US Consulate in Karachi and another outside the Marriott Hotel. On 7 March, Varanasi felt the scourge with bombs leaving fifteen dead and more than fifty injured. I got through to Buddha babu immediately to ask him to alert the state's security apparatus. He had not heard of the outrage but swung alerted security at once, as did Nitish babu in Patna when I spoke to him, too.

Assembly elections were held in West Bengal in five phases between 17 April and 8 May. The votes were counted three days later, on 11 May 2006, with all the results out by the end of that day.

The Left Front won the election with an overwhelming majority. It had been ruling the state of West Bengal for the last three decades. Buddha babu was set to lead the world's longest-running democratically elected Communist government for a second time. It was a joy to swear his ministry in, with Jyoti babu attending. I was a little uncomfortable with the request that a pandal be erected in the Raj Bhavan lawns for the ceremony instead of it being held in the Throne Room, as per custom. And the cost—if I remember right, of Rs 11 lakhs—seemed to me unethical, but it was Buddha babu's day, and I decided to say nothing except to suggest that the pandal not be dismantled immediately after the ceremony but kept going for a free entry recital that evening of Hindustani music by Ustad Rashid Khan (1968–2024). The maestro excelled himself, singing at my request a Tilak Kamod mesmerically.

Mamata Banerjee was not going to be an easy loser, though.

She spotted an opportunity in the disaffection created by the state government's acquisition under the Land Acquisition Act of nearly 1,000 acres in Singur, for the Nano or small car project of the Tatas. This was an industrial model project of the government, and it wanted to give prime land located along a highway to the company. But the point is that the Act is meant for acquiring lands for a public purpose, not for a private company's profit-making venture, and was difficult to contest. She went on a warpath, demanding that lands acquired from them be returned to them. On being prevented from entering the venue, she, with many of her MLAs, stormed into the assembly. The rampaging MLAs brought disgrace to the solemn house by their wanton violence to the assembly's property, as Buddha babu, with great restraint, watched the event in stony silence.

Mamata started towards the end of December a fast in solidarity with the 'unwilling' farmers. President Kalam, on a visit to Kolkata at that very time, asked both me and Buddha babu if something could not be done to help Mamata end her fast and bring the dispute to an amicable end. Medha Patkar (b. 1954), the stormy petrel, had meanwhile arrived and given President Kalam a vivid account of the protesters' feelings and the government's and Tatas' lack of feelings.

It was decided that I should go to the fasting leader's venue and ask her to end her fast as the chief minister was ready to discuss the whole issue threadbare. This was my first 'proper' interaction with her. She was most attentive and respectful but would not budge. She would fast, she said, until the lands concerned were returned. It took a letter from the prime minister after four more days for her to agree to end her ordeal and enter discussions.

I was given undeserved credit for having brought about a thaw in her.

Reading letters from 'the general public' was a delightful pastime for me. I received a beautifully handwritten one in August from a school student in Madhyamgram written perhaps with help from a parent or a teacher, which said : '...your words are great, music phrases in the style of Beethoven, stirring rhythms like the March of Handel...I can't touch these phrases without receiving a thrill through my body like Gallick Electric shocks....' I could not figure out then and have not tried to check later what Gallick Electric Shocks meant but the letter reminded me of a famous letter to the editor of a Calcutta newspaper* carrying a verse penned by a Bengali gentleman upon the death of Queen Victoria:

> Dust to dust, ashes to ashes,
> Into the grave the Great Queen dashes.

Letters of a very different strain came with equal velocity as well. One said:

> You have always encashed the Gandhi cheque and wangled plum cushy postings...you are a very mediocre average Jt Secy level officer... don't you have any self respect?

---

*Cited by Sarvepalli Gopal in 'English Language in India', *Imperialists, Nationalists, Democrats: The Collected Essays Sarvepalli Gopal*, Srinath Raghavan (ed.), Ranikhet: Permanent Black, p. 375.

2007
A YEAR TO WISH AWAY

The Ides of March is an expression used mechanically to denote a period of impending misfortune without an understanding of its origins. It is, in fact, a particular day, the 15th of March, in the ancient Roman calendar that, for historical reasons, is associated with doom. Not on that day but on just the previous day, 14 March, Nandigram in the district of Purba Medinipur erupted in violence. I had been told of tension building up there ever since notices had appeared, without little if any discussion on the acquisition of as many as 10,000 acres in that region for the setting up of a chemical hub. The dock complex of Haldia, with its partnership with Kolkata port being close, made such a hub a sound idea—in theory. But sound ideas need sound consulting when they involve the taking over of land from its natural and traditional owners and users. This is what did not happen in Nandigram.

The affected peasants got organized to resist the acquisition even as the state government and the Haldia Development Authority went ahead with their plans for a chemical hub with foreign—Indonesian—participation. Early on the Ides—14 March—my secretary Dilip Rath informed me of a large protest demonstration being organized and a matching check being set in place by police. I asked him to convey to the government my concern that this could lead to violence and bloodshed. He did so at once and was assured that the police had been instructed to exercise every caution and not to act impulsively on being provoked. But by evening, what I had feared and warned the government about had happened. The protesters were fired upon, with fourteen killed on the spot and their bodies identified. Many were reported missing, presumably killed, with their bodies disposed of in the rivers nearby, Haldi, Rupnarayan.[1] I discounted the report, but the fact the missing persons had been in the protest demonstration when the firing started and had not been seen since was undeniable. Staggered by the firing and deaths and even more by the complete indifference shown to my warnings, I issued a statement to the press expressing my anguish.

This turned me, overnight, from a governor the state government and the Left were happy with and was praised by into a governor who was disliked by them. Approval from the general public and, of course, from the opposition was overwhelming. the chief minister maintained a stoic silence, but some of his ministers and party MLAs more than made up for that.

The next day brought in more details of the outrage. I could see that Buddha babu really was unaware of what had happened. The party cadres had taken over, infiltrated the police ranks, wore police uniforms minus police shoes which did not fit them, got hold of police arms, and went berserk.

I went to the area and saw the corpses laid out in the local hospital for post-mortem. The people, benumbed, spoke in whispers. An outrage had been perpetrated in the name of the state by men in police uniform and without the CM, who was also home minister, knowing.

April and May had me being adulated by one set and berated by another. It was clear that the huge majority of the people of West Bengal had been as appalled as their governor by what had happened, but while that for me was important the fact that the powerful Left was now ostracizing me when it was not criticizing me, was even more so. A governor's is a lonesome position. An ostracized governor's is many times so.

My brother Ramu turned seventy on 9 June. He was more than a teacher of philosophy; he was a philosopher. But to me, he was a mentor. Ramu's daughter Leela, a teacher of no small renown in her chosen field of post-colonial literature, came to India around this time from Australia, where she was teaching at the time and arranged for a small gathering at New Delhi's India International Centre to celebrate Ramu's birthday. All three of Ramu's siblings—Taru, Mohan, and I—were there, as were many of their children. The evening was an uncommonly happy one, for it was an uncommonly rare one.

Back in Kolkata, I had a strange experience on the night of 11/12 June. I got up in the middle of the night feeling uneasy, and when I stood up, I felt the ground was slipping from under my feet. A few moments later, I knew there was nothing the matter with me. And so, rattled by my experience, went back to sleep. On the 13th, I got a call from the IIC to say Ramu had died. I went numb. I had experienced a clear sign in the very moments when Ramu was crossing over. As I got into the car to head for the airport to take the first available flight to Delhi, Buddha babu rang to condole. He had been informed by someone.

If I am recording these details about my brother's death, it is because while his death instantly impoverished us, his family, and friends, it robbed the country of a thinker of the rarest refraction, whose mind was at home on the terrain Wittgenstein and Spinoza occupied and equally on that of the Buddha, Sri Ramakrishna, Sri Aurobindo, and Sri Ramana Maharshi. But more significantly, India had lost in Ramu's death a philosopher of India's spiritual intelligence who saw Advaita as a unique wisdom in that it demolished the divisions of creed and caste. Ramu was Ramana's disciple and Gandhi's messenger in their land, as it turned away from that active Advaita to restlessly active dualities, dissonances, and discord.

Shortly before he died, Ramu had sent me an email to say he was sorry I had been 'denied' the office of rashtrapati. He had assumed (or been told by someone) that post-Nandigram I had been thought unsafe for such a position. Be all that as it may, in the event, India got Pratibha Patil for president, the first woman to occupy that post. She was governor of Rajasthan, and when I told her I, as a fellow governor, was proud that she had ascended to the highest office in the land, she said to me, simply, 'I thought you were becoming rashtrapati and was very happy about it.' Pratibha Patil was good and kind to me throughout her five years in office, and I admired her for steadfastly declining to approve a single recommendation for the death penalty, commuting the sentences to life imprisonment. No other president has that record. But that said, it has to be admitted that there were several women far more deserving than her of the honour of being India's first woman president. She was selected by the Congress-Left combine by default after it was suggested at the relevant meeting that it was time India had a woman heading the state. The Congress, which meant Sonia Gandhi, thought of her not for outstanding ability but for outstanding loyalty to 'the family'. This test has been the bane of Congress politics. Loyalty is a great quality, but when it comes as a form of servitude, it becomes something else.

Nandigram notwithstanding, Sitaram Yechury asked me if I would consider being the coalition's candidate for vice president. I found it astonishing that the CPI(M) should ask me this, overcoming all its irritation with me over Nandigram. He accepted with a sigh my declining. The nation was fortunate in getting instead Hamid Ansari, former diplomat and scholar, to occupy that office for two consecutive terms, the only vice president after Dr S. Radhakrishnan to do so. And what a boost that gave to India's secularism!

Tehzeeb is an untranslatable Arabic word meaning etiquette but much more. It has in its grace, humility, and culture. When I rang Ansari sahib to congratulate him, he said, 'Hum to soch rahe the ki aap banenge' (I thought you would become vice president). I said God knew better.

Feroz Abbas Khan's film *Gandhi, My Father*, on the tragic life of Gandhi's eldest son Harilal, was being screened, on 4 August. Tara and I took Netaji's nephew Subrata Bose (1932–2016) and his wife, Nandita, good friends of ours, to see it. Akshaye Khanna, playing Harilal, did the character full justice, and all of us had lumps in our throats for much of the screening's duration. We should have taken descendants of Deshbandhu Chittaranjan Das (1870–1925) with us as well, for Harilal and Deshbandhu's son Chiraranjan were close friends, the Das scion clearing the Gandhi scion's many debts.

But our much larger debts as a people remained uncleared, staring us in the face. On 15 August, the 'actual' anniversary, a thousand people came by invitation to Raj Bhavan for an At Home. The customary event was saved from assured tedium by our screening of a documentary with footage on Gandhi's time in Bengal and Rajaji's swearing-in as the first governor on this day in 1947. Many veterans of the freedom struggle were present, as was Siddhartha Shankar Ray, former chief minister and grandson of the Deshbandhu. His wife, Maya Ray (1927–2013), told me later that Siddhartha babu was moved to tears by the film. But what lifted the anniversary to the skies for me was the inauguration later in the evening at Hydari Manzil, Beliaghata, the house where Gandhi was, on 15 August 1947. A new museum was inaugurated there by Jyoti babu, who had visited Gandhi right there that landmark year when, after the festivities of Independence had barely given over, vicious riots broke out.

Governor–chief minister relations—The author with Buddhadeb Bhattacharjee, chief minister of West Bengal, at an exhibition of historical photographs, Raj Bhavan, Kolkata, 2007. (State Information Department, Government of West Bengal).

It was fear of a recurrence of the riots, of violence, triggered now by terrorism, that predominated all other thoughts. I was not celebratory. I was fearful. The Manmohan Singh coalition government was under strain, which meant secular India was under threat. The irony was that the strain on the government was being caused by its natural partner in secularism, the Left. The support being given to the Manmohan Singh government by the CPI(M) and CPI seemed likely to be withdrawn over the Indo-US agreement being worked out on nuclear cooperation for civilian purposes—energy, basically. Was this wise? Would not a fall of the Manmohan Singh government lead to another election that would weaken secularism?

Eid fell on 14 October, and grim thoughts of the slaughter of goats that must be taking place assailed me. The wretched animals are decapitated in common places and in homes, children watching the gory scene. But being in Kolkata, I could not forget that the sacrificing of goats in the great Kali temple was also routine. The poor ungulate knew only the sharp edge of the knife on its throat and saw no Hindu or Muslim in the man who held it down but its killer. Both religions were at par in Kolkata and West Bengal when it came to the slaughter of goats. Gandhi's ringing words in his autobiography on the hideous cruelty of this rite had been preceded by a most moving play—*Visarjan*—by Rabindranath Tagore, in which he denounces the practice. Those two men have written as they have written and have gone into the mist. The goats continue to bleed to death at the altar of religion.

Perhaps one day, not far from now, in India, rather than anywhere else, a Muslim divine will rise to say killing animals for food straightforwardly is all right, but please, let us not bring religion into it. And likewise, a Hindu sage will say, 'From now on, let no animal be killed, not even fowl, in the name of gods and goddesses. They do not want to taste blood.'

Putting the goats and other animals being slaughtered out of my mind, I decided to visit on that Eid day, the Muslim orphanage on Zakaria Street. The institution and building had been set up in 1895—over 110 years ago. How many orphans had passed through its portals from childhood to adulthood…? Mohammed Salim (b. 1957), CPI(M) MP, and Abdus Sattar, the minister for Minority Affairs, joined me to spend that morning with the home's forty children who had no home to go to for Eid. They were a bright and beaming lot, reminding me of Swayam in Darjeeling. Aping President Abdul Kalam, I asked one what he would like to be growing up. He said he would like to be a zakir, a professionally trained reciter of the Holy Quran. Another said soldier. I noted that none of them was timid, none tentative. They showed me, with pride, their dorms, which were clean and the bathrooms spotless. They were, in their home, better off perhaps than many children, not orphans, in their family homes.

I have never understood why Islam is believed to prohibit adoption. The Muslim 'yatim' (orphan) cannot be given or taken in adoption. This has hindered wholesome adoption initiatives started internationally for orphans. Reasoning has been cited to say that Muslim orphans do not need adoption, for their relatives are enjoined to take care of them. If so, why this and similar Muslim orphanages?

Festivals are a blessing and a bane in India. They are a celebration and a provocation. The criss-cross nature of its community's divisions makes the joy of one the irritation of the other. The lights and sounds of one are smoke and din for the other, the colours of one, smears for the other. And, for the law enforcers, festivals meant high tension. It was Ramzan time, the month of fasting and feasting, in turn, for Muslims, and in Bengal, the annual pageantry of Durga Puja, with throngs crowding the makeshift shrines at every street corner, was approaching.

A blast occurred in Ludhiana the very next day, 15 October. Terrorists were not going to give India any respite. I sent word to the government to say, with the Ajmer experience in mind, that maximum alertness was called for. Having had that word of caution sent, I felt bad about feeling good over having done my bit. Regardless of any warning coming or not from the governor under his tinkling chandeliers, the chief minister had to keep a hundred eyes and ears open, guns at the ready. And this was not just about spotting bombs or stopping terrorists in their tracks but also keeping communal fires down. Kolkata was a city with the widest possible outlook on the human condition, the broadest sympathy with the liberal sentiments of an evolving humanity. But it was also home to subconscious suspicions, narrow prejudices and insecurities which, like the plague, could erupt in rat sewers without warning. So, while I got onto 'the line' with my words, Buddha babu's men had to put their lives on the line.

Diwali was approaching when, on 27 October, I got intimation of things flaring up in Nandigram again. Six months after the first outbreak of violence, which saw the villagers rise against the land acquisition project and its perceived CPI(M) initiators, now the 'repulsed' cadres of the party were giving it back. The pro-project and anti-project groups were all Nandigrami, people of the same soil. Politics had separated them from each other, making them adversaries. Areas from which the pro-project CPI(M) supporters had been ejected were now termed in Nandigram's political vocabulary 'the liberated zone'. The cadres were now intent on reversing the 'liberation' by entering in large numbers the homes of the villagers there and pushing them out. Violence was abroad once again. From the government's point of view, administration had been brought to a standstill in the 'liberated zone', and it proposed to deploy the CRPF in Nandigram. I had said to Buddha babu that the CRPF should be used impartially and with no one accusing it of bias towards the supporters of the ruling party. My messages to the chief minister and his to me were becoming telegraphic, in swiftness and brevity. He was, as I had always known him to be, a man of civility and inscrutability.

Tara was, at this point, in Chennai, recovering from a serious illness, and Buddha babu's solicitude for her health was a strength to me. He offered to fly down doctors and any help that she needed. He told me, with the earnest tones of a family member, I should not let my preoccupation with Nandigram come in the way of doing my bit for her recuperation. I was more than touched by this. But on Nandigram itself, he was now totally insuggestible. Mahasweta Devi rang me: 'Do something,' she said. Mamata came with thirty political and non-political persons, touched my feet, and said, 'Please do something to stop this state-sponsored terror.'

Buddha babu had veritably stopped meeting me. But he did take phone calls. I rang him at 8 p.m. that (27 October) night to get his analysis. He conceded the situation was bad but could be brought under control provided he got CRPF support. He said the union home secretary had told the state government that the CRPF could not be spared as it was required elsewhere and asked me if I could speak to the union home minister to reconsider. I said the minister would not do so and that he (Buddha babu) should act, starting with 'clear directions to his party cadres to cease all intrusive activity in Nandigram'. A man of few words, at any time, he said almost nothing to this except to tell me what was most plausible, that is, that Maoists were taking advantage of the situation and making it extremely complicated.

A governor has to be and be seen to be impartial between adversarial groups and between the government and the opposition. This is not difficult when the grey area between the black and white is wide. But when it is almost non-existent, when the black and white are clearly demarcated, such neutrality is not only difficult but is wrong. I had to issue a statement to the press that evening, saying the news of deaths in police firing in Nandigram had filled me with a sense of cold horror.

'Governor's Fireworks' ran a headline in *The Telegraph* the next morning. I had asked for what I got within hours. Describing me as partial, unconstitutional and provocative, the CPI(M) general secretary in West Bengal and a person with whom I had enjoyed a particularly warm equation, Biman babu, made some scathing remarks on me as a person as well. My diary notes: '*I do not mind. He is doing his political dharma. He also reads a resolution of the CPI(M) Politburo calling my statement "un-called for". That, too, does not disturb me. The Politburo has to say something about my statement. Silence would amount to acknowledging guilt.*'

Buddha babu was now ice.

I motored to Jyoti babu's home to urge him to resume the efforts he had initiated to bring some sanity to the situation. Amazingly well-informed and up-to-date, he said to me he was sorry I made the statement and also sorry it was rebutted. I said I would not retract one word in it, but it was necessary to bring normalcy back quickly. I was to see him again a few days later. Biman babu was with him. 'I do not hold what you said about me in my mind,' I told the party veteran, 'life is too short for that.' Taking my hand in his, Biman babu then said, 'Please, please don't take it personally.' I was not doing so, I told him.

Buddha babu met me on 13 November, four days after my statement. It was most civil of him to do so. He was frank. As was I. He said he had come with 'a heavy heart'. I said I had no political baggage, no political 'from' address, no political destination, and only did what I thought was right. And then I said, 'You can, if you want, ask Delhi to get you another governor.' This was no ordinary statement to make, as the Congress and the Left were still in coalition, and just as the Left had proposed my name to Manmohan Singh for the governorship of West Bengal, it could ask him for a change. Buddha babu's response was something I will never forget. 'I am not that type of a person. I will never do such a thing.'

I then told him he must sack a particular person from a position he occupied for his role in Nandigram. Buddha babu's response to this was elegant and dignified. It reflected political etiquette and, in a sense, educated me. 'We are not a Nazi party. We are the Communist Party. We follow procedure.' That is called stature.

Some minutes after CM left, I got a call from the PM. He had just spoken to the CM over the mobile, as the CM was in his car returning from Raj Bhavan. 'Gopal,' the PM said, 'I have just told the CM that he cannot have a better governor than you and that he must satisfy your concerns.'

Why am I recounting this? The following from my diary for 13 November 2007 explains why:

> *Advaniji comes with Sushma Swaraj and many NDA leaders, including Sharad Yadav. They give me vivid accounts of what they saw in Nandigram—the panic and the terror. I am praised for my stand. I say I did what I did because I have a certain philosophy about governorships, viz., that they (and all those appointed to public offices) should be accountable to the people no less than those elected. Also, there have been other events in the country's recent history where the governor of the day should have spoken up. I do not name Gujarat (2002) or Delhi (1984), but they understand. I add that I*

have been influenced by President K. R. Narayanan, who did not hesitate to speak his mind on many issues that were inconvenient to the government of the day.

The 14th of November is red-lettered as Nehru's birthday. I went to his statue and placed a wreath. There was almost no one around, certainly no Congressman. A few flowers had been placed there by the authorities mechanically. Indira Gandhi's statue in Kolkata, in comparison, is bedecked by flowers on her anniversaries, and Congress volunteers flock to it. I wondered at the why and wherefore of this difference. Why in independent India is a freedom fighter and palpably greater democrat and statesman in Nehru less of a draw than his autocratic and inscrutable daughter (except in Punjab, one might add)? And I concluded, somewhat hazily and sadly, that this has to be because she is nearer to us in time than Nehru and has been likened with much appeal to the pious and patriotic in us, as a Durga who dismembered Pakistan. And then, of course, as a prime minister who was assassinated. But beyond these reasons for two others. One, to use her self-description, she is perceived as a doer and her father as a thinker, the 'doer' being 'tough,' and the 'thinker' being akin to a 'dreamer'. Two, Indians, by nature, valorize victors and martyrs. Nehru was neither; Indira was both. The one who can spill the villain's blood and has his or her own spilled in the process becomes a demi-God in India. Others take their place on different plinths of the pantheon. For me, this was infinitely sad.

The Calcutta High Court delivered on 16 November a major judgment vindicating my stand on Nandigram totally—calling the 14 March incidents as unconstitutional, ordering compensation within a month, and asking for criminal proceedings to be initiated against those responsible. Predictably, the state government said it would appeal against the judgment in the Supreme Court. The newspapers flashed the judgment. Representatives of the BJP and TMC, along with many others, came and asked for Article 356 to be imposed on the state, replacing the Buddhadeb government with President's Rule. There was no case; I told all of them unambiguously. The constitutional machinery in the state had not broken down, and though the state had behaved unacceptably and unlawfully in Nandigram, the legitimacy of the Buddhadeb government was beyond question.

The year 2007 ended for me on a lovely musical note. Pandit Ravi Shankar and his daughter Anoushka played on the sitar of which he is master at the Calcutta Club for its centenary. The eighty-seven-year-old and his twenty-six-year-old daughter played magically—he with a maestro's genius, she with calm confidence. His Jogeshwari was serious, sedate, his Maaj

Khamaaj, playful. In the audience was his twenty-eight-year-old daughter Norah Jones, the superbly gifted singer and songwriter. Beside her was her father's wife, Sukanya Shankar, with a lapdog on the seat. Was this—bringing a dog into the concert hall—a good thing to do? Pet lovers would say, 'Of course, yes, what is wrong?' Music lovers might demur. Pet lovers who are also music lovers would be in a dilemma. As one who adored our family's pet dog, a London-born mongrel, Chiku, I too was in a dilemma. But this dilemma was nothing compared to another that confronted me. The maestro's sister-in-law Amala Shankar (1919–2020), widow of the great and matchless dancer Uday Shankar (1900–77) and a distinguished dancer herself, met me shortly thereafter to speak about her great distress at the persistent neglect by just about everybody of Uday Shankar and his legacy. Amala di was far too elevated a person and evolved to as much whisper resentment against her husband's younger brother getting global recognition.

Bengal is the seat of music, of the arts. But it is also, more than any place that I know of, the stage of dilemmas.

2008
JE PATHE JETE HOBEY.... (ON THE ROAD YOU HAVE TAKEN....)

And the new year—2008—opened for me with another concert on the sitar. Shujaat Khan, then forty-eight, was the son of Ustad Vilayat Khan (1928–2004), the other great sitarist of our times. Both the Pandit (Ravi Shankar) and the Ustad (Vilayat Khan) were sons of Bengal, both contemporaries, the Ustad dying at age seventy-five in 2004 when Ravi Shankar was eighty-four. The two were diamond-cutting-diamonds. Ravi Shankar had stature and renown; Vilayat had stature and a loyal following. The first was a maestro, the second a virtuoso. Ravi Shankar had been awarded the Bharat Ratna in 1999—the second musician after M. S. Subbulakshmi to receive the nation's highest civilian honour. When Vilayat Khan was offered the nation's second highest honour, the Padma Vibhushan, the following year, he declined. Stature declined to be second to renown.

All this swirled in my mind as I heard Shujaat, the virtuoso's stunningly gifted son, play the sitar with effortless ease. He was of a heavy build but had the lightest of light touches on the strings. Melody frolicked on those. This was a huge relief, used as one had become to hearing sitarists and sarodists play as if they are tearing the entrails of some screaming animal.

Bengal has been prodigal in giving India its genius in the arts in pairs. If it gives us Ravi Shankar, it also gives us Vilayat Khan. If it produces a Satyajit Ray, it also makes a Mrinal Sen (1923–2018). If it gives us Uttam Kumar (1926–80), it also gifts us Soumitra Chatterjee (1935–2020). Likewise, I would like to mention Suchitra Sen (1931–2014) and Aparna Sen (b. 1945). I cannot fail to mention another 'double'. If Bangla has given us a great rendering of 'We Shall Overcome' in 'Amra Korbo Joy' through the translation of Hemanga Biswas (1912–87) and the music of Bhupen Hazarika (1926–2011), it has also given us 'Ek Din Surjer Bhor' organized by Ruma Guha Thakurta (1934–2019). No surprise, therefore, that Bengal should have given India the two songs, Bankim's 'Vande Mataram' and Tagore's 'Jana Gana', both evenly matched for their evocation of India, to become our national song and national anthem, respectively.

For its artistic vitality, India independent is Bengal dependent. And a felicity, that is.

If I was grateful for this musical interlude, I was to be shaken out of it before I could say Aa-san-sol by what can only be called the fury of fire.

Having heard of the problem of illegal mining in the state, I had long wanted to go to that area to see the problem for myself. Apart from the scandalous loss of revenue to both the centre and the state by those rat-holes as they are graphically and realistically described, there was also the issue of human lives being imperilled by fires that grow from the unscientific operations in those methane-filled cavities. Unbeknownst to them, passengers in their countless numbers hurtle over those death-traps when they travel on the Shatabdi and Rajdhani express trains. I went down the 'normal' mine-shafts to their 400 feet depth to just get an idea of the problem. Emerging, I found my nose and throat clogged by fine black coal dust. How miners spend eight hours or more in those dungeons every day was beyond imagining. If peasants in independent India were facing problems due to thoughtless industrialization, miners were not getting compensated enough for what they were doing. And now, a miners' mafia, perhaps in collusion with corrupt staffers in companies, was abducting the mineral for illegal profit and putting human lives in jeopardy. Asansol showed me a howling truth about India in its development mode: our natural resources are being used by the rightful users and also abused by abusers of the opportunity for crass and illegal profit. Industrial development is the cradle of India's future; it is also its crucifix.

And there is then, looming over India's coal story, the question of fossil fuels and carbon debits and credits and climate change in which the developed world, China joining it, wants India to 'cap' its coal output and use. Do they not know of Shakespeare's lines in *Cymbeline*: 'Golden lads and girls all must as chimney-sweepers come to dust...'? The globe is not going to burn up in parts.

The tall and tough Haryanvi Congressman Balram Jakhar, confident of step and speech in his mid-eighties, came on an official visit. He was the governor of Madhya Pradesh at the time. He knew all that farms and farming meant and, as union agriculture minister, had won the admiration of Dr M. S. Swaminathan. I asked him to educate me on the state of agriculture in India. 'Gopal, look,' he said, 'the agriculture scene is grim. The days of conventional farming are over in India. Farm sizes are shrinking; their topsoil is in trouble. Farms and farmers now do not need romantic activists to make some kind of "cause" of agriculture. They need practical ideas. The fact is that agriculture now needs to be rescued from itself. I am a farmer myself, so I know what I am saying. Debt waivers will not help them. They will harm them. Farming has to diversify. It has to do so with and not against industrialization. We have to farm, and we have to industrialize. The question is: how do we do both together? We cannot industrialise like Europe. Our industrialization has to suit our needs and our nature. It has to be farm-based; that is, we must rely now on agro-industries. In India, it cannot be an agriculture versus industry thing. Our agriculture must become part of our industry and vice versa. This is how I see the future of India, agro-industry, with technology playing its role.' More common sense I had not heard in a long time. It had in it the rugged wisdom of the land of the five rivers.

Meanwhile, Darjeeling was now in ferment. And the concept of 'desh' was at the heart of this ferment. Subhash Ghisingh and his Gorkhaland National Liberation Front (GNLF) were being upstaged by Bimal Gurung (b. 1964), a relatively unknown politician until then, who set up the Gorkha Janmukti Morcha. Gorkhaland, without Ghising's 'National' adjective, was now being put forward as the goal. Posters ridiculing Ghising and eulogizing Gurung appeared in many places in Darjeeling. The nuanced arrangements of the Sixth Schedule for greater devolution suddenly began to look like a children's picnic.

Gurung's rise from being one of Ghising's foot soldiers to a significant disrupter of political equilibrium in the hills was, incidentally, about a technological reality in India. Ghising, with all his canniness, could not have thought of this. In 2008, a TV reality Indian Idol show with a music contest had two contenders for the prize—a Shillong-based Meghalayan youth, Amit Paul (b. 1973), and a Darjeeling-born police constable, Prashant Tamang (b. 1983). Gurung got the bright idea that in the popular vote segment of the choice, he would have thousands of Nepali-speaking Darjeeling mobile phone users SMS their vote for Tamang. The young Darjeelinger was good, but the Shillong youth was not any less as a singer, perhaps even better. But thanks to the power of the mobile phone and the SMS votes it generated, Tamang won the last round of the contest decisively, getting about ten times more votes (70 million votes) than Paul in the final and went on to win. Tara and I watched the contest, absorbed by the singing, and while I was parochial enough to want Tamang to win, she said, the Meghalayan was by far the better singer and deserved idolhood. And so, by a strange concatenation of technology, music and desh prem, the Gorkhaland demand for its own desh within the Indian desh, got a shot in the arm. That Prashant moved on from his place in the West Bengal police to a film career and failed there is another sad story. Social media can lift one sky high and fling him down from there into an abyss.

I did not realize then, nor am I sure did most, that this SMS score was a sign of the emerging power of social media, its ability to sway minds and votes and put talent or merit in second place after manipulation. India's future would be tied to how social media can be used and misused to influence feelings, choices, and, therefore, destinies.

This was a time when the state was passing through an acute electricity crunch. Long hours of load-shedding had engulfed us. The state power minister, Mrinal Banerjee (1938–2010), was an impressive man, serious to the point of seeming grave. An engineer, he was more of a trade unionist, having been secretary of the West Bengal unit of the Centre of Indian Trade Unions (CITU). Mrinal babu had warned the state, honestly and frankly, about the impending crisis caused by coal supply bottlenecks: 'The existing block at Tara (Paschim Bardhaman district) was allotted sometimes in the 90s, and its reserves are set to get exhausted any day. The Panchwara North coal block was allotted in the year 2002, but we managed to receive environmental clearance only in July 2008. The block can now start operation only during 2011. In the interim, we will require additional supplies to run the new capacities that have come on stream, or we will have to face massive loadshedding.'[1]

I was motoring on the evening of 6 May in the air-conditioned comfort of my limousine along the Maidan when I rang my valued friend, the historian Barun De (1932–2013), from my mobile phone for 'just a chat'. Ramabai, his wife, answered the call. To my cliched question, 'How are you doing?' she responded, 'How are we doing? Well, with the rest of the city, we are sweating it out with no fan, no bijli.... It has been gone for hours.... We have been suffering for days now under this horrible power cut. And God knows how long it will go on for.' There was little I could say or do to help. The car was taking me back to Raj Bhavan, and as we turned into the massive gate, the magnificent building dazzled. Lights were on in every room, and the 'brilliants' on the chandeliers in the banquet hall glittered through the high doors. The palace (for that is what it is) looked like a diamond shower. To mix metaphors, I decided in a flash that I would have the lights in Raj Bhavan dimmed by a voluntary power cut for two hours at peak-use time, that is, in the late evenings, till the power position improved. Power saving was an indirect form of power generation, and I wanted Raj Bhavan to participate in and experience the city's (and state's) load-shedding and, in the process, set an example for other heavy-duty users. It was one of those instinctive things. Ramabai, of course, had suggested no such thing, or even, I am sure, thought of it. She had, however, catalysed the thought in me.

But when does the imp in us called ego let go?

While calling in the Raj Bhavan engineer, another Mrinal—Mrinal Kundu—a fine technocrat, and the comptroller—Susanta Upadhaya, one of god's good men, to ask for this plan to be put in force, I did something more, something egregious. I had a small statement issued that Raj Bhavan was going to self-impose a power cut. Issuing this was a bad step. In all propriety, I should have invited the good minister Mrinal babu over and apprised him of the decision before switching the power off.

Media was, as it invariably is in West Bengal, eloquently divided. Through interviews, most newspapers and TV channels hailed the move, and those belonging to the Left establishment criticized it roundly. Jyoti babu, with the humour and sarcasm he was master of, using a telling Bangla expression, said I was being childish, adding that if I wanted to help the state, I should have had a discussion on the matter with the concerned minister. He was, of course, right. Mrinal babu himself said, 'If a person chooses to have a single meal because of food crisis, what can we do?' Dialectically speaking, this statement was unarguable. The chief minister, to his great credit, kept silent. What he felt and may have said in private to his small family and intimates is another matter. But he said not a word against the step in public.

In its public expressions of disapproval, the Left's performance was a study in contrasts, designed or accidental, I could not say. Prakash Karat, Sitaram Yechury, and Buddha babu, not having put good taste to any strain, *Aajkaal*, the CPI(M)-supporting daily more than made up for it. The Bangla daily carried an article on me by the amazingly versatile writer, musician, and painter Buddhadeb Guha (1936–2021) entitled 'Raja tomar kapad kothay?' (King, where are your clothes?), followed by a letter to the editor captioned 'Ullanga Raja' (Naked King). The stripping was done with deliberation in graduated stages.

But the popular response was overwhelmingly positive. I was quite inundated with messages of appreciation, confirming me in my guilt over having done what I did because I wanted appreciation rather than wanting to reduce Raj Bhavan's draw on the grid to set a salutary example.

The little 'power-cut' episode in Kolkata and the Left's anger were a 'trailer' for Kolkata audiences of the much larger issue of India's nuclear power generation to augment its severely constrained thermal and hydel power resources. Manmohan Singh's government, in a highly contentious move, was clinching with the USA the bilateral agreement, which was to pass into the USA and Indian systems on nuclear cooperation. The idea was that India, which had been blacklisted for nuclear commerce after its nuclear tests, should be enabled by a special, perhaps unique, dispensation to buy and sell nuclear material needed for its energy requirements. The US, with its concerns, was, of course, going to impose some conditionalities for this, which the Left and many others in India saw as affronts to Indian sovereignty.

By mid-June, the Left was openly and strongly threatening to withdraw support to the Manmohan Singh government on account of the India–US nuclear parleys. In Kolkata, it appeared that the Left was thinking of toppling the government and installing a Third Front government minus the Congress within the life of the then Lok Sabha—a childish (to use Jyoti babu's phrase) fantasy. But dangerous for the country.

While all this was happening on the political stage, terrorists were busier than ever. They know when and where to strike. And political preoccupations of the leadership and of governments were an ideal setting for their malevolence. On 25 July, a series of bomb blasts went off in Bengaluru. They were described as low-intensity gelatine devices. But what was terrifying about them was that they had timers fixed on them, triggered by mobile phones. And were placed in crowded areas. Before the implications of this could sink in, Ahmedabad reported horrible serial blasts the very next day. The devices used were similar to those in Bengaluru, but the intensity was higher. As many as twenty-one blasts hit Ahmedabad within a span of seventy minutes. Reports of the number killed mounted from one to three, to five, to nearly fifty by night-time. In the final count, fifty-six were dead and over 200 injured. These bombings were said to have been the work of the Pakistani Islamic terrorist group Harkat-ul-Jihad al-Islami.

The situation was now that of war. My diary for the day notes: '*It is now time for a global initiative with the UNO perhaps setting up a multi-country force with an intelligence hub (or scattered centres) that think/s as terrorists think, and by following their thinking imagines what they may do at their worst, and then being one step ahead of the terrorists, "shoot" at a future target as per the laws of parallax.*'

Kashmir was hotting up, meanwhile. Jammu and the Valley were like two nations at war, with the Indian state having to use force against both, inflaming both sides. The 'march' of traders in the valley towards the PoK border to sell produce, which they claimed was not getting an outlet because of an alleged blockade, led to violence and firing in which fifteen were killed and hundreds injured. Fortunately for all concerned, the governor of Jammu and Kashmir was the seasoned civilian and my senior in the IAS by several years, N. N. Vohra (b. 1936), whose balanced maturity saved the situation from embroiling a much larger segment of the population.

It is a myth that only political appointees to Raj Bhavans understand the politics of a state and that retired officials are out of their depths as governors. Vohra sahib's sharp appreciation of the nuances of the India–Pakistan scene from Srinagar was spot-on. Peace talks between Delhi and Islamabad were their privilege; handling war-like situations in the state and along its borders had to be his prerogative, and that of the administration in the state, as these situations evolved not by the hour, not by the minute but in fractions of seconds.

The disinterested interest of a governor whose DNA is by definition neutral can act as he should, undeflected by hopes of preferment, undeterred by fears of interference. Vohra sahib understood his state, and Delhi understood that he understood. As one who had seen the horrors of partition, every single kind of those, and been at the helm of the administrative edifice of independent India, with the additional asset of knowing to speak, read, and write Urdu and, by extension Urdu's sister-language Kashmiri, he was where he needed to be, and ready to act as the situation needed, prepared to do so for as long as necessary, and ready also to quit if so required at a moment's notice.

Mine was a far less onerous set of challenges in Kolkata and a far less set of qualifications for handling those. But it was tested to its maximum. The tribal-rich districts of Purba and Paschim Medinipur had gone under flood waters in June 2008—'flash floods, triggered by heavy rains caused by a depression in the Bay of Bengal and southwest monsoon' are an almost annual feature. But this time around, the fury of the swollen waters of the Keleghai and Subarnarekha was worse than any flood in recent memory. After the waters had receded and I could not be accused of interfering with relief operations by landing in the middle, I went to see how help had been reached to the affected.

District officers, like governors, can be hugely effective if they are neutral and are also work-addicts. Anoop Agarwal, district magistrate of Purba Medinipur, made a statement, the candour and objectivity of which made me feel very reassured: 'The flood condition is worsening at Egra, Bhagwanpur, Patashpur, and Panskura. There is much political bias going on in the name of relief distribution. I have requested all political parties at Sunday's meeting to see that no flood victim is deprived of relief. We will put up a notice at every block and village stating the quantity and kind of relief distributed there.' Likewise, Paschim Medinipur's district magistrate N. S. Nigam said, '...the situation is improving in the district, except in Pingla and Janchak I and II blocks. Pingla and Janchak I and II are still waterlogged. But we can handle the situation now. Waters of the Keleghai and Subarnarekha rivers have gone below the danger level.' This had just the right blend of honesty and hope. There is no such thing as complete satisfaction among the recipients of disaster relief. In Purba Medinipur's Lalchak village, an old woman came up to me, took my hands, and said with the entitlement of age: 'Tumi Raajyasarkaar...' (you are the state government), I loved the intimacy and the breeziness of her 'tumi' as different from the formal 'aapni' and her creative fluxing of raajya with sarkaar was masterly. Then followed a withering comment. 'Dekhun tomar raajyer durbyabasthaa....' (Just see your raj's maladministration.) This was what is called an alert citizenry, West Bengal's pride.

On 8 July, as we were reeling under the monsoon's furies, CPI(M)'s general secretary, the intellectuals' intellectual Prakash Karat, announced that the Left Front was withdrawing its support to the government over the decision by the government to go ahead with the US–India Peaceful Atomic Energy Cooperation Act. All things considered, placing my trust of tiny worth in the Manmohan Singh government's wisdom and integrity, I bemoaned the Left withdrawing support from the UPA government, a step which many at the time believed would hasten the fall of the UPA ministry.

But if Karat was the very personification of pertinacity, Manmohan Singh was the very epitome of tenacity. On 22 July, he faced his first confidence vote, winning it with 275 votes to the opposition's 256. Ten members abstained from the vote to record a nineteen-vote victory, which also saw the Left expelling Somnath Chatterjee, Lok Sabha's speaker, for his refusal to join the Left's opposition to the Act. Delhi and Kolkata now had deeply conflicted and uncooperative governments, making my governor's work in West Bengal that much more complex.

And Singur was at the heart of that complexity.

After checking with Buddha babu, I wrote to Mamata Banerjee, suggesting intermediation and a dialogue to similarly bring the Singur imbroglio to an end. Buddha babu showed astonishing conciliation and, with great patience, in my presence, stayed completely unprovoked by Mamata's temper spikes, and miraculously, discussions started. With the benign and sobering presence as adviser of Justice Chittatosh Mookerjee (b. 1929) at sessions that were held in Raj Bhavan, Kolkata, my making it clear that I would play a role in bringing the two sides together for a preliminary confluence of energies, but in any discussions on details that would follow, I would not take part.

With several glitches and pullbacks threatening to derail the process, the discussions did happen only to break down at the substantive stage over the actual area that the Tatas would relinquish. At a crucial point, Ratan Tata (1937–2024) made it known that they were 'near to leaving' the site and the project. Mamata was continuing to demand a return of 400 acres from the 1,100 acres acquired for the Nano project from unwilling farmers. The Tatas showed no inclination to oblige and seemed all packed and ready to exit, the government unwilling or unable to discuss the issue any further. Fresh from a 'siege of Singur', she came on 24 August to see me. My diary notes of that date: '*If anyone in West Bengal has grit, MB has. She may be stubborn (is the government not? Is Ratan Tata not?), she may be strident (is CPI(M) not?), she may be street-struck (does the Left not call bandhs, does BJP not?), but she is with the people "out there". I hope she keeps the agitation on the peaceful path she vows.*'

The next day was a black day, a day of horrors for Odisha and for India. According to government reports, the violence started after the murder of a Hindu monk, Lakshmanananda Saraswati[2] and going on for four full days, resulted in at least 39 Christians killed and 3,906 Christian houses completely destroyed. More than 395 churches were reportedly razed or burnt down, over 5,600—6,500 houses plundered or burnt down, over 600 villages ransacked and more than 60,000—75,000 people left homeless. Other reports put the death toll at nearly 100 and suggested more than 40 women were sexually assaulted.[3] Unofficial reports placed the number of those killed to many times that number, most of them burnt alive. What was one to feel, say to a barbarism like this? Nothing. One was to just curl up and wail. Prime Minister Manmohan Singh called the Kandhamal murders a 'shame'. What else could he say? But the world condemned it also, starting with His Holiness the Pope Benedict, who did not omit to condemn 'the reprehensible murder' of the Swami.

On 7 September, a way forward was agreed upon, and Mamata called off her agitation. But the devil lay waiting in the details, and hard-lining within the government by some led to a return of the logjam. Buddha babu and Mamata had come within an inch of an agreement only to break up in a collapse when she found that only 70 acres within the project site would be returned. She left the meeting in high dudgeon. I am convinced that left to himself, Buddha babu would have offered a bigger acreage for being returned to the 'unwilling' farmers but was restrained by party and government hardliners.

I had tried to effect a mediation, Buddha babu had gone up to the last mile that his circumstances allowed, Mamata climbed down from her agitating high horse, and the wise Chittatosh Mookerjee had guided the process with detached sagacity. I could not fault Ratan Tata for wanting to take his small car, which, I could see, he loved as dearly as one would love one's own offspring, to where it could bring in large profits smoothly, unencumbered by disgruntled peasants and agitating politicians. I think he had imagined, ironically enough, that the CPI(M) government would, like the Peoples' Democratic Republic of China, insulate his factory from all difficulties. He had not reckoned for the tone and temper of democracy in West Bengal. Industry's natural home is a congenial manufacturing environment, its goal: a fair return on the investment or, in other words, profit. A politician's natural home is an electorally promising turf, her or his goal: a good chance of widening influence or, in other words, power. A government's natural home is a stable polity, its goal: sustained incumbency or, in other words, permanence. These three were at variance in Singur.

On 23 November, Buddha babu rang me to say that the Industries minister had learnt from the Tatas that they had decided, internally, to pull out. Mamata came to see me with forty persons the next day. They must persevere in dialogue, I told them, and say and do everything they say and do in a democratic, peaceful and law-abiding manner. Thinking aloud, I said the failure of the initiative was on account of my ego wanting to bask in the glory of a successful mediation. I said I still wanted to hope and tried to recall a line from Tagore: 'Je pathe jete hobey…' (On the road you have taken…) Mamata completed it for me

…she pathe tumi ekaa
nayane aandhaar robe
dhyaane alo-rekhaa…

(you walk by yourself, your eyes see only darkness
But your mind glimpses a streak of radiant light)

Buddha babu would, politics notwithstanding, have silently responded to this moment with Tagore. But Ratan Tata? No. His alo rekha was by this time in Sanand in Gujarat where, he was to say later, that it was his 'fortune and good luck' to have moved.

On 10 October, External Affairs Minister Pranab Mukherjee (1935–2020) and Secretary of State Condoleezza Rice (b. 1954) signed, the Indo-US nuclear civilian agreement. The forty-eight-nation NSG had granted a waiver to India on 6 September 2008, allowing it to access civilian nuclear technology and fuel from other countries, making India the only known country with nuclear weapons which was not a party to the Non-Proliferation Treaty (NPT) being allowed to carry out nuclear commerce with the rest of the world. The Manmohan Singh government had veritably achieved the unbelievable and against severe resistance not just from the Indian Left, with its traditional scepticism about the USA, but also from NGOs and anti-nuclear energy activists, apart from other nations.

I understood little of the technicalities of the deal and was by no means an admirer of George Bush's intellectual resources, but the fact that the agreement would help India meet its goal of adding 25,000 MW of nuclear power capacity through imports of nuclear reactors and fuel by 2020, seemed to my inexpert mind a sensible step in the interests of India's energy security.

On 24 October, India launched Chandrayaan. Given that every news item, whether national or international, was about a crisis or a catastrophe, this was welcome. It literally lifted one's spirits, though I was yet to fully grasp the utility to India of knowing the moon's terrain in such detail. But the launch was, to use Neil Armstrong's famous expression, a giant leap for India.

The news that truly thrilled me, with countless millions the world over, was the election on 5 November of Barack Obama (b. 1961) as president of the United States of America. Irrespective of what history may have to say on his presidency, the fact of it had taken the world forward in one 'giant leap' towards equity and hope. The president of the USA was arguably the most powerful person in the world, whereas the president of India was only a constitutional head. Nevertheless, in terms of symbolism, our president was no ordinary entity. And so we could be proud of the fact that the marginalized in India had made it to the 'top job' quicker than their counterparts in the US—India's third president was a Muslim, the fifth president was a Muslim, the seventh a Sikh, the tenth a Dalit, the eleventh a Muslim and the twelfth, a woman. That made 50 per cent of the total. It had taken the US forty-three presidents to find a black man to be the forty-fourth President.

But symbols are, at the end of the day, only symbols.

On 26 November, independent India was put through its worst experience of terror, straining its secular nerve as never before. The ghoulish audacity of the terrorists who sneaked into Mumbai by sea had left us gasping in disbelief. Ten members of the LeT carried out twelve meticulously planned and coordinated shooting and bombing attacks across Mumbai, leaving 135 dead, including 9 of the 10 attackers. The police officers—Hemant Karkare (1954–2008), Ashok Kamte (1965–2008), Vijay Salaskar (1957–2008) and constables who died under terrorist fire and the brave-hearted firemen who fought the inferno—united the country in a renewed bond of anguished rage. Among the killed were Hindus, Muslims, rich, and poor, all utterly innocent caught in the ballistic barbarism. Who won and who lost in the attack? No one. Certainly not the terrorists.

Mahesh Bhatt (b. 1948), the film director, said, 'We ain't seen nothin' yet.' That sounded chillingly true. Bhatt's prognostication was shared by many, including, of course, the agencies in charge of internal security. Of the many agonies of India, the ever-present danger of terrorists dealing death in the name of Islam is the vilest. It not only performs its hideous act but leaves a trail of hate, fear and suspicion.

This was also the time when the financial meltdown, which had started somewhat inconspicuously in 2007 in the USA's housing credit sector, led to a sharp decline in economic activity that began to affect other economies. By the end of 2008, India was worried about the slump affecting our financial health. Former president Abdul Kalam came to Kolkata on a visit in December. At a quiet dinner in Raj Bhavan with just Tara and me, he answered a barrage of questions that I put to him uninhibitedly, now that he was not president.

On the economic meltdown: We will be affected but will be protected by the fact that our banks have been cautious and our people save.

On Pakistan: War with Pakistan will be foolish because it will set us back by ten years, and Pakistan, having lost four consecutive wars against us, will be tempted to try the nuke option this time, which would be disastrous.

On terror: Terror may not stop with war.

On a nuclear strike: First, 10 kilometres around the drop—all out. Next, 2-3 kms radiation. Another 5 kms, slow radiation.

I was impressed by his commonsensical prognosis on the economic slump fears but amazed at his cool description of the nuclear disaster. He spoke of it as one might of a street fire. He said what he said about a nuclear holocaust as he ate frugally, vegetarian food, as always, slowly but enjoying what little he ate. I felt then and have felt ever since that if President Kalam had, like J. Robert Oppenheimer, expressed his abhorrence of nuclear war and, in some form that accorded with his personality, also said that he had played a key role in building India's defence capability through measures that included the delivery of nuclear warheads, and that he thought that capability went against the grain of human civilization and then devoted himself to the cause of global disarmament, he would have risen to a great stature and would even have been seen as deserving of the Nobel Peace Prize.

By now, any bomb blast anywhere in India was axiomatically linked to 'Muslim terror', a broad assumption that stemmed from narrow mental conditioning. But Guwahati, the capital of the Northeast's most prominent state, Assam, showed an exception. Three blasts, again 'low intensity', went off in the city's busy segments on new year day, shortly before Home Minister P. Chidambaram was about to land on a visit and on the route, he was to take. Carried out by the United Liberation Front of Asom (ULFA), the bombings left six people dead and a further sixty-seven injured. The perpetrators and the victims belonged to the same social and ethnic 'stock'. This was indiscriminate violence against one's own kind. Chidambaram had had a narrow escape, but ethnic divisiveness had dug another flagpole, for ULFA's aims of an Assam independent of the Republic of India (to be dropped later) did not contain an equal space for Muslims and non-Assamese Indians.

Deafening to all others, these blasts were music to the ears of the morcha in Darjeeling led by Bimal Gurung. Their agitation had more than ordinary merit to it in terms of its aspirations for the people of Darjeeling. Still, it had much greater demerit in terms of what it was doing to the fabric of society and the structure of the administration. That, of course, was the 'problem' with all the movements for self-expression in the Northeast. Northeasterners' grievances had been sidelined by the powers that be for long years till the only sound that could not be ignored was the sound of bombs. North Bengal is geopolitically in West Bengal, but ecologically, it is a cousin of Northeast India. Its forests are agnatically related to the forests of the Northeast. Its flora and fauna are similar. And it can provide hideouts to just the kind of disaffection that has marked life in those hill states.

2009
WELCOME HOME, FORMER GOVERNOR

Tara and I were in Buxa Tiger Reserve on 7 January, and a Scorpio drove us noiselessly into its deep density. But we could see only a dancing peacock and a herd of ten elephants that included two young tuskers. The older one, said to be fifteen years old, was impressive, and our guides said, had 'leadership qualities'. The younger one (two-three years old) was a loner that loved foraging in craters dug by older elephants. He did not join the others and, as we watched from the security of our Scorpio, wandered off on his own. May he be safe, I prayed, and may he prosper. The youth of the Northeast, Darjeeling included, were like this pre-adult tusker, roaming the wilds of their aspiration and at great risk from the tigers of violence and power-wars in the name of democracy. Those with leadership qualities needed to bestir themselves and protect the vulnerable. But how many had such qualities?

Later the same week, I was in that all-important north Bengal city of Siliguri, where security vulnerability is at its highest. A group of engineers from the National Hydroelectric Power Corporation met me to say Gurung's agitation was affecting the Teesta Project and would escalate its cost. The engineers told me the per unit tariff for power from the project will increase and must be borne by the people. Did Gurung not realize this?

Indian politics is about the short term. Indian culture is about the medium term, while Indian philosophy is about the long term and, more, tells us how to prepare for life after all these terms. Life, being short-spanned, is sodden by politics and culture.

Mamata Banerjee came with a jumbo delegation of ninety persons on 18 February, astonishing me by introducing almost each one of them to me by name. She then gave me a ten-minute 'presentation' on what she called the 'misdeeds' of the Left Front government in the state and closed with a question that was both rhetorical and not. 'Sir, you tell me, is there any state in the country that has not seen a change in government for thirty-two years? Are the communists so great? No, sir...it is their rule by terror.' There was no need for me to comment on the comment, but I could sense the change that was imminent in the politics of the state.

Not wanting to speculate on Mamata's description of the 'rule of terror' as such, I did reflect on why the Left was now, three decades and more after it was swept into power in 1977, in retreat. There was the distance that had grown between it and the people. There were several generations of CPI(M) youth cadres that had never known a time when their party was not in power. Smugness is independent of ideology. The spartan can become arrogant, austere, and conceited. A few days later, I called on the veteran communist Ashok Mitra, as I did regularly, and I got invaluable insight. Ashok babu said, answering a question of mine, that he had not met Jyoti babu for some six years now. (He had been finance minister in Jyoti Basu's first ministry.) 'I would love to go and see him, but there is always someone sitting there with him.' And then added, ruefully, 'I hope he does not have to live through the coming debacle.' He meant the defeat of the Left Front in the 2011 elections to the state assembly.

Elections were held in India in five phases between 16 April 2009 and 13 May 2009 to elect the fifteenth Lok Sabha. An electorate of 716 million was to give to itself the chance to participate in what was going to be the largest democratic election held so far in the world. In the event, 58 per cent of the registered voters turned out to vote, which is not a bad tally. Should a governor vote? Should the president? A moot point. Going by the example set by President Narayanan, I was inclined to do so. I reasoned that I should not vote in the elections to the state assembly, where I would be called upon to play a role in government formation. But this was an election to parliament where, as a voter-citizen, I could not be faulted for exercising my franchise. Not wanting to use a Raj Bhavan car to go to the booth, Tara and I walked across to the polling booth, which was just across the Raj Bhavan gates. We went very early, and very few voters had come by then. Tara asked me who the candidates were, and I told her who they were, leaving her choice to herself.

The polling personnel knew who I was and were courteous, but just that and nothing more. This was Kolkata. I was not sure of what the results would be like, though I sensed that the Left's Third Front gambit was not likely to do well. Later that evening, I called on Jyoti babu, who, I gathered, had suffered a fall. He was sitting up in his bed, wearing a simple shirt. With his glasses perched on the tip of his nose, he looked like a little bird. He clasped his frail and fragile palms in my podgy ones.

GG: How are you doing, sir?

JB: I am finished. This is my fourth fall.... What is your assessment?

GG: My assessment of what, sir?

JB: Elections.

GG: It will be a confused picture, each segment voting according to local goals.

JB (laughing): We are trying a Third Front...(and then laughing again, a short, soft, pained laugh)...Third Front.... The slogan of a Third Front...people won't understand....'

On 14 April, President Patil presented the Padma awards in Rashtrapati Bhavan's Ashoka Hall. It was, as always, a glittering affair. Seated with Tara among the invitees, I applauded with all my heart the conferment of the Padma Bhushan on Ramachandra Guha, historian of historians, friend of friends. I could not but feel that my two elder brothers, Rajmohan and Ramchandra, who have contributed so much to scholarship, public affairs, and to India's civilizational stature, have remained undecorated.

The conferment on the same day of the Padma Bhushan on Sarojini Varadappan (1921–2013), the distinguished social worker and feminist from Chennai, was deeply gratifying. When she moved forward to receive the pendant from President Patil, I said to Jayanthi Natarajan (Mrs Varadappan's niece) seated next to us, 'Your aunt should have been conferring it, not receiving it.' The self-effacing worker for gender justice deserved to be president no less than President Patil did. The loudest applause started, I might add, by Tara and me, of the day, went to the great cinema artiste Helen Richardson (b. 1938), now Helen Khan. Helen was a star, a dancer. Helen was a person who danced, had become a star. Her life had been hard, her achievements wrung out of adversity through sheer talent. As we applauded, her dancing to Geeta Dutt's great song in *Howrah Bridge* ran through my mind certainly: 'Merra naam Chin Chin Chu, arre Chin Chin Chu'... with the 'r' erotically rumbled on the tongue. Qamar Jalalabadi (1917–2003) was at his best as the song's lyricist, as was O. P. Nayyar (1926–2007) as its creative tuner. Helen's selection for the Padma Shri (she deserved a Bhushan) was a recognition of not just the outstanding dancer and actress in her but of the genre of cabaret artistes and the far less recognized and highly disparaged community of 'bar dancers' and the even more benighted community of girls in Tamil Nadu who are known as 'record dancers', dancing to cinema songs on makeshift platforms in suburban and rural settings for miserable earnings and inevitable exploitation.

Helen-style dancing, and its many forms, does not have its origins in venerated texts containing shastraic instructions, but their practitioners don't dance 'just like that'. They are like acrobats schooled in a rigour of its own, needing confidence, training, and energy. Only more, for they also have to be inured to the gaze of those not interested in the dancer's art but in the dancer's body. The average male seeing Helen dance as a gypsy to the song 'Mehbooba' in *Sholay* has the eyes of a hyena hunting for sex. I have no idea how much Helen was paid for a guest appearance in that film, but I should imagine the lead actors Amitabh Bachchan (b. 1942), Dharmendra (b. 1935), and even Hema Malini (b. 1948) must have been paid more. If the earnings of that film at the box office were to be co-related to the value of its separate segments, I have no doubt that the single dance sequence by Helen would emerge as the magnet that drew the biggest haul.

Helen belongs to the Anglo-Indian community, one of India's very small minority groups and one of the most misunderstood, misrepresented, and mistreated ones. An Anglo-Indian being neither the one nor the other is denied the strength of numbers and also the confidence that comes from a line of populous consanguinity.

Most figures for the Anglo-Indian population in India place it around 125,000-150,000, with Kolkata and Chennai as its main 'centres'. But the community's own estimates place it at around 400,000. Anglo-Indians are said to have numbered about one million at the time of Independence. Post-Independence, Anglo-Indians left India for the United Kingdom, Australia, and other destinations in significant numbers. That speaks poorly of the sense of 'home' they felt in the new republic. And this despite the fact that the Constitution of India in its Article 366(2) made it the only ethnic community to be given its own representatives in the Lok Sabha (two members) and to several state assemblies (14 of the 29 states have one nominated member each). This reservation of two seats in the Lok Sabha was used with varying effects for some seven decades. Frank Anthony (1908–93), the intrepid educator, was a notable figure both within the community and in parliament. But since the reservation in parliament was open to revocation if the president or governor felt that the need for that was over, it was done away with in 2020—an unfortunate step, not just because the community needed a voice in the Indian Parliament but because its presence there showed India's republican soul—it has space in its legislative fora for the demographically unelectable and numerically minuscule segments of its family. And also, because having the Anglo-Indian there gave India the satisfaction of being not just fair politically and ethnographically but civilizationally. The fall of an imperial dice on the chequerboard of colonial satrapy has created the Anglo-Indian. It was not just fair but civilized of the thinking mind that was our constituent assembly to have made a space on the canvas of India for the chance of fate to etch its presence.

The reservation was no favour done to the community; it was a duty performed to the foundational mandate underlying in the concept of 'We the People of India'. I believe a reservation on the same lines was thought of for the Parsi community as well but was not pressed—or waved away by its own leaders—as being patronizing. I respect the pride underlying that but must say that the self-confidence of the tusked leader can let the herd down, for it has in it the calf, the weak, the lone, the aged, and hunted by 'nature red in tooth and claw'. India's parliament has known outstanding Parsi MPs of whom the tallest is Feroze Gandhi. Others include Minoo Masani, Piloo Mody (1926–83), and, more recently, nominated by the president, Anu Aga (b. 1942). Given the tiny size of their base, their work has been remarkable.

It so happened that I was talking a few days later to the ninety-three-year-old Russi Mody (1918–2014), once the head of Tata Steel and virtual king of Jamshedpur. Russi had contested the Jamshedpur seat for the Lok Sabha in 1998 as an independent candidate and lost badly to a greenhorn. Such is the whimsical spirit of the popular ballot. The Parsi industrialist would have made a great contribution to the debates there but even more than the debates, to the eclectic spirit of parliament. But he lost.
Russi was ruminating when he came to meet me.

RM: When a man is on his deathbed....

GG: Russi you are not in any deathbed...and like Morarji Desai have to reach and cross 100.

RM: No, you see, I wonder these days what death will be like.... It is so near.

GG: Of one thing, I am sure, Russi. When death faces Russi Mody, it will be interrogated about its nature.

RM: Death is a godly thing, and you do not question God.

I had never known the big man to be so philosophical. His end was still five years away. But he had sailed into the great sea in his mind. Tara and I called him over for dinner with a few friends shortly thereafter. Russi was distant and talked little. But when he spotted the Raj Bhavan piano, he took his seat at it as a natural-born pianist and started to sing and play with rapture—'Buona Sera', followed by 'Lara's Theme'. It was the highest possible impromptu music one can have. The next day, he dropped by, unannounced, with a large basketful of avocados from his garden. 'It was a lovely evening last night over dinner, wasn't it, Russi?' I said. 'Dinner? What dinner?' He had forgotten.

The handling of dementia and Alzheimer's disease in India is a big and inadequately addressed challenge. By 2050, it has been calculated by economics professor Jinkook Lee and her colleagues in a study funded in part by the National Institute on Aging at the University of Southern California, India's share of seniors is poised to increase to nearly 20 per cent of its population—319 million individuals. According to Lee and her co-authors, with age the strongest risk factor for Alzheimer's and related disorders, India faces an alarming potential increase in the number of people with dementia. India's success story in raising its figure for life expectancy at birth requires to be saved from itself on the Alzheimer's disease and related dementias (ADRD) front.

In the May of 2009, at Cooch Behar railway station, I came face to face with a Great Indian Reality at the other end of the age spectrum—lost children. Destitute parents in India are known to abandon children on railway trains and stations. And kids—boys mainly—from families that are unable to look after them wander into railway stations and jumping onto passing trains, find themselves in strange and strangely attractive venues with strangers, very often criminally minded, 'taking them over'. India's railway system is a wonder. Given the volume of passengers and goods it carries from one end of the country of continental size, it is a miracle. But it is also a tale with many smaller tales within it that has not been written. A remarkable NGO, with the caring involvement of the Railway Police, was trying to find a new life for such children who had run away from (or been thrown out of) homes mired in drudgery. They had found in the Indian railways a mobile home, not without dire risks and brutal experiences. I met seven such boys who were as innocent as their young ages, but I could tell had seen more of life in aspects I neither knew nor could imagine. They were students in the kindergarten of time but also in the university of life. 'I want to study,' one of the smartest among them told me. He was hooked on Dendrite, a glue sniffed for a 'high'. I was told by his carers that he was getting out of it. I nodded at this information, sagely. Is he really getting out of it? And even if he was, what about the others? I admired the dedication of the NGO and the Railway Police. But I could see that the volume of the problem was oceanic. India is holy, mystic, serene, yogic, sacred, and all of that. But it is also the home of howling misery, sickening exploitation, and utter hopelessness to countless little children who live precariously across railway tracks. If boys, they rough it out. If girls, I dare not even begin to think of their fate. The independent India that has surfed the moon holds dark craters in its soul.

By this time, the polling was over, and exit polls gave the UPA a slight edge. It was a relief for me that the UPA won a second term and a great satisfaction that a person I respected unequivocally was going to be prime minister a second time—the only one till that point after Nehru to have that honour. From the West Bengal angle, the Left Front's candidates did badly, while Congress and Trinamool did splendidly. Mamata became a union minister, not a new thing for her, but for the first time under Manmohan Singh.

On coming home to Kolkata as a minister, she called on me and asked if I would give her some advice. Since she asked, I said to her: 'You are now a senior minister. Think of yourself now as a national-level leader who can give rather than one who is forever asking. Be conscious of your giving strength and give when occasion demands it, strategic and selective support to the state government.' I do not think she was fully convinced.

Bengal puts one's intellect to rigorous tests. At—of all events—an Air Force Day celebration at Fort William on 7 October, an invitee came up and asked me: 'Sir, one Gujarat town—Dwarka—is famous for Krishna who said (to Arjuna): "The end is what matters, let the thought of means not confuse you." Another Gujarat town—Porbandar—is famous for Mohan, who said, "Means are as important as ends." What do you go by?' A veteran speechifier by now, I was rendered quite speechless by this question and muttered something inconsequential to the querist's clear disappointment (and also a sense of victory).

But I could see in this brief encounter of mine another clear sign of where educated India was headed, conceptually and theologically, on the subject of ends and means. The end is what was important to India now, not the means. And one major 'end' was success, victory, triumph. Be it in sports, investments, or science. And, of course, in war. India was now restless not to be great, just, noble, but strong, powerful, 'super'. Not a nation but a 'power'. And a major power at that. In fact—and why not?—a superpower. 'Super' as an adjective is derived from the Latin super, which means 'above' and 'above the rest'. No place for humility there. No room for modesty. Gone were the times when we were taught to be humble, even if 'great' in achievement. Now you were expected to pin the epaulette of 'super' on your shoulder yourself before you even started out on the field of whatever you wanted to be.

On my last visit to Darjeeling as governor, in mid-October, Tara and I visited the museum dedicated to Tenzing Norgay (1914–86) and called on the great man's family. Ayyo! What humility lay in that summiteer, what infinite calm in his dizzy peak! Did he think of himself as a superman, a hero even? We were shown three coats that were presented to him by Jawaharlal Nehru from his own modest wardrobe, just before Tenzing went with Edmund Hillary on his first visit to the United Kingdom after the ascent of Everest. Finding Tenzing had no suitable jacket for the visit, Nehru gave him these three, reflexively.

At the Tenzing home, we were astonished and sobered to learn that nineteen of Tenzing's relatives have summitted Everest since his 'first', including his son Jamling Tenzing Norgay (b. 1965). I asked the worthy son a question which has been put to him times without number. 'Who got there first—Hillary or your father?' Jamling said that many years after the summiting, he had asked his father about this. The mountain's top, incidentally, is not like one cone. It is more of a flat surface with some projections, like a pointed cone, one of which has been made immortal by the photograph of Hillary taken by Tenzing, with the great New Zealander's foot planted firmly and triumphantly on it. Tenzing told Jamling: 'For us Buddhists, the summit of Everest is holy. Do you think I would put my foot on it?' The truly superior do not speak of being super. They do not need to.

I had sent word by now that I would not be staying a day longer when my five-year term comes to a close. But I would, of course, welcome and be grateful for a second term in West Bengal or a governorship anywhere else. Staying as a daily wager after the fifth year was, to me, anathema. Again, sure, inverted ego this was. But there it was. And no word came from Delhi. Towards the 10th of December, I asked Chandan Sinha, my able secretary, to ask the Ministry of Home Affairs if my message about leaving had registered with it. 'Is he really set to go?' Chandan was asked. 'He is, of course,' he replied. 'On the 14th, when he completes five years.' There was silence to that.

Tara and I hosted a farewell reception on the 13th for a select few, which included a rather silent and unsmiling Buddhadeb Bhattacharjee and an equally taciturn but smiling Biman Basu. Buddha babu gave me as a farewell gift a copy of Tagore's *Red Oleanders*—a thoughtful gesture. In the rush of things, I forgot to ask him to inscribe it to me.

On the 14th, as we left Raj Bhavan for the last time, amid very touching scenes which I kept reminding myself were not special for us, I noticed that the row of photographs of former governors, starting with that of Rajaji, my 'Anna'. Bowing low before that and the large painting of Bapu's in the throne room, as inconspicuously as I could, I sped through the rows of staff and their children who had come to say goodbye. The departure was quick enough, but the car had necessarily to turn slowly at the exit, and as it did so, a perfect stranger standing at the kerb said with a wave, 'Aabaar aashun!' (Come again). That did it. I wept uncontrollably, Tara holding my hand and ADC Pankaj Pande checking his own emotions in the front seat.

The chief minister had sent a minister, his chief secretary, and the director general of police to see me off—a calculated short-changing of sorts. Mamata had sent her lieutenant Partha Chatterjee. 'Sir,' he said, 'if Delhi again asks you to return to Kolkata as governor, please do not refuse.'

My last sentence in the diary for that day has: '*We are in Chennai by 4 p.m. I unpack at once. Welcome home, former governor.*'

BOOK EIGHT

2010–25
INTO THE MODI ERA

Towards the end of 2009, when my wife and I were back in Chennai, we hoped to live in some quiet, reflecting on things past, the present and the unforeseeable future. We intended to live on my pension, with some writing thrown in, perhaps, to augment what I received as a pensioner. But while India venerates its hermits; it does not encourage reclusion in ordinary mortals.

Our morning routine of opening *The Hindu* over good brown filter coffee was a very 'Chennai' pleasure, but it also meant receiving multiple shocks by way of news on the conflicted truths of India. When I was employed, these bits of news did not affect me as much as they did now when my mind had more time to absorb them. Of these disturbing signals, violence headed the list and when seen on television as Breaking News was distinctly unfriendly to cardiac stability.

On 13 February 2010, came reports of a bomb going off in the city of Pune at a popular eatery called German Bakery, killing 17 people and injuring at least 60 others.[1] Bombs in a bakery! Anathema. Two outfits one had never heard of—the Lashkar-e-Taiba Al Alami and the Indian Mujahideen Kashmir—claimed they were behind the bomb attack.[2] But who could tell if they were indeed the real masterminds or merely fictitious names for the real perpetrators lurking behind them? This attack was not on any governmental or political target but on innocent civilians, a devilish act meant to foment disbelief, revulsion, hatred, and trigger riots and thereby further polarize society. Terrorism feeds fundamentalism of either variety.

In the June of 2010, ballistics erupted in the Kupwara region of the valley of Kashmir between the military in an encounter some saw as 'fake'. The Hurriyat Conference* in Kashmir called for the impossible—a 'complete demilitarization' of Jammu and Kashmir, with a spontaneous movement rallying to the call. The state's chief minister at the time was the young Omar Abdullah. The state's forces then did what any administration would, in such circumstances: retaliate with force. And the retaliation did what it would have to do. It left, over the coming days, 112 including an eleven-year-old boy, dead.

*A coalition of 26 associations formed in 1993, all united in their quest for an 'independent Kashmir', the word itself meaning 'liberty' or 'independence'.

Prime Minister Manmohan Singh, shocked, offered compensations (which were declined) and an unconditional dialogue with just one requirement: the eschewal of violence. Nothing less could have been expected of that man of honour. And he directed the appointment of a group of interlocutors to begin a conversation with the people of the state so as to ascertain their complex feelings, aspirations, and fears. When I heard of the plan, I thought my friend and batchmate Wajahat Habibullah, with the advantage of belonging to the Jammu and Kashmir cadre, would be ideal as chair of the panel. Also that the interlocutors would make Governor N. N. Vohra than whom a more seasoned and mature officer could not be found, their sounding board. A couple of friends put it to those that decide things in Delhi that I be included among the interlocutors, in fact, the principal, if not only one. 'He knows Hindi and can understand Urdu,' it was said, 'and being apolitical, will be trusted by all or at least not distrusted by any.' The suggestion did not, luckily for me and even more so for Kashmir, go any further. I would have been a disaster there. Radha Kumar, the amazingly sharp historian of post-colonial agonies the world over, such as ethnic strife and partition, was appointed to it, the sole woman member, with Information Commissioner M. M. Ansari as member, and the distinguished journalist Dileep Padgaonkar, senior journalist, being its chair. The group met some 600 deputationists in intensive consultations, many of them held in confidence, and held public meetings in every district of Jammu and Kashmir. But there were rifts within the group, Radha Kumar attempting to resign midway. She was far too honest with her views and candid with her recommendations. The one for 'meaningful autonomy' was pretty much fraught from the word go. The exercise was unable to achieve its larger goals of steps towards a solution to the conflict, but it did 'buy the administration three years of relative peace', in Chief Minister Omar Abdullah's words. After 2014, the polarization in the state was to resurface, growing in intensity.

Another issue over which India itself stood polarized—Ayodhya and the demand that a temple to Ram be installed where the Babri Masjid had stood—rose toweringly over the country in the September of 2010. The Allahabad High Court ruled a three-way division of the disputed area in an exercise in compromise through the maze of legal rights and wrongs. Sickened as I was by the demolition of the Babri Masjid and its trail of blood-letting, I thought the pronouncement could have one good result: it would ensure the transfer of the matter to the Supreme Court, where it would—and did—lie for long and, I hoped, long enough for the 'keyed-up' public to lose all interest in it. I was to be proved wrong, naïve, stupid. The matter did go up to the highest court in the land, but the public did not lose interest in it or, rather, was not allowed to do so.

The Ram temple issue was to loom over India for the next many years, colouring all politics and marginalizing important issues like the tightening stranglehold of corruption on the nation's governance. The urgent in India always gets the better of the important.

Corruption enjoys an endemicity in India that may be likened to that of jaundice and typhoid. It is accepted, sullenly, as a fact of life until some utterly egregious instance of it comes to light and disgusts the nation by its scale or by the audacity of the persons implicated in it. The XIX Commonwealth Games were held in Delhi from 3 to 14 October 2010, bringing a total of 4,352 athletes from 71 Commonwealth nations and dependencies competing in 21 sports and 272 events. In sports terms, India did well, finishing second overall with 38 gold medals and 101 total medals. But the gold in the medals sank under the muck of scandal. Preparations for the games had started months earlier, as they had to. But so did money-spinning. Findings showed the 'award of work contracts at higher prices, poor quality assurance and management, and work contracts awarded to ineligible agencies'. Also noted was widespread corruption in 'procurement and awarding of contracts for constructing the game's infrastructures.' News agency reports spoke of 'shadowy off-shore firms, forged emails, inexplicable payments to bogus companies and inflated bills—for every purchase from toilet paper to treadmills'[3].

Congress leader Suresh Kalmadi (b. 1944) was president of the Organizing Committee. He was booed at the opening with 80,000 spectators, and the games' joint inaugurators, HRH the Prince of Wales and HE President Pratibha Patil watching. From being a major celebration, CWG became a major embarrassment for India, its government, and Prime Minister Manmohan Singh. The world-class economist heading the government of India was a lion in a jungle full of rapacious canines and libidinous simians.

Two years later, another VIP-related scandal was to break, embarrassing the Congress-led UPA-II government. It was about a multimillion-dollar corruption case relating to 2006 and 2007 during UPA-I. Controversy over the contract came to light on 12 February 2013 with the arrest in Italy by Italian authorities of Giuseppe Orsi, the CEO of Finmeccanica, AgustaWestland's parent company, over corruption and bribery charges. Money was alleged to have been paid to middlemen and Indian officials to purchase a new fleet of twelve helicopters for VIP and VVIP duties. The amount involved was said to be ₹2.5 billion (US$ 31 million), transferred through bank accounts in the UK and UAE. On 25 March 2013, Defence

Minister A. K. Antony confirmed corruption allegations by stating with admirable, if unavoidable honesty: 'Yes, corruption has taken place in the helicopter deal, and bribes have been taken. The CBI is pursuing the case very vigorously.'[4] The UPA-II government was to cancel the contract and effect recoveries of the amounts it had paid to AgustaWestland, but the stain on its reputation was deep. The days of UPA-II under the same prime minister now seemed numbered.

Behind the collapse of individual reputations, the real casualty was public trust in the occupiers of high office. Known as nambikkai in Tamil, vishvas and bharosa in Hindi or aitbar in Hindustani or Urdu, trust had become one of independent India's 'war wounded'. It walked on crutches.

Elections depended on the trust of the electors in the fairness of the election machine. Among the nations that became independent around the middle and end of the twentieth century, India's electors had shown themselves to be masters of electoral expertise. Watched over by the nation's judicial system, it elected governments and ejected them with aplomb. State assembly elections took place in 2011 in two states I was intimately connected with: West Bengal and Tamil Nadu. Mamata Banerjee became chief minister of West Bengal and Jayalalithaa of Tamil Nadu; the former because West Bengal, after thirty-four years of the CPI(M)-led coalition government, was in need of a change, and the latter largely because the DMK had begun to be perceived as corrupt and its prominent leader A. Raja, then union minister of Communication and Information Technology, had been charged (wrongly, as it later turned out) of corruption. Mamata and Jayalalithaa had, without doubt, been elected by a massive popular vote.

This is when Anna Hazare (b. 1937) presented himself.

In 2011, the Maharashtrian activist was relatively unknown outside his state and the circles of rural NGOs. And in those circles, too, he was known more for his personality traits, such as an authoritative and arbitrary style of functioning, which included punishing the 'guilty' and doing so in public.

On 5 April, Hazare started a hunger strike on the issue of state corruption and demanding the establishment, through an Act of parliament, of an ombudsman-type authority, the Lok Pal (meaning people's protector) something that had long been discussed from the time that nomenclature had been first suggested by the legal luminary and parliamentarian L. M. Singhvi. People flocked to the venue of Hazare's fast in New Delhi's Jantar Mantar as to a suddenly arrived Messiah, and to watch him exert pressure on the government. No one missed the presence near the fasting Hazare of his principal associate, the strong and silent Arvind Kejriwal.

Arvind Kejriwal addressing the public at Jantar Mantar, New Delhi, July 2011, with his then leader Anna Hazare fasting beneath a photograph of the Mahatma. The fast was directed against the Manmohan Singh government to press for an inquiry against cabinet ministers whom the protesters had accused of corruption. (*Hindustan Times* archives).

Anna Hazare blesses Arvind Kejriwal, New Delhi, 2011. (*Hindustan Times* archives).

Late on 8 April, under mounting calls from civil society and the media, especially social media, the Manmohan Singh government accepted each one of Hazare's demands. My diary notes for 9 April:

> *He has won a signal victory. A joint committee comprising 50% activists and 5% Ministers will draft the Lok Pal Bill. I join thousands gathered at Jantar Mantar to see AH break his fast. The 'mix' of young and old, middle class and poor (some perhaps rich as well) in the throng is impressive. No cop controls it; volunteers do. I see opportunists aplenty and (as I realise only later) experience one as well—a pickpocket who relieves me of Rs 200 or so. AH on the stage is an image of determination and empowered contentment. I notice self-seeking among some on the stage.... Several 'cranks' are around—Limca Book of Records type of weirdos, sadhus and sannyasis, who in India descend like flies on any free gathering. But all in all it is a most interesting and even exhilarating experience.*

The Lokpal Bill, 2011, as modified in the Jan Lokpal Bill, instituted an ombudsman with the powers to deal with corruption in public institutions. But if anything is achieved in the letter and squandered in spirit, Hazare's movement is its great example. We have a Lok Pal. But ask anyone who the incumbent Lok Pal is, and you will get 'Lok what....?'

At a discussion on 'India, Gandhi, and leadership', around this very time in Chennai, when it looked like India had found and lost a leader in the sudden popping up and equally fast vanishing from the popular imagination of Anna Hazare, I was asked by a visiting Dutchman: 'What is the difference between a guru and a leader?' I was at a loss for an answer.

Life is not without its compensations. Shortly after the rise and subsiding of the Lok Pal movement, its dissipation and cracking-up with Kejriwal moving away from Hazare and Hazare moving away from just about everyone, I was to meet a true 'leader' who had already made a difference—in medical science.

TNQ Technologies in Chennai, a globally valued source of knowledge and inputs for medical science research, invites annually a scholar or medical expert to speak in at least three venues in India on her or his chosen field of specialization. This year, it was Shinya Yamanaka (b. 1962), the Japanese path-breaking expert on stem cells, speaking in one of Chennai's great halls. Yamanaka is a gentle speaker with a subtle sense of humour. After his lecture on 1 February, thanks to the generosity of Mariam Ram, TNQ's moving spirit, I found myself seated next to the speaker at dinner and felt encouraged to ask him: what are the areas that are likely to benefit the most from stem-cells application? He said 'diabetes and ophthalmic (especially retinal) conditions'. This was great to know. My father had died at age fifty-seven of a heart attack while undergoing treatment for severe diabetes. And my mother, also diabetic, had succumbed to complications after cataract surgery at seventy-one. So, Yamanaka was saying something that went straight to my brain-heart.

Later that very year, Yamanaka was to get the Nobel Prize for Medicine. But prize or no prize, his contribution was phenomenal, and for India, which is home to the world's second highest number of diabetic patients and where one out of every seven diabetic adults worldwide resides, and one in every third household has diabetic patients. According to the 2020 figures from the International Association for the Prevention of Blindness, India has 9.2 million blind persons, followed by China at 8.9 million, and Indonesia in third place with 3.7 million. A grim truth.

Within a few days of Yamanaka's visit to Chennai, India had another Japanese visitor. Fuki Yoshimoto, a forty-three-year-old Japanese national, was on her first visit to New Delhi and was given, apart from the dubious offerings of Paharganj, where she opted to stay, a quick taste of the criminal talents of urban India. She was in an autorickshaw, rounding the circle between Aurangzeb Road and Tughlaq Road, when thieves adept at bag-snatching winged past on a two-wheeler and lunged for the bag that she was carrying. The bag contained her passport, notebook, iPod, mobile phone, two ATM cards, and 50,000 Japanese yen. Yoshimoto was not one to give up easily. Resisting the bag snatchers, she was flung out of the vehicle, badly injured. The wounds on her head and face after she fell off the moving autorickshaw were not minor.

Yamanaka and Yoshimoto, unknown to each other, saw two Indias and would remember each vividly, the first to our credit and the second to our shame.

Tara and I had, over 2011 and 2012, been given the ineffable gift by our daughters of a grand-daughter each. It was a relief to be promoted from being a 'forever grandson' to being a grandfather. I was elated beyond description. But I was still not above wanting more of life's material opportunities.

Over May, June, and July, until August, 2011, India was into election mood again—for the offices of president and prime minister. As last time around, this time too, media speculation was rife about names, and mine kept being taken as a 'likely' one and a 'likely consensus one'. I knew better, as the UPA leadership was saying nothing of the sort to me. Only Mamata and Naveen Patnaik, chief minister of Odisha, seemed keen on my candidature. She was in regular touch, saying I was 'the most credible man' and he saying the country needed a 'father figure'.

Did I want to become president or vice president? Of course, yes. I knew my failings, of which hankering for high positions (such as these two or 'at least' a nomination to the Rajya Sabha) was the greatest failing. Ambition, like lust, intoxicates before it leads you to crash. And age-seniors are the most pathetic of 'crashers'. And in a moment of honesty with myself I noted the following in my diary:' *I do not know if I am liberal or conservative, a socialist or a believer in free enterprise. I am not patriotic enough, not learned enough, not earnest enough, not knowledgeable or experienced enough. I have lived on the capital of my surname.*'

My diary got this for 13 June 2011: '*A day to be remembered. The morning is placid, afternoon full of vim! Mamata is in Delhi to meet Sonia amidst a TV blitz about me as MB's preferred choice. I am besieged by about the maximum number of phone calls I have received in any half an hour for that half hour. Then—anti-climax. MB emerges from that meeting to say Sonia Gandhi's first choice is Pranab, second Hamid Ansari.... The phones stop ringing at once!*'

Pranab Mukherjee had put up with not being prime minister. He was not going to put up being side-lined again. He got what he wanted.

Pranab Mukherjee brought to Rashtrapati Bhavan the temperament of the diligent student who is cleverer than all the others in his class, but the 'others' being 'posher' than him, he is long denied his due. And so he decides to use his cleverness to outsmart all the others in the nuts and bolts and screws of systems. He decides to 'show them' how agility is also an ability and how when others may spend hours thinking, he can within minutes 'do it'. Our thirteenth president 'did it' in one major area. He took one look at the death penalty files pending on his desk, cases recommended to his predecessor, President Pratibha Patil, who had not approved even one. Pranab babu approved each and every one of them with robotic finesse.[5] The gallows had, for some years, dangled between appeal and doubt. They were now swinging. And there was little or no public disapproval. The land of the Buddha, Mahavira, Nanak, and Gandhi is not pro-abolition. It generally is 'okay' with the death penalty. Ironical.

If I was asked to say what is independent India's essential 'rasa', I would say it is irony. India is about contrasts, yes. It is about contradictions, of course. And, of course, it is a land of extremes. But more than any of these, it is essentially home to ironies. And ironically, the word 'irony' has no real equivalent in the languages of India.

The nation's endorsement of capital punishment got a wholly understandable voltage that year with the brutal gang-rape of a physiotherapy student on a bus that she boarded with a male companion. The four perpetrators were of varying ages, one of them a minor. The outrage caused a sensation and shame across the country and led to many protests which targeted the authorities for the poor state of protection for women. The government was on the back foot, doing its utmost to save the life of the battered woman, but it was too late. It must not be forgotten that while there was outrage over the episode, it was also true that for quite some time, as Nirbhaya (as the media came to call her) lay senseless on the roadside, many people had passed her by. Before she became 'news', Nirbhaya was alone in her agony. Civil society in India must not forget that.

On the same day as Nirbhaya's, another brutal rape was reported from Tura district of Meghalaya. The victim was a minor and allegedly raped by sixteen people. Like Nirbhaya, who had gone to watch a movie with her friend and was assaulted on her way back home, the Meghalaya victim had gone to watch the Winter Festival at Williamnagar with her friends.

There were demands immediately after Nirbhaya for the law to be amended to hand the death sentence for rape convicts. Now, under certain circumstances, rape convicts can hang. Have rape cases, as reported, fallen as a result? The National Crime Records Bureau (NCRB) report 'Crime in India 2012' was to give the alarming information that 'the singular crime of rape is the fastest growing crime in India' and has increased by 902 per cent over the four decades from 1971 to 2012. This was reported rape cases. The actual number has to be many times that number. Incidents of rapes reported had, according to this report, increased from 24,206 in 2011 to 24,923 in 2012, including Nirbhaya's. This meant sixty-eight cases of rape were registered, on an average, every day. If sixty-eight girls and women were raped every day in India in 2012, the daily average number of reported rapes was to increase to eighty-six in 2021, according to the same and sole source of crime information—NCRB data.

So, has awareness among potential victims and, basically, among women in India about this criminal disease increased? Yes, it has. Has that made the Indian girl and woman less vulnerable to rape? No. Why? Because the potential rapist has not gone away. He is very much around us.

The readers will say of this writer: 'Can he think of nothing better than recounting one national setback after another, one horror story after another?' She might well say, 'Here is another Katherine Mayo.' And I would not blame her for thinking so. But this book is not a 'history of India' which must itemize all things, the happy and the sad, the good and the wicked, like an encyclopaedia of events. It is my glimpsing of events, and if the sad and the saddening have outweighed the happy and the gladdening in my mind, that is how I am. I did say, at the start of the book, that my earliest memories are overcast with images of the violent end of a man of peace. So, if read you must these pages, dear reader, bear with my grim bag of impressions.

We have considered Naxalism earlier in these pages.

On 25 May 2013, Naxalism showed its fangs in the tribal-rich state of Chhattisgarh. Naxalite insurgents of the CPI(M) attacked a convoy of Indian National Congress leaders in the Jhiram Ghati, Darbha Valley, in the Sukma district. At least twenty-seven men lay dead, including a former state minister, Mahendra Karma, and Chhattisgarh's Congress chief Nand Kumar Patel. A former union minister and senior Congressman, Vidya Charan Shukla, succumbed to his injuries after a few days.[6] Karma had a violent reputation himself, with many charges chasing him, including some very sinister ones.[7] He had earned the particular hatred of Naxalites for having masterminded an anti-Naxal vigilante group, the Salwa Judum, which spread its own counter-terror. Karma's guards and the attackers exchanged fire, but his defenders running out of bullets; Karma came forward, identified himself and surrendered. The Naxals then took him away, beat him, stabbed him several times and sprayed him with bullets. They beat him again about the head with the butts of their guns. Autopsy revealed seventy-eight wounds on his body. India is not Libya, and may it never be, but the bludgeoners of Mahendra Karma matched in their ferocity the butchers of Muammar Gaddafi.

In the final analysis, the Jhiram Ghati dead were tragic figures, dying at the hands of their murderers but inviting their deaths by reason of policy mistakes, political misjudgements and sheer hubris. The vigilantism that Karma unleashed had been taken up by the Supreme Court in a landmark case filed by Nandini Sundar and others and argued by the exceptionally gutsy Ashok Desai. On 5 July 2011, the Supreme Court had declared the militia to be illegal and unconstitutional and ordered its disbanding. The court had also directed the government of Chhattisgarh to recover all of its firearms, ammunition, and accessories. But Karma was a marked man.

The state's absorption with 'development' over 'justice' and the upwardly mobile classes' preoccupation with 'progress' over 'equality' has sharpened the edge of resentment's razor and slid the bullets of anger into the barrels of want. Are these images smooth metaphors, self-fulfilling abstractions?

Not for someone like P. Sainath, a cherished friend, for whom life-throttling droughts were not a subject for meteorologists but an existential reality as real as a war. His 1996 masterpiece *Everybody Loves a Good Drought* based on despatches he had written from 1990 to 1992 for the *Times of India*, while staying in destitute villages in the interiors of India, had given me a picture I had not received earlier, except in Premchand's stories, of how life is eked out in rural India, how various government projects do and do not work at the ground level, and how development theories are far from reality. It was again from him that I saw with disbelief the stunningly high levels of corruption in so called development projects.

For Sainath, the phenomenon of farmers' suicides in the wake of collapsing farm incomes was not about the statistics for unnatural deaths among farmers but a reality to be faced four square and tackled if the rage was not going to move to different levels of violence.

Nor was 'justice' an abstraction for Aruna Roy and her husband Bunker Roy, even older friends, with whom Tara and I spent quality time that year, 2013. Aruna, my 'batchmate' in the IAS, had left the codified world of the civil service for real work among the people of Rajasthan (and beyond) where her husband Bunker Roy, my contemporary at college, had set up in Tilonia, a village in Ajmer district, Barefoot College. Reaching there, and after being shown to our room, which, as we learnt to our awe, the Dalai Lama himself had stayed in, and going around the premises, I asked Bunker, 'The college started with you, didn't it?' He nodded absent-mindedly as if confirming something—his role—which was of no importance. Aruna, likewise, made light of the austerity of their Tilonia home as she served up bajra and makai rotis even as she frowned on her associate for 'unnecessarily making a second vegetable curry'. We then went to Aruna's 'own' village, Dev Dungri, where her own hut, scarcely bigger in size than a bullock cart, hosted us. Interns from the National Law School, Bengaluru, no less, were in the village as well, as also college students from elsewhere in India, experiencing life in that part of India, which had no piped water supply or toilets in homes and just about one precarious power line.

We were all served rotis again, and no one wanted a second, for the one that we got was so full of 'meal' that our appetites were totally satiated. With Aruna's remarkable colleague Nikhil Dey, who had walked out of a high-powered executive job in a US-based firm to work among India's marginalized people, we met people in the vicinity, all being helped by Aruna's movement Mazdoor Kisan Shakti Sangathan (MKSS), to claim their due, their rights, and reclaim their voices in the running of their lives. Aruna had pioneered the Right to Information Act, now a household enactment in India. It was giving people with no 'hold' on the authorities a 'hold' over their rights as citizens to 'just know'. If the spirit of Tilonia and Dev Dungri had reached the districts where Naxalism thrived, the story would have been different.

Aruna gave Tara and me another blessing of an experience. She enabled us to visit Ajmer and its great dargah of Khwaja Moinuddin Chishti, at the site famed as Ajmer Sharif. Sufi singers were enthralling the gathering that comprised both Hindus and Muslims. Here again, the thought was irresistible: if only the spirit of Ajmer Sharif was to be seen and felt in every place of worship, Hindu and Muslim, would the other scourge of independent India—communal tension and terror thrive? Ghazi Khan, the chief Sufi singer and kartal player, was singing or saying: *Ajmer vahi jata hai, jise Khwaja bulata hai* (Only he goes to Ajmer who has, by the Khwaja, been 'called' to Ajmer). Completely enraptured by the atmosphere of the venue, I had forgotten to switch my mobile phone off, and as Tara and I sat down among the congregation, the phone rang. It was the peerless Carnatic vocalist and friend of friends, T. M. Krishna. I told the young vidvan in a soft voice where we are. 'Please pray for me,' he said and disconnected. The vidvan, believed to be an agnostic, had called, but surely, he had also been 'called'? Similarly, I believe his foundational book *A Southern Music* with its startling insights into the inner life of Carnatic music, but had been written by him to the dictation of a muse. Exactly like his music. He sings, possessed. By what? The deities his 'classical' songs invoke? Or by what W. B. Yeats in his poem on an Irish airman calls a 'lonely impulse of delight?' Neither, I should say, because when lost to his music's swirl he is in something that can only be called rapture. That is it: his music is rapturous and he transmits it, unbeknownst to himself to his listeners. I rejoiced, therefore, in the announcement in the summer of 2024, of the conferment on him of the Madras Music Academy's cherished decoration of Sangita Kalanidhi, a recognition of his musical genius. And admired his unruffledness at the carping comments of some displeased by his 'activism' on dismantling upper-caste predominance in the world of the arts. Krishna's concert at the Music Academy on Christmas day, 2024, was spectacular, not just for the beauty of his singing but also for the rapture of the overflowing audience, mainly of young music enthusiasts, who filled the hall with sheer joy. At the 'investiture' on 1 January 2025, at which he formally became a Sangita Kalanidhi, the scholar of multiple Indian languages David Shulman said Carnatic music was about a 'passionate introspection'. Seated in the audience was the extraordinary 'Bombay' Jayshree Ramnath who had been presented the Sangita Kalanidhi the previous year, an embodiment of that form of inner meditation.

Ramachandra Guha was central to the intellectual ecology of this period in my life. His being described now very rightly but, in my view, inadequately, as India's most celebrated historian gave me no ordinary happiness. Ram's interest in Gandhi is only part historical. It is, essentially civilizational because he sees in the bania-turned-barrister-turned-political-game changer the work of a global phenomenon. His Gandhi-sited books, *India After Gandhi* (2007),

Gandhi Before India (2013), and *Gandhi: The Years that changed the World: 1914-1948* (2014) form a trilogy or a triptych in three genres—history, biography, and political science, framed in what may be called humanity's spiritual intelligence. I read all three in this 'post-governorship' phase of mine, gripped by both the recounting as well as the messaging. They tell us what Gandhi attempted for his people, his country, and his times in a way that is chastening for he neither despairs nor dons a fake optimism.

I drew strength from Guha's writings as I had from my brother Rajmohan's when, on 8 June 2014, a great new turn was given to the nation's life. Elections being around the corner, the BJP named Gujarat's chief minister Narendra Modi as its prime ministerial candidate. Here was a leader who owed nothing to the Gandhi–Nehru era, who was born after India became independent and who was now offering his services to a nation that seemed to have tired of the ethos of the freedom-of-fighters' I referred to at the start of this book.

By January, election fever climbed, and candidates were being speculated about. Aam Aadmi Party's (AAP) ideologue and incisive thinker Yogendra Yadav rang to ask me to join the fray in Gujarat with AAP's backing. He was later to leave AAP on grounds of principle, a step in conscience, which I respected, but that is another story. I told Yogendra I was not a political animal but would give his kind suggestion careful thought. I knew if I were to do this, irrespective of whether I won or lost, my life would not be the same again. A month later, he mailed to say AAP would like me to contest Narendra Modi, and if I did that, they would back me even if I stood as an Independent. But if I agreed to join AAP and contest as an AAP candidate, the party would back me wherever I stood from, including Delhi. I consulted close friends and, of course, family. My instinct was against the idea, and I told Yogendra as much. He got in touch two days later to ask if I would not reconsider and said AAP would like me to stand on a party ticket from Delhi, an AAP stronghold.

AAP's trust in my ability to put up 'a strong fight' even if I were to not win, touched me. But I was not ready for such a risk. I was, basically, what I know myself to be: strong-sounding in my political views, timid when it comes to political action. Keen on public office but of the constitutional, non-combative kind, not ones that come as a result of battle. I admire battlers but will not bear the arms of protest myself. Basically, I am a wimp.

As Narendra Modi's candidature from Varanasi was announced, Yogendra made another final attempt: will I not agree, please, to stand from Varanasi? No, I said, no, Yogen, thank you.

More than party fortunes were at stake in the election. The secular ethos of the Constitution was. In a wonderful concatenation, *Samvidhaan: The Making of the Constitution of India*, a ten-part television mini-series based on the making of the Constitution of India, directed by Shyam Benegal, appeared now, the great sequence being premiered on 2 March 2014 on Rajya Sabha TV, with an episode scheduled to air every Sunday morning. This was not going to become the craze that Ramanand Sagar's *Ramayana* serial was, but it was something to be grateful for.

I had declined to enter the elections, but my brother Rajmohan, then eighty, battle-scarred three times over three general elections fought from UP, Madhya Pradesh, and Gujarat, stood from East Delhi as an AAP candidate. After the polls, while he was reflectively silent, not ruling out a win though the 'air' said 'you have lost', his wife Usha was clear. There was no chance of winning, she said and gave an interesting reason: Mahatma Gandhi has lost all relevance for India's urban electorate. Rajmohan lost—handsomely. The seat, as indeed all seats in Delhi, were regarded as 'safe', but no one had quite sensed the strength and sweeping power of the Modi wave. I was more saddened by his defeat than I would have been by my own. Our father had held the highest hopes for him, including his becoming an MP. And our grandfather Rajaji had expected Rajmohan, who bore his name in its first three letters, to play an important part in Indian politics. My own child's eye had seen in him a successor to our father in the *Hindustan Times*, a follower of Rajaji in politics, a worthy example of all Gandhi stood for in overarching national values. I had always believed Rajmohan is the best prime minister India never had. A little-known political entity had bested him.

Another defeat I lamented was that of Nandan Nilekani in Bengaluru. Brighter than the brightest, sharp as a blade, and of Himalayan personal integrity, he had it in him to be a minister, a prime minister who, like Rajiv Gandhi, would have used technological tools to leverage India's economic strengths. He, too, had been defeated by a BJP election-repeater who was wafted from a bored defeat to an emphatic victory by the same wave.

Narendra Modi had secured for his party a victory on its own. My diary noted: '*Congress decimated, the Left vanquished. Mohan and Nandan defeated. But somehow, I am not as shattered as I might have been.*'

As in the first election to the Lok Sabha, which saw less than half of India instal a Nehru-led Congress government in office, less than half of India installed Narendra Modi-led NDA in office. Be the nation's guardian, I said to him through an 'open letter' in *The Hindu*. As much of that India which did not vote for you as the India that did. Be the Savarkar in your heart if you must be, I said to him, but be the Ambedkar in your mind that India needs you to be. I did not refer him to Gandhi. I should have. I should have said, 'Place Gandhi in your soul.'

Had the fast and regular clip of polls in India seen the process become cleaner, less manipulable by the old and new interests that abound in the country to short-change the voter and strike gold for themselves? No. Had the hold of money over elections abated? No way! Had the intimidation of voters been reduced, if not banished? Heavens, no. Had the distribution of liquor and cash as last-minute incentives been abandoned? Ayyo, far from it. Has slander, mud-slinging and character assassination in election campaign rhetoric ended? They had only increased in foulness and frequency. Had the insidious introduction of religious sentiment in campaigns been given up? On the contrary, leaflets appealing for votes had now come to be given with the images of gods and goddesses attached to them. Had all violence before, during, and after the polls ceased? It had only increased.

India's electoral democracy was moving higher and higher, not in the science of electoral finesse but in the art of electoral sleights of hand, a process that subverted the system without the system realizing that it was being subverted.

So, was the Indian voter now beginning to take malpractice as standard practice?

The prime minister's announcement on Independence Day—his first from the turreted heights of Delhi's Red Fort—abolishing the Planning Commission seemed to me to defy reasoning. True, Yojana Bhavan had its 'passengers', and much paper had rolled in the idle ink of reports no one read, much less acted on, but still, who would doubt or deny that some of India's finest minds had given from that organization, a sense of the nation's integrated progress towards set goals in poverty alleviation and self-reliance? The step was, for me, the lobotomy of a vital organ of the state.

And what was to take the place of planning by experts? Intuiting by a new elite?

Stray pieces of news kept coming around this time of moves to instal statues of Gandhi's assassin and, more disturbingly, of groups doing 'shooting practice' on pictures of Gandhi. Asked by the media to write on the subject, I chose to not react.

In the March of 2015, however, London saw a truly beautiful thing happen. On its leafy Parliament Square, a statue was installed of Gandhi, sculpted by Philip Jackson, one of the most gifted sculptors of our time. The moving spirit behind this was Meghnad Desai, a Labour peer and economist, guided by India's high commissioner in London, Ranjan Mathai, who was keen that the statue should bear a true likeness. Doing the honours were

Britain's Prime Minister David Cameron and India's Finance Minister Arun Jaitley. Amitabh Bachchan was invited to speak at the event and so was I. It was, as I have said, a beautiful event because here was Gandhi, a dismantler of the British Raj, being honoured by a statue to him being placed in front of Britain's Parliament House, and unveiled by the country's prime minister, right beside the statues of two men who had opposed him—Winston Churchill and Field Marshal Smuts. That there also stood in the same square, statues of Abraham Lincoln and Nelson Mandela, was a felicity I could not but notice and be glad of. I will not take the reader's time by repeating what I said at the event, but I must record that I did say that while London was having this Gandhi statue come up, there were those in India who wanted a statue of his assassin to be raised. After the event was over, Jaitley said to me, 'Gopal, be assured we will never let that happen.' I found that reassurance coming from one as responsible as him, most gratifying. Jaitley's premature death not long thereafter grieved me. His mind was committed to the BJP, but with its autonomy to think, intact. He was no bonded labourer.

In the wake of the election, on 25 July 2017, of Ram Nath Kovind, a little-known former member of the Rajya Sabha and the then governor of Bihar, as the fourteenth president of India, the election also fell due for the office of the vice president of India, just vacated by Hamid Ansari who had done that office proud over two five-year terms. I was driving up to my class at Ashoka University in Sonepat, where, thanks to the generous invitation of its first vice chancellor and now chancellor, the historian Professor Rudrangshu Mukherjee, I had been teaching a course on the civilizations of India, when Sonia Gandhi rang on my mobile phone to ask if I would agree to be the combined opposition's candidate for that office. I asked her for a little time to consult my wife, my sister, and brother. 'Of course,' she said and indicated that the time left for me to decide was something like an hour. The entire opposition was in conclave at that very time and was waiting for my response, she said. An hour! Tara asked if I had any chance of winning, and I said none, none at all, zero, and that the ruling party had the numbers and its candidate will sail in. In that case, why? she asked. Why, indeed, I said rhetorically but then added there is something to be said for 'a good, strong, symbolic contest'. After speaking to my sister and brother—all within the same hour—I decided I would wait to see what 'the combined opposition' was about.

Sure enough, during the course of the class, my phone, which I had put on 'silent', vibrated. I took my students' permission to step out of the class to take the call, saying it was something urgent. Every major opposition party, then in conclave, 'spoke' to me in that one call—Ghulam Nabi Azad from the Congress, Derek O'Brien from the Trinamool, and Sitaram Yechury from the CPI(M), among others. A more galactic formation could not have been imagined. I conveyed my acceptance to their collective happiness. The call over, I spent about five minutes staring into the open lawn in front of me, reflecting on what I had led myself into before returning to my class. I had barely repositioned myself at the lectern when a student sitting in the middle of the rows said, 'Congratulations, professor. You are going to be the opposition's candidate for vice president.' I could have been in good Wodehouse-style, 'knocked down by a feather'. The young man then explained that social media had been speculating for much of that morning about the candidate and that around the time I got my call, instead of attending to my lecture, he had been surfing the net and lo, even as I was ruminating for those five minutes, the meeting had announced my acceptance and he had heard it before I had fully absorbed it.

Ashoka University's vice-chancellor at the time, Pratap Bhanu Mehta, most graciously said I could take it that the university had no objection to my contesting and that while he would like me to succeed, the university would be ready and happy to see me return to the faculty after the contest!

The next few days were tumultuous for me, various persons and parties swamping my phone with felicitatory calls and 'we know you are up against the NDA's bigger numbers.... But it is important to take a stand...you may not win, but you would have made a point....' and so on. There were also those who said I was being made a sacrificial goat. But most interestingly, missiles were suddenly manufactured and hurled at me for having joined, several weeks earlier, many public figures and legal luminaries in urging President Mukherjee to commute the death sentence on the 1993 Mumbai serial blast convict, Yakub Memon. Predictably, the word 'traitor' was flung at me, reminding me at once and vividly, of JP's letter to me of 28 October 1964 in which he had said, '*When abuses were being hurled from every side and the word "traitor" was being thrown into the face, your letter, the letter of a fine...*'

At a press conference held outside Parliament House immediately after I filed my nomination papers, I was again asked about this, and I said I was, on a point of principle, against capital punishment and had written, in the same vein, to the president of Pakistan to not execute Kulbhushan Jadhav, the Indian held captive there.

The NDA took more time than I would have expected to announce its candidate—the seasoned BJP veteran Venkaiah Naidu. Some Congressmen promptly got some data to accuse him of corrupt practice—something which was totally unacceptable to me, and I rang Rahul Gandhi to ask him to have the thing stopped. To my relief, he agreed at once, and no one heard anything more on the subject. Nitish Kumar's JDU, which had joined the opposition's identification of me for the candidature, did a somersault midway into the election season, switching from UPA to NDA, but the Bihar chief minister told me in no uncertain terms himself over the phone that the alliance switch would make no difference to his and his party's support of my candidature. And he remained true to his word, except for three of his MPs marking the ballot paper wrong so that they had to be deemed invalid. Naveen Patnaik, chief minister of Odisha, announced his and his party's support to me as well.

Election day, 5 August 2017, was an experience. As a candidate, I was allowed access, up to a point, to the election venue in Parliament House and saw a good number of the MPs from both camps filing in to vote. Home Minister Rajnath Singh was particularly cordial as he was brought up to where I stood by Ananth Kumar, a BJP MP I had long known. Two MPs nominated to the Rajya Sabha in UPA times and hence, presumably, voting for me I saw but could not meet: Sachin Tendulkar came in, walking briskly, and I looked forward to a handshake with the great cricketer, but he turned into one of the circular corridors before I could do that. Another was the glamour diva of the Hindi screen, Rekha. She wafted in like a cool breeze in summer, wearing sunglasses though indoors, so none could see her eyes or see what her eyes were seeing; unsmiling, expressionless, she slid into and out of the voting chamber after voting, as I hoped, for me. But I will never know. Two other MPs from the world of cinema who spoke long and warmly with me were Jaya Bachchan, who not only voted for me but was vocal in support from the Samajwadi Party and Hema Malini of the BJP, who, of course, voted for Venkaiah Naidu, was amazingly cordial. I spoke to the popular actress in the language our mothers were born into—Tamil.

GG: Namaskaram. Yen peyar Gopalkrishna Gandhi (Namaskaram, I am Gopalkrishna Gandhi)

HM: Oh...Neenga Tamil pesarangala.... Eppadi? (Oh...You speak Tamil...how come?)

GG: Aamaam, adhu yen thaiyin mozhi (That is so, it is my mother's language...)

HM: Adhu eppadi? (How is that?)

GG: Ninga Rajajiyin peyar kettirpinga.... (You might have heard the name Rajaji)

HM: Aamaam.... (Yes....)

GG: Avar yen Ammaavin Appa aavaar (He was my mother's father....)

Hema Malini was altogether disarming. I will always remember that pleasant banter.

A rock-solid friend, Sitaram Yechury, stood by my side throughout as MPs moved in and out, all very pleasant to each other, whatever be their politics. This was democracy, India's democracy, at work. As the votes were counted, I could see the tray holding my opponent's ballot papers climb from base to slope to summit, while mine laboured up to a very modest base camp, with the tray for invalid votes getting not a few ballots—surprising for each voter was an MP expected to know how to mark the ballot.

Venkaiah Naidu won the election with 516 votes against my tally of 244. I rang him to offer felicitations. 'Sir,' he said, 'I have long been an admirer of your grandfather, Rajaji... I will call on you in Chennai.'

The 24th of August 2017 saw and heard and read in the news the delivering of a major judgment, perhaps one of the most significant in the entire life of the Republic of India's judicial history. A nine-judge bench of the Supreme Court in *Justice K. S. Puttaswamy vs Union of India* declared by majority opinion, privacy to be an integral component of Part III of the Constitution of India, which lays down the fundamental rights of the citizens of India. Writing the plurality opinion, Justice Chandrachud held that the right to privacy was an element of human dignity and constituted an inalienable natural right. This was, to use contemporary figures of speech, 'big', 'huge', 'awesome'. It was defining.

India's history has been traditionally as also unrigorously seen in terms of eras named after rulers or dynasties, like the Maurya, Gupta, Chola, Chera, Lodhi, Mughal and the like. In modern times, the first four decades of independent India have been broadly characterized, not incorrectly, as those of the Nehru–Gandhis. By that 'rough-and-ready' method, it could now be said that India, after 2014, was in the Modi era. No two questions about that. Narendra Modi was the elected leader of the elected majority in Parliament, and it was, to use a Hindi colloquialism, his 'baari', his turn, to govern this vast and complex land. And to use another current phrase, this time an English one, he was not just the leader of his party but its supremo.

And a supremo, not in the colours of electoral politics but in the chiaroscuro of ideological politics, professing an ideology that had its being in the seedbeds of religious belief and the protoplasm of cultural self-identity. He was not a new captain in the old boat, SS *India*, but a new helmsman at the stern of a new boat, SS *Bharat*. The older vessel had been powered by two jets of steam: democratic republicanism and secularism, the new one by those of majoritarian nationalism and Hindutva.

He had the numbers, the numbers had him.

He was perceived by his electors and later by a much larger arc of society as a man who had risen from utter non-privilege, with no ancestry to flaunt, no estate, factory or enterprise to display. It was just his consistent adherence to the philosophy of the RSS and his services to his political party through its highs and its lows, that appealed to this Bharat, which was now his Bharat. Born after independence was won by India, he was not of the generation of freedom fighters but of that which had, in its perception, been let down by free India's leading party, the Indian National Congress. His triumph pedestaled him and depedestaled a galaxy of Congress names—except one, that of Sardar Vallabhbhai Patel, whom the Modi era now saw and proclaimed as its own role model and inspiration. This was all too easy; in the years after Patel's death, he had been rapidly forgotten by the Congress. His disappropriation by the Congress made his reappropriation by the BJP simple. A larger-than-life statue of Patel on the banks of the Narmada in Gujarat had been announced by Narendra Modi even when he was chief minister, and it was now unveiled by him as the world's tallest statue, with a height of 182 metres (597 feet) and at a total construction cost of ₹3,000 crore. That a detailed 3D scan of the approved model formed the basis for the bronze cladding cast in a foundry in China was an Indian irony of great proportions. But this was noted by only those who knew of Patel's strong warnings about China's geopolitical goals sent by him to Prime Minister Nehru.

In 2018, a statue of Vladimir Lenin was knocked down in Belonia, Tripura, following the end of the twenty-five-year-long CPI(M) rule in the state. No statues of Gandhi or Nehru were knocked down anywhere in Modi's India, but their spirit stood bruised and even battered. Nowhere more disturbingly (to the adherents of Gandhi–Nehru) than when dissidents were arrested and confined for seemingly interminable durations.

'Dissent is a safety valve of democracy. If you don't allow dissent, the pressure valve of democracy will burst,' Justice Chandrachud had said in his landmark observation in 2018. Independent India could not have asked for more by way of fundamentals. Whatever else that singular judge is going to be remembered for, or not, this remark of his, is and will always be his equivalent of Gladstone's 'Justice delayed is justice denied', Martin Luther King Jr.'s 'Injustice anywhere is a threat to justice everywhere' and William Blackstone's 'Where there is a right, there is a remedy.'

By the time India entered 2019, the Modi era was firm and strong, its supporters a heaving ocean and its critics a still pond. And the elections to the Lok Sabha that year were, for the BJP, almost a mere formality. When a convoy of vehicles carrying security personnel on the Jammu–Srinagar National Highway was attacked by a suicide bomber near Pulwama District, Jammu and Kashmir, and then the Balakot airstrike was carried out by the Indian Air Force crossing the LoC directed against a terrorist training camp in Pakistan, Narendra Modi winning his second national election and taking his oath a second time as prime minister of India was foregone.

And so, when the president of the United States, Donald Trump and India's prime minister, Narendra Modi, addressed 50,000 Indian Americans at the Howdy Modi: Shared Dreams Bright Futures rally in NRG Stadium in Houston, Texas, a mega-film based on spectator popularity was aired to the euphoric delectation of its watchers. It was like Orson Welles and Walt Disney had combined to make that giant of a film.

The revocation of the special status accorded to Jammu and Kashmir and its being downsized to two union territories came as a surprise even to those who were advocating it. No liberal in twenty-first-century India and no rationalist in secular India, whether Hindu or Muslim, could cavil at the doing away of all that made Kashmir an exception to the rule of India's Indianness. But the uniqueness of the state, its three segments with distinct Hindu, Muslim, and Buddhist features and the extreme sensitivity of the people of the Valley to 'rule from Delhi', and the wars fought over and on it had invested it with an altogether distinct character. Doing away with that at some point or the other was not something that could be described as 'wrong'. Nor could the doing away, legally, of the odious practice of 'triple talaq'.

Increasingly heard now was the on-the-anvil proclamation of a Uniform Civil Code. Who can possibly object to the position that there should be no differences in civil rights and responsibilities between community and community? But the point was: were these reforms being brought in for the love of liberalism, for faith in justice, for rationality and equity, or for something else? Something called finger-pointing at the Muslims of India? And if the Citizenship Amendment Act of 2019 was the result of concern for persecuted minorities in our neighbourhood, why should Muslims from all those countries (e.g. the Rohingya from Myanmar), Tamil from Sri Lanka, and Tibetan Buddhists not be included?

But liberal and rational India, which included good-but-silent types like I, did not ask these questions loudly or regularly enough. Why? For Tagore's immortal song 'Where the mind is without fear, and the head held high' had been rescripted over these years as 'Where the mind is filled with fear, and the head droops low....'

'Sedition' as a crime recognized and placed in the codes of independent India's penology is, after the English language and parliamentary democracy, the British Raj's most abiding bequest to its former colony. Hubris made the Raj see sedition in dissent and treason in protest. Intolerance did the same during Indira Gandhi's national Emergency, and now, it was doing the same like a second wave of that virus.

That Anand Teltumbde is married to Babasaheb Ambedkar's granddaughter, and, thereby, the great man's grandson-in-law is the least of his 'introductions'. Scholar, teacher, writer, and human rights activist, he was among several others arrested in 2018 for having Maoist links and had attracted the provisions of the Unlawful Activities Prevention Act. The charges and the ways in which the arrests were made were criticized by, among many others, Supreme Court Justice D. Y. Chandrachud (later Chief Justice of India), who questioned the nature of the investigation by the Maharashtra police when hearing a plea for bail. Teltumbde remained incarcerated with many others similarly indicted until, in November 2022, he was released from Taloja Central Prison after the Bombay High Court granted him bail. The order was upheld by the Supreme Court, which found no prima facie evidence that Teltumbde had been involved in a terrorist act under the Unlawful Activities Prevention Act.

I have no knowledge of the interstices of the many cases of such detenus. It is possible and indeed probable that some of them harboured violent emotions and intentions and were associated with persons and outfits that were a danger to the nation's security. But the net effect of these actions of the state was that fear descended like a haze over the country's thinking mind. Independent India's press, television channels, and social media platforms not only had their vocal cords go silent but be transplanted by new ones that sang like a school choir, new songs in praise of the Modi era.

Of the Covid-bitten years 2020 to 2023, what I would like to remember are two things.

First, the heroic work of nurses and doctors in India, whose work was no different from that of firemen entering and fighting a giant blaze. Their example is beyond description, beyond praise. They were stoic; they were Stoics.

Second, the agony—and the number—of migrant workers who after the lockdown, were suddenly out of work and out of such homes as they were living in. Invisible until the lockdown, they loomed overnight at railway stations and bus terminals and, when those sites had no space for them, on the highways, trudging. Migration for finding work (in other words, underemployment or unemployment), a major reason for it, is a giant fact of Indian life. Maharashtra, UP, and West Bengal are the big hosts, UP is the big 'source', followed by Maharashtra, West Bengal, and Bihar. India is, in its freedom, the theatre for what is perhaps the largest internal migration in the world, unique in being wholly 'fluid' for it is itinerant, with features of vagrancy and, of course, insolvency. Migrant workers are invariably underpaid (which is better than being without wages), overworked, unorganized, and generally forlorn. The last census—held in 2011—showed that 453.6 million people in India were internal migrants, which amounted to 37 per cent of the country's entire population. They are one of India's most admirable people for their perseverance and their never-say-die spirit, but they are also one of India's most immiserated people. Were they, in late Covid times, vaccinated? Unlikely. Vulnerable economically, and fragile socially, they were and remain highly precarious medically. Only the mobile phone saves them from total neglect.

Many views float on how effective the vaccines that entered our lives faster than expected, were. I went down with the virus shortly after my 'shot' and was told that can happen if the 'load of the inoculum' is so high that the vaccine stands defeated. All that be as it may, the virus, after two and possible three waves, receded. This was perhaps because we had all, as a mass, got infected and therefore immunized. But were any lessons learnt about the why and wherefore of the pandemic and on ways of preventing its recurrence? Sadly, no. The Indian passion for crowding and its reluctance to self-regulate in basics like masking up remain standing invitations to Covid and its mutants. I will be surprised if this beast does not recur and with greater ferocity, carrying away the old and vulnerable among the poor first and turn to others next. As Dr Srinath Reddy has pointed out, other viruses emanating from zoonotic sources under the pressure of climate change and human interference with wild tracts are chafing to get loose and swamp human societies.[8]

Whether China was behind the Covid-19 spread or not, the fact is that Wuhan equivalent festers in every city, town, and mohalla in India. Sewers are an inextricable part of India's bloodstream, filth integral to its body, and our understanding of zoonotic imperatives as flat and slippery as green moss. Between now and 2047, when independent India turns a hundred, we may expect India's public health to give us jolts we are unprepared for. This is not a Nostradamus prediction but a probability projection made in sadness. When I heard of thousands of dead bodies found floating or washing up the shore of the river Ganga, and it was surmised that the corpses include people who had died due to Covid-19, I recalled the autobiographical story by Suryakant Tripathi 'Nirala', entitled 'Kulli Bhaat' when he describes an identical scene from the 1919 'Spanish' flu epidemic in which his entire family was wiped out. I recalled too, that my aunt Gulab and her little son Shanti (Gandhi's eldest daughter-in-law and grandson) had died of the same flu.

While the epidemic was at its height, the massive protest by farmers in North India against three farm laws that were seen as being pro-corporates, reached a crescendo. Masses of farmers braved the heat, cold, rain, and the epidemic over their one-year-long protest in what was an unprecedented act of satyagraha, almost wholly peaceful. Though in public health, it was most unwise, the ambitious in me saw in the protest and in Prime Minister Modi's retraction of the laws and his apology to the farmers a sign that the pall of fear was not permanent.

EPILOGUE

In July 2024, a veteran economist and teacher of economics, C. T. Kurien, passed away. V. K. Ramachandran, himself one of India's senior economists, in a tribute to him, said of Kurien: '...he maintained that three related questions were required to understand an economy: 'Who owns what?', 'Who does what?' and 'Who gets what?'.[1]

Like Gandhi's 'talisman'—'Whenever you are in doubt, or when the self becomes too much with you, apply the following test: recall the face of the poorest and the weakest man whom you may have seen and ask yourself if the step you contemplate is going to be of any use to him. Will he gain anything by it?'—the late economist's three questions are a key to understanding not just independent India's economic condition, but its life as a whole.

Who owns what in independent India? I cannot quite answer that wide question, but I can answer a variant of the question: Who is it that does not own that basic thing, economic security, in India? Thanks to old hierarchies and new priorities, some 220 million Indians subsist below the poverty line.[*] They may be said to own nothing by way of saleable, heritable, not to speak of profitable property. There are many estimates of the number of the wretchedly poor and destitute in India. And it should be noted, with more than ordinary relief, that according to a United Nations report—no less—as of 12 July 2023, India 'lifted' approximately 415 million individuals out of poverty between 2005–06 and 2019–21, 'with notable progress seen among the most impoverished states and marginalised populations, including children and disadvantaged caste groups'.[†]

But along with this statistic, must be seen another: As per the last census of 2011, India is, to mix metaphors, 'home' to 450 million who have left home, who are internal migrants[‡]. A sizeable section of these may not have migrated in distress, and yet there is no doubt that the bulk of them have opted to exit home and homestead to find work as what they had by way of

---

*A 2020 study from the World Economic Forum found 'Some 220 million Indians sustained on an expenditure level of less than Rs 32 / day—the poverty line for rural India—by the last headcount of the poor in India in 2013', 'How India remains poor: "It will take 7 generations for India's poor to reach mean income".', *Downtoearth.org.in.*, 21 January 2020.

†'India registers remarkable reduction in poverty; 415 million exit in 15 years', *Mint*, 11 July 2023.

‡Supriyo De, 'Internal Migration in India Grows, But Inter-State Movements Remain Low', *World Bank Blogs*, 18 December 2019.

livelihood was either monetarily inadequate or professionally untenable, the dynamics of mechanized development having compromised the availability of basic resources like land, water and timber and all but killed the market for many low-cost products.

And over and above this, the 'owning' of resources and opportunities has had to contend with the crippling effects of climate change and the bizarre phenomenon of zoonotic diseases on livelihoods. We, the people of India, who, according to the UN's World Population dashboard, now stand at slightly over 1.428 billion, edging past China's population of 1.425 billion, exceeding China's at 1.42 billion, are now a house divided—between the urban population of upwardly mobile aspirants who want to and dream of living in towns that are morphing into cities, cities into metropolises and metropolises into Singapore or Hong Kong on the one hand, and another, largely rural population, seeing migration and lurching from under-employment at home to uncertain wage-earning mass 'out under the sky'.

Who does what in India? India stands at 134 out of 193 countries in the United Nations Human Development Index 2022.[2] It ranks, shockingly, at 111 out of 125 nations in the Global Hunger Index 2023.[3] In the Global Gender Gap Report 2024, we are at 129 out of 146 countries surveyed.[4] That is, eighteenth from the bottom. In the Environmental Performance Index 2024, India stands at 176 out of 180 nations surveyed.[5] Fifth from the bottom. 'We do rank,' as Sainath tells us, 'at No. 3, though, in the Forbes Billionaires list.'

So, to the question 'Who does what?' One answer is there are Indians who celebrate pre-wedding events, weddings, and post-wedding events at a scale that beats world records. They are doing what they are doing without self-consciousness, and the rest of India watches that, as it would a film, without resentment or recrimination—a wonder in itself. And there are Indians who, a street's turn away from the extravaganzas just described, wash themselves and their utensils and clothes in hand-operated pumps that yield water erratically at best, reluctantly at worst.

Who gets what in India? Not what is deserved or in the right proportion, but in chaotic haphazardness, which taxation does not quite correct, state interventions have not been able to rectify, and politics has been unable to mend.

And 'getting' what includes getting punishments under the law.

Sainath, the unfailing observer of facts, as opposed to narratives, says:*

---

*In an essay entitled 'The Top Court and the Troubled Countryside' for a book on 75 years of the Supreme Court, ed. By Justice (Red.) S. Muralidhar. For references in the quotation from

'Look at India's giant army of undertrials. What are their backgrounds? In the media, barring a brilliant series in *The Wire*, there have mostly only been a few one-off stories. And those often lack the depth and punch required to place the issue on the national agenda.

Here's what we learned in 2022 from a minister's reply in Parliament. Out of 5,54,034 prisoners in our jails, 4,27,165 of them, or 77 per cent, were undertrial prisoners. And that the Prison Statistics Report India, 2022, recorded that Dalits, Adivasis and other marginalised castes from OBC groups accounted for 66 per cent of all the undertrials. In Uttar Pradesh, that figure is over 75 per cent. The undertrials tend to be mainly rural people with little access to legal aid.

To counter this sequence of India's travails is the great story of India's electoral democracy. Why is it great? It is great first of all, for the sheer numbers involved, making our elections the seventh wonder of the world. But India's electoral democracy is great for another more important reason. It just cannot be taken for granted.

The 2024 election results were not the same thing as the liberating mandate of 1977. But they gave the polity something where there had been next to nothing by way of real-life questions being asked of those who were preoccupied with the building of temples and the bulldozing of what were seen as unauthorized dwellings, invariably belonging to ethnic minorities. What the electorate in India did in the 2024 elections to the Lok Sabha showed what an instrument in its hands—the ballot—could do: measure the extent of the government's performance and its failures and thereby—stun.

If the ambitious in me saw in the 2024 election results a reduction of fear, and the re-emergence from low numbers to respectable ones by opposition parties, the Congress in particular, the elections that followed five months later to the state assemblies of Haryana and Maharashtra, did the opposite. It brought the incumbent government back and with a much wider margin of seats. Almost everyone I knew was confident until a few days before polling day, that there was an anti-BJP wave in those two states and that the opposition would displace the incumbents. No such things happened. The victories of India's democratic spirit in the elections to the Lok Sabha had been celebrated too soon.

Sainath above see Rohini Roy, 'Undertrial Prisoners in India: Why Are 66% From Marginalised Castes?', *The Quint*, 24 December 2022; Shreehari Paliath IndiaSpend.com, 'Despite Campaign, India Saw Number of Prisoners Increase in 2022', *Scroll.in*, 15 December 2023; The Wire Staff, 'Over 75% of Undertrials in UP from SC, ST, OBC Groups, Centre Tells Parliament', *The Wire*, 15 March 2023.

The people of India are no fools; they can be fooled. By the crafty and the crooked. But only for a while. The people of India are not children; they can be beguiled. By the cunning and the conspiratorial. But again, only for a while.

They can and do find out what is good for them and what is harmful for them. My fear now is not that the duration of being fooled and beguiled might increase but that political and techno-commercial manipulations, with the aid of artificial intelligence and its deft agencies, will try to alter public value-systems at their seedbeds, making false Godhoods a new pantheon, turning fake Robin Hoods into new heroes and confer Epichood on fraudulent narratives. As a people, Indians adore the legendary, revere the mythical and worship the fabulous. This is a form of trusting, believing in and depending on the seemingly great. As a people, we long for the theatre of the unbelievable and are therefore impatient with the history of credible events. We make of the historical figures we love, superhuman phantasms. We turn the great transactions of Time into overwhelming dramatic lore.

Knowing that the market of politics and the politics of the market can contrive to nudge our subconscious predilections and vulnerabilities to the advantage they seek. Rewriting history becomes, in such a situation, a professional ploy and who cares if it is an academically dishonest exercise?

When I contemplate the future of India becoming a manipulable toy, I shudder, but then only for a while.

There is such a thing as volume. The sheer volume and the massive reality of India cannot be overtaken by a miasma of manipulation for all time or in a large capture of space.

Floods, famine, and disease cannot engulf all of India; fakery, fraud, and dramatics cannot either. Somewhere, truth survives and, through invisible vents, reaches the heartbeats of India.

The imaginative in me recalled Subedar Neeraj Chopra's winning gold at the Tokyo Olympics in 2021 for his javelin throw and a silver medal in the Paris Olympics in 2024. Neeraj is non-political and may he remain so! But there was something about the accomplishment, something that linked the Tokyo and Paris moments to the ancient practice of precise aiming, measured strength, and sheer will-power that moved me. Moved? Yes, exactly that. Neeraj was quintessentially rural, from village India, a part of India—Haryana–Punjab—a tract that has, for centuries, millennia, in fact, known rivers to course through it, change course, even disappear. The very tract from which the farmers' protest had originated. Neeraj's javelin measured a distance reached by the power of an arm's throw. And it showed the working of skill in that throw, not by technologically-backed computings of aerodynamic speed and distances but by a combination of biochemical instincts that can assess the muscular packing needed for the launch so that it covers the span aimed at.

Vinesh Phogat's failing the weight test by a wafer-thin margin before the women's wrestling segment in the same 2024 Paris Olympics reminded me of the opposition INDIA bloc's close fight and defeat at the 2024 elections. 'Up but out' is how *The Hindu* described her losing out when the medal was almost in her clasp.

The winners and losers in political or commercial battles for India's soul cannot and need not wither exult or despair. They need to only be humble. Can they learn that India is bigger than its largest party, its tallest leader, and its strongest majority? Greater than its biggest corporate, its highest market ratings, its strongest stake?

Statesmanship, of the sinews of not sparing, not forgiving oneself.

Manmohan Singh, I believe, is the last living Indian statesman I have known. When he died, in the demising days of 2024, I could not but think civility in Indian public life had shrivelled, decency withered. He was in office, not in a war-room. His table was a desk, not a battle-board. His pen wrote, it did not decree. Siyasat is a Hindustani word for politics. And sharafat for honesty, decency. Manmohan Singh had shown there was space in siyasat for sharafat and for sharafat in siyasat. The Indian sky had decidedly darkened at the departure of this good man.

The sun sank on 2024, disappointed.

Disappointed in us, earthlings. In the way we are treating the earth, treating each other.

The sun that rose on 2025 did so in uncertain hope.

Plumes of hate rise from the mounds of death. These have formed into dense clouds over our own, our own precariously precious patch of the earth. Bigotry tries to drive science, and intolerance to prescribe the nostrums of faith in the India that is Bharat.

The simmering turbulence in Bangladesh portends no ordinary danger. Noakhali and Bihar in 1946, Bengal and Punjab in 1947 ask 'Will 2025 protect India?'

The answer comes in a seventy-nine-year old's prayer in the months before his voice was stilled: *Sabko sanmati de Bhagavan* (Grant, please, God, good sense to all).

There was something to the man Subhas Bose had described as the 'Father of our Nation', which made Nehru say spontaneously after the assassination, 'the light has gone out of our lives'. Photographs captured Nehru, Patel, and Kripalani on the cortege as it moved with thousands upon thousands of ordinary folk grieving along its path. Not so well known is the fact that at the funeral, there walked for a distance, unnoticed, unphotographed and unwell, the man who had crafted India's Constitution, Babasaheb Ambedkar, law minister at the time and the spirit of our laws, ensuring freedom and justice for all. He had his differences with Gandhi, which must be noted and acknowledged with respect. As did Gandhi, whose differences with Ambedkar were always in the open for all to see and judge. But all of them—Bose, Nehru, Patel, Kripalani, Azad, Ambedkar, and Gandhi—together stood for an India where unity did not mean uniformity, love of country or community did not translate into hatred of another, and liberty meant the right to seek and get justice without robbing another's.

When Nehru said, the same evening, in a spontaneous broadcast, he had no time to prepare, that 'the light has gone out of our lives', he was, of course, thinking of the man who had just died. But when he added: 'That light will be seen...the world will see it and it will give solace to innumerable hearts, for that light represented something more than the immediate present; it represented the living, the eternal truths, reminding us of the right path, drawing us from error, taking this ancient country to freedom' he was speaking of the light that he felt was India.

Has that light brightened or dimmed over the seventy-five-plus years that India has been independent?

I will not ask an imagined Gandhi that question. He needs, I believe, to be given some rest from India's many lives. He has done enough in his lifetime and is entitled to tell India to do what best it can for itself. Now, will I deflect it to his associates, Nehru and Patel in particular. I will not trouble his independent follower, Subhas Bose, with the question. Nor his most important critic, B. R. Ambedkar. To ask what would Gandhi, Nehru, Patel, Bose, and Ambedkar say, what they would feel and do today is to be worse than cowardly. India has not become independent to clutch at its founders' shadows.

So, asking myself the question, I must be true to myself and say I cannot say the light of India has brightened after Independence. Five situations, above all others, show that light getting dimmed by the hour, situations that I can best describe by the only means I know, which is to ask myself questions and reflect in consternation:

1. India and its natural assets: Are we headed to a water crisis the like of which has not been seen? Our satellites can see, and our space teams probably sense it, but as a people, we do not know if, with Himalayan glaciers melting, how much water from our snow-fed rivers we and our progeny can be sure of. There is talk of linking rivers. Are our

rivers so flush with water as to join others? Will river-linking create a grid of dry river beds or rivers? Are we, therefore, also headed for a hydel energy crisis and its fallout—a sharp food crisis? Forest fires are on the rise. Why? Again, our space machines can guide us, but is their high eye showing us the truth of our forests? No. And we go ahead with plans for 'developing' the Great Nicobar Islands into a ₹72,000 crore extravaganza, which will annihilate its unique and fabulous forests. But we are going to compensate for that by growing trees elsewhere.... Where? Robbing islands of what they hold and giving someone else what their ecology does not know of. Independent India is not meant to act as an imperial colonial power to run its writ over the natural bent of its soil and the natural pulse of its soul.

2. India and its people: We are an uneasy plurality. We have always been that, for sure, but now, into our eighth decade as an independent nation, more so than before. And with those bent on sharpening the unease into the fissures of suspicion, fumes of hatred and flames of violence, astir. Colours have turned political; temples and mosques, churches, and gurdwaras are now magnetic fields for identity assertion, not spiritual devotion, religious symbols meant to soothe, elevate, now scare, and alienate. Is our 'majority of minorities' going to be replaced by the authority of majorities?
3. India and its covenants: The Constitution's guarantees and democracies nostrums meant to safeguard our plurality seem easy prey to those who can subvert them. The courts have their limits, suggest the high seats of legislative privilege. Do they mean to reverse the maxim 'Laws are like spider webs: strong enough to trap the weak, but fragile enough to be torn apart by the strong' and throw overboard Thoreau's timeless words: 'The law will never make men free; it is men who have got to make the law free.'
4. India and its past: Will India's past change from being available for study, analysis, and self-development into being a territory for re-enacting religious combats and political score-settlings, in other words, the territory for eternal conflict? Will history be used in India as a tool for control, for political aggrandisement, by creating new myths of victimhood and tools for vendetta? Is India becoming the theatre for a post-modern tragedy and, worse—for the pantomimes of imagined villainy and staged heroisms?
5. India and its future: Is India, which has known intolerance but taught tolerance, known antagonism but suggested as an alternative, mutual respect, known turf wars but prized a shared life in struggles and

> successes, now going to see Artificial Intelligence overtake the organic wisdoms of the Buddha, Mahavira, Adi Sankara, Guru Nanak, Akbar, Sarmad, and Dara Shukoh? Are cutting-edge technology and digitally-powered commerce going to become the handmaidens of a new behemoth called 'progress'? Is India going to work for a civilized world order that begins to dismantle its death machines and help slow down global heating? Or wear blinkers that will continue to take it into what the astronomer-philosopher Martin Rees has called the earth's 'final century'?

And yet, the 'kuchh baat' about India will not leave me in doubt or in dejection. Sonam Wangchuk of Ladakh has become an indistinguishable part of Ladakh's geophysical heartbeat. He, with the late Sunderlal Bahuguna, Chandiprasad Bhatt, Gaura Devi and Shekhar Pathak of Uttarakhand, is now part of India's ecological conscience.

His protests go beyond saying yes or no to this or that project. They are about what Ladakh's soil, its rocks, its people need and desire, what their hopes and anxieties are about. They are about consultation. We may invoke concepts like federalism, democracy, and consensus. And we would be right in doing so. But life is about the sense of touch, about tactility. Does Ladakh need a giant of a tunnel (Zojila, 14–25 km), or a national highway (Kargil–Zanskar, 230 km)? Will the Himalaya there bear the disembowelling that this will involve? Does not the Joshimath experience tell us something is wrong about those interventions? Are we doing what we should be doing to protect life in the Himalaya, along with whatever we are doing to promote tourism? Wangchuk holds out hope.

Another extraordinary Indian who has worked for and striven for peace and reconciliation in his part of India is eighty-nine-year-old Niketu Iralu of Nagaland. If wisdom, courage, and calm have coalesced in someone, they have in this amazing Indian. To most Indians—let us accept this truth—'Northeast India' is a blur, a distant part of the country 'somewhere up there near China' from where 'contingents' come in colourful clothes and headgear to the Republic Day parade in New Delhi. Men like Niketu tell us that the 'blur', which includes his Nagaland is where some 400 ethnic groups live, within touching distance of five, no less, countries—Myanmar, China, Bhutan, Nepal, and Bangladesh. History, geography, and destiny have placed the Northeast of India in India. But has India placed India in Northeast India's heart and mind ? Ask a Northeast Indian.

At India's other extremity, Great Nicobar, the intrepid champion of the Andamans' ecosystem, its forests and marine life, Pankaj Sekhsaria's *The*

Great Nicobar Betrayal, chronicles the devastation that awaits that fragile and unique ecosystem as a result of the ₹72,000 crore project to 'develop' it. Narrated in thirteen essays on various aspects of the project and the island, the book says the havoc that the project is bound to cause to one of the world's rare island habitations and its singularly distinct people. The argument that the airport and sea-monitoring establishments proposed in the project are necessary on account of China's growing presence and ambitions in the region is not to be dismissed. But security can come surely without this magnitude of disfigurement. Here again, the raising of a voice offers hope for 'kuchh baat'.

And then, my despair at the weakening of secular traditions in India and its neighbourhood, found relief—not from any political quarter but from a simple woman. When Neeraj Chopra's javelin throw was bettered in the Paris Olympics by that of Pakistan's Arshad Nadeem, Neeraj's mother—Saroj Devi—said that Nadeem was also like a son to her. Nadeem, responding, said that he was grateful for the fact that she prayed for him as well and said that she is also like a mother to him.

When, on 12 December 2024, eighteen-year-old Gukesh became the world chess champion, India was ecstatic, and Tamil Nadu was over the moon. And Chennai, where Gukesh was born, celebrated the victory like it had celebrated few things in recent memory.

I know next to nothing of the game. But knew enough to see, like anyone else that Gukesh had won more than a game and a title. He had won a moment of epiphanic rapture.

I have not heard in recent times, or even in more than recent times, in a long time, a statement like his about Ding: 'He is a true champion.' Wow. I felt proud as an Indian, as a Chennaivasi, that Gukesh should show what being Indian means. Victories have come to be celebrated with fireworks, dance, and delirium. And with that singularly unlovely, self-righteous sign held up before cameras—V.

Watching the two, I could not forget the fact that here were two young men representing two of the world's greatest civilizations—those of China and India. And in a sense representing the cultures of Hiuen Tsang, seventh-century Chinese Buddhist monk, scholar, traveller, and translator, and Nagarjuna, adviser to a king of the Satavahana dynasty which ruled the Deccan Plateau in the second century.

All sports in their competitive moments have become miniature battles. Cricket on the subcontinent of India has become ballistic. Not because the teams want them to be so but because we make them that. Be it said to the credit of south Indian cities that their cheering is more for cricket than for the countries represented by the playing teams.

And of politics and politicians in hours of victory and defeat, I shall say nothing because I do not want to spoil the purity of the 'rasa' created by the chess tournament just concluded. Except to say that in the chaturanga of elections today we are not likely to hear the victor call the vanquished 'a true champion'.

How right Ramchandra Gandhi was when he said that Gandhi was not stopped by three bullets. He stopped those three bullets on their tracks of suspicion, hate, and vendetta

His dying word was Ram.

Calling out to him, he merged his entire self in Ram, which was no different for him from what he called his 'inner voice', which was all that God meant for him. Ram, inner voice, God were for him, one and the same. And all three were subsumed in one word: truth.

Truth, he said, was God.

Not 'God is Truth', but Truth is God.

This new meaning freed God from custom and creeds. It made truth the one and only guide. Your, my and India's guide. The guide for its majorities and its minorities.

A dog, a mere dog, showed Gandhi the truth in Dattapara.

Let no one stoop to the polemic 'What is Truth?'. You and I know what it is in our hearts. As clearly as we know, do we not, what lies are when we hear them, get fooled awhile by them, let them go unchallenged, connive with them, and why, even speak them.

There is no mistaking lies.

Lies can and do win in bazaars, courts and elections.

Blades, bullets and bombs can and do stain India's dawns, stun its days, scare the wits out of its nights.

They cannot touch India's human truth which is its very soul.

India's light can dim; it cannot, will not die.

ACKNOWLEDGEMENTS

I commence my expression of thanks with acknowledging Rudrangshu Mukherjee, friend and scholar for two favours: one, as Chancellor of Ashoka University, for giving me, as one of the university's faculty, the latitude in terms of time for the making of this book, and two, for having identified Megha Sharma, for initial help as a research assistant.

To Anurag Behar, CEO of Azim Premji Foundation and Chancellor of Azim Premji University, Bhopal, my deep gratitude for having so spontaneously and generously supported my study for this work, and having facilitated thereby, my engaging Murtaza Gandhi, meticulous researcher and text-comber, for that most vital assistance. To S. Giridhar, Chief Operating Officer of Azim Premji University and to the Azim Premji Foundation itself, my thanks are due for having been instrumental in the setting up of that support.

Without Murtaza Gandhi's pivotal assistance, work on this book would have been hard to take up, even as without the intricate copy-editing by Pujitha Krishnan and Aienla Ozukum, Aleph Book Company's expert specialists in book production, it would have been impossible to complete.

For thought-partnering, encouragement, invaluable strike-a-lights and leads to archival records, I am beholden to my sister Tara Gandhi Bhattacharjee, my brother Rajmohan Gandhi and my sister-in-law Usha Gandhi. For invaluable assistance, my thanks are owed and gratefully given to the archivists, biographers, historians, and teachers Deepa Bhatnagar, Kinnari Bhatt, Sugata Bose, Venu Madhav Govindu, Ramachandra Guha, Anil Nauriya, Jairam Ramesh, Vinay Sitapati, Tridip Suhrud, A. R. Venkatachalapathy. To two scholars, Samanth Subramaniam who searched records at the British Museum, London, for me and to Vikram Raghavan, whose generous and most crucial help in accessing records at the Library of Congress and the archives containing John F. Kennedy's papers, has been invaluable, and to his research assistant, Parv Tyagi, my special thanks. Huge thanks are due and given to Vikram Raghavan, again, and to Kerrie Cotten Williams and Joshua A. Levy for their phenomenal help in accessing Oppenheimer papers at the Library of Congress, Washington DC. And for their help in providing various leads, permissions, verifications, confirmations and corrections, S. Theodore Baskaran, Indira Chowdhury, Dan O'Connor, Uma Dasgupta, Vikram Doraiswami, Eric Gonsalves, Wajahat Habibullah, Nasreen Munni Kabir, Nayanjot Lahiri, Sarwar Lateef, Philip Lutgendorf, Ranjan Mathai, Dalip Mehta, Shivshankar Menon, P. S. Raghavan, Srinath Raghavan, T. C. A

Raghavan, Aruna Roy, L. S. Shashidhara, Krishnan 'Kris' Srinivasan, Suhrith Parthasarathy, P. Sainath, Upinder Singh, Rupert Snell, R. Sudarshan, Vijay Tankha, and Sharda Ugra.

The amazing archives in the offices of two of India's flagship newspapers—*The Hindu* (Chennai) and the *Hindustan Times* (New Delhi)—have been generosity itself in furnishing access to reports and articles carried by them in the years covered by the book. I thank their editors and, very specifically their archivists Sujoy Das of the *Hindustan Times*, and Naresh Kumar and Vibha Sudarshan of *The Hindu* for their prompt and amazingly precise help.

My great appreciation to my daughter Divya for invaluably timely comments. To my daughter Amrita, the same, for sustained thought-partnering. To both, gratitude, for wanting the best for their father's narrative of earlier times in today's day and age.

To my wife, Tara, whose patience with my preoccupations is rivalled only by her active support to it in ways at once too large to describe, and too subtle to define, my everlasting gratefulness.

ENDNOTES

PRELUDE

1 Fintan O'Toole, *We Don't Know Ourselves: A Personal History of Modern Ireland*, New York: Liveright, 2022.

THE 1940S: FRIENDS, FAMILY, AND THE FURIES

1 *Hindustan Times,* 18 August 1946, editorial entitled 'Simla Outrage'.
2 J. B. Kripalani, *Gandhi: His Life and Thought*, New Delhi: Publications Division, 1970, p. 255
3 Ibid., p. 254.
4 Ibid.
5 J. B. Kripalani, *Gandhi: His Life and Thought*, New Delhi: Publications Division, 1970, pp. 255–56.

1947: THE DAWN SO STAINED, SO STAINED—FAIZ AHMED FAIZ

1. N. K. Bose, *Lectures on Gandhism*, Ahmedabad: Navajivan Trust, 1971. p. 63.
2. Rajmohan Gandhi, *Mohandas*, New Delhi: Penguin/Viking, 2006, p. 601.
3. P. N. S. Mansergh, 'The Inter-Asian Relations Conference', 28 April 1947, in CO 537/2092, The National Archives (TNA), Kew, United Kingdom.
4. Tridip Suhrud (ed.), *The Diary of Manu Gandhi 1946-48,* Ahmedabad: Navajivan Trust, 2024, p. 229.
5. Louis MacNeice, 'Prayer Before Birth', poetryarchive.org.
6. Chaudhry Khaliquzzaman, *Pathway to Pakistan*, Longmans, Pakistan, 1961.
7. Pyarelal's *Mahatma Gandhi: The Last Phase*, Vol. II, p. 364
8. Alan Cambell-Johnson, *Mission with Mountbatten*, London: Robert Hale Ltd., 1951, p. 156.
9. A. R. Venkatachalapathy, *Tamil Characters: Personalities, Politics and Culture*, New Delhi: Pan Macmillan India, 2018.
10. Rajmohan Gandhi, *The Rajaji Story 1937-1972,* Bombay: Bharatiya Vidya Bhavan, 1984, p. 143.
11. *Hindustan Times*, 17 September 1947.
12. Margaret Bourke-White, *Halfway to Freedom,* New York: Simon & Schuster, 1949, p. 91.
13. Ibid., p. 193 and pp. 210–11.

1948: STOPPING THREE BULLETS IN THEIR TRACKS

1. Khushwant Singh, *Train to Pakistan,* London: Chatto & Windus, 1956, opening page.
2. Jay Livingston, Ray Evans, 'Que Sera, Sera', 1955.
3. Translation of Rajinder Krishan's lines done by Rupert Snell at the author's request.
4. Bakhtiar K. Dadabhoy, *Homi J. Bhabha: A Life*, New Delhi: Rupa Publications, 2023, p. 434.
5. For a discussion on Nehru's position on India's nuclear options, see *Homi Bhabha killed a Crow* by Zia Mian and Ashis Nandy, Regional Centre for Strategic Studies, Colombo, Sri Lanka, 1998.

1950: NO REGRETS?

1. Rajmohan Gandhi, *The Rajaji Story 1937-1972*, Bharatiya Vidya Bhavan, 1984, p. 193.
2. 'Reordering a Border Space: Relief, rehabilitation, and nation-building in northeastern India after the 1950 Assam earthquake', Berence Guyot-Rechard, Emmanuel College and History Faculty, University of Cambridge, United Kingdom.
3. *Modern Asian Studies*, London: Cambridge University Press, 2015, pp. 1–32.
4. Ibid.
5. 'Dammed in the Himalaya', article by Gopakumar Menon in *Frontline*, 23 August 2024, cites an August 2020 paper published in *Seismological Research Letters* by Stephen G. Wesnousky, Professor of Geology and Seismology, University of Nevada, USA, entitled 'Great Pending Himalayan Earthquakes'.
6. Rajmohan Gandhi, *Patel: A Life*, Ahmedabad: Navajivan Trust, 1990.

1951: THE GAMES OF POWER

1 Detailed report in *Hindustan Times*, 12/13 October 1951, entitled 'Interruptions Mark Debate on Hindu Code Bill'.
2 Ibid.

1952: THE MOST IMPORTANT MAN ALIVE

1 Ashok Gopal, *A Part Apart—The Life and Thought of B. R. Ambedkar*, New Delhi: Navayana Publishing, 2023.

1953: HINDUSTAN CALLS

1 Jayaprakash Narayan, *Selected Works*, Vol. V, 2005, NMM&L, p. 361.
2 Sheikh Mohammad Abdullah, *The Blazing Chinar: Autobiography*, Srinagar: Gulshan Books 2013.

1955: REMAPPING INDIA

1 Gandhi, *The Rajaji Story 1937-1972*, p. 25.
2 Ibid., p. 263.

1956: APSARA—DANCER IN THE COURT OF INDRA

1 'A Serious Menace to Security': British Intelligence, V.K. Krishna Menon and the Indian High Commission in London, 1947-52 Paul M. McGarr.
2 Allan and Wendy Scharfe, *J.P. His Biography*, Hyderabad: Orient Longman India, 1998 edition.
3 Dadabhoy, *Homi J. Bhabha*, Chapter Apsara.

1957: A THRONE AMIDST THORNS

1 This portion is derived from *Grappling with the Bomb: Britain's Pacific H-bomb tests*, by Nic Maclellan, published 2017 by ANU Press, The Australian National University, Canberra, Australia.

1958: SCIENCE, SECRETS, AND SCANDALS

1 Dadabhoy, *Homi J. Bhabha*, pp. 496-97.

1959: SWATANTRA

1 Monica Felton, *I Meet Rajaji,* London: Macmillan & Co. Ltd., 1968.
2 *Freedom in Exile: The Autobiography of the Dalai Lama of Tibet*, London: Hodder and Stoughton, 1990, pp. 156–57.
3 Ibid., p. 161.
4 Srinath Raghavan, *War and Peace in Modern India: A Strategic History of the Nehru* Years, Ranikhet: Permanent Black, 2010, p. 236.
5 Rafiq Zakaria (ed.), *A Study of Nehru*, Bennett Coleman & Co., 1959, pp. 222–26.

1961: TH' EXPENSE OF SPIRIT IN A WASTE OF SHAME—WILLIAM SHAKESPEARE, SONNET 129

1 Gandhi, *The Rajaji* Story, p. 297.
2 *ItsGoa*, 'Manuel António Vassalo e Silva – The guy who didn't burn Goa'.
3 Ibid.
4 Ibid.

1962: PERFIDY

1 Shaoli Debnath, 'Gayatri Devi Birth Centenary: The lady who rocked the Lok Sabha Election with her landslide victory', *Indian Express*, 23 May 2019.
2 Gandhi, *The Rajaji Story*, p. 309.
3 Ibid., p. 311.
4 Ibid., pp.311–12.
5 McGeorge Bundy, *Danger and Survival*, Random House, NY, 1988, p. 329.
6 Sidney D. Drell in NATURE, Vol. 383, 10 October 1996.
7 'Menon must go, CR says', *Hindustan Times*, 26 October 1962.
8 S. Gopal, *Radhakrishnan: A Biography*, New Delhi: Oxford University Press, 1989.

1963: I SPY WITH MY LITTLE EYE

1 Dadabhoy, *Homi J. Bhabha,* pp. 568–69.
2 Ibid.
3 Paul M. McGarr, 'A Serious Menace to Security': British Intelligence, V.K. Krishna Menon and the Indian High Commission in London, 1947–52, *Journal of Imperial and Commonwealth History,* September 2010.

1964: ...A FLAME VANISHES

1. Abdullah, *The Blazing Chinar: Autobiography*, p. 501.
2. Rajya Sabha debates 29 May 1964,
3. Walter Crocker, *Nehru: A Contemporary's Estimate*, George Allen & Unwin, 1966.
4. S. Gopal, *Radhakrishnan: A Biography*, New Delhi: Oxford University Press, 1989, p. 329.
5. Balachandra Rajan, *The Dark Dancer*, New York: Simon and Schuster, 1958.
6. Balachandra Rajan, *Too Long in the West,* New York: Atheneum, 1962.
7. Brahmanand Papers (NMML).
8. Wilson Center Digital Archive Record ID 114337, Talk by Mao Zedong at an Enlarged Meeting of the Chinese Communist Party Central Committee Politburo (Excerpts).
9. Speech on AIR, cited in George Perkovich, *India's Nuclear Bomb: The Impact on Global Proliferation*, Berkeley: University of California Press, 1999, p. 67.

1965: FIVE FEET TWO AND SO TALL

1 I. Malhotra, 'Remains of the day When India and Pakistan thrashed their issues out in Tashkent', *Indian Express*, 9 January 2009.
2 *South Asia in World Politics*, Bowman & Littlefield Publishers Inc., 2005, part I, Chapter 1.
3 Dadabhoy, *Homi J. Bhabha*, pp. 587–88.

1966: 'AYYO, AYYAYYIYYO !'

1 'Tashkent Declaration', 10 January 1966, Media Center, MEA, Government of India.
2 Dadabhoy, *Homi J. Bhabha*, p. 595.

1967: GOODNESS TO GOODNESS.

1 Statistical Report on General Elections 1967 to the Fourth Lok Sabha, Volume 1 (National and State Abstracts & Detailed Results), Election Commission of India, New Delhi, 1968.

1968: WHOSE SERVICE?

1 B. Kolappan, '55 years on, scars of the gruesome Keezhvenmani massacre run deep', *The Hindu*, 21 December 2023.

1969: TO BRAHM OR NOT TO BRAHM

1 Arvind Elangovan, 'BN Rau: An idealist and a staunch constitutionalist', *Hindustan Times*, 26 November 2024.

1970: NO LESS HIDEOUS THAN RAPE

1 Aadira Perinchery, 'From Kerala to Tamil Nadu, a Good Week for Elephants', *The Wire*, 2 March 2023.

1971: SIR...LOOK AT THESE BALLOTS...STUFFED INTO THE BOX...

1 Ayodhya Kand, Stanza 27.1. Translation by Philip Lutgendorf, Tulsidas: *The Epic of Ram*, Volume 3, Murty Classical Library of India, 2016.
2 Press Trust of India, 'Mother's Praise', *Hindustan Times*, 24 September 1970.
3 Nayantara Sahgal, *Indira Gandhi: Tryst with Power*, New Delhi: Penguin Books, 2012, p. 336.

1973: SOMETHING ASHOKA WOULD HAVE LAUDED, LINCOLN SEEN AS NOBLE

1 Jairam Ramesh, *Intertwined Lives: P.N. Haksar and Indira Gandhi*, New Delhi: Simon & Schuster, 2018, pp. 318–20.

1974: WATCHING WITH ANXIETY

1 Ibid., p. 329.
2 Jairam Ramesh, *A Chequered Brilliance: The Many Lives of V.K. Krishna Menon*, New Delhi: Viking, 2019, pp. 662–63.
3 Sucheta Kripalani correspondence (NMML).
4 Keshav Desiraju, *Of Gifted Voice: The Life and Art of M.S. Subbulakshmi*, Gurugram: HarperCollins Publishers India, 2021, p. 215.

1975: LIFE NORMAL IN DELHI

1 Sahgal, *Indira Gandhi*, p. 211 and p. 216.
2 R. Rangaraj TNN updated in *Times of India*, 13 March 2019.

1976: WALLS ACQUIRE EARS, SPEECH DISAPPEARS

1 Nambi Marthandan, 'Over one million people throng Marina Beach in Madras to hear PM Indira Gandhi', *India Today*, 29 February 1976.
2 Michael Henderson, *Experiment with Untruth*, Macmillan, 1977, p. 66.
3 *Indian Express*, 19 November 1976.

1977: EPIPHANY

1 *Indian Express*, 2 November 1976.
2 Sagarika Ghose, *Indira: India's Most Powerful Prime Minister*, New Delhi: Juggernaut, 2017.
3 *Indira Gandhi: A Biography*, New Delhi: Penguin Books, 1997.
4 Ghose, *Indira*, p. 193.
5 Ibid., p. 196.
6 Sahgal, *Indira Gandhi*, p. 294.

1980: KARMA

1 Report in *The Hindustan Times*, 2 December 1980 entitled 'Walk-out over jail-blinding'.
2 Ibid.

1981: AS IF GOD DID NOT EXIST

1 Farzand Ahmed, 'Communal violence in Biharsharif leaves 48 people dead, 68 injured', *India Today*, 31 May 1981.
2 Ibid.

1984: SARE JAHAN SE ACHHA?

1 K. C. Singh, *The Indian President: An Insider's Account of the Zail Singh Years*, Gurugram: HarperCollins Publishers India, 2023.
2 Justice Nanavati Commission of Inquiry (1984 Anti-Sikh Riots).

1986: WHO RULES INDIA?

1 Mani Shankar Aiyar, *The Rajiv I Knew*, Juggernaut, 2024, pp. 49–66.
2 Wajahat Habibullah, *My Years with Rajiv: Triumph and Tragedy*, New Delhi: Westland Books, 2020.
3 Chinmaya R. Gharekhan, *Centres of Power*, Rupa Publications, 2023, p. 87.
4 Hawksley Humphrey, 'Massacre in Akkaraipattu', *The Guardian*, 22 February 1986.
5 BBC on this Day, 1986: Bomb kills 21 in Sri Lanka, 3 May 1986.

1987: THE RIGHT MAN IN THE RIGHT PLACE

1 PTI, 'Hashimpura massacare: Rifles given to PAC', *Times of India*, 27 July 2006.
2 Habibullah, *My Years with Rajiv*.
3 Ajitha Karthikeyan, TNN, 'Self-immolation entwined in Dravidian movement', *Times of India*, 30 January 2009.

1989: JUSTICE

1 'Sawant, two others sentenced to death', *Hindustan Times*, 23 January 1986.
2 Jyoti Punwani, 'Why it's wrong to hang Yakub Memon', rediff.com, 20 July 2015.
3 *The Review*, International Commission of Jurists, Special Edition No. 57, December 1996, p. 59.
4 Barbara Crossette, 'Panel Throws Out Vote Result in Gandhi's District', *New York Times*, 26 November 1989; Dilip Awasthi, 'Both Rajiv Gandhi's and V.P. Singh's constituencies were affected by poll malaise', *India Today*, 15 December 1989.
5 Bashaarat Masood, Explained: The 1989 Rubaiya Sayeed abduction case and jailed JKLF chief Yasin Malik's role, *Indian Express*, 19 July 2022.
6 Moosa Raza, *Kashmir: Land of Regrets*, New Delhi: Context, 2019.
7 R. Venkataraman, *My Presidential Years*, New Delhi: Indus, 1994, p. 350.

1990: IF THERE BE A FIELD OF WAR ON EARTH, IT IS HERE, IT IS HERE, IT IS HERE

1 Habibullah, *My Years with Rajiv*, p. 270.
2 Neerja Chowdhury, *How Prime Ministers Decide*, New Delhi: Aleph Book Company, 2023.

1991: 'YEH KYA HUA HAI?'

1 *My Presidential Years*, p. 54.
2 Vinay Sitapati, *Half-Lion: How P.V. Narasimha Rao transformed India*, New Delhi: Penguin Viking, 2016, p. 108.
3 Bernard Weinraub, Economic Austerity Vowed for India, *New York Times*, 23 June 1991.
4 Ibid.

1992: A CIVILIZATIONAL COLLAPSE?

1 *The Hindustan Times*, 15 October, 1992.
2 J. N. Dixit, *India-Pakistan in War and Peace*, Taylor and Francis Group, London, 2002.
3 Ibid, p. 292
4 *Half-Lion: How P.V. Narasimha Rao transformed India.*
5 J. N. Dixit, *India-Pakistan in War & Peace*, London and New York: Routledge, 2002, p. 282.
6 Rajiv Dogra, *Where Borders Bleed: An Insider's Account of Indo-Pak Relations,* New Delhi: Rupa Publications, 2015.

1993: THE QUAKING EARTH

1 Dixit, *India-Pakistan in War and Peace*, p. 283.

1994: WHY IS OUR LAND THE THEATRE OF TRAUMA AFTER TRAUMA?

1 Kashmir Law & Justice Project, 'Kupwara Massacre 1994', 23 November 2023.
2 UK Parliament website, Visit of the Indian Prime Minister, EDM (Early Day Motion) 796: tabled on 09 March 1994.
3 CDC, International Notes Update: Human Plague—India, 1994.
4 John F. Burns, 'With Old Skills and New, India Battles the Plague', *New York Times*, 29 September 1994.

1995: MYSTIFYING MILK

1 Report in *The Hindustan Times*, 22 September 1995 entitled 'Deities 'drink' milk in tonnes'.
2 Dadabhoy, *Homi J. Bhabha*, p. 255.
3 *Half-Lion*, pp. 266–68.

1996–97: RAINBOWING A NATION

1 T. N. Seshan, *Through the Broken Glass: An Autobiography*, New Delhi: Rupa Publications, 2023, p. 339.
2 Kathleen Raine, 'A Spell for Creation', allpoetry.com.
3 Treaty of Pelindaba, un.org.
4 Sitapati, *Half-Lion*, pp. 290–95.
5 Chowdhury, *How Prime Ministers Decide*, p. 345.
6 HIV/AIDS in South Africa, published online: 28 March 2018.
7 Henry J. Kaiser Foundation HIV AIDS Fact Sheet, May 2005.
8 *Mandela, Luthuli, and Nonviolence in the South African Freedom Struggle,* paper by Vinay Lal, UCLA Ufahamu: A Journal of African Studies, 2014.
9 Timothy Franklin Othienio, 'Contending Issues in South Africa's Foreign Policy: Universalism Versus Economic National Interest—The Case of South Africa's Arms Sales to "Pariah States"1994-1999, August 2004 pp. 170–71.
10 Chris Barron, 'Leo "Rusty" Evans: Nat-era diplomat who won the trust of Mandela 1943-2017', *Sunday Times*, 11 November 2017.
11 South Africa: Question of Principle: Arms Trade and Human Rights, Human Rights Watch, 1 October 2000.
12 Ruchita Beri, 'Indo-South Africa Defence Cooperation: Potential and Prospects', *Strategic Analysis: A Monthly Journal of the IDSA*, January 2000, Vol. XXIII No. 10.

1999: BLOODY, BLOODY BEASTS. BLOODY BEASTS

1 Suchitra Kalyan Mohanty, 'Bajrang Dal activist convicted for murder of Christian missionary Graham Staines moves SC seeking remission', *Indian Express*, 9 Jul 2024.
2 Sagarika Ghose, *Atal Bihari Vajpayee*, New Delhi: Juggernaut, 2021, pp. 276–78.
3 'The last time Sonia Gandhi said we have the numbers', *Times of India*, 19 July 2018.
4 Chowdhury, *How Prime Ministers Decide*, p. 380.
5 A. G. Noorani, 'A tale of shattered credibility', *Frontline*, 22 January 2000.

2000: THE CONSTITUTION, DEMOCRACY, SECULARISM, AND FUNDAMENTAL RIGHTS

1 HT Correspondent, 'How the bargain was clinched', *Hindustan Times*, 31 December 1999.
2 *Indian Express*, 8 January 2000.
3 Robert D. Mcfadden, 'Madeleine Albright, First Woman to Serve as Secretary of State, Dies at 84', *New York Times*, 25 March 2022.
4 Chittisinghpura massacre, *Times of India*, 4 May 2017.
5 *Perceptions and purpose of the bomb: Explaining India's nuclear restraint against China*, Yogesh Joshi, published online by Cambridge University Press, 16 November 2021.
6 The Rediff Special/K R Narayanan, rediff.com.
7 N. Ram in *Frontline*, 10 June,2000.
8 In a personal communication to the author dated 9 November 2023.
9 Report by Nirupama Subramaniam, *The Hindu*, 11 Sep 2002.
10 'Suicide Attacks by the LTTE', satp.org.
11 'Narasimha Rao, Buta Singh Found Guilty In Jmm Bribery Case', *Business Standard*, 30 December 2000.

12 Sitapati, *Half-Lion*, p. 202.
13 'Sri Lanka: Failure of Justice for Victims of Massacre', Human Rights Watch, 2 June 2005.
14 '15 years since Bindunuwewa prison massacre', *Tamil Guardian*, 23 October 2015; Sri Lanka: The Bindunuwewa Massacre, Asian Human Rights Commission.
15 'Tamil Tigers announce ceasefire', *The Tribune*, 22 December 2002.

2001: WORDS AS DIPLOMACY—SRI LANKA

1 *Values in Foreign Policy*, Rowman & Littlefield, 2019, (ed.) Krishnan Srinivasan et al.
2 Asian Disaster Reduction Center, The Gujarat Earthquake 2001.
3 'Profile: Yoshiro Mori', BBC, 20 November 2002.
4 Swapan Dasgupta, 'Gujarat earthquake: Gujarat CM Keshubhai Patel hardpressed to explain sluggish response', *India Today*, 12 February 2001.
5 Toral Varia Deshpande, 'Boomtown: Can anything put India's defence middlemen out of business?', *The Caravan*, 1 September 2013.
6 Celia W. Dugger, '16 Indian Soldiers Are Victims in Bangladesh Border Skirmish', *New York Times*, 26 April 2001.
7 'Jayalalithaa is First Serving Chief Minister to Be Convicted for Corruption', All Gov India, 27 September 2014.
8 'The roar of the Tigers', *Aljazeera*, 4 April 2007.
9 'India/Jammu and Kashmir (1947-present)', University of Central Arkansas.
10 ANI, 'Leaders pay floral tributes to victims of 2001 Parliament attack', *The Hindu*, 13 December 2022.

2002: WHEELS WITHIN WHEELS—NORWAY

1 'Vikrant Massey's The Sabarmati Report released: All about 2002 Godhra tragedy', *India Today*, 15 November 2024.
2 'Gulberg Society massacre case: A timeline', *The Hindu*, 4 December 2021.
3 'Prime Minister, Atal Behari Vajpayee on Gujarat', *Outlook*, 22 December 2002.
4 Shishir Gupta, 'Twice in 2002, India was on the verge of striking against Pakistan. Here's why it didn't', *India Today*, 23 December 2002.
5 Praveen Donthi, 'How Mufti Mohammad Sayeed Shaped the 1987 Elections in Kashmir', *The Caravan*, 23 March 2016.

2003: SURJEET, SHATRUGHAN, AND SHIV SHARMA IN OSLO

1 'The Cabinet Committee on Security Reviews operationalization of India's Nuclear Doctrine, 4 January 2003, Media Center, MEA, Government of India; Antoine Levesques, IISS Research Fellow for South Asia with Desmond Bowen, IISS Associate Fellow for South Asia John H. Gill, IISS Associate Fellow for South Asia, 'Nuclear Deterrence and Stability in South Asia: Perceptions and Realities', International Institute for Strategic Studies, May 2021.
2 See PMO, 'Cabinet Committee on Security Reviews Progress in Operationalizing India's Nuclear Doctrine', 4 January 2003, pin.gov.in.; PTI, 'Pakistan does not adhere to "no first use" of nuclear weapons policy: ex-Army official', *The Hindu*, 30 May 2024; Baqir Sajjad Syed, 'Pakistan doesn't have No First Use policy', *DAWN*, 30 May 2024; Kanti Bajpai, 'No First Use in the India-Pakistan Context', Pugwash Conferences on Science and World Affairs, 15-17 November 2002.
3 Pradeep Magazine, 'Azharuddin and 4 Others Are Punished for Cricket Match Fixing: Former India Captain Banned', *New York Times*, 6 December 2000.
4 HT Correspondent, Lucknow, 'Taj corridor case: CBI gets sanction to prosecute the then NPCC GM', *Hindustan Times*, 25 April 2023.
5 'Statoil admits bribe for Iran oil rights', *Financial Times*, 13 October 2006.

6 Safwat Zargar, 'The death of a Pakistani militant near LoC leaves lingering questions about a massacre in Kashmir', *Scroll.in*, 2 November 2021.
7 '25 August 2003 Mumbai bombing', *Times of India*, 7 March 2017.
8 Naseer Ganai, 'Foreigner kidnap case returns to haunt Jammu and Kashmir after 17-years', *India Today*, 8 April 2012.
9 Shirin Ebadi Nobel Lecture, nobelprize.org.

2005: RAJ BHAVAN, KOLKATA

1 Avishek Rakshit, 'Darjeeling tea to cost more abroad', *Business Standard*, 11 March 2016; Peter GW Keen, 'Tea in Germany & its Darjeeling Connection', Teabox, 8 December 2016.

2006: RAJ BHAVAN, PATNA

1 'Kalam wanted to quit after Bihar Assembly dissolution was quashed', *The Hindu*, 17 November 2021.
2 'Joint Press Conference by Prime Minister Dr. Manmohan Singh and US President Mr. George W. Bush, 2 March 2006', Media Center, MEA, Government of India.

2007: A YEAR TO WISH AWAY

1 '2007: Nandigram protest', *Frontline*, 15 August 2022.

2008: JE PATHE JETE HOBEY.... (ON THE ROAD YOU HAVE TAKEN....)

1 'Coal shortage may trigger power crisis in W Bengal', *Economic Times*, 20 January 2009.
2 'In photos: Damaged churches, broken homes are the lingering scars of the 2008 Kandhamal riots', Scroll.in, 5 September 2019.
3 India: EFICOR responds to Communal Violence in Kandhamal, Orissa - Update 4, relief web, 12 February 2009.

2010–2025: INTO THE MODI ERA

1 PTI, '10 years on, German Bakery blast continues to haunt relatives of victims', *The Hindu*, 12 February 2020.
2 TNN, 'Lashkar's breakaway "group" claims Pune blast, *Times of India*, 12 February 2010.
3 Mehul Srivastava, 'Toilet-Paper Scandal in India "Shames" Commonwealth Games Host', *Bloomberg Business Week*, 19 August 2010.
4 A. Harikumar, 'Bribes were taken in the VVIP helicopter deal, admits AK Antony', *India Today*, 25 March 2013.
5 Amartya Kanjilal, 'The Quality of Mercy', *The Caravan*, 1 July 2017.
6 Nileena MS, 'Why are BJP and Congress at odds over the investigation into the 2013 Maoist attack?', *The Caravan*, 19 October 2019.
7 Sudeep Chakravarti, 'Mahendra Karma and his cynical form of vigilantism', *Mint*, 28 May 2013; Suvojit Bagchi, 'The rise and fall of Mahendra Karma – the Bastar Tiger', *The Hindu*, 12 November 2021.
8 Article by Dr K.Srinath Reddy 'Nipah, Chandipura, are only the tip of the iceberg', *Hindustan Times*, 1 August 2024.

EPILOGUE

1 V. K. Ramachandran, 'C.T. Kurien: A notable life of a scholar-economist of distinction and social conscience', *The Hindu*, 25 July 2024.

2 'India ranks 134th in global human development index, says UNDP report', *The Hindu*, 15 March 2024.

3 Klaus von Grebmer et al., '2023 Global Hunger Index: The Power of Youth in Shaping Food Systems', Bonn: Welthungerhilfe, 2023.

4 Kusum Kali Pal, Kim Piaget, and Saadia Zahidi, 'Global Gender Gap Report 2024', World Economic Forum, June 2024.

5 Sebastián Block et al., '2024 Environmental Performance Index', (New Haven, CT: Yale Center for Environmental Law & Policy, 2024).

INDEX

Also by Gopalkrishna Gandhi

Fiction

Refuge

Non-fiction

Of a Certain Age: Twenty Life Sketches

Abolishing the Death Penalty: Why India Should Say No to Capital Punishment

Plays

Dara Shukoh: A Play

Translations

The Tirukkural

Koi Achha Sa Ladka (Translation of *A Suitable Boy* by Vikram Seth into Hindustani)

Books edited by Gopalkrishna Gandhi

Restless as Mercury: My Life as a Young Man by M. K. Gandhi

I am an Ordinary Man: Or India's Struggle for Freedom (1914–1948) by M. K. Gandhi

Gandhi and South Africa (with E. S. Reddy)

Gandhi and Sri Lanka

Nehru and Sri Lanka

India House, Colombo: Portrait of a Residence

Gandhi Is Gone: Who Will Guide Us Now?

A Frank Friendship: Gandhi and Bengal: A Descriptive Chronology

The Oxford India Gandhi: Essential Writings

My Dear Bapu: Letters from C. Rajagopalachari to Mohandas Karamchand Gandhi

Scorching Love: Letters from Mohandas K. Gandhi to his son Devadas (edited with Tridip Suhrud)